Fibber McGee and Molly

ON THE AIR 1935-1959
Second Revised and Enlarged Edition

CLAIR SCHULZ

Fibber McGee and Molly: On the Air 1935-1959
© 2021 Clair Schulz. All Rights Reserved.

No part of this book may be reproduced in any form or by any means, electronic, mechanical, digital, photocopying or recording, except for the inclusion in a review, without permission in writing from the publisher.

Published in the USA by:
BearManor Media
1317 Edgewater Dr #110
Orlando FL 32804
www.bearmanormedia.com

ISBN 978-1-62933-813-2

Printed in the United States of America.

Table of Contents

Preface to Second Revised Edition 5
Introduction 7
Overview of *Fibber McGee and Molly* 19
Format of Episode Entries 23

EPISODE GUIDE
   Thirty-Minute Episodes 37
   Fifteen-Minute Episodes 313
   Monitor Series 479

Appendix A: Alphabetical List of Episodes 501
Appendix B: Ratings and Rankings Summary 539
Appendix C: Hall Closet Gags 541
Appendix D: Notable Occurrences 547
Appendix E: Guest Appearances 551

Selected Bibliography 557
Index 559

A 1937 Parmount publicity photograph for *This Way Please* showing a young Jim and Marian Jordan.

Preface to Second Revised Edition

This updated edition adds over 80 episodes to the earlier volume published by Bear Manor Media. Most of these episodes are from 1935, 1936, and 1937 which were not available to collectors when that book was being prepared. Titles assigned to some of the early shows may differ from those frequently cited to more precisely describe the events which often took place in two separate locations with disparate story lines. Writer Don Quinn was consciously creating the facet of Fibber's character as a fabulous fabulist in the latter portion of these misadventures.

Information on 1939-1944 episodes for which no recording exists came from scripts on microfilm at the Wisconsin State Historical Society Library. Those shows are designated in the entries after the date as (Script). The (Script) designation has been removed from six episodes which have become available to listeners in recent years.

In preparing this revision, all episodes published in the earlier edition have been played again to correct errors, update information, and make additional comments.

For the old-time radio fans who wonder what programs aired in the *Fibber McGee and Molly* spot during the summers, a notation in the comments section of the final episode each season indicates the performers and title of the replacement series.

Because the hall closet running gag remains one of the most memorable aspects of *Fibber McGee and Molly*, Appendix C enumerates all the openings in order and a tally of the openings through the years. Appendix D lists dates of first and last appearances of regular cast members and running gags as well as other notable occurrences on one of radio's most famous programs.

Just Plain Folks. Written on the back of this photograph: "Appeared in person in Oshkosh Jan. 22, 1937 at Oshkosh Theatre. Entertained in my car same day."

Introduction: An Appreciation

Verbose Fibber McGee might have described this book as "A lengthy log listing the legendary shows of the loquacious leader and his laudable lady who landed loads of laughable lines in the laps of lots of lads and lasses who loved listening in locales from the lofty ledges of Leadville to luscious Lake Louise."

More concisely, this book is a guide to the episodes of *Fibber McGee and Molly* whose recordings have survived and are currently available to collectors. It is designed primarily to be used by people as they listen to the recordings to enhance their enjoyment of the shows. An alphabetical list of the episodes by title is provided in Appendix A for those readers who are looking for the date of a particular show.

Comments that accompany each episode are intended to help readers and listeners appreciate the show for what it was, one of radio's best programs and a fixture on NBC for over twenty years. Tuesday evening was *Fibber McGee and Molly* night in millions of homes during most of the 1940s when the program could be found consistently near the top of the ratings. A measure of the popularity of *Fibber McGee and Molly* is that it is one of the very few shows to be the source of two spinoffs, *The Great Gildersleeve* and *The Beulah Show*. Appendix B lists the ratings and rankings of *Fibber McGee and Molly* from 1935 to 1956.

Another purpose in writing a book that examines the episodes in chronological order is to correct misconceptions that have been circling *Fibber McGee and Molly* for a long time. Postings about the program on the Internet or in catalogs listing copies of the show for sale often use phrases like "Audiences exploded with laughter when Fibber opened the hall closet each week." Newspaper accounts have been perpetuating this myth for decades. The Associated Press obituary for Marian Jordan published nationwide on

April 8, 1961 reported "Whenever McGee opened it–at least once a show–hundreds of articles spilled thunderously onto the floor–a sure laugh from coast to coast." A 1970 newspaper article indicated that "on every radio show McGee would open the closet door and every week a pile of junk stored inside would come clattering out on top of him." The staff writer who interviewed Jim Jordan for the January 5, 1982 *Los Angeles Times* stated that the hall closet "became a weekly occurrence, one of the most familiar sounds in radio." Authors of *Final Curtain* published in 1996 claimed the show's "favorite running joke was Fibber's closet which was constantly being opened by someone who had no idea what was coming. The unsuspecting innocent would be subjected to the McGees' howls of 'Don't!' before being buried by two minutes of falling, clattering and clanging junk that Fibber had packed into it." The noise accompanying the opening of the closet door never exceeded twenty seconds. Readers who study the pattern of running gags listed in this book will see that sometimes two months or longer passed between openings of the famous door and that others besides McGee touched the doorknob that triggered the clamorous avalanche. A comprehensive list of the hall closet gags is provided in Appendix C. Listeners who love to hear the Old Timer say, "That ain't the way I heered it" will discover that his catch phrase disappeared completely from the program years before the codger's last appearance. Fans who insist that the voice of Myrt was never heard on the show will learn that she did appear one time at 79 Wistful Vista to wish the McGees well for the summer.

The spelling of Nick Depopolis in this book is the way it appears in scripts. The writers preferred to start the names of the druggist and the patient Doc Gamble talked to over the phone exactly as they sounded so they are spelled as Kremer and Mrs. Kladderhatch.

For years some collectors have assumed that because a complete transcription of the March 9, 1943 episode does not exist that a seven-minute excerpt being circulated is from that broadcast. That "fragment" is actually from different sides of 78 RPM records in the Top Ten *Fibber McGee and Molly* album released in 1947 of specially-recorded sketches performed before a live audience. Jim Backus, who appears as Waterman on the recording, did not make his first appearance on *Fibber McGee and Molly* until 1946.

Comments included with each episode should also shed some light on memories that have become cloudy. Jim Jordan's assertion in interviews recorded in his later years that the episode with Gildersleeve acting as butler (December 26, 1939) was the funniest in the series is questioned when an actual listening to that show reveals it to be just fair *Fibber McGee and Molly* fare. A January 5, 1982 *Los Angeles Times* interview with Jim reported that "He owns no tapes of the Fibber shows, but does have about 78 records, which he never plays. 'The last show I heard,' he says, 'was the last one I did.'" The ability of anyone to judge the comparative quality of episodes decades after hearing them is problematical. Susan Leslie Peters, daughter of Phil Leslie, who co-wrote the series from 1943 to 1956, stated in an article printed in the August 1992 issue of *The Catholic Digest* that "Nobody ever asked Fibber what he did for a living." Comments in the episode entries reveal that this claim is not true for McGee was asked that embarrassing question several times over the years.

But the primary function of the comments is not to bury questionable claims and correct errors but to praise the talents of the writers and Jim and Marian Jordan. The influence of the program reached far beyond the city limits of Wistful Vista. A visit from Fibber and Molly could boost the ratings of any program (Appendix E itemizes guest appearances by Jim and Marian from 1937 to 1957). A measure of the popularity of *Fibber McGee and Molly* can be gauged just by noting references to its characters or their pet expressions on other shows. In February 1945 alone both Shorty Lewis on *Amos 'n' Andy* and Rochester Van Jones on *The Jack Benny Program* adopted Beulah's catch phrase "Love that man." The following month, upon hearing "I betcha, I betcha" spoken by one young actress, Jack compared her to "the little girl on *Fibber McGee and Molly*." The October 10, 1943 episode opened the Benny bag of gags for the new season with a pilot engaging in a Myrt bit with someone in the control tower. On May 9, 1948 Benita Colman repudiated Benny's fanciful story of how he lost her husband's Oscar by invoking the Old Timer's playful declaration of disbelief, which Dennis Day also employed on September 20, 1950 in skeptical response to the claim that Jack had been a big hit at the London Palladium that summer. The Benny bunch knew that allusions to Fibber and Molly were like money in the vault. That legendary vault, first heard on January 7, 1945, could be considered a noisy stepchild of the McGee closet.

The surefire formula that writers Don Quinn and Phil Leslie concocted changed little during the vintage years, yet they added many new spices to keep it fresh. The principal ingredients stayed the same: give Fibber a problem, let him simmer for a while, drop in three or four bits and as many outside characters, and then get him out before the tag. Fibber sometimes had a bitter pill to swallow at the end, but things finally came to rest at the McGee house.

And what a house it was: 79 Wistful Vista, the most famous address in radio. We know that property as well as our own: the hall where they welcomed their guests; the closet; the horsehair sofa and Fibber's well-worn chair; the living room rug spotted with paint and ink from ill-fated projects; a kitchen which was the scene of misguided efforts to make vase, fudge, and cake; and the yard, site of fights with Gildersleeve, aborted barbeques, and a singular attempt to extract maple syrup from an elm tree.

The parade of characters who walked through the front door of that house contributed no small part to the charm of the program. The Old Timer had more old gags than a gang of kidnappers. Nick and Ole regularly donated their time and their jokes. Windbag Gildersleeve blew in long enough to ignite his short fuse. Horatio K. Boomer could find his way in and out of the house but seemed incapable of locating that missing card or paper among all the gewgaws he carried with him. Doctor Gamble and Teeny might stop by just to tease or aggravate Fibber. Henpecked Wallace Wimple used the house as a refuge from his formidable stronger half. The McGees trimmed more than a little of the upper crust off Mmes. Uppington and Carstairs. Try as he would to remain calm, LaTrivia usually could not refrain from flying off the handle (or hying off the fandle, as he might say at the height of his tantrum).

Fibber McGee and Molly boasted one of the strongest line-ups of any comedy program. Harold Peary, Bea Benaderet, Gale Gordon, Dick LeGrand, and Arthur Q. Bryan possessed some of the better-known voices on the air; Bill Thompson alone owned a handful of them. The teasing introductions by Harlow Wilcox whet our appetite and then the visitors were shuffled in and out between bouncy musical numbers. Even the middle commercial was painless because we, like the McGees, were drawn into Harlow's web and it was over before we knew it.

The program was both fun *and* funny. Some sitcoms of past and present are as mirthless as *Murder at Midnight*, but Fibber and Molly were always good for a laugh. Presented with a smorgasbord of word play, sarcasm, hyperbole, banter, riddles, shaggy dog stories, malapropisms, running gags, wheezes and twists on wheezes, one-liners, and non sequiturs, there had to be *something* listeners liked.

The mighty Quinn was a gifted wordsmith, well-suited to the aural medium because he liked rearranging phrases and twisting sayings around for humorous gain. A number of the memorable epigrams he and other writers devised are designated as "quotes of note" in the comments for appropriate episodes. The writers kept us off-balance by varying the pitch they delivered, emphasizing, for example, aphorisms on the May 30, 1944 broadcast and punching out puns on the next regular broadcast (after the D-Day musical special broadcast June 6th) on June 13th.

A belated nod of recognition should be directed toward Len Levinson, whose name appears below Quinn's on many of the 1940-1941 scripts and Bill Danch, who assisted Quinn on numerous 1942-1943 scripts right up until Leslie came onboard in March 1943 but who did not receive on-air credit until they co-wrote some of the fifteen-minute episodes with Phil.

Quinn, Leslie, and other writers were masters of taking a simple idea and building a whole script out of it. Fibber seeking a ride to the Elks Club is all the April 24, 1945 episode is about, yet the short trip is worth it. Writing checks for bills and posting them should be a simple matter but not for McGee as his writers send him downtown three times for ink, envelopes, and a stamp on February 5, 1952. During the November 4, 1947 show, which consisted of nothing more than McGee's efforts to weigh himself at the drugstore to verify the reading of the scale at home, listeners become so engaged in his misadventures they do not even care that it is never revealed what the store's scale showed his weight to be.

Except for some topical references to styles or political events, the show ages well due to the skill of the writers in conceiving funny situations which are still pertinent. Even many of references to World War II rationing are still amusing because of the way the lines are phrased such as Molly's comment about Fibber on November 10, 1942: "He's as proud and happy as a man who doesn't own a car, can't eat sugar, and hates coffee."

The creation of the most picturesque humorous similes and other comparisons on the air make Quinn and Leslie unique among those who toiled on writer's row. Some examples: "He's as hard to pin down as a sunburned wrestler" (March 12, 1946); "The bars in there [a jail] are farther apart than they are in Kansas" (March 26, 1946); "He's so two-faced he could dance cheek-to-cheek in a broom closet" (May 28, 1946); "You got about as much chance of sharing Fifi as a blindfolded Bulgarian with the seven-year itch and a busted garter riding a high-wheeled bicycle across quicksand in a forty mile gale" (November 26, 1946); "He goes to pieces like a club sandwich with a loose toothpick" (March 9, 1948); Gamble suggests that anything crafted by McGee would look like it was made by "a blindfolded Potawatomi with the hiccups while riding full gallop on a railroad trestle on a lame camel in the dark of the moon" (April 20, 1948).

When the writers piled on the comparisons one after another, the most vivid images of a character emerged. On January 7, 1947 Doctor Gamble assessed Fibber's physical condition for free: "You yourself have the fresh, ruddy complexion of a soiled golf ball. Your chest is flatter than a sharecropper's wallet. Your lungs are so full of nicotine they won't let you blow up the balloons for the Elks party. Your arches are flatter than yesterday's beer and, if you were ever boiled down for fat, you'd make enough cheap soap to scour the Lincoln Highway from Turkey Run, Indiana to Buffalo Hump, Wyoming. Little Scorpion Face here has about as much resilience as a flophouse mattress and the dynamic energy of cold oatmeal." The kicker to the list is Fibber's comment after Doc leaves: "They will *too* let me blow up the balloons at the Elks party," the only one of the insults McGee chooses to contest.

The descriptions were often as hilarious to the ear as they still are to the eye such as Gamble's appraisal of McGee's dancing on December 28, 1948: "You are about as graceful as a three-toed sloth creeping across a bed of hot horseshoes or, in a faster tempo, you look like you just got into a pair of trousers which had been put to dry on an anthill."

Quinn was quoted in *There's Laughter in the Air!*, a book of sample scripts from some of radio's comedy programs published in 1945, as saying, "We do not go in for sarcasm or meanness." The doctor's litany of cutting remarks seems to refute that statement, but, as is illustrated in a number of episodes, good pals McGee and Gamble took pot shots at each other for their amusement, not with any malicious intent.

Coming up with new plots to build a foundation of amusing lines around must have been a challenge, yet Quinn and Leslie accomplished it at a time when at least 37 scripts had to be written every season. Even when choosing the same themes like McGee's magic act (June 12, 1945 and January 6, 1948), a special McGee recipe (May 27, 1947 and December 16, 1947), and a newspaper interview (May 20, 1947 and December 9, 1947), they made the story lines so different each episode seems unique.

Writers of comedy shows are rarely commended for the construction of their scripts. People may picture a smoke-filled room of cigar-chompers tossing jokes back and forth in the manner of "And then let's have him do a switch on the gag about…" Artful Quinn and Leslie often planted clues along the way which pointed toward the outcome. Many of the episodes have a symmetry to them, ending with the McGees back at a point alluded to early in the script. One example is the April 11, 1950 escapade that begins with Fibber commenting about getting rid of pickles in a barrel and ends with him revealing why that goal is an obsession with him.

As with all good writers, Quinn and Leslie (and Keith Fowler who came along when Quinn left the show) knew how to let the actions and words of their characters deliver the message without moralizing. One instance of this is evident in the "Some Like It Hot" episode (November 20, 1951) with Fibber and Molly, after bickering about the temperature in the house and moving the thermostat back and forth to regulate a furnace they later find is inactive, demonstrating they have learned something about compromise and understanding at a restaurant by both ordering hot mince pie with ice cream on top. In what may very well be the best back-to-back episodes of the series (December 25, 1951 and January 1, 1952), lessons on the true spirit of giving and the value of friendship are presented but not preached.

Tom Koch, who wrote the vignettes performed by just Jim and Marian for NBC *Monitor*, is not given enough credit for his late contribution to the *Fibber McGee and Molly* legacy, perhaps because many people have not heard these funny sketches. Actually, a number of those three-minute bits are more amusing than the fifteen-minute shows written by Leslie with help from Levinson, Danch, Ralph Goodman, or Joel Kane.

Any comedy writer could learn from studying Koch's ability to set the scene in ten seconds and then tell a story in less time than it takes to make two slices of toast. It is remarkable how some of these skits are like condensed three-act plays such as the December 22, 1957 vignette in which the concept of getting prosperous is set in the first minute, the McGees take stock of salable items in the attic in the second minute, and Fibber places a phone call to determine the value of the relics in the third minute.

Over the years the writers did have a few misfires like briefly introducing Uncle Dennis and Myrt when they were better left offstage, but they had many more hits than errors like the hilarious exchanges between the McGees and the characters played by Cliff Arquette in the early 1950s which feature the badinage of confusion at its best. Although some of the predicaments McGee found himself in were downright silly, they never seemed as contrived as those entangling the Aldrich and Bumstead families. Once listeners bought Fibber, they bought the whole package.

What sold the show were Fibber and Molly and, in Jim and Marian Jordan, the writers had two of the best comic actors on the air to bring their dialogue to life and get the maximum effect from the lines.

Marian's portrayal of a long-suffering, amiable housewife was just as believable as her role as Teeny, the little girl who consistently outwitted Fibber. When some actors assume another character other than their principal one, listeners can tell immediately, but absolutely nothing in Teeny's speech sounded like Marian's normal voice. The illusion was only broken once when, at the close of the June 10, 1941 program, Marian purposely switched parts in mid-sentence. (Another illusion is that listeners probably assumed that Marian and Jim read their lines side-by-side. Throughout most of the program's run, Marian sat at a table with her own microphone facing Jim and other members of the cast who came up to his microphone to speak their lines.) Other characters played by Marian (especially during the formative years of the show) included drawling Mrs. Wearybottom, jabbering Geraldine, and a sprightly old woman (sometimes referred to as Old Lady Wheedledeck.)

But it was Jim's Fibber that was the program's sine qua non. Fibber McGee is sui generis; there never has been anyone like him. There is a line of descent from Chester Riley to Ralph Kramden to Archie Bunker. Irma, Lucy, and Gracie could have been sisters. But there was only one Fibber, a garrulous know-it-all and lovable bungler, an inveterate teller of tales and dreamer of dreams with no visible means of support. He certainly remains one of the most distinctive characters to have appeared on any comedy program on radio or television.

Fibber really was the indispensable half of the team for without him there was no show. On the two occasions when Jim's illness prevented him from appearing, Molly was also not present as Gildersleeve and Leroy filled in on March 28, 1944, and the rest of the cast took over on March 27, 1951. During Marian's long absence from the 1937 to 1939 and on several occasions in later years when she did not appear, Fibber and company carried on as the prime mover kept things moving along smoothly until she returned. Plainly put, Molly was too sensible and kindly to be funny all alone whereas impetuous, short-tempered Fibber could be a riot just talking to himself.

What made Molly stay with this strong-willed klutz all those years must have been the variety with which he spiced up her life for, as he declared on

December 9, 1947, "I've never had an average day in my life. There's always something." On April 28, 1942 she could not even get angry with him after he misused one of her brushes by saying, "I can get another hairbrush but amusing husbands are hard to get." On December 11, 1945 Molly boldly stated she married him for the million laughs he had provided. Fibber recognized the high standard of fun he had set for her by declaring on January 6, 1948 that "You've heard so many good jokes around here, a gag has to be dynamite to make you smile."

On April 4, 1950 when Molly called her fun-loving hubby Fibber a natural curiosity, Marian could have been talking about her fun-loving hubby Jim who stepped into the skin of an extraordinary character extraordinarily well. Just as the man Jack Benny succeeded in becoming the parsimonious, vain character Jack Benny to a degree of perfection no imitator could achieve, so Jim Jordan convincingly became the jesting four-flusher Fibber McGee.

Jim has never received adequate recognition for his skills as a comic actor. Fred Allen's status as a witty ad-libber is well-documented, yet Jim could fire off a spontaneous line with the best of them. It is this talent of the quick quip that is noted in the comments of numerous episodes in this book.

If the part called for Fibber to have no pep (April 6, 1943), Jim was down to the task. If hyperactive McGee had excess energy (January 23, 1945), Jordan sounded like he was bouncing all over the studio. Confronted by a man he believes to be notorious criminal Briefcase Bronson on May 1, 1945, Jim made Fibber seem more nervous than Don Knotts at his shakiest.

In the course of one episode Fibber could be in high dudgeon over a bill, affectionate toward Molly, impatient with Wilcox, playful with the Old Timer, exasperated with Teeny, rude with Mrs. Uppington, and wistful when reminiscing about his days in vaudeville, yet be totally believable in each mood because Jim imbued each of the mercurial McGees with verisimilitude.

Careful listening to the shows reveals vocal touches that Jim added which cannot be written into a script. On the May 30, 1944 show in the midst of describing his bamboo fishing rod to Molly, Fibber's frustration vented itself when Jim's voice cracks in delivering "It's *supposed* to be split." When stabbed by a spring on November 9, 1948 or zapped by electricity on several occasions, Fibber's yelps of pain sounded so realistic we wondered if someone had jabbed Jim with a needle at the microphone. Similarly, the nervous giggles we heard on the March 22, 1949 show sounded as if they came while Jim was tickling himself. On December 18, 1951 Jim went from a boast on his lips to a gulp in his throat in a flash as McGee the braggart became McGee the stammerer. Other actors sounded like they were pinching their noses or grabbing their throats for desired effects, but Jim made it seem like McGee did take a punch in the puss on October 17, 1950 and that the hoarse Fibber could barely squeak out his words on April

7, 1953. The abashed reactions to conversations with other women about lingerie on May 5, 1953 and December 16, 1953 fit perfectly with the character of McGee who we have come to know and the actor we should come to admire more.

Listeners for decades have come to admire and love the common folks, Jim and Marian, who made us feel like guests. When Harlow Wilcox opened the show with "Fibber and Molly join us in a moment" and closed with "Join us again next week, won't you?," we felt like we had been invited into their living room just as much as we had welcomed them into our homes.

Whenever the Jordans stepped to the footlights at the end to speak from the heart about buying war bonds or donating to a charity, the words carried a sincerity that could come only from our kind of people, not from stars reading a mimeographed sheet handed to them just before the broadcast. (Even during the period of fifteen-minute shows when many episodes were sustaining, the Public Service Announcements for groups like the Red Cross, American Cancer Society, CARE, and March of Dimes carried on the close association between the Jordans and charitable organizations.) When they talked about a matter like carpooling to save gas as they did on April 24, 1945, the solid arguments they presented in calm tones made sense. Listeners could not help being attracted to an unpretentious couple who closed shows with sentiments such as "Until McGee and I see all of you nice people again..." (June 22, 1943); "[about blessings]... among which we count the friendship of all you who have been so loyal to us these many years" (December 25, 1945); and "Our grateful thanks to all our friends who have let us visit their homes each Tuesday night. I hope we have been pleasant guests" (June 12, 1951).

What made the Jordans and the McGees so attractive and almost impossible to dislike was the self-mocking tone that ran through the shows which invited us in on the jokes. Rather than parody other shows as some comedy programs did, Fibber and Molly made fun of themselves. There really was no fourth wall between us and the performers for we were inside 79 Wistful Vista with the McGees. Fibber turned to us knowingly on May 27, 1941 to say, "Now get this, folks. It's the crux of the whole program." The McGees and their visitors often made remarks about the age of their jokes, the unkindest cut of all probably coming on December 5, 1950 when Fibber admitted that a gag they used that night came from a book published in 1873 and, after promising a new joke the following week, invited listeners to tune in to see if they could tell which one it was. Even on the special hour-long program that began the 1949-1950 season by celebrating the fifteenth anniversary of *Fibber McGee and Molly*, the Jordans, instead of concentrating on their accomplishments at the end, conclude the proceedings with a crack about them telling a lot of awful jokes. Whether the line came from Molly informing us on November 19, 1946 that she knew the phone that just rang was for Fibber because she was reading ahead or Fibber on January 27, 1948 stating that Wilcox appeared "right on time, page thirteen," we felt like we were part of the action reading right along with Jim and Marian as they played Fibber and Molly for all those years.

The best of those years were certainly those during the thirty-minute period, particularly from 1940 through the end in 1953. (One oddity listeners notice is that for all those years the sponsor's name came first when Wilcox opened the show, e.g. "The Johnson's Wax Program with Fibber McGee and Molly.") A change in time and format can dramatically alter a program's chemistry. *Lum and Abner* and *Vic and Sade* thrived in a quarter-hour environment with just the players present. The thirty-minute shows at the ends of their runs are somewhat painful to hear because the writing is geared not in the direction of character interaction but rather toward lines that generate laughs from an audience. With the need to "write funny" no longer present because the episodes were prerecorded in a studio, too many of the fifteen-minute *Fibber McGee and Molly* shows seem more intent on developing a story that would be continued the next day instead of making each episode amusing and rewarding. More satisfying are the bits done for *Monitor* from 1957 to 1959 for therein one catches glimpses of the humor that made us sometimes laugh until the tears came during the golden years. Thanks to tapes and CDs that have preserved most of the episodes of *Fibber McGee and Molly* for our enjoyment, we can still sing its praises.

Every time this writer hears the theme "Wing to Wing" open *Fibber McGee and Molly*, he sings his praises with the verse he wrote that fits the melody somewhat snugly: "The greatest program there ever was/Was this one with Fib and Mol/With Bill and Gale and all the rest/This was the best." To misquote the Old Timer, "That's the way I hear it."

Admirers of Fibber and Molly should not be concerned if others consider them out of touch with the current popular culture. Our hero, McGee, never let harsh reality get in the way of living the good life. Molly pinpointed her husband's mindset accurately on November 5, 1940 when she asked for a present of "a big, beautifully-colored, handsomely-framed Rand McNally map of the dream world you live in."

That dream world is ours each time we press "play." When it opens before us, we see a magical place where every business is located at 14th and Oak, all calls have to go through a smooth operator named Myrt, streetcar conductors speak in garbled tongues, and the only drink in town is hot-buttered root beer. Over on the back steps there's a short man saying, "Oh, no you don't" and a little girl replying, "Oh, yes I do." But isn't that him by the side of the house telling his wife that if their neighbor doesn't keep his dadratted lawn mower in better shape, he'll borrow one from someone else? And that's the same gabby fellow on the front sidewalk who is boring a portly gent holding a doctor's bag about some Fred Nitney that he used to have a vaudeville act with back in nineteen-aught-sixteen. It seems that no matter which way we turn we can't get away from Fibber McGee and Molly. May it always be so.

The *Fibber McGee and Molly* crew in the fall of 1945: Frank Pittman, Bea Benaderet, Gale Gordon, Jim Jordan, Harlow Wilcox, Marian Jordan, Phil Leslie, Billy Mills, Don Quinn, Shirley Mitchell, Arthur Q. Bryan. Bill Thompson had not yet returned from the Navy.

Overview of
Fibber McGee and Molly

When Fibber McGee would say, "I was born in a little white house on top of Kickapoo Hill back in Peoria of poor but honest parents," he could have been speaking about James Jordan who was born near Peoria on November 16, 1896. (On the December 12, 1939 episode of *Fibber McGee and Molly* Teeny correctly guesses Fibber's birthday of November 16th.) Marian Driscoll was born not far away from Jim's birthplace on April 15, 1898. The couple dated while teenagers and were married August 31, 1918. After Jim returned from brief service with the army at the end of World War I (which, Fibber would always insist, was the Big War), the pair began touring as a musical act with Marian as pianist and Jim assisting on the singing.

Jim and Marian's audition at Chicago station WIBO developed into a string of radio jobs in that city: *The O'Henry Twins, Marian and Jim in Songs, The Air Scouts, Luke and Mirandy,* and *Smackout.* By the time the Jordans were performing in *Smackout* on WMAQ, Don Quinn had joined the Jordans as writer and the couple were mixing comedy with the musical numbers. Among other characters Jim played Luke Gray, proprietor of the Smackout General Store, a spinner of tall tales who was the forerunner of Fibber McGee. Marian also assumed a variety of roles, including the little girl Teeny as well an assortment of haughty, flirty, and sluggish women.

When Johnson's Wax expressed interest in sponsoring a show featuring the Jordans, Quinn fashioned what might be considered a *Luke and Mirandy* on wheels which allowed the nomadic couple a chance to travel about and peddle auto wax simultaneously. *Fibber McGee and Molly* debuted on April 16, 1935. During the early years the Jordans dressed the parts, Jim as bespectacled yokel and Marian as plain housewife in patterned dress and feathered hat.

By September 1935 the McGees had settled into their house at 79 Wistful Vista. Fibber's tall tales, an integral part of the early shows, gradually gave way to situational comedy and interchanges with other characters who visited their home. The show was heard on Mondays until March 1938 when it settled into its familiar spot on Tuesday evenings at 9:30 Eastern.

The addition of Bill Thompson in 1936 gave the show a boost because in his kit bag of voices he brought forth the most memorable characters heard on the program, namely the Old Timer, Horatio K. Boomer, and Nick Depopolis. Later in 1941 Wallace Wimple joined the mirthful menagerie.

During Marian's extended absence from the show from November 1937 to April 1939 when the show was known as *Fibber McGee and Company*, Hugh Studebaker, Betty Winkler, and ZaSu Pitts appeared frequently to help or hinder Fibber in his weekly dilemmas. Isabel Randolph and Harold Peary assumed various parts before settling into the well-known roles of Mrs. Uppington in 1937 and Throckmorton P. Gildersleeve in 1939. Likewise, Gale Gordon played doctors, clerks, and other bits until assuming the mantle of Mayor LaTrivia on October 14, 1941.

When military service during WWII subtracted Thompson and Gordon from the cast, Arthur Q. Bryan began making house calls as Doctor Gamble in 1943, and Shirley Mitchell as Alice Darling moved in with the McGees the same year. Ransom Sherman took a few bows as pompous Sigmund Wellington and tipsy Uncle Dennis during the 1943-1944 season. Short-term residents at 79 Wistful Vista were Beulah (Marlin Hurt) in 1944-1945 and Lena (Gene Carroll) in 1947.

In 1945 Bea Benaderet as Millicent Carstairs brought in the voice of the upper class absent since Mrs. Uppington's departure in 1943. The last recurring character appeared in 1949 with the arrival of Ole Swenson played by Dick LeGrand.

Music in the early years was provided by the orchestras of Ulderico (Rico) Marcelli and Ted Weems with songs by Perry Como and Donald Novis. However, the tuneful sounds most closely associated with *Fibber McGee and Molly* came from the music makers under the direction of Billy Mills and the four-part harmonies of The King's Men.

Billy Mills, a member of the *Fibber McGee and Molly* family from January 17, 1938 to the end of the 1952-1953 season, also wrote some of the numbers heard on the show including the long-running "Wing to Wing" theme and "The Sound Effects Man." Billy's unheralded contributions to the program as a skillful arranger are frequently evident, particularly late in the thirty-minute period as evidenced on three consecutive Tuesdays in 1952 when he treated audiences to uptempo versions of "Grand Central Station" (January 29), "Always" (February 5), and "Anytime" (February 12). Given just 90 seconds of airtime on December 23, 1952, Mills strung together a yuletide garland of "Sleigh Ride," "Here Comes Santa Claus," "Santa Claus Is Comin' to Town," "Jingle Bells," and "White Christmas." This updated edition identifies many of the brief melodies the Billy Mills Orchestra played near the end of shows before the Jordans returned for some final words to their devoted listeners.

The King's Men, who came on board February 6, 1940, consisted of Ken Darby, Rad Robinson, Bud Linn, and Jon Dodson. Darby won several Oscars for his musical work on motion pictures and his connection with Walt Disney films is probably one reason why a number of songs like "Zip-a-Dee-Doo-Dah" and "The Cinderella Work Song" were performed by the quartet on *Fibber McGee and Molly*.

The men responsible for the noisy closet and the other distinctive sound effects included Virgil Reimer, Monty Fraser, Bud Tollefson, and Frank Pittman. Cecil Underwood served as director during the formative years of the show, followed by Pittman through the end of the 1949-1950 season, and finally by Max Hutto who directed from September 1950 through March 1956.

The program remained a listener favorite throughout the 1940s, finishing in the top five shows until the end of the decade. After the 1949-1950 season, Johnson's Wax decided to move more of its advertising to television and dropped the show. Pet Milk took over the program for the next two seasons. Reynolds Aluminum sponsored the show during 1952-1953, the final year of the thirty-minute broadcasts, the last episode airing on June 30, 1953.

From October 5, 1953 through March 23, 1956 *Fibber McGee and Molly* was heard five times a week in fifteen-minute episodes. John Wald took over as announcer from Harlow Wilcox who had been with the show since the first episode. Bill Thompson and Arthur Q. Bryan were the only supporting players carried over from the earlier series with radio reliables like Herb Vigran, Elvia Allman, and Parley Baer helping to open up the action of the scripts even though there was no audience present to respond to that action. Sponsorship was sporadic with a number of shows featuring Public Service Announcements and promotions for NBC programs.

The final act for Jim and Marian was played out in sketches between Fibber and Molly heard on weekend *Monitor* broadcast from June 1, 1957 to September 6, 1959. Five of these bits lasting about three minutes each were aired most Saturdays and Sundays.

From September 15, 1959 through January 19, 1960 *Fibber McGee and Molly* was seen on NBC television Tuesday evenings with Bob Sweeney as Fibber and Cathy Lewis as Molly. Harold Peary played Mayor LaTrivia on the short-lived series.

When Marian was diagnosed with ovarian cancer, the Jordans in essence retired and closed the hall closet for good. She died on April 7, 1961. Jim lived to be 91, succumbing on a date in 1988 that seems appropriate for one of radio's best jokers: April 1st.

A visual equivalent of the "'Tain't funny, McGee" squelch showing a beaming Fibber and a skeptical Molly on the cover of the December 12-18, 1942 *Movie-Radio Guide*.

Format of Episode Entries

Date: Month, day, and year episode was broadcast. (Script) by certain entries indicates information is from a script because no recording exists for that episode.

Title: The theme of the episode, sometimes shortened to key words. Because most episodes are concerned with actions started by Fibber, titles used do not begin with *Fibber* or *McGee*. An exception is "Fibber's Tune" for that is the title of McGee's song which is also the subject of the episode.

Cast: A list of the identifiable performers followed by the character's name in parentheses.

Summary: A one-sentence synopsis of the plot without giving away the ending.

Music: Orchestra leader appears first followed by the titles of identifiable musical numbers and vocalists in parentheses. Snatches from compositions like "The William Tell Overture," "Let's Have Another Cup of Coffee," "Time on My Hands," and "Sleep" used to denote passage of time or change of scene are not noted nor are the brief bridges to the first or last commercials which are not announced by Wilcox.

Running Gags: Sayings, routines, or actions which are designed to generate laughter or serve as a response to an amusing line followed by the speaker in parentheses. Common phrases repeated as a part of regular conversation such as "Heavenly days" by Molly and "Stuff like that there" by Fibber are not noted. The running gags cataloged are:

> "*'Tain't funny, McGee*": usually spoken by Molly in response to a witticism from Fibber who often asks for the sharp retort with his teasing "Don't you get it, Molly?"
>
> "*Gotta get them brakes fixed*": usually spoken by Fibber following the sound effect of squealing tires.

"That ain't the way I heered it": usually spoken by the Old Timer following a wisecrack by Fibber and preceding another joke by the Old Timer.

Tongue twister: a string of alliteration spoken by Fibber after he gives a name he "was knowed [known] as in those days." A variant is a tongue twister of a different sort with a string of words that rhyme rather than start with the same letter. An example appears in the comments for the April 30, 1940 episode.

"Where'd I put that…?": usually spoken by Horatio K. Boomer as he looks for (and rarely finds) some object on his person. Instead he usually comes across the tools of the trade he uses in his shady pursuits.

Myrt bit: usually spoken by Fibber as he relates what the telephone operator tells him with a line that leads listeners to think of one interpretation before pulling a switch on that word or phrase.

"You're a harrrrd man, McGee": Gildersleeve's comeback to a criticism or cutting quip delivered by Fibber.

Hall closet: who opens the door letting all the noisy contents spill out and the reason for opening it.

Cigar routine: involving Fibber and another male. The bit took the form of "Have a cigar?" "No, thanks. I have one." "You got two? Thanks."

Word confusion: usually a series of words used improperly that sound somewhat alike like *optimist/optometrist/bigamist* in which Fibber and Molly and perhaps a visitor offer corrections.

LaTrivia blowup: usually initiated by Fibber and Molly who take a term or saying like "Skating on thin ice" used by the mayor literally and frustrating him until he explodes in a string of spoonerisms.

"Love that man": spoken by Beulah after one of Fibber's jokes. Her response can be considered the opposite to Molly's "'Tain't funny, McGee" reactions to Fibber's gags.

"Bird book": the alliterative phrase spoken by Wallace Wimple with exaggerated lip movement. Fibber or Molly frequently asked him to repeat it to milk some more laughs.

Mrs. Kladderhatch bit: a variation of Fibber's conversations with Myrt in that Doctor Gamble revealed some information while on the phone that required amplification after the conversation was over.

"Yust donating my time": spoken by Ole Swenson in response to work requests or situations at home.

Name game: confused exchanges between the McGees and characters assumed by Cliff Arquette in which he addresses them using terms like *clairvoyant* and *tuckered*.

Comments: Remarks on that particular episode indicating character/writer/sponsor changes, notable commercials, memorable lines, bloopers, ad-libs, etc.

Fibber appears to setting up a Myrt bit with Molly in this photograph promoting the new season to begin September 19, 1950 on NBC.

Front cover of the 1947 Top Ten album of four 78 RPM records issued by Audience Records, New York City. Copyright holders are "James and Marian Jordan and Don Quinn," not NBC or Johnson's Wax.

One of the caricatures by Sam Berman for a 1947 promotional kit spotlighting the NBC Parade of Stars.

In 1977 Golden Age Records adapted Berman's artwork on the cover of an album with phrasing which conjoined Fibber's fabrications and the overstuffed closet.

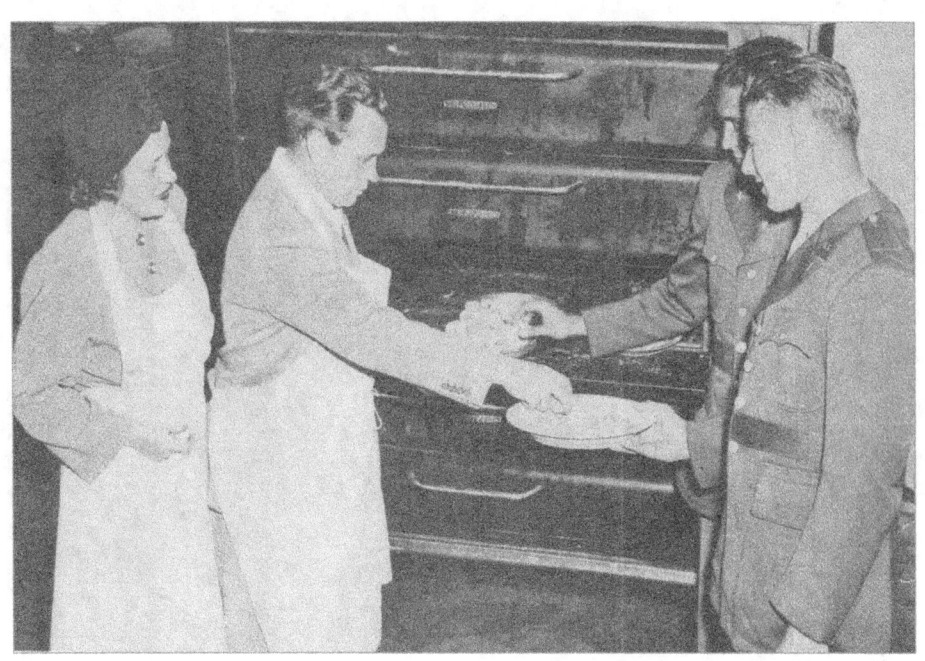

Doing their part: Marian and Jim serve hot biscuits and moral support at Lemoore Field near Fresno, California during World War II.

Marian and Jim test one of Fibber's inventions for the press in the summer of 1943.

Jim Jordan and Bill Thompson offer advice to writer Don Quinn in this 1943 gag shot.

A premium suitable for framing offered to purchasers of Johnson's Wax products in the fall of 1941.

Proof that Fibber McGee and Molly were tops even in 1936 when this set was offered as a premium.

More fun from 1936 with an unbiased endorsement from Fibber himself.

A 1946 can of Glo-Coat showing the sparkling smiles of radio's royal couple.

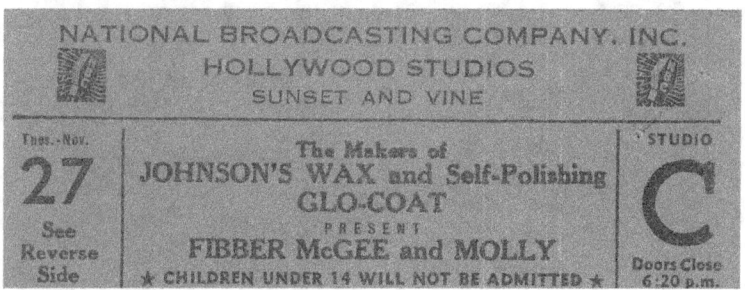

This ticket is for the November 27, 1945 episode, "Chopping Down the Oak Tree." No ticket is needed by modern listeners to gain admittance to Wistful Vista. This way please…

Episode Guide

THIRTY-MINUTE EPISODES

Date: April 16, 1935
Title: Motorcycle Cop and Judge
Cast: Jim Jordan (Fibber McGee), Marian Jordan (Molly McGee), Harlow Wilcox (gas station attendant)
Summary: Fibber and Molly are stopped by a motorcycle cop for running a red light and appear before a justice of the peace.
Music: Rico Marcelli's Orchestra: "Save Your Sorrow for Tomorrow" (theme song at the beginning of episodes), "Rhythm in the Rain," "Smooth Sailing" (Ronnie and Van, vocal), "Flossie Farmer, the Snake Charmer" (Jim and Marian, vocal), "If the Moon Turns Green" (Kathleen Wells, vocal), "Love Is Just Around the Corner"
Running Gag: "'Tain't funny, McGee" (Molly)
Comments: Sponsor is Johnson's Wax which sponsors the program through the May 23, 1950 episode. Writer is Don Quinn. The first four shows were broadcast from New York, then from Chicago through the January 24, 1939 episode except for ten weeks in 1937 when the shows came from Hollywood where the Jordans were making their first motion picture. This first episode shows its age with creaky gags and labored puns. Harlow's laughter seems forced and out of register with the quality of the jokes. Fibber's tall tale about Ermintrude the camel is a shaggy dog bit that may have been showing its whiskers already in 1935. The early programs featuring the nomadic McGees seem like vaudeville on the air with a heavy reliance on music and frequent bridges between bits as if bringing on the next act.

Date: April 30, 1935
Title: Hot Dogs and a Blowout
Cast: Jim Jordan (Fibber), Marian Jordan (Molly), Harlow Wilcox (gas station attendant)
Summary: The McGees grab a bite at a trailer court and deal with a flat tire.
Music: Rico Marcelli: "March Winds and April Showers" (Ronnie and Van, vocal), "Blue Room," "Every Day" (Kathleen Wells, vocal), "Feel Like Sweet Sixteen (Jim and Marian, vocal), "Lost My Rhythm, Lost My Music, Lost My Man" (Ronnie, Van, Kathleen, vocal)
Running Gag: "Gotta get them brakes fixed" (Fibber)
Comments: The show is still getting its legs with Jim speaking in an older man's dialect and Marian acting a bit like an Irish harridan who harangues her husband more than helps him. Molly unleashes an awful pun about chili con carnival and Fibber unfolds another tall tale, this one about an elephant named Myrtle. Unlike the later shows in which the action flows seamlessly between the commercials and the musical interludes, the routines are isolated and seem almost like spoken bridges between the musical numbers.

Date: May 7, 1935
Title: Out of Gas on Broadway
Cast: Jim Jordan (Fibber), Marian Jordan (Molly), Harlow Wilcox
Summary: The McGees incur the wrath of a policeman who threatens to arrest them after they run out of gas on a busy street.
Music: Rico Marcelli: "Strike Up the Band," "Lovely to Look At" (Ronnie, vocal), "Life is a Song" (Kathleen Wells, vocal), "Fare Thee Well, Annabelle" (Ronnie and Van, vocal)
Running Gag: "Gotta get them brakes fixed" (Fibber)
Comments: Molly does a clever switch with "Neon rays/Rayon knees" to suggest Fibber might be more distracted by legs than lights. For purposes of this episode Molly indicates her maiden surname was Mahoney. This is the last show from New York.

Date: May 21, 1935
Title: Tire Trouble and Gondola Tale
Cast: Jim Jordan (Fibber), Marian Jordan (Molly), Harlow Wilcox
Summary: The McGees try to return a faulty tire, then they stop near a balloon ascension airfield where Fibber uncorks hot air of his own.
Music: Rico Marcelli: "A Shine on Your Shoes" (Three Kings, vocal), "You and the Night and the Music," "Throwing Stones at the Sun" (Gale Page, vocal), "Whose Honey Are You?" (Three Kings, vocal)
Running Gags: "Gotta get them brakes fixed" (Fibber), "'Tain't funny, McGee" (Molly)
Comments: This is the first extant episode broadcast from Chicago. Typical of the early shows, there is as much melody as there is mirth. McGee, so often

caught with his head in the clouds, takes off on a flight of fancy that lives up to his first name.

Date: June 11, 1935
Title: Toll Bridge and Diving Tale
Cast: Jim Jordan (Fibber), Marian Jordan (Molly), Harlow Wilcox
Summary: Fibber balks at paying 30 cents to cross a bridge, then at a gas station he unfolds a tale about diving for pearls.
Music: Rico Marcelli: "New Sun in the Sky" (Three Kings, vocal), "In the Twinkling of an Eye" (Gale Page, vocal), "When You've Got a Little Springtime in Your Heart" (Gale Page, vocal), "Living in a Great Big Way"
Running Gags: "Gotta get them brakes fixed" (Fibber), "'Tain't funny, McGee" (Molly)
Comments: Jim and Marian harmonize on a rhythmic "History in a few, few words." Fibber sounds like dickering Jack Benny as he weighs the cost of paying a toll versus the price of gas for driving to another spot. The Mudcat McGee patter foreshadows lyrical tongue twisters which will come later. During the tall tale, Fibber invents a unit of currency using bandleader Rico's last name.

Date: June 18, 1935
Title: River Moonlight and Circus Tale
Cast: Jim Jordan (Fibber), Marian Jordan (Molly), Harlow Wilcox
Summary: The McGees bask in the glow of a moonlit night, then Fibber attempts to get a theatrical rate at a hotel with a story about his days in the circus.
Music: Rico Marcelli: "Rise and Shine" (Three Kings, vocal), "In the Middle of a Kiss" (Gale Page, vocal), "Polly," "In Caliente" (Three Kings, vocal)
Running Gags: "'Tain't funny, McGee" (Molly), "Gotta get them brakes fixed" (Fibber)
Comments: Words and expressions such as "Dadratted" and "Like that there" are entering Fibber's speech patterns with increasing regularity. On this and other early episodes the Three Kings provide a coda to Fibber's blarney with "The Greatest Story Ever Told." The number of the highway Fibber and Molly have been traveling on for several weeks will shortly become their house number.

Date: July 8, 1935
Title: Visiting Washington and G-Man Tale
Cast: Jim Jordan (Fibber), Marian Jordan (Molly), Harlow Wilcox
Summary: The McGees talk politics with a man on the street in the nation's capital, then Fibber tells a bellboy about his days working as an undercover agent.
Music: Rico Marcelli: "An Old Southern Custom," "I'm Just an Ordinary Human" (Lynn Martin, vocal), "A Morning in May," "Hooray for Love" (Three Kings, vocal)

Running Gags: "'Tain't funny, McGee" (Molly), "Gotta get them brakes fixed" (Fibber)

Comments: *Fibber McGee and Molly* is now being broadcast on Mondays at 7:00 PM Central, 8:00 PM Eastern. A WLS ID precedes this episode. Wilcox still objects to being called Harpo by Fibber, but he will get used to the name.

Date: July 15, 1935
Title: Swimming by Ocean and Lifeguard Tale
Cast: Jim Jordan (Fibber), Marian Jordan (Molly), Harlow Wilcox
Summary: After their plan to swim in the Atlantic is stymied, the McGees move to a public beach where Fibber recounts a story about his lifesaving skills.
Music: Rico Marcelli: "At about a Quarter to Nine" (Three Kings, vocal), "Hunkadola," "Paris in the Spring" (Lynn Martin, vocal), "Crazy Rhythm" (Johnson Waxtette, vocal)
Running Gags: "Gotta get them brakes fixed" (Fibber), "'Tain't funny, McGee" (Molly)
Comments: Listeners get two peeks into the past as the McGees change clothes in the car with the mention of side curtains and the top of Fibber's bathing suit. An extended version of "Save Your Sorrow for Tomorrow" is heard at the end.

Date: July 29, 1935
Title: Crackshot McGee and Swordfish Tale
Cast: Jim Jordan (Fibber), Marian Jordan (Molly), Harlow Wilcox
Summary: Under the big top the McGees try their luck at a shooting gallery, then Fibber tells a story about dueling with a swordfish.
Music: Rico Marcelli: Circus Music Medley (Johnson Merrymen, vocal), "Little Things You Used to Do" (Lynn Martin, vocal), "La Cucaracha," "Jungle Drums" (Johnson Merrymen, vocal)
Running Gags: "Gotta get them brakes fixed" (Fibber), "'Tain't funny, McGee" (Molly), "'Tain't funny, Molly" (Fibber)
Comments: Jim and Marian harmonize on a novelty number "She Was an Acrobat's Daughter." This episode has more unity of place than some of the others during the vagabond days in that both the first half action and the tall tale section occur at the circus sideshows.

Date: August 12, 1935
Title: Fortune Told and Furniture Tale
Cast: Jim Jordan (Fibber), Marian Jordan (Molly), Harlow Wilcox, Hugh Studebaker (gas jockey)
Summary: The McGees get Fibber's fortune told, then Fibber tells a filling station attendant about his days of growing furniture.

Music: Rico Marcelli: "Page Miss Glory," "Every Little Moment" (Lynn Martin, vocal), "When a Gypsy Makes His Violin Cry" (Audrey Call, violinist), "Hallelujah' (Johnson Merryman, vocal)
Running Gags: "Gotta get them brakes fixed" (Fibber), "'Tain't funny, McGee" (Molly), "'Tain't funny, Molly" (Fibber)
Comments: Audrey Call was married to orchestra leader Rico Marcelli. Madame Astrolo is at least correct in predicting that the journeys of the McGees will come to an end soon because they will land in Wistful Vista on August 26. Harlow invites listeners back for more hokum and hotcha.

Date: August 26, 1935
Title: Win House in Wistful Vista
Cast: Jim Jordan (Fibber), Marian Jordan (Molly), Harlow Wilcox, Charlie Wilson (Hagglemeyer)
Summary: Fibber and Molly win their dream house when the ticket they hold in a real estate raffle (number 131313) is selected.
Music: Rico Marcelli: "The Weatherman" (Johnson Merrymen, vocal), "I Wished on the Moon," "And Then My Heart Stood Still" (Ronnie Mansfield, vocal), "Of Thee I Sing" (Johnson Merrymen, vocal)
Running Gag: "Gotta get them brakes fixed" (Fibber)
Comments: Fibber tells a tall tale about banana splits. Realtor Mr. Hagglemeyer engages in a string of spoonerisms in much the same style as Doodles Weaver used later. This is the sixteenth episode broadcast from Chicago.

Date: September 16, 1935
Title: Hanging Curtains and Shoe Tree Tale
Cast: Jim Jordan (Fibber), Marian Jordan (Molly), Harlow Wilcox
Summary: The McGees receive a visitor from the Chamber of Commerce and phone calls from businesses welcoming them to Wistful Vista the same day Fibber adds another tall tale to his repertoire.
Music: Rico Marcelli: "Fine and Dandy," "Body and Soul," "I'm in the Mood for Love" (Lynn Martin, Johnson Merrymen, vocal), "And Then Some" (Johnson Merrymen, vocal)
Running Gags: "Gotta get that pipe fixed" (Fibber), cigar routine (Fibber, visitor), "'Tain't funny, McGee" (Molly, twice)
Comments: The place where McGee's shoe trees were supposedly grown is certainly appropriate: Santa Baloney. Fibber's response to a bakery sending a sample is also in tune: "Lookie, Lookie, Lookie, Here Comes Cookie."

Date: September 23, 1935
Title: Avoids Scrubbing the Back Porch
Cast: Jim Jordan (Fibber), Marian Jordan (Molly), Harlow Wilcox

Summary: Fibber prefers to dabble with the doorbell and read the newspaper rather than scrub the porch as Molly has requested him to do.
Music: Rico Marcelli: "Strike Me Pink" (Johnson Merrymen, vocal), "I've Got to Pass Your House" (Lynn Martin, vocal), "Cheek to Cheek" (Johnson Merrymen and Lynn Martin, vocal), "Double Trouble" (Johnson Merrymen)
Running Gag: "'Tain't funny, McGee" (Molly, twice)
Comments: This episode is distinctive in that Molly calls McGee by his first name and she delivers the "'Tain't funny, McGee" squelch twice. This is the first instance of Fibber addressing someone he has just met colloquially ("Withy"). This is also the first time Fibber battles electricity and comes out a loser.

Date: October 7, 1935
Title: Bicycle Ride and Cannibal Tale
Cast: Jim Jordan (Fibber), Marian Jordan (Molly), Harlow Wilcox, Betty Lou Gerson (Helen)
Summary: After Fibber proves to be unsteady on a little girl's bike, he tells her a story about being captured in Africa.
Music: Rico Marcelli: "A Bicycle Built for Two," "My Dreams" (Clef Dwellers, vocal), "You're All I Need" (Lynn Martin, vocal), "Broadway Rhythm" (Clef Dwellers, vocal)
Running Gag: "'Tain't funny, McGee" (Molly)
Comments: One would almost expect Fibber to pull a switch as he is wobbling on the bicycle by exclaiming "Gotta get brakes!" The grocery boy provides mirthful counterpoint to Fibber's fable by periodically naming foods like horse radish, applesauce, nuts, and boiled ham.

Date: October 14, 1935
Title: Amateur Show
Cast: Jim Jordan (Fibber, Stuffy O'Toole, Mort Toops), Marian Jordan (Molly, Geraldine, Teeny), Harlow Wilcox, Rico Marcelli, Audrey Call
Summary: Fibber and Molly host a program of amateur talent for a radio station.
Music: Rico Marcelli: "No Strings," "In My Solitude" (Audrey Call, violin), "Animal Crackers in My Soup" (Teeny, vocal), "Sweet Sue" (Clef Dwellers, vocal)
Running Gags: "'Tain't funny, McGee" (Molly), "'Tain't funny, Molly" (Fibber)
Comments: Marian and Jim give listeners a taste of what *Smackout* was like by playing several characters. This show marks the first appearance of Teeny and Mort Toops.

Date: October 21, 1935
Title: Courtroom of McGees
Cast: Jim Jordan (Fibber), Marian Jordan (Molly), Harlow Wilcox

Summary: After being arrested for going through a red light, Fibber pleads his case in court.
Music: Rico Marcelli: "I'm on a Seesaw," "The Girl with the Dreamy Eyes" (Clef Dwellers, vocal), "Poor Butterfly" (Clef Dwellers, vocal), "Top Hat, White Tie and Tails" (Charles LaVere, vocal)
Running Gags: "Gotta get that case fixed "(Fibber), "'Tain't funny, McGee" (Molly)
Comments: In addition to the courtroom being packed with McGees, the audience for this broadcast consists of many people having that surname living in the Chicago area. Testimony delivered under oath by a user of Johnson's Wax adds credence to the efficacy of the product.

Date: October 28, 1935
Title: Halloween Party
Cast: Jim Jordan (Fibber, Mort Toops), Marian Jordan (Molly, Teeny, Geraldine), Harlow Wilcox
Summary: The McGees entertain friends at a party, highlighted by Fibber's punch and his eerie ghost story.
Music: Rico Marcelli: "Rhythm and Romance (Clef Dwellers, vocal), "Hobgoblin" (Audrey Call, violin), "I've Got a Feeling You're Fooling" (Kay Donna, vocal), "From the Top of Your Head to the Tip of Your Toes" (Clef Dwellers, vocal)
Running Gags: "'Tain't funny, McGee" (cast), tongue twister starting with Haunt Hunter McGee using H's (Fibber)
Comments: Jim plays Mort Toops in a voice not unlike the one Edgar Bergen employed later with Mortimer Snerd. With Jim and Marian playing almost all the parts, this is another episode that gives listeners a taste of what *Smackout* sounded like.

Date: November 18, 1935
Title: Lighting Furnace with Gasoline
Cast: Jim Jordan (Fibber), Marian Jordan (Molly), Harlow Wilcox, Hugh Studebaker (Silly Watson)
Summary: Fibber attempts to get the furnace working with advice and assistance from Silly Watson and Molly.
Music: Rico Marcelli: "Fine and Dandy," "No Other One" (Kay Donna, vocal), "Treasure Island," "I Wish I Were Aladdin" (Charles LaVere, vocal)
Running Gag: "'Tain't funny, McGee' (Molly)
Comments: Hugh Studebaker gets credit at the beginning of the show. As sometimes happened, McGee gets sidetracked from addressing a pressing current matter with recollections from his fabled past. In this episode Silly seems to have more common sense than McGee at least when it comes to flammable liquids.

Date: November 25, 1935
Title: Buying Vegetables at Roadside Stand
Cast: Jim Jordan (Fibber), Marian Jordan (Molly, Teeny, Geraldine), Harlow Wilcox
Summary: Fibber, Molly, and Teeny drive into the country to purchase vegetables for Thanksgiving dinner.
Music: Rico Marcelli: "You Do Something to Me," "Them There Eyes" (Kay Donna, vocal), "Up the Lazy River" (Joe Bolen, vocal), "You Know That I Know"
Running Gags: "'Tain't funny, McGee" (Molly once, Fibber once), "Gotta get them brakes fixed" (Fibber)
Comments: Harlow, who had earlier objected to be called Harpo, refers to himself as Groucho Wilcox, one of the Wax Brothers. Fibber, instead of switching Molly's squelch of his jokes, is now sometimes dousing his own lame gags with "'Tain't funny, McGee."

Date: December 2, 1935
Title: Street Interview
Cast: Jim Jordan (Fibber), Marian Jordan (Molly, Teeny, Geraldine), Harlow Wilcox, Hugh Studebaker (Silly Watson), Tom Post (officer)
Summary: The McGees ask citizens on the street various questions for a radio station.
Music: Rico Marcelli: "Soon" (Kay Donna, vocal), "I Want to Be Happy"
Running Gags: "Tain't funny, McGee" (Molly, twice)
Comments: 14th and Oak, the busiest corner in Wistful Vista, will be mentioned many times in the future. Hugh Studebaker, who had taken unbilled parts earlier, is now given credit by Wilcox.

Date: December 9, 1935
Title: Christmas Shopping
Cast: Jim Jordan (Fibber), Marian Jordan (Molly), Harlow Wilcox
Summary: Much to Molly's displeasure, Fibber gets involved with a number of toys at the Wistful Vista Department Store.
Music: Rico Marcelli: "Liza," "Red Sails in the Sunset," (Kay Donna, vocal), "You Are My Lucky Star"
Running Gag: "'Tain't funny, McGee" (Molly)
Comments: Fibber is still living up to his name with another tall tale about tobacco and rubber trees. Fibber's character often tended toward the childish and Molly's scolding attitude indicates she is treating him more like a mother than a wife.

Date: December 16, 1935
Title: Bridge Game
Cast: Jim Jordan (Fibber), Marian Jordan (Molly, Geraldine), Harlow Wilcox, Hugh Studebaker (Silly Watson)

Summary: Fibber and Watson are more of a hindrance than a help as Molly tries to learn how to play bridge from an instructor.
Music: Rico Marcelli: "When My Baby Smiles at Me," "Why Shouldn't I?" (Kay Donna, vocal), "Take Me Back to My Boots and Saddles "(Emery D'Arcy, vocal)
Running Gags: "'Tain't funny, McGee" (Fibber), tongue twister starting with Two-Draw McGee (Fibber)
Comments: Harlow is found lurking in the closet, which in 1935 had an open door policy. There is as much playing with words as there is card playing in this episode with terms such as *suitable bid* and *biddable suit*.

Date: December 30, 1935
Title: New Year's Celebration
Cast: Jim Jordan (Fibber), Marian Jordan (Molly, Geraldine), Harlow Wilcox (head waiter), Hugh Studebaker (Silly Watson)
Summary: The McGees get dressed in their best clothes, then go to the Wistful Vista Nightclub to celebrate the onset of 1936.
Music: Rico Marcelli: "Lady Be Good," "When Day is Done" (Audrey Call, violin), "Here's to Romance" (Emery D'Arcy), "I Found a Dream"
Running Gags: Tongue twister starting with Broadcloth McGee (Fibber), "Gotta get them brakes fixed" (Fibber), "'Tain't funny, McGee" (Fibber)
Comments: Molly's voice for Geraldine is quite a bit different than her natural voice. Quinn is already using clever ways to make people listen to the integrated commercial like having the cigarette girl's voice change to Harlow's. The full name of Studebaker's character, first introduced on the November 4th episode, bears the Quinn stamp of eccentricity: Silvius Leviticus Deuteronomy Watson.

Date: January 13, 1936
Title: Dog Trainer/Tutor Mixup
Cast: Jim Jordan (Fibber), Marian Jordan (Molly), Harlow Wilcox (mailman, butler), Hugh Studebaker (Silly Watson), Isabel Randolph (Mrs. Kuppenheim)
Summary: At Molly's urging Fibber goes to an employment agency which leads to them being sent to the wrong address in search of a job.
Music: Rico Marcelli: "Cosi Cosa," "Lady of the Evening," "I Feel a Song Coming On"
Running Gags: "Gotta get them brakes fixed" (Fibber), "'Tain't funny, McGee" (Molly once, Fibber once), tongue twister starting with Pedigree McGee (Fibber)
Comments: Isabel Randolph appears for the first time. This is the first instance of the humor of confusion resulting from parties talking about two different subjects. Harlow gets a chance to try an affected voice that even amuses him to the breaking point. Appropriately, a man named Fibber receives an award as the World's Champion Liar from O.C. Hewlitt of the Burlington Liar's Club.

Date: January 20, 1936
Title: Managing Drugstore
Cast: Jim Jordan (Fibber), Marian Jordan (Molly, Geraldine), Harlow Wilcox, Isabel Randolph (hiccupping woman), Tommy Tucker (gruff man, horse)
Summary: When the owner of the Wistful Vista Drugstore steps out, Fibber and Molly step in to dispense remedies and advice to customers.
Music: Rico Marcelli: "High on a Hilltop," "Alone"
Running Gags: "'Tain't funny, McGee" (Fibber), "Better get them brakes fixed" (Fibber)
Comments: Though Geraldine is a motor-mouthed marvel, her words whizz by so fast the effect of some of the gags are lost. The contagious hiccups even carry over to "Hardglow" Wilcox.

Date: January 27, 1936
Title: Learning the Restaurant Business
Cast: Jim Jordan (Fibber), Marian Jordan (Molly), Harlow Wilcox, Bill Thompson (Nick Depopolis)
Summary: In the All-American Restaurant Fibber wreaks havoc in the dining area and kitchen.
Music: Rico Marcelli: "Say It with Music," "With All My Heart" (Audrey Call, violin)
Running Gags: "'Tain't funny, McGee" (Molly once, Fibber once), "'Tain't funny, Molly" (Fibber), tongue twisters starting with Hi-Ho McGee and Hammerlock McGee (Fibber)
Comments: Bill Thompson appears for the first time. This is one time Fibber really does the dishes...absolutely no good.

Date: February 3, 1936
Title: Crime Solver McGee
Cast: Jim Jordan (Fibber), Marian Jordan (Molly), Harlow Wilcox, Hugh Studebaker (Silly Watson)
Summary: A visit to the Wistful Vista police station results in the McGees accompanying officers to interrogate a suspected shoplifter.
Music: Rico Marcelli: "Alexander's Ragtime Band," "Broken Record" (Charles LaVere, vocal), "Cheek to Cheek"
Running Gags: "'Tain't funny, McGee" (Molly once, Fibber once), "'Tain't funny, Molly" (Fibber), "You better get them brakes fixed, Sarge" (Fibber), tongue twister starting with Peacock McGee (Fibber)
Comments: This is an episode in which the fingerprints of the sponsor are all over the place. An announcement of the winner of Rico's song contest points to the following week's show.

Date: February 10, 1936
Title: Job in Grand Rapids
Cast: Jim Jordan (Fibber), Marian Jordan (Molly, Geraldine, child, mother), Harlow Wilcox, Bill Thompson (Nick Depopolis, taxi driver)
Summary: After seeing an ad offering employment in the furniture business, the McGees board a train bound for Grand Rapids.
Music: Rico Marcelli: "I Can't Give You Anything but Love," "Life Begins When You're in Love," "The Old Kitchen Clock" (Clark Dennis, vocal), "Saddle Your Blues to a Wild Mustang"
Running Gag: Tongue twister starting with Overstuffed McGee (Fibber)
Comments: Naturally the number of Fibber and Molly's train car is 79. Like Mary's little lamb, wherever the McGees go Harlow is sure to follow to plug the product. "The Old Kitchen Clock" is the prize-winning song in Rico's contest.

Date: February 17, 1936
Title: Visiting Fire Station
Cast: Jim Jordan (Fibber), Marian Jordan (Molly, Geraldine, old lady), Harlow Wilcox, Bill Thompson (Nick Depopolis)
Summary: Fibber and Molly, after stopping at a fire station, accompany firefighters as they go to extinguish a blaze.
Music: Rico Marcelli: "I'm Shooting High," "Moon Over Miami," "Yours" (Annette King, vocal)
Running Gags: "'Tain't funny, McGee" (Molly), tongue twister starting with Helmet McGee (Fibber),
Comments: Harlow's introduction is quite futuristic as he locates the McGees via a television screen at the fire station, which is naturally located at 14th and Oak. The old lady character taken by Marian is sometimes known as Old Lady Wheedledeck. Newcomer Annette King sings one of the compositions in Rico's song contest.

Date: February 24, 1936
Title: Waiting for Radio Repairman
Cast: Jim Jordan (Fibber), Marian Jordan (Molly, Mrs. Wheedledeck, Geraldine), Harlow Wilcox, Bill Thompson (Nick Depopolis, hospital keeper)
Summary: The McGees receive a number of unexpected visitors while waiting for a man to repair their radio.
Music: Rico Marcelli: "Midnight in Paris," "I Found You in the Moonlight" (Bob Hanan, vocal), "Dinner for One, Please James" (Audrey Call, violin), "I'll See You in My Dreams"
Running Gag: "'Tain't funny, McGee" (Molly)

Comments: This episode contains an early instance of Fibber singing a verse to himself as he putters about the house. The show's writer takes a jab at himself by naming the deranged man Mr. Quinn.

Date: March 2, 1936
Title: Encyclopedia Salesman
Cast: Jim Jordan (Fibber), Marian Jordan (Molly, Mrs. Wheedledeck, little girl), Harlow Wilcox, Bill Thompson (disgruntled man at door, Nick Depopolis)
Summary: Fibber and Molly go door to door selling encyclopedias with no success.
Music: Rico Marcelli: "Whose Honey Are You?," "I'll Feast My Eyes on You" (Charlie LaVere, vocal), "March Winds and April Showers"
Running Gags: None
Comments: Wilcox mentions "Marian and Jim" in the opening credits. The closing commercial offers a pair of Fibber and Molly tops, one of the few premiums offered by Johnson's Wax on this program.

Date: March 9, 1936
Title: Pickpockets on the Bus
Cast: Jim Jordan (Fibber), Marian Jordan (Molly, Geraldine, Mrs. Wheedledeck, little girl), Harlow Wilcox, Hugh Studebaker (Silly Watson), Bill Thompson (con man)
Summary: After being warned about pickpockets, Fibber fears the worst on a bus headed for Jamestown.
Music: Rico Marcelli: "You Are My Lucky Star," "Please Believe Me," "You Hit the Spot," "Cheek to Cheek"
Running Gags: None
Comments: Molly's Aunt Sarah is mentioned for the first time. In his role as the swindler, Bill Thompson uses the W.C. Fields voice that will eventually become bombastic Horatio K. Boomer.

Date: March 16, 1936
Title: Checkroom Attendants
Cast: Jim Jordan (Fibber), Marian Jordan (Molly, old lady, Geraldine, little girl), Harlow Wilcox, Bill Thompson (train inquirer)
Summary: The McGees accept a gallimaufry of items and a bit of guff at the checkroom of the Wistful Vista railroad station.
Music: Rico Marcelli: "We Saw the Sea," "When a Gypsy Makes His Violin Cry" (Audrey Call, violin), "Margie"
Running Gags: "'Tain't funny, McGee" (Molly once, parrot once), tongue twister starting with Paraguay McGee (Fibber)
Comments: Naturally the most important check number is 79 and the address on Oak Street has a 14 in it. A trombone is the instrument of choice so Quinn can insert the wheeze about keeping an eye on the derby.

Date: March 23, 1936
Title: Spring Cleaning
Cast: Jim Jordan (Fibber), Harlow Wilcox, Hugh Studebaker (Silly Watson), Bill Thompson (Nick Depopolis, con man), Rico Marcelli
Summary: While Molly is visiting Aunt Sarah, Fibber cleans the house with the help of friends.
Music: Rico Marcelli: "Bugle Call Rag," "Alone," "Let Yourself Go," "No Other One"
Running Gags: None
Comments: Rico has a rare speaking part so he can exchange some banter with Fibber about being alone. At the end of the show Wilcox explains Molly's absence is due to Marian's laryngitis.

Date: March 30, 1936
Title: Hospital Room
Cast: Jim Jordan (Fibber), Marian Jordan (Molly, old lady), Harlow Wilcox, Hugh Studebaker (Silly Watson), Bill Thompson (Nick Depopolis), Cliff Arquette (old man, doctor)
Summary: Because rooms in Pinecrest are scarce, Fibber pretends to be ill so the McGees can stay the night at a hospital.
Music: Rico Marcelli: "Wake Up and Sing," "Melancholy Baby," "Let's Face the Music and Dance"
Running Gag: "'Tain't funny, McGee' (Molly)
Comments: Cliff Arquette appears in a dual role. The old man says at one point "That ain't the way I heered it" because the character is virtually deaf, not as a lead-in to a gag as told by the Old Timer played by Bill Thompson in future programs.

Date: April 6, 1936
Title: Trading in Car
Cast: Jim Jordan (Fibber), Marian Jordan (Molly, little girl), Harlow Wilcox (car salesman), Hugh Studebaker (Silly Watson), Bill Thompson (J. Widdicomb Blotto)
Summary: The McGees offer their car to dealers to see how much it might be worth.
Music: Rico Marcelli: "Wah! Hoo!," "Alone at a Table for Two" (Audrey Call, violin), "I Love You"
Running Gag: "'Tain't funny, McGee" (Fibber)
Comments: Wilcox does a fair job as the tony Rolls Nice dealer. Blotto by any other name will be known as Horatio K. Boomer.

Date: April 13, 1936
Title: Taking Over Hotel Desk

Cast: Jim Jordan (Fibber), Marian Jordan (Molly, old lady), Harlow Wilcox, Rico Marcelli, Bill Thompson (Nick Depopolis), Cliff Arquette (Walliford Tuttle Gildersleeve, man in hall), Isabel Randolph (Mrs. Gildersleeve)
Summary: Fibber and Molly take over a hotel desk after McGee inadvertently locks the clerk in a vault.
Music: Rico Marcelli: "Lost," "Cosi Cosa," "Sleepy Time Gal"
Running Gag: Tongue twister starting with Hi Ho McGee (Fibber)
Comments: This marks the first time *Gildersleeve* is used for characters on the show. Harlow again reminds listeners how to get the Fibber and Molly tops.

Date: April 20, 1936
Title: Streetcar Motorman McGee
Cast: Jim Jordan (Fibber), Marian Jordan (Molly, passenger, little girl), Harlow Wilcox (man on street), Bill Thompson (passenger, John), Hugh Studebaker (Silly Watson)
Summary: When the motorman abandons the streetcar, the McGees take over the running of the car but take in very few fares.
Music: Rico Marcelli: "Goody, Goody," "Let Yourself Go," "Old Rockin' Chair" (Audrey Call, violin), "You"
Running Gags: "'Tain't funny, McGee" (Fibber), tongue twister starting with Motorman McGee (Fibber)
Comments: This is another early instance of Bill Thompson using the W.C. Fields voice that will become Horatio K. Boomer. He asks the question "What did I do with my star?," but doesn't start searching his person and pull out objects as he will shortly.

Date: June 22, 1936
Title: Employment Agency
Cast: Jim Jordan (Fibber, Mort Toops), Marian Jordan (Molly), Harlow Wilcox, Bill Thompson (Chinese restaurateur, Angus McPherson McTavish, man), Hugh Studebaker (Silly Watson), Isabel Randolph (woman), Ted Weems
Summary: Fibber and Molly question a number of people who come to the employment agency they are temporarily running (into the ground).
Music: Ted Weems: "She Shall Have Music," "Twilight on the Trail" (Perry Como, vocal), "Great Big Man from the South"
Running Gags: None
Comments: Elmo Tanner whistles part of "Save Your Sorrow for Tomorrow" on this and a number of other subsequent episodes. It is significant that the Chinese restaurant is located at 14 W. Oak Street as that number and street name will be used often in the coming years. Quinn cleverly induces listeners to attend to the integrated commercial as they have to follow Harlow's fractured French. The laughing bit by Mort actually slows down the show instead of enlivening it.

Date: July 20, 1936
Title: Trailer Camp
Cast: Jim Jordan (Fibber), Marian Jordan (Molly, little girl), Harlow Wilcox, Bill Thompson (Horatio W. Boomer), Ted Weems, Red Ingle
Summary: The McGees borrow trouble in a tourist camp where almost everyone they meet is in a borrowing mood.
Music: Ted Weems: "Cross Patch," These Foolish Things" (Perry Como, vocal), "I'm a Lone Cowhand" (Red Ingle, vocal), "Nobody's Sweetheart"
Running Gags: "Gotta get them brakes fixed" (Fibber), "'Tain't funny, McGee" (Molly)
Comments: The flamboyant light-fingered character portrayed by Bill Thompson identifies himself as Horatio W. Boomer. Liza Muggin, the name of the camp's flighty recreational director, is a play on a popular song of the day "I'se a Muggin.'"

Date: July 27, 1936
Title: Great Lakes Exposition
Cast: Jim Jordan (Fibber), Marian Jordan (Molly, Mrs. Wheedledeck, little girl), Harlow Wilcox, Bill Thompson (weight guesser)
Summary: Fibber hopes to meet an old friend when the McGees walk the grounds of the Great Lakes Exposition in Cleveland.
Music: Ted Weems: "San Francisco," "There Isn't Any Limit to My Love" (Perry Como, vocal), "I Take to You" (Parker Gibbs, vocal), "Some of These Days"
Running Gag: "'Tain't funny, Molly" (Fibber)
Comments: This episode takes place in the convention hall at the Exposition Center in Cleveland. Fibber and Molly's affection for fairs and carnivals mentioned by Harlow also applies to writer Don Quinn because those venues present endless opportunities for gags.

Date: August 3, 1936
Title: Captain of Ship
Cast: Jim Jordan (Fibber), Marian Jordan (Molly, old lady, little girl), Bob Brown, Bill Thompson (Scotsman, lighthouse keeper), Red Ingle
Summary: As Fibber fills in for the captain of a yacht with his usual bravado, he throws caution to the wind.
Music: Ted Weems: "He Saw the Sea," "No Regrets' (Perry Como, vocal), "On the Beach at Bali-Bali" (whistling by Elmo Tanner)
Running Gags: "'Tain't funny, McGee" (Fibber), tongue twister starting with Whaler McGee (Fibber), "Gotta get them brakes fixed" (Fibber)
Comments: The mighty Quinn loads this vessel with numerous nautical puns. Just as McGee replaces the head of the ship, Bob Brown substitutes for Harlow Wilcox.

Date: August 10, 1936
Title: Militia Camp
Cast: Jim Jordan (Fibber), Marian Jordan (Molly, old lady), Bob Brown, Hugh Studebaker (Silly Watson), Bill Thompson (Scotsman, guard, Horatio K. Boomer), Ted Weems, Red Ingle (Private Ingle)
Summary: The McGees inspect the summer encampment of the Wistful Vista militia where Fibber is put in charge by a colonel.
Music: Ted Weems: "There's Something about a Soldier," "Take My Heart' (Perry Como, vocal), "Hey Straw"
Running Gag: Tongue twister starting with Caliper McGee (Fibber)
Comments: Bob Brown pitches for the Johnson's Wax team in relief of Harlow Wilcox who was sidelined with appendicitis. Horatio now has the familiar K middle initial.

Date: August 17, 1936
Title: Flying Lessons
Cast: Jim Jordan (Fibber), Marian Jordan (Molly, old lady, little girl), Bob Brown, Hugh Studebaker (Silly Watson), Bill Thompson (Scotsman, Horatio K. Boomer)
Summary: At the Wistful Vista Airport Fibber prepares to take his first flight as a pilot.
Music: Ted Weems: "Bye Bye, Baby," "Dance My Way to Heaven" (Perry Como, vocal), "Knock, Knock"
Running Gags: None
Comments: Bob Brown again subs for Harlow Wilcox. The principal action takes place at the end which unfolds like one of Fibber's tall tales.

Date: August 24, 1936
Title: Solving a Mystery as Detectives
Cast: Jim Jordan (Fibber), Marian Jordan (Molly, old lady), Harlow Wilcox, Bill Thompson (Horatio K. Boomer, officer, Ah Sing), Ted Weems (Butch Weems), Red Ingle (Sargent)
Summary: The McGees attempt to find the missing Chester Checkstub.
Music: Ted Weems: "After You're Gone," "Canadian Capers," "Rendezvous with a Dream" (Perry Como, vocal), "Them There Eyes"
Running Gag: Cigar routine (Fibber, Horatio)
Comments: Harlow gets a warm welcome upon his return to the program. The Checkstub mansion is located at that Wistful Vista hot corner, 14th and Oak.

Date: August 31, 1936
Title: Eighteenth Wedding Anniversary
Cast: Jim Jordan (Fibber), Marian Jordan (Molly, Geraldine, little girl), Harlow Wilcox, Hugh Studebaker (Silly Watson), Bill Thompson (Horatio K.

Boomer), Red Ingle (mailman), Parker Gibbs, Perry Como, Elmo Tanner, Ted Weems
Summary: Fibber and Molly clean a vacant lot next door in preparation for a garden party celebrating their anniversary.
Music: Ted Weems "Sing, Baby, Sing," "When I'm with You" (Perry Como, vocal), "Rose Room," "Dinah"
Running Gag: "'Tain't funny, McGee" (Molly)
Comments: The number of years and the date are for real as James Jordan and Marian Driscoll were actually married August 31, 1918. Members of the Weems team have small parts to reinforce the impression that a fair number of people will be attending the party. The carnival atmosphere present in the early shows is punctuated by the surprise ending of this adventure.

Date: September 7, 1936
Title: Judge of Domestic Relations Court
Cast: Jim Jordan (Fibber), Marian Jordan (Molly, Mary, old lady), Harlow Wilcox, Hugh Studebaker (Silly Watson), Bill Thompson (McTavish, Horatio K. Boomer), Ted Weems
Summary: Fibber and Molly quickly adjudicate a number of disputes involving money and marriages.
Music: Ted Weems: "Sing, Sing, Sing," "Did I Remember?" (Perry Como, vocal), "Ida"/"Sweet Sue," "Sweet Georgia Brown"
Running Gags: None
Comments: The orchestra works a goofus and bazooka into the novelty number. Don Quinn plants a courtroom full of puns into the script. Marian steps down from the bench to take the parts of Mary Doe and Peggy Hotchkiss.

Date: September 14, 1936
Title: Dance Hall
Cast: Jim Jordan (Fibber, Mort Toops), Marian Jordan (Molly, old lady), Harlow Wilcox, Hugh Studebaker (Silly Watson), Bill Thompson (ticket taker, Scotsman, Mike Houilhan), Ted Weems
Summary: At the Palais de Hoof Ballroom the McGees look for a definition of swing music while Fibber looks out for a roughneck who threatened him.
Music: Ted Weems: "Linger Awhile," "The Stars Fell Out of Heaven" (Perry Como, vocal), "Sing Me a Swing Song," "That's A Plenty"
Running Gag: Tongue twister starting with Featherfoot McGee (Fibber)
Comments: The ticket taker with the Boomer voice slips in a terse definition of Mae West: "Two hips and a hooray." Fibber turns Popeye in the finish that's a real knockout.

Date: September 28, 1936
Title: At the Racetrack
Cast: Jim Jordan (Fibber), Marian Jordan (Molly, little girl), Harlow Wilcox, Bill Thompson (Scotsman, Horatio K. Boomer)
Summary: Fibber and Molly receive tips on various horses from people they meet at the track before deciding to place their bet.
Music: Ted Weems: "Mr. Bojangles of Harlem," "Through the Courtesy of Love" (Perry Como, vocal), "When My Baby Smiles at Me"
Running Gags: "'Tain't funny, McGee" (Molly), tongue twister starting with Turf Topper McGee (Fibber)
Comments: The ending of this episode is clipped and some of the dialogue between the little girl and Fibber is absent. Horatio delivers a segment of the "Where I'd put that" routine which will be extended in later shows. There is a neat tie-in between a horse and the final musical number.

Date: October 5, 1936
Title: Shopping for Clothes
Cast: Jim Jordan (Fibber), Marian Jordan (Molly, old lady), Harlow Wilcox, Bill Thompson (Russian, Scotsman, Chief of Police)
Summary: Buying a fall outfit for Fibber reaps a bountiful harvest for Molly.
Music: Ted Weems: "You Know That I Know," "My Kingdom for a Kiss" (Perry Como, vocal), "A Five-Piece Band"
Running Gags: "Gotta get them brakes fixed" (Fibber), "'Tain't funny, McGee" (Molly)
Comments: The Bon Ton department store, cornerstone of the Wistful Vista commercial district, is mentioned for the first time. "Who made your bows?" is just one of the punny gags that ring the gong in this episode.

Date: October 12, 1936
Title: Dude Ranch
Cast: Jim Jordan (Fibber), Marian Jordan (Molly, little girl, old lady), Harlow Wilcox, Bill Thompson (Chinese cook, Indian, bellhop), Ted Weems
Summary: Fibber finds western ranch life too tame for his liking.
Music: Ted Weems; "I Got Rhythm," "The Way You Look Tonight" (Perry Como, vocal), "Whoopie Ti Yi Yo"
Running Gags: "'Tain't funny, McGee" (Molly), tongue twister starting with Coyote Killer McGee (Fibber)
Comments: G-Bar-C, the name of the ranch, is a subtle way of slipping in a plug for Glo-Coat. Bill Thompson's Indian sounds just like Horatio K. Boomer.

On October 19 the McGees took their show on the road to Detroit before returning to Chicago for episodes heard on November 2, 9, 16, and 23. On November 30 the broadcast was from Minneapolis. The following week the cast of *Fibber McGee and Molly* returned to Chicago.

Date: December 7, 1936
Title: Managing Jewelry Store
Cast: Jim Jordan (Fibber), Marian Jordan (Molly, Mrs. Wearybottom, little girl, old lady), Harlow Wilcox, Hugh Studebaker (Silly Watson), Bill Thompson (Scotsman, Horatio K. Boomer, officer)
Summary: The McGees wait on customers while the owner of a jewelry shop is out for the day.
Music: Ted Weems: "Do You Mean It?" "Who Loves You?" (Perry Como, vocal), "Say It with Music"
Running Gag: Tongue twister starting with Clock Doctor McGee (Fibber)
Comments: Boomer mentions "a short beer" for the first time, words that will become part of his routine when he pats himself down looking for various items. Harlow's two brief plugs at the shop are really shoehorned in as no pretense is made that he even enters or leaves the building. Molly's Uncle Dennis is mentioned for the first time.

Date: December 14, 1936
Title: Bucking Bronco Contest
Cast: Jim Jordan (Fibber), Marian Jordan (Molly, little girl, old lady), Harlow Wilcox, Hugh Studebaker (Silly Watson), Bill Thompson (rodeo manager), Ted Weems
Summary: At the rodeo Fibber gradually gains confidence that he can stay on a horse for three minutes to win $100.
Music: Ted Weems: "My Red Letter Day," "It's De-Lovely" (Perry Como, vocal), "It Ain't Right," "Who?"
Running Gags: "'Tain't funny, McGee" (Molly), tongue twister starting with Lightning McGee (Fibber)
Comments: A stadium where the rodeo is held suddenly looms up as another structure on the Wistful Vista map. The *folk/joke/yolk* patter is an early example of the shrewd little girl outsmarting McGee.

Date: December 21, 1936
Title: Post Office Job
Cast: Jim Jordan (Fibber), Marian Jordan (Molly, Mrs. Wearybottom, little girl), Harlow Wilcox, Hugh Studebaker (Silly Watson), Bill Thompson (Horatio K. Boomer, Russian clerk), Ted Weems, Perry Como
Summary: Fibber and Molly manage a busy post office window during the Christmas rush.
Music: Ted Weems: "With Plenty of Money and You," "I've Got You Under My Skin" (Perry Como, vocal)
Running Gag: "'Tain't funny, McGee" (Molly)
Comments: The Wistful Vista Post Office is located at 14th and Oak. Boomer offers a precursor to the "Where I'd put that" bit as he looks for credentials.

The "Farley Good" response is a nod toward Postmaster General James A. Farley. Scriptwriter Don Quinn receives credit at the end along with Thompson, Weems, and Studebaker.

Date: December 28, 1936
Title: Chicken Soup for Fibber
Cast: Jim Jordan (Fibber), Marian Jordan (Molly, little girl, Mrs. Wearybottom), Harlow Wilcox, Hugh Studebaker (Silly Watson), Bill Thompson (McTavish, Doctor Boomer), Elmo Tanner
Summary: After Fibber pretends to be ill and Molly puts him to bed, visitors stop by to offer remedies to help him get well.
Music: Ted Weems: "You Know That I Know," "In the Chapel in the Moonlight" (Perry Como, vocal), "From Coast to Coast," "All's Fair in Love and War"
Running Gag: Tongue twister starting with Ski Skipper McGee (Fibber)
Comments: For the second week Harlow's introduction places Fibber and Molly in the studio. Perceptive Molly sees through Fibber's malingering when she twists his bedbound line into "You just rest there and lie."

Date: March 1, 1937
Title: Pickpockets on the Bus (revised version)
Cast: Jim Jordan (Fibber), Marian Jordan (Molly, Geraldine, little girl, old lady), Harlow Wilcox, Hugh Studebaker (Silly Watson), Bill Thompson (Scotsman, Russian, deaf man, Horatio K. Boomer), Ted Weems
Summary: After being warned about pickpockets, Fibber fears the worst on a bus headed for Johnstown.
Music: Ted Weems: "Ridin' High," "Rainbow on the River," (Perry Como, vocal), "Finesse" (whistling by Elmo Tanner)
Running Gags: "'Tain't funny, McGee" (Molly), tongue twister starting with Piggyback McGee (Fibber)
Comments: The story is an amended version of the March 9, 1936 episode. Among the changes are the addition of running gags, more characters played by Bill Thompson, destination altered from Jamestown to Johnstown, and relative to be visited from Aunt Sarah to Uncle Dennis.

Date: March 8, 1937
Title: Telegram to Sponsor
Cast: Jim Jordan (Fibber), Marian Jordan (Molly), Harlow Wilcox, Bill Thompson (Russian, Horatio K. Boomer), Ted Weems, Perry Como, Elmo Tanner
Summary: At a telegraph office the McGees consider how best to thank their sponsor on the occasion of their 100th broadcast.
Music: Ted Weems: "He Ain't Got Rhythm," "Dancing to Love's Call" (Perry Como, vocal), "The Telegraph Song" (Parker Gibbs, vocal)

Running Gags: "'Tain't funny, McGee" (Molly), Tongue twister starting with Morse Code McGee (Fibber)
Comments: Blowhard Boomer pats himself down looking for 42 cents and comes up with an empty proposal to send a telegram collect. Fibber and Molly poke fun at the sound effect of a door slam after the early exchange with Wilcox. Fibber addresses the Russian character as Vodka as he has in passing on a number of episodes.

Date: March 15, 1937
Title: Managing Hardware Store
Cast: Jim Jordan (Fibber), Marian Jordan (Molly, old lady, little girl), Harlow Wilcox, Hugh Studebaker (Silly Watson), Bill Thompson (Russian, Horatio K. Boomer), Isabel Randolph (Mrs. J. Uppington Upson)
Summary: While temporarily in charge of the hardware store, the McGees handle a variety of customers while Fibber cuts a bench down to size.
Music: Ted Weems: "Good Night My Lucky Day" "Moonlight and Shadows" (Perry Como, vocal), "Twinkle, Twinkle, Little Star" (whistling by Elmo Tanner), "Oh, Say Can You Swing"
Running Gag: Tongue twister starting with Faucet Fixer McGee (Fibber)
Comments: The Wistful Vista Hardware Store is located at 14th and Oak. The door slam sound effect mentioned by the McGees the previous week really gets a workout on this episode. Isabel Randolph's haughty socialite Mrs. J. Uppington Upson will become Abigail Uppington later in 1937.

Date: March 22, 1937
Title: Interviewing Vaudeville Talent
Cast: Jim Jordan (Fibber), Marian Jordan (Molly, little girl), Harlow Wilcox, Hugh Studebaker (Silly Watson), Bill Thompson (Ivan, Horatio K. Boomer), Perry Como, Ted Weems, Elmo Tanner
Summary: Fibber and Molly judge the merits of various performers in preparation for putting on a vaudeville show.
Music: Ted Weems: "My Red Letter Day," "Summer Night" (Perry Como, vocal), "Floating on a Bubble" (whistling by Elmo Tanner)
Running Gag: "'Tain't funny, McGee" (Molly)
Comments: The Bijou Theater is mentioned for the first time. The closing alerts the audience in a jocular manner that the program will be changing time in several weeks.

Date: March 29, 1937
Title: Presenting Vaudeville Show
Cast: Jim Jordan (Fibber, Mort Toops), Marian Jordan (Molly, old lady, Mrs. Wearybottom), Harlow Wilcox, Hugh Studebaker (Silly Watson), Bill Thompson (Donald McDonald, Serge, Horatio K. Boomer)

Summary: As the McGees introduce acts at the talent show, Fibber and Molly prove they can take a hint while taking hits from a persistent heckler.
Music: Ted Weems: "Give a Little Thought to Me," "Funiculi Funicula," "When the Poppies Bloom Again" (Perry Como, vocal), "The Girl on the Police Gazette" (whistling by Elmo Tanner), "One in a Million"
Running Gag: "'Tain't funny, McGee" (Molly)
Comments: It is not surprising that Jim and Marian account for most of the non-musical talent because they are the talent listeners tuned in to hear every week. Boomer seems to mend his ways, though it is only a matter of time before he returns to form.

Date: April 5, 1937
Title: Gardening Urge
Cast: Jim Jordan (Fibber), Marian Jordan (Molly, little girl), Harlow Wilcox, Hugh Studebaker (O'Shea), Bill Thompson (Nicolas), Isabel Randolph, Ted Weems
Summary: Fibber solicits advice about gardening before planting a variety of seeds in the yard with grim results.
Music: Ted Weems: "This Year's Kisses," "Smoke Rings" (Perry Como, vocal), "I'm Bubbling Over," "April Showers" (whistling by Elmo Tanner)
Running Gag: Tongue twister starting with Calla Lily McGee (Fibber)
Comments: The first act almost seems like a continuation from the vaudeville episodes with the McGees asking people to speak into a microphone. Emphasis on the time change to take place April 12 interrupts one of the musical numbers and also is the focus of bits by Thompson, Isabel Randolph, and the little girl which close the program.

Date: April 12, 1937
Title: Managing Night Club
Cast: Jim Jordan (Fibber), Marian Jordan (Molly, Mrs. Wearybottom), Harlow Wilcox, Isabel Randolph (lady), Hugh Studebaker (Silly Watson), Bill Thompson (Chef, hood, Scotsman, Horatio K. Boomer)
Summary: Fibber gets unwanted protection from unsavory sources after he opens a night club.
Music: Ted Weems: "Boo Hoo," "My Last Affair" (Perry Como, vocal), "The Love Bug Will Bite You," "12th Street Rag"
Running Gags: None
Comments: *Fibber McGee and Molly* is now being broadcast at 8:00 Central, 9:00 Eastern. Gangster Mulligan seems more of square shooter than shifty Boomer, who leaves Fibber holding the bag.

Date: April 19, 1937
Title: Officer of the Bank
Cast: Jim Jordan (Fibber), Marian Jordan (Molly, little girl), Harlow Wilcox, Hugh Studebaker (Silly Watson), Bill Thompson (Teller, H. Post), Elmo Tanner, Ted Weems
Summary: Fibber assumes the position of an official in an empty bank office where he handles legal matters with his usual braggadocio.
Music: Ted Weems: "Jamboree," "September in the Rain" (Perry Como, vocal), "Fiddle Dee" (whistling by Elmo Tanner), "You Can Tell She Comes from Dixie," "Margie"
Running Gags: "'Tain't funny, McGee (Molly), tongue twister starting with Cash Counting McGee (Fibber)
Comments: The First National Bank is located at 14th and Oak. For the client H. Post Bill Thompson assumes the voice that will become that of the Old Timer. At one point Molly utters a warning that could be issued to her husband on many a night: "I think you better find out just what you're doing here."

Date: April 26, 1937
Title: Preparing to Leave for Hollywood
Cast: Jim Jordan (Fibber), Marian Jordan (Molly, Geraldine, Mrs. Wearybottom), Harlow Wilcox, Hugh Studebaker (Barrymel Lionmore), Ted Weems
Summary: Prior to leaving for Hollywood to make the film *This Way Please*, Fibber gets some acting tips from a dramatic teacher.
Music: Ted Weems: "Love Is News," "There's Something in the Air" (Perry Como, vocal), "When Hearts Are Young" (whistling by Elmo Tanner), "Slap That Bass"
Running Gag: "'Tain't funny, McGee" (Molly)
Comments: The McGees and Wilcox drop lots of names of Hollywood stars in this episode including that of Buddy Rogers, who has a featured role in *This Way Please*. The mention of Tuffy Goff is an in-joke referring to the man who played Abner Peabody on *Lum and Abner*. The show will be broadcast from Hollywood until July 12th when it returns to Chicago.

Date: May 3, 1937
Title: Indian Trouble
Cast: Jim Jordan (Fibber), Marian Jordan (Molly, little girl, old lady), Harlow Wilcox, Bill Thompson (prospector, Indian), Jimmy Grier, Joy Hodges
Summary: On their way to Hollywood Fibber and Molly are seized by Indians.
Music: Jimmy Grier: "That's A Plenty," "Raggin' the Scale," "Southern Hospitality" (Joy Hodges, vocal)
Running Gags: "Gotta get them brakes fixed "(Fibber), "'Tain't funny, McGee" (Molly), tongue twister starting with Death Dealer McGee (Fibber)

Comments: The program will be broadcast from Hollywood until completion of work on *This Way Please* with Jimmy Grier's Orchestra providing the music. Bill Thompson uses his Old Timer voice for the prospector and Boomer voice for the Indian Chief.

Date: May 10, 1937
Title: Patrolman McGee
Cast: Jim Jordan (Fibber), Marian Jordan (Molly, little girl), Harlow Wilcox, Bill Thompson (Director, Japanese man, Horatio K. Boomer), Tommy Harris
Summary: After Fibber preens too much in preparation for his movie role, Molly makes him get a job as a patrolman which leads to both of them being taken for a ride.
Music: Jimmy Grier: "They All Laughed," "It's the Mood That I'm In" (Tommy Harris, vocal), "Doing the Suzie Q," "Nagasaki," "Swing High Swing Low"
Running Gags: "'Tain't funny, McGee (Molly), tongue twister starting with Jerry Jitzu McGee (Fibber), "Where I'd put that" looking for keys (Boomer)
Comments: Boomer puts all the pieces together on his routine for this con job. Jim punctuates one of his longer tongue twisters with "I made it."

Date: May 17, 1937
Title: School of Dramatic Arts
Cast: Jim Jordan (Fibber), Marian Jordan (Molly, Mrs. Wearybottom, little girl), Harlow Wilcox, Bill Thompson (Scotsman, ventriloquist, Russian), Jimmy Grier, Tommy Harris
Summary: Fibber opens the Fibber McGee Academy of Dramatic Art, Acting, and Bagpipe Instruction on Hollywood Blvd. where he is less than a ripping success.
Music: Jimmy Grier: "52nd Street," "Mr. Ghost Goes to Town," "Too Marvelous for Words" (Tommy Harris, vocal), "After You're Gone," "I'm Bubbling Over"
Running Gags: "'Tain't funny, Mrs. McGee "(Fibber), "'Tain't funny, McGee" (Molly)
Comments: Molly's pointed warning about the contract on the desk prepares listeners for the denouement.

Date: May 24, 1937
Title: Picnic Outing
Cast: Jim Jordan (Fibber), Marian Jordan (Molly, Geraldine, old lady, little girl), Harlow Wilcox, Bill Thompson (Irishman, Russian)
Summary: Fibber and Molly get the runaround as they move from one place to another trying to enjoy a picnic lunch.

Music: Jimmy Grier: "I'm Hatin' This Waitin' Around," "The Goona Goo," "They Can't Take That Away from Me" (Tommy Harris, vocal), "Limehouse Blues," "Boo Hoo"

Running Gags: "Gotta get them brakes fixed" (Fibber), "'Tain't funny, McGee" (Molly), tongue twister starting with Timber McGee (Fibber)

Comments: Fibber and Molly, though still in Hollywood, seem to have been magically transported out of urban California back to Wistful Vista for this adventure in the green, green grass of home. The final scene takes place in their backyard and Molly pointedly answers the phone with the familiar "79 Wistful Vista." Although the first person to move the McGees along is not identified as an officer, everyone senses that when Bill Thompson gets his Irish up, he is about to lower the boom of authority.

Date: June 14, 1937
Title: Searching for Summer Cottage
Cast: Jim Jordan (Fibber, Mort Toops), Marian Jordan (Molly, little girl, old lady), Harlow Wilcox, Bill Thompson (old man, Indian, Russian), Jimmy Grier
Summary: As Fibber and Molly traipse though the woods looking for a cottage, they receive little help from people they ask for directions.
Music: Jimmy Grier: "Dreamy Eyes," "Heat Wave," "Sweet Heartaches" (Tommy Harris, vocal), "I Know That You Know," "'Cause My Baby Says It's So"
Running Gags: "Gotta get my brakes fixed" (Fibber), "'Tain't funny, McGee" (Molly), tongue twister starting with Pole Toter McGee (Fibber)
Comments: The old man character is now becoming a regular in Bill Thompson's repertoire. Jim's muff of the Paramount line when playing Mort Toops might have passed by the audience had not he mentioned it.

Date: June 28, 1937
Title: Human Cannonball
Cast: Jim Jordan (Fibber, Mort Toops), Marian Jordan (Molly, Geraldine, Mrs. Wearybottom, landlady, little girl), Harlow Wilcox, Bill Thompson (grouchy concessionaire, Russian, old man), Hugh Studebaker (Mayor Egbert Applepuss), Bea Benaderet (woman looking for husband)
Summary: As the McGees tour the carnival grounds, Fibber expresses his apprehension about being shot out of a cannon.
Music: Jimmy Grier: "Get Happy," "My Last Affair" (Tommy Harris, vocal), "Who's Sorry Now?"
Running Gags: "'Tain't funny, McGee" (Molly), tongue twister starting with Boom Boom McGee (Fibber)
Comments: This is another episode that takes place in the atmosphere of an amusement Park or a carnival. This is the most number of characters

Marian will assume on any Episode of *Fibber McGee and Molly*. The hard-of-hearing codger has some of the Mannerisms that will become part of the enduring character who will be known as the Old Timer including addressing Fibber as Johnny.

Date: July 5, 1937
Title: Getting Out of Lease
Cast: Jim Jordan (Fibber), Marian Jordan (Molly, Mrs. Wearybottom, little girl), Harlow Wilcox, Bill Thompson (Russian), Hugh Studebaker (Edward Hassbeck), Jimmy Grier, Tommy Harris
Summary: The McGees, ready to leave Hollywood, try to break a six-month lease.
Music: Jimmy Grier: "Toodleloo," "Bye Bye, Blackbird," "Was It Rain?" (Tommy Harris, vocal), "Johnny One Note," "Let's Call the Whole Thing Off"
Running Gags: "'Tain't funny, McGee" (Molly), tongue twister starting with Hotel McGee (Fibber)
Comments: The title of the last musical number is also the attitude of landllord and tenants at the conclusion of this episode. Even in Hollywood Molly answers the phone formally by giving the number just as she gives the address when she picks up the receiver in Wistful Vista. Harlow's entrances are shoehorned in without so much as a door opening; he just appears to give a quick pun and plug.

Date: July 12, 1937
Title: Streamliner Back to Wistful Vista
Cast: Jim Jordan (Fibber), Marian Jordan (Molly, Geraldine, Mrs. Wearybottom), Harlow Wilcox, Hugh Studebaker (Silly Watson, Barrymel Lionmore), Bill Thompson (conductor, cardsharp, Russian), Isabel Randolph (inquiring woman), Charlie Sears
Summary: Their movie work completed, the McGees grab an empty room aboard a fast train back home.
Music: Henry Busse: "Honey Bunch," "Bingo," "A Sailboat in the Moonlight" (Charlie Sears, vocal), "Alexander's Ragtime Band," "Stop, You're Breaking My Heart"
Running Gag: "'Tain't funny, McGee" (Molly)
Comments: The program is again being broadcast from Chicago. Henry Busse and his Orchestra fill in this week for the Ted Weems band. For the time being Fibber and Molly are making funnies on the air *and* being seen in the Sunday funnies.

Date: July 19, 1937
Title: Homecoming after Making Movie
Cast: Jim Jordan (Fibber), Marian Jordan (Molly, little girl), Harlow Wilcox, Hugh Studebaker (Silly Watson), Bill Thompson (telegram messenger, old man), Isabel Randolph (woman), Harold Peary (exuberant man, suggestion man), Ted Weems, Perry Como, Elmo Tanner
Summary: Fibber and Molly answer pointed and sometimes barbed questions about the film industry.
Music: Ted Weems: "The Camera Doesn't Lie," "Happy Birthday to Love," "Blue Hawaii" (Perry Como, vocal), "Say It with Music" (whistling by Elmo Tanner)
Running Gag: Tongue twister starting with Director McGee (Fibber)
Comments: Harold Peary's characters are as up and down in temperament as mercurial Gildersleeve will be in later episodes.

Date: July 26, 1937
Title: Managing Food Store
Cast: Jim Jordan (Fibber), Marian Jordan (Molly, Geraldine, old lady, little girl), Harlow Wilcox, Hugh Studebaker (Silly Watson), Bill Thompson (Schmierkase, old man, Chinaman), Isabel Randolph (customer), Harold Peary (customer), Perry Como
Summary: Fibber's attempt to turn a grocery shop into a health food store proves to be not very healthy for the cash register.
Music: Ted Weems: "Shall We Dance," "That's A Plenty," "What is Love?" (Perry Como, vocal), "When Hearts Are Young" (whistling by Elmo Tanner)
Running Gags: Tongue twister starting with Provision McGee (Fibber), "'Tain't funny, McGee" (Molly)
Comments: The food shop is located at 14th and Oak. Isabel Randolph adopts the hoity-toity tone that will be ingrained into the Uppington characterization. Fibber gives listeners a mental image of this pompous poser with his "glasses on a stick" description.

Date: August 2, 1937
Title: Life on a Modern Farm
Cast: Jim Jordan (Fibber), Marian Jordan (Molly), Harlow Wilcox, Hugh Studebaker (Silly Watson), Bill Thompson (Nick Depopolis, Scotsman), Isabel Randolph (lady), Harold Peary (man)
Summary: The McGees are surprised to find that life on Idlewild Farm is very up-to-date with the latest machinery and conveniences.
Music: Ted Weems: "High, Wide and Lonesome," "Love is on the Air Tonight," "It Looks Like Rain in Cherry Blossom Lane' (Perry Como, vocal)
Running Gags: "Gotta get them brakes fixed" (Fibber), "'Tain't funny, McGee" (Molly), tongue twister starting with Moo Moo McGee (Fibber)

Comments: This visit to the country seems very futuristic for 1937, convincing the McGees that things to come are already here. Molly does get some of the needed rest mentioned in Harlow's introduction as Marian plays just one character.

Date: August 16, 1937
Title: Newspaperman McGee
Cast: Jim Jordan (Fibber), Marian Jordan (Molly, little girl), Harlow Wilcox, Hugh Studebaker (Edward C. Uppercase), Bill Thompson (man buying paper, suspected robber, old man, Irishman), Isabel Randolph (woman on street), Harold Peary (man in police station)
Summary: After promising to increase circulation, Fibber sells newspapers on the street where the McGees encounter a possible bank robber.
Music: Ted Weems: "You Can't Have Everything," "Wild Rose" (whistling by Elmo Tanner), "Strangers in the Dark" (Perry Como, vocal)
Running Gags: Cigar routine (Uppercase, Fibber), tongue twister starting with Loud Lung McGee (Fibber)
Comments: *The Wistful Vista Gazette* is mentioned for the first time. Fibber doesn't stand on formality; he tramples all over it by addressing his potential employer as Uppy and by shooting half-baked proposals all over the place.

Date: August 23, 1937
Title: Resort Hotel Visit
Cast: Jim Jordan (Fibber), Marian Jordan (Molly, little girl), Harlow Wilcox, Hugh Studebaker (Silly Watson), Bill Thompson (bellboy, Nick Depopolis), Harold Peary (Fitzmaurice Smoothbore), Ted Weems
Summary: Fibber and Molly are treated well at the Breakers Hotel, though members of the staff seem unable to stop addressing them by the wrong last name and bombarding them with copies of their hometown newspaper.
Music: Ted Weems: "Wake Up and Live," "Is it Love or Infatuation?" (Perry Como, vocal), "I'm in a Dancing Mood" (whistling by Elmo Tanner), "Who?"
Running Gags: "Gotta get them brakes fixed" (Fibber), tongue twister starting with Resort Running McGee (Fibber)
Comments: The inflexibility of fancy hotels is extensively lampooned in this episode. This the first time Fibber resurrects "Pretty Red Wing" from his romantic past. The fancy moniker given to Peary's character is a precursor to Throckmorton P. Gildersleeve.

Date: August 30, 1937
Title: Sports Reporter
Cast: Jim Jordan (Fibber), Marian Jordan (Molly, little girl), Harlow Wilcox (Spike), Hugh Studebaker (Silly Watson), Bill Thompson (Nick Depopolis, officer), Isabel Randolph (cook)

Summary: McGee interviews two boxers before a fight that delivers a double knockout.
Music: Ted Weems: "This Way Please," "Slap That Bass," "Whispers in the Dark" (Perry Como, vocal), "I Got Rhythm"
Running Gags: "'Tain't funny, McGee" (Molly), tongue twister starting with Mixmaster McGee (Fibber)
Comments: The tongue twister, usually delivered much earlier in the program, turns out to be a closer this time.

Date: September 6, 1937
Title: Acting School Principal
Cast: Jim Jordan (Fibber), Marian Jordan (Molly, old lady, little girl), Harlow Wilcox, Hugh Studebaker (Silly Watson), Bill Thompson (Nick Depopolis), Isabel Randolph (Mrs. Whipperman), Harold Peary (J. Elmer Guffy), Ted Weems, Elmo Tanner
Summary: When the principal at Public School #14 steps out, Fibber steps in with unsolicited advice.
Music: Ted Weems: "Hallelujah," "Yours and Mine," "The Loveliness of You" (Perry Como, vocal), "The Things I Want to Do" (whistling by Elmo Tanner), "Good Night My Lucky Day"
Running Gags: Tongue twister staring with Curriculum McGee (Fibber), "'Tain't funny, McGee" (Molly)
Comments: McGee, who suffered fore last week, takes a beating aft this time out. Nick reveals the names of all his children for the first time.

Date: September 13, 1937
Title: Play about Julius Caesar
Cast: Jim Jordan (Fibber), Marian Jordan (Molly, little girl), Harlow Wilcox, Bill Thompson (Old Timer, Nick Depopolis, Irishman), Hugh Studebaker (Silly Watson), Isabel Randolph (Abigail Uppington), Harold Peary (actor), Ted Weems, Perry Como
Summary: Fibber rehearses a cast and then performs in his play about ancient Rome.
Music: Ted Weems: "Stop, You're Breaking My Heart," "Goodbye, Jonah," "That Old Feeling" (Perry Como, vocal), "Cross Your Heart" (whistling by Elmo Tanner)
Running Gags: "'Tain't funny, McGee" (Molly), tongue twister starting with Thespian McGee (Fibber)
Comments: The elderly character played by Bill Thompson is now called the Old Timer. The haughty character played by Isabel Randolph is now referred to as Mrs. Uppington.

Date: September 20, 1937
Title: Buried Money in Backyard
Cast: Jim Jordan (Fibber), Marian Jordan (Molly, little girl), Harlow Wilcox, Hugh Studebaker (Silly Watson), Bill Thompson (Old Timer, Nick Depopolis, Irish worker), Harold Peary (man), Isabel Randolph (Abigail Uppington), Ted Weems, Elmo Tanner
Summary: After a bank robbery, Fibber plants seeds in the minds of Wistful Vista residents that the loot is buried on his property which results in a crowd of diggers cropping up on his property.
Music: Ted Weems: "Your Broadway and My Broadway," "Love is On the Air Tonight," "Don't Ever Change" (Perry Como, vocal), "Have You Got Any Castles, Baby?" (whistling by Elmo Tanner), "Ridin' High"
Running Gags: None
Comments: Fibber knows the best spot to hear and spread gossip is at 14th and Oak. Mrs. Uppington is now living next to the McGees. Promotion of a personal appearance by Fibber and Molly in St. Louis closes the program.

Date: October 4, 1937
Title: Supervisor at State Fair
Cast: Jim Jordan (Fibber, Mort Toops), Marian Jordan (Molly, Mrs. Wearybottom, offended woman, little girl), Harlow Wilcox, Hugh Studebaker (Applepuss, Silly Watson), Bill Thompson (Old Timer, Doctor Dentyne, Nick Depopolis), Harold Peary (exhibitor)
Summary: The McGees tour the Midway as Fibber searches for a badge that will entitle him to be supervisor of the fair.
Music: Ted Weems: "Things Look Brighter Again," "Night Ride," "The Moon Got in My Eyes" (Perry Como, vocal), "Nola" (whistling by Elmo Tanner), "High, Wide, and Handsome"
Running Gag: Tongue twister starting with Ballyhoo McGee (Fibber)
Comments: Molly's apt description of Mort's irksome chortle as a horse laugh leads to more equine humor. The lure of a blue ribbon, which attracts many entrants to fairs, also sells Fibber on the idea of going to this event.

Date: October 11, 1937
Title: Auto Show and an Appraisal
Cast: Jim Jordan (Fibber), Marian Jordan (Molly, little girl), Harlow Wilcox, Harold Peary (auto salesman), Bill Thompson (Nick Depopolis, Horatio K. Boomer), Hugh Studebaker (Silly Watson)
Summary: Fibber and Molly visit the auto show to look for a new car, then Horatio visits their home to appraise their car.
Music: Ted Weems: "Overnight," "Cabin of Dreams" (Perry Como, vocal), "Josephine" (whistling by Elmo Tanner)
Running Gags: "'Tain't funny, McGee" (Molly), tongue twister starting with Honk Honk McGee (Fibber), "Where'd I put that [business] card?" (Horatio)

Comments: Jim milks a laugh when he echoes Harold's slight mispronunciation of *revolutionized*. The sound effects man gets a good workout in this episode, making the McGee car sound like the sputtering vehicle belonging to Jack Benny.

Date: October 18, 1937
Title: Man on the Street Interview
Cast: Jim Jordan (Fibber), Marian Jordan (Molly, little girl, Mrs. Wearybottom), Harlow Wilcox, High Studebaker (Silly Watson), Bill Thompson (Nick Depopolis), Harold Peary (Cicero Clod), Betty Winkler (Dimples LaRue), Ted Weems
Summary: Fibber talks to people on the street in hopes of impressing the mayor and thus getting a permanent job.
Music: Ted Weems: "Laugh Your Way Through Life," "I Like to Make Music," "Roses in December" (Perry Como, vocal), "Afraid to Dream" (whistling by Elmo Tanner)
Running Gags: None
Comments: McGee naturally does his "vox popping" at 14th and Oak. It is out of character for Fibber to be such an obsequious apple-polisher for Applepuss just as it is unusual for the little girl to appear in two separate sequences of the program.

Date: October 25, 1937
Title: Managing Candy Company
Cast: Jim Jordan (Fibber), Marian Jordan (Molly, little girl), Harlow Wilcox, Betty Winkler (Miss Wood), Hugh Studebaker (Silly Watson), Bill Thompson (Nick Depopolis), Harold Peary (boiler room worker, candy employee)
Summary: Fibber takes on the sweet but sticky task of running things at the Cuttlekirk Candy Company.
Music: Ted Weems: "Sing and Be Happy," "Dixieland One-Step," "Stardust on the Moon" (Perry Como, vocal), "I Know Now" (whistling by Elmo Tanner), "You Can't Have Everything"
Running Gags: "'Tain't funny, McGee" (Molly), tongue twister starting with Confection McGee (Fibber)
Comments: Fibber's chest-pounding as a human dynamo prompts Molly's witty definition of a dynamo: "Something that goes round and round, never gets anyplace, and wouldn't be worth a hoop if it didn't have good connections."

Date: November 1, 1937
Title: Trimming Drugstore Window
Cast: Jim Jordan (Fibber), Marian Jordan (Molly, little girl), Harlow Wilcox, Hugh Studebaker (Silly Watson), Bill Thompson (angry man, Nick Depopolis), Harold Peary (Kremer, turkey), Isabel Randolph (Mrs. Uppington), Ted Weems, Elmo Tanner

Summary: After Fibber agrees to decorate a storefront window for thirty dollars, he throws himself into the job with a harvest plan.
Music: Ted Weems: "San Francisco," "She's Tall...She's Tan...She's Terrific," "Blossoms on Broadway" (Perry Como, vocal), "On with the Dance" (whistling by Elmo Tanner), "The Lady Is a Tramp"
Running Gag: Tongue twister starting with Trimmer McGee (Fibber)
Comments: The stores viewed by the McGees are located at 14th and Oak. This is one of the few times Fibber agrees to a specific salary for a job, and the reason becomes apparent at the end. This is the first time Kremer's Drugstore is mentioned on the show.

Date: November 8, 1937
Title: Auditioning for New Singer
Cast: Jim Jordan (Fibber), Marian Jordan (Molly, little girl), Harlow Wilcox (emcee), Hugh Studebaker (Silly Watson), Bill Thompson (Hennessey, taxi driver), Harold Peary (photographer), Betty Winkler (interviewer), Ted Weems
Summary: The McGees audition several candidates to replace Perry Como before finding a new tenor at the Wistful Vista Night Club.
Music: Ted Weems: "Who Put That Moon in the Sky?" "Mama's Gone Goodbye," "Vieni, Vieni" (whistling by Elmo Tanner), "Once in a While" (Clark Dennis, vocal), "I'm in my Glory"
Running Gags: "'Tain't funny, McGee' (Molly), "Cabbie oughta get them brakes fixed" (Fibber)
Comments: Weems, Hennessey, and Wilcox offer deliberately dreary versions of "It Looks like Rain in Cherry Blossom Lane." Many night spots then and now fit Fibber's description: "Grope your way in, gripe your way out."

Date: November 15, 1937
Title: Football Ringer
Cast: Jim Jordan (Fibber), Harlow Wilcox (sports announcer), Hugh Studebaker (Silly Watson), Bill Thompson (Nick Depopolis, student, professor), Harold Peary (heckler, Butch), Betty Winkler (Margie), Ted Weems
Summary: After Fibber takes a test for Wistful Vista University's star player, he takes the student's place on the football field.
Music: Ted Weems: "Thanksgiving," "Varsity Sue," "Summertime" (Clark Dennis, vocal), "Good Night Kisses" (whistling by Elmo Tanner)
Running Gags: Tongue twister starting with Pigskin McGee (Fibber), "'Tain't funny, McGee" (hecklers)
Comments: Although Marian is mentioned by Wilcox at the start of the program, she will not be back until April 18, 1939. Studebaker and Thompson have larger parts starting with this episode.

Date: November 22, 1937
Title: Scandinavian Sweepstakes Winner

Cast: Jim Jordan (Fibber), Harlow Wilcox (Jones), Hugh Studebaker (Silly Watson), Bill Thompson (Nick Depopolis, Oscar Erp), Harold Peary (car salesman, mendicant), Betty Winkler (woman)
Summary: Impulsive McGee spends money recklessly after learning he won $100,000 in a sweepstakes.
Music: Ted Weems: "Swing is Here to Sway," "Remember Me" (whistling by Elmo Tanner), "If It's the Last Thing I Do" (Clark Dennis, vocal), "Lucky Day"
Running Gag: Tongue twister starting with Blow Me Down McGee (Fibber)
Comments: Attentive listeners suspect before the ending there is a reason why McGee signs for all the merchandise with his own new pen. At the close Jim expresses hope that Molly will soon be back on the program.

Date: November 29, 1937
Title: College of Santa Clausing
Cast: Jim Jordan (Fibber), Harold Wilcox, Hugh Studebaker (Reginald, Silly Watson), Bill Thompson (Santa, Scotsman, Old Timer, Nick Depopolis), Isabel Randolph (lady), Betty Winkler (customer), Harold Peary (Santa, child, sugar daddy)
Summary: Fibber teaches a class on the art of being Santa Claus before donning a costume himself to act as St. Nicholas at a store.
Music: Ted Weems: "Goodbye Jonah," "I've Got My Heart Set on You" (Clark Dennis, vocal), "Rosalie" (whistling by Elmo Tanner), "Who Knows?"
Running Gag: Tongue twister starting with Kris Kringle McGee (Fibber)
Comments: Hugh adopts his Lionmore voice for the part of Reginald and also alludes to the radio version of *A Christmas Carol*. Director Cecil Underwood has a bit as one of the student Santa Clauses.

Date: December 6, 1937
Title: Making Dinner for 30 People
Cast: Jim Jordan (Fibber), Harlow Wilcox, Hugh Studebaker (Silly Watson), Bill Thompson (Old Timer, Nick Depopolis), Isabel Randolph (Mrs. Uppington, questioner)
Summary: Fibber and Silly Watson prepare a meal for members of the Wistful Vista Drama and Literary Club despite knowing little about the art of cooking.
Music: Ted Weems: "Be a Good Sport," "I Can't Be Bothered Now," "Farewell, My Love" (Clark Dennis, vocal), "You Took the Words Right Out of My Heart" (whistling by Elmo Tanner), "You Can't Stop Me from Dreaming"
Running Gag: Tongue twister starting with Pot Luck McGee (Fibber)
Comments: Titles of musical selections one, two, and five relate to this and many a McGee misadventure. The parade of people coming to 79 Wistful Vista gives listeners a taste of what shows will be like after Molly's return to the program.

Date: December 13, 1937
Title: Matrimonial Bureau
Cast: Jim Jordan (Fibber), Harlow Wilcox, Hugh Studebaker (Silly Watson), Bill Thompson (Old Timer, McKenzie, officer, Nick Depopolis), Harold Peary (suitor), Betty Winkler (woman), Ted Weems
Summary: Fibber offers advice to the lovelorn and loveworn after opening a matrimonial bureau.
Music: Ted Weems: "Who Put That Moon in the Sky?" "Paris in Swing," "I Still Love to Kiss You Good Night" (Clark Dennis, vocal), "Nice Work If You Can Get It" (whistling by Elmo Tanner), "Laugh Your Way Through Life"
Running Gag: Tongue twister starting with Matchmaker McGee (Fibber)
Comments: For the second consecutive week a loud sound effect closes the action. "Here comes the bride" becomes a warning call in this episode.

Date: December 20, 1937
Title: Detective McGee
Cast: Jim Jordan (Fibber), Harlow Wilcox, Hugh Studebaker (Silly Watson), Bill Thompson (Old Timer, officer, Nick Depopolis), Harold Peary (Chinese man, guilty party)
Summary: After taking a correspondence school course in detection, McGee attempts to solve the case of a kidnapped Pekinese held for $10,000 ransom.
Music: Ted Weems: "Jubilee," "Rockin' the Town," "Home Sweet Home" (Clark Dennis, vocal), "Canadian Capers" (whistling by Elmo Tanner)
Running Gags: None
Comments: Wilcox now introduces the program as *Fibber McGee and Company*. Sherlockians will appreciate the wit in Fibber's request for Silly to play a record: "Quick, Watson, the needle."

Date: December 27, 1937
Title: Heir to Estate with Oil Wells
Cast: Jim Jordan (Fibber), Harlow Wilcox, Bill Thompson (Old Timer), Hugh Studebaker (Silly Watson), Harold Peary (Conductor), Betty Winkler (Lulu, Daisy), Clark Dennis
Summary: Fibber and Silly travel to Kentucky to claim a legacy which McGee hopes with be sizeable.
Music: Ted Weems: "I Double Dare You," "The Martins and the Coys," "When the Mighty Organ Played 'Oh Promise Me'"(Clark Dennis, vocal), "I'm Bubbling Over"
Running Gag: Tongue twister starting with Bullet Bouncer McGee (Fibber)
Comments: Peary's part involved stretching out monosyllables whereas Harlow's brief intrusion into the Kentucky setting stretched credibility to the breaking point. The first and fourth musical selections capture McGee's enthusiasm in rhythm, although his disappointment at the end is no surprise.

Date: January 3, 1938
Title: Managing Travel Bureau
Cast: Jim Jordan (Fibber), Harlow Wilcox, Hugh Studebaker (Silly Watson, Reginald), Bill Thompson (Old Timer, Nick Depopolis), Isabel Randolph (customer), Betty Winkler (customer, new bride), Harold Peary (new groom, Gildersleeve W. Fiditch), Ted Weems, Clark Dennis, Elmo Tanner
Summary: Fibber and Silly Watson encounter an assortment of people wishing information about faraway places with strange sounding names.
Music: Ted Weems: "The Lady is a Tramp," "The Snake Charmer," "A Foggy Day in London Town" (Clark Dennis, vocal), "When Hearts Are Young" (whistling by Elmo Tanner), "Be a Good Sport"
Running Gags: None
Comments: This is the first time a character played by Peary uses the name *Gildersleeve*. In this adventure McGee wins a tussle with an opponent.

Date: January 10, 1938
Title: Doing the Laundry
Cast: Jim Jordan (Fibber), Harlow Wilcox, Hugh Studebaker (Silly Watson), Bill Thompson (Old Timer, Nick Depopolis), Isabel Randolph (Mrs. Dillyham-Skunkle), Betty Winkler (artist's model, giggling woman), Harold Peary (China Boy, Slink), Clark Dennis
Summary: McGee wants to wash the dirty clothes that have been piling up either by hiring a laundress or by doing the job himself with a new machine.
Music: Ted Weems: "In Old Chicago," "Rockin' the Town," "True Confessions" (Clark Dennis, vocal), "Nola" (whistling by Elmo Tanner)
Running Gags: Myrt bits involving old man out/90 days and sister/how soon she expect/coupe (Fibber), tongue twister starting with Soft Soap McGee (Fibber)
Comments: The first Myrt bits are introduced with a double dose of misinterpretations. Searsmont and Wardbuck are real merchandising wizards for they deliver phone orders right away and follow that up with a prompt visit from a maintenance man.

Date: January 17, 1938
Title: Real Estate Agent
Cast: Jim Jordan (Fibber), Harlow Wilcox, Hugh Studebaker (Silly Watson), Bill Thompson (Old Timer, Nick Depopolis), Harold Peary (customer, Denver Louie), Betty Winkler (Mrs. Crawford, Rosalie), Billy Mills, Clark Dennis
Summary: McGee handles some housing matters in his office before going to the railroad yard to investigate opportunities there.
Music: Billy Mills: "Fifi," "Bob White," "There's a Gold Mine in the Sky" (Clark Dennis, vocal), "Rosalie"
Running Gag: Tongue twister starting with Boom Boom McGee (Fibber)

Comments: Harlow's introduction intimates that Billy Mills will be just a temporary replacement while Ted Weems is on tour when actually the Billy Mills Orchestra will remain with the program until the end of the 30-minute series in 1953. The name *Gildersleeve* is again used as Fibber talks to a customer on the phone.

Date: January 24, 1938
Title: Minding the Baby
Cast: Jim Jordan (Fibber), Harlow Wilcox, Hugh Studebaker (Silly Watson), Bill Thompson (Old Timer, Nick Depopolis), Harold Peary (Chris Anthemum), Betty Winkler (Mrs. Fiditch, baby)
Summary: Mrs. Fiditch leaves baby Rose in the care of Fibber and Silly which turns out to be a wearysome task for both men.
Music: Billy Mills: "Fine and Dandy," "Whistle While You Work," "Easy to Remember (Clark Dennis, vocal), "I Double Dare You," "That Moon's Here Again"
Running Gag: Tongue twister starting with Coo Coo McGee (Fibber)
Comments: Fibber and Chris engage in a phone conversation in which there is confusion over a day nursery and a plant nursery. Don Quinn uses this device of two parties meaning different things a number of times to great comic effect.

Date: February 7, 1938
Title: Building a Fireplace
Cast: Jim Jordan (Fibber), Harlow Wilcox (carpenter), Bill Thompson (contractor, Old Timer, Nick Depopolis), Hugh Studebaker (Silly Watson), Harold Peary (Chinese character, plasterer, plumber), Betty Winkler (woman, Mrs. Fiditch)
Summary: After receiving a package of marshmallows, Fibber decides to build a fireplace to roast them in with disastrous results.
Music: Billy Mills: "'S Wonderful"
Running Gags: Myrt bit involving her sister and a tomcat (Fibber), "That ain't the way I heered it" (Old Timer), tongue twister starting with Firefly McGee (Fibber)
Comments: The recording of this episode lacks the opening and most of the music. Other musical numbers scheduled for this show were "Jubilee," "Every Day's a Holiday," and the Clark Dennis vocal "You Took the Words Right Out of My Heart."

Date: February 14, 1938
Title: Justice of the Peace
Cast: Jim Jordan (Fibber), Harlow Wilcox, Bill Thompson (Old Timer, officer, Nick Depopolis), Hugh Studebaker (Silly Watson), Harold Peary (Chinese character), Betty Winkler (complainant)

Summary: Fibber, acting as a temporary justice of the peace, pronounces judgment on various cases brought before him.
Music: Billy Mills: Just a few notes from a number exist.
Running Gag: Tongue twister starting with Pin Pointer McGee (Fibber)
Comments: Only a portion of this broadcast currently exists. Musical numbers scheduled for that evening were "I've Taken a Fancy to You," "Heigh Ho," and the Clark Dennis vocal "In the Still of the Night."

Date: March 7, 1938
Title: Pawn Broker
Cast: Jim Jordan (Fibber), Bill Thompson (Indian, Old Timer), Hugh Studebaker (Silly Watson), Harold Peary (gruff customer)
Summary: Fibber and Silly temporarily run Mr. Solomon's pawn shop.
Music: Billy Mills: "Whistle While You Work" (fragment)
Running Gag: "That ain't the way I heered it" (Old Timer)
Comments: Only a portion of this broadcast currently exists. Harlow Wilcox appeared on this show but is not in this fragment. Other musical numbers scheduled for this broadcast included "Love is Sweeping the Country," "Sunny Side of the Rockies," and the Clark Dennis vocal "I Can Dream, Can't I?"

The program moves to Tuesday evenings at 8:30 Central, 9:30 Eastern beginning March 15, 1938. *Attorney at Law* is the summer replacement series from July 5 through August 30, 1938.

Date: November 29, 1938
Title: Masquerade
Cast: Jim Jordan (Fibber), Harlow Wilcox (radio dispatcher), Bill Thompson (Clarence, Mulligan, Horatio K. Boomer, Old Timer, Nick Depopolis), Hugh Studebaker (Silly Watson), Harold Peary (O'Toole, man in police costume), Isabel Randolph (Abigail Uppington), Mel Blanc (cab driver), Ken Christy (police lieutenant)
Summary: Fibber gets arrested while going to a masquerade dressed as a convict.
Music: Billy Mills: "Anything Goes," "Changes" (Four Notes, vocal), "All Ashore" (Donald Novis, vocal)
Running Gags: "'Tain't funny, McGee" (O'Toole), "Where'd I put my identification?" (Horatio), "That ain't the way I heered it" (Old Timer)
Comments: Wilcox delivers the Johnson's Wax commercial in jail in a gruff voice using the argot of crooks. Don Quinn skillfully integrated the middle commercial into the program, often using the circumstances and situations of the story as a transition to "sell the stuff." Nick tells the tale of King Arthur and the Round Table in his fractured English.

Date: December 20, 1938
Title: Christmas Shopping for Nephew
Cast: Jim Jordan (Fibber), Harlow Wilcox, Bill Thompson (officer, man on streetcar, Old Timer, Horatio K. Boomer, Nick Depopolis), Hugh Studebaker (Silly Watson), Harold Peary (streetcar conductor), Isabel Randolph (Abigail Uppington), Sam Hearn (Shlepperman), Billy Mills, Ken Christy (floorwalker, deep-voiced man on streetcar), Betty Winkler (clerk, woman on streetcar), Mel Blanc (customer)
Summary: Fibber purchases a tricycle for his nephew, then takes it home on the streetcar.
Music: Billy Mills: "I Hit a New High," "Mutiny in the Nursery" (Four Notes, vocal), "Deep in a Dream" (Donald Novis, vocal)
Running Gags: "That ain't the way I heered it" (Old Timer), "Where did I put that transfer?" (Horatio), tongue twister starting with Candy Cane McGee (Fibber)
Comments: During this period of Molly's absence, Bill Thompson sometimes appears as five different characters. Abigail's startled response of "Watch out where you put those handlebars!" is one of those lines that allows the imaginations of listeners to picture her being jabbed right where she sits.

Date: January 24, 1939
Title: Lost Collar Button
Cast: Jim Jordan (Fibber), Harlow Wilcox, Bill Thompson (Old Timer, Nick Depopolis), Hugh Studebaker (Silly Watson), Harold Peary (Gooey Fooey, store clerk), Isabel Randolph (Abigail Uppington), Betty Winkler (actress), Billy Mills, Donald Novis
Summary: Invited to a formal dinner at the Uppington mansion, Fibber's search for a lost collar button leads him on a wild goose chase.
Music: Billy Mills: "There's a New Sun in the Sky," "Ferdinand the Bull" (Four Notes, vocal), "Thanks for Everything" (Donald Novis, vocal), "This Is It"
Running Gag: "That ain't the way I heered it" (Old Timer)
Comments: Fibber delivers the best line of the show after Wilcox reveals his shirt size: "17½? Wow! That ain't a shirt. That's a step-in." Rather than catch a cold with an open collar, Fibber announces he is moving the show to Hollywood where he "won't be the only one out there who hasn't lost all his buttons." Hugh Studebaker does not make the trip and does not appear again on the series. "Stuff like that there" will be used with greater frequency in future shows. The appeal for the March of Dimes is just one of many messages for charitable organizations that will be made at the end of episodes.

Date: January 31, 1939
Title: Military Maneuvers
Cast: Jim Jordan (Fibber), Harlow Wilcox, Bill Thompson (Colonel Hackamore, Old Timer, Nick Depopolis, Horatio K. Boomer), Harold Peary

(general, Gooey Fooey), Isabel Randolph (Abigail Uppington), Mel Blanc (sentry), Donald Novis

Summary: Fibber, touting himself as Major McGee, offers the military brass unsolicited advice which tosses a foul ball into the army games.

Music: Billy Mills: "Anything Goes," "Only a Rose" (Donald Novis, vocal), "Patty Cake, Patty Cake" (Four Notes, vocal), "Zing Went the Strings of My Heart"

Running Gags: Tongue twister starting with Carpet Tactics McGee (Fibber), "That ain't the way I heered it" (Old Timer), cigar routine (Fibber and general), "Where'd I put that authorization?" (Horatio)

Comments: *Fibber McGee and Molly* is now being broadcast from Hollywood. After a door slam sound effect, Fibber says, "Nice of them to put that door on this tent. Otherwise, nobody could I tell I was entering." Don Quinn and Jim Jordan were both fond of knocking down the fourth wall and telling the audience "We're all in on the gag."

Date: February 7, 1939
Title: Window Shade
Cast: Jim Jordan (Fibber), Harlow Wilcox, Bill Thompson (Old Timer), Isabel Randolph (Abigail Uppington), Harold Peary (Gus the Grunt, interior decorator), ZaSu Pitts (woman selling books), Walter Tetley (Wilbur), Billy Mills, Donald Novis
Summary: Fibber consults with an interior decorator to help with a window shade that won't stay down.
Music: Billy Mills: "Drums in My Heart," "Have You Forgotten?" (Donald Novis, vocal), "Paul Revere" (Four Notes, vocal)
Running Gags: Myrt bit about her old man doing ninety days (Fibber), "That ain't the way I heered it" (Old Timer), cigar routine (Fibber and decorator), "Where'd I put that sonnet?" (Horatio)
Comments: Fibber indicates at one point he is looking ahead a few pages to see what wrestler Gus the Grunt does to him. Mrs. Uppington announces she is in love with Horatio. Fibber reveals his skepticism of Boomer's motives in a speech indicative of Don Quinn's love of punning dialogue: "You may think you're getting away with something for a while, Kipling, but it won't be for long, fellow." After pausing for the laugh Fibber adds, "I should have made that Whittier." Bill Thompson's knockoff of the W.C. Fields voice he used for Boomer is evident in the line he uses when talking about siphoning gas as the only time "a sucker gets an even break."

Date: February 14, 1939
Title: Frozen Water Pipes
Cast: Jim Jordan (Fibber), Harlow Wilcox, Bill Thompson (Old Timer, Joe, Nick Depopolis, Horatio K. Boomer), Harold Peary (Van Meter), Isabel Randolph (Abigail Uppington), Mel Blanc (plumber's helper), Bea Benaderet (Miss Cadwell), Billy Mills, Donald Novis

Summary: Fibber tries to keep warm after forgetting to order coal and pay the water bill.
Music: Billy Mills: "This Is It," "I Have Eyes" (Donald Novis, vocal), "Sing for Your Supper" (Four Notes, vocal)
Running Gags: "That ain't the way I heered it," (Old Timer), Myrt bit about General Grant statue coming alive (Fibber), cigar routine (Fibber and Van Meter), "Where'd I put that valentine?" (Horatio)
Comments: There is a mirthful exchange between the squeaky-voiced plumber's helper and Fibber with Mel Blanc's "What are you talking about?" laying them in the aisles after catching Jim in a small blooper. The best line of the show, though, is Fibber's sarcastic response to the Old Timer's inquiry of where the basement was: "Underneath the house. We used to have it up on the roof, but it was too far for the mice to walk." There are more playful moments with sound effects when McGee mentions the elements and, instead of howling winds, the sound of a trumpeting elephant is heard.

Date: February 21, 1939
Title: Club Banquet
Cast: Jim Jordan (Fibber), Harlow Wilcox, Bill Thompson (Horatio K. Boomer, Old Timer, doorman), Harold Peary (Homer Gildersleeve), Isabel Randolph (Abigail Uppington), Walter Tetley (bellboy), Verna Felton (Homer's wife), ZaSu Pitts (housekeeper)
Summary: Fibber inveigles a free meal at the Rotawannis supper by offering to be the featured speaker.
Music: Billy Mills: "It's All Yours," "My Heart Stood Still" (Donald Novis, vocal), "I Must See Annie Tonight" (Four Notes, vocal)
Running Gags: Tongue twister starting with Ad Glib McGee (Fibber), "That ain't the Way I heered it" (Old Timer)
Comments: Tetley's part is mainly to deliver a twist on the popular cigarette call when the bellboy hollers for a man named Morris Phillips. This is another instance of the name Gildersleeve being used by a character assumed by Harold Peary. Wilcox's commercial is delivered in a crying tone. Harlow's presumed devotion to Johnson's Wax at almost any cost is a theme that will run through many pitches for the product.

Date: February 28, 1939
Title: Mouse Frightens Big Game Hunters
Cast: Jim Jordan (Fibber), Harlow Wilcox, Bill Thompson (Old Timer, gunman, Nick Depopolis, Horatio K. Boomer), Harold Peary (Lord Bingham), Isabel Randolph (Abigail Uppington), Mel Blanc (store clerk), Billy Mills, Donald Novis
Summary: Bingham and Fibber exchange tall tales about hunting big game, yet cower at the sight of a mouse.

Music: Billy Mills: "Of Thee I Sing," "Phil the Fluter's Ball" (Donald Novis, vocal), "Chopsticks" (Four Notes, vocal)
Running Gags: Tongue twister starting with Card Trek McGee (Fibber), "That ain't the way I heered it" (Old Timer), "Where'd I put that mousetrap?" (Horatio), cigar routine (Fibber and Bingham)
Comments: Nick tells the story of the Pied Piper in fractured English. An example of Quinn's vivid descriptions is heard in Fibber's assessment of Horatio's level of integrity: "There's a crack in that guy's conscience so wide it would make the Grand Canyon look like the dimple in a golf ball."

Date: March 7, 1939
Title: Hamburger Stand
Cast: Jim Jordan (Fibber), Harlow Wilcox, Bill Thompson (disgruntled customer, Old Timer, Horatio K. Boomer), Isabel Randolph (Abigail Uppington), ZaSu Pitts (applicant for cashier), Mel Blanc (cook), Frank Nelson (repeat customer), Donald Novis
Summary: Fibber, temporarily in charge of a sandwich parlor, dispenses some corn along with the beef.
Music: Billy Mills: "Don't Ever Leave Me," "I Promise You" (Donald Novis, vocal), "There's a Hole in the Old Oaken Bucket" (Four Notes, vocal), "Last Night"
Running Gags: "That ain't the way I heered it" (Old Timer), Myrt bit involving father/stitches/pants (Fibber), "Where'd I put that $100 bill?" (Horatio)
Comments: Wilcox's integrated commercial designed to create sympathy comes with sappy music of the "hearts and flowers" school. Playful commercials made this program one of the few on the air in which the sponsor's message was as enjoyable as the action of the script. The cashier part, like most of those written for ZaSu Pitts, cast her as a man-hungry spinster. Pitts was a semi-regular during the absence of Marian, probably to give the show a female presence for bantering with Fibber, but the two characters never really connected or varied much from the interviewer-interviewee mode.

Date: March 14, 1939
Title: Memory Course
Cast: Jim Jordan (Fibber), Harlow Wilcox, Bill Thompson (Old Timer, Horatio K. Boomer), Harold Peary (Cyrus L. Dalrymple), Isabel Randolph (Abigail Uppington), Mel Blanc (robber with hiccups), Billy Mills
Summary: Fibber takes a memory course that is of no help in remembering what he did with Uppy's ten-carat diamond ring.
Music: Billy Mills: "I Gotta Get Some Shuteye," "Penny Serenade" (Donald Novis, vocal), "Blue Skies" (Four Notes, vocal)
Running Gags: Tongue twister starting with Forget Me Knot McGee (Fibber), "That ain't the way I heered it" (Old Timer), "Where did I put that note?" (Horatio)

Comments: Quinn jogs the memories of listeners by having Fibber mention where the ring is at the start of the final act to set up the climax.

Date: March 21, 1939
Title: Getting Bald
Cast: Jim Jordan (Fibber), Harlow Wilcox, Bill Thompson (Old Timer, horse delivery man, Nick Depopolis), Harold Peary (barber), Isabel Randolph (Abigail Uppington), ZaSu Pitts (nurse), Mel Blanc (tattoo artist), Billy Mills, Donald Novis
Summary: After a barber indicates Fibber's hair is thinning, McGee goes to scalp specialist Harry Storer who gives him an old Indian remedy.
Music: Billy Mills: "Life Begins When You're in Love," "I Kiss Your Hand, Madame" (Donald Novis, vocal), "The Funny Old Hills" (Four Notes, vocal), "Rainbow Round the Moon"
Running Gag: "That ain't the way I heered it" (Old Timer)
Comments: Nick tells the story of Ferdinand the Bull in his fractured English during which Jim calls him Dick once by mistake. As the barber Harold Peary uses the hearty laugh that will become his trademark as Gildersleeve. In the exchange with ZaSu's character, Don Quinn gives Fibber the pun about "Someday your prints will come" which may have been fresh then after the release of *Snow White and the Seven Dwarfs*.

Date: March 28, 1939
Title: World Cruise Plans
Cast: Jim Jordan (Fibber), Harlow Wilcox, Bill Thompson (Old Timer, Scotsman, Horatio K. Boomer), Harold Peary (Ogden Fiditch), Isabel Randolph (Abigail Uppington), Mel Blanc (goat), Frank Nelson (clerk), Billy Mills, Donald Novis
Summary: After learning that his late uncle Ticonderoga McGee has left him the boat Billy B, Fibber makes plans to sail around the world.
Music: Billy Mills: "Liza," "Deep Purple" (Donald Novis, vocal), "Umbrella Man" (Four Notes, vocal), "No Wonder"
Running Gags: Cigar routine (Fibber and Fiditch), "That ain't the way I heered it" (Old Timer), Myrt bit about brother/whaling expeditions/woodshed (Fibber), "Where'd I put those navigation papers?" (Horatio), tongue twister starting with Sea Urchin McGee (Fibber)
Comments: There is a witty exchange when the nautical clerk says, "We have a special sale today on silent foghorns for clear weather" and Fibber replies, "That so? You got any cork anchors for people who just want to drift?" When Fibber asks Wilcox how he saved a woman, he admits sheepishly, "I got a feeling I shouldn't have asked that, folks," one of many times when he winks at us as if to say, "Here comes the pitch, folks."

Date: April 4, 1939
Title: Antique Furniture
Cast: Jim Jordan (Fibber), Harlow Wilcox (Sergeant Wilcox), Bill Thompson (Old Timer, Nick Depopolis), Isabel Randolph (Abigail Uppington), Harold Peary (Wallaby), Elvia Allman (stocking saleslady), Billy Mills, Donald Novis
Summary: Upon learning that an antique dealer is in town, Fibber abuses his furniture to "age" them.
Music: Billy Mills: "A Shine on Your Shoes," "This Night" (Donald Novis, vocal), "The Cuckoo in the Clock" (Four Notes, vocal)
Running Gags: "That ain't the way I heered it" (Old Timer), tongue twister starting with Canadian Capers McGee (Fibber), Myrt bit about brother/Harvard College/House of Corrections (Fibber), cigar routine (Fibber and Wallaby)
Comments: Wilcox appears as a Canadian Mountie during the commercial to honor the stations of the Canadian Broadcasting Corporation which are now carrying the program. Fibber again treats us as one of the family after a door knock, telling us that it isn't the antique dealer because "We ain't built up enough suspense yet."

Date: April 11, 1939
Title: Delivering the Mail
Cast: Jim Jordan (Fibber), Harlow Wilcox, Bill Thompson (Angus McTavish, telegram delivery man, Old Timer, Horatio K. Boomer, Nick Depopolis), Isabel Randolph (Abigail Uppington), Harold Peary (resident), Mel Blanc (resident with hiccups), ZaSu Pitts (resident), Billy Mills, Donald Novis
Summary: While the regular mailman is on vacation, Fibber takes his place.
Music: Billy Mills: "You Do Something to Me," "Heaven Can Wait" (Donald Novis, vocal), "I Cried for You" (Four Notes, vocal), "That Ain't the Way I Heered It" (Fibber, Uppington, Old Timer, Novis, Nick, Mel Blanc's character with hiccups)
Running Gags: "That ain't the way I heered it" (Old Timer), "Where'd I put that power of attorney?" (Horatio)
Comments: Because this is the 200th program in the series, mock telegrams of congratulations from comedians Jack Benny, Bob Hope, and Eddie Cantor arrive at timely intervals. More gentle self-kidding is evident in the song Billy Mills wrote, "That Ain't the Way I Heered It," which allows most of the cast to chime in with a verse. Quinn's ability to make a slightly racy line seem innocently amusing is apparent in the postcard Fibber reads from a man who has a room adjacent to a room occupied by a couple on their honeymoon: "Having fine time. Wish you could hear."

Date: April 18, 1939
Title: Bills and a Budget
Cast: Jim Jordan (Fibber), Marian Jordan (Molly, Teeny), Harlow Wilcox, Bill Thompson (Old Timer, Horatio K. Boomer), Isabel Randolph (Abigail Uppington), Harold Peary (laughing artist), Mel Blanc (insurance man, passenger on streetcar, mendicant), Billy Mills
Summary: Because Molly is dismayed by the bills accrued during her absence, Fibber acquires a budget book to help manage their finances.
Music: Billy Mills: "Fine and Dandy," "You're the Only One for Me" (Donald Novis, vocal), "Hawaiian War Chant" (Four Notes, vocal), "Wishing"
Running Gags: "'Tain't funny, McGee" (Molly), "That ain't the way I heered it" (Old Timer), "Where'd I put that budget book?" (Horatio)
Comments: Marian receives a warm response from the audience when she is introduced at the beginning of the program. The contrast between the title characters is dramatic: Fibber speaks in the colloquial, jocular tone that will be his norm throughout the rest of the series while Molly is still harping away as a scold, asking "Who's Myrt?" in a jealous tone after answering the phone and referring to her husband in derogatory terms like *igernitz*. The little girl who will appear regularly at the McGee doorstep identifies herself as Teeny. Fibber gets off a rib-tickler with "I don't know any red-hot mamas. All I know is smolder women." For a change Boomer, who is posing as a clerk in the stationery store, actually finds what he is looking for, the budget book, before making a hasty retreat.

Date: April 25, 1939
Title: Glasses
Cast: Jim Jordan (Fibber), Marian Jordan (Molly, Teeny, Mrs. Wheedledeck), Harlow Wilcox, Bill Thompson (Old Timer, man at doctor's door, Nick Depopolis), Harold Peary (Doctor Donald Gildersleeve), Isabel Randolph (Abigail Uppington), Mel Blanc (patient), Bea Benaderet (receptionist), Billy Mills
Summary: After Fibber experiences difficulty reading a newspaper, he visits an optometrist.
Music: Billy Mills: "The Best Things in Life Are Free," "My Reverie" (Donald Novis, vocal), "Basin Street Blues" (Four Notes, vocal), "I've Taken a Fancy to You"
Running Gags: Myrt bit involving cousin getting swallowed by a goldfish (Fibber), "That ain't the way I heered it" (Old Timer), "'Tain't funny, McGee" (Molly)
Comments: Doctor Gildersleeve's office is at 14th and Oak, the prime commercial property in Wistful Vista where most businesses are located. Fibber indicates that Uppy belongs to the upper crust "but she's beginning to crumble," a variation of a joke Quinn inserts occasionally using bread. The tag mentions the recent opening of the Johnson's Wax building in Racine which was designed by Frank Lloyd Wright.

Date: May 2, 1939 (Script)
Title: Driving Used Car Home
Cast: Jim Jordan (Fibber), Marian Jordan (Molly, Teeny), Harlow Wilcox, Bill Thompson (Horatio K. Boomer, Old Timer, officer), Harold Peary (car salesman), Isabel Randolph (Abigail Uppington), Frank Nelson (Joe)
Summary: Fibber and Molly, after purchasing a used car, are stopped several times by policemen asking for various licenses.
Music: Billy Mills: "Rosalie," "If There Is Someone Lovelier Than You" (Donald Novis, vocal), "I'll See You in My Dreams"
Running Gags: "Now where is that address?" (Horatio), "That ain't the way I heered it" (Old Timer), tongue twister starting with Gas Bag McGee (Fibber)
Comments: McGee aptly describes Boomer's character as "shadier than a coal mine during a total eclipse." In the tag Marian thanks listeners for the many wires, letters, and postcards she received since her return to the show.

Date: May 9, 1939 (Script)
Title: World's Fair Plans
Cast: Jim Jordan (Fibber), Marian Jordan (Molly, Teeny), Harlow Wilcox, Bill Thompson (Old Timer, Nick Depopolis), Harold Peary (plumber), Isabel Randolph (Abigail Uppington), Billy Mills
Summary: After receiving a $200 check from Aunt Sarah, the McGees try to recover a coin flipped to determine whether they will go to New York or San Francisco to see the World's Fair.
Music: Billy Mills: "I Know That You Know," "Bury Me Not on the Lone Prairie" (Donald Novis, vocal), "Three Little Fishes" (Four Notes, vocal)
Running Gags: "'Tain't funny, McGee" (Molly), "That ain't the way I heered it" (Old Timer), Myrt bit involving taxicab/boy or girl/doll (Fibber)
Comments: This is one of the few episodes that gives listeners an idea of where in the country Wistful Vista is when Molly indicates they live midway between California and New York. The McGees do not even leave their property with their windfall because the $200 is needed to pay the plumber's bill for retrieving the flipped coin from a drainpipe.

Date: May 16, 1939
Title: Zither
Cast: Jim Jordan (Fibber), Marian Jordan (Molly, Teeny), Harlow Wilcox, Bill Thompson (Old Timer, Nick Depopolis), Harold Peary (neighbor), Isabel Randolph (Abigail Uppington), Donald Novis
Summary: While Fibber picks away on a zither, he gets picked on by those who disparage his musical ability.
Music: Billy Mills: "Sing, My Heart," "Our Love" (Donald Novis, vocal), "Way Down Yonder in New Orleans" (Four Notes, vocal)
Running Gags: Tongue twister starting with Tune Twister McGee (Fibber), "That ain't the way I heered it" (Old Timer), cigar routine (Fibber and neighbor)

Comments: The May 2nd and May 9th episodes mentioned the expected arrival of a zither Fibber had ordered so listeners were prepared for the backyard picking and grinning. Molly's voice and manner are becoming more tolerant and natural in her exchanges with Fibber. Molly excuses herself before Teeny's appearance as she will do often during the series so Fibber and Teeny can banter freely without Marian having to jump back and forth between the two characters. Teeny's precocious sassiness, one of her most endearing traits, is apparent in her statement after Fibber's lengthy tongue twister: "Are you the old windbag!" However, the biggest laugh of the evening occurs when Isabel stumbles over her pronunciation of *zither*, which Jim follows up with "We do all right accidentally." McGee accurately describes Nick's mangled tales as "feeble fables." This episode is distinctive in that all the action takes place *around* the house (on the back porch, in the backyard, or at the neighbor's front door) rather than *in* the house.

Date: May 23, 1939
Title: Parrot or Stork?
Cast: Jim Jordan (Fibber), Marian Jordan (Molly, Teeny), Harlow Wilcox, Bill Thompson (Nick Depopolis, Horatio K. Boomer), Harold Peary (Gooey Fooey, motorcycle cop), Isabel Randolph (Abigail Uppington), Mel Blanc (hiccupping telegram delivery man), Donald Novis
Summary: Fibber awaits the delivery of a bird being sent by Mort Toops.
Music: Billy Mills: "Rise and Shine," "The Way You Look Tonight" (Donald Novis, vocal), "And the Angels Sing" (Four Notes, vocal)
Running Gags: Myrt bit involving grandfather/bullet/Gettysburg (Fibber), "Where I'd put that punchboard?" (Horatio), "Gotta get them brakes fixed" (Fibber)
Comments: Nick recounts his version of the Robinson Crusoe story in fractured English. Teeny delivers a Quinn quote of note when she repeats her father's description of Wynken, Blynken, and Nod as two producers and a yes man.

Date: May 30, 1939
Title: Convicts in the House?
Cast: Jim Jordan (Fibber), Marian Jordan (Molly, Teeny, old lady on roller skates), Harlow Wilcox, Bill Thompson (Old Timer, Nick Depopolis, voice of second convict, Murphy), Harold Peary (voice of first convict, policeman), Isabel Randolph (Abigail Uppington), Mel Blanc (newspaper hawker), Donald Novis
Summary: McGee buys cigars, then returns home to discover that Molly is apparently being held captive by escaped convicts.
Music: Billy Mills: "Hallelujah," "I'm Building a Sailboat of Dreams" (Donald Novis, vocal), "Jonah and the Whale" (Four Notes, vocal), "Zing Went the Strings of My Heart"
Running Gag: "That ain't the way I heered it" (Old Timer)

Comments: Nick gives his take on Paul Revere's ride in fractured English. Fibber states a Quinn quote of note with his claim that women in Uppy's club remind him of a dollar alarm clock: "Full of good works, sound awful busy, and never quite on time."

Date: June 6, 1939
Title: Wrestler McGee
Cast: Jim Jordan (Fibber), Marian Jordan (Molly, Teeny), Harlow Wilcox, Bill Thompson (Horatio K. Boomer, Old Timer, Gabby), Harold Peary (manager), Isabel Randolph (Abigail Uppington), Mel Blanc (man at door, Jerky), Donald Novis
Summary: When a handwriting expert informs Fibber he is the athletic type, McGee decides to become a wrestler.
Music: Billy Mills: "The Lady's in Love with You," "A New Moon and an Old Serenade" (Donald Novis, vocal), "When You and I Were Young" (Four Notes, vocal)
Running Gags: "Where'd I put those floor plans?" (Horatio), "That ain't the way I heered it" (Old Timer), tongue twister starting with Book Match McGee (Fibber)
Comments: A clever Egyptian skit involving Jim, Marian, and Harlow sells the CarNu auto wax in a pleasant fashion. Self-deprecating gags appear in many scripts and this episode abounds in them, including Molly's retort to Fibber's claim there are too many comedians on the show: "Name one."

Date: June 13, 1939
Title: Advice Column
Cast: Jim Jordan (Fibber), Marian Jordan (Molly, Mrs. Wearybottom), Harlow Wilcox, Bill Thompson (man at door, Old Timer, Horatio K. Boomer), Harold Peary (J. Bumble Busby, Ransom), Isabel Randolph (Abigail Uppington), Bea Benaderet (stenographer), Donald Novis
Summary: The McGees take over the advice to the world-weary column for *The Wistful Vista Gazette*.
Music: Billy Mills: "Of Thee I Sing," "I Never Knew Heaven Could Speak" (Donald Novis, vocal), "Mississippi Mud" (Four Notes, vocal)
Running Gags: "'Tain't funny, McGee" (Molly), "That ain't the way–" (Old Timer interrupts himself), "Where'd I put that item?" (Horatio)
Comments: All of the action occurs in the newspaper office with no scenes at the McGee residence. The Old Timer admits to having a 62-year-old son named Ransom who does a bit here and never appears again in the series.

Date: June 20, 1939
Title: Toothache Sends Fibber to Dentist
Cast: Jim Jordan (Fibber), Marian Jordan (Molly, Teeny), Harlow Wilcox, Bill Thompson (Old Timer, Greek voice in flashback), Isabel Randolph

(Abigail Uppington, Miss Fiditch), Harold Peary (Doctor Wilberforce Gildersleeve), Mel Blanc (man at door, hiccupping newspaper salesman), Donald Novis

Summary: Fibber goes to Doctor Gildersleeve to cure his toothache.

Music: Billy Mills: "Don't Ever Leave Me," "The One Rose" (Donald Novis, vocal), "Hooray for Spinach" (Four Notes, vocal), "Hang Your Heart on a Hickory Limb"

Running Gag: "That's just about the way I heered it" (Old Timer)

Comments: The episode features a flashback in which Gildersleeve and Fibber were rivals for Molly's affections and Fibber gets Gildy in trouble with the teacher. Quinn tossed in a switch on the Old Timer's famous line now and then to provide a little variety.

Date: June 27, 1939 (Script)
Title: Loan for Summer Trip
Cast: Jim Jordan (Fibber), Marian Jordan (Molly, Teeny), Harlow Wilcox, Bill Thompson (Old Timer, Nick Depopolis), Harold Peary (Hamilton J. Sharkey), Isabel Randolph (Abigail Uppington), Billy Mills, Alec Templeton
Summary: The McGees go to the Lendahand Loan Company to borrow $500 for their summer vacation.
Music: Billy Mills: "Love Is Sweeping the Country," "Phil the Fluter's Ball" (Donald Novis, vocal), "Goodbye, My Love, Goodbye" (Four Notes, vocal)
Running Gags: "'Tain't funny, McGee" (Molly), "That ain't the way I heered it" (Old Timer), tongue twister starting with Polka Chip McGee (Fibber)
Comments: This "lost episode" contains an exchange between the loan officer and Fibber that pointedly answers the question of our hero's occupation when Sharkey asks, "What kind of work do you do?" and McGee replies, "We do a radio show, *Fibber McGee and Molly.*" Although Fibber repeatedly professes his belief that Teeny is a pint-sized adult, on this occasion he mutters "she's a forty-year-old midget" because she would have to be that old to remember the hoary gag she recites before her exit. Alec Templeton makes a brief appearance to promote the summer replacement series, *The Alec Templeton Show.*

Date: September 5, 1939
Title: Fish Fry for Friends
Cast: Jim Jordan (Fibber), Marian Jordan (Molly, Teeny), Harlow Wilcox, Bill Thompson (Old Timer, Horatio K. Boomer, Nick Depopolis), Isabel Randolph (Abigail Uppington), Harold Peary (pollster), Mel Blanc (laundryman), Billy Mills, Donald Novis
Summary: The McGees invite their friends to a fish fry to commemorate their return from summer vacation.
Music: Billy Mills: "Don't Ever Leave Me," "Over the Rainbow" (Donald Novis, vocal), "Back to Back," "Good Morning"

Running Gags: "That ain't the way I heered it" (Old Timer), "'Tain't funny, McGee" (Molly), "Where'd I put that entry blank?" (Horatio)

Comments: Bill Thompson is now mentioned in the opening credits. McGee and Teeny engage in "Oh, Yes"–"Oh, No" badinage for the first time. The brogue in Molly's speech and the harshness in her attitude are virtually gone now. Fibber is introduced as "Squire of 79 Wistful Vista," a title he will be given a number of times in the coming years.

Date: September 12, 1939
Title: Elope on Fifteenth Anniversary
Cast: Jim Jordan (Fibber), Marian Jordan (Molly, Teeny), Harlow Wilcox, Bill Thompson (Mike, radio dispatcher, Horatio K. Boomer, Old Timer), Harold Peary (salesman, Callahan), Isabel Randolph (Abigail Uppington), Frank Nelson (police lieutenant), Donald Novis
Summary: Fibber and Molly's decision to elope to celebrate their anniversary leads to their arrest for breaking and entering.
Music: Billy Mills: "Sing, My Heart," "My Wild Irish Rose" (Donald Novis, vocal), "White Sails"
Running Gags: Tongue twister starting with Pinhead McGee (Fibber), "Where'd I I put that thousand bucks?" (Horatio), "That ain't the way I heered it" (Old Timer)
Comments: Horatio does find what he is looking for, albeit a counterfeit $1,000 bill. The Old Timer admits he married the McGees in 1924, an impossibility given the program's continuity which has the couple meeting him for the first time in 1937.

Date: September 19, 1939
Title: Gossip Column
Cast: Jim Jordan (Fibber), Marian Jordan (Molly, Teeny), Harlow Wilcox, Bill Thompson (Old Timer, Horatio K. Boomer), Harold Peary (watchman, waiter), Isabel Randolph (Abigail Uppington), Mel Blanc (nightclub MC), Frank Nelson (man with whip), Sara Berner (Miss Print)
Summary: Fibber takes over when the gossip columnist for *The Wistful Vista Gazette* goes on vacation.
Music: Billy Mills: "The Best Things in Life Are Free," "An Apple for the Teacher," "Melancholy Mood" (Donald Novis, vocal)
Running Gags: "'Tain't funny, McGee" (Molly), "That ain't the way I heered it" (Old Timer), "Where'd I put that tidbit?" (Horatio)
Comments: Isabel tries to pick up Jim's fumble on *festivities* and gain some extra comic yardage. Fibber delivers a Quinn quote of note in this definition: "A scoop is when you get there first to give some second-rater the third degree for the fourth estate."

Date: September 26, 1939
Title: Faking an Illness
Cast: Jim Jordan (Fibber), Marian Jordan (Molly, Teeny), Harlow Wilcox, Bill Thompson (Old Timer, Nick Depopolis), Harold Peary (doctor), Isabel Randolph (Abigail Uppington), Mel Blanc (exterminator), Donald Novis, Frankie Zaputo
Summary: Fibber pretends to be ill to avoid taking down the window screens.
Music: Billy Mills: "A New Sun in the Sky," "Pagan Love Song," "The Man with the Mandolin" (Donald Novis, vocal), "I Long to Belong to You" Frankie Zaputo performs "Lazybones"
Running Gags: "'Tain't funny, McGee" (Molly), "That ain't the way I heered it" (Old Timer)
Summary: Another of the self-mocking gags occurs when Teeny voices the Old Timer's famous line of skepticism after Fibber provides the straight line of "I don't lay eggs." A Quinn quote of note occurs when Fibber describes a wrinkle as "just a dimple that got up to stretch and never sat down again."

Date: October 3, 1939
Title: Killer Canova's Autograph
Cast: Jim Jordan (Fibber), Marian Jordan (Molly, Teeny), Harlow Wilcox, Bill Thompson (Old Timer, Canova's servant, Horatio K. Boomer), Harold Peary (Throckmorton P. Gildersleeve), Isabel Randolph (Abigail Uppington), Donald Novis
Summary: In hopes of collecting a $500 finder's fee, the McGees seek the autograph of public enemy Killer Canova.
Music: Billy Mills: "Embraceable You," "Little White Lies," "The Lamp is Low" (Donald Novis, vocal) Teeny sings a portion of "We're Off to See the Wizard"
Running Gags: Tongue twister starting with Plug Ugly McGee (Fibber), "That ain't the way I heered it" (Old Timer), "Where'd I put that autograph?" (Horatio)
Comments: This episode marks the first use of Throckmorton P. Gildersleeve, the name that will be applied shortly to Fibber and Molly's neighbor. Within seconds of meeting Gildersleeve, Fibber calls him Throcky, a McGee characteristic of assigning folksy nicknames to new acquaintances immediately after meeting them.

Date: October 10, 1939
Title: Charity Bazaar
Cast: Jim Jordan (Fibber), Marian Jordan (Molly, old lady at bazaar), Harlow Wilcox, Bill Thompson (Old Timer, Horatio K. Boomer, bidder at bazaar), Harold Peary (man at door, bidder at bazaar), Isabel Randolph (Abigail Uppington), Frankie Zaputo
Summary: Fibber is reluctant to donate his old overcoat to the charity bazaar.

Music: Billy Mills: "A Shine on Your Shoes," "South of the Border" (Donald Novis, vocal), "It Had to Be You," "Goody, Goodbye" "You Go to My Head" performed by Frankie Zaputo
Running Gag: "That ain't the way I heered it" (Old Timer)
Comments: Frankie Zaputo's off-key, stop-and-start singing was a novelty that wore thin after two appearances, a showstopper in the wrong sense. The tag includes a sincere appeal to give to charity invoking Quinn's love of puns: "A city's heart beats loudest in its Community Chest."

Date: October 17, 1939
Title: Lawn Care
Cast: Jim Jordan (Fibber), Marian Jordan (Molly, Teeny), Harlow Wilcox, Bill Thompson (man at door, Old Timer, Nick Depopolis), Harold Peary (Throckmorton P. Gildersleeve), Isabel Randolph (Abigail Uppington)
Summary: Fibber and Gildersleeve argue about raking leaves to keep their lawns tidy.
Music: Billy Mills: "Fine and Dandy," "Comes Love," "Diane" (Donald Novis, vocal), "All in Favor Say Aye"
Running Gags: Myrt bit involving sister/pinched/revolving door (Fibber), "That ain't the way I heered it" (Old Timer), tongue twister starting with Prune Whip McGee (Fibber)
Comments: An inventive introduction opens the program with Wilcox employing a variation of "When the Frost is on the Punkin." Fibber and Gildersleeve are at loggerheads from their first words as neighbors, a rivalry of the best of enemies that will continue throughout their relationship. Nick provides a version of Aesop's fable of the north wind and the sun in his fractured English. Fibber tells a fanciful version of why leaves turn colors in the fall to Teeny followed by her scientific explanation, a prelude of numerous exchanges between the pair that will leave Fibber flabbergasted at the youngster's precocity. Another example of the memorable gags that remain with one long after the hearing occurs after Molly asks her husband how the geese know which way is south and is told that they just follow the robins. "How do the robins know?" she asks and Fibber replies, "They look back and see the geese."

Date: October 24, 1939
Title: Gildersleeve's Party
Cast: Jim Jordan (Fibber), Marian Jordan (Molly, Teeny), Harlow Wilcox, Bill Thompson (Horatio K. Boomer, Old Timer), Harold Peary (Throckmorton P. Gildersleeve), Isabel Randolph (Abigail Uppington)
Summary: The McGees attend a buffet supper and party next door at the Gildersleeves.
Music: Billy Mills: "Life Begins When You're in Love," "Are You Having Any Fun?," "With a Song in My Heart" (Donald Novis, vocal), "Ding Dong, the Witch is Dead"

Running Gags: "Where'd I put that $5.00 bill?" (Horatio), "That ain't the way I heered it" (Old Timer), tongue twister starting with Graveyard McGee (Fibber)

Comments: Gildersleeve's wife is too busy preparing the food to be seen by the guests. She is mentioned but does not appear on *Fibber McGee and Molly*, and Gildersleeve is a bachelor throughout the years of *The Great Gildersleeve*. Jim's teasing chortle and Bill's answering cackle make for delightful comic harmony. Wilcox's commercial told as a spooky ghost story is an effective way of getting listeners to pay attention. A Quinn quote of note is Fibber's description of a ghost and a sailor with a sprained ankle: "One's a hobgoblin and the other's a gob hobblin'."

Date: October 31, 1939
Title: Auto Show
Cast: Jim Jordan (Fibber), Marian Jordan (Molly, Teeny), Harlow Wilcox, Bill Thompson (Old Timer, salesman, customer, Horatio K. Boomer), Harold Peary (Throckmorton P. Gildersleeve), Isabel Randolph (Abigail Uppington)
Summary: The McGees visit the auto show where they meet car salesman Gildersleeve.
Music: Billy Mills: "Who?," "Blue Room," "Good Night, My Love" (Donald Novis and Paul Taylor Choristers, vocal), "Put That Down in Writing"
Running Gags: "That ain't the way I heered it" (Old Timer), "Where'd I put that trinket?" (Horatio)
Comments: Quinn's kit bag of material was so extensive that he could take a show that had a similar story line as an earlier broadcast (October 11, 1937) and make new gags out of old. The tag is a parody of soap opera teasers with Fibber and Molly offering leading questions about Uppy, Teeny, Boomer, Wilcox, and the Old Timer designed to lure listeners back for another week of merriment.

Date: November 7, 1939
Title: Hiawatha
Cast: Jim Jordan (Fibber), Marian Jordan (Molly, Teeny), Harlow Wilcox, Bill Thompson (Old Timer, Horatio K. Boomer), Harold Peary (Throckmorton P. Gildersleeve), Isabel Randolph (Abigail Uppington)
Summary: The McGees, Gildersleeve, and Boomer perform in Fibber's dramatic version of *The Song of Hiawatha*.
Music: Billy Mills: "Great Day," "Lady Be Good," "Last Night" (Donald Novis and Paul Taylor Choristers, vocal), "Make with the Kisses"
Running Gags: Tongue twister starting with Box Office McGee (Fibber), "That ain't the way I heered it" (Old Timer), "Where'd I put that tomahawk?" (Horatio)

Comments: There is more of the story of Pocahontas than the tale of Hiawatha in the play, but the fun is in the rhyming puns and the parody of Longfellow's verses. A Quinn quote of note is delivered in Teeny's definition of a stage door Johnny: "A sap who hangs around with orchids in his hand and dough in his jeans waiting for a chorus girl with knots in her legs and larceny in her heart." Jim and Marian announce in the tag that Donald Novis is leaving the program.

Date: November 14, 1939
Title: Parking Ticket
Cast: Jim Jordan (Fibber), Marian Jordan (Molly, Teeny), Harlow Wilcox, Bill Thompson (Officer Donahue, Old Timer, Horatio K. Boomer), Harold Peary (Throckmorton P. Gildersleeve), Frank Nelson (policeman)
Summary: After Fibber receives a parking ticket, he decides to fight it in court.
Music: Billy Mills: "Good Morning," "Ding Dong, the Witch is Dead," "Begin the Beguine" (Jimmy Shields, vocal), "It's a Hap-Hap-Happy Day"
Running Gags: "'Tain't funny, McGee" (Molly), "Gotta get them brakes fixed" (Fibber), "That ain't the way I heered it" (Old Timer), "Where'd I put that bailiff?" (Horatio)
Comments: Molly suggests that Teeny may be a midget, a belief that Fibber will espouse a number of times in the coming years after losing battles of wits with the child. Molly gives Marian's actual maiden name of Driscoll to Donahue. This is the first appearance of Jimmy Shields as vocalist on the program. The tag includes an appeal for the Red Cross so listeners can show "where the heart is."

Date: November 21, 1939
Title: Library Book Overdue
Cast: Jim Jordan (Fibber), Marian Jordan (Molly, Teeny), Harlow Wilcox, Bill Thompson (Old Timer, Nick Depopolis, Jake), Harold Peary (Throckmorton P. Gildersleeve, Chinese man on phone), Isabel Randolph (Abigail Uppington)
Summary: After receiving a letter about an overdue library book, Fibber cannot remember the title or where he left it.
Music: Billy Mills: "All in Favor say Aye," "Scatterbrain," "Good Night, My Beautiful" (Jimmy Shields, vocal)
Running Gags: "That's not the way I heered it" (Old Timer), Myrt bit involving brother/shot/movie (Fibber), "Gotta get them brakes fixed" (Fibber), "'Tain't funny, McGee" (Molly)
Comments: Fibber alerts us that Wilcox is about to deliver the commercial pitch by saying, "Loosen your collar, folks, I'm about to stick your necks out." In this episode the sound effect of the McGee car chugging along resembles that of the Maxwell on *The Jack Benny Program*.

Date: November 28, 1939
Title: Finance Company
Cast: Jim Jordan (Fibber), Marian Jordan (Molly, Teeny), Harlow Wilcox, Bill Thompson (Old Timer, Horatio K. Boomer), Harold Peary (Throckmorton P. Gildersleeve), Isabel Randolph (Abigail Uppington), Frank Nelson (Perkins)
Summary: The McGees try to avoid the man from the Wistful Vista Finance Company.
Music: Billy Mills: "Goody Goodbye," "Ciribiribin," "Lilacs in the Rain" (Jimmy Shields, vocal)
Running Gags: "That ain't the way I heered it" (Old Timer), tongue twister starting with Loophole McGee (Fibber), "Where'd I put that notebook?" (Horatio)
Comments: Fibber delivers a Quinn quote of note explaining why he is not fond of mistletoe: "There's too many guys that stand under and not enough gals that understand." Perkins, who is named by Teeny as her daddy in this episode, really knows the ropes: on June 6, 1939 she claimed her father grappled in the ring as Gus the Gorilla.

Date: December 5, 1939
Title: Store Adjusters
Cast: Jim Jordan (Fibber), Marian Jordan (Molly, Teeny), Harlow Wilcox, Bill Thompson (Old Timer, Santa Claus, Horatio K. Boomer), Harold Peary (Throckmorton P. Gildersleeve), Isabel Randolph (Abigail Uppington), Sara Berner (Mrs. Goldfarb)
Summary: Gildersleeve hires the McGees as adjusters at the Bon Ton Department Store.
Music: Billy Mills: "Anything Goes," "South of the Border," "A Pretty Girl is Like a Melody" (Jimmy Shields, vocal)
Running Gags: "Where'd I put that sales slip?" (Horatio), "That ain't the way I heered it" (Old Timer)
Comments: Quinn's ability to milk every possible pun on a subject is evidenced in Boomer's description of his nephew Wyandotte: "Feather-brained, chicken-hearted, foul-mouthed, and a cluck in general." Fibber's reaction to Harlow's sales pitch demonstrates how subtlety and imagination went a long way on radio: "Well, I'll be a rude expression." The routine in which Fibber is talking about red flannel underwear while Uppy thinks they are talking about dining room chairs also indicates how the medium could be slightly racy without being vulgar. This week Teeny reveals to the audience that the Santa Claus at the Bon Ton is her father.

Date: December 12, 1939
Title: Jewelry Store Robbery

Cast: Jim Jordan (Fibber), Marian Jordan (Molly, Teeny), Harlow Wilcox, Bill Thompson (Old Timer, Horatio K. Boomer), Isabel Randolph (Abigail Uppington), Sara Berner (Mrs. Titelbaum), Harold Peary (officer)
Summary: Fibber attempts to recover a stolen diamond necklace.
Music: Billy Mills: "Hallelujah," "Digga Digga Do," "My Prayer" (Jimmy Shields, vocal)
Running Gags: Tongue twister starting with Get the Lead Out McGee (Fibber), Myrt bit with cousin/razor/grin (Fibber), "You gotta get them brakes fixed" (Fibber), "'Tain't funny, McGee" (Molly), "That ain't the way I heered it" (Old Timer)
Comments: After a small fluff by Jim, he responds to the line "You're talking" with "I was wondering for a minute." After speaking with Myrt, Fibber suggests that "one of these days I'm gonna really get a number and spoil everything." Fibber responds to Teeny's list of facts she knows about him by stating, "Well, I'll be a censored exclamation," a variation of the line he delivered a week before. Teeny provides an accurate portrait of both Jim Jordan *and* Fibber McGee: Height: 5'7" Weight: 147 Waist: 37 inches Birthday: November 16. Boomer reveals that his middle name is Kilpatrick and his current address is Kremer's Drugstore.

Date: December 19, 1939
Title: Package from Uncle Sycamore
Cast: Jim Jordan (Fibber), Marian Jordan (Molly, spirited old lady), Harlow Wilcox, Bill Thompson (Old Timer, Horatio K. Boomer, telegram delivery man), Harold Peary (cab driver, Throckmorton P. Gildersleeve), Isabel Randolph (Abigail Uppington), Bea Benaderet (Miss Abernathy)
Summary: The McGees are anxious to discover the contents of a package sent by Fibber's Uncle Sycamore.
Music: Billy Mills: "It's a Hap-Hap-Happy Day," "Dark Eyes," "I'll Take You Home Again, Kathleen" (Jimmy Shields, vocal), "Laugh Your Way Through Life"
Running Gag: "That ain't the–" (Old Timer interrupts himself)
Comments: Molly delivers a Quinn quote of note: "A heel never gets anywhere without some good soul to lead the way." Fibber continues his string of "bite my tongue" remarks with "Well, I'll be a naughty comment." Peary utters a blooper when he asks for his "show snovel" back.

Date: December 26, 1939
Title: Butler Gildersleeve
Cast: Jim Jordan (Fibber), Marian Jordan (Molly, Teeny), Harlow Wilcox, Harold Peary (Throckmorton P. Gildersleeve), Isabel Randolph (Abigail Uppington), Mel Blanc (hiccupping information clerk), Gale Gordon (Otis Cadwallader)

Summary: To help the McGees impress an old beau of Molly's, Gildersleeve agrees to act as their butler.
Music: Billy Mills: "Heigh Ho," "Stop! It's Wonderful," "I Didn't Know What Time It Was" (Jimmy Shields, vocal)
Running Gags: None
Comments: Gale Gordon appears for the first time. Jim reprises the "show snovel" fluff from the previous week. Otis must be clairvoyant because, after agreeing to come to dinner at the McGees, he shows up at their door without ever being given the address or directions to their house.

Date: January 2, 1940
Title: New Tools
Cast: Jim Jordan (Fibber), Marian Jordan (Molly, Teeny, spirited old lady), Harlow Wilcox, Harold Peary (Throckmorton P. Gildersleeve), Isabel Randolph (Abigail Uppington), Mel Blanc (hiccupping census taker)
Summary: At Molly's urging Fibber makes a doghouse with tools she gave him for Christmas.
Music: Billy Mills: "Love Is Sweeping the Country," "Oh, Johnny, Oh," "When Day Is Done" (Jimmy Shields, vocal)
Running Gags: Myrt bit with drunk/police/root beer (Fibber), "'Tain't funny, McGee" (Molly), tongue twister starting with Bowwow McGee (Fibber)
Comments: Jim opens the show with a playful announcement: "Hi, folks. The program originally cancelled for this time will now be heard." Fibber stifles the urge to swear with "I'll be a series of dashes." It is not unusual for McGee to end up in the doghouse, but it is uncommon for Molly to call her mate by his first name as she does in the tag.

Date: January 9, 1940
Title: Gildersleeve's Suit
Cast: Jim Jordan (Fibber), Marian Jordan (Molly, Teeny), Harlow Wilcox, Bill Thompson (Old Timer, Horatio K. Boomer), Harold Peary (Throckmorton P. Gildersleeve, ticket taker), Isabel Randolph (Abigail Uppington)
Summary: After the McGees receive tickets to a showing of *Gone With the Wind*, Fibber "borrows" Gildy's suit.
Music: Billy Mills: "Liza," "Fascinating Rhythm," "All the Things You Are" (Jimmy Shields, vocal)
Running Gags: "'Tain't funny, McGee" (Molly), "That ain't the way I heered it" (Old Timer), tongue twister starting with Hypocritical McGee (Fibber), "Good thing I got them brakes fixed" (Fibber, after the usual sound effect of squealing tires), "Where'd I put put that ticket stub?" (Horatio)
Comments: Fibber continues his series of statements showing his stifled emotions with "Well, I'll be a censored cognomen." The Bijou Theater joins Kremer's Drugstore and the Bon Ton as the major downtown attractions in Wistful Vista. Teeny's peripatetic papa is now manager of the Bijou.

Date: January 16, 1940
Title: Car Reported Stolen
Cast: Jim Jordan (Fibber), Marian Jordan (Molly, Teeny), Harlow Wilcox, Bill Thompson (Old Timer, Horatio K. Boomer, Irish cop), Harold Peary (Gus, Throckmorton P. Gildersleeve), Isabel Randolph (Abigail Uppington), Mel Blanc (Lieutenant Brorby), Gale Gordon (man on the street)
Summary: After reporting their car stolen, the McGees are arrested for stealing it themselves.
Music: Billy Mills: "Rise and Shine," "Indian Summer," "Over the Rainbow" (Jimmy Shields, vocal)
Running Gags: "'Tain't funny, McGee" (Molly), Myrt bit involving brother/leg/shoot him (Fibber), "That ain't the way I heered it" (Old Timer), "Gotta get them brakes fixed" (Fibber), "Where'd I put that address book?" (Horatio)
Comments: Fibber concludes his stifled statements with "Well, I'll be a gap in the dialogue." Jim provides an ad-lib in response to the Old Timer's inquiry about what the McGees have been doing: "Waiting for a sound effect." The name of the police lieutenant is a wink at the name of the show's advertising agency, Needham, Louis and Brorby. This is a rare episode in which Teeny does not appear until the tag, maybe because Quinn could not fit a gag about a candy rabbit anywhere else in the script.

Date: January 23, 1940
Title: Gildersleeve Girdle Quiz Show
Cast: Jim Jordan (Fibber), Marian Jordan (Molly, woman on tour), Harlow Wilcox, Bill Thompson (Old Timer, Horatio K. Boomer), Harold Peary (Throckmorton P. Gildersleeve, Milton J. Prentwhistle), Isabel Randolph (Abigail Uppington), Gale Gordon (tour guide), Mel Blanc (hiccupping contestant), Sara Berner (Patricia Goldfarb)
Summary: After completing a tour of the Wistful Vista Broadcasting Company studio, the McGees host a quiz show.
Music: Billy Mills: "Goody Goodbye," "Stardust" (Jimmy Shields, vocal), "Three Little Words"
Running Gags: "That ain't the way I heered it" (Old Timer), tongue twister starting with for the Love of Mike McGee (Fibber), "Where'd I put that Taj Mahal?" (Horatio)
Comments: A sample of the fun present in the audience warm-up spills over into some of the openings such as this episode in which Jim jumps into Harlow's introduction to credit Wilcox. Abigail reveals that her middle name is Farthingale and her address is 97 Wistful Vista. Fibber unveils his "nothing that any red-blooded, clean-living American boy" line of false humility for the first time. The tag includes a plea for donations to fight infantile paralysis.

Date: January 30, 1940
Title: Old Suit
Cast: Jim Jordan (Fibber), Marian (Molly, Teeny), Harlow Wilcox, Bill Thompson (Old Timer, Nick Depopolis, Officer Kelly), Harold Peary (Throckmorton P. Gildersleeve), Isabel Randolph (Abigail Uppington), Gale Gordon (man on the street), Billy Mills
Summary: Fibber discovers that getting rid of his old blue serge suit is no easy matter.
Music: Billy Mills: "Make With the Kisses," "Somebody Loves Me," "Careless" (Jimmy Shields, vocal)
Running Gags: Myrt bit invoving father/broke and polluted/water (Fibber), "That ain't the way I heered it" (Old Timer), "'Tain't funny, McGee" (Molly)
Comments: Quinn begins the episode with a funny "he said, she said" bit with Fibber's reading from the newspaper dovetailing with Molly's comments on his pants. Quinn also sets up a commercial that makes listeners pay attention to the message when Molly bets Fibber a dollar that Wilcox will not use the words "Johnson's Wax" during his sales pitch. Jimmy Shields appears for the final time.

Date: February 6, 1940
Title: Everyone Nice to Fibber
Cast: Jim Jordan (Fibber), Marian Jordan (Molly, Teeny), Harlow Wilcox, Bill Thompson (Old Timer, Horatio K. Boomer), Harold Peary (Throckmorton P. Gildersleeve), Isabel Randolph (Abigail Uppington)
Summary: Fibber wonders why everyone is treating him with kindness.
Music: Billy Mills: "Holy Smoke, Can't You Take a Joke?" (The King's Men, vocal), "Give a Little Whistle," "Old MacDonald Had a Farm (The King's Men, vocal), "Pinch Me"
Running Gags: "That's exactly the way I heered it" (Old Timer switches his line), tongue twister starting with Buglenose McGee (Fibber), "Where'd I put those tickets for *Pinocchio*?" (Horatio)
Comments: The King's Men appear for the first time. Boomer actually finds the tickets he is looking for and presents them to a startled Fibber. Teeny precociously calls Confucius the "little mandarin who wasn't there." That Fibber's birthday is February 6th contradicts information on the December 12, 1939 show which identified his birthday as November 16th.

Date: February 13, 1940
Title: Egyptian Good Luck Ring
Cast: Jim Jordan (Fibber), Marian Jordan (Molly, Teeny), Harlow Wilcox, Bill Thompson (Old Timer, Nick Depopolis), Harold Peary (mail carrier, Throckmorton P. Gildersleeve), Isabel Randolph (Abigail Uppington), Gale Gordon (Corpus), Sara Berner (Charity, Miss Goldfarb)
Summary: After Fibber puts on a good luck ring, his luck is anything but good.

Music: Billy Mills: "Ma, He's Making Eyes at Me," "Night After Night After You," "The Lamp Is Low" (The King's Men, vocal), "How High the Moon"
Running Gag: "You're a harrrrd man, McGee" (Throckmorton)
Comments: One week after dealing all the right cards to Fibber, Quinn turns the tables and shows what happens when everything goes wrong. Molly's comment about Fibber precedes Pogo's famous quote by several decades: "McGee, the things that happen to you shouldn't happen to your worst enemy, and that's you, too."

Date: February 20, 1940
Title: To Tell the Truth
Cast: Jim Jordan (Fibber), Marian Jordan (Molly, Teeny), Harlow Wilcox, Bill Thompson (Old Timer, Nick Depopolis), Harold Peary (Throckmorton P. Gildersleeve), Isabel Randolph (Abigail Uppington)
Summary: Molly bets Fibber that he cannot tell the truth for an hour.
Music: Billy Mills: "I Know That You Know," "The Little Red Fox," "Confucius Say" (The King's Men, vocal), "I've Got My Eyes on You"
Running Gags: "That ain't the way I heered it" (Old Timer), "'Tain't funny, McGee" (Molly)
Comments: Fibber actually fibs less than twenty seconds after the cuckoo starts the countdown, but Molly gives him a mulligan. McGee leads into the integrated commercial with a playful question followed by "Said he, with a sly wink at Racine, Wisconsin." This is one of a number of episodes in which the title of the final musical selection by Billy Mills relates to the action which preceded it.

Date: February 27, 1940
Title: Chinchilla Coat
Cast: Jim Jordan (Fibber), Marian Jordan (Molly, Teeny), Harlow Wilcox, Bill Thompson (Horatio K. Boomer, Nick Depopolis), Harold Peary (Throckmorton P. Gildersleeve), Isabel Randolph (Abigail Uppington), Gale Gordon (Doctor Cyclops)
Summary: Fibber seeks a remedy for his sneezing.
Music: Billy Mills: "Louisiana Hayride," "He's a Lucky Guy," "Lazy Rolls the Rio Grande" (The King's Men, vocal)
Running Gags: Tongue twister starting with Dapper Diaper McGee (Fibber), "Where'd I put Grandma Beulah's cold cure?" (Horatio), "'Tain't bunny, McGee" (Molly, doing a clever switch)
Comments: There is plenty of playful humor in this episode right from Fibber's request that Molly keep their scripts and their eggs in different places early in the show to the tag in which Fibber hints that the names of Lincoln and Cadillac might be mentioned on the next week's program in hopes of getting some free cars as gifts for the plugs.

Date: March 5, 1940
Title: Dictionary in the Closet
Cast: Jim Jordan (Fibber), Marian Jordan (Molly, Teeny), Harlow Wilcox, Bill Thompson (Old Timer), Harold Peary (Throckmorton P. Gildersleeve), Isabel Randolph (Abigail Uppington), Mel Blanc (man at the door), Gracie Allen
Summary: Molly opens a can of worms when she opens the hall closet door.
Music: Billy Mills: "Shine," "Gaucho Serenade," "Kapuzalem" (The King's Men, vocal), "It's a Hap-Hap-Happy Day"
Running Gags: Hall closet opened once by Molly, once by Fibber, both of them looking for a dictionary, "That ain't the way I heered it" (Old Timer), Myrt bit involving uncle/body/car (Fibber), "'Taint funny, McGee" (Molly)
Comments: Gracie's appearance is one she made while on her tour of radio shows promoting her presidential bid running on the Suprise Party ticket. One of radio's best-known sound effects debuts in this episode when the hall closet erupts twice. Only in Wistful Vista do telephone operators dial wrong numbers as a matter of routine.

Date: March 12, 1940
Title: Pal of Your Wife
Cast: Jim Jordan (Fibber), Marian Jordan (Molly, Teeny, Mrs. Wearybottom), Harlow Wilcox, Bill Thompson (Old Timer, Nick Depopolis), Harold Peary (Throckmorton P. Gildersleeve), Isabel Randolph (Abigail Uppington), Gale Gordon (head waiter), Billy Mills
Summary: Fibber treats Molly to lunch at Nick's restaurant.
Music: Billy Mills: "Jericho," "I've Got My Eyes on You," "Dinah" (The King's Men, vocal), "How High the Moon"
Running Gags: Tongue twister starting with Kitchenette McGee (Fibber), "That ain't the the way I heered it" (Old Timer)
Comments: Abigail has switched beaus from con man Boomer to baton man Billy. When the McGees spot Uppy with Billy Mills at the hash house, she is caught beneath her station, a plot device Quinn will use several times.

Date: March 19, 1940
Title: Dog License
Cast: Jim Jordan (Fibber), Marian Jordan (Molly, Teeny), Harlow Wilcox (license clerk), Bill Thompson (Old Timer, Nick Depopolis, officer), Harold Peary (Throckmorton P. Gildersleeve, cab driver), Isabel Randolph (Abigail Uppington), Gale Gordon (snoopy mailman)
Summary: Fibber contests a notice he receives in the mail requesting him to buy a dog license when he does not even own a dog.
Music: Billy Mills: "I Got Rhythm," "Ooh! What You Said," "Old King Cole" (The King's Men, vocal)

Running Gags: "'Tain't funny, McGee" (Molly), Myrt bit involving brother/pie-eyed/eating contest (Fibber), "That ain't the way I heered it" (Old Timer)

Comments: This is an early instance of McGee taking on city hall. Another example of self-deprecating humor occurs when Fibber mentions that the couple started working for Johnson's Wax in 1935, pauses a beat, then adds, "Got our first belly laugh in 1938."

Date: March 26, 1940
Title: Planting a Hedge
Cast: Jim Jordan (Fibber), Marian Jordan (Molly, Teeny), Harlow Wilcox, Bill Thompson (Old Timer, Nick Depopolis, Cap Stivers), Harold Peary (Throckmorton P. Gildersleeve), Isabel Randolph (Abigail Uppington)
Summary: After Fibber and Gildersleeve argue over their property line, they decide to hire a surveyor to settle the issue.
Music: Billy Mills: "I Want to Be Happy," "Give a Little Whistle," "All the Things You Are" (The King's Men, vocal)
Running Gags: "That ain't the way I heered it" (Old Timer), tongue twister starting with Party of the First Pot McGee (Fibber)
Comments: More pot shots are directed at the McGees in the tag, concluding with Molly's assertion that they can only please all the people "for a couple months in the summer."

Date: April 2, 1940 (Script)
Title: Watching Gildersleeve's House
Cast: Jim Jordan (Fibber), Marian Jordan (Molly, Teeny), Harlow Wilcox, Bill Thompson (Old Timer, Horatio K. Boomer), Harold Peary (Throckmorton P. Gildersleeve), Isabel Randolph (Abigail Uppington), Gale Gordon (man from collection agency)
Summary: The McGees play house sitters while the Gildersleeves are away.
Music: Billy Mills: "Say Si Si," "Wouldst Could I But Kiss Thy Hand, O Babe," "Fu Manchu" (The King's Men, vocal)
Running Gags: "That ain't the way I heered it" (Old Timer), "[Where'd I put those] personal cards?" (Horatio)
Comments: There is no hall closet gag in this episode but plenty of other sound effects as Fibber and Molly wreck havoc in Gildersleeve Manor. Teeny delivers a witty comparison between the print and screen versions of *Gone With the Wind*: In the book after 1000 pages the reader learns the Blue and Grey come together in the Deep South while after sitting through four hours of the movie "the audience discovers the Black and Blue come together in the same vicinity." The Jordans genially promote their upcoming appearance on *Lux Radio Theatre* in the tag.

Date: April 9, 1940
Title: Homecoming after Lux
Cast: Jim Jordan (Fibber), Marian Jordan (Molly, Teeny), Harlow Wilcox, Bill Thompson (Old Timer, cab driver), Harold Peary (Throckmorton P. Gildersleeve), Isabel Randolph (Abigail Uppington), Ken Christy (bus driver), Billy Mills
Summary: The McGees plan for a warm welcome after returning home from a performance on *Lux Radio Theatre*.
Music: Billy Mills: "Ooh! What You Said," "The Woodpecker Song," medley from *Pinocchio* (The King's Men, vocal)
Running Gags: "'Tain't funny, McGee" (Molly), "But I heered a slightly different version" (Old Timer does a switch)
Comments: The couple had performed in "Mama Loves Papa" on *Lux* just the evening before this broadcast. This episode contains another infrequent instance of Molly addressing her husband as Fibber. Another good-natured slap at themselves is delivered at the end when Fibber reads a message stating that "we never go anywhere on Tuesday night and neither does your program."

Date: April 16, 1940
Title: Ink on the Rug
Cast: Jim Jordan (Fibber), Marian Jordan (Molly, Teeny), Harlow Wilcox, Bill Thompson (Old Timer, Horatio K. Boomer), Harold Peary (Throckmorton P. Gildersleeve), Isabel Randolph (Abigail Uppington)
Summary: The McGees try to remove ink stains from a rug with milk and salt.
Music: Billy Mills: "This Can't Be Love," "Let's All Sing Together," "Mad Dogs and Englishmen" (The King's Men, vocal)
Running Gags: "That ain't the way I heered it" (Old Timer), Myrt bit involving brother/lost at sea/Morse code (Fibber), "Where'd I put Grandma Boomer's stain-removing recipe?" (Horatio), tongue twister starting with Housebroke McGee (Fibber), "'Tain't funny, McGee" (Molly)
Comments: Mention is made several times during the show that April 16th marks the fifth anniversary of the program. The McGees express their gratitude in the tag and credit Don Quinn for much of their success. This episode is the forerunner of the fine messes that Fibber will create in various rooms of 79 Wistful Vista during the coming years.

Date: April 23, 1940
Title: Hanging a Picture
Cast: Jim Jordan (Fibber), Marian Jordan (Molly, Teeny, Geraldine), Harlow Wilcox, Bill Thompson (Old Timer, Jed, Horatio K. Boomer), Harold Peary (Clem, Throckmorton P. Gildersleeve), Isabel Randolph (Abigail Uppington), Mel Blanc (petitioner, man at museum, hiccuping artist Twerp), Guard (Ken Christy), Verna Felton (museum employee)

Summary: Fibber and Molly seek advice on settling a dispute over the proper height to hang a picture.
Music: Billy Mills: "Of Thee I Sing," "You Little Hearbreaker You," "Back Home Again in Indiana" (The King's Men, vocal)
Running Gags: Myrt bit involving uncle/Claude/tiger (Fibber), "That ain't the way I seen it" (Old Timer doing a switch), "'Tain't funny, McGee" (Molly), "Where'd I put that miniature?" (Horatio), "You're a harrrrd man, McGee" (Throckmorton)
Comments: Gildersleeve again appears in the final act as he does in a number of the episodes in which a conflict between Fibber and Gildy is not the main focus, allowing him to comment on the proceedings and stir up some action with bickering gags before the closing commercial.

Date: April 30, 1940
Title: Stage Director
Cast: Jim Jordan (Fibber), Marian Jordan (Molly, Teeny), Harlow Wilcox, Bill Thompson (Old Timer, Nick Depopolis, telegram delivery man), Harold Peary (Throckmorton P. Gildersleeve), Isabel Randolph (Abigail Uppington)
Summary: Fibber downplays the upcoming women's club pageant while waiting for word on a stage director's job.
Music: Billy Mills: "Bojangles of Harlem," So Far, So Good," "With the Wind and the Rain in Your Hair" (The King's Men, vocal), "Night After Night After You"
Running Gags: "That ain't the way I heered it" (Old Timer), "'Tain't funny, McGee" (Molly), tongue twister starting with Script Ease McGee (Fibber)
Comments: The voice used by Bill Thompson as the man who delivers a telegram is the one that will eventually become associated with the character Wallace Wimple. The tongue twister is one of the better ones with Jim developing a singsong cadence and concluding with a cute lead-in to the next musical selection: "Script Ease McGee I was knowed as in those days. Script Ease McGee, the sensational and super-sophisticated showman of stage and screen, schooling sappy cinema stars in the subtle science of screaming and scowling, smiling and smirking, sneering and snorting, sniffing and snickering, sneering and sneezing, shouting and shooting, skillfully supervising stupendous spectacles, shooting smooth and sustained scenarios, shaming Shakespeare and showing up Shaw for his shabby shoddiness, soundly seasoned by storms and stresses, but take it, King's Men, it's tough with these S's."

Date: May 7, 1940
Title: Women's Club Play
Cast: Jim Jordan (Fibber), Marian Jordan (Molly, Teeny), Harlow Wilcox, Bill Thompson (officer, Horatio K. Boomer, Old Timer), Harold Peary (Throckmorton P. Gildersleeve), Isabel Randolph (Abigail Uppington)

Summary: After performing in a play about knights of old, Fibber wears his suit of armor home.
Music: Billy Mills: "Crazy Rhythm," "You, You Darlin'," "We Play Hoops" (The King's Men, vocal)
Running Gags: "'Tain't funny, McLancelot" (Molly), "What did I do with that little gem?" (Horatio), "That ain't the way I heered it" (Old Timer), "You're a harrrrd man, McGee" (Throckmorton)
Comments: Like the play about Hiawatha in which Quinn used rhyme for parody, he employs archaic terms like *forsooth* for great comic effect. The tag includes a sincere plea to remember National Hospital Day and the "men and women in white we turn to when everything looks black."

Date: May 14, 1940
Title: Water Fight
Cast: Jim Jordan (Fibber), Marian Jordan (Molly, Teeny), Harlow Wilcox, Bill Thompson (Nick Depopolis, Old Timer, Horatio K. Boomer), Harold Peary (Throckmorton P. Gildersleeve), Isabel Randolph (Abigail Uppington)
Summary: Fibber and Gildersleeve's bickering over a hose threatens to escalate into fisticuffs.
Music: Billy Mills: "I'm Just Wild about Harry," "My! My!," "Swing Low, Sweet Chariot" (The King's Men, vocal), "Believing"
Running Gags: "It still ain't the way I heered it" (Old Timer), tongue twister starting with Punchbowl McGee (Fibber), "[Where'd I put that] insurance policy?" (Horatio), You're a harrrrd man, McGee" (Throckmorton)
Comments: Fibber's fanciful explanation of why grass is green is countered by Teeny's scientific explanation with words like *photosynthesis* and *chlorophyll* and her sassy closer telling Fibber he can spread his theory on the grass to make it grow.

Date: May 21, 1940
Title: Running a Hardware Store
Cast: Jim Jordan (Fibber), Marian Jordan (Molly, Teeny, spirited old lady), Harlow Wilcox, Bill Thompson (Old Timer, two gun inquirer bits), Harold Peary (Throckmorton P. Gildersleeve), Isabel Randolph (Abigail Uppington), Gale Gordon (Mr. Plumber)
Summary: After a week of playing checkers with Gildersleeve, Fibber agrees to manage a hardware store for one day.
Music: Billy Mills: "Liza," "Playmates," "Coming Through the Rye" (The King's Men, vocal), "Where Do I Go From You?"
Running Gags: "You're a harrrrd man, McGee" (Throckmorton), tongue twister starting with Killer Driller McGee (Fibber), "'Tain't funny, McGee" (Molly), Myrt bit involving sister/vertebrate/spelling bee (Fibber), "That ain't the way I heered it" (Old Timer)

Comments: Fibber and Uppy have a mirthful exchange when she wants a bathtub and he thinks she is talking about bathing. Mrs. Wilcox (played by an unidentified actress) arrives at the hardware store during the integrated commercial to say a few lines about the efficacy of Johnson's Wax. Harlow's wife never appears again in the series.

Date: May 28, 1940
Title: Circus
Cast: Jim Jordan (Fibber), Marian Jordan (Molly, Teeny), Harlow Wilcox, Bill Thompson (Old Timer, Horatio K. Boomer), Harold Peary (Throckmorton P. Gildersleeve), Isabel Randolph (Abigail Uppington), Gale Gordon (Buster Dawson)
Summary: The McGees go to the circus with free tickets.
Music: Billy Mills: "Why?," "You Can't Brush Me Off," "The Singing Hills" (The King's Men, vocal), "I Forget"
Running Gags: Myrt bit involving aunt/beat up by uncle/bed (Fibber), "That's very good, McGee" (Molly), "It ain't the way I heered it" (Old Timer), "You're a harrrrd woman, Mrs. McGee" (Throckmorton), "Where'd I put that sheriff's badge?" (Horatio)
Comments: Buster brings Uppy down off her high horse by reminding her that she used to get up on the horses in the circus as Tootsie LaTour, a bareback rider. Quinn subtly contrasts the childishness of Fibber and Gildy who bicker over a bauble like schoolboys with the maturity of Teeny who is concerned that her father will overeat at the concession stands. The integrated commercial is effectively done with Wilcox acting as a barker on the midway to attract passersby and listeners to his message about Johnson's Wax.

Date: June 4, 1940
Title: Spaghetti Dinner
Cast: Jim Jordan (Fibber), Marian Jordan (Molly, Teeny), Harlow Wilcox, Bill Thompson (Old Timer, Nick Depopolis), Harold Peary (Throckmorton P. Gildersleeve), Isabel Randolph (Abigail Uppington), Sara Berner (Mrs. Goldfarb)
Summary: Fibber makes spaghetti for a stag dinner.
Music: Billy Mills: "Don't Hold Everything," "Too Romantic," "The Leader Doesn't Like Music" (The King's Men, vocal), "How Can I Ever Be Alone?"
Running Gags: "That ain't the way I heered it" (Old Timer), tongue twister starting with Son of a Sea Cook McGee (Fibber), Myrt bit involving family/terrible/nothing happened (Fibber), "You're a harrrrd man, McGee" (Throckmorton)
Comments: Fibber's "flung a fang into" becomes his way of describing tasty food. The pass-it-along request for Jell-O is a variation of the relay question and answer routine heard on *The Jack Benny Program*. Quinn's ability to

switch sayings humorously is evident in most scripts and is used so frequently they are almost throwaway lines. In this episode Molly delivers two of them related to eating: "One if by land, two if bicarbonate" near the beginning and later, after Fibber asks "Stomach gone back on him?" about Wilcox, she replies, "No, it's gone front on him."

Date: June 11, 1940
Title: Paperhanging
Cast: Jim Jordan (Fibber), Marian Jordan (Molly, Teeny), Harlow Wilcox, Bill Thompson (Horatio K. Boomer, Old Timer), Harold Peary (Throckmorton P. Gildersleeve), Isabel Randolph (Abigail Uppington)
Summary: After buying wallpaper at an auction, Fibber decides to paper the living room.
Music: Billy Mills: "You," "Meet the Sun Half Way," "Say It" (The King's Men, vocal), "Where Do I Go From You?"
Running Gags: "'Tain't funny, McGee" (Molly), "That ain't the way I heered it" (Old Timer), Myrt bit involving brother/pinched/wedding train (Fibber), tongue twister starting with Double Bill McGee (Fibber), "You're a harrrrd man, McGee" (Throckmorton)
Comments: Gildy and Fibber again behave childishly, bickering and throwing wallpaper paste at each other. Wilcox's warning to hurry up because the show was just about over brings a sigh from Fibber who wondered how they would get out of the mess. Teeny is indeed a wise child, already being named valedictorian of her class in the second grade.

Date: June 18, 1940
Title: Modeling a Dress
Cast: Jim Jordan (Fibber), Marian Jordan (Molly, Teeny), Harlow Wilcox, Bill Thompson (man at door, Old Timer, cab driver), Harold Peary (Throckmorton P. Gildersleeve), Isabel Randolph (Abigail Uppington)
Summary: Because Fibber helped ruin a dress form, Molly makes him model the dress she is making.
Music: Billy Mills: "Do It Again," "Outside of That, I Love You," "Ezekiel Saw the Wheel" (The King's Men, vocal)
Running Gags: Myrt bit involving skirts longer (Molly), "'Tain't funny, McGee" (Molly), "That ain't the way I heered it" (Old Timer), "You're a harrrrd man, McGee" (Throckmorton)
Comments: The appearance by Thompson as the man at the door that leads into a joke about Bob Hope's program marks the second time the Wallace Wimple voice is used. Quinn's wonderfully descriptive language leaves us with a picture of Uppy as painted by Fibber: "She's about as close-mouthed as a steam shovel and she digs up more dirt, too."

Date: June 25, 1940
Title: Gildersleeve Helps Pack
Cast: Jim Jordan (Fibber), Marian Jordan (Molly, Teeny), Harlow Wilcox, Bill Thompson (Old Timer, Horatio K. Boomer), Harold Peary (Throckmorton P. Gildersleeve), Isabel Randolph (Abigail Uppington), Billy Mills, Meredith Willson
Summary: While Molly and Gildersleeve pack the car for a trip, Fibber creates a musical composition.
Music: Billy Mills: "Shine," "Kiss Me Again," "Old MacDonald Had a Farm" (The King's Men, vocal)
Running Gags: "You're a harrrrd man, McGee" (Throckmorton), tongue twister starting with Bandylegs McGee (Fibber), "Where'd I put those World's Fair tickets?" (Horatio)
Comments: This is the first of numerous episodes in which Fibber plays the artiste with a haughty demeanor as he earnestly works at composing, painting, sculpting, writing, etc. The results of his endeavors are similar to what emerges from the instruments in this episode, a discordant conglomeration of sounds in the Spike Jones manner. Willson, host of the summer replacement series *Meredith Willson's Revue*, is a guest.

Date: October 1, 1940
Title: Back from Vacation
Cast: Jim Jordan (Fibber), Marian Jordan (Molly, Teeny), Harlow Wilcox, Bill Thompson (man at door, Nick Depopolis, Old Timer, warning man), Harold Peary (Throckmorton P. Gildersleeve), Isabel Randolph (Abigail Uppington), Billy Mills
Summary: After the McGees return from summer vacation, Fibber has a feeling he forgot something on the trip.
Music: Billy Mills: "Get the Moon Out of Your Eyes," "I'm Nobody's Baby," "The House That Jack Built" (The King's Men, vocal)
Running Gags: "Gotta get them brakes fixed" (Fibber), "You're a harrrrd man, McGee" (Throckmorton), word confusion involving *paprika/papoose/caboodle* (Fibber and Molly), tongue twister starting with Bullhead McGee (Fibber), Myrt bit involving old man man/shot in leg/cartridges (Fibber)
Comments: With the beginning of the new season, the bridge before the action begins is dropped as Wilcox moves into the introduction right away after completion of the first commercial and opening musical number.

Date: October 8, 1940
Title: Gives Up Cigars
Cast: Jim Jordan (Fibber), Marian Jordan (Molly), Harlow Wilcox, Bill Thompson (Flanagan, Old Timer, Horatio K. Boomer), Harold Peary (Throckmorton P. Gildersleeve), Isabel Randolph (Abigail Uppington), Gale Gordon (doctor), Bea Benaderet (clerk)

Summary: After a doctor advises him to give up cigars, Fibber's will power is put to the test.
Music: Billy Mills: "There's a Great Day Coming Mañana," "That's For Me," "The Breeze and I" (The King's Men, vocal)
Running Gags: "That ain't the way I heered it" (Old Timer), "'Tain't funny, McGee" (Molly), "Where'd I put that sterilized stogie? (Horatio), "You're a good man, McGee" (Throckmorton doing a switch)
Comments: Quinn again lets the audience feel like insiders several times in this episode, most notably with Fibber's lead-in to Wilcox's pitch ("'Why?,' said he innocently, knowing very well he was giving Wilcox an opening he could drive a truck through") and McGee's reaction to a knock on the door ("It's gotta be either Gildersleeve or the little girl unless they rung in another character on us").

Date: October 15, 1940
Title: Missing Screwdriver
Cast: Jim Jordan (Fibber), Marian Jordan (Molly, Teeny, spirited old lady), Harlow Wilcox, Bill Thompson (Old Timer, Flanagan, Horatio K. Boomer), Harold Peary (Throckmorton P. Gildersleeve), Isabel Randolph (Abigail Uppington), Walter Tetley (Cedric Boomer), Gale Gordon (hardware store clerk)
Summary: Fibber's search for a screwdriver leads him all over the house and even downtown.
Music: Billy Mills: "The World Is in My Arms," "Blueberry Hill," "Sawing a Woman in Half" (The King's Men, vocal)
Running Gags: "That ain't the way I heered it" (Old Timer), "Where'd I put that screwdriver?" (Horatio), hall closet opened by Fibber looking for screwdriver
Comments: The highlight of this episode is the bit in which Walter Tetley as Boomer's nephew not only replicates the W.C. Fields voice of his uncle but also extracts from his person juvenile equivalents of the nefarious knickknacks that Horatio carries with him. The tag includes an appeal for the Community Chest.

Date: October 22, 1940
Title: Gildersleeve's Diary
Cast: Jim Jordan (Fibber), Marian Jordan (Molly, Teeny), Harlow Wilcox, Bill Thompson (Nick Depopolis), Harold Peary (Throckmorton P. Gildersleeve), Isabel Randolph (Abigail Uppington)
Summary: When Fibber is a finder and a keeper of Gildersleeve's diary, Gildy is a sore loser who almost becomes a weeper.
Music: Billy Mills: "Our Love Affair," "Little Boy Love," "I Dream of Jeannie" (The King's Men, vocal), "Where Do You Keep Your Heart?"

Running Gags: Hall closet opened by Fibber looking for gloves, "That ain't the way I h–" (Nick before realizing it was the wrong character), word confusion involving *zephyr/zither/heifer/hoofer/zebra* (Fibber, Molly, Nick), "You're a harrrrd man, McGee" (Throckmorton), cigar routine (Fibber and Throckmorton)

Comments: Fibber delivers the equivalent of "to be or not to be" in his "be that as it may or may not be or not" line which he will use a number of times over the years. Gildy reveals that his middle name is Philharmonic.

Date: October 29, 1940
Title: Driving to Football Game
Cast: Jim Jordan (Fibber), Marian Jordan (Molly, Teeny), Harlow Wilcox, Bill Thompson (Old Timer, Nick Depopolis, Horatio K. Boomer, officer), Harold Peary (Throckmorton P. Gildersleeve), Isabel Randolph (Abigail Uppington), Gale Gordon (motorcycle cop), Billy Mills
Summary: The McGees take the entire gang to South Bend for a football game.
Music: Billy Mills: "The Sun'll Be Up in the Morning," medley of college fight songs, "McNamera's Band" (The King's Men, vocal), "Let's Be Buddies"
Running Gags: Hall closet opened by Fibber looking for road maps, "Where'd I put those identification papers?" (Horatio), "'Tain't funny, McGee" (Molly), word confusion involving *furnished/famished/famous/notorious/notary/rotary* (Fibber, Molly, Nick, Throckmorton, Harlow, Abigail), "That ain't the way I heered it" (Old Timer), "You're a hired man, McGee" (Throckmorton), tongue twister starting with Blockhead McGee (Fibber)
Comments: With nine adults jammed in the vintage vehicle, it is surprising that Fibber doesn't declare at some point "Gotta get them springs fixed." The tongue twister is one of the longest in the series. The message at the end reminding listeners to vote serves as an indirect teaser for the subject of the following week's episode.

Date: November 5, 1940
Title: Get Out the Vote
Cast: Jim Jordan (Fibber), Marian Jordan (Molly, giggling woman), Harlow Wilcox, Bill Thompson (Nick Depopolis, Flanagan, Old Timer, man voting, Horatio K. Boomer, Irish city official), Harold Peary (Throckmorton P. Gildersleeve), Isabel Randolph (Abigail Uppington)
Summary: The McGees preside over the polling place inside their home.
Music: Billy Mills: "So You're the One," "Bojangles of Harlem," "You Can't Tell a Man by His Hat" (The King's Men, vocal), "You Walk By"
Running Gags: Word confusion involving *cantaloupe/calamity/antelope* (Fibber, Molly), hall closet opened by Abigail looking for voting booth, Myrt bit involving sister/chopped off/chorus (Fibber), tongue twister starting

with Pretty Please McGee (Fibber), "Where'd I put those instructions?" (Horatio), "You're a harrrrd man, McGee" (Throckmorton)

Summary: Thompson uses the milquetoast voice for the third time when playing a man preparing to vote. Election returns which interrupt the show blend in nicely as if Fibber is tuning in for updates on the radio. The integrated commercial is cleverly done as if Wilcox is electioneering. Fibber's putdown of an Uppy gag hits the spot: "You ought to save that material–indefinitely."

Date: November 12, 1940
Title: Black Eye
Cast: Jim Jordan (Fibber), Marian Jordan (Molly, Teeny), Harlow Wilcox, Bill Thompson (Old Timer, Flanagan, Horatio K. Boomer), Harold Peary (Throckmorton P. Gildersleeve), Isabel Randolph (Abigail Uppington), Gale Gordon (doctor)
Summary: After Fibber gets a black eye, no one believes it happened from bumping into a door.
Music: Billy Mills: "You and Your Kiss," "Loch Lomond," "Biding My Time" (The King's Men, vocal)
Running Gags: Word confusion involving *genius/genie/fractional/frictional* (Fibber, Molly), "That ain't the way I heered it" (Old Timer), "Where'd I put those sunglasses?" (Horatio), hall closet opened by Fibber to hide from Uppy
Comments: This episode contains another switch on a cliché which emerges as a throwaway from Molly assessing Fibber's version of the black eye: "Maybe your story is too true to be good."

Date: November 19, 1940
Title: Visiting Uncle Dennis
Cast: Jim Jordan (Fibber), Marian Jordan (Molly, Teeny), Harlow Wilcox, Bill Thompson (Old Timer, joke teller, Horatio K. Boomer), Harold Peary (Throckmorton P. Gildersleeve), Isabel Randolph (Abigail Uppington)
Summary: The McGees travel by train to see Molly's Uncle Dennis.
Music: Billy Mills: "Why?," "My Heart at Thy Sweet Voice," "Easy Go Slim" (The King's Men, vocal)
Running Gags: "That ain't the way I heered it" (Old Timer), "'Tain't funny, McGee" (Harlow), "Where'd I put that deck of cards?" (Horatio)
Comments: An amusing exchange involving mistaken ideas occurs between Uppy and Fibber when she is talking about babies and he thinks they are discussing quilts. The tag includes an appeal for the American Red Cross. Snippets of "Wing to Wing" are played after the tags until December 24th when it becomes the main theme.

Date: November 26, 1940
Title: Uncle Dennis Visits
Cast: Jim Jordan (Fibber), Marian Jordan (Molly, Teeny), Harlow Wilcox, Bill Thompson (Old Timer, Horatio K. Boomer), Harold Peary (Throckmorton P. Gildersleeve), Isabel Randolph (Abigail Uppington)
Summary: The unseen Uncle Dennis is a hit with everyone else but a miss with the McGees who return to 79 Wistful Vista and discover a disorderly house.
Music: Billy Mills: "Don't Hold Everything," "Fascinating Rhythm," "Moonglow" (The King's Men, vocal)
Running Gags: "That ain't the way I heerd it" (Old Timer), Myrt bit involving brother/knocked down/snowman, "Where'd I put that address?" (Horatio), "You're a harrrrd man, McGee" (Throckmorton), tongue twister starting with Slap Pappy McGee (Fibber)
Comments: Wonderful word play that continues the self-mocking tradition occurs in an exchange when Fibber states that if he had a face like Uncle Dennis has, he wouldn't show it and Teeny tops him with "Yeah, and he said if he had a show like yours, he couldn't face it."

Date: December 3, 1940
Title: Five Tons of Coal
Cast: Jim Jordan (Fibber), Marian Jordan (Molly, Teeny), Harlow Wilcox, Bill Thompson (Old Timer, Nick Depopolis), Harold Peary (Throckmorton P. Gildersleeve), Isabel Randolph (Abigail Uppington)
Summary: Fibber helps Gildersleeve shovel coal into Gildy's basement.
Music: Billy Mills: "Liza," "Ferryboat Serenade," "The Bad Humor Man" (The King's Men, vocal), "How High the Moon"
Running Gags: Word confusion involving *typhoon/tycoon/Ty Cobb/typhoid/siphon/python* (Fibber, Molly), "You're a harrrrd man, McGee" (Throckmorton), hall closet opened by Fibber looking for coat, "That ain't the way I heered it" (Old Timer), "'Tain't funny, McGee" (Molly)
Comments: The best moments in this episode are when Fibber and Gildy try to explain to Teeny how coal is converted into steam heat. Quinn again uses word play for a dig at the program when the Old Timer gives a response to his own question of whether a man was going to listen to *Fibber McGee and Molly* the next week at this time: "Not if they're this weak next time." The childishness of McGee and Gildy is reemphasized in the gifts they plan to give to each other: a Daisy air rifle and a Boy Scout knife.

Date: December 10, 1940
Title: Mailing Christmas Packages
Cast: Jim Jordan (Fibber), Marian Jordan (Molly, Teeny, Nellie), Harlow Wilcox, Bill Thompson (man at door, Old Timer, Horatio K. Boomer), Harold Peary (Throckmorton P. Gildersleeve, Pedro), Isabel Randolph (Abigail Uppington)

Summary: The McGees wait in line at the post office to mail their Christmas packages.

Music: Billy Mills: "Crazy Rhythm," "Our Love Affair," "Hilda" (The King's Men, vocal), "Some of Your Sweetness"

Running Gags: Myrt bit involving sister/face-lifted/false face (Fibber), word confusion involving *camisole/casserole/castor oil* (Fibber, Molly), "You're a harrrrd man, McGee" (Throckmorton), tongue twister starting with Stamping at the Savoy McGee (Fibber), "'Tain't funny, McGee" (Molly), "Where'd I put Mother's letter?" (Horatio)

Comments: Jim's ad-lib after the Myrt bit fizzles is better than the gag: "Yes, it laid there." Teeny's response to Fibber's question of "What juvenile peccadillo aroused his antipathy?" is "What's the matter with you?" which brings about a quick apology. Apparently there were limits to the little girl's audaciousness toward her elders and Marian/Teeny knew when she stepped over that line. Quinn himself steps out on a limb in this episode by bringing into the post office the Old Timer's long-lost sister Nellie (Marian) riding on a horse who stops long enough to address her brother as Roy and haul him aboard for a ride. It is a surreal scene that might have left Fibber muttering the exclamation he sometimes employed after hearing a labored joke or pun: "Whoa, Nellie!" The tag includes an appeal to buy Christmas Seals to fight tuberculosis.

Date: December 17, 1940 (Script)
Title: Chamber of Commerce Presidency
Cast: Jim Jordan (Fibber), Marian Jordan (Molly, Teeny), Harlow Wilcox, Bill Thompson (Old Timer, Nick Depopolis), Harold Peary (Throckmorton P. Gildersleeve), Isabel Randolph (Abigail Uppington), Gale Gordon (chamber chairman), Sara Berner (Mrs. Goldfarb)
Summary: The McGees seek support of Wistful Vista residents after Gildersleeve asks them to help him become president of the chamber of commerce.
Music: Billy Mills: "Of Thee I Sing," "The Carioca," "A Little Close Harmony" (The King's Men, vocal)
Running Gags: Hall closet opened by Fibber looking for hat and coat, "That ain't the way I heered it" (Old Timer), tongue twister starting with Pain in the Knack McGee (Fibber)
Comments: In this episode, the only one in which the McGees cross the threshold of the Uppington manse, it takes Fibber less than two minutes to wreck various precious objects. Gildersleeve confesses that he weighs 232 pounds. In a bizarre twist at the end, McGee's stirring speech in front of business leaders is misinterpreted, resulting in him and not Gildy being elected president. At this time Jim actually served as president of the Encino Chamber of Commerce.

Date: December 24, 1940
Title: Record Player
Cast: Jim Jordan (Fibber), Marian Jordan (Molly, Teeny), Harlow Wilcox, Harold Peary (Throckmorton P. Gildersleeve), Isabel Randolph (Abigail Uppington), Gale Gordon (store clerk), Mel Blanc (delivery man, hiccupping floorwalker)
Summary: The McGees break a radio-phonograph they think belongs to Gildersleeve, then try to replace it before he stops at their house.
Music: Billy Mills: "Keep an Eye on Your Heart," "Skater's Waltz," "Home, Sweet Home" (The King's Men, vocal)
Running Gags: Hall closet opened by Fibber looking for scissors, "'Tain't funny, McGee" (Molly), "You're a harrrrd man, McGee" (Throckmorton)
Comments: "Wing to Wing" replaces "Save Your Sorrow for Tomorrow" as the show's theme song and will remain so through the rest of the series except for three months in 1946. Jim Jordan possessed the wonderful gift of ad-libbing which turned fluffs into lines that generated more laughter than the scripted words. In this episode, after he does not pronounce *succession* exactly correct, he has a great comeback to Molly's remark that they don't have any records to play: "We got that broken one we just did." Bill Thompson's valuable contribution to the show is casually noted in the tag when Molly asks where Nick, the Old Timer, and Boomer are and Fibber replies, "Oh, him. He went to Chicago to spend the holidays with his folks."

Date: December 31, 1940
Title: Finds a Watch
Cast: Jim Jordan (Fibber), Marian Jordan (Molly, Teeny), Harlow Wilcox, Harold Peary (Throckmorton P. Gildersleeve), Isabel Randolph (Abigail Uppington), Gale Gordon (Mr. Wolf), Mel Blanc (claimant for watch)
Summary: Fibber hopes to locate the person who lost the gold watch he found at 14th and Oak.
Music: Billy Mills: "There's a Great Day Coming Mañana," "The Winter Song" (The King's Men, vocal)
Running Gags: Word confusion involving *mollycoddle/molecule/reticule/ridicule* (Fibber, Molly), "'Tain't funny, McGee" (Molly)
Comments: Fibber and Gildy again act like children as they climb in a bathtub to take the watch apart. There is some foreshadowing of the days when toys related to characters on radio and television shows would be commonplace in Teeny's announcement that for Christmas she received a Molly dolly that says, "Heavenly days" and a game called Dadratit, one of Fibber's favorite expressions.

Date: January 7, 1941
Title: Hundred Dollar Bill
Cast: Jim Jordan (Fibber), Marian Jordan (Molly, Teeny), Harlow Wilcox, Bill Thompson (attendant, Old Timer, clerk, Horatio K. Boomer), Harold Peary (Throckmorton P. Gildersleeve), Isabel Randolph (Abigail Uppington), Gale Gordon (cashier)
Summary: Fibber finds that money isn't everything when he has no money on him smaller than a $100 bill.
Music: Billy Mills: "My Mind's on You," "Frenesi," "I Hear a Rhapsody" (The King's Men, vocal), "You Walk By"
Running Gags: Word confusion involving *impeculiar/impecunious/impetuous/non-competitive* (Fibber, Molly), tongue twister starting with Vaude-De-Owed Dough McGee (Fibber), Myrt bit involving brother/hair/rabbit hutch (Fibber), "Where'd I put those small bills?" (Horatio), "You're a harrrrd man, McGee" (Throckmorton), "'Tain't funny, McGee" (Molly), hall closet opened by Fibber looking for slippers
Comments: Jim tosses in another witty ad-lib when Marian's voice cracks as she overacts a bit while trying to emphasize that she is cold and hungry: "Tomorrow night, *East Lynne*," a reference to the sentimental melodrama. Another ad-lib slips by amid the laughter after Marian fluffs "last quarter" instead of "lost quarter" when Jim chimes in with "Lost it in the first quarter [of the show]." The voice of the cigar clerk used by Thompson is again that of the wimp who will become Wallace Wimple. Bill's return after a two-week absence is a welcome one for his contribution to the comic rhythm of the show is inestimable.

Date: January 14, 1941 (Script)
Title: Babysitting Teeny
Cast: Jim Jordan (Fibber), Marian Jordan (Molly, Teeny), Harlow Wilcox, Bill Thompson (Horatio K. Boomer, Old Timer), Harold Peary (Throckmorton P. Gildersleeve), Isabel Randolph (Abigail Uppington)
Summary: Fibber has his hands full when he tries to keep Teeny entertained and fed after the tyke is left in his care.
Music: Billy Mills: "So Sweet," "Two Guitars," "Oh, Susanna" (The King's Men, vocal)
Running Gags: "Where did I put that excuse for dropping in?" (Horatio), "That ain't the way I heered it" (Old Timer), tongue twister starting with Sinker Swim McGee (Fibber), hall closet opened by Fibber looking for pipe
Comments: This week Quinn drags in Thompson's characters rather obtrusively as Horatio confesses he has no reason for being there and the Old Timer shows up with an offer to mow the lawn in mid-January when the ground is covered with four inches of snow.

Date: January 21, 1941
Title: Plays the Piano
Cast: Jim Jordan (Fibber), Marian Jordan (Molly), Harlow Wilcox, Bill Thompson (Old Timer, Charlie), Harold Peary (Throckmorton P. Gildersleeve), Isabel Randolph (Abigail Uppington), Gale Gordon (clerk, Percy), Sara Berner (Helen Highwater)
Summary: After attending a concert, Fibber wants to become a pianist.
Music: Billy Mills: "Love Is," "Perfidia," "Old Rockin' Chair" (The King's Men, vocal)
Running Gags: "That ain't the way I heered it" (Old Timer), tongue twister starting with Long Under Ware McGee (Fibber), "You're a harrrrd man, McGee" (Throckmorton), Myrt bit involving 9999/6666/standing on head (Fibber)
Comments: The integrated commercial includes numerous musical terms such as *treble, sharp, measures, flat, bar, chorus, key, major, overture, counterpoint,* and *duet* which keeps listeners attuned to the sponsor's message. Jim recovers from his fluff on the word *now* with an apposite ad-lib: "It's hard to play piano and talk at the same time."

Date: January 28, 1941 (Script)
Title: Hand Stuck in Bottle
Cast: Jim Jordan (Fibber), Marian Jordan (Molly, Teeny), Harlow Wilcox, Bill Thompson (Horatio K. Boomer, Nick Depopolis, Old Timer), Harold Peary (Throckmorton P. Gildersleeve), Isabel Randolph (Abigail Uppington)
Summary: After Fibber gets stuck in another fine mess while attempting to retrieve coins Molly put in a milk bottle, he seeks the advice of visitors to get him out of his predicament.
Music: Billy Mills: "What This Country Needs Is More Love," "Say Si Si," "It All Comes Back to Me Now" (The King's Men, vocal)
Running Gags: "You're a harrrrd woman, Mrs. McGee" (Fibber), 'Tain't funny, McGee" (Molly), "Where'd I put that glass cutter?" (Horatio), "Where did I put that guarantee?" (Isabel), hall closet opened by Fibber looking for heating pad, "That ain't the way I heered it" (Old Timer)
Comments: This episode features a few clever switches such as Abigail reprising Horatio's running gag and Fibber delivering the pitch in the integrated commercial after being hypnotized by Wilcox.

Date: February 4, 1941
Title: Buying a New Suit
Cast: Jim Jordan (Fibber), Marian Jordan (Molly, Teeny), Harlow Wilcox, Bill Thompson (Old Timer, Horatio K. Boomer), Harold Peary (Throckmorton P. Gildersleeve), Isabel Randolph (Abigail Uppington), Ken Christy (clerk), Frank Nelson (clerk)

Summary: At Molly's urging Fibber decides to buy a new outfit.
Music: Billy Mills: "Let's Break the Ice," "Orientale," "Clementine" (The King's Men, vocal)
Running Gags: "That ain't the way I heered it" (Old Timer), word confusion involving *Chevrolet/cheviot/Soviet/serviette* (Fibber, Molly), "Where'd I put that complaint?" (Horatio), tongue twister starting with Glow Coat McGee (Fibber)
Comments: Gildy's level of regression to puerile behavior is almost complete in this episode when, after a fight with McGee over a hat, he exits in tears and is aptly labeled a crybaby by Fibber.

Date: February 11, 1941
Title: Watch Salesman
Cast: Jim Jordan (Fibber), Marian Jordan (Molly, Teeny), Harlow Wilcox, Bill Thompson (Old Timer, officer, Horatio K. Boomer, time watcher), Harold Peary (Throckmorton P. Gildersleeve), Isabel Randolph (Abigail Uppington), Frank Nelson (judge), Sara Berner (Rebecca Callahan)
Summary: Fibber gets arrested while trying to sell watches.
Music: Billy Mills: "Here's My Heart," "When You and I Were Young, Maggie," "Coming Through the Rye" (The King's Men, vocal)
Running Gags: "That ain't the way I heered it" (Old Timer), hall closet opened by Fibber looking for spats, "Where did I put that clipping?" (Horatio), "You're a harrrrd man, your honor" (Throckmorton)
Comments: This may not be the funniest episode in the series, but it is certainly one of the punniest with lots of word play beginning with the man who, as he delivers the watches, declares that the package is for Mr. Fragile from Use No Hooks to which Fibber adds "Where will this end up?" Fibber provides a reason for not straightening out the closet and thus the rationale for continuing with the bit: "It still gets a laugh."

Date: February 18, 1941
Title: Early to Bed
Cast: Jim Jordan (Fibber), Marian Jordan (Molly, Teeny), Harlow Wilcox, Bill Thompson (Old Timer, Horatio K. Boomer), Harold Peary (Throckmorton P. Gildersleeve), Isabel Randolph (Abigail Uppington)
Summary: Fibber and Molly's resolution to get a good night's sleep is repeatedly thwarted by friends and neighbors.
Music: Billy Mills: "It's High Time," "Keep an Eye on Your Heart," "In the Gloaming" (The King's Men, vocal)
Running Gags: Tongue twister starting with Biggs Tinker McGee (Fibber), "What did I do with that star?" (Horatio), hall closet opened by Fibber looking for dictionary, "That ain't the way I heered it" (Old Timer)
Comments: This is one of the best episodes from the pre-war years as Fibber battles forces from without (visitors who knock at the front door) and

within (a cedar chest) that prolong his agony and enrich our enjoyment. Molly receives the biggest laugh of the night with her succinct response to her husband's statement that at his age he is not going to chase any more fires: "Nor anything else." Uncle Dennis is heard for the first time via skittish snores as he takes a cat nap.

Date: February 25, 1941
Title: Redeeming Bottles
Cast: Jim Jordan (Fibber), Marian Jordan (Molly, Teeny), Harlow Wilcox, Bill Thompson (Old Timer, Nick Depopolis, clerk), Harold Peary (Throckmorton P. Gildersleeve), Isabel Randolph (Abigail Uppington), Gale Gordon (Mr. Sale), Bea Benaderet (clerk, lady in lead commercial)
Summary: Fibber takes the bottles he has collected for three years to stores to collect the deposit money.
Music: Billy Mills: "I See the Moon at Noon," "Song of the Volga Boatman," "The Covered Wagon Rolled Right Along" (The King's Men, vocal), "You Should Be Set to Music"
Running Gags: "That ain't the way I heered it" (Old Timer), "Gotta get them brakes fixed" (Fibber)
Comments: The banter between Fibber and Teeny over the word *rebate* provides some of the best comic moments in this episode. When Gale Gordon as the owner of the grocery store explodes in anger after McGee breaks some glass, it is a foretaste of the outbursts that will become a hallmark of his role as Mayor LaTrivia.

Date: March 4, 1941
Title: Supper Party for Friends
Cast: Jim Jordan (Fibber), Marian Jordan (Molly, Teeny), Harlow Wilcox, Bill Thompson (Nick Depopolis, Old Timer, Horatio K. Boomer), Harold Peary (Throckmorton P. Gildersleeve), Isabel Randolph (Abigail Uppington), Gale Gordon (doctor), Billy Mills
Summary: The McGees host a buffet supper to prove they are not in financial need.
Music: Billy Mills: "My Mind's on You," "Villa," "Ezekiel Saw the Wheel" (The King's Men, vocal), "No Fooling"
Running Gags: Myrt bit involving brother/broken back/broke and back (Fibber), "That ain't the way I heered it" (Old Timer), tongue twister starting with Rumba Seat McGee (Fibber), "Where'd I put that $20 bill?" (Horatio)
Comments: Over the years Quinn will pull a switch on many sayings and quotations and in this episode he renders unto Caesar when Fibber says, "I came, I saw, and I congaed."

Date: March 11, 1941
Title: Measles Quarantine
Cast: Jim Jordan (Fibber), Marian Jordan (Molly, Teeny), Harlow Wilcox, Bill Thompson (Nick Depopolis, Old Timer, Horatio K. Boomer), Harold Peary (Throckmorton P. Gildersleeve), Isabel Randolph (Abigail Uppington), Billy Mills
Summary: Tempers flare among the guests at the McGee house after a week of being quarantined.
Music: Billy Mills: "Love Is," "Scheherazade," "There Is a Tavern in the Town" (The King's Men, vocal), "Because of You"
Running Gags: Hall closet opened by Gildersleeve who was seeking the front door, "That ain't the way I heered it" (Old Timer), "Where did I put that notice?" (Horatio), word confusion involving *epidermis/hypodermic/epidemic* (Fibber, Molly, Abigail), Myrt bit involving brother/caught a spy/caught his pie (Fibber)
Comments: As happened on a number of occasions, the title of the last musical selection by Billy Mills relates to the action that preceded it. Teeny's plaintive cry of "I'm hungry," heard for the first time in this episode, will be milked for more laughs in the coming weeks. Because a game of poker is being played, Wilcox skillfully employs the card terms *trey, full house, deuce, aces, jack, discards,* and *dealer* to pitch the sponsor's product. As he frequently did, Quinn teases the audience with hints about some secret knowledge a character has early in the show which is then mentioned once or twice more before the climax (in this case, what a doctor told McGee about quarantining for measles).

Date: March 18, 1941
Title: Drafted
Cast: Jim Jordan (Fibber), Marian Jordan (Molly), Harlow Wilcox, Bill Thompson (Old Timer, taunter), Harold Peary (Throckmorton P. Gildersleeve), Isabel Randolph (Abigail Uppington), Gale Gordon (Mr. Bagworthy, colonel), Frank Nelson (bank clerk)
Summary: Friends greet Fibber's announcement that he has been drafted with skepticism and scoffing.
Music: Billy Mills: "So Sweet," "La Golondrina," "Genevieve, Sweet Genevieve" (The King's Men, vocal), "I Can't Remember to Forget"
Running Gags: Myrt bit involving brother/shot at sunrise/comes home like that (Fibber), "That ain't the way I heered it" (Old Timer), tongue twister starting with Pigeon-Toed McGee (Fibber)
Comments: The device of playing bits of "The William Tell Overture" to indicate change of scene is used for the first time. Quinn occasionally spoofed the titles of juvenile books and the one Fibber returns to the library in this episode is the raciest of the lot: *The Rover Boys at Earl Carroll's*. In the

tag Jim strikes a serious note as he observes what is taking place overseas: "We're lucky to be living to a country where they have guards around the camp to keep people *out.*"

Date: March 25, 1941
Title: Changes Name to Ronald McGee
Cast: Jim Jordan (Fibber), Marian Jordan (Molly, Teeny), Harlow Wilcox, Bill Thompson (Old Timer, bailiff), Harold Peary (Throckmorton P. Gildersleeve), Isabel Randolph (Abigail Uppington), Gale Gordon (judge), Lurene Tuttle (Clara)
Summary: Because he is regarded as a prevaricator, Fibber tries to have his name legally changed to Ronald McGee.
Music: Billy Mills: "What This Country Needs Is More Love," "The Peanut Vendor," "The Wise Old Owl" (The King's Men, vocal), "Time of Your Life"
Running Gags: Hall closet opened by Fibber looking for his birth certificate, "That ain't the way I heered it" (Old Timer), "You're a harrrrd man, Ronald" (Throckmorton)
Comments: Fibber reveals to Molly that his real first name is Fimmer and that he is saddled with his current name because the minister who christened him had a cold in his head. Molly attributes his stretching of the truth to having a memory that is too good, allowing him to remember things that never happened. Bill Thompson rehearses the wimp voice one more time as the bailiff before assuming the character of Wallace Wimple in three weeks.

Date: April 1, 1941
Title: Car Missing a Fender
Cast: Jim Jordan (Fibber), Marian Jordan (Molly, Teeny), Harlow Wilcox, Bill Thompson (Horatio K. Boomer), Harold Peary (Throckmorton P. Gildersleeve), Isabel Randolph (Abigail Uppington)
Summary: Gildy and Uppy convince Molly that it is best to keep Fibber from finding out about a missing fender on the McGee automobile.
Music: Billy Mills: "I Struck a Match on the Moon," "Anitra's Dance," "Abdul Abulbul Amir" (The King's Men, vocal), "Just Give Me Music in the Evening"
Running Gags: "Where'd he put them subpoenas?" (Fibber assisting Horatio), Myrt bit involving stork/lays egg (Fibber)
Comments: Molly's taking over the integrated commercial serves the double function of taking Fibber's mind off the car and keeping the minds of the audience on the sponsor's message she is co-opting from Wilcox. Great teamwork on the part of Jim and Harold in the correction of the last syllable of *nincompoop* results in a quick burst of *pip-pop-poop* that does, as Molly suggests, sound like a bunch of firecrackers.

Date: April 8, 1941
Title: Telescope
Cast: Jim Jordan (Fibber), Marian Jordan (Molly, Teeny), Harlow Wilcox, Bill Thompson (Nick Depopolis, newspaper hawker), Harold Peary (Throckmorton P. Gildersleeve), Isabel Randolph (Abigail Uppington), Gale Gordon (Hercules Witikind), Frank Nelson (radio newscaster), Verna Felton (lady in lead commercial)
Summary: Fibber hopes to discover a new heavenly body while using his telescope.
Music: Billy Mills: "It's High Time," "Kerry Dance," "The Reluctant Dragon" (The King's Men, vocal)
Running Gag: "'Tain't funny, McGee" (Molly)
Comments: Jim rebounds when he fluffs "I wanna do—" with a handy ad-lib, "As the man said when he stuck his hand in the alphabet soup, I'm groping for words." He also breaks up Wilcox when he spontaneously calls him "you Omaha flash." Teeny gets the upper hand on Fibber again when she counters his whimsical interpretation of the man on the moon with an astronomically correct explanation.

Date: April 15, 1941
Title: Visit to Oculist
Cast: Jim Jordan (Fibber), Marian Jordan (Molly, Teeny), Harlow Wilcox, Bill Thompson (Old Timer, Wallace Wimple), Harold Peary (Throckmorton P. Gildersleeve), Isabel Randolph (Abigail Uppington), Gale Gordon (oculist)
Summary: After Fibber sees an oculist, he cannot see much else as he conducts a bleary-eyed search for his missing coat.
Music: Billy Mills: "Let's Break the Ice," "Martha," "Let's Get Away from It All," (The King's Men, vocal)
Running Gags: "That ain't the way I heered it," (Old Timer), word confusion involving *teepee/frappé/coupe* (Fibber, Molly), tongue twister starting with Eyes-a-Mugging McGee (Fibber), "You're a harrrrd man, McGee" (Throckmorton)
Comments: Wilcox mentions at the beginning of the show this is the sixth anniversary broadcast and the McGees thank listeners for their support during those years in the tag. Jim delivers an apt ad-lib after he stumbles on a compliment to Abigail and she returns the favor by saying he always says such sweet things: "I have a tough time doing it though." Wallace Wimple appears for the first time as the man who inadvertently switches coats with McGee. Wilcox, through Quinn's craftiness, unleashes a drawn-out plug like a sentence in a Henry James novel just to say he does not know Wimple.

Date: April 22, 1941
Title: Night Out with Gildersleeve
Cast: Jim Jordan (Fibber), Marian Jordan (Molly, Teeny), Harlow Wilcox, Bill Thompson (Old Timer, Nick Depopolis, Wallace Wimple), Harold Peary (Throckmorton P. Gildersleeve), Frank Nelson (Peabody)
Summary: Fibber and Gildersleeve find that the night out they planned turns out to be mild instead of wild.
Music: Billy Mills: "Here's My Heart," "Lucia," "The Hut Sut Song" (The King's Men, vocal), "You Should Be Set to Music"
Running Gag: "That ain't the way I heered it" (Old Timer), "You're a harrrrd man, McGee" (Throckmorton)
Comments: The high point of this episode is Gildy and Fibber's futile attempt to explain metabolism to Teeny. That being henpecked will be Wimple's predominant characteristic is apparent as early as this second appearance in which he is hiding because his wife is mad at him.

Date: April 29, 1941
Title: Stuck in Pavement
Cast: Jim Jordan (Fibber), Marian Jordan (Molly, Teeny), Harlow Wilcox, Bill Thompson (Joe, Old Timer, Wallace Wimple), Harold Peary (Throckmorton P. Gildersleeve), Isabel Randolph (Abigail Uppington)
Summary: As Fibber crosses the street to mail a letter, he is double-crossed by the freshly surfaced pavement.
Music: Billy Mills: "I Struck a Match on the Moon," "Poupee Valsante," "Little Brown Jug" (The King's Men, vocal)
Running Gags: "That ain't the way I heered it," (Old Timer), Myrt bit involving cousin/overturned canoe/turned over to brother (Molly reporting phone call indirectly to Fibber)
Comments: In the midst of his "stuck in the middle" dilemma Fibber releases a lament he will utter a number of times over the years: "Why does everything have to happen to me?" Fibber and Teeny do a deft switch of their "I'm hungry" and "Oh, pshaw!" lines. Wimple refers to his wife as Cornelia, the woman listeners will come to know as Sweetie Face.

Date: May 6, 1941
Title: Games for the Army
Cast: Jim Jordan (Fibber), Marian Jordan (Molly), Harlow Wilcox, Bill Thompson (Nick Depopolis, Wallace Wimple, Old Timer) Harold Peary (Throckmorton P. Gildersleeve), Isabel Randolph (Abigail Uppington), Gale Gordon (Captain Gordon)
Summary: The McGees collect games and reading matter from their friends to donate to the army.
Music: Billy Mills: "Sweet Dreaming," "Rustle of Spring," "Polly, Put the Kettle On" (The King's Men, vocal)

Running Gags: Hall closet opened by Fibber looking for ping pong set, "'Tain't funny, McGee" (Molly), tongue twister starting with Son of a Sea Cook McGee (Fibber), "That ain't the way I heered it" (Old Timer)

Comments: Wallace again calls his wife Cornelia, the last time he will use her first name. The character of Teeny does not actually appear in this episode, though Marian caps the vocal selection with the moppet's "I'm hungry." The tag includes an appeal to donate recreational items to army camps, the first of many pitches on behalf of the military that Jim and Marian will make over the next five years.

Date: May 13, 1941
Title: Salmon Dinner
Cast: Jim Jordan (Fibber), Marian Jordan (Molly, Teeny), Harlow Wilcox, Bill Thompson (telegram delivery man, Old Timer, Wallace Wimple), Harold Peary (Throckmorton P. Gildersleeve), Isabel Randolph (Abigail Uppington), Verna Felton (mother in lead commercial)
Summary: The McGees invite friends for a dinner after Otis Cadwallader, Molly's old flame, informs them he is sending them a large salmon.
Music: Billy Mills: "It's High Time," "With a Twist of the Wrist," "Mush Mush" (The King's Men, vocal), "All I Desire"
Running Gag: Myrt bit involving sister/three of them/blowouts (Fibber)
Comments: Jim covers his fluff of the line "Not even if I thought so" by claiming that Otis has "got me talking like a salmon." Fibber paints a vivid image of Wilcox's tenacity in the comment "He rides a plug harder than Eddie Arcaro." The tag includes an appeal to buy savings bonds.

Date: May 20, 1941
Title: Bakes a Cake
Cast: Jim Jordan (Fibber), Marian Jordan (Molly, Teeny), Harlow Wilcox, Bill Thompson (Wallace Wimple, Old Timer), Harold Peary (Throckmorton P. Gildersleeve), Isabel Randolph (Abigail Uppington)
Summary: Fibber bakes a birthday cake for Molly.
Music: Billy Mills: "Love Is," "Dark Eyes," "Three Blind Mice" (The King's Men, vocal), "Because of You"
Running Gags: Tongue twister starting with Dead Beet McGee (Fibber), hall closet opened by Fibber in disbelief after Molly opened it noiselessly
Comments: This episode features a rare instance of Fibber going to Teeny's house and knocking on her door. McGee will later use *lard bucket* as an epithet employed almost endearingly when addressing Doctor Gamble.

Date: May 27, 1941
Title: Gildersleeve's Ladder
Cast: Jim Jordan (Fibber), Marian Jordan (Molly), Harlow Wilcox, Bill Thompson (Old Timer, Wallace Wimple), Harold Peary (Throckmorton

P. Gildersleeve), Isabel Randolph (Abigail Uppington), Gale Gordon (Asa Tate)

Summary: After he causes Gildy to fall off a ladder, Fibber decides to make a record of his apology and send it to his neighbor.

Music: Billy Mills: "So Sweet," "Adios," "Open Your Heart and Say 'Ah'" (The King's Men, vocal),

Running Gags: Myrt bit involving sister/new teeth/kicked out (Fibber), "That ain't the way I heered it" (Old Timer)

Comments: In the days before *backside* and its more vulgar equivalents were in common usage in the media, Quinn still got the point across as noted in this episode when Fibber's declaration to Uppy that "You couldn't take a joke if it was tattooed-" is interrupted by Molly's "McGee!" which still allows the imagination of listeners to fill in the rest. Quinn also does a nice switch on the cliché about buddies when Fibber admits that down deep Gildy and he hate each other, but on the surface there never were two finer friends.

Date: June 3, 1941 (Script)
Title: Policeman's Ball
Cast: Jim Jordan (Fibber), Marian Jordan (Molly, Teeny), Harlow Wilcox, Bill Thompson (Wallace Wimple), Harold Peary (Throckmorton P. Gildersleeve), Isabel Randolph (Abigail Uppington), Gale Gordon (Lieutenant Fitzgerald)
Summary: Problems the McGees encounter on the way to a dance sponsored by the police have them wondering if they will arrive after the ball is over.
Music: Billy Mills: "Here's My Heart," "Amapola," "Old Dan Tucker" (The King's Men, vocal)
Running Gags: Hall closet opened by Fibber who has been hiding there, Myrt bit involving cat got her tongue/cat fed cold meat (Abigail)
Comments: Gale Gordon gets to employ an Irish brogue and make three separate appearances as the officer who sells the tickets, makes an arrest, and steals a dance. In the tag Harlow announces that Jim Jordan has been named the outstanding radio father of 1941 by the National Father's Day Committee.

Date: June 10, 1941
Title: Getting Photo Taken
Cast: Jim Jordan (Fibber), Marian Jordan (Molly, Teeny), Harlow Wilcox, Bill Thompson (Old Timer, Wallace Wimple), Harold Peary (Throckmorton P. Gildersleeve), Isabel Randolph (Abigail Uppington), Gale Gordon (bill collector), Frank Nelson (Bachrach), Lurene Tuttle (Miss Jones)
Summary: After taking some shots at the old mugs in the family album, the McGees visit a photographer for new shots of them mugging.
Music: Billy Mills: "I See the Moon at Noon," "Just a Little Bit South of North Carolina," "The Chool Song" (The King's Men, vocal), "Hi There, Mr. Moon"

Running Gags: None

Comments: Teeny frustrates Fibber in this episode with the monosyllabic question that children have been pestering their elders with for centuries: "Why?" During the tag Bill Thompson, Isabel Randolph, Harold Peary, and even Teeny are recognized for their contributions to the success of *Fibber McGee and Molly*. "The Chool Song," a bit of nonsense penned by Ken Darby perhaps to capitalize on the success of "The Hut Sut Song," would be the subject of a soundie released in 1942 in which the bewigged King's Men sing in a drawing room setting while a couple toss aside their stately minuet in favor of a fevered jitterbug.

Date: June 17, 1941
Title: Amusement Park
Cast: Jim Jordan (Fibber), Marian Jordan (Molly, Teeny), Harlow Wilcox, Bill Thompson (Old Timer), Harold Peary (Throckmorton P. Gildersleeve), Isabel Randolph (Abigail Uppington), Gale Gordon (RKO representative), Billy Mills
Summary: Teeny eats while Fibber treats on the midway.
Music: Billy Mills: "Let's Break the Ice," "She'll Be Coming Round the Mountain," "The Sound Effects Man" (The King's Men, vocal), "Poor Moon"
Running Gag: Hall closet opened by Fibber during song by King's Men
Comments: This program commemorates Billy Mills 10,000th radio broadcast. Virgil Reimer is saluted during the song about sound effects as are the King's Men and Harlow Wilcox in the tag.

Date: June 24, 1941
Title: Leaving for Hollywood
Cast: Jim Jordan (Fibber), Marian Jordan (Molly, Teeny), Harlow Wilcox, Bill Thompson (Old Timer, Wallace Wimple), Harold Peary (Throckmorton P. Gildersleeve), Isabel Randolph (Abigail Uppington), Gale Gordon (Doctor Davenport)
Summary: Fibber undergoes a physical examination before the McGees leave for Hollywood to make *Look Who's Laughing*.
Music: Billy Mills: "Sweet Dreaming," "Scheherazade," "The Reluctant Dragon" (The King's Men, vocal), "Give Me Music in the Evening"
Running Gags: Myrt bit involving sister/train wreck/wedding dress (Fibber), "That ain't the way I heered it" (Old Timer), hall closet opened by Fibber looking for bill of sale
Comments: There is some witty crosstalk from the different conversations being conducted between Fibber and Davenport and between Molly and Uppy. In the tag Jim offers sincere words of thanks to listeners at the end of another season, concluding with "It's people like you who make people like us like people like you." The summer replacement series is *Hap Hazard*

starring Ransom Sherman, who will join the *Fibber McGee and Molly* cast for the 1943-1944 season.

Date: September 30, 1941
Title: Back from Vacation to Alaska
Cast: Jim Jordan (Fibber), Marian Jordan (Molly, Teeny), Harlow Wilcox, Bill Thompson (Wallace Wimple, Old Timer), Harold Peary (Throckmorton P. Gildersleeve), Isabel Randolph (Abigail Uppington), Billy Mills
Summary: Fibber repeatedly tries to tell friends about his hunting adventures in Alaska during the summer.
Music: Billy Mills: "I'm Not in the Mood," "Yes, Indeed" (Martha Tilton, vocal), "Little Liza Jane" (The King's Men, vocal)
Running Gags: "'Tain't funny, McGee" (Molly), hall closet opened by Gildersleeve looking for his lawn mower, "That ain't the way I heered it" (Old Timer)
Comments: Two Quinn quotes of note are heard, the first when Fibber defines home as "a four-letter word meaning no tipping" and then Molly indicates that girls "love menus when they're young and they love used men when they're old." The tag includes well wishes to Harold Peary who had already begun *The Great Gildersleeve* series.

Date: October 7, 1941
Title: Fifty Thousand Dollar Deal
Cast: Jim Jordan (Fibber), Marian Jordan (Molly, Teeny), Harlow Wilcox, Bill Thompson (Wallace Wimple, Old Timer), Isabel Randolph (Abigail Uppington), Gale Gordon (Hamilton Quigley), Frank Nelson (court reporter), Billy Mills
Summary: The McGees frantically attempt to decipher a shorthand message regarding a sum of $50,000.
Music: Billy Mills: "Hi, Neighbor," "Ching Ling Lo Is Feeling High," (Martha Tilton, vocal), "The Cowboy Serenade" (The King's Men, vocal)
Running Gags: Hall closet opened by Fibber looking for shorthand book, "That ain't the way I heered it" (Old Timer)
Comments: The combination of Quinn's writing and Jim Jordan's delivery created lines that remain funny no matter how many times one hears them, notable in Fibber's response to Molly's admission that she is rusty at shorthand: "Rusty? You're corroded!" Fibber speaks the truth when he claims to know Jim Jordan, "a guy in Kansas City" who has "got a bottling works," because Jim and his brother owned a Hires Root Beer franchise in that city. Wimple calls his wife Sweetie Face for the first time in this episode. The tag includes an appeal for the Community Chest, concluding with "There's no closed season on generosity."

Date: October 14, 1941
Title: Fire Commissioner McGee
Cast: Jim Jordan (Fibber), Marian Jordan (Molly, Teeny), Harlow Wilcox, Bill Thompson (Nick Depopolis, Wallace Wimple), Isabel Randolph (Abigail Uppington), Gale Gordon (Mayor LaTrivia), Frank Nelson (Conley), Billy Mills
Summary: The mayor appoints McGee as temporary fire commissioner.
Music: Billy Mills: "It's High Time," "Tapioca" (The King's Men, vocal), "Easy Street" (Martha Tilton, vocal)
Running Gag: Myrt bit involving old man/shot off/mouth over Yankees (Fibber)
Comments: This episode marks the first appearance of Gale Gordon as Mayor LaTrivia. A good laugh occurs when Fibber says his admonition to a policeman who had been growing a beard was to "quit bushing around the beat" which is almost topped by the ad-lib "Imagine that! We almost took that out, too." In the closing commercial Wilcox promotes a premium accompanying the purchase of Johnson's Wax products, a photograph of the cast, which was already out-of-date because it featured a shot of Peary (as Gildersleeve) who left the show to be the star of his own program.

Date: October 21, 1941
Title: Fall House Cleaning
Cast: Jim Jordan (Fibber), Marian Jordan (Molly), Harlow Wilcox, Bill Thompson (Old Timer, Wallace Wimple), Isabel Randolph (Abigail Uppington), Gale Gordon (house hunter)
Summary: While cleaning the house the McGees discover love letters written to Molly.
Music: Billy Mills: "Sing a Song of Spring," "Little Brown Jug" (The King's Men, vocal), "Bayou By-O," (Martha Tilton, vocal)
Running Gags: "That ain't the way I heered it" (Old Timer), hall closet opened by Fibber to lock himself in, word confusion involving *missile/missive/massive/masseur/ monsieur* (Fibber, Molly), Myrt bit involving brother/cut off his feet/Boy Scout show (Fibber)
Comments: As the man who gets hit by the love letters thrown out the window Gordon, who has not yet been assigned a continuing role as LaTrivia, demonstrates some of the hot-tempered behavior that will be the most distinctive characteristic of the mayor.

Date: October 28, 1941 (Script)
Title: Protection Begins at Home
Cast: Jim Jordan (Fibber), Marian Jordan (Molly), Harlow Wilcox, Bill Thompson (Old Timer, Wallace Wimple), Isabel Randolph (Abigail Uppington), Gale Gordon (Mayor LaTrivia), Billy Mills

Summary: After a man offers to sell them protection and promises to return, the McGees assume he is a racketeer and seek legal protection from LaTrivia and the police.
Music: Billy Mills: "A Romantic Guy, I," "I Don't Want to Set the World on Fire" (Martha Tilton, vocal), "The Gay Ranchero" (The King's Men, vocal)
Running Gags: "That ain't the way I heered it" (Old Timer), "'Tain't funny, McGee" (Molly)
Comments: A fair portion of the humor is derived from Fibber's cowardly behavior. There is plenty of self-promotion as the Old Timer jocularly plugs the Tuesday night NBC lineup and their sponsors as part of his running gag and later Fibber and Molly use the tag to mention the premiere of *Look Who's Laughing* plus an appearance with Edgar Bergen and Charlie McCarthy.

Date: November 4, 1941
Title: New Furniture
Cast: Jim Jordan (Fibber), Marian Jordan (Molly, Teeny), Harlow Wilcox, Bill Thompson (Horatio K. Boomer, Wallace Wimple), Isabel Randolph (Abigail Uppington), Gale Gordon (Twombley)
Summary: When Uppy gives them a new smoking stand, the McGees decide to buy new furniture to go with it.
Music: Billy Mills: "There's a Great Day Coming Mañana," "Louisiana Hayride" (The King's Men, vocal), "Blue Champagne" (Martha Tilton, vocal)
Running Gag: Myrt bit involving sister/broke her nose/her broker knows (Fibber),
Comments: The highlight of this episode is Fibber's detailed explanation to Molly and Uppy how men need thirteen pockets to take care of women's needs. The biggest laugh occurs when Wimple says he does "some of my best work while I'm...Well, almost anywhere in the house," which could be considered the closest Quinn ever got to bathroom humor.

Date: November 11, 1941
Title: Bergen and McCarthy Visit
Cast: Jim Jordan (Fibber), Marian Jordan (Molly, Teeny), Harlow Wilcox, Bill Thompson (Old Timer, man near phone), Isabel Randolph (Abigail Uppington), Gale Gordon (man in theater lobby, Mayor LaTrivia), Frank Nelson (flight announcer, man in theater lobby), Edgar Bergen (Charlie McCarthy)
Summary: Edgar and Charlie stay with the McGees before attending the premiere of *Look Who's Laughing*.
Music: Billy Mills: "Be Young Again," "I Like a Balalaika" (The King's Men, vocal), "I See a Million People" (Martha Tilton, vocal)
Running Gags: "That ain't the way I heered it" (Old Timer), Myrt bit involving brother/thrown in hoosegow/throne (Fibber)

Comments: During her verbal sparring match with Charlie, Teeny holds her own against the wooden wisecracker. LaTrivia will now appear as a continuing character throughout the thirty-minute shows except, of course, for the time Gordon was serving in the Coast Guard and the 1947-1948 season when Gale played a weatherman instead of the mayor.

Date: November 18, 1941
Title: Mayor Doesn't Leave
Cast: Jim Jordan (Fibber), Marian Jordan (Molly, Teeny), Harlow Wilcox, Bill Thompson (Old Timer, Wallace Wimple), Isabel Randolph (Abigail Uppington), Gale Gordon (Mayor LaTrivia)
Summary: Interruptions have the McGees wondering if LaTrivia will ever leave their home.
Music: Billy Mills: "Great Day," "My Silent Love" (Martha Tilton, vocal), "Thirty More Shopping Days Till Christmas" (The King's Men, vocal), "Do I Love You?"
Running Gags: Myrt bit involving grandmother/plastered again/pleurisy (Fibber), hall closet opened by LaTrivia seeking the front door
Comments: The reasons for opening the hall closet are usually plausible, but this is one of the times when credibility is stretched more than a bit. How can LaTrivia mistake the closet door for the front door when he has been standing in the entryway watching people enter and exit for almost the entire episode?

Date: November 25, 1941
Title: Clay Investment Scheme
Cast: Jim Jordan (Fibber), Marian Jordan (Molly, Teeny), Harlow Wilcox, Bill Thompson (man at door, Old Timer, Wallace Wimple), Isabel Randolph (Abigail Uppington), Gale Gordon (Mayor LaTrivia), Billy Mills
Summary: Fibber believes Molly and their friends have been victimized by a con man.
Music: Billy Mills: "Sing, My Heart," "Katy Did" (The King's Men, vocal), "Jim" (Martha Tilton, vocal), "How High the Moon"
Running Gags: Myrt bit involving sister/threw husband out the window/kiss (Fibber), "'Tain't funny, McGee" (Molly)
Comments: The gag with Myrt had a few whiskers on it even in 1941. Another wheeze receives this comment from Fibber: "A joke as old as that is at least entitled to respect."

Date: December 2, 1941
Title: Mustache
Cast: Jim Jordan (Fibber), Marian Jordan (Molly, Teeny), Harlow Wilcox, Bill Thompson (Old Timer, delivery man), Isabel Randolph (Abigail Uppington), Gale Gordon (Mayor LaTrivia)

Summary: After seeing Ronald Colman in a movie, Fibber cultivates a mustache and foppish mannerisms.
Music: Billy Mills: "Who Cares?," "Kiss the Boys Goodbye" (Martha Tilton, vocal), "Rose O'Day" (The King's Men, vocal), "How About You?"
Running Gags: Tongue twister starting with Mill Dude McGee (Fibber), Myrt bit involving sister/pinched/revolving door (Fibber), "That ain't the way I heered it" (Old Timer)
Comments: This is the first episode in which Fibber adopts an affected English accent that will make him insufferable to everyone. Molly suggests that one day Fibber will get his party right off when he picks up the phone and they will not have time for one of his routines with Myrt.

Date: December 9, 1941
Title: Forty Percent Discount
Cast: Jim Jordan (Fibber), Marian Jordan (Molly), Harlow Wilcox, Bill Thompson (Wallace Wimple), Isabel Randolph (Abigail Uppington), Gale Gordon (Mayor LaTrivia), Billy Mills
Summary: After Fibber promises to acquire needed items at a deep discount for friends, he gets less than he bargained for at a wholesale store.
Music: Billy Mills: "Don't Ever Leave Me," "The Chool Song" (The King's Men, vocal), "The Last Time I Saw Paris" (Martha Tilton, vocal), "My Country, 'Tis of Thee" (All)
Running Gags: "'Tain't funny, McGee" (Molly), hall closet opened by Fibber looking for checkbook
Comments: Broadcast just two days after the attack on Pearl Harbor, this episode provides ample evidence that everyone involved with *Fibber McGee and Molly* is behind the war effort, from Wilcox's reading a telegram from Johnson's Wax authorizing NBC to break in with any news bulletins to Harlow's appeal to buy defense bonds at the close which leads into a stirring version of the first verse of a patriotic hymn sung by everyone in attendance.

Date: December 16, 1941
Title: Cutting Christmas Tree
Cast: Jim Jordan (Fibber), Marian Jordan (Molly, Teeny), Harlow Wilcox, Bill Thompson (Wallace Wimple, Old Timer), Isabel Randolph (Abigail Uppington), Gale Gordon (Mayor LaTrivia)
Summary: Fibber cuts his own Christmas tree, then keeps cutting it down to size after he brings it home.
Music: Billy Mills: "The National Emblem March," "Thank Your Lucky Stars and Stripes" (Martha Tilton, vocal), "Coming Through the Rye" (The King's Men, vocal), "Zing Went the Strings of My Heart"
Running Gags: "Gotta get them brakes fixed" (Fibber), Myrt bit involving niece/grabbed and kissed/blackout (Fibber), "'Tain't funny, McGee" (Molly)

Comments: The Old Timer's joke about Hitler is the first of many to be delivered in the coming months. A Quinn quote of note Fibber hopes will make *Reader's Digest* is an explanation of why nature is always referred to as she: "Nature is inconsistent, unstable, unpredictable, beautiful, mean, gorgeous, appealing, nasty, and nobody yet has ever understood her."

Date: December 23, 1941
Title: Door Chimes
Cast: Jim Jordan (Fibber), Marian Jordan (Molly, Teeny), Harlow Wilcox, Harold Peary (Throckmorton P. Gildersleeve), Isabel Randolph (Abigail Uppington), Gale Gordon (Mayor LaTrivia), Mel Blanc (hiccupping telegram delivery man)
Summary: The McGees receive door chimes for a gift and a visit from Gildersleeve for a tiff.
Music: Billy Mills: "Love Is," "He's 1-A in the Army and He's A1 in my Heart" (Martha Tilton, vocal), "What Do I Want for Christmas?" (The King's Men, vocal), "Let's Be Buddies"
Running Gag: Tongue twister starting with Get That Dope McGee (Fibber)
Comments: LaTrivia gets the longest laugh and even applause with his response to Fibber's declaration that he is a man of a thousand faces: "You had your choice of a thousand faces and went back to your own?" There are also some funny moments in Fibber's banter with Teeny who tries to to sell him what she calls miserabletoe. At one point Fibber says, "Well, that was a short ride, but I enjoyed it. Let's go around again," which probably echoed the sentiments of the listeners who were lapping and laughing it up. Martha Tilton appears for the last time in the series. Mel Blanc's bit falls into the "Wouldn't it be nice?" category of radio employment for supporting players. After a similar brief appearance Blanc made on *The Abbott and Costello Show,* Lou expressed a desire to have the kind of part that would allow to him say one speech, get paid, wash up, and go home.

Date: December 30, 1941
Title: Fix-It McGee
Cast: Jim Jordan (Fibber), Marian Jordan (Molly, Mrs. Wearybottom), Harlow Wilcox, Isabel Randolph (Abigail Uppington), Gale Gordon (Mayor LaTrivia), Billy Mills
Summary: McGee works on a secret repair project for Molly.
Music: Billy Mills: "Of Thee I Sing." "American Patrol," "Old Dan Tucker" (The King's Men, vocal), "How About You?"
Running Gags: "'Tain't funny, McGee" (Molly), cigar routine (Fibber and Billy)
Comments: Door chimes or the door bell now replaces the knocking on the door. For this episode the melody of the chimes matches the visitor: "Where Did You Get That Hat?" (Abigail); "The Old Gray Mare" (LaTrivia); "On

Wisconsin" (Harlow); "Lazybones" (Wearybottom); "Down by the Old Mill Stream" (Billy); "How Dry I Am" (Dennis). Uncle Dennis makes his first appearance of sorts as he is heard staggering up the stairs to his room.

Date: January 6, 1942
Title: Preparing for a Night Out
Cast: Jim Jordan (Fibber), Marian Jordan (Molly, Teeny), Harlow Wilcox, Bill Thompson (Wallace Wimple, Old Timer), Isabel Randolph (Abigail Uppington), Gale Gordon (Mayor LaTrivia)
Summary: Fibber makes plans to take Molly dancing at the Cuba Libre nightclub.
Music: Billy Mills: "Anything Goes," "Why Don't We Do This More Often?," "Zana Zeranda" (The King's Men, vocal), "For the Life of Me"
Running Gags: "'Tain't funny, McGee" (Molly), Myrt bit with Clara involving brother/hanging over a what/hanging over (Harlow), tongue twister starting with Slewfoot McGee (Fibber)
Comments: Although Wilcox gets Clara when he calls instead of Myrt, Fibber's usual silent partner proves to be a smooth operator after hours as well when the Old Timer reveals that she has been his dancing partner. In the tag Jim plays off the "keep 'em flying" motto by stating that the cast's job is to "keep 'em smiling" before concluding the show with an appeal for the Red Cross.

Date: January 13, 1942
Title: Broken Window, Part 1
Cast: Jim Jordan (Fibber), Marian Jordan (Molly), Harlow Wilcox, Bill Thompson (Old Timer, Wallace Wimple), Isabel Randolph (Abigail Uppington), Gale Gordon (Mayor LaTrivia), Frank Nelson (Officer Frink)
Summary: Fibber thinks he threw a rock through Mrs. Uppington's window while sleepwalking.
Music: Billy Mills: "Who Knows?," "Volga Boatman," "The Old Man of the Mountain" (The King's Men, vocal)
Running Gags: None
Comments: The tag includes an appeal to buy defense bonds and to support the Red Cross.

Date: January 20, 1942
Title: Broken Window, Part 2
Cast: Jim Jordan (Fibber), Marian Jordan (Molly, Teeny), Harlow Wilcox, Bill Thompson (Wallace Wimple), Isabel Randolph (Abigail Uppington), Gale Gordon (Mayor LaTrivia)
Summary: The McGees recreate Fibber's habits on the night Uppy's window was broken to see if he will return to the scene of the crime in his sleep.
Music: Billy Mills: "Be Young Again," "Toselli's Serenade," "Lydia" (The King's Men, vocal), "I Love You More and More"

Running Gags: None

Comments: The comic highlight of this episode is the confusion between the McGees and Abigail regarding a girdle/turtle mixup, another instance of how Quinn ably handled situations like the flannel underwear confusion on the December 5, 1939 program that could be slightly naughty with gentle humor and knowing when to stop before the lines became offensive. The tag includes an appeal for funds to fight infantile paralysis.

Date: January 27, 1942
Title: Blizzard
Cast: Jim Jordan (Fibber), Marian Jordan (Molly), Harlow Wilcox, Bill Thompson (Old Timer, Wallace Wimple), Isabel Randolph (Abigail Uppington), Gale Gordon (Mayor LaTrivia), Frank Nelson (George Spelvin)
Summary: A man with an important message regarding a governor finds his way to the McGee residence during a snowstorm.
Music: Billy Mills: "Free for All," "Souvenir," The Gay Ranchero" (The King's Men, vocal), "Who Could Be Lonely?"
Running Gags: "'Tain't funny, McGee" (Molly), cigar routine (Fibber, Spelvin), hall closet opened by Fibber looking for shovel
Comments: Quinn asks listeners to freeze their disbelief as Spelvin, the Old Timer, Uppy, Wilcox, LaTrivia, and Wimple visit the McGees during the worst blizzard in 76 years, but we are willing to go along with the gags. *George Spelvin* is a show business pseudonym used by an actor in lieu of his real name. Fibber's lyrical description of a winter wonderland casts a spell on LaTrivia in a way Tom Sawyer would envy, causing the Mayor to grab a shovel and clear the sidewalk. The tag includes an appeal to help Uncle Sam with dollars, work, and support.

Date: February 3, 1942
Title: Lost Engagement Ring
Cast: Jim Jordan (Fibber), Marian Jordan (Molly, Teeny), Harlow Wilcox, Bill Thompson (Old Timer), Isabel Randolph (Abigail Uppington), Gale Gordon (Mayor LaTrivia)
Summary: The McGees clean the house while looking for Molly's missing diamond ring.
Music: Billy Mills: "I Love Louisa," "Blue Room," "The White Cliffs of Dover" (The King's Men, vocal)
Running Gag: "That ain't the way I heered it" (Old Timer)
Comments: Teeny debunks the Groundhog Day myth with a scientific explanation that leaves Fibber sputtering at her impudence. The tag includes a request to support wartime restrictions.

Date: February 10, 1942
Title: Valentine's Day Candy

Cast: Jim Jordan (Fibber), Marian Jordan (Molly), Harlow Wilcox, Bill Thompson (delivery man, Old Timer, Wallace Wimple), Isabel Randolph (Abigail Uppington), Gale Gordon (Mayor LaTrivia)
Summary: When Molly receives a box of candy delivered to the house, she assumes it is from Fibber, who does not remember sending it.
Music: Billy Mills: "Hallelujah," "She Didn't Say Yes," "Don't Tetch It" (The King's Men, vocal), "I Love You More and More"
Running Gag: LaTrivia blowup because Fibber fibbed about their relationship to try to get a parking ticket fixed
Comments: Later explosions of temper by LaTrivia will be more prolonged with sputtering and spoonerisms, but this was a good preview of what was to come. The integrated commercial is devoted to bringing attention to the pledge Johnson's Wax was promoting for consumers to buy carefully, use wisely, and waste nothing.

Date: February 17, 1942
Title: Home Movies
Cast: Jim Jordan (Fibber), Marian Jordan (Molly, Teeny), Harlow Wilcox, Bill Thompson (Old Timer, Wallace Wimple), Isabel Randolph (Abigail Uppington), Gale Gordon (Mayor LaTrivia), Frank Nelson (clerk), Shirley Mitchell (delivery woman)
Summary: Fibber's amusing amateur movies threaten to fracture more of his bones than the funnybones of filmgoers.
Music: Billy Mills: "It's High Time," "You Ought to be in Pictures," "What's Buzzin' Cousin?" (The King's Men, vocal)
Running Gags: "'Tain't funny, McGee" (Molly), "That ain't the way I heered it" (Old Timer), "Fooled"
Comments: Two heads are not necessarily better than one as Fibber and LaTrivia make little progress in explaining to Teeny why she should not write on the sidewalk. Shirley Mitchell appears for the first time. The funniest line of the episode, delivered by Molly after Fibber plans to jump off the roof with an umbrella for a parachute and in response to his claim that a new umbrella only costs three dollars, demonstrates how much rubber restrictions were on the minds of Americans: "Yes, but can you get a retread on your sacroiliac?"

Date: February 24, 1942
Title: Horse in the Garage
Cast: Jim Jordan (Fibber), Marian Jordan (Molly, Teeny), Harlow Wilcox, Bill Thompson (Old Timer, Wallace Wimple), Isabel Randolph (Abigail Uppington), Gale Gordon (Mayor LaTrivia)
Summary: Fibber buys a horse, then tries to convince Molly they need one.
Music: Billy Mills: "Liza," "Blue Skies," "Gay Caballero" (The King's Men, vocal)

Running Gags: "That ain't the way I heered it" (Old Timer), tongue twister starting with Horse's Neck McGee (Fibber)
Comments: Fibber's reason for buying the horse, to save what rubber is left on auto tires, is patriotic, but a bit far-fetched as it is hard to imagine the McGees going to the grocery store or visiting friends on a saddle built for two.

Date: March 3, 1942
Title: Boomer's Suitcase
Cast: Jim Jordan (Fibber), Marian Jordan (Molly, Teeny), Harlow Wilcox, Bill Thompson (Horatio K. Boomer), Isabel Randolph (Abigail Uppington), Gale Gordon (Mayor LaTrivia)
Summary: The McGees cannot contain their curiosity regarding the contents of a suitcase left in their care.
Music: Billy Mills: "New Sun in the Sky," "United States Field Artillery March," "Deep in the Heart of Texas" (The King's Men, vocal), "Once in a Lovetime"
Running Gags: Myrt bit involving sister/taking off too much/income taxes (Fibber), "'Tain't funny, McGee" (Molly)
Comments: Wilcox announces that *Fibber McGee and Molly* will be broadcast to the armed forces overseas via shortwave. Boomer explains that during his extended absence he has been working as an Arkansas geologist taking big rocks and making them into little rocks.

Date: March 10, 1942
Title: Footstool
Cast: Jim Jordan (Fibber), Marian Jordan (Molly, Teeny), Harlow Wilcox, Bill Thompson (Old Timer, Wallace Wimple), Isabel Randolph (Abigail Uppington), Gale Gordon (Mayor LaTrivia)
Summary: Fibber turns the living room into his shop as he makes a footstool for Molly.
Music: Billy Mills: "Oh Gee, Oh Joy," "Perfidia," "Army Air Corps March" (The King's Men, vocal), "Some of Your Sweetness"
Running Gag: "That ain't the way I heered it" (Old Timer)
Comments: Fibber's explanation of why he classifies Uppy as the salt of the earth is a Quinn quote of note: "You can't take too much of her at a time and it takes a good shaking to get her to come out in wet weather." Fibber unfolds one of his tall tales in explaining how a truckload of sponges soaked up all the water in a river. Fibber and Teeny engage in some banter a la Abbott and Costello over the word *awl*.

Date: March 17, 1942 Public service program on war production. No *Fibber McGee and Molly* broadcast.

Date: March 24, 1942
Title: Songwriter McGee
Cast: Jim Jordan (Fibber), Marian Jordan (Molly), Harlow Wilcox, Bill Thompson (Wallace Wimple), Isabel Randolph (Abigail Uppington), Gale Gordon (Mayor LaTrivia), Frank Nelson (radio station manager), Billy Mills
Summary: With the help of Billy Mills and Wallace Wimple, Fibber composes "The War Stamp Stomp."
Music: Billy Mills: "'S Wonderful," "Tea for Two," "Lanigan's Shillelagh" (The King's Men, vocal), "Everything I Love"
Running Gags: LaTrivia blowup over Phi Beta Kappa key, Myrt bit involving brother/shot it out with cops/milk (Fibber)
Comments: LaTrivia's outburst of temper is the first blowup in which Fibber and Molly team up to frustrate him and the first one in which he stumbles over words in the midst of his fit. Fibber uses *scoff* and *deride* together for the first time, a repetitive lament he will employ with some frequency in the coming years to express his "me against the world" feelings.

Date: March 31, 1942
Title: Soap Contest
Cast: Jim Jordan (Fibber), Marian Jordan (Molly, Teeny), Harlow Wilcox, Bill Thompson (Old Timer, Wallace Wimple), Isabel Randolph (Abigail Uppington), Gale Gordon (Mayor LaTrivia)
Summary: Fibber takes over dishwashing chores from Molly to get inspiration for entering a slogan in the Latherino Soap contest.
Music: Billy Mills: "There's a Great Day Coming Mañana," medley of military songs, "Old Uncle Fud" (The King's Men, vocal), "How About You?"
Running Gags: "That ain't the way I heered it" (Old Timer), hall closet opened by Old Timer looking for the front door, "'Tain't funny, McGee" (Molly), LaTrivia blowup over *derby*
Comments: After Jim stumbles out of the gate with "I'm riley—I'm really trying to think of a good reason" for entering the contest, Marian quickly ad-libs, "Well, good luck, Riley." During the weeks when the horse in the garage has been in the background but still in the conversation occasionally, Quinn invokes just about every nag gag imaginable including Fibber's declaration in this episode that he knew LaTrivia "ran for office on a promise of a stable government, but I thought it was just a stall."

Date: April 7, 1942
Title: Scrap Drive
Cast: Jim Jordan (Fibber), Marian Jordan (Molly, Teeny), Harlow Wilcox, Bill Thompson (Wallace Wimple), Isabel Randolph (Abigail Uppington), Gale Gordon (Mayor LaTrivia)
Summary: The McGees respond with action after Mrs. Uppington urges them to find material for the scrap drive.

Music: Billy Mills: "Great Day," "Sometimes I'm Happy," "The Village Blacksmith" (The King's Men, vocal), "Full Moon"

Running Gags: Hall closet opened twice by Fibber (looking for scrap and later to show Wimple result of the cleaning), LaTrivia blowup regarding glee club that does not unfold completely because Fibber and Molly get sidetracked

Comments: Even the kitchen sink is found lurking in the hall closet in this episode. In lieu of the final commercial Wilcox delivers an appeal for listeners to turn in paper, rubber, and scrap metal so those items can be used for military purposes. This is the first of numerous episodes that will air over the next four years in which the focus of the entire show is on a wartime concern.

Date: April 14, 1942
Title: Parade Plans
Cast: Jim Jordan (Fibber), Marian Jordan (Molly, Teeny), Harlow Wilcox, Bill Thompson (Old Timer, Wallace Wimple), Isabel Randolph (Abigail Uppington), Gale Gordon (Mayor LaTrivia), Frank Nelson (clerk)
Summary: Fibber plans to ride his horse while acting as grand marshal in the spring parade.
Music: Billy Mills: "Blow, Gabriel, Blow," "Two Guitars," "Keeping Our Big Mouth Shut" (The King's Men, vocal), "Tangerine"
Running Gags: "That ain't the way I heered it" (Old Timer), LaTrivia blowup over directions of the parade route
Comments: Whether the words come in the form of a joke about war stamps from the Old Timer, a rousing speech by LaTrivia concerning the superiority of American know-how, or a song by the King's Men addressing the importance of keeping mum on military manuevers, the message is clear: This is everybody's war.

Date: April 21, 1942
Title: Take Me Out to the Ball Game
Cast: Jim Jordan (Fibber), Marian Jordan (Molly), Harlow Wilcox, Bill Thompson (Old Timer, Wallace Wimple), Isabel Randolph (Abigail Uppington), Gale Gordon (Mayor LaTrivia)
Summary: Fibber promises Molly to get her into the ball game free, then puts his plan into action by throwing a few curves at LaTrivia.
Music: Billy Mills: "Who Cares?," "Somebody Else Is Taking My Place," "Blues in the Night" (The King's Men, vocal), "Everybody But Me"
Running Gags: LaTrivia blowup concerning *lit*, hall closet opened by Fibber looking for mitt and ball
Comments: The war touches all classes as Uppy joins the patriotic parade when Molly reveals that the matron has put her money where her mouth is by buying $40,000 in bonds in addition to her service as a volunteer worker

for the Red Cross. Wilcox's commercial deftly employs baseball terms such as *shortstop, bat, first base, home run, pop fly, diamond,* and *innings* to pitch the product.

Date: April 28, 1942
Title: Straw Hat
Cast: Jim Jordan (Fibber), Marian Jordan (Molly, Teeny), Harlow Wilcox, Bill Thompson (Old Timer, Wallace Wimple), Isabel Randolph (Abigail Uppington), Gale Gordon (Mayor LaTrivia)
Summary: Fibber decides to clean his straw hat rather than buy a new one.
Music: Billy Mills: "Rise and Shine," "Tangerine," "Hey, Mabel" (The King's Men, vocal), "Let's Be Buddies"
Running Gags: Myrt bit involving uncle/face smashed and broke his hand/watch (Fibber, Molly), LaTrivia blowup over Army/Navy confusion
Comments: Teeny demonstrates that even children have a part in the war effort by selling seeds for victory gardens and spouting the message that, whether planting vegetables or buying bonds, the watchword is the same: "Dig, dig, dig."

Date: May 5, 1942
Title: Sugar Substitute
Cast: Jim Jordan (Fibber), Marian Jordan (Molly, Teeny), Harlow Wilcox, Bill Thompson (Old Timer, Wallace Wimple), Isabel Randolph (Abigail Uppington), Gale Gordon (Mayor LaTrivia)
Summary: Fibber creates a smelly concoction while trying to find a chemical equivalent for sugar.
Music: Billy Mills: "Dark Eyes," "Open Your Heart and Say, 'Ah'" (The King's Men, \vocal), "Do I Love You?"
Running Gag: "That ain't the way I heered it" (Old Timer)
Comments: When Bill badly fluffs the scientific name for aspirin, he blames it on his upper plate slipping, a ready excuse he will use whenever the Old Timer gets tongue-tied. The identity of the person who broke Mrs. Uppington's window in January is revealed in this episode. At the end Jim asks people to register for sugar rationing to ensure fair distribution of that commodity.

Date: May 12, 1942
Title: Photographer a Spy?
Cast: Jim Jordan (Fibber), Marian Jordan (Molly), Harlow Wilcox, Bill Thompson (Horatio K. Boomer, Wallace Wimple), Isabel Randolph (Abigail Uppington), Gale Gordon (Mayor LaTrivia), Frank Nelson (FBI agent)
Summary: Fibber suspects that the man following him around town snapping photographs is a foreign agent.

Music: Billy Mills: "A Shine on Your Shoes," "How About You?," "America is Calling" (The King's Men, vocal), "Once in a Lovetime"

Running Gag: "Where did I put those credentials?" (Horatio)

Comments: The cleverest line is delivered by Fibber as he reveals that the result of a triple cross involving a homing pigeon, a woodpecker, and a parrot would be a bird who could fly to the right place, knock on the door, and speak the message. Just as children latch on to an expression they recite all day long, Fibber keeps repeating his catch phrase of "Click, click, click. All day long" until he gets his comeuppance at the end.

Date: May 19, 1942

Title: Going to Be Rich

Cast: Jim Jordan (Fibber), Marian Jordan (Molly, Teeny), Harlow Wilcox, Bill Thompson (Old Timer, Wallace Wimple), Isabel Randolph (Abigail Uppington), Gale Gordon (Mayor LaTrivia)

Summary: Fibber tells everyone the McGees will be wealthy next year but refuses to reveal how this miracle will occur.

Music: Billy Mills: "Who Knows?," "Carioca," "Steamboat Bill" (The King's Men, vocal), "Some of Your Sweetness"

Running Gags: Myrt bit involving brother/intelligence/didn't have any (Fibber), "That ain't the way I heered it" (Old Timer), LaTriva blowup over *Wright/wrote/right*

Comments: Some of Quinn's witty lines almost get lost in the shuffle off to Buffalo leading into the musical numbers, Fibber's citing Dun and Bradstreet and Teeny's declaration that she is done on this street being just one example. LaTrivia's complaint that the McGees have him talking like Abbott and Costello is just one of the allusions made on recent shows to the pair of comedians who were riding high in 1941 and 1942.

Date: May 26, 1942

Title: Uncle Dennis is Missing

Cast: Jim Jordan (Fibber), Marian Jordan (Molly), Harlow Wilcox, Bill Thompson (Old Timer, Wallace Wimple), Isabel Randolph (Abigail Uppington), Gale Gordon (Mayor LaTrivia), Billy Mills

Summary: While Molly is anxious to find her missing uncle, Fibber is concerned with recovering his gray suit Dennis was wearing at the time of his disappearance.

Music: Billy Mills: "A Million Miles from Manhattan," "Jealous," "The Sound Effects Man" (The King's Men, vocal), "Memory of This Dance"

Running Gags: Myrt bit involving grandmother/playing for Brooklyn Dodgers/piano (Fibber), hall closet opened by Fibber during song by King's Men

Comments: This is one of the few episodes during this period in which, except for Harlow's reminder about the consumer victory pledge near the end, there is no mention of the war or any concern related to it. A man in the audience with a distinctive laugh not unlike the recorded chortle which emanated from midway funhouses can be heard several times during this program. Quinn taps into the playful *drag out the thrownet/throw out the dragnet* banter between Fibber and Molly that he has mined before and will again with rich results.

Date: June 2, 1942
Title: Uncle Dennis Still Missing
Cast: Jim Jordan (Fibber), Marian Jordan (Molly, Teeny), Harlow Wilcox, Bill Thompson (officer, Wallace Wimple), Isabel Randolph (Abigail Uppington), Gale Gordon (Mayor LaTrivia)
Summary: The McGees continue to monitor the search for Uncle Dennis at home and achieve better results than the previous week when they hunted all over town for him.
Music: Billy Mills: "You Do Something to Me," "Fascinating Rhythm," "Chucklehead" (The King's Men, vocal)
Running Gags: "'Tain't funny, McGee" (Molly), Myrt bit involving niece/knees skinned up (Fibber), LaTrivia blowup over Patrick Henry and Jimmy Doolittle
Comments: There is an in-joke near the beginning in which Fibber cites a police report with a twist on the names of Chester Lauck and Norris Goff, the stars of *Lum and Abner*. The exchange of medical double talk between McGee and Teeny is just the right dosage: short, silly, and savory. The need for 55,000 nurses is voiced first by Teeny, then reinforced by LaTrivia's more explicit appeal.

Date: June 9, 1942
Title: Pot Roast
Cast: Jim Jordan (Fibber), Marian Jordan (Molly), Harlow Wilcox, Bill Thompson (Old Timer), Isabel Randolph (Abigail Uppington), Gale Gordon (Mayor LaTrivia), Shirley Mitchell (waitress)
Summary: Fibber tries to make LaTrivia the man who left without dinner so the McGees can enjoy a pot roast Molly has prepared for themselves.
Music: Billy Mills: "New Sun in the Sky," "One Dozen Roses," "The Bombadier Song" (The King's Men, vocal), "Full Moon"
Running Gags: Myrt bit involving bones/algebra teacher (Fibber), LaTrivia blowup over "a stitch in time saves nine," "That ain't the way I heered it" (Old Timer)
Comments: This episode marks one of the Old Timer's shining moments as he steals the show with his inability to comprehend that the LaTrivia he is talking to and the mayor he is talking about are the same person, topped off by his accomplishment of getting LaTrivia to sign a petition to impeach himself. The tag includes an appeal from Jim and Marian to young men to fill the vacancies for 30,000 Navy pilots.

Date: June 16, 1942
Title: Mouse in the House
Cast: Jim Jordan (Fibber), Marian Jordan (Molly, Teeny), Harlow Wilcox, Bill Thompson (Old Timer, Wallace Wimple), Isabel Randolph (Abigail Uppington), Gale Gordon (Mayor LaTrivia)
Summary: The McGees attempt to catch and dispose of a mouse without killing it.
Music: Billy Mills: "Oh Gee, Oh Joy," medley of songs by George M. Cohan, "I Like a Balalaika" (The King's Men, vocal), "Everything I Love"
Running Gags: Myrt bit involving brother/blew his brains out/tuba (Fibber), word confusion involving *invisible/invincible* (Fibber, Molly), "That's very funny, McGee" (Molly doing a switch), "That ain't the way I heered it" (Old Timer), LaTrivia blowup over his dislike of cabbage
Comments: Just like the mice gag on the February 14, 1939 show that is funny no matter how many times one listens to the show, so Fibber's response to Molly's insistence they do not kill the mouse tickles the funnybone even when Jim fluffs part of the punch line: "What am I supposed to do? Feed him caramels till his teeth go bad and hope he gets run down on his way over to the dentist?" One of Fibber's suggestions for capturing the rodent sounds like a Rube Goldberg invention.

Date: June 23, 1942
Title: Packing for Summer Vacation
Cast: Jim Jordan (Fibber), Marian Jordan (Molly, Teeny), Harlow Wilcox, Bill Thompson (Old Timer, Wallace Wimple), Isabel Randolph (Abigail Uppington), Gale Gordon (Mayor LaTrivia), Meredith Willson, John Nesbitt
Summary: The McGees' plans for their vacation are delayed by a locked suitcase.
Music: Billy Mills: "Fine and Dandy," "Stompin' at the Savoy," "The Blacksmith Song" (The King's Men, vocal)
Running Gags: "That ain't the way I heered it" (Old Timer), Myrt bit involving doorstep/rattle and bottle/Uncle Dennis (Fibber), hall closet opened by Meredith because he asked for it
Comments: Wilcox brings attention to a spread in the current issue of *Life* which features Fibber & Molly and what Johnson's Wax is doing for the war effort and (not coincidentally) what the use of Johnson's Wax on household items can do for the cause. The tag includes Jim and Marian's thanks for another year of support from listeners. Willson and Nesbitt will host the summer replacement series.

Date: September 29, 1942
Title: Camera Left on Train
Cast: Jim Jordan (Fibber), Marian Jordan (Molly, Teeny), Harlow Wilcox, Bill Thompson (Old Timer, clerk at Lost and Found, Wallace Wimple), Isabel

Randolph (Abigail Uppington), Gale Gordon (Mayor LaTrivia), Frank Nelson (information clerk)

Summary: The McGees spend more time looking for their lost camera than they do unpacking from their vacation.

Music: Billy Mills: "Of Thee I Sing," "Praise the Lord and Pass the Ammunition" (The King's Men, vocal)

Running Gags: "That ain't the way I heered it" (Old Timer), Myrt bit involving brother/government garage, collie/jeep herder (Fibber), LaTrivia blowup over "highly incensed"

Comments: Marian steps forward during the tag to deliver a heartfelt appeal to housewives about buying wisely, reminding them of the V for Victory slogan and concluding with a reminder that in the alphabet "the only way to reach V is through U." Beginning this new season, Bill Thompson receives recognition in the closing credits.

Date: October 6, 1942
Title: Otis Cadwallader Calls
Cast: Jim Jordan (Fibber), Marian Jordan (Molly, Teeny), Harlow Wilcox, Bill Thompson (Old Timer, Wallace Wimple), Isabel Randolph (Abigail Uppington), Gale Gordon (Mayor LaTrivia)
Summary: A phone call from Otis Cadwallader to Molly puts Fibber in a bad humor.
Music: Billy Mills: "It's Fun to be Free," "This is the Army, Mr. Jones" "Please Won't You Leave My Girl Alone?" (The King's Men, vocal), "Until I Live Again"
Running Gags: "The way I heered it is even worse" (Old Timer doing a switch), word confusion involving *incinerating/insinuating/extenuating/extending* (Fibber, Molly), LaTrivia blowup over "kicking a puppy off the sidewalk"
Comments: Fibber says, "Fine old family, my clavicle!," the first of numerous times he will invoke his favorite part of the anatomy in a tone of ridicule. In the tag promoting the opening of *Here We Go Again* Jim unselfishly credits Gildersleeve, Uppington, and Wimple for their roles in the film.

Date: October 13, 1942
Title: Converting Furnace
Cast: Jim Jordan (Fibber), Marian Jordan (Molly, Teeny), Harlow Wilcox, Bill Thompson (Old Timer, Wallace Wimple), Isabel Randolph (Abigail Uppington), Gale Gordon (Mayor LaTrivia)
Summary: Molly is in agreement with Fibber's decision to convert the furnace from oil to coal but not with his plans to do the job himself.
Music: Billy Mills: "Bojangles of Harlem," "I Get the Neck of the Chicken," "I Got a Touch of Texas" (The King's Men, vocal), "I'm Old Fashioned"

Running Gags: "I heered an interesting variation of it" (Old Timer), LaTrivia blowup over using Latin

Comments: This is one of the WWII episodes in which the entire show plays upon a pertinent issue, abetted by undertones of Uppy's entering Fifi in a dog show to benefit the USO and Molly's donating some of Fibber's clothing to the Red Cross, all of which points to the recurrent theme of "Let's keep on laughing and let's keep on giving."

Date: October 20, 1942
Title: Family Tree
Cast: Jim Jordan (Fibber), Marian Jordan (Molly), Harlow Wilcox, Bill Thompson (Old Timer, Wallace Wimple), Isabel Randolph (Abigail Uppington), Gale Gordon (Mayor LaTrivia)
Summary: After hearing Abigail brag about her ancestry, Fibber decides to trace his genealogy.
Music: Billy Mills: "Great Day," "I Got a Girl in Kalamazoo," "It Ain't Necessarily So" (The King's Men, vocal)
Running Gags: Hall closet opened by Fibber looking for his hat, "That ain't the way I heered it" (Old Timer), Myrt bit involving sister/sporting an anchor/hope chest (Fibber), McGee blowup when LaTrivia turns the tables over the expression "a wink is as good as a nod to a blind horse"
Comments: For those wondering what happened to Lillian the horse, the subject of several episodes last season, Fibber picks up that loose thread by telling LaTrivia that the McGees sold her.

Date: October 27, 1942
Title: Old Timer on the Lam
Cast: Jim Jordan (Fibber), Marian Jordan (Molly, Teeny), Harlow Wilcox, Bill Thompson (Old Timer), Isabel Randolph (Abigail Uppington), Gale Gordon (Mayor LaTrivia), Billy Mills
Summary: The Old Timer seeks refuge with the McGees but won't divulge the reason he is hiding from the police and FBI.
Music: Billy Mills: "Who Cares?," "Everything I've Got," "Conchita Lopez" (The King's Men, vocal), "Full Moon"
Running Gag: Hall closet opened by Old Timer looking for a hiding place
Comments: Bill Thompson makes the most of the biggest part he will ever get in the series. Quinn puts the Old Timer at center stage from his interruption of Wilcox's introduction to the closing line. The Old Timer repeatedly confesses that he was born in Terre Haute, Indiana, Thompson's actual birthplace.

Date: November 3, 1942
Title: Duck Hunting with LaTrivia

Cast: Jim Jordan (Fibber), Marian Jordan (Molly, Teeny), Harlow Wilcox, Bill Thompson (Old Timer, Wallace Wimple), Isabel Randolph (Abigail Uppington), Gale Gordon (Mayor LaTrivia)
Summary: When Fibber returns home from duck hunting with the Mayor, the score is LaTrivia 9, McGee 1.
Music: Billy Mills: "There's a Great Day Coming Mañana," "Manhattan Serenade," "It's Clabberin' Up for Rain" (The King's Men, vocal), "Zing Went the Strings of My Heart"
Running Gag: "That ain't the way I heered it" (Old Timer)
Comments: The hilarity caused by Jim's blooper of "shut with my eyes shut" leads to more unintentional fun when Isabel stumbles over "anyone who survived." Fibber's slant on how leaves turning colors are like traffic lights is the stuff that children's books are made of, though realist Teeny is not buying any of the "heavy-handed whimsy" as she counters his tale with a biological explanation. In the tag Jim and Marian emphasize the need to waste less and buy more bonds.

Date: November 10, 1942
Title: Counselor McGee
Cast: Jim Jordan (Fibber), Marian Jordan (Molly, Teeny), Harlow Wilcox, Bill Thompson (Old Timer, Wallace Wimple), Isabel Randolph (Abigail Uppington), Gale Gordon (Mayor LaTrivia)
Summary: After Fibber promises to serve as advisor and role model for Abigail's nephew, the McGees undertake a search for the wayward fellow.
Music: Billy Mills: "Blow, Gabriel, Blow," "I Met Her on a Monday," "This Is Worth Fighting For" (The King's Men, vocal)
Running Gag: LaTrivia blowup over misinterpretation of phone conversation
Comments: Quinn keeps listeners glued to each word of the integrated commercial with the device of Fibber reciting (supposedly from memory) all the wording on a can of Glo-Coat. The song by The King's Men contains some of the most inspiring lyrics of the period with stirring images of American life that can still raise goose pimples.

Date: November 17, 1942
Title: Money Hidden in Sofa
Cast: Jim Jordan (Fibber), Marian Jordan (Molly, Teeny), Harlow Wilcox, Bill Thompson (Wallace Wimple), Isabel Randolph (Abigail Uppington), Gale Gordon (Mayor LaTrivia)
Summary: While cleaning the attic, the McGees discover a letter from Fibber's grand-uncle about $20,000 in a sofa which sets off a frantic hunt for the hidden loot.
Music: Billy Mills: "This is the Army, Mr. Jones," "Daybreak," "Abraham" (The King's Men, vocal), "I'm Old Fashioned"

Running Gag: LaTrivia blowup over "help the underdog"
Comments: Abigail indicates that her husband wants their snow shovel returned, suggesting at least for the nonce she is again a married woman. Like a skillful author of mysteries, Quinn deftly drops an important clue when the action begins (the date 1867 on the letter) that points toward the revelation in the denouement. In typical fashion, Fibber puts on airs before finding any money and adopts a tony, phony accent when addressing Wilcox. The tag ties the theme of the show, the prospect of finding a fortune, with the best place for such a windfall: buying war bonds.

Date: November 24, 1942
Title: Getting in Shape
Cast: Jim Jordan (Fibber), Marian Jordan (Molly, Teeny), Harlow Wilcox, Bill Thompson (Wallace Wimple), Isabel Randolph (Abigail Uppington), Gale Gordon (Mayor LaTrivia), Frank Nelson (exercise man heard on the radio)
Summary: Fibber's passion for fitness cools considerably when Wimple volunteers his wife for McGee's personal trainer.
Music: Billy Mills: "Who Knows?," "Mister Five by Five," "By the Light of the Silvery Moon" (The King's Men, vocal)
Running Gags: "'Tain't funny, McGee" (Molly), Myrt bit involving brother/bar on shoulder/shoulder on bar (Fibber)
Comments: Gale Gordon demonstrates that he has more comedic tricks than just igniting his short fuse as he stumbles from one faux pas to another in his observations about McGee's bathrobe.

Date: December 1, 1942
Title: Gas Rationing
Cast: Jim Jordan (Fibber), Marian Jordan (Molly, Teeny), Harlow Wilcox, Bill Thompson (Wallace Wimple), Isabel Randolph (Abigail Uppington), Gale Gordon (Mayor LaTrivia), Virginia Gordon (Mrs. Simpson)
Summary: Fibber's strident griping about gas rationing falls on deaf ears of all who come within shouting distance of him.
Music: Billy Mills: "Hallelujah," "Carioca," "Yea, Man" (The King's Men, vocal), "Everything I Love"
Running Gag: Myrt bit involving brother/stung by a black widow/pulled down shade (Fibber)
Comments: Fibber's self-centered rant is contrasted with LaTrivia's enlistment in the Coast Guard, one grumbling over a minor imposition and the other volunteering to put himself in harm's way. Gordon will not return on a regular basis until the beginning of the 1945-1946 season. Virginia Gordon, who appears for the first time on the program, was Gale's wife. The themes of rationing and conserving rubber dominate this episode to the point where the middle commercial is omitted.

Date: December 8, 1942
Title: Women in the Workforce
Cast: Jim Jordan (Fibber), Marian Jordan (Molly), Harlow Wilcox, Bill Thompson (Old Timer, Wallace Wimple), Isabel Randolph (Abigail Uppington), Verna Felton (hardware store manager), Virginia Gordon (paperboy)
Summary: Fibber is dismayed to learn that women are doing many of the jobs formerly performed by men.
Music: Billy Mills: "New Sun in the Sky," "Swampfire," "No More Coffee in the Pot" (The King's Men, vocal), "Out of This World"
Running Gags: Myrt bit involving uncle/over 38, can't get back in/high school (Fibber), "That ain't the way I heered it" (Old Timer)
Comments: Fibber is still fighting the battle of the sexes while everyone else is focused on the battle against the Axis. The song by the King's Men reinforces the theme of all Americans doing their part to win the war. Signs of those times that are rarely seen in these times: Fibber mentions poems on Burma Shave signs, Molly pays for a part for the vacuum cleaner with a half dollar.

Date: December 15, 1942
Title: Missing Fifteen Dollars
Cast: Jim Jordan (Fibber), Marian Jordan (Molly), Harlow Wilcox, Bill Thompson (Old Timer, Wallace Wimple), Isabel Randolph (Abigail Uppington), Ken Christy (Tolliver), Virginia Gordon (Madame X)
Summary: Fibber cannot remember where he hid money for Molly's Christmas present.
Music: Billy Mills: "Oh Gee, Oh Joy," "Road to Morocco," "I'm Dreaming of a White Christmas" (The King's Men, vocal), "It Can't Be Wrong"
Running Gags: None
Comments: Fibber delivers one of those amusing lines that does not make sense, yet everyone senses the meaning: "Uppy, you sound ozzier than Nelson." The appearance of Tolliver as a new neighbor may have been a test to see if this gruff character would replace LaTrivia as a recurring cast member.

Date: December 22, 1942
Title: Grumpy McGee at Christmastime
Cast: Jim Jordan (Fibber), Marian Jordan (Molly, Teeny), Harlow Wilcox, Isabel Randolph (Abigail Uppington), Billy Mills
Summary: Fibber acts like Scrooge regarding Christmas customs so people will not discover that he is a sentimental softie.
Music: Billy Mills: "Who?," "Dark Eyes," "'Twas the Night Before Christmas" (The King's Men and Teeny, vocal), "Silent Night"
Running Gag: Myrt bit involving brother/fishing through the ice/planter's punch (Molly)

Comments: "'Twas the Night Before Christmas," adapted by Ken Darby from "A Visit from St. Nicholas" by Clement Clarke Moore, is performed for the first time. It will be featured on the show closest to Christmas nearly every year through the end of the thirty-minute episodes.

Date: December 29, 1942 (Script)
Title: Gildersleeve as Supper Guest
Cast: Jim Jordan (Fibber), Marian Jordan (Molly), Harlow Wilcox, Harold Peary (Throckmorton P. Gildersleeve), Isabel Randolph (Abigail Uppington), Billy Mills
Summary: Molly makes Fibber promise to behave when former neighbor Gildersleeve returns to Wistful Vista for a meal.
Music: "High Time," "You'd Be So Nice to Come Home To," "I Like a Balalaika" (The King's Men, vocal)
Running Gags: Myrt bits involving father/old skunk/skunk coat, Uncle Dennis/pinched for parking parallel to curb/not in car, Cousin Cecil/shot in back/butcher shot him in back way, half sister/worked for magician/sawed in half (Fibber)
Comments: Gildersleeve delivers a message about the new Victory withholding tax that will start in January to encourage buying more bonds to finance the mounting costs of the war. The four Myrt routines come one after the other in a torrent that Molly is powerless to stop. She vents most of her displeasure at Gildy after learning that he ate little of the food she prepared because he had already dined at a restaurant.

Date: January 5, 1943
Title: Cutting Down Suit
Cast: Jim Jordan (Fibber), Marian Jordan (Molly, Teeny), Harlow Wilcox, Isabel Randolph (Abigail Uppington), Ken Christy (Tolliver)
Summary: The McGees take a pinstripe men's suit to the tailor so it can be altered to fit Molly.
Music: Billy Mills: "Sing, My Heart," "I Had the Craziest Dream," "Hitch Old Dobbin to the Shay Again" (The King's Men, vocal)
Running Gags: "'Tain't funny, McGee" (Molly), Myrt bit involving nephew/Book of the Month Club/ration book (Fibber)
Comments: The example of Teeny's family putting their car up on blocks and the message of the song by the King's Men point listeners in the direction of alternate means of transportation which do not use gas or rubber.

Date: January 12, 1943
Title: Billy Mills in the Hospital
Cast: Jim Jordan (Fibber), Marian Jordan (Molly), Harlow Wilcox, Bill Thompson (Old Timer, Wallace Wimple), Isabel Randolph (Abigail Uppington), Elvia Allman (nurse), Virginia Gordon (nurse), Billy Mills

Summary: While the McGees visit with Billy Mills to cheer him up, Fibber proceeds to fill himself up.
Music: Billy Mills: "Be Young Again," "Brazil," "Lullaby of the Herd" (The King's Men, vocal), "Do I Love You?"
Running Gag: Myrt bit involving cousin/1,500 pounds of horsemeat/riding to work (Fibber)
Comments: The treatment of "Brazil" is distinctive, and in future shows Mills will develop an affinity for Latin rhythms. Billy gets more than his fair share of lines in this episode, one of which is the hoary "took a turn for the nurse" gag.

Date: January 19, 1943
Title: Uppy Wants to Join the WACs
Cast: Jim Jordan (Fibber), Marian Jordan (Molly, Teeny, woman on second record), Harlow Wilcox, Bill Thompson (Horatio K. Boomer, Wallace Wimple), Isabel Randolph (Abigail Uppington), Elvia Allman (woman on first record), Virginia Gordon (Lieutenant Gordon)
Summary: After Abigail announces her intention to enlist, Molly agrees to go with her for moral support, causing Fibber to fear that his wife will sign up, too.
Music: Billy Mills: "Love Is," "Just One of Those Things," "Would You Rather Be a Colonel With an Eagle on Your Shoulder Than a Private With a Chicken on Your Knee?" (The King's Men, vocal), "Out of This World"
Running Gag: "Where'd I put that badge?" (Horatio)
Comments: Writing more than three dozen introductions every season would tax the creativity of any writer, even a gifted one like Don Quinn who could only manage a quick sentence for Wilcox to start this one. Thus, this episode which does not have any memorable sequences except for the *vou/you/who* banter between Fibber and Teeny, is noteworthy for having the shortest opening and the song with the longest title.

Date: January 26, 1943
Title: Author McGee
Cast: Jim Jordan (Fibber), Marian Jordan (Molly, Teeny), Harlow Wilcox, Bill Thompson (Old Timer, Wallace Wimple), Isabel Randolph (Abigail Uppington), Virginia Gordon (Virginia Cheltenham)
Summary: Fibber writes part of a novel, then pays an agent to peddle the manuscript.
Music: Billy Mills: "Free for All," "Could It Be You?" "And Still the Volga Flows" (The King's Men, vocal), "Let's Get Lost"
Running Gags: Word confusion involving *manacle/monocle/barnacle/binacle/clavicle* (Fibber, Molly) and involving *pelican/predicate/pretzel/pistol/hospital/hospitable* (Fibber, Molly, Old Timer)

Comments: Abigail reluctantly picks up the plot thread left dangling the previous week regarding her intention to enlist in the Women's Army Corps. When Fibber puts on airs with his phony English accent, the fun steps up a notch as listeners climb aboard for the ride, waiting for the moment when he will get knocked off his high horse.

Date: February 2, 1943
Title: Cleaning the Hall Closet
Cast: Jim Jordan (Fibber), Marian Jordan (Molly, Teeny), Harlow Wilcox, Bill Thompson (Wallace Wimple, Old Timer), Arthur Q. Bryan (pollster), Virginia Gordon (irate lady), Rosita Moreno (neighbor)
Summary: Fibber and Molly are repeatedly interrupted while trying to the clean the closet.
Music: Billy Mills: "It's Fun to Be Free," "Hey, Good Lookin'," "Hit the Road to Dreamland" (The King's Men, vocal)
Running Gags: Hall closet opened by Wimple looking for typewriter and linen cabinet opened by Molly looking for tablecloth, word confusion involving *arthritis/arbutus/ Brutus/puss and Brutus* (Fibber, Molly)
Comments: Arthur Q. Bryan makes his first appearance as a man asking questions about a radio program. Quinn, who had earlier taken pot shots at the cliffhanger endings of soap operas, parodies the genre in this episode with the fictitious title *David's First Wife's Second Husband*.

Date: February 9, 1943 (Script)
Title: Auto License
Cast: Jim Jordan (Fibber), Marian Jordan (Molly, Teeny), Harlow Wilcox, Bill Thompson (Old Timer, Wallace Wimple), Isabel Randolph (Abigail Uppington), Virginia Gordon (clerk)
Summary: The McGees scramble to scrape up the necessary funds when they learn that February 9th is the last day to purchase a license for their car.
Music: Billy Mills: "Of Thee I Sing," "Tico Tico," "The Chool Song" (The King's Men, vocal)
Running Gags: Myrt bit involving brother/shot it out with cops/craps (Fibber), word confusion involving *allegory/alligator/navigator/narrator/aviator* (Fibber, Molly)
Comments: Listeners are asked to accept the very implausible situation that the McGees, short five cents of the necessary $8.60 for the license, cannot raise that trival amount. Apparently the more recent used car purchased on May 2, 1939 has been scrapped because Fibber tells the clerk their current vehicle is a 1923 Chandler with five cylinders (the sixth one must have gone to war, too). Folks who consider Wimple a 98-pound weakling are giving him the benefit of his doubts because on this broadcast Wimple admits he weighs 78 pounds.

Date: February 16, 1943
Title: Skilled War Workers Needed
Cast: Jim Jordan (Fibber), Marian Jordan (Molly), Harlow Wilcox, Bill Thompson (Old Timer, Wallace Wimple), Gale Gordon (Mayor LaTrivia), Virginia Gordon (mail woman)
Summary: After learning that the government is looking for tack welders and plate hangers, Fibber decides to recruit some of these workers even though he does not know what these occupations are.
Music: Billy Mills: "Great Day," "Happy Go Lucky," "Phil the Fluter's Ball" (The King's Men, vocal)
Running Gags: Word confusion involving *pewter pigeon/potter pigeon/putty pigeon* (Fibber, Molly), LaTrivia blowup over *furlong*
Comments: This episode marks two firsts: the Old Timer mentions Bessie who will become his girl friend of long standing and LaTrivia's blowup is finished by singling out McGee which will be standard practice later. Real-life husband and wife Gale and Virginia have well-wrought blowups in separate scenes. The name of Fibber's old pal, Fred Nitney, will be used with increasing frequency in weeks to come. When Molly mentions that she would not like to miss *Vic and Sade*, Quinn is tipping his hat to the players on that show and its creator, Paul Rhymer, who belongs in the same pantheon of radio writers as Quinn and the team penning *The Jack Benny Program*.

Date: February 23, 1943
Title: Poker Game
Cast: Jim Jordan (Fibber), Marian Jordan (Molly, Teeny), Harlow Wilcox, Bill Thompson (Old Timer, Wallace Wimple), Isabel Randolph (Abigail Uppington), Rosita Moreno
Summary: Although Fibber tells Molly he has to attend a meeting at the Elks Club, he actually is planning on playing poker with the boys.
Music: Billy Mills: "This Is the Army, Mr. Jones," "I've Heard that Song Before," "Murder, He Says" (The King's Men, vocal)
Running Gags: None
Comments: Like the episode of March 11, 1941 which featured a game of poker in the basement of the house, Quinn again employs card terms such as *deal, royal flush, ante, full house, trey, deuce,* and *aces* in Wilcox's commercial. Rosita Moreno, a transitional character who will not survive beyond the current season, was married to Mel Shauer, producer of Jim and Marian's first film, *This Way Please*. Rosita, like Nick Depopolis, speaks English that is so broken Fibber, Molly, and even the King's Men cannot put it together again.

Date: March 2, 1943
Title: Breakfast in Bed for Molly
Cast: Jim Jordan (Fibber), Marian Jordan (Molly), Harlow Wilcox, Bill Thompson (Old Timer, Wallace Wimple), Isabel Randolph (Abigail Uppington), Virginia Gordon (mail woman)
Summary: Fibber, while making breakfast for Molly, does his best and soon the kitchen is looking its worst.
Music: Billy Mills: "A Shine on Your Shoes," "Weep No More, My Lady," "Rosie the Riveter" (The King's Men, vocal), "What's the Good Word, Mr. Bluebird?"
Running Gags: None
Comments: The integrated commercial is one of those in which the McGees literally take the words out of Harlow's mouth and deliver the pitch themselves.

Date: March 9, 1943 (Script)
Title: Visiting the Dairy
Cast: Jim Jordan (Fibber), Marian Jordan (Molly, Teeny), Harlow Wilcox, Bill Thompson (Old Timer), Isabel Randolph (Abigail Uppington), Arthur Q. Bryan (Waterman), Virginia Gordon (secretary), Rosita Moreno
Summary: Fibber and Molly take the Wistful Vista Dairy up on its offer after reading on a milk bottle label that the business welcomes visitors.
Music: Billy Mills: "Hallelujah," "Taking a Chance on Love," "Well I Swan" (The King's Men, vocal)
Running Gag: Word confusion involving *calsomine/calomel/camel* (Fibber, Molly)
Comments: No recording of this broadcast has survived. The shortened version currently in circulation is taken from the Top Ten *Fibber McGee and Molly* album released in 1947 with Jim Backus playing the part of Waterman. Teeny indicates her feminine cat's name is Edward, a worthy companion for her male dog Margaret. The Old Timer, who arrives with Wilcox, delivers the Johnson's Wax pitch in his usual breezy manner. This is the first script with the names of both Don Quinn and Phil Leslie on it, although Leslie will not receive consistent credit as co-writer at the beginning of episodes until November of 1944. A contemporary article by Quinn explained that the idea for this adventure came one day when he and Phil were in the Jordans' kitchen. As Jim poured himself a glass of milk, he noticed the inscription "Come out and visit our sanitary dairy" on the bottle and wondered aloud if anyone ever accepted the invitation. Quinn replied, "Fibber would," and the two writers had the plot for the next episode.

Date: March 16, 1943
Title: Horoscope
Cast: Jim Jordan (Fibber), Marian Jordan (Molly, Teeny), Harlow Wilcox, Isabel Randolph (Abigail Uppington), Arthur Q. Bryan (Stuffy Stillwell), Virginia Gordon (mail woman)
Summary: Fibber, suddenly infatuated with astrology, believes what his horoscope predicts.
Music: Billy Mills: "Bojangles of Harlem," "Caxinga," "Ve Don't Like It" (The King's Men, vocal), "Don't Cry"
Running Gag: Myrt bit involving grandmother/plastered/ceiling fell in (Fibber)
Comments: Molly gets more than her usual share of jokes in this episode because, with Bill Thompson absent and Fibber on his best behavior with Uppy, it was up to her to deliver the goods (and the bad gags as well). McGee drops another piece on the game board of local geography, the Ritz Vista Hotel. Intentional or not, the title of the last musical selection is most fitting after Stillwell connects solidly with McGee.

Date: March 23, 1943
Title: Red Cross Volunteer
Cast: Jim Jordan (Fibber), Marian Jordan (Molly, Teeny), Harlow Wilcox, Bill Thompson (Wallace Wimple), Isabel Randolph (Abigail Uppington), Arthur Q. Bryan (MacDonald), Virginia Gordon (mail woman)
Summary: Fibber appoints himself as a fundraiser for the Red Cross, then finds himself contributing most of the funds.
Music: Billy Mills: "You Do Something to Me," "Please Think of Me," "Sky Anchors Away" (The King's Men, vocal), "It Can't Be Wrong"
Running Gags: Word confusion involving *escort/escrow/Esquire/eskimo* (Fibber, Molly), hall closet opened by Fibber trying to prove to Wimple the closet has been cleaned
Comments: Apparently Uppy but not Fibber had heard or seen Abbott and Costello do the dice routine as she pulls a variation of it on the astounded McGee. Recordings skip from a conversation between McGee and Wimple right into the vocal selection so modern listeners miss Fibber losing his bet with Wimple when the closet he thought was cleaned erupts as usual.

Date: March 30, 1943
Title: Washing Machine
Cast: Jim Jordan (Fibber), Marian Jordan (Molly, Teeny), Harlow Wilcox, Bill Thompson (butler, Old Timer, Wallace Wimple), Isabel Randolph (Abigail Uppington), Arthur Q. Bryan (Jimmy Sales), Virginia Gordon (mail woman)
Summary: After Fibber breaks their washing machine, the McGees search all over town to find a woman who is advertising one for sale.

Music: Billy Mills: "Anything Goes," "Don't Get Around Much Any More," "I'm an Old Cowhand" (The King's Men, vocal), "Keep That Smile"
Running Gag: Myrt bit involving sister/studying to be gunner/gunner's mate (Fibber)
Summary: This episode contains another instance of Jim's ad-libbing to punch up the joke that preceded it. After Molly's gag about crooked parts and her uncle's barber shop gets a mild reaction, he has a ready response to her question of "What do we do now?": "Just stand here and wait I guess." There is some unintentional fun when Harlow loses track of which voice he is using when he doubles as his twin brother. Assigning Bryan the part of a laughing grocer may have been another test role.

Date: April 6, 1943
Title:: No Pep
Cast: Jim Jordan (Fibber), Marian Jordan (Molly, Teeny), Harlow Wilcox, Bill Thompson (Old Timer, Wallace Wimple), Isabel Randolph (Abigail Uppington), Arthur Q. Bryan (Doctor Gamble)
Summary: Fibber calls for a doctor to cure his lethargy.
Music: Billy Mills: "Thank Your Father," "What's the Good Word, Mr. Bluebird?," "Oceana Roll" (The King's Men, vocal), "Take It from There"
Running Gags: Myrt bit involving mother/beat the rap/evening wrap (Fibber), Myrt bit involving cousin/hiccups for weeks/riveter (Molly), word confusion involving *collie/colic/cowlick* (Fibber, Molly)
Summary: In his first appearance as Doctor Gamble, Arthur Q. Bryan is a gag-a-minute extrovert, a far cry from the cynic who will later greet Fibber's presence with insults and McGee's ideas with skepticism. Quinn, now with the able assistance of Phil Leslie, develops cadences on the repeated phrases so that by the time Fibber says, "I got no pep, I got no energy" for the sixth time, the audience is joining in the chorus. It is like following the bouncing ball when listening to the sing-song patter of the Old Timer's recitation of the lineage of the cure for spring fever ("Mother to daughter, daughter to daughter, daughter to son...") The antipode of the listless McGee heard here is the hyperactive one who tears through the house on January 23, 1945.

Date: April 13, 1943
Title: Uncle Sycamore on the Radio
Cast: Jim Jordan (Fibber), Marian Jordan (Molly, Teeny), Harlow Wilcox, Bill Thompson (Old Timer, Wallace Wimple), Isabel Randolph (Abigail Uppington), Frank Nelson (radio announcer), Virginia Gordon (pollster), Rosita Moreno, Claudette Colbert
Summary: The McGees experience technical difficulties while trying to listen to a radio program about the western exploits of Fibber's uncle.

Music: Billy Mills: "High and Low," "Brazil Moreno," "Everybody Every Payday" (The King's Men, vocal), "Let's Get Lost"
Running Gag: Word confusion involving *encylopedia/velocipede/centipede/centigrade* (Fibber, Molly, Teeny)
Comments: Fibber and Molly may have trouble with the reception on their receiver, but the message about radio comes in loud and clear from Harlow's quoting letters from servicemen expressing gratitude for the shortwave broadcasts of *Fibber McGee and Molly* to Claudette's appeal for bonds to meet the second war loan drive to Jim and Marian's declaration of thanks to listeners for their support during the previous eight years.

Date: April 20, 1943
Title: Making a Dress for Molly
Cast: Jim Jordan (Fibber), Marian Jordan (Molly, Teeny), Harlow Wilcox, Bill Thompson (Old Timer, Wallace Wimple), Isabel Randolph (Abigail Uppington), Arthur Q. Bryan (Doctor Gamble)
Summary: Molly takes Fibber up on his boast that anyone can make a dress and soon the living room is a mess of patterns.
Music: Billy Mills: "Blow, Gabriel, Blow," "Do I Know What I'm Doing," "Song of the Merchant Marine (The King's Men, vocal), "I'm Old Fashioned"
Running Gag: Myrt bit involving grandfather/clipped on the puss/cat (Fibber)
Comments: Molly creates a lasting image of Fibber's ineptitude when she describes a sock Fibber darned once: "You bunched it up around the hole and you tied a string around it and pounded it down with a hammer." Jim's fluff of "clack his cravicle" instead of "crack his clavicle" is a comic highlight that really amuses Marian. This time when Fibber mentions Fred Nitney it is connected with their days in vaudeville, an allusion that will bore people for years to come. When Molly is trying to reach the doctor on the phone, she asks for J. Ramsey Gamble, the only time he will be referred to by that name. Throughout the rest of the series his name is George Gamble.

Date: April 27, 1943
Title: Black Market Meat
Cast: Jim Jordan (Fibber), Marian Jordan (Molly, Teeny), Harlow Wilcox, Bill Thompson (Old Timer, Wallace Wimple), Isabel Randolph (Abigail Uppington), Arthur Q. Bryan (Doctor Gamble)
Summary: Fibber buys a steak from a back alley butcher, then begins to wonder if both the decision and the meat are bad.
Music: Billy Mills: "Oklahoma," "People Will Say We're in Love," "Clementine" (The King's Men, vocal), "A Change of Heart"
Running Gags: "'Tain't funny, McGee" (Molly), Myrt bit involving uncle/caught a spy/caught his pie (Fibber), hall closet opened by Teeny seeking the front door, word confusion involving *representative/reprehensible/prehensile/utensil/tonsil* (Fibber, Molly)

Comments: Listeners' devotion to the show readily accepts both Fibber's selfish decision and shortsightedness for laughs *and* Jim's deadly serious message that such actions as McGee's are unwise and unhealthy.

Date: May 4, 1943
Title: Changes Name to Homer K. Frink
Cast: Jim Jordan (Fibber), Marian Jordan (Molly), Harlow Wilcox, Bill Thompson (Old Timer, Wallace Wimple, Officer Clancy), Isabel Randolph (Abigail Uppington), Arthur Q. Bryan (Doctor Gamble), Ken Christy (police chief)
Summary: Fibber visits a numerologist who suggests that he change his name to Homer K. Frink.
Music: Billy Mills: "There's a Great Day Coming Mañana," "It Started All Over Again," "I Got Plenty of Nothin'" (The King's Men, vocal)
Running Gag: Word confusion involving *incognito/incommunicado/avocado/obligato* (Fibber, Clancy, chief)
Comments: It is a credit to Quinn and Leslie that the theme of this episode is identical to that of the one aired March 25, 1941 when Fibber wanted to become Ronald McGee, yet the flow of the action and interplay of secondary characters make each show distinctive.

Date: May 11, 1943
Title: Barometer
Cast: Jim Jordan (Fibber), Marian Jordan (Molly, Teeny), Harlow Wilcox, Bill Thompson (Old Timer, Wallace Wimple), Isabel Randolph (Abigail Uppington), Arthur Q. Bryan (Doctor Gamble), Virginia Gordon (Miss Oglethorpe)
Summary: Fibber's prediction of snow in May is met with derision and disbelief.
Music: Billy Mills: "But Not for Me," "Right Kind of Love," "Steamboat Bill" (The King's Men, vocal), "Out of This World"
Running Gags: Word confusion involving *simoleon/chameleon/comedian/compendium/ companion* (Fibber, Molly, Old Timer) Myrt bit involving brother/invasion/packing them in (Fibber)
Comments: Teeny unleashes another poodle, a "riddle you can't get through your noodle." These concatenations of often disparate parts travel a long way to get to mild payoffs which, in the words of Molly after hearing lame wheezes by Fibber, are "hardly worth the effort."

Date: May 18, 1943
Title: Borrows Uppy's Car
Cast: Jim Jordan (Fibber), Marian Jordan (Molly, Teeny), Harlow Wilcox, Bill Thompson (Nolly Pross, Old Timer, police sergeant), Isabel Randolph (Abigail Uppington), Arthur Q. Bryan (Doctor Gamble), Virginia Gordon (bailiff), Ken Christy (Clancy)

Summary: Fibber takes Abigail's car to go downtown without telling her and, after the auto is stolen, fears that he will be accused of the crime.
Music: Billy Mills: "Sing, My Heart," "Let's Get Lost," "Coming in on a Wing and a Prayer" (The King's Men, vocal), "What's the Good Word, Mr. Bluebird?"
Running Gags: None
Comments: Bill Thompson's mastery of different voices is on display in this episode. There are no vocal giveaways in the delivery of Pross the lawyer, the Irish sergeant, and the Old Timer so that one unfamiliar with *Fibber McGee and Molly* would likely assume three different actors assumed the roles.

Date: May 25, 1943
Title: Train Tickets Difficult to Get
Cast: Jim Jordan (Fibber), Marian Jordan (Molly), Harlow Wilcox, Bill Thompson (Wallace Wimple, Old Timer, foreigner), Isabel Randolph (Abigail Uppington), Arthur Q. Bryan (Doctor Gamble), Virginia Gordon (information clerk), Frank Nelson (ticket agent)
Summary: Fibber plans to travel by train to Middleton to explain his idea regarding post-war transportation.
Music: Billy Mills: "Who?," "You'll Never Know," "In My Arms" (The King's Men, vocal), "It Can't Be Wrong"
Running Gags: "'Tain't funny, McGee" (Molly), word confusion involving *anonymous/synonymous/cinema/cinnamon/salmon* (Fibber, Molly)
Comments: In this episode about civilians forgoing unnecessary travel as in previous shows with war-related themes, Fibber stubbornly stands alone until the repeated chastisements of friends such as Wilcox, the Old Timer, Uppington, and Gamble open his eyes so he can see his selfishness.

Date: June 1, 1943
Title: Bowling Ball
Cast: Jim Jordan (Fibber), Marian Jordan (Molly, Teeny), Harlow Wilcox, Bill Thompson (Wallace Wimple), Isabel Randolph (Abigail Uppington), Arthur Q. Bryan (Doctor Gamble), Virginia Gordon (nurse), Ken Christy (owner of bowling alley)
Summary: While showing Molly how to bowl, Fibber gets his thumb stuck in the ball so they go to Doc Gamble to get his hand free.
Music: Billy Mills: "It's High Time," "Oh Say, Don Jose," "Riding Herd on a Cloud" (The King's Men, vocal), "Don't Worry"
Running Gag: Myrt bit involving brother/Balkan expert/mules (Fibber)
Comments: Fibber delivers an explanation in awful English that nevertheless gets the point across in his description of the purpose of bowling: "The more you knock down with the less balls the better you are at winning more games faster." The Myrt gag in the tag is the latest that routine appears in

any episode, an indication that it might have been a filler because no other jokes came to mind to close the show.

Date: June 8, 1943
Title: Happy Face McGee
Cast: Jim Jordan (Fibber), Marian Jordan (Molly, Teeny), Harlow Wilcox, Bill Thompson (Old Timer), Isabel Randolph (Abigail Uppington), Arthur Q. Bryan (Doctor Gamble), Virginia Gordon (magazine saleslady)
Summary: After reading that a happy appearance leads to a healthy lifestyle, Fibber becomes a Pollyanna who tries to cheer up everyone he meets.
Music: Billy Mills: "Gee, But It's Fun to Sing a Song," "Nevada," "McNamera's Band" (The King's Men, vocal)
Running Gags: None
Comments: The promising idea of turning Frowning Fibber into Smiley McGee for one week is a change of pace that fizzles more than sizzles. The denouement that finds McGee returning to normal even hits a sour note as listeners are expected to believe Fibber would not know the identity of a man he has played pinochle with for two years.

Date: June 15, 1943
Title: Repairing Doc's Car
Cast: Jim Jordan (Fibber), Marian Jordan (Molly, Teeny), Harlow Wilcox, Bill Thompson (Old Timer, Wallace Wimple, radio announcer), Gale Gordon (Mayor LaTrivia), Arthur Q. Bryan (Doctor Gamble)
Summary: When McGee starts to tinker with Gamble's car left in his care, he soon finds himself in a fine fix.
Music: Billy Mills: "Love Is," "She's From Missouri," "The Man with the Big Sombrero" (The King's Men, vocal), "People Will Say We're in Love"
Running Gags: Word confusion involving *hernia/hermit/derby/helmet/hammock/hummock* (Fibber, Molly, Old Timer), "'Tain't funny, McGee" (Molly)
Comments: The Old Timer has temporarily dropped Bessie in favor of a woman named Piggy. LaTrivia beats the drum a bit for the Coast Guard. Gamble accepts the sight of his wrecked auto rather passively, then rejoices at the positive war news coming from the car radio, the implicit message being, as cogently stated onscreen by Rick Blaine, that the problems of "little people don't amount to a hill of beans in this crazy world."

Date: June 22, 1943
Title: Planning Vacation at Dugan's Lake
Cast: Jim Jordan (Fibber), Marian Jordan (Molly), Harlow Wilcox, Bill Thompson (Old Timer, Wallace Wimple), Isabel Randolph (Abigail Uppington), Gale Gordon (Mayor LaTrivia), Arthur Q. Bryan (Doctor Gamble), Virginia Gordon (Myrt)

Summary: The McGees shop for camping equipment prior to leaving for their summer vacation.
Music: Billy Mills: "Great Day," "A Little Close Harmony," (The King's Men, vocal), "If You Please"
Running Gags: "'Tain't funny, McGee" (Molly), hall closet opened by Abigail seeking the front door to make a "graceful exit," "That ain't the way I heered it" (Old Timer), LaTrivia blowup over "petty officer"
Comments: Myrt is heard for the first and last time while Mrs. Uppington makes her final appearance. With Isabel Randolph leaving the show to concentrate on work in movies and Bill Thompson joining the Navy during the summer, the program would have a new but not necessarily improved look in the fall and for the duration of the war. *The Passing Parade* featuring John Nesbitt replaces *Fibber McGee and Molly* for the summer.

Date: September 28, 1943
Title: Movies Mix-up
Cast: Jim Jordan (Fibber), Marian Jordan (Molly, Teeny), Harlow Wilcox, Gale Gordon (Mayor LaTrivia), Arthur Q. Bryan (Doctor Gamble), Ransom Sherman (Sigmund Wellington), Shirley Mitchell (cashier)
Summary: In a case of mistaken identity Fibber manages to turn the McGees' night at the theater into an adventure more lively than anything showing on the screen.
Music: Billy Mills: "Oklahoma," "Nevada," "Pistol Packin' Mama" (The King's Men, vocal), "Don't Worry"
Running Gags: Myrt bit involving saddle of mutton/stolen/saddle sore (Fibber), "'Tain't funny, McGee" (Molly)
Comments: Ransom Sherman appears for the first time as Wellington. To give the theater manager some distinctive characteristic, the writers created a unique style of speaking in which he hestitates between syllables of certain words. Molly's hints about taking in a boarder lay the groundwork for the following week's episode.

Date: October 5, 1943
Title: New Roomer
Cast: Jim Jordan (Fibber), Marian Jordan (Molly, Teeny), Harlow Wilcox, Gale Gordon (Mayor LaTrivia), Arthur Q. Bryan (Doctor Gamble), Ransom Sherman (Uncle Dennis), Shirley Mitchell (Alice Darling)
Summary: The McGees clean up a spare room in preparation for taking in a war worker as a boarder.
Music: Billy Mills: "Fun to Be Free," "Thank Your Lucky Stars," "The Best of All" (The King's Men, vocal), "My Heart Tells Me"
Running Gags: Hall closet opened by Fibber to get his hat, LaTrivia blowup over barber college

Comments: The oft-mentioned Uncle Dennis finally gets to say some slurred words. This is the first appearance of the character Alice Darling. *Fibber McGee and Molly* eschewed off-color humor, yet this episode contains two bits about infidelity and hanky-panky that pass by harmlessly because there could be another meaning to the lines. One is Fibber's "He used to pick 'em up all over the country" about Fred Nitney and the other is the "There'll be none of that stuff in this house!" response to Wilcox's "rest in the arms of Morpheus."

Date: October 12, 1943
Title: Commission in WACs
Cast: Jim Jordan (Fibber), Marian Jordan (Molly), Harlow Wilcox, Arthur Q. Bryan (Doctor Gamble), Ransom Sherman (Uncle Dennis), Shirley Mitchell (Alice Darling), Virginia Gordon (Anita Nitney)
Summary: Fibber finds that getting a military commission for a friend's daughter is easier said than done.
Music: Billy Mills: "Blow, Gabriel, Blow," "People Will Say We're in Love," "I've Got Sixpence" (The King's Men, vocal), "How Sweet You Are"
Running Gags: None
Comments: The bickering between McGee and Gamble shows them in fine form already and provides a foretaste of the verbal brawls to come. The part where Fibber stops reading Nitney's letter because Fred went out to sharpen his pencil is one of those comic moments that will either cause listeners to crack a smile or scatch their heads.

Date: October 19, 1943
Title: Bad Luck with Mirrors
Cast: Jim Jordan (Fibber), Marian Jordan (Molly, Teeny), Harlow Wilcox, Arthur Q. Bryan (Doctor Gamble), Ransom Sherman (Uncle Dennis), Shirley Mitchell (Alice Darling), Virginia Gordon (clerk)
Summary: Superstitious Fibber is filled with trepidation when Molly asks him to take a mirror downtown to be resilvered.
Music: Billy Mills: "But Not for Me," "They're Either Too Young or Too Old," "The Infantry Song" (The King's Men, vocal), "For the First Time"
Running Gag: Myrt bit involving three terms/not want fourth/brother repeating third grade (Fibber)
Comments: Alice's luck at attracting suitors is far from bad and will improve in the coming weeks. The name of the mirror shop, Here's Looking at You, casts a nice reflection thrown all the way from Casablanca.

Date: October 26, 1943
Title: Cigar Ashes
Cast: Jim Jordan (Fibber), Marian Jordan (Molly, Teeny), Harlow Wilcox, Arthur Q. Bryan (Doctor Gamble, fireman), Ransom Sherman (Uncle Dennis, fireman), Shirley Mitchell (Alice Darling)

Summary: Fibber bets Gamble $5.00 he can keep three inches of ash on his cigar.
Music: Billy Mills: "Of Thee I Sing," "If You Please," "Key-Toky-I-O" (The King's Men, vocal)
Running Gag: Word confusion involving *croquette/croquet/cocaine/cocoon/tycoon* (Fibber, Molly)
Comments: Listeners are asked to believe that Fibber considers winning a trivial bet more important than the danger and damage caused by a blazing fire in the kitchen, a very long stretch of credibility even in the preoccupied world McGee lives in. Teeny adroitly works in titles of some popular songs of the day while delivering a message about saving waste paper for the war effort.

Date: November 2, 1943
Title: Ants in Doc's House
Cast: Jim Jordan (Fibber), Marian Jordan (Molly, Teeny), Harlow Wilcox, Arthur Q. Bryan (Doctor Gamble), Ransom Sherman (Uncle Dennis), Shirley Mitchell (Alice Darling)
Summary: After deciding to help rid Gamble's home of ants, the McGees put their feet in it in more ways than one.
Music: Billy Mills: "Love Is," "How Sweet You Are," "Riding Herd on a Cloud" (The King's Men, vocal)
Running Gags: None
Comments: Molly mentions several occasions when Gamble came to McGee's aid (turkey leg in the eye, broken arm while doing a trick, sitting on a hornet) that might have been just as memorable as the bowling ball adventure the previous June.

Date: November 9, 1943
Title: Chili Sauce
Cast: Jim Jordan (Fibber), Marian Jordan (Molly, Teeny), Harlow Wilcox, Arthur Q. Bryan (Doctor Gamble), Ransom Sherman (Uncle Dennis), Shirley Mitchell (Alice Darling)
Summary: Acting on a challenge from Molly, Fibber makes his own chili sauce.
Music: Billy Mills: "I Know That You Know," "The Surrey With the Fringe on Top," "Sourwood Mountain" (The King's Men, vocal), "Zing Went the Strings of My Heart"
Running Gag: Myrt bit involving you don't tell me/she don't tell me (Fibber)
Comments: When Fibber is isolated from Molly in or around the house as in this episode, it is almost a sure sign he will meet Teeny. Jim's fluff of *oaf/of* gets the biggest laugh of the night.

Date: November 16, 1943
Title: Paying Water Bill
Cast: Jim Jordan (Fibber), Marian Jordan (Molly, Teeny), Harlow Wilcox, Arthur Q. Bryan (Doctor Gamble), Ransom Sherman (Uncle Dennis), Shirley Mitchell (Alice Darling), Virginia Gordon (clerk)
Summary: The McGees, somewhat embarrassed after their water is shut off because Fibber forgot to the mail the check for the bill, attempt to set things straight by going to the utility office and making a payment there.
Music: Billy Mills: "Sing, My Heart," "My Heart Tells Me," "Sunshine of Virginia," (The King's Men, vocal), "I'd Like to Set You to Music"
Running Gags: Word confusion involving *epidermis/epidemic/hypo/Harpo* (Fibber, Molly), hall closet opened by Fibber looking for hat
Comments: In the midst of one of his rants against the utility Fibber mentions his "hard-earned dough," which anyone familiar with his lack of meaningful employment might correct to "hardly-earned dough." One source of income is mentioned in this episode: Alice's weekly rent is $12.

Date: November 23, 1943
Title: Etiquette Book
Cast: Jim Jordan (Fibber), Marian Jordan (Molly, Teeny), Harlow Wilcox, Arthur Q. Bryan (Doctor Gamble), Ransom Sherman (Uncle Dennis), Shirley Mitchell (Alice Darling)
Summary: After finding an 1877 book on etiquette, Fibber becomes mindful of manners much to the annoyance of everyone he encounters.
Music: Billy Mills: "Gee, But It's Fun," "The Volga Boatman," "The Lullaby of Broadway" (The King's Men, vocal), "Do I Love You?"
Running Gags: None
Comments: The conclusion provides evidence that under all the huffing and puffing of insults Fibber and Doc are best of friends. In the tag Jim shows how a skilled radio performer can say the same phrase three times to express three different moods.

Date: November 30, 1943
Title: Teeny's Missing Dog
Cast: Jim Jordan (Fibber), Marian Jordan (Molly, Teeny), Harlow Wilcox, Arthur Q. Bryan (Doctor Gamble), Ransom Sherman (Sigmund Wellington), Shirley Mitchell (Alice Darling)
Summary: The McGees look all over town for Teeny's blue-eyed dog.
Music: Billy Mills: "Why Not?," "She Didn't Say Yes," "Lena from Palestina" (The King's Men, vocal), "My Heart Tells Me"
Running Gags: Myrt bit involving red litter day/Irish Setter puppies (Fibber), word confusion involving *possum/posse/passé/parsley/paisley* (Fibber, Molly)

Comments: Leaving Teeny behind is necessary for the wild pooch chase, but it does stretch credulity a bit to leave a little girl by herself in a house especially when she is the only one who can identify the dog.

Date: December 7, 1943
Title: Wins Drawing
Cast: Jim Jordan (Fibber), Marian Jordan (Molly), Harlow Wilcox, Gale Gordon (Mayor LaTrivia), Arthur Q. Bryan (Doctor Gamble), Ransom Sherman (Sigmund Wellington), Shirley Mitchell (Alice Darling), Virginia Gordon (Crenshaw)
Summary: After Fibber wins money at a drawing at the Bijou, he and Molly have different views on how to spend the windfall.
Music: Billy Mills: "This is the Army, Mr. Jones," "American Patrol," An American Medley (The King's Men, vocal), "National Emblem March"
Running Gags: Myrt bit involving brother/shot it off/his mouth (Fibber), LaTrivia blowup over parents/teachers
Comments: When Fibber says that LaTrivia looks like Flash Gordon, the comparison is most appropriate for Gale Gordon played the space hero on radio in 1935. The tag reinforces the theme of the episode: buy bonds because the war is far from over.

Date: December 14, 1943 (Script)
Title: Handcuffed
Cast: Jim Jordan (Fibber), Marian Jordan (Molly, Teeny), Harlow Wilcox, Arthur Q. Bryan (Doctor Gamble), Ransom Sherman (Sigmund Wellington), Shirley Mitchell (Alice Darling)
Summary: After getting locked in a pair of handcuffs, Fibber attempts to hide the embarasing predicament from visitors.
Music: Billy Mills: "Great Day," "The Carioca," "The Daughter of Mademoiselle from Armentières" (The King's Men, vocal)
Running Gags: Word confusion involving *Geronimo/dominos/dynamo/dynamite* (Fibber, Molly, Alice), Myrt bit involving grandfather/took it on lam/mint sauce (Molly)
Comments: The site of this broadcast is March Field near Riverside, California. Because Fibber cannot use the phone, he provides step-by-step instructions for Molly on performing the Myrt routine. The writers, who often illustrated the folly of not practicing what is preached, use Gamble as the guilty party this week when they show the doctor vociferously berating McGee for juvenile pursuits before having him confess he was able to extricate Fibber because he also owns the Wizard Magic Model Number 22.

Date: December 21, 1943
Title: Shopping for a Christmas Tree
Cast: Jim Jordan (Fibber), Marian Jordan (Molly, Teeny), Harlow Wilcox, Arthur Q. Bryan (Doctor Gamble), Ransom Sherman (Uncle Dennis), Shirley Mitchell (Alice Darling)
Summary: Because Fibber has waited until the last minute to find a Christmas tree, it looks like the McGees will not have one this year.
Music: Billy Mills: "Oklahoma," "Jingle Bells," "Twas the Night Before Christmas" (The King's Men and Teeny, vocal)
Running Gags: None
Comments: Jim milks his *pock picking* blooper for three laughs. The concluding request by the Jordans that listeners include their sincere best wishes in letters to relatives in the service is fitting for by now most families considered Jim and Marian part of the family.

Date: December 28, 1943
Title: Ribbon on Finger
Cast: Jim Jordan (Fibber), Marian Jordan (Molly), Harlow Wilcox, Arthur Q. Bryan (Doctor Gamble), Ransom Sherman (Sigmund Wellington), Shirley Mitchell (Alice Darling)
Summary: Fibber performs a variety of tasks, hoping that one of them is the reason for the ribbon on his finger.
Music: Billy Mills: "Who?," "Blue Skies," "Only 12 More Shopping Months Till Christmas" (The King's Men, vocal), "You're the Rainbow"
Running Gags: Hall closet opened by Fibber looking for hat, Myrt bit involving aunt/lost afghan/went back to Afghanistan (Fibber)
Comments: At least two wonderful comic images linger in the mind from this episode. One is Molly's description of it being so dark without a light outside that Fibber threw the garbage in the cellar window and went in the garage hollering that someone had stolen the back steps. Another is Fibber's description of the mismatched wallpaper which has resulted in the odd pairing of a horse jumping over a chrysanthemum.

Date: January 4, 1944
Title: Businessman McGee
Cast: Jim Jordan (Fibber), Marian Jordan (Molly), Arthur Q. Bryan (Doctor Gamble), Shirley Mitchell (Alice Darling), Harry Von Zell
Summary: Gabby Fibber takes numerous large orders over the phone but remains tight-lipped about the nature of the business.
Music: Billy Mills Orchestra (sans Billy): "There's a Great Day Coming Mañana," "Could It Be You?," "The Time is Now" (The King's Men, vocal)
Running Gags: None
Comments: Harlow Wilcox, Billy Mills, and Ransom Sherman are all absent, battling the flu. Although it bears no date of broadcast, portions of the

script for this episode appear in *There's Laughter in the Air!*, a collection of comedy radio scripts published in 1945. The six pages of excerpts convey little of the wartime flavor of the broadcast as all but one of the pointed remarks about conserving paper are omitted. Quinn and Leslie repeatedly dangle the initials of the company, the huge numbers of orders, and the colors in front of the audience so that they should either beat Fibber to the finish line or at least not be surprised at how he got there.

Date: January 11, 1944
Title: Income Tax Return
Cast: Jim Jordan (Fibber), Marian Jordan (Molly, Teeny), Harlow Wilcox, Arthur Q. Bryan (Doctor Gamble), Ransom Sherman (Sigmund Wellington), Shirley Mitchell (Alice Darling), Harry Von Zell
Summary: The McGees grapple with the instructions of the 1943 tax form which prove to be almost as painful as paying the money owed.
Music: Billy Mills: "High and Low," "No Love, No Nothing," "Skip to My Lou" (The King's Men, vocal)
Running Gags: Myrt bit involving bottle/behind each ear/Teacher's (Fibber), hall closet opened by Fibber looking for phone book
Comments: Jim deftly covers a late door effect by telling Alice "I thought you were never going to get here." There is a nod to another program announced by Von Zell or Wilcox when Fibber mentions "Sally Patica" (*The Eddie Cantor Show*) or whistles the melody for "Rinso white" (*Amos 'n' Andy*).

Date: January 18, 1944
Title: Flowers from Ralph
Cast: Jim Jordan (Fibber), Marian Jordan (Molly, Teeny), Harlow Wilcox, Arthur Q. Bryan (delivery man, Doctor Gamble), Ransom Sherman (Uncle Dennis), Shirley Mitchell (Alice Darling)
Summary: When Molly receives flowers from a man named Ralph, a jealous Fibber spews out threats toward the unknown admirer.
Music: Billy Mills: "High and Low," "Thou Swell," "Don't Tetch It" (The King's Men, vocal), "The Music Stopped"
Running Gags: Word confusion involving *Austin/bantam/phantom* (Fibber, Molly, Dennis), Myrt bit involving going to run again/Whirlaway (Fibber)
Comments: Ransom's slip on *phantom/bantam* is one of those errors when an actor says the right word in context but the wrong word comically and therefore blows the gag.

Date: January 25, 1944
Title: Dining Out
Cast: Jim Jordan (Fibber), Marian Jordan (Molly), Harlow Wilcox, Arthur Q. Bryan (doorman, Doctor Gamble), Ransom Sherman (Uncle Dennis),

Shirley Mitchell (Alice Darling), Marlin Hurt (Beulah), Ken Christy (owner of nightclub)

Summary: The McGees go out for a night on the town to celebrate the return of their laundry.

Music: Billy Mills: "Who Knows?," "My Heart Stood Still," "Deacon Jones" (The King's Men, vocal), "You're the Rainbow"

Running Gag: Hall closet opened by Fibber to get derby hat

Comments: Surprisingly Marlin Hurt's first appearance as a woman speaking in dialect does not get as much of a reaction from the audience as it will in weeks to come. Molly delivers one of the most vivid descriptions of boogie woogie: "The kind of piano playing that sounds like rain on the roof with the left hand and somebody playing the flute in the attic with the right hand."

Date: February 1, 1944
Title: Diamond Ring for $20.00
Cast: Jim Jordan (Fibber), Marian Jordan (Molly, Teeny), Harlow Wilcox, Arthur Q. Bryan (Doctor Gamble), Ransom Sherman (Sigmund Wellington), Shirley Mitchell (Alice Darling), Marlin Hurt (Beulah)
Summary: Fibber begins to wonder if the diamond ring he bought for $20.00 is bogus.
Music: Billy Mills: "Anything Goes," "I'm Just Wild about Harry," "The Surrey With the Fringe on Top" (The King's Men, vocal)
Running Gags: None
Comments: Alice's weekly rent has apparently increased from $12 in November 1943 to $15 in 1944. Of all his confrontations with Teeny, Fibber's blood pressure rises to its highest level in this episode with the aid of a bicycle pump. Jim and Marian's sincere plea to buy bonds in the tag is an offer no American in good conscience could refuse.

Date: February 8, 1944
Title: Ice Cream
Cast: Jim Jordan (Fibber), Marian Jordan (Molly, Teeny), Harlow Wilcox, Arthur Q. Bryan (Doctor Gamble), Ransom Sherman (Sigmund Wellington), Shirley Mitchell (Alice Darling), Marlin Hurt (Beulah)
Summary: After Fibber is unsuccessful in making ice cream at home, the McGees hope to find the object of their confection at Kremer's Drugstore.
Music: Billy Mills: "New Sun in the Sky," "Sunday," "Billy Boy" (The King's Men, vocal), "For the First Time"
Running Gags: Myrt bit involving flat in front of post office/sister singing (Fibber), "'Tain't funny, McGee" (Molly)
Comments: Like the conclusion of the the pot roast episode of June 9, 1942, the last morsel of a tasty treat is gobbled up by a friend, leaving Fibber

hungry and huffy. Lest listeners think the network has forgotten there is a war on, "Buy war bonds" replaces the NBC chimes at the end.

Date: February 15, 1944
Title: Handwriting Analysis
Cast: Jim Jordan (Fibber), Marian Jordan (Molly, Teeny), Harlow Wilcox, Arthur Q. Bryan (Doctor Gamble), Ransom Sherman (Sigmund Wellington), Shirley Mitchell (Alice Darling), Marlin Hurt (Beulah)
Summary: When Fibber learns that his handwriting reveals he has the common touch of a physician, he begins diagnosing with abandon but without a degree.
Music: Billy Mills: "Thank You, Father," "Softly As in a Morning Sunrise," "Johnny One-Note" (The King's Men, vocal), "Someday I'll Meet You Again"
Running Gag: Myrt bit involving uncle/lost pair of rubbers/went in army (Fibber)
Comments: Beulah delivers what may be the funniest line in her tenure on the show when she says that, after Mort Toops indicated that her biscuits are just like a feather, Mort asked if he could have one that is more like a biscuit. Fibber also gets a good response with his quip about having a "gift for diagno-sis," but the line that gets no reaction which in retrospect tickles as much as any delivered in this episode is his request to Molly and Alice for "less levity...if we can have any less." The heartfelt thanks delivered in the tag for recent support of the 4th War Loan Drive is delivered with such sincerity that listeners are certain Jim and Marian have the common touch.

Date: February 22, 1944
Title: School Pal Visits
Cast: Jim Jordan (Fibber), Marian Jordan (Molly), Harlow Wilcox, Arthur Q. Bryan (Doctor Gamble), Ransom Sherman (Sigmund Wellington), Shirley Mitchell (Alice Darling), Marlin Hurt (Beulah)
Summary: The McGees welcome a man into their home who appears to be a classmate from their childhood days in Peoria.
Music: Billy Mills: "Bojangles of Harlem," Temptation," "Mairzy Doats" (The King's Men, vocal)
Running Gags: None
Comments: Other men look back on herculean feats accomplished on athletic field or court; Fibber remembers being second blade on the mumblety-peg team. "Sourwood Mountain" by The King's Men is inserted in lieu of the integrated commercial in the AFRS rebroadcast of this episode. The tune "Sunday" is also played on the AFRS show.

Date: February 29, 1944
Title: Campfire in Fireplace
Cast: Jim Jordan (Fibber), Marian Jordan (Molly, Teeny), Harlow Wilcox, Arthur Q. Bryan (Doctor Gamble), Ransom Sherman (Sigmund Wellington), Shirley Mitchell (Alice Darling), Marlin Hurt (Beulah), Eddie Cantor
Summary: After reading a story about the Old West, McGee gets a burning desire to recreate a prairie campfire in the fireplace.
Music: Billy Mills: "Who Cares?," "Where or When," "The Polka Dot Polka" (The King's Men, vocal), "My Heart Tells Me"
Running Gags: Word confusion involving *tarantula/tarantella/panatella/patella/ peccadillo/dill pickle* (Fibber, Molly), tongue twister starting with Panamint McGee (Fibber), hall closet opened by Eddie Cantor seeking the front door
Summary: Marian has more than her share of good lines with some clever twists on common sayings. Wilcox gets in the western swing of things with some twangy talk about the "JW spread." "The Surrey With the Fringe on Top" by the King's Men and a portion of "Carioca" by the orchestra fills out the AFRS rebroadcast of this episode.

Date: March 7, 1944
Title: Speech for the Red Cross
Cast: Jim Jordan (Fibber), Marian Jordan (Molly), Harlow Wilcox, Arthur Q. Bryan (Doctor Gamble), Ransom Sherman (Sigmund Wellington), Shirley Mitchell (Alice Darling), Marlin Hurt (Beulah)
Summary: Fibber prepares a speech on behalf of the Red Cross to be delivered on station WVIS.
Music: Billy Mills: "Long Ago and Far Away," "When They Ask About You," "The Kid with the Rip in his Pants" (The King's Men, vocal)
Running Gag: "Love that man" (Beulah)
Comments: Harlow's middle commercial with sound effects is a splendid audio rebus. As in earlier appeals for the Community Chest, Marian's request for donations to the Red Cross gets right to the heart of the matter.

Date: March 14, 1944
Title: Beulah Is Hired
Cast: Jim Jordan (Fibber), Marian Jordan (Molly, Teeny), Harlow Wilcox, Arthur Q. Bryan (Doctor Gamble), Ransom Sherman (Sigmund Wellington), Shirley Mitchell (Alice Darling), Marlin Hurt (Beulah)
Summary: The McGees host a supper to celebrate the hiring of Beulah as their new cook and housekeeper.
Music: Billy Mills: "Oh Gee, Oh Joy," "I Love You," "It's Love, Love, Love" (The King's Men, vocal), "My Shining Hour"

Running Gags: Myrt bit involving sister/contract with 20th Century/brakewoman (Fibber), "Love that man" (Beulah), cigar routine (Fibber, Doc Gamble)
Comments: Jim milks a few extra laughs with his pronunciation of *Woodbury*. Fibber and Molly try to get Wellington's goat on his use of *wont* and *carriage* like they did with LaTrivia, but it does not go very far because Sigmund is not the explosive type. Fibber's recitation of the Indian tribes will be reprised later in the year on the December 12th episode.

Date: March 21, 1944
Title: Mandolin
Cast: Jim Jordan (Fibber), Marian Jordan (Molly), Arthur Q. Bryan (Doctor Gamble), Ransom Sherman (Sigmund Wellington), Shirley Mitchell (Alice Darling), Marlin Hurt (Beulah), Harry Von Zell
Summary: Fibber, at first elated with finding his old mandolin in the closet, becomes dismayed when he discovers that everyone plays it better than he does.
Music: Billy Mills: "Sing, My Heart," "Besame Mucho," "Put on Your Old Gray Bonnet" (The King's Men, vocal)
Running Gags: Hall closet opened by Fibber to find electric cord for iron, then opened a second time to see where the mandolin will fall, "Love that man" (Beulah)
Comments: Harry Von Zell substitutes for Harlow Wilcox. Doc Gamble gets the best line of the night after he listens to Fibber's warbling: "I've heard prettier music than that coming from a beer truck running over a manhole cover." In a number of episodes Fibber wants to sing or play "Red Wing" in the worst way, and he does just that.

Date: March 28, 1944
Title: Gildersleeve Returns
Cast: Harlow Wilcox, Harold Peary (Throckmorton P. Gildersleeve), Arthur Q. Bryan (Doctor Gamble), Ransom Sherman (Sigmund Wellington), Shirley Mitchell (Alice Darling), Marlin Hurt (Beulah), Walter Tetley (Leroy Forrester)
Summary: Gildersleeve returns to Wistful Vista with his nephew Leroy, only to find that the McGees are not home.
Music: Billy Mills: "Rise and Shine," "Take It Easy," "You Can't Say No to a Soldier" (The King's Men, vocal), "So Dumb But So Beautiful"
Running Gags: "Love that boy" (Beulah), hall closet opened by Leroy looking for basement, Myrt bit involving terrier/breaches of peace/piece of breaches (Throckmorton)
Comments: The Jordans are absent due to Jim's bout with pneumonia. Phil Leslie receives co-writer credit with Don Quinn. The idea for Gildy and Leroy to take over this week may have come at late notice with little

rehearsal because the show is rough in spots with Peary fluffing *buggy* and he and Tetley stepping on each other's lines. Gildersleeve treats Wellington and Gamble like old friends, although Gildy left for Summerfield in 1941 and the other two did not appear until 1943. Shirley *is* Hal's old pal so the flirting between the boarder and the guest is as natural as the romantic byplay between Leila and Throcky on *The Great Gildersleeve*.

Date: April 4, 1944
Title: Recovering from Pneumonia
Cast: Jim Jordan (Fibber), Marian Jordan (Molly), Harlow Wilcox, Arthur Q. Bryan (Doctor Gamble), Ransom Sherman (Sigmund Wellington), Shirley Mitchell (Alice Darling), Marlin Hurt (Beulah)
Summary: Fibber tries to tell each of his visitors about his stay in the hospital.
Music: Billy Mills: "Sure Thing," "Speak Low," "San Fernando Valley" (The King's Men, vocal), "You're the Rainbow"
Running Gags: Myrt bit involving brother/1944 convertible/$19.44 (Fibber), "Love that man" (Beulah)
Summary: Fibber and the writers effectively dangle the carrot of a nurse in front of listeners ten times before the payoff. Another subtle tip of the hat is given to *Vic and Sade*. The mention in the tag of the many cards, flowers, and telegrams Jim received during his illness is another indication of how well-loved he was by friends and fans.

Date: April 11, 1944
Title: Whipped Cream
Cast: Jim Jordan (Fibber), Marian Jordan (Molly), Harlow Wilcox, Arthur Q. Bryan (Doctor Gamble), Ransom Sherman (Sigmund Wellington), Shirley Mitchell (Alice Darling), Marlin Hurt (Beulah)
Summary: McGee takes his sudden craving for whipped cream into the countryside.
Music: Billy Mills: "Love Is Sweeping the Country," "Don't Sweetheart Me," "Old MacDonald Had a Farm" (The King's Men, vocal), "Goodnight, Wherever You Are"
Running Gags: "Love that man" (Beulah), word confusion involving *infinitive/alternative/fraternity/maternity* (Fibber, Molly), hall closet opened by Fibber looking for thermos bottle, "'Tain't funny, McGee" (Molly)
Comments: To convey the message about increasing farm production, the writers ask the listeners to stretch their forbearance a country mile so Fibber and Molly can run into their acquaintances *very* coincidentally: theater manager Wellington on a rural road in search of mint to make juleps for his grandmother, pitchman Wilcox riding by on a horse, pouring it out and spreading it around the landscape like Racine's version of Paul Revere, and Alice Darling popping out of a door at the farmhouse of her uncle, Henry MacDonald, whose last name leads into the number by The King's Men.

Date: April 18, 1944
Title: Spy Across the Street
Cast: Jim Jordan (Fibber), Marian Jordan (Molly, Teeny), Harlow Wilcox, Arthur Q. Bryan (Doctor Gamble), Ransom Sherman (Sigmund Wellington), Shirley Mitchell (Alice Darling), Marlin Hurt (Beulah)
Summary: Fibber is convinced that his neighbor is a German spy, although no one except Teeny agrees with his belief.
Music: Billy Mills: "Rustle of Spring," "It's Love, Love, Love" (The King's Men, vocal), "My Shining Hour"
Running Gags: Myrt bit involving cousin/chief pretty officer/Petty (Fibber), word confusion involving *Atlas/alias/Alice/antlers* (Fibber, Molly, Harlow), "Love that man" (Beulah)
Comments: This episode might be called apundant with word play (e.g. *Leica, Gay Abandon, cote/coat*). One funny line that slips by quickly after there is a knock on the front door is Fibber's request for Molly to get in front of him so he can shoot over her shoulder, a comment in the vein of those delivered by Bob Hope in one of his screen roles as cowardly jester. The tag includes a thank you for nine years of support and a nod to Don Quinn for his writing. (Phil Leslie, who has been onboard for over a year as co-writer, has not yet earned consistent weekly naming rights.)

Date: April 25, 1944
Title: Cannery Job Offer
Cast: Jim Jordan (Fibber), Marian Jordan (Molly, Teeny), Harlow Wilcox, Arthur Q. Bryan (Doctor Gamble), Ransom Sherman (Sigmund Wellington), Marlin Hurt (Beulah)
Summary: Fibber makes plans to leave Wistful Vista after receiving a letter from Cousin Roy asking him to take over his canneries in Oregon.
Music: Billy Mills: "The Best Things in Life Are Free," "Here It Is Monday," "The Sound Effects Man" (The King's Men, vocal)
Running Gags: Myrt bit involving kid sister/Sidney/Sid kissed her (Fibber), hall closet opened by Fibber during the song about the sound effects man, "Love that man" (Beulah)
Comments: The writers let Myrt have it with fourteen rapid-fire figures of speech indicating how gabby the telephone operator is. Precocious Teeny again counters a fanciful story of Fibber's (this one about salmon) with a scientific explanation that seems more than a little advanced for a little girl, but anything is possible for a child who, as she will admit on next week's show, is six years old but has dropping in on the McGees for nine years.

Date: May 2, 1944
Title: Aunt Sarah's Portrait
Cast: Jim Jordan (Fibber), Marian Jordan (Molly, Teeny), Harlow Wilcox, Arthur Q. Bryan (Doctor Gamble), Ransom Sherman (Sigmund Wellington), Shirley Mitchell (Alice Darling), Marlin Hurt (Beulah)

Summary: Expecting a visit from Aunt Sarah, the McGees retrieve her portrait from storage and prepare to hang it in the living room.
Music: Billy Mills: "Of Thee I Sing," "Anitra's Dance," "Sure Thing" (The King's Men, vocal), "You Will, Won't You?"
Running Gags: Word confusion involving *stalemate/stagnant/stalactite* (Fibber, Molly, Alice), hall closet opened by Alice looking for portrait, "Love that man" (Beulah)
Comments: Quinn and Leslie have a way with figurative language that brings up images which are apt and funny. Two examples from this episode: Fibber describes Sarah as "closer than Scotch tape" and Molly says that the portrait "tips like a counterfeiter in a nightclub." A joke that probably launched a thousand quips at bars over the next few weeks is Teeny's admission that her father called her Martini as a baby because she "was never dry enough to suit him."

Date: May 9, 1944
Title: Alice's Boyfriend
Cast: Jim Jordan (Fibber), Marian Jordan (Molly), Harlow Wilcox, Arthur Q. Bryan (Robert Richards), Ransom Sherman (Sigmund Wellington), Shirley Mitchell (Alice Darling), Marlin Hurt (Beulah)
Summary: After a rainstorm prevents Alice and her date from leaving the house, Fibber entertains the captive couple who wish that he, like the weather, would dry up.
Music: Billy Mills: "You Do Something to Me," "Poinciana," "The Enchilada Man" (The King's Men, vocal), "Look for the Silver Lining"
Running Gags: "'Tain't funny, McGee" (Molly), "Love that man" (Beulah)
Comments: The introduction of Richards with Bryan employing the Elmer Fudd voice he used in cartoons may have been a test to create a new character in the neighborhood to give the show some variety. When Roberts asks Fibber what he does for a living, it is the $64 question listeners have been asking themselves since 1935.

Date: May 16, 1944
Title: Charity Ends at Home
Cast: Jim Jordan (Fibber), Marian Jordan (Molly), Harlow Wilcox, Arthur Q. Bryan (Doctor Gamble), Ransom Sherman (Sigmund Wellington), Shirley Mitchell (Alice Darling), Marlin Hurt (Beulah), Ken Christy (Hogan), Dick LeGrand (Dubinsky)
Summary: The McGees get the third degree from a pair of toughs selling tickets to the policemen's benefit.
Music: Billy Mills: "Be Young Again," "I'll Get By," "Old Dan Tucker" (The King's Men, vocal), "So Dumb But So Beautiful"
Running Gags: Word confusion involving *macaroon/masquerade/mascara/Moscow* (Fibber, Molly, Alice), "Love that man" (Beulah), hall closet opened by Hogan looking for clues

Comments: Molly refers to a FHA payment of $30.00 and on a few other episodes a mortgage payment is mentioned which contradicts the fact that the McGees won their house on a raffle. Harlow gives his middle name as Moffat. Dick (Richard) LeGrand appears for the first time. When asked to buy tickets, Fibber unleashes a scornful reply that only he, of all the characters on radio, could deliver with the appropriate sarcasm: "Do I look dumb enough to pay any part of a fin to see a bunch of tavern-tummied, muscle-bound, handcuff-rattlers shaking their fallen arches around a third-class ballroom?"

Date: May 23, 1944 (Script)
Title: Beauty Parlor Palaver
Cast: Jim Jordan (Fibber), Marian Jordan (Molly, Teeny), Harlow Wilcox, Arthur Q. Bryan (Doctor Gamble), Ransom Sherman (Sigmund Wellington), Shirley Mitchell (Alice Darling), Marlin Hurt (Beulah)
Summary: While Molly has her hair done at the beauty shop, Fibber eavesdrops on the ladies boisterously talking in an adjoining room.
Music: Billy Mills: Script simply indicates "Selection" rather than specifying the titles of the two orchestra numbers. "Umbriago" (The King's Men, vocal)
Running Gags: "Love that man" (Beulah), word confusion involving *bombardier/ pompadour/troubadour/cuspidor/toreador* (Fibber, Molly, beautician)
Comments: In the conclusion Gamble and McGee are overheard engaging in their own brand of chit-chat. The war message on this occasion is recruitment for the WACs in the casual conversation between the beautician and Molly, between Alice and Fibber, and also in the direct appeal by Jim and Marian in the tag.

Date: May 30, 1944
Title: Fishing License
Cast: Jim Jordan (Fibber), Marian Jordan (Molly), Harlow Wilcox, Arthur Q. Bryan (Doctor Gamble), Sherman Ransom (Sigmund Wellington), Shirley Mitchell (Alice Darling), Marlin Hurt (Beulah), Lurene Tuttle (secretary)
Summary: Fibber plans to use a contact at city hall to get his fishing license the easy way.
Music: Billy Mills: "Make Way for Tomorrow," "Holiday for Strings," "27 Times Around the Block" (The King's Men, vocal), "Red Grow the Roses"
Running Gags: Word confusion involving *intercede/intercept/inept/apt* (Fibber, Molly), "Love that man" (Beulah)
Comments: Old Muley, a fabled bass who will become a part of Lake Dugan fishing lore in the same league with the Loch Ness monster, is mentioned for the first time. This is a night for punny epigrams, notably Fibber's observation on politics ("If you start to run, you can't stop till Gallup says you'll win in a walk") and his take on money ("The Romans did their figuring with chisels; we do our chiseling with figures").

Date: June 6, 1944
Title: Salute to D-Day Invasion
Cast: Jim Jordan, Marian Jordan, Harlow Wilcox
Summary: With no audience or commercials, the Jordans and Harlow introduce musical numbers which are interrupted by news about the invasion.
Music: Billy Mills: George M. Cohan medley, "Song of the Merchant Marine" (The King's Men, vocal), "U.S. Field Artillery March," "*Semper Paratus*," "The Time Is Now" (The King's Men, vocal), "This Is the Army, Mr. Jones" "This Is Worth Fighting For" (The King's Men, vocal), "National Emblem March," "Song of the Bombardier" (The King's Men, vocal), "American Patrol," Salute to the armed forces medley, "Army Hymn" (The King's Men, vocal)
Running Gags: None
Comments: This episode is a strong candidate for the most patriotic half-hour of radio broadcast during the war, capped by Marian's declaration that the weapon the Allies have that their enemies do not is "the knowledge that God is on our side," a statement that would cause controversy if spoken on a top-rated network show today but which was widely regarded as accurate by most listeners then.

Date: June 13, 1944
Title: Porch Swing
Cast: Jim Jordan (Fibber), Marian Jordan (Molly, Teeny), Harlow Wilcox, Arthur Q. Bryan (Doctor Gamble), Ransom Sherman (Sigmund Wellington), Shirley Mitchell (Alice Darling), Marlin Hurt (Beulah)
Summary: Fibber assembles a collection of borrowed tools that he doesn't really need to hang the porch swing.
Music: Billy Mills: "I Feel a Song Coming On," "Besame Mucho," "She Broke My Heart in Three Places" (The King's Men, vocal), "In a Moment of Madness"
Running Gags: Word confusion involving *remorse/reminisce/remiss/remit* (Fibber, Molly), hall closet opened by Doc looking for chains for the swing, "Love that man" (Beulah)
Comments: Puns take over the comedy spotlight in this episode, most of them related to the tools (*all/awl/punch, pliers in a pinch*) or the swing (*it squealed*). This is also a busy night for the sound effects man who, in addition to supplying the usual closet noise, produces the sounds of a hacksaw blade breaking four times, a squeaky swing, and a train whistle. The vignette on the swing with the McGees and the old mandolin captures a time when homes had front porches and people felt the desire to spend time relaxing on them observing the sights and sounds around them rather than insulating themselves from neighbors behind closed doors to watch manufactured entertainment.

Date: June 20, 1944
Title: Planning for Ranch Life
Cast: Jim Jordan (Fibber), Marian Jordan (Molly, Teeny), Harlow Wilcox, Arthur Q. Bryan (Doctor Gamble), Ransom Sherman (Sigmund Wellington), Shirley Mitchell (Alice Darling), Marlin Hurt (Beulah)
Summary: Molly gets a kick out of plans for a summer on a cattle ranch while Fibber just gets kicked.
Music: Billy Mills: "Who Cares?," "I Get a Kick Out of You," "Swinging on a Star" (The King's Men, vocal), "Red Grow the Roses"
Running Gags: Cigar routine (Fibber, Harlow), "Love that man" (Beulah)
Comments: The clever device of Molly kicking Fibber in the shins in the middle of his exaggerations results in truthful punch lines that are funnier than his tall tales would have been. It is probably not a coincidence that the title of the second song is the theme of the episode. Ransom Sherman appears for the last time. *Words at War*, hosted by Carl Van Doren, is the summer replacement series.

Date: October 10, 1944
Title: Hip Boots
Cast: Jim Jordan (Fibber), Marian Jordan (Molly, Teeny), Harlow Wilcox, Arthur Q. Bryan (Doctor Gamble), Shirley Mitchell (Alice Darling), Marlin Hurt (Beulah)
Summary: Fibber tears the house apart looking for his hip boots.
Music: Billy Mills: "Flying Down to Rio," "The Continental," "The Three Caballeros" (The King's Men, vocal), "If I Knew Then"
Running Gags: Hall closet opened by Fibber looking for boots, Myrt bit involving uncle/tank commander/water wagon (Fibber), "Love that man" (Beulah)
Comments: The closet effect has become so identified with *Fibber McGee and Molly* that it opens the broadcast of the new season. For a change McGee addresses the little girl as Teeny when she enters, then drops back to his term of familiarity, Sis. The writers skillfully keep the reason for the search hidden until the "futility of it all" finale. Fibber's Frankie and Tommy allusion has a double bite which includes both the musical twosome Sinatra/Dorsey and the political pair Roosevelt/Dewey.

Date: October 17, 1944
Title: Maple Syrup
Cast: Jim Jordan (Fibber), Marian Jordan (Molly), Harlow Wilcox, Arthur Q. Bryan (Doctor Gamble), Shirley Mitchell (Alice Darling), Marlin Hurt (Beulah)
Summary: Fibber plans to tap the tree in the front yard so he will have his own supply of maple syrup.

Music: Billy Mills: "Oklahoma," "Cheek to Cheek," "The Trolley Song" (The King's Men, vocal), "In the Middle of Nowhere"
Running Gags: Word confusion involving *glid/glided/slid/slided/slid/rode/rid* (Fibber, Molly, Beulah), "Love that man" (Beulah), Myrt bit involving grandfather/corn/basement (Fibber)
Comments: Molly defines vaudeville as "a form of entertainment where the same people used the same joke for fifteen or twenty years," then the writers let Alice take a slap at themselves when she says, "Just like on the radio." Fibber's pun on *surreptitiously* may prove their point about hoary gags, but it certainly fits the occasion.

Date: October 24, 1944
Title: Four Dollar Debt
Cast: Jim Jordan (Fibber), Marian Jordan (Molly, Teeny), Harlow Wilcox, Arthur Q. Bryan (Doctor Gamble), Shirley Mitchell (Alice Darling), Marlin Hurt (Beulah), Ken Christy (T. Orville Drake)
Summary: A man who returns $4.00 he borrowed from McGee is focused more on making a score than evening one.
Music: Billy Mills: "Hurray for Hollywood," "Dance with the Dolly," "Baiao" (The King's Men, vocal), "Strange Music"
Running Gags: Cigar routine (Fibber, Drake), hall closet opened by Fibber to hang up Drake's hat, "Love that man" (Beulah), word confusion involving *veterinarian/ veteran/vegetarian/octogenarian/octopus* (Fibber, Molly, Orville)
Comments: One clue to Drake's character is the six-year-old check McGee does not question but which will likely be refused by the bank. In recent shows Fibber has been using a number of terms (e.g. *naked eye, landing strip, lower drawers*) that might have an indelicate meaning which he follows with "If you'll pardon the expression." This bit does not generate much audience reaction and will not become a regular feature after this year.

Date: October 31, 1944
Title: Duck Hunting with Gamble
Cast: Jim Jordan (Fibber), Marian Jordan (Molly), Harlow Wilcox, Arthur Q. Bryan (Doctor Gamble), Shirley Mitchell (Alice Darling), Marlin Hurt (Beulah)
Summary: McGee and Gamble wisely take Molly along when they go hunting because she has remembered to bring everything they forgot.
Music: Billy Mills: "Bojangles of Harlem," "How Many Hearts Have You Broken?"
Running Gag: "Love that man" (Beulah)
Comments: Wilcox mentions The King's Men in the introduction ("And Her Tears Flowed Like Wine" was supposed to be their song on this date), but there is no vocal selection in extant recordings of this broadcast. As part of the pitch to write to servicemen Alice delivers a painless plug for Jim and

Marian's film *Heavenly Days*. Harlow phones in the middle commercial, yet he doesn't miss a beat even when interrupted. Molly may have the funniest line of the night when, in response to two of Fibber's discordant duck calls, she compliments him on his repertoire and asks, "Can you play the Webfoot Boogie?"

Date: November 7, 1944
Election Returns—No *Fibber McGee and Molly* broadcast.

Date: November 14, 1944
Title: Night School
Cast: Jim Jordan (Fibber), Marian Jordan (Molly, Teeny), Harlow Wilcox, Arthur Q. Bryan (Doctor Gamble), Shirley Mitchell (Alice Darling), Marlin Hurt (Beulah)
Summary: After embarrassing himself in front of friends over his ignorance about inflation, Fibber intends to improve his education by attending night school.
Music: Billy Mills: "It's High Time," "I'll Walk Alone," "Sing a Tropical Song" (The King's Men, vocal), "And Then You Kissed Me"
Running Gags: Hall closet opened by Fibber looking for leather strap, word confusion involving *curlicue/curriculum/Corinthian/chrysanthemum* (Fibber, Molly), "Love that man" (Beulah)
Comments: Phil Leslie now will receive co-writing credit on a consistent basis. Curbing inflation is really the theme of the show with Beulah, Gamble, and the Jordans in the tag punching home the message. Doc's reaction to hearing that Fibber is going to night school is ungrammatical but appropriate: "Well, hypo my dermic!" The affection that Gamble and McGee have for each other that is under the name-calling is revealed when Doc tells Molly, "You don't know what it does to me to be able to drop in and take turns pinning each other's ears back."

Date: November 21, 1944
Title: Broken Rib?
Cast: Jim Jordan (Fibber), Marian Jordan (Molly), Harlow Wilcox, Arthur Q. Bryan (Doctor Gamble), Shirley Mitchell (Alice Darling), Marlin Hurt (Beulah), Virginia Gordon (nurse)
Summary: Fibber has x-rays taken to see if he has a broken rib.
Music: Billy Mills: "Why?," "It Had to Be You," "Singing Down the Road," (The King's Men, vocal), "Just Close Your Eyes"
Running Gags: Myrt bit involving nylons/cigarettes (Molly), "Love that poor sick man" (Beulah), word confusion involving *calcium/calcimine/palomino/ knickerbocker/ pantaloons* (Fibber, Molly)
Comments: The x-ray machine sounds like it was made from objects expelled from the hall closet. Gamble promotes the feature now playing (*Heavenly Days*) and a coming attraction (Wimple's visit the following Tuesday).

Date: November 28, 1944
Title: Wimple Home on Leave
Cast: Jim Jordan (Fibber), Marian Jordan (Molly), Harlow Wilcox, Bill Thompson (Old Timer, Wallace Wimple), Arthur Q. Bryan (Doctor Gamble), Shirley Mitchell (Alice Darling), Marlin Hurt (Beulah)
Summary: The McGees, awaiting a visit from Wallace Wimple, cannot believe he is teaching bodybuilding to men in the Navy.
Music: Billy Mills: "New Sun in the Sky," "Come With Me, My Honey," "This Little Bond Went to War" (The King's Men, vocal)
Running Gags: Hall closet opened by Old Timer seeking the front door, Myrt bit involving brother/lieutenant junior grade/full after dinner (Fibber), "Love that man" (Beulah)
Comments: In keeping with this broadcast from Chicago's Navy Pier the middle commercial is replaced by Harlow's appeal on behalf of the sixth war loan drive which contains emotional lines like "if we let up over here, we're letting our men down over there" and "tie a string around your heart to remind you" to buy bonds that are sure to hit home. Among the Navy personnel Marian expresses gratitude for services rendered is Lieutenant Clinton Stanley, a rank and name shared by the hero of many a volume of vigorous fiction read by Rush on *Vic and Sade*.

Date: December 5, 1944
Title: Pressing a Pair of Pants
Cast: Jim Jordan (Fibber), Marian Jordan (Molly, Teeny), Harlow Wilcox, Arthur Q. Bryan (Doctor Gamble), Shirley Mitchell (Alice Darling), Marlin Hurt (Beulah)
Summary: Fibber makes a mess of the house trying to press his pants.
Music: Billy Mills: "Anything Goes," "Tico Tico," "Why Don't You Kiss Me?" (The King's Men, vocal)
Running Gags: Myrt bit involving uncle/vegetable, deli/sweet potato (Fibber), "Love that man" (Beulah)
Comments: This episode contains another example of how the writers let the imaginations of the listeners fill in the blanks when, in response to Molly's question of what the tailor said after McGee told him off, Fibber says, "Never mind what he said. It would have been a physical impossibility anyway."

Date: December 12, 1944
Title: Quiz Program
Cast: Jim Jordan (Fibber), Marian Jordan (Molly, Teeny), Harlow Wilcox, Arthur Q. Bryan (Doctor Gamble), Shirley Mitchell (Alice Darling), Marlin Hurt (Beulah)
Music: Billy Mills: "There's a Great Day Coming Mañana," "There Goes That Song Again," "Too-Ra-Loo-Ra-Loo-Ra" (The King's Men, vocal), "Any Moment Now"

Summary: Fibber becomes a contestant on *Smokes for Folks* in an effort to win cigarettes for Doc Gamble.
Running Gags: "'Tain't funny, McGee" (Molly), Myrt bit involving sister/waves/fell out of boat (Fibber), "Love that man" (Beulah)
Comments: This *Fibber McGee and Molly* take on "Ten Little Indians" is similar to Fibber's recitation on the March 14, 1944 episode except Molly's sneeze helps him out on the last tribe to win the prize. Molly makes a declaration that could be the title of her autobiography: "I married a million laughs."

Date: December 19, 1944
Title: Presents in the Closet
Cast: Jim Jordan (Fibber), Marian Jordan (Molly, Teeny), Harlow Wilcox, Arthur Q. Bryan (Doctor Gamble), Shirley Mitchell (Alice Darling), Marlin Hurt (Beulah)
Summary: Fibber's peeking in the closet leads to his getting to unwrap some of his gifts before Christmas.
Music: Billy Mills: "Make Way for Tomorrow," "Jingle Bells," "'Twas the Night Before Christmas" (The King's Men and Teeny, vocal)
Running Gags: Hall closet opened by Fibber looking for presents, "'Tain't funny, McGee" (Molly), "Love that man" (Beulah)
Comments: When Alice's joke about a hairdo "that is more trouble than it's worth" fizzles, Jim's ad-lib about the misfire is instantaneous: "Yes, I think so, too." Harlow mentions Big Bill Wilcox, one of numerous "big" relatives he will namedrop from time to time who might be in a position to render a service for the McGees.

Date: December 26, 1944
Title: Temper Under Control
Cast: Jim Jordan (Fibber), Marian Jordan (Molly), Harlow Wilcox, Arthur Q. Bryan (Doctor Gamble), Shirley Mitchell (Alice Darling), Marlin Hurt (Beulah)
Summary: Fibber's resolution to stop his angry outbursts is put to the test with everyone he encounters.
Music: Billy Mills: "The Best Things in Life Are Free," "The Parade of the Wooden Soldiers," "Accentuate the Positive" (The King's Men, vocal)
Running Gag: "Mad about that little character" (Beulah)
Comments: Surprisingly for a show aired so close after Christmas there is no mention of the holiday and, except for the second number by Billy Mills, would not have out of place any week of the year. The writers could count on newspaper ads with sloppy syntax like the one Fibber reads in this episode ("Wanted: Man to work around small farm with six cows and one horse who can drive half-ton truck and help with housework") always being good for laughs, especially from Marian.

Date: January 2, 1945
Title: Gift from Aunt Sarah
Cast: Jim Jordan (Fibber), Marian Jordan (Molly), Harlow Wilcox, Arthur Q. Bryan (Doctor Gamble), Shirley Mitchell (Alice Darling), Marlin Hurt (Beulah), Virginia Gordon (mail woman), Ken Christy (Big Barney Wilcox)
Summary: When the McGees receive a diamond stickpin from Aunt Sarah, Fibber changes his tune from "What a skinflint!" to "What a grand old gal!"
Music: Billy Mills: "The Carioca," "Don't Fence Me In" (The King's Men, vocal), "If I Knew Then"
Running Gag: "Love that man" (Beulah)
Comments: Alice, Fibber, and the Jordans in the tag promote the use of V mail. Doc's Rumpelstiltskin gag and Fibber's rejoinder about pistol pockets go right to the seat of their affections.

Date: January 9, 1945
Title: Mushrooms
Cast: Jim Jordan (Fibber), Marian Jordan (Molly, Teeny), Harlow Wilcox, Arthur Q. Bryan (Doctor Gamble), Shirley Mitchell (Alice Darling), Marlin Hurt (Beulah)
Summary: Everyone but Fibber believes that what he brought back from a day in the woods are lethal toadstools, not edible mushrooms.
Music: Billy Mills: "Hallelujah," "Right as Rain," "Evalina" (The King's Men, vocal), "There's Beauty Everywhere"
Running Gags: Myrt bit involving old man/higher than a kite/hire a kite (Fibber), hall closet opened by Fibber looking for cookbook, "Love that man" (Beulah)
Comments: Alice mentions having a date with Monty Fraser, the name of the sound effects man who will shortly answer the call when McGee opens *that* door. Fibber demonstrates there is organization even in a cluttered closet as he places the items back in order: snowshoes, moose head, tennis racket, ice skates, camera tripod, skid chains, little stuff, and mandolin. A Quinn and Leslie quote of note is uttered by Gamble: "More people die from a fork in the mouth than from a knife in the back."

Date: January 16, 1945
Title: No Hot Water
Cast: Jim Jordan (Fibber), Marian Jordan (Molly), Harlow Wilcox, Arthur Q. Bryan (Doctor Gamble), Shirley Mitchell (Alice Darling), Marlin Hurt (Beulah)
Summary: After storming out of the barber shop to protest the cost of a shampoo, Fibber finds that for once in his life getting into hot water isn't so easy.
Music: Billy Mills: "I Feel a Song Coming On," "Fascinating Rhythm," "The Whistler's Song" (The King's Men, vocal), "I Walked In"

Running Gags: "'Tain't funny, McGee" (Molly), "Love that man" (Beulah), Myrt bit involving brother/dropped 1500 feet/projectionist (Fibber), word confusion involving *exonerated/exasperated/expiration/exploration* (Fibber, Molly)

Comments: This episode contains one of the few instances in which someone (Doc Gamble) about to open the closet door is called off (by Molly) which must have disappointed those waiting for the cacophony. Another mild letdown is Fibber's closing line of "It wasn't even loaded" which leaves listeners wondering how the gun could then have shot a hole in the water heater. The all-purpose "This is ridiculous," idle for weeks, would have been a more appropriate endnote.

Date: January 23, 1945
Title: Too Much Energy
Cast: Jim Jordan (Fibber), Marian Jordan (Molly, Teeny), Harlow Wilcox, Arthur Q. Bryan (Doctor Gamble), Shirley Mitchell (Alice Darling), Marlin Hurt (Beulah)
Summary: Molly tries to find projects for Fibber to do while he is playing Mr. Fix-It.
Music: Billy Mills: "Who Cares?," "Broadway Rhythm," "The Oceana Roll" (The King's Men, vocal)
Running Gags: "Love that man" (Beulah), "'Tain't funny, McGee" (Molly), hall closet opened by Fibber looking for plans for jet-propelled bicycle
Comments: This episode offers the flip side of the lethargic McGee who shuffled his way through the April 6, 1943 broadcast. The appeal for the March of Dimes in the tag effectively causes feelings of guilt to create a desire to donate funds.

Date: January 30, 1945
Title: Merchant Marine
Cast: Jim Jordan (Fibber), Marian Jordan (Molly), Harlow Wilcox, Arthur Q. Bryan (Doctor Gamble), Shirley Mitchell (Alice Darling), Marlin Hurt (Beulah)
Summary: The McGees take in a seaman for a night.
Music: Billy Mills: "Poor Little Rhode Island," "Stompin' at the Savoy," "Oh, Moitle" (The King's Men, vocal), "Only Another Boy and Girl"
Running Gag: "Love that man" (Beulah)
Comments: Fibber throws out enough nautical gibberish to sink a ship. The recurring theme in the broadcast is not just a clarion call for the merchant marine but a reminder that the war is not over.

Date: February 6, 1945
Title: Reading *The Case of the Cross-Eyed Cat*
Cast: Jim Jordan (Fibber), Marian Jordan (Molly, Teeny), Harlow Wilcox, Arthur Q. Bryan (Doctor Gamble), Shirley Mitchell (Alice Darling), Marlin Hurt (Beulah), Virginia Gordon (Mrs. Tolliver, lady on the street), Ken Christy (police officer)
Summary: Fibber, intrigued with the novel he is reading, is oblivious to almost everything happening around him.
Music: Billy Mills: "Oklahoma," "On the Sunny Side of the Street," "The Chool Song" (The King's Men, vocal), "Just Close Your Eyes"
Running Gag: "Love that little lady" (Beulah)
Comments: By giving Teeny a lead quarter in exchange for her silence, Fibber for once at least breaks even in a tête-à-tête with the moppet.

Date: February 13, 1945
Title: Tunes the Piano
Cast: Jim Jordan (Fibber), Marian Jordan (Molly, Teeny), Harlow Wilcox, Arthur Q. Bryan (Doctor Gamble), Shirley Mitchell (Alice Darling), Marlin Hurt (Beulah)
Summary: Fibber dismantles the piano while ham-handedly trying to tune it.
Music: Billy Mills: "Blow, Gabriel, Blow," "I Won't Dance," "Skip to My Lou" (The King's Men, vocal)
Running Gags: "Love that man" (Beulah), hall closet opened by piano tuner thinking it was the back door
Comments: In a revelation by Molly we learn that the piano, like the house, cost nothing because Fibber won the instrument as a prize in a magazine contest. Harlow's comment about putting money saved from using Johnson's Wax into war bonds and Jim's salute to the Boy Scouts which is tied to the virtues of courage, loyalty, and devotion to duty are two more examples of how efficiently the writers could sell messages with a patriotic twist.

Date: February 20, 1945
Title: To Catch a Train
Cast: Jim Jordan (Fibber), Marian Jordan (Molly), Harlow Wilcox, Arthur Q. Bryan (Doctor Gamble), Shirley Mitchell (Alice Darling), Marlin Hurt (Beulah), Virginia Gordon (Mrs. George Abercrombie), Ken Christy (George Abercrombie)
Summary: The McGees hurry to Union Station so they can be there when a train called the Squaw leaves.
Music: Billy Mills: "Liza," "I Dream of You," "Poor Little Rhode Island" (The King's Men, vocal)
Running Gag: "Love that man" (Beulah)
Comments: Harlow's introduction suggests that the oft-mentioned 14th and Oak is only four blocks from 79 Wistful Vista. The well-wishing after the

name-calling between Gamble and McGee again illustrates that the raillery is all in fun.

Date: February 27, 1945
Title: Red Cross Drive
Cast: Jim Jordan (Fibber), Marian Jordan (Molly), Harlow Wilcox, Arthur Q. Bryan (Doctor Gamble), Shirley Mitchell (Alice Darling), Marlin Hurt (Beulah), Bea Benaderet (Mrs. Gunderson), Virginia Gordon (Mrs. Smith), Lurene Tuttle (Mrs. Dixon), Ken Christy (Sarpus)
Summary: Fibber goes along with Molly to collect funds for the Red Cross *and* to round up business for his Magnifico icebox.
Music: Billy Mills: "Love Is Sweeping the Country," "Two Guitars," "The Typewriter Serenade" (The King's Men, vocal), "Someday, Somewhere"
Running Gags: "'Tain't funny, McGee" (Molly), "Love that tired man" (Beulah)
Comments: The American Red Cross found the ideal way to promote its services by having this highly-rated show devote the full half-hour to beating the drums for funds.

Date: March 6, 1945
Title: Early 50th Anniversary
Cast: Jim Jordan (Fibber), Marian Jordan (Molly, Teeny), Harlow Wilcox, Arthur Q. Bryan (Doctor Gamble), Shirley Mitchell (Alice Darling), Marlin Hurt (Beulah), Joseph Kearns (dentist)
Summary: The McGees celebrate their golden wedding anniversary about twenty-five years ahead of time.
Music: Billy Mills: "Flying Down to Rio," "Perfidia," "Accentuate the Positive" (The King's Men, vocal), "I Should Care"
Running Gag: "Love that golden wedding couple" (Beulah)
Comments: Fibber's tale of Miss Fiditch is one of a number of reminiscences in which he was present to record peccadilloes of teachers, some of which he used to his advantage.

Date: March 13, 1945
Title: Going Western
Cast: Jim Jordan (Fibber), Marian Jordan (Molly), Harlow Wilcox, Arthur Q. Bryan (Doctor Gamble), Shirley Mitchell (Alice Darling), Marlin Hurt (Beulah)
Summary: While waiting for a western chum to arrive, the McGees get in the spirit by talking like cowpokes.
Music: Billy Mills: "But Not for Me," "Magic Is the Moonlight," "I'm an Old Cowhand" (The King's Men, vocal), "I Wish I Knew"
Running Gags: Myrt bit involving brother/first man to reach the Rhine/watermelon contest (Fibber), word confusion involving *barnacle/*

binocular/binnacle/pinnacle/ pinochle (Fibber, Molly, Gamble), "Love that man" (Beulah)

Comments: The cast seems to be genuinely having fun speaking in dialect and pulling cowboy gags. At over four minutes the banter between the McGees and Wilcox constitutes one of the longest and most mirthful of the integrated commercials. The seamless flow into and out of "I'm an Old Cowhand" is masterfully done, concluding with a tip of the ten-gallon hat to each member of the quartet. A salute to Bob Hope in the tag appears to come from the heart rather than from the typewriter of the NBC publicity department.

Date: March 20, 1945
Title: Fixing the Radio
Cast: Jim Jordan (Fibber), Marian Jordan (Molly, Teeny), Harlow Wilcox, Arthur Q. Bryan (Doctor Gamble), Shirley Mitchell (Alice Darling), Marlin Hurt (Beulah), Mel Blanc (radio announcer), Elvia Allman (Gloria Pizzicato)
Summary: Fibber tries to fix the radio so he can listen to singer Gloria Pizzicato.
Music: Billy Mills: "Great Day," "Sleigh Ride in July," "Leave the Dishes in the Sink, Ma" (The King's Men, vocal), "The More I See You"
Running Gags: Hall closet opened by Fibber looking for tire tape, "Love that man" (Beulah)
Comments: Harlow's theory about a radio speaker repeating what is spoken into it is a crafty way to get listeners to follow his sales pitch. Alice, always sweetness and light to this point, reaches her breaking point in the put-down at the end. People who to this day do not understand how radios work will find that Fibber's version given to Teeny makes as much sense as the correct explanation.

Date: March 27, 1945
Title: Clothing Drive for European Relief
Cast: Jim Jordan (Fibber), Marian Jordan (Molly), Harlow Wilcox, Arthur Q. Bryan (Doctor Gamble), Shirley Mitchell (Alice Darling), Marlin Hurt (Beulah), Bea Benaderet (Millicent Carstairs)
Summary: The McGees sort through their clothes for items they can donate to the United National Clothing Collection.
Music: Billy Mills: "New Sun in the Sky," "I'm Beginning to See the Light," "You Belong to My Heart" (The King's Men, vocal), "Any Moment Now"
Running Gags: Myrt bit involving mother/paratroopers/pair of troopers (Fibber), "Love that-Love everybody" (Beulah), word confusion involving *macaroon/marooned/Maureen* (Fibber, Molly)
Comments: "The moths chewed the L out of it" escapes the censor's pencil because of its innocuous meaning in context. After a cereal gag fizzles, Jim adroitly ad-libs a take-off on a popular Cole Porter lyric by singing

"Every joke I make tonight I die a little." Like the program devoted to the Red Cross broadcast four weeks earlier, this episode focuses on a humanitarian cause in which everyone gives including the sponsor who replaces the middle commercial with Harlow's appeal for those people in war-torn countries in need of warm clothing. Bea Benaderet appears for the first time as Mrs. Carstairs, a welcome addition who would provide some variety to *Fibber McGee and Molly* since Gamble was the only regular visitor to 79 Wistful Vista after the departure of LaTrivia, the Old Timer, and Wimple.

Date: April 3, 1945
Title: Poet McGee
Cast: Jim Jordan (Fibber), Marian Jordan (Molly, Teeny), Harlow Wilcox, Arthur Q. Bryan (Doctor Gamble), Shirley Mitchell (Alice Darling), Marlin Hurt (Beulah), Bea Benaderet (Millicent Carstairs)
Summary: When Fibber learns that he has won a limerick contest, he decides to make versifying his life work.
Music: Billy Mills: "Love Is, "La Golondrina," "Walk a Little, Talk a Little" (The King's Men, vocal), "The More I See You"
Running Gag: "Love that man" (Beulah)
Comments: This episode picks up the loose thread left at the end of the February 20th show when Fibber made certain his letter for the contest was on the train. Although Quinn and Leslie did not delve into social satire often, they occasionally slipped a dig in now and then like Millicent's remark about Americanism and prohibiting the flying of the flag in front of shops that cater to the lower classes.

Date: April 10, 1945
Title: No Newspaper
Cast: Jim Jordan (Fibber), Marian Jordan (Molly), Harlow Wilcox, Arthur Q. Bryan (Doctor Gamble), Shirley Mitchell (Alice Darling, sobbing woman in comic strip department of newspaper), Marlin Hurt (Beulah), Bea Benaderet (Millicent Carstairs), Ken Christy (Canfield), Jim Jordan Jr. (circulation manager)
Summary: The McGees take the matter of a missing newspaper directly to the offices of *The Wistful Vista Gazette*.
Music: Billy Mills: "High and Low," "Candy," "The Three Caballeros" (The King's Men, vocal), "It Doesn't Cost You Anything to Dream"
Running Gags: Myrt bit involving uncle/digging/confederate money (Fibber), "Love that man" (Beulah)
Comments: After meeting Millicent only twice before, Fibber is already referring to her familiarly as Carstie just as he called his former rich neighbor Uppy.

Date: April 17, 1945
Title: Alice on the Phone
Cast: Jim Jordan (Fibber), Marian Jordan (Molly), Harlow Wilcox, Arthur Q. Bryan (Doctor Gamble), Shirley Mitchell (Alice Darling), Marlin Hurt (Beulah), Bea Benaderet (Millicent Carstairs), Jim Jordan Jr. (Charlie)
Summary: Fibber cannot use the telephone to call the bank about his monthly statement because Alice is engaged in a gabfest with a boyfriend.
Music: Billy Mills: "Who Knows?," "Siboney," "Iowa" (The King's Men, vocal), "Someday, Somewhere"
Running Gags: "'Tain't funny, McGee" (Molly), "Love that man" (Beulah)
Comments: The writers chose a gem of an image reflecting the duration of Alice's talkathon, that of Wilcox planting a redwood which will get to the sawmill before she relinquishes the phone. In their respectful closing the Jordans extend best wishes to Harry Truman who became president after Roosevelt's death five days before this broadcast.

Date: April 24, 1945
Title: Ride to Elks Club
Cast: Jim Jordan (Fibber), Marian Jordan (Molly), Harlow Wilcox, Arthur Q. Bryan (Doctor Gamble), Shirley Mitchell (Alice Darling), Marlin Hurt (Beulah), Bea Benaderet (Millicent Carstairs)
Summary: When Molly wants Fibber out of the house so she can do her spring cleaning, McGee has difficulty finding someone to drive him to the Elks Club.
Music: Billy Mills: "Poor Little Rhode Island," "The Sweetheart of All My Dreams," "The Choo Choo Polka" (The King's Men, vocal), "I Hope to Die If I Told a Lie"
Running Gag: "Love that man" (Beulah)
Comments: This episode is an example of how the writers could take a simple idea (McGee needs a ride), wrap a package of jokes around it, and tie it up with a message of public interest so listeners learn while they laugh, capped by Jim and Marian's sensible appeal for carpooling in the tag.

Date: May 1, 1945
Title: Briefcase Bronson
Cast: Jim Jordan (Fibber), Marian Jordan (Molly, Teeny), Harlow Wilcox, Arthur Q. Bryan (Doctor Gamble), Marlin Hurt (Beulah), Bea Benaderet (Millicent Carstairs), Joseph Kearns (Davis)
Summary: After examining wanted posters at the post office, Fibber hopes to collect the $6,000 reward offered for an escaped criminal.
Music: Billy Mills: "Bojangles of Harlem," "Evalina," "The Martins and the Coys" (The King's Men, vocal), "Someday, Somewhere"

Running Gags: Myrt bit involving grandmother/got a sock/sewing basket (Fibber), tongue twister starting with Mildewed McGee (Fibber), "Love that man" (Beulah), hall closet opened by Davis as directed by Fibber

Comments: A report citing a Hamburg radio announcement regarding the death of Adolph Hitler precedes Harlow's introduction. The tongue twister returns after a long absence, last used on the February 24, 1942 broadcast. In his blow-by-blow account of an imaginary encounter with Bronson, McGee gets the worst of it but listeners get to enjoy the best of it.

Date: May 8, 1945
Title: Housing Survey
Cast: Jim Jordan (Fibber), Marian Jordan (Molly), Harlow Wilcox, Arthur Q. Bryan (Doctor Gamble), Shirley Mitchell (Alice Darling), Marlin Hurt (Beulah), Bea Benaderet (Millicent Carstairs)
Summary: Molly cannot understand how Fibber is going to complete a survey of people needing housing for the mayor of Wistful Vista by just sitting in the living room doing crossword puzzles.
Music: Billy Mills: "Blow, Gabriel, Blow," "Tico Tico," "His Rocking Horse Ran Away" (The King's Men, vocal), "Army Hymn" (The King's Men, vocal)
Running Gag: "Love that man" (Beulah)
Comments: No commercials are heard on this broadcast. It is clear, from Harlow's announcement about the end of the war in Europe before the program begins to the reminder by the Jordans in the tag that the job is not finished, that commerce and comedy take a back seat to the state of the world. Jim again shows his quick wit with an ad-lib when he extends the tie joke by bringing back the Drawrof gag and breaks up Shirley Mitchell in the process.

Date: May 15, 1945
Title: Trunk of Trouble
Cast: Jim Jordan (Fibber), Marian Jordan (Molly), Harlow Wilcox, Arthur Q. Bryan (bidder, Doctor Gamble), Shirley Mitchell (Alice Darling), Marlin Hurt (Beulah), Bea Benaderet (Millicent Carstairs)
Summary: After purchasing a trunk at an auction, the McGees try to find a way to open it because they do not have a key that fits the lock.
Music: Billy Mills: "Meet the People," "Dream," "Ya-Ta-Ta, Ya-Ta-Ta," (The King's Men, vocal), "I Walked In"
Running Gag: "Love that man" (Beulah)
Comments: This episode is notable in that it contains what Fibber considers the perfect straight line (Millicent's statement that "Mr. Carstairs is extremely fond of antiques") and also Fibber's declaration to Molly which could serve as his epitaph: "There's a right way and a wrong way to do things, Tootsie, and I haven't used up the wrong ways yet."

Date: May 22, 1945
Title: Seventh War Loan Drive
Cast: Jim Jordan (Fibber), Marian Jordan (Molly), Harlow Wilcox, Arthur Q. Bryan (Doctor Gamble, heckler), Shirley Mitchell (Alice Darling), Marlin Hurt (Beulah), Bea Benaderet (Millicent Carstairs), Jim Jordan Jr. (Charlie, announcer), Billy Mills
Summary: Fibber takes over the show for the bond rally, much to the consternation of Mrs. Carstairs and Billy Mills.
Music: Billy Mills: "Welcome to the Diamond Horseshoe," "Kiss Me Again," "This Little Bond Went to Battle" (The King's Men, vocal), "There's Beauty Everywhere"
Running Gags: Tongue twister starting with Long Under Ware McGee (Fibber), "Love that man's wife" (Beulah), cigar routine (Fibber, Gamble)
Comments: The writers have given Alice a distinctive speech pattern, that of jumbled antecedents (e.g. "the boy that his father that owns the airplane plant"), so she can generate laughs on her own or set up responses from the McGees.

Date: May 29, 1945
Title: Lawn Mower a No-Goer
Cast: Jim Jordan (Fibber), Marian Jordan (Molly, Teeny), Harlow Wilcox, Arthur Q. Bryan (Doctor Gamble), Shirley Mitchell (Alice Darling), Marlin Hurt (Beulah), Bea Benaderet (Millicent Carstairs)
Summary: Fibber cannot get the lawn mower he borrowed to run for more than a few seconds.
Music: Billy Mills: "I Begged Her," "In Acapulco," "Kentucky Babe" (The King's Men, vocal), "I Don't Care Who Knows It"
Running Gag: "Love that man" (Beulah)
Comments: *There's Laughter in the Air!*, the book Molly is reading while Fibber tussles with the mower, contains excerpts from two *Fibber McGee and Molly* shows and portions of scripts from twenty other comedy programs. This episode features two extended similes that linger because of their descriptiveness: Fibber says the mower "runs like an iron deer being pursued by a stuffed dog through a petrified forest" and asserts that he is "making as much progress as a punch-drunk caterpillar trying to follow the white line around a revolving barber pole."

Date: June 5, 1945
Title: Cleaning Closet for Millicent's Visit
Cast: Jim Jordan (Fibber), Marian Jordan (Molly), Harlow Wilcox, Arthur Q. Bryan (Doctor Gamble), Shirley Mitchell (Alice Darling), Marlin Hurt (Beulah), Bea Benaderet (Millicent Carstairs), Jim Jordan Jr. (Jimmy)
Summary: The McGees empty the hall closet in preparation for a house call from Mrs. Carstairs.

Music: Billy Mills: "The Best Things in Life Are Free," "The More I See You," "The Fireman's Bride" (The King's Men, Marian), "I Wish I Knew"

Running Gags: Myrt bit involving brother/judge gave him twenty years/twenty ears of corn (Fibber), "Love that man" (Beulah), back stairs door opened by Millicent and contents formerly in hall closet tumble out

Comments: Jim gets the biggest laugh of the night when he tells Harlow "I could break your little heart," a perfect example of how delivery by an accomplished radio performer reaped rewards far exceeding the inherent value of the words spoken.

Date: June 12, 1945
Title: Magic Act
Cast: Jim Jordan (Fibber), Marian Jordan (Molly, Teeny), Harlow Wilcox, Arthur Q. Bryan (Doctor Gamble), Shirley Mitchell (Alice Darling), Marlin Hurt (Beulah), Bea Benaderet (Millicent Carstairs)
Summary: Fibber tries out tricks for Molly that he hopes to perform at a smoker.
Music: Billy Mills: "Hallelujah," "There Must Be a Way," "Singing Down the Road" (The King's Men, vocal), "I Hope to Die If I Told a Lie"
Running Gags: Word confusion involving *raccoon/cocoon/lagoon/leghorn/leggings* (Fibber, Molly, Gamble), "Love that man" (Beulah)
Comments: Shirley Mitchell, a capable actress, also proved to be a good audience as her laughter can be heard several times during the patter between Fibber and Molly before Alice makes her appearance. This is one of the few episodes that runs long with the NBC ID heard over the tag.

Date: June 19, 1945
Title: Deal with Mr. Carstairs
Cast: Jim Jordan (Fibber), Marian Jordan (Molly), Harlow Wilcox, Arthur Q. Bryan (Doctor Gamble), Shirley Mitchell (Alice Darling), Marlin Hurt (Beulah), Bea Benaderet (Millicent Carstairs), Jim Jordan Jr. (Mr. Carstairs)
Summary: Fibber won't reveal to Molly the details of a financial transaction he plans to make with wealthy Mr. Carstairs.
Music: Billy Mills: "Who Cares?," "Good, Good, Good," "Buy a Bond" (The King's Men, vocal), "I Hope to Die If I Told a Lie"
Running Gag: Word confusion involving *adversary/emissary/commissary/dromedary* (Fibber, Molly), "Love that man" (Beulah)
Comments: Harlow pitches war bonds in lieu of the middle commercial. What this program meant to radio listeners is best conveyed in the wording of the citation from Catholic War Veterans read near the end of the show: "To the beloved Fibber McGee and Molly of America's millions in recognition of their successful efforts to lighten the burdens of American people in a time of great ordeal through understanding and clean comedy and in acknowledgement of their accomplishment in portraying the

American home through gentle humor in true dignity as a great source of our national strength."

Date: June 26, 1945
Title: Houseboat on Dugan's Lake
Cast: Jim Jordan (Fibber), Marian Jordan (Molly, Teeny), Harlow Wilcox, Arthur Q. Bryan (Doctor Gamble), Shirley Mitchell (Alice Darling), Marlin Hurt (Beulah), Bea Benaderet (Millicent Carstairs), Jim Jordan Jr. (Harvey Knox), Victor Borge
Summary: The McGees make plans for spending the summer on Mrs. Carstairs' houseboat.
Music: Billy Mills: "But Not for Me," "Love," "You Belong to My Heart" (The King's Men, vocal), "The More I See You"
Running Gag: "Love that man" (Beulah)
Comments: At least for this week the price of sodas drops from a quarter to a dime as Teeny plans to turn one simple simoleon into ten treats. Marlin Hurt, who appears for the last time, will be heard on *The Beulah Show* over CBS beginning in July. The Jordans close the season by expressing heartfelt thanks to listeners for their loyal support. Borge is introduced as the host of the summer replacement series, *The Victor Borge Show*.

Date: October 2, 1945
Title: Welcoming LaTrivia Home
Cast: Jim Jordan (Fibber), Marian Jordan (Molly), Harlow Wilcox, Gale Gordon (Mayor LaTrivia), Arthur Q. Bryan (Doctor Gamble), Shirley Mitchell (Alice Darling), Bea Benaderet (Millicent Carstairs), Jim Jordan Jr. (train announcer)
Summary: Fibber feels he has been left out of the plans for greeting their old friend when Mayor LaTrivia returns to Wistful Vista from his service in the Coast Guard.
Music: Billy Mills: "Flying Down to Rio," "Along the Navajo Trail" (The King's Men, vocal), "Atchison, Topeka, and the Santa Fe," "You Came to Me"
Running Gag: Hall closet opened by Fibber looking for helmet
Comments: Gamble, often kidded about having too much around the middle by McGee, is gently ribbed about having too little on top when LaTrivia affectionately greets the physician as "you baldheaded old midwife." This will not be the last time a train is referred to as the Cinder Bucket. Salutes to Perry Como, Spike Jones, Harold Peary, and Marlin Hurt in the tag indicate what a launching pad the popular *Fibber McGee and Molly* was for talented performers.

Date: October 9, 1945
Title: Shopping for a Used Car

Cast: Jim Jordan (Fibber), Marian Jordan (Molly, Teeny), Harlow Wilcox, Gale Gordon (Mayor LaTrivia), Arthur Q. Bryan (Doctor Gamble), Bea Benaderet (Millicent Carstairs), Ken Christy (Stanley Stutz)
Summary: The McGees have their eyes on a green sedan but find the car salesman reluctant to sell it to them.
Music: Billy Mills: "But Not for Me," "No Can Do," "There, I've Said It Again," (The King's Men, vocal), "I Wish I Knew"
Running Gags: "'Tain't funny, McGee" (Molly), LaTrivia blowup over Chief Gunner's Mate, word confusion involving *liver/livid/Olivia/Bolivia* (Fibber, Molly)
Comments: Perhaps the cleverest line of the show goes by with hardly a ripple when Fibber responds to one of Teeny's witticisms with "If I ever want to saw my way out of a radio program, Sis, I'll borrow your gag file."

Date: October 16, 1945
Title: No Train Reservations
Cast: Jim Jordan (Fibber), Marian Jordan (Molly), Harlow Wilcox, Gale Gordon (Mayor LaTrivia), Arthur Q. Bryan (Doctor Gamble), Shirley Mitchell (Alice Darling), Bea Benaderet (Millicent Carstairs)
Summary: After Fibber vows to get Millicent a spot on a train to Florida, he phones everyone he can think of to make good on his promise.
Music: Billy Mills: "I Feel a Song Coming On," "Atchison, Topeka, and the Santa Fe," "In the Middle of May" (The King's Men, vocal)
Running Gag: Myrt bit involving sister/Miss America/married man in England (Fibber)
Comments: Part of being a good ad-libber is being a good listener and Jim proves himself to be both in this episode as he counters Marian's and Arthur's stop-and-starts with "You betcha, kid, you betcha, kid" and "3:40, 3:41." Molly's definition of *derriere* as "a French word meaning the back of the lap" demonstrates how subtlety in humor tops vulgarity every time.

Date: October 23, 1945
Title: Cousin Ernest
Cast: Jim Jordan (Fibber), Marian Jordan (Molly), Harlow Wilcox, Gale Gordon (Mayor LaTrivia), Arthur Q. Bryan (Doctor Gamble), Shirley Mitchell (Alice Darling), Bea Benaderet (Millicent Carstairs), Jim Jordan Jr. (Joe), Tommy Cook (Ernest)
Summary: Fibber plans a dinner in honor of a visit from a cousin he has never seen.
Music: Billy Mills: "Oklahoma," "I'm Gonna Love That Guy," "A Kiss Good Night" (The King's Men, vocal)
Running Gags: Word confusion involving *artichoke/architect* (Fibber, Molly), hall closet opened by Fibber looking for Parcheesi board, LaTrivia blowup over officer's messes

Comments: Sometimes even a small fluff of an extra word like *with* generates a response far exceeding anything scripted as exemplified by Fibber's question to Wilcox: "How come your wife don't know any more about Glo-Coat than that after living with all these years with you?" For the second consecutive week Molly provides a daffynition when she describes crepe suzettes as "four-alarm pancakes." The AFRS rebroadcast opens the show with "The More I See You" and closes with "I'm Beginning to See the Light."

Date: October 30, 1945
Title: Sculptor McGee
Cast: Jim Jordan (Fibber), Marian Jordan (Molly, Teeny), Harlow Wilcox, Gale Gordon (Mayor LaTrivia), Arthur Q. Bryan (Doctor Gamble), Bea Benaderet (Millicent Carstairs), Virginia Gordon (neighbor)
Summary: Fibber sculpts a bust of himself so he can win the first prize of $100 in an art contest.
Music: Billy Mills: "Make Way for Tomorrow," "It's a Grand Night for Singing" (The King's Men, vocal), "Good, Good, Good," "Out of Nowhere"
Running Gags: Tongue twister starting with Skinnermerink McGee (Fibber), "'Tain't funny, McGee" (Molly), hall closet opened by Fibber looking for wrapping paper, LaTrivia blowup over bridle path
Comments: That this broadcast takes place in a large venue (The Maple Leaf Gardens in Toronto) is evident in the echo effect, particularly when Harlow is setting the scene and when Fibber is talking to himself. Shirley Mitchell did not accompany the cast on their three-week sojourn from Hollywood. Four surefire running gags associated with *Fibber McGee and Molly* are included to ensure that purchasers of bonds as part of the Ninth Canadian Loan Drive get their money's worth.

Date: November 6, 1945
Title: Fudge
Cast: Jim Jordan (Fibber), Marian Jordan (Molly, Teeny), Harlow Wilcox, Gale Gordon (Mayor LaTrivia), Arthur Q. Bryan (Doctor Gamble), Virginia Gordon (neighbor)
Summary: McGee concocts what he calls Fibber's Fine Fudge because he thinks Molly craves the confection.
Music: Billy Mills: "Some Sunday Afternoon," "Gotta Be This or That," "Tampico" (The King's Men, vocal), "In the Valley"
Running Gags: Myrt bit involving sister/interesting condition/foot behind neck (Fibber), LaTrivia blowup over "chips on their shoulders"
Comments: This broadcast is from New York. An abundance of riches occurs when two images with colorful descriptions follow so closely that listeners cannot fully appreciate either on the first hearing, namely Fibber's assertion that Kremer's "idea of a bargain is to give you two of something you don't want with something you gotta have for half again what you'd have to pay

if you went someplace you'd rather go to if it wasn't raining" countered by Molly's contention that telling her husband something "is like trying to lie on your back and play badminton with hailstones." Marian gets to deliver several of those reliable "I haven't smelled so much..." and "I haven't seen so many..." lines that joke writers have been invoking in countless variations since the heyday of vaudeville.

Date: November 13, 1945
Title: Driving Lesson
Cast: Jim Jordan (Fibber), Marian Jordan (Molly, Teeny), Harlow Wilcox, Gale Gordon (Mayor LaTrivia), Arthur Q. Bryan (Doctor Gamble), Virginia Gordon (neighbor)
Summary: Fibber learns almost as much as he teaches when he shows Molly how to drive a car.
Music: Billy Mills: "Ridin' High," "But I Did," "In the Valley"
Running Gags: Word confusion involving *swine/swain/swan/swami/salami* (Fibber, Molly, Gamble), hall closet opened by Gamble looking for a hat to wear, "'Tain't funny, McGee" (Molly)
Comments: This broadcast is from New York. In this episode Fibber is asked by a policeman what his business is, a question that "for twelve years I've been afraid somebody would ask..." The King's Men are absent for this broadcast. The reason for opening the closet is one of the flimsiest ever: Doc, who did not wear a hat for his visit, is invited to open the closet and take one of Fibber's to wear on his trip home as if being caught bareheaded on the streets of Wistful Vista is a misdemeanor.

Date: November 20, 1945
Title: Architect McGee
Cast: Jim Jordan (Fibber), Marian Jordan (Molly), Harlow Wilcox, Gale Gordon (Mayor LaTrivia), Arthur Q. Bryan (Doctor Gamble), Shirley Mitchell (Alice Darling), Bea Benaderet (Millicent Carstairs), Ken Christy (neighbor), Virginia Gordon (neighbor), Jim Jordan Jr. (foreman)
Summary: Brassy Fibber becomes bossy Fibber as he supervises the construction of a house next door.
Music: Billy Mills: "Who Cares?," "The Carioca," "The Typewriter Serenade" (The King's Men, vocal), "I'd Do It All Over Again"
Running Gags: Word confusion involving *palooka/pagoda/Pomona/kimono* (Fibber, Molly, Alice), LaTrivia blowup over "code in my head"
Summary: The Jordans and company have returned to Hollywood so Shirley Mitchell rejoins the cast as Alice Darling. After a joke misfires, Jim ad-libs that he and Molly "won't have to go to Carstie's Thanksgiving. We're having our turkey now." Fibber's take on architects is a quote worth noting: "They spend six years in Italy studying Greek architecture so they can come home and build Spanish bungalows with French windows for a lot of Yankees

who don't know an English basement from a Turkish bath." There is a pause after Gamble's remark that his cousin died of one (i.e. a rump roast) at Sing Sing as if the audience is stunned by the frankness of the remark.

Date: November 27, 1945
Title: Chopping Down the Oak Tree
Cast: Jim Jordan (Fibber), Marian Jordan (Molly), Harlow Wilcox, Gale Gordon (Mayor LaTrivia), Arthur Q. Bryan (Doctor Gamble), Bea Benaderet (Millicent Carstairs), Virginia Gordon (neighbor)
Summary: After a tree surgeon pronounces their oak tree as dead, the McGees decide to cut it down themselves.
Music: Billy Mills: "There's a Great Day Coming Mañana," "I Can't Believe You're in Love with Me," "Come to Baby Do" (The King's Men, vocal), "Tell It to a Star"
Running Gags: Hall closet opened by tree surgeon looking for his hat, tongue twister starting with Big Mouth McGee using B's (Fibber), "'Tain't funny, McGee" (Molly)
Comments: Jim follows Fibber's comment that a punchy fighter "uses up more seconds than a Fred Allen ad-lib" with an ad-lib of his own, "Fred Allen, that is," an echo of Senator Claghorn's catch phrase. The savvy audience is one step ahead of the plot at the climax when they laugh as soon as Fibber announces that he is going to drive downtown because they know where the tree landed.

Date: December 4, 1945
Title: Walk to Dugan's Lake
Cast: Jim Jordan (Fibber), Marian Jordan (Molly), Harlow Wilcox, Gale Gordon (Mayor LaTrivia), Arthur Q. Bryan (Doctor Gamble), Shirley Mitchell (Alice Darling), Bea Benaderet (Millicent Carstairs)
Summary: Fibber resolves to take a long walk in the brisk evening air, then uses visits from friends as excuses for not venturing outside.
Music: Billy Mills: "The Last Time I Saw You," "Ya-Ta-Ta, Ya-Ta-Ta" (The King's Men, vocal), "Love Me"
Running Gag: LaTrivia blowup over a commission for a commissioner
Comments: McGee matches Alice's garbled sentence construction with a dandy of his own. Fibber lives up to his name with tall tales of frozen smoke being made into igloos and cows giving ice cream instead of milk. The "welcome back" extended to Red Skelton in the tag is neatly tied to a pitch to buy bonds.

Date: December 11, 1945
Title: Governor's Pal
Cast: Jim Jordan (Fibber), Marian Jordan (Molly), Harlow Wilcox, Gale Gordon (Mayor LaTrivia), Arthur Q. Bryan (Doctor Gamble), Shirley Mitchell

(Alice Darling), Bea Benaderet (Millicent Carstairs), Jim Jordan Jr. (elevator operator)

Summary: Fibber gets himself into another fine mess when, after bragging that he is a friend of the governor to Gamble, he talks himself into a meeting with the state kingpin, a man he has never met.

Music: Billy Mills: "You Haven't Changed at All," "It's Only a Paper Moon," "Chickery Chick" (The King's Men, vocal), "You're Nobody Till Somebody Loves You"

Running Gags: Myrt bit involving grandmother/pinched in Bon Ton/revolving door (Fibber), hall closet opened by Millicent looking for the front door, LaTrivia blowup over "you strike me"

Comments: Doc's comments about aging (trying to eat steak with false teeth, needing bifocals to read and ear trumpets to hear, and being too tired to go places and unable to do things) seem as apropos today as in 1945 if one substitutes hearing aids for ear trumpets. After the lukewarm response to the shock absorbers gag, Jim enthusiastically ad-libs a welcome to Wilcox which generates more than enough laughter to make up for lost ground.

Date: December 18, 1945
Title: White Christmas Tree
Cast: Jim Jordan (Fibber), Marian Jordan (Molly, Teeny), Harlow Wilcox, Arthur Q. Bryan (Doctor Gamble), Shirley Mitchell (Alice Darling), Bea Benaderet (Millicent Carstairs), Jim Jordan Jr. (Fred Corrigan)
Summary: Rather than pay $10 to have someone paint his Christmas tree white, Fibber undertakes the job himself in the front yard with the help of a vacuum cleaner attachment.
Music: Billy Mills: "Welcome Home," "The Parade of the Wooden Soldiers," "'Twas the Night Before Christmas" (The King's Men and Teeny, vocal), "The First Noel"
Running Gags: None
Comments: Quinn and Leslie repeatedly showed themselves to be experts at build-a-gag in which related elements were parlayed together for comic effect, and in this episode they play the numbers game as Gamble describes how during the silly season "200-pound men start climbing 49-cent stepladders to wire dime store angels to the tops of three-dollar Christmas trees and wind up in a $500 plaster cast." By having Wilcox deliver the middle commercial in the flamboyant language of a hammy Shakespearean actor, the writers get the sponsor's message across and serve up some yuks as well.

Date: December 25, 1945
Title: Doc's Present to McGee
Cast: Jim Jordan (Fibber), Marian Jordan (Molly), Harlow Wilcox, Gale Gordon (Mayor LaTrivia), Arthur Q. Bryan (Doctor Gamble), Shirley Mitchell (Alice Darling), Bea Benaderet (Millicent Carstairs)

Summary: The McGees would appreciate the gift they received from Doctor Gamble more if they could just determine what it is.
Music: Billy Mills: "Day by Day," "Symphony," "Jingle Bells" (The King's Men, vocal)
Running Gags: Hall closet opened by Alice looking for a present for a friend, LaTrivia blowup over "keep an eagle eye about me"
Comments: Harlow's announcement that it is not very often that *Fibber McGee and Molly* was heard on Christmas was understating the case. It had not happened before and would occur only once more (in 1951) during the period of half-hour broadcasts. Gamble's phone conversation, a variation of the Myrt bit, receives a very favorable reception from the audience.

Date: January 1, 1946
Title: Tall Story Contest
Cast: Jim Jordan (Fibber), Marian Jordan (Molly), Harlow Wilcox, Gale Gordon (Mayor LaTrivia), Arthur Q. Bryan (Doctor Gamble), Shirley Mitchell (Alice Darling), Bea Benaderet (Millicent Carstairs), Jim Jordan Jr. (radio announcer)
Summary: To the amazement of everyone, Fibber seems unable to think of a tall story to enter in a contest.
Music: Billy Mills: "New Sun in the Sky," "Two Guitars," "I Don't Care if I Never Go to Bed" (The King's Men, vocal), "Here Comes Heaven Again"
Running Gags: None
Comments: Shirley Mitchell appears for the last time as Alice Darling. With Bill Thompson's return to the show in two weeks, *Fibber McGee and Molly* would again have a full house of visitors and Alice was the odd character out. The audience had come to know Fibber so well that after Molly says to Millicent, "You have a wonderful seat on a horse" and follows that with "McGee!," their imaginations supplied the implied wisecrack. Jim echoes Gale's small fluff with a stutter on *building*, again demonstrating how attentive he was to the script-reading and how quick his responses were.

Date: January 8, 1946
Title: Bean Contest
Cast: Jim Jordan (Fibber), Marian Jordan (Molly, woman on the street, Teeny), Harlow Wilcox, Gale Gordon (Mayor LaTrivia), Arthur Q. Bryan (Doctor Gamble), Bea Benaderet (woman on the street, Millicent Carstairs), Joseph Kearns (Kremer)
Summary: Fibber finds that his plan for winning the "guess the number of beans" contest being sponsored by Kremer's Drugstore is not one he can count on.
Music: Billy Mills: "Of Thee I Sing," "Let it Snow," "Doctor, Lawyer, Indian Chief" (The King's Men, vocal)
Running Gag: LaTrivia blowup over *pi/pie*

Comments: "What's that gotta do…" now becomes Fibber's futile cry when he attempts to stop the Wilcox Express that rolls over him like a locomotive during the middle commercial. Millicent adds the accordion to the bagpipes and trumpet in her personal orchestra. Harlow concludes the broadcast with an appetizing carrot on the end of the stick by announcing that Bill Thompson will rejoin *Fibber McGee and Molly* the following Tuesday.

Date: January 15, 1946
Title: Treasure Map
Cast: Jim Jordan (Fibber), Marian Jordan (Molly), Harlow Wilcox, Bill Thompson (Wallace Wimple), Gale Gordon (Mayor LaTrivia), Arthur Q. Bryan (Doctor Gamble), Bea Benaderet (Millicent Carstairs)
Summary: After Fibber finds a map in a book borrowed from the library, he plans a clandestine midnight digging party with Molly to find a buried treasure.
Music: Billy Mills: "Some Sunday Morning," "The Bells of St. Mary's," "Hubba, Hubba, Hubba" (The King's Men, vocal), "Love Me"
Running Gag: LaTrivia blowup over *catboat*
Comments: With Bill Thompson's return to the program, the regular cast members now receive credit during Harlow's opening remarks. Jim gets the biggest laugh of the night when, after his fit of fear elicits a tepid response, he ad-libs, "All that effort for that."

Date: January 22, 1946
Title: Pioneer Day
Cast: Jim Jordan (Fibber), Marian Jordan (Molly), Harlow Wilcox, Bill Thompson (Old Timer, Wallace Wimple, man on the street), Gale Gordon (Mayor LaTrivia), Arthur Q. Bryan (Doctor Gamble), Bea Benaderet (Millicent Carstairs, woman on the street)
Summary: Fibber, acting as sheriff on Pioneer Day, plans to arrest two residents pretending to be desperadoes in a reenactment of an historical bank robbery.
Music: Billy Mills: "Ridin' High," "My Shawl," "Which Way They Go?" (The King's Men, vocal), "Pin Marin"
Running Gags: "That ain't the way I heered it" (Old Timer), LaTrivia blowup over Much and Bart Younger
Comments: The wild west theme, so full of abundant treasure the previous March, is mined again here with rich results. The Old Timer receives a warm welcome and his catch phrase is greeted with applause. Guitarist Perry Botkin gets a quick nod before the number by The King's Men and more proper credit at the end of the broadcast.

Date: January 29, 1946
Title: Molly's Card Party
Cast: Jim Jordan (Fibber), Marian Jordan (Molly), Harlow Wilcox, Bill Thompson (Old Timer, Wallace Wimple), Gale Gordon (Mayor LaTrivia), Arthur Q. Bryan (Doctor Gamble),Bea Benaderet (Millicent Carstairs), Lurene Tuttle (Fordelia Blakewell Butler)
Summary: As Molly prepares to host a card party, she wants to make certain everything is right for the honored guest who is the society editor of *The Wistful Vista Gazette*.
Music: Billy Mills: "I'm No Angel," "Aren't You Glad You're You?," "Tampico" (The King's Men, vocal), "Forever"
Running Gags: LaTrivia blowup over bachelor's degree, hall closet opened by LaTrivia looking for his hat
Comments: A measure of the popularity of *Fibber McGee and Molly* at this time is the show's number one ranking among commercial programs in a poll of almost 1,100 radio editors conducted by *Radio Daily*. After the Old Timer reveals that his real name is Rupert Blasingame, we realize why it is a good thing everyone calls him the Old Timer. Jim's repeated "Hi, Doc" is another instance of the cast enjoying their roles and inviting the audience in on the fun.

Date: February 5, 1946
Title: Ice Skating
Cast: Jim Jordan (Fibber), Marian Jordan (Molly), Harlow Wilcox, Bill Thompson (Old Timer, Wallace Wimple), Gale Gordon (Mayor LaTrivia), Arthur Q. Bryan (Doctor Gamble)
Summary: At Fibber's urging, Molly agrees to go ice skating at Dugan's Lake.
Music: Billy Mills: "You Haven't Changed at All," "Atlanta, GA," "Let it Snow" (The King's Men, vocal), "Skater's Waltz"
Running Gags: "That ain't the way I heered it" (Old Timer), LaTrivia blowup over *bobsledding*
Comments: The Old Timer's "Eh?" injects a new note of levity into his exchanges with the McGees. The writers occasionally give Gamble some words of wisdom befitting a man of his education and experience so there is reason to listen to his wish that "every boy when he reaches the age of 18 could see his own obituary and then either correct it or live up to it." The closing vignette at the lake when Fibber and Molly are by themselves is likely the most romantic scene ever heard on the series.

Date: February 12, 1946
Title: New Suits for Fibber and Friends
Cast: Jim Jordan (Fibber), Marian Jordan (Molly), Harlow Wilcox, Bill Thompson (Old Timer, ambulance man), Gale Gordon (Mayor LaTrivia),

Arthur Q. Bryan (Doctor Gamble), Bea Benaderet (Millicent Carstairs), Jim Jordan Jr. (Gusset)
Summary: Fibber tries to get ten customers for a tailor so his suit will be free.
Music: Billy Mills: "Love Is," "Pin Marin," "Old Rockin' Chair" (The King's Men, vocal), "Here Comes Heaven Again"
Running Gags: LaTrivia blowup over knot tying, Myrt bit involving cut his tail right off/uncle/telling story (Fibber)
Comments: Jim Jordan Jr., who began appearing in uncredited roles the previous spring, receives credit for the first and only time. Perhaps the decision to keep their son's identity hidden most of the time was so Jim and Marian would not be accused of nepotism. Fibber's excuse for the size of his expanded waistline is as good as any: "I got low lungs." McGee drops the names of members of the show's advertising agency as acquaintances he has recruited for new suits.

Date: February 19, 1946
Title: Dining Out with Doc Gamble
Cast: Jim Jordan (Fibber), Harlow Wilcox, Bill Thompson (Old Timer, irate diner), Gale Gordon (Mayor LaTrivia), Arthur Q. Bryan (Doctor Gamble), Bea Benaderet (Millicent Carstairs, Suzy, irate diner)
Summary: In order to give Molly some rest so she can recover from the flu, Gamble takes Fibber out for supper at Joe's Gravy Bowl.
Music: Billy Mills: "The Best Things in Life Are Free," "I Can't Begin to Tell You," "Personality" (The King's Men, vocal)
Running Gags: "That ain't the way I heered it" (Old Timer), LaTrivia blowup over *tuba*
Comments: Marian is not there due to illness, but Bea is here, there, and everywhere as she plays three parts. Fibber's pronouncement on the dry weather is one of those statements which seem to have a kernel of sense to it, yet is a hard nut to crack: "Half an hour of this rain right now would do them more good now in five minutes than a month of it would do in a week at any other time." Jim gets a big laugh with an ad-lib by following a fluff on *joint* with "Maybe we should do the one about the Coast Guard," an allusion to an earlier gag by LaTrivia that flopped.

Date: February 26, 1946
Title: Missing Pen
Cast: Jim Jordan (Fibber), Marian Jordan (Molly, Teeny), Harlow Wilcox, Bill Thompson (Old Timer, Wallace Wimple), Arthur Q. Bryan (Doctor Gamble), Bea Benaderet (Millicent Carstairs, Miss Fregelhorn), Jim Backus (Houtentrout)
Summary: Incensed Fibber takes his search for a missing fountain pen to the cleaners.

Music: Billy Mills: "But Not for Me," "Three Little Words," "One-Zy, Two-Zy" (The King's Men, vocal), "Tomorrow Is Forever"
Running Gag: "That ain't the way I heered it" (Old Timer)
Comments: This episode is a good example of how the writers could take a common occurrence like a pen that appears to be missing, mix in a simmering McGee, let him stew for about twenty minutes, and then finish up with his just desserts. Fibber's reaction to Harlow's take on *Romeo and Juliet*, "Ain't this awful, folks?," makes him sound a bit like Goodman Ace reacting to one of Jane's malapropisms on *Easy Aces*.

Date: March 5, 1946
Title: Car Reported Stolen Again
Cast: Jim Jordan (Fibber), Marian Jordan (Molly), Harlow Wilcox, Bill Thompson (Old Timer), Gale Gordon (Mayor LaTrivia), Arthur Q. Bryan (Doctor Gamble), Bea Benaderet (Millicent Carstairs), Jim Backus (police sergeant), Jim Jordan Jr. (officer)
Summary: After the McGees mistakenly report their car stolen, they are arrested while driving home.
Music: Billy Mills: "The Last Time I Saw You," "Baiao" (The King's Men, vocal), "Here Comes Heaven Again"
Running Gags: LaTrivia blowup over "tying flies," "Gotta get them brakes fixed" (Fibber)
Comments: Fibber's tirade to LaTrivia about the police force ("Why don't your whistle-blowing, tavern-tummied bunch of Keystone Cops get busy?") is reminiscent of his longer rant on the May 16, 1944 episode. When the McGees enter Kremer's Drugstore, the audience not only pictures the merchandise in their imaginations but, thanks to Molly's description, they also smell the licorice, peppermint, carbolic acid, mayonnaise, tobacco, and wet umbrellas.

Date: March 12, 1946
Title: Flying a Kite
Cast: Jim Jordan (Fibber), Marian Jordan (Molly, Teeny), Harlow Wilcox, Bill Thompson (Wallace Wimple), Gale Gordon (Mayor LaTrivia), Arthur Q. Bryan (Doctor Gamble), Bea Benaderet (Millicent Carstairs)
Summary: Everything is not on the up-and-up after Fibber and Doc make a wager as to which of them can build the better kite.
Music: Billy Mills: "Some Sunday Morning," "Take Care," "Money Is the Root of All Evil" (The King's Men, vocal), "Wait and See"
Running Gags: Hall closet opened by Molly looking for writing paper, "Gotta get them brakes fixed" (Fibber), McGee blowup over "smack the old horsehide"
Comments: Jim's birthday greeting to Wilcox is no joke: Harlow was born March 12, 1900. Even though his method of getting his kite to fly is underhanded, Fibber has a sense of fair play which he acknowledges when

LaTrivia turns the tables on him. Others who get a chance to step into another character's shoes are Gamble when he voices Fibber's often-stated assessment that Teeny is a midget and Teeny herself who delivers the "This is ridiculous" clincher.

Date: March 19, 1946
Title: Red Cross Captain
Cast: Jim Jordan (Fibber), Marian Jordan (Molly), Harlow Wilcox, Bill Thompson (Old Timer, Roebuck), Gale Gordon (Mayor LaTrivia), Arthur Q. Bryan (Doctor Gamble), Bea Benaderet (Millicent Carstairs), Earle Ross (MacDonald), Virginia Gordon (donor)
Summary: Fibber, who is surprised at how eager people are to donate to the Red Cross before he delivers his spiel, fears that an earlier argument with wealthy MacDonald will decrease the size of the bank president's contribution.
Music: Billy Mills: "Day by Day," "Laughing on the Outside," "Make Mine Music" (The King's Men, vocal), "I'm Glad I Waited for You"
Running Gag: LaTrivia blowup over *dray horse*
Comments: Just as all businesses in Wistful Vista seem to be located near 14th and Oak, most clocks in that community seem fixed at about half past some unspecified hour as MacDonald notes in this episode and the McGees in many others. Jim's small fluff of using *Shears* instead of *Sears* is overlooked when the audience fills in the missing part about the room where he spent "many a long summer afternoon reading" catalogs. You couldn't think of a better fundraising slogan for the Red Cross than Molly's "You couldn't think of a better cause to save your life."

Date: March 26, 1946
Title: Bullets Brannigan
Cast: Jim Jordan (Fibber), Marian Jordan (Molly), Harlow Wilcox, Bill Thompson (Harry in pre-show bit, Wallace Wimple), Gale Gordon (Mayor LaTrivia), Arthur Q. Bryan (Doctor Gamble), Bea Benaderet (Millicent Carstairs), Jim Backus (Bullets Brannigan), Jim Jordan Jr. (Officer Leslie)
Summary: Escaped convict Brannigan, pretending to be a police officer, takes refuge in the McGee house.
Music: Billy Mills: "Swamp Fire," "Patience and Fortitude" (The King's Men, vocal), "Tomorrow Is Forever"
Running Gag: LaTrivia blowup over *setter/sitter*
Comments: Fibber's comment about catching the Pittman Gang single-handedly is an in-joke because the cast was the Pittman Gang under the direction of Frank Pittman. Jim again turns a gag that lays an egg into the biggest laugh of the evening with the ad-lib "I'd have sworn that was a joke." In the tag Jim and Marian pay tribute to Marlin Hurt who died suddenly of a heart attack on March 21st.

Date: April 2, 1946
Title: Ignition Release Invention
Cast: Jim Jordan (Fibber), Marian Jordan (Ma in pre-show bit, Molly), Harlow Wilcox, Bill Thompson (Old Timer, Horatio K. Boomer), Gale Gordon (Mayor LaTrivia), Arthur Q. Bryan (Doctor Gamble), Bea Benaderet (Millicent Carstairs)
Summary: Fibber works on the Perfecto Rejecto ignition lock, a device he hopes will make the McGees rich.
Music: Billy Mills: "I'm No Angel," "We'll Gather Lilacs," "There Is a Tavern in the Town" (The King's Men, vocal), "All Through the Day"
Running Gags: Hall closet opened by Gamble to exit the house, "That ain't the way I heered it" (Old Timer), LaTrivia blowup over *raffle/rifle*, "Where'd I put those springs?" (Horatio)
Comments: Fibber indicates that his invention is going to pay off the mortgage which faithful listeners note is an error in the McGee family history because the couple won the house in a raffle. Jim breaks up when giving the name of his gadget to the Old Timer, a rare occurrence for him. Boomer appears for the first time since January 19, 1943.

Date: April 9, 1946
Title: Painter McGee
Cast: Jim Jordan (Fibber), Marian Jordan (Molly, Teeny), Harlow Wilcox, Bill Thompson (Wallace Wimple), Gale Gordon (Mayor LaTrivia), Arthur Q. Bryan (Doctor Gamble), Bea Benaderet (Millicent Carstairs), Jess Kirkpatrick (Salvador McGee)
Summary: Expecting a visit from an artistic cousin, Fibber gets into the painting mood complete with smock, beret, and hauteur.
Music: Billy Mills: "You Haven't Changed at All," "Villa," "The Bluetail Fly" (The King's Men, vocal), "I Love You This Morning"
Running Gag: LaTrivia blowup over *Muriel/mural*
Comments: Wilcox usually drops in to deliver the middle commercial alone so his entrance with Mrs. Carstairs may have been the result of a long script. As in past shows in which painting is the main theme, modern expressionistic art is ridiculed both in incidents cited (the mule winning a competition, Harlow buying a rag) and ludicrous titles (e.g. "Seven Razor Blades in Search of a Girl's Bicycle").

Date: April 16, 1946
Title: Salvador Fixes Furniture
Cast: Jim Jordan (Fibber), Marian Jordan (Molly), Harlow Wilcox, Bill Thompson (Wallace Wimple), Gale Gordon (Mayor LaTrivia), Arthur Q. Bryan (Doctor Gamble), Bea Benaderet (Millicent Carstairs), Jess Kirkpatrick (Salvador McGee)
Summary: Between calls for food Cousin Salvador restores an antique table for Molly.

Music: Billy Mills: "Make Way for Tomorrow," "The Warsaw Concerto," "Shoo Fly Pie and Apple Pan Dowdy" (The King's Men, vocal), "Make Mine Music"

Running Gags: "'Tain't funny, McGee" (Molly), LaTrivia blowup over no vacancy signs

Comments: A clever way the writers make the audience attend to every word in the commercial is to have Wilcox mispronounce a key word like *linoleum*. The two biggest laughs come as a result of fluffs, Jim's "The sinking steamer sunk" and Gale's improvised "by George be ready..."

Date: April 23, 1946
Title: Health Foods
Cast: Jim Jordan (Fibber), Marian Jordan (Molly), Harlow Wilcox, Bill Thompson (Wallace Wimple), Gale Gordon (Mayor LaTrivia), Arthur Q. Bryan (Doctor Gamble), Bea Benaderet (Millicent Carstairs).
Summary: After reading *Be Middle-Aged at 100,* Fibber lays out his plan for eating healthful foods.
Music: Billy Mills: "Who Cares?," "One More Dream" (The King's Men, vocal), "Ezekiel Saw the Wheel" (The King's Men, vocal), "Pin Marin"
Running Gag: Myrt bit involving brother/job at UN/opens doors for Russians (Fibber)
Comments: When visiting the McGees, LaTrivia's appearances almost always come after the middle commercial so when he arrives as the second guest in this episode it is notable enough for Molly to remark "And so early in the program." LaTrivia adds a bit to the listener's picture of Wistful Vista geography by stating that he lives just two blocks from the McGee residence.

Date: April 30, 1946
Title: Barbershop Quartet
Cast: Jim Jordan (Fibber), Marian Jordan (Molly), Harlow Wilcox, Bill Thompson (Wallace Wimple), Gale Gordon (Mayor LaTrivia), Arthur Q. Bryan (Doctor Gamble), Bea Benaderet (Millicent Carstairs)
Summary: Fibber, upset that Gamble is going to a convention of barbershop quartets instead of him, seems to sing a different tune when he eagerly coaches Doc on the fine points of music.
Music: Billy Mills: "When We Meet Again," "Souvenir," medley consisting of "Kentucky Babe," "You Tell Me Your Dream" and "I Want a Girl" (The King's Men, vocal), "I Love You This Morning"
Running Gag: LaTrivia blowup over *stagecoach*
Comments: Cagey Fibber's stratagem for straining Doc's voice is similar to the method he employed to wear out LaTrivia's arm on the April 21, 1942 program. Musical Millicent, feeling the pinch of her accordion, now slides down the scale with a trombone In keeping with the theme of the show, The King's Men sing their medley in barbershop style with no musical accompaniment except a barely perceptible piano.

Date: May 7, 1946
Title: Old Muley Caught?
Cast: Jim Jordan (Fibber), Marian Jordan (Molly), Harlow Wilcox, Bill Thompson (Wallace Wimple), Gale Gordon (Mayor LaTrivia), Arthur Q. Bryan (Doctor Gamble), Bea Benaderet (Millicent Carstairs), Jim Jordan Jr. (Gordon Jordan)
Summary: Fibber is eager to let everyone know that he caught the fabled Old Muley at Dugan's Lake until he learns that he landed his prize hours before the fishing season officially opened.
Music: Billy Mills: "I Feel a Song Coming On," "All the Cats Join In," (The King's Men, vocal), "My Fickle Eye" (The King's Men, vocal), "Make Mine Music"
Running Gag: Cigar routine (Fibber, Gordon)
Comments: Molly plays off of Mr. Kitzel's catch phrase from *The Jack Benny Program* with her joke about the "pickerel in the middle and the mustard, etc." Millicent's story about the octopus playing bridge, along with earlier fanciful anecdotes about smoke becoming tires and about her dog using the telephone, indicates that she could rival Fibber in the category of spinning tall tales.

Date: May 14, 1946
Title: Clay Morgan for Council
Cast: Jim Jordan (Fibber), Marian Jordan (Molly), Harlow Wilcox, Bill Thompson (Wallace Wimple), Gale Gordon (Mayor LaTrivia), Arthur Q. Bryan (Doctor Gamble), Bea Benaderet (Millicent Carstairs)
Summary: After LaTrivia asks Fibber to help with an election, McGee spearheads the campaign to get Clay Morgan on the city council.
Music: Billy Mills: "Flying Down to Rio," "Atlanta, GA" (The King's Men, vocal), "Harriet" (The King's Men, vocal), "Tomorrow Is Forever"
Running Gags: Tongue twister starting with Baby Kisser McGee (Fibber), Myrt bit involving nylon hose/25 feet at hardware store (Fibber)
Comments: The three bloopers (two by Jim, one by Harlow) add to the fun of the show with Jim's "Don't you start doing it" suggesting that the fluffs had become contagious. Molly's "Oh, this is wonderful!" is a switch on the "Oh, this is ridiculous!" ending and aptly describes the outcome in which Fibber, though a loser, still comes out a winner due to the successful campaign for Morgan.

Date: May 21, 1946
Title: Fireball McGee
Cast: Jim Jordan (Fibber), Marian Jordan (Molly), Harlow Wilcox, Bill Thompson (Wallace Wimple), Gale Gordon (Mayor LaTrivia), Arthur Q. Bryan (Doctor Gamble), Bea Benaderet (Millicent Carstairs), Jim Jordan Jr. (announcer), John Wald (sports editor)

Summary: McGee, who is to pitch for the Elks against the Rotarians, is worried that he will not be able to find his control before the game begins.
Music: Billy Mills: "Coax Me a Little Bit," "Casey, the Pride of Them All" (The King's Men, vocal)
Running Gags: Hall closet opened by Wallace looking for the front door, LaTrivia blowup over "struck out from home"
Comments: John Wald, who will become the announcer on the fifteen-minute episodes broadcast from 1953-1956, appears for the first time. Fibber's comment to Doc that he hadn't had a baseball in his hand for twenty years is not in accord with his game of catch with LaTrivia on the April 21, 1942 show. The writers are careful with a key element in this episode by having Fibber specifically state "My right arm feels like it is made of concrete" just before the game begins to set up the reversal of fortune at the end.

Date: May 28, 1946
Title: Forgotten Wedding Anniversary
Cast: Jim Jordan (Fibber), Marian Jordan (Molly, Teeny), Harlow Wilcox, Bill Thompson (Old Timer, florist delivery man), Gale Gordon (Mayor LaTrivia), Arthur Q. Bryan (Doctor Gamble), Bea Benaderet (Millicent Carstairs)
Summary: Despite Molly's steady stream of hints, Fibber remains blissfully unaware that May 28th is their wedding anniversary.
Music: Billy Mills: "But Not for Me," "Seems Like Old Times," "Out California Way" (The King's Men, vocal), "I'm Glad I Waited for You"
Running Gag: LaTrivia blowup over *batter cakes*
Comments: Instead of ignoring his minor flub on Otis's coat and going right on, Jim accentuates it by calling it a "skincoon coat" to try to generate something out of nothing. That the audience was let in on the workings of the show is again evident when, after Fibber asks Teeny where she has been the last couple weeks, she replies, "Cut for time." (The Old Timer might have answered that question the same way.)

Date: June 4, 1946
Title: Aviation Show
Cast: Jim Jordan (Fibber), Marian Jordan (Molly), Harlow Wilcox, Bill Thompson (Wallace Wimple), Gale Gordon (Mayor LaTrivia), Arthur Q. Bryan (Doctor Gamble), Bea Benaderet (Millicent Carstairs), Jim Jordan Jr. (airport engineer)
Summary: Fibber becomes an instant authority on flying after reading a couple magazines, then puts his expertise to the test at an aviation show.
Music: Billy Mills: "Love Is," "They Say It's Wonderful" (The King's Men, vocal), "Old Dan Tucker" (The King's Men, vocal), "I Love You This Morning"
Running Gag: LaTrivia blowup over "stick to his last"
Comments: Fibber, who sometimes slavered over the straight lines he had been thrown by Uppington and Carstairs, leaves himself as wide open as he will

in the entire series when he tells Gamble that "I learned to fly by the seat of my pants and that was a big thing in them days." Molly joins George Bailey and countless others in the "I didn't know how well off I was" department when she implores Fibber and Doc to be nice to each other, soon grows sick of their syrupy compliments, and begs them to revert to their former selves.

Date: June 11, 1946
Title: Summer Fishing Plans
Cast: Jim Jordan (Fibber), Marian Jordan (Molly), Harlow Wilcox, Bill Thompson (Wallace Wimple, telegram delivery man), Gale Gordon (Mayor LaTrivia), Arthur Q. Bryan (Doctor Gamble), Bea Benaderet (Millicent Carstairs), Jim Jordan Jr. (clerk)
Summary: Fibber tries to convince Molly to accompany him on a fishing trip through the Ozarks.
Music: Billy Mills: "There's a New Day Coming Mañana," "The Gypsy" (The King's Men, vocal), "It's a Grand Night for Singing" (The King's Men, vocal)
Running Gag: LaTrivia blowup over "old hat"
Comments: When Jim gets himself into a flub, he dives in all the way to make waves as in "be coming in a T shirt in a T shirt to tea." Gamble's remark that he has nothing "against humanity except that there are too many people mixed up in it" rings true to his cynical nature and his sagacity. *The Fred Waring Show*, featuring Waring and his Pennsylvanians, is the summer replacement series.

Date: October 1, 1946
Title: Whims Cured with Placebos
Cast: Jim Jordan (Fibber), Marian Jordan (Molly, Teeny), Harlow Wilcox, Bill Thompson (Old Timer), Gale Gordon (Mayor LaTrivia), Arthur Q. Bryan (Doctor Gamble), Bea Benaderet (Elsie Merkle)
Summary: Malingering Fibber, following doctor's orders, takes placebos every thirty minutes to cure his whims.
Music: Billy Mills: "Doin' What Comes Naturally" (The King's Men, vocal), "I Got the Sun in the Morning," "Make Mine Music"
Running Gag: "That ain't the way I heered it" (Old Timer)
Comments: A new theme, "Ride, Ride, Ride," temporary replaces "Wing to Wing." Another temporary change is that Bea Benaderet, following writers' orders, sends Millicent Carstairs off on her high horse for a while so she can play beautician Elsie Merkle, a variation of her part as Gertrude Gearshift on *The Jack Benny Program*. The name of Fifi Tremaine, an unseen character who will serve as the focus of a romantic rivalry between LaTrivia and Gamble, is mentioned for the first time. The credits have been moved to the end of the show for this episode. Two of the featured songs are from the same source, a rarity for *Fibber McGee and Molly*, but not a shocking occurrence considering that *Annie Get Your Gun* was the hottest musical on Broadway at the time.

Date: October 8, 1946
Title: Bull Moran
Cast: Jim Jordan (Fibber), Marian Jordan (Molly), Harlow Wilcox, Bill Thompson (Clancy, Bull Moran), Gale Gordon (Mayor LaTrivia), Arthur Q. Bryan (Doctor Gamble), Bea Benaderet (Elsie Merkle)
Summary: Fibber, believing that Bull Moran is in town to pay him back for a childhood prank, acts like a hunted man on the run for his life.
Music: Billy Mills: "Ole Buttermilk Sky," "My Darling Clementine" (The King's Men, vocal)
Running Gag: Hall closet opened by Fibber looking for glasses
Comments: The credits return to the beginning of the program. Although Bill Thompson had played Irish policemen on occasions that brought the McGees in touch with the law, this season he will assume the parts of mush-mouthed officers on a regular basis.

Date: October 15, 1946
Title: Examining the Water
Cast: Jim Jordan (Fibber), Marian Jordan (Molly, Teeny), Harlow Wilcox, Bill Thompson (Wallace Wimple), Gale Gordon (Mayor LaTrivia), Arthur Q. Bryan (Doctor Gamble), Bea Benaderet (Elsie Merkle)
Summary: Fibber is shocked to discover strange creatures lurking in the water sample he spies through his microscope.
Music: Billy Mills: "Give Me Five Minutes More" (The King's Men, vocal), "It's a Pity to Say Good Night" (The King's Men, vocal)
Running Gags: None
Comments: Like good mystery authors who drop clues along the way, the writers have Fibber state early in the show in a matter-of-fact way that he is going to spread a newspaper out before he begins his research which should prepare listeners for the climax. It is also a significant plot element that none of the adults question McGee's incredible assertions by looking in the microscope.

Date: October 22, 1946
Title: Shopping for Shoelaces
Cast: Jim Jordan (Fibber), Marian Jordan (Molly), Harlow Wilcox, Bill Thompson (McIlhenny, clerk), Gale Gordon (Mayor LaTrivia), Arthur Q. Bryan (Doctor Gamble), Bea Benaderet (Elsie Merkle), Jim Backus (floorwalker), Virginia Gordon (clerk)
Summary: After Molly comments on his sloppy appearance, Fibber agrees to start from the ground up by going with her to the Bon Ton for new shoelaces.
Music: Billy Mills: "South America, Take It Away," "Out California Way" (The King's Men, vocal)
Running Gags: "'Tain't funny, McGee" (Molly), hall closet opened by Fibber looking for muffler, LaTrivia blowup over *Oklahoma* in Yonkers

Comments: A joke about Palm Springs is inserted to take advantage of the friendly audience in that city, the site of this broadcast. The "everything but what we needed" plot device, long a comic staple, is used again with good results.

Date: October 29, 1946
Title: Dinner with Miss Tremaine
Cast: Jim Jordan (Fibber), Marian Jordan (Molly), Harlow Wilcox, Bill Thompson (Wallace Wimple, McClanahan), Gale Gordon (Mayor LaTrivia), Arthur Q. Bryan (Doctor Gamble), Bea Benaderet (Elsie Merkle)
Summary: Molly plans the meal while Fibber prepares the fireworks for a dinner with Fifi Tremaine and her two beaus, LaTrivia and Gamble.
Music: Billy Mills: "Nola," "On the Boardwalk in Atlantic City" (The King's Men, vocal)
Running Gag: Myrt bit involving mother/hand caught/playing bridge (Fibber)
Comments: After a flub Jim parries Molly's question "Is there some chapter in your life I skipped?" with the ad-lib "I think *I* skipped one." For those wondering why Fibber repeatedly wants Molly to hand him the phone (including Molly who asks, "Why don't you just reach over and pick it up?"), Fibber provides the answer in this episode: "Better dialogue this way." There is some evidence the ubiquitous Kilroy was there, but he is nowhere to be seen (or heard).

Date: November 5, 1946
Title: Visit to Racine
Cast: Jim Jordan (Fibber), Marian Jordan (Molly, weary-voiced woman), Harlow Wilcox, Bill Thompson (cab driver, Wallace Wimple), Gale Gordon (Mayor LaTrivia), Arthur Q. Bryan (Doctor Gamble), Virginia Gordon (Miss Morris)
Summary: The McGees visit Racine to celebrate S.C. Johnson & Son's 60th anniversary.
Music: Billy Mills: "Zip-a-Dee-Do-Dah" (The King's Men, vocal)
Running Gags: LaTrivia blowup over *itinerary*, closet of president's office opened by Fibber to hang up hats and coats
Comments: In this broadcast from Racine, Wilcox has one of his largest parts in the series as he serves as guide for the McGees. No commercials are read by Harlow and none are necessary because the list of Johnson's Wax products are spoken by a number of characters. LaTrivia's overt plug for capitalism might have made Atlas shrug but would have pleased Ayn Rand. Election results follow the tag.

Date: November 12, 1946
Title: Expecting Ronald Colman
Cast: Jim Jordan (Fibber), Marian Jordan (Molly, Teeny), Harlow Wilcox, Bill Thompson (O'Shea), Gale Gordon (Mayor LaTrivia), Arthur Q. Bryan (Doctor Gamble), Walter Tetley (telegram delivery boy), Ed Max (Ronald)

Summary: Anticipating a visit from Ronald Colman, Fibber puts on his high hat and English accent while putting off the skeptical reactions of Molly and friends.
Music: Billy Mills: "Why Does It Get So Late So Early?," "Sooner or Later" (The King's Men, vocal), "The Whole World Is Singing My Song"
Running Gag: Word confusion involving *lumpet/crumpet/trump it* (Fibber, Molly, LaTrivia)
Comments: O'Shea's question could have served as a campaign slogan decades later: "And what's the matter with a fine Irish lad like Ronald Reagan?" Corrupting the name of a serious actress into Ingrid O'Bergman is a stretch, but Bill's admission that he tripped over his brogue on the way makes the delivery worthwhile.

Date: November 19, 1946
Title: Football Play
Cast: Jim Jordan (Fibber), Marian Jordan (Molly), Harlow Wilcox, Bill Thompson (Wallace Wimple), Gale Gordon (Mayor LaTrivia), Arthur Q. Bryan (Doctor Gamble), Bea Benaderet (Elsie Merkle), John Wald (announcer)
Summary: Fibber devises a complicated play that he hopes will enable Wistful Vista Prep to win their football game against Mohawk Military.
Music: Billy Mills: "You Keep Coming Back Like a Song," "Buckle Down, Winsocki" (The King's Men, vocal), "But Not for Me"
Running Gags: LaTrivia blowup over winning his letter at Harvard, "'Tain't funny, McGee" (Molly)
Comments: Some of the names Fibber calls out as he moves the ball from player to player are members of the Billy Mills Orchestra. Jim follows Molly's declaration that she would not miss the game for all the corn in radio with the ad-lib "Taking in a lotta territory."

Date: November 26, 1946
Title: Prowler at Fifi's House
Cast: Jim Jordan (Fibber), Marian Jordan (Molly, Teeny), Harlow Wilcox, Bill Thompson (Mahooney), Gale Gordon (Mayor LaTrivia), Arthur Q. Bryan (Doctor Gamble), Bea Benaderet (Elsie Merkle), Ken Christy (upset neighbor)
Summary: Gamble solicits the aid of the McGees in tracking down a prowler lurking near Fifi Tremaine's house at night.
Music: Billy Mills: "Soliloquy," "Cindy" (The King's Men, vocal), "What More Can I Ask For?"
Running Gags: Hall closet opened by Fibber looking for air raid helmet, "'Tain't funny, McGee" (Molly), "Gotta get them brakes fixed" (Mahooney)
Comments: The writers insert a wedge of social satire into the proceedings when Teeny asks Fibber what the Indians have to be thankful about on

Thanksgiving. The audience should be thankful Fibber is there to add "So I hear" to Molly's comment that there is no money in old jokes.

Date: December 3, 1946
Title: Offer from 4th National Bank
Cast: Jim Jordan (Fibber), Marian Jordan (Molly), Harlow Wilcox, Bill Thompson (Wallace Wimple), Gale Gordon (Mayor LaTrivia), Arthur Q. Bryan (Doctor Gamble), Bea Benaderet (Elsie Merkle)
Summary: Fibber, angry because he believes the bank has lost his account, takes the matter to the president of the institution.
Music: Billy Mills: "My Sugar Is So Refined," "The Coffee Song" (The King's Men, vocal), "For You, For Me, For Evermore"
Running Gag: LaTrivia blowup over *ermine stole*
Comments: The contrived appearances of Elsie, connected with a missing compact, end with this episode. The *Fibber McGee and Molly* audience was a tolerant lot, willing to accept the flimsy excuses for a character showing up at 79 Wistful Vista and also for recipients of phone calls to be guests who had recently arrived (on this program after the phone rings Molly blithely says, "Most likely for you, Doctor" and, to no one's surprise, it is). Jim rolls a tiny laugh into a big one when *tiara* ties him up a little and so he answers Molly's comment that "Doctor Gamble didn't say that" with "Certainly not. Not like that anyway." Another in-joke occurs when MacDonald, conversing with a Mr. Leslie on the phone, asks, "Was this your idea?" (Phil Leslie was the writer who usually supplied the story lines for *Fibber McGee and Molly*).

Date: December 10, 1946
Title: Promoting a Feud
Cast: Jim Jordan (Fibber), Marian Jordan (Molly, Teeny), Harlow Wilcox, Bill Thompson (Wallace Wimple), Gale Gordon (Mayor LaTrivia), Arthur Q. Bryan (Doctor Gamble), Bea Benaderet (Millicent Carstairs)
Summary: Fibber stirs up the rivalry between Gamble and LaTrivia for Fifi's affections by telling half-truths about each suitor.
Music: Billy Mills: "Red River Valley" (The King's Men, vocal), "The Gal in Calico," "And So to Bed"
Running Gags: None
Comments: Bea Benaderet resumes her role as Mrs. Carstairs. Molly's description of a chateau could hardly be bettered: "Architecture by Louis XIV and plumbing by Dracula." The plot thread of repairing toys will be dangled before the listeners for three consecutive weeks.

Date: December 17, 1946
Title: Sun Lamp
Cast: Jim Jordan (Fibber), Marian Jordan (Molly, Teeny), Harlow Wilcox, Bill Thompson (Wallace Wimple), Gale Gordon (Mayor LaTrivia), Arthur Q. Bryan (Doctor Gamble), Bea Benaderet (Millicent Carstairs)

Summary: Fibber spends most of the day basking under a sun lamp in the expectation of developing a healthy tan.
Music: Billy Mills: "The Best Man," "Ole Buttermilk Sky" (The King's Men, vocal), "I'll Close My Eyes"
Running Gags: "'Tain't funny, McGee" (Molly), "Bird book" (Wallace), LaTrivia blowup over *spelling bee*
Comments: Wimple's hobby of bird watching is mentioned for the first time. Millicent mentions Hubert Updike III, a character on *The Alan Young Show*, so Fibber can slip in a plug for the NBC program. A sense of decorum reflecting the times is present in that Fibber has to slip on a pair of pants each time a guest arrives lest he be seen in swimming trunks.

Date: December 24, 1946
Title: Fixing Christmas Toys
Cast: Jim Jordan (Fibber), Marian Jordan (Molly, Teeny), Harlow Wilcox, Bill Thompson (Wallace Wimple), Gale Gordon (Mayor LaTrivia), Arthur Q. Bryan (Doctor Gamble), Bea Benaderet (Millicent Carstairs)
Summary: Fibber, running out of time to fix toys for underprivileged children by Christmas, devises a plan to save the day.
Music: Billy Mills: "The Parade of the Wooden Soldiers," "'Twas the Night Before Christmas" (The King's Men and Teeny, vocal)
Running Gag: "Bird book" (Wallace)
Comments: Harlow indicates this is the third time *Fibber McGee and Molly* has been on the air on Christmas Eve. (The other two shows were broadcast in 1940 and 1944.) Even when Jim does not have an ad-lib ready, he plunges ahead to make something out of nothing, namely singing "Jingle Bells" after the joke about barn swallows pecking the grain out of the wood lays an egg. The twist on "Gift of the Magi" in which the McGees use money they were going to spend on each other on the toys leaves them and listeners with a renewed appreciation of the true spirit of Christmas.

Date: December 31, 1946
Fred Waring and the Pennsylvanians Special—No *Fibber McGee and Molly* broadcast.

Just as Harlow Wilcox appeared at 79 Wistful Vista about halfway through broadcasts to deliver his sales pitch, we pause here for some messages by those companies responsible for keeping *Fibber McGee and Molly* on the air.

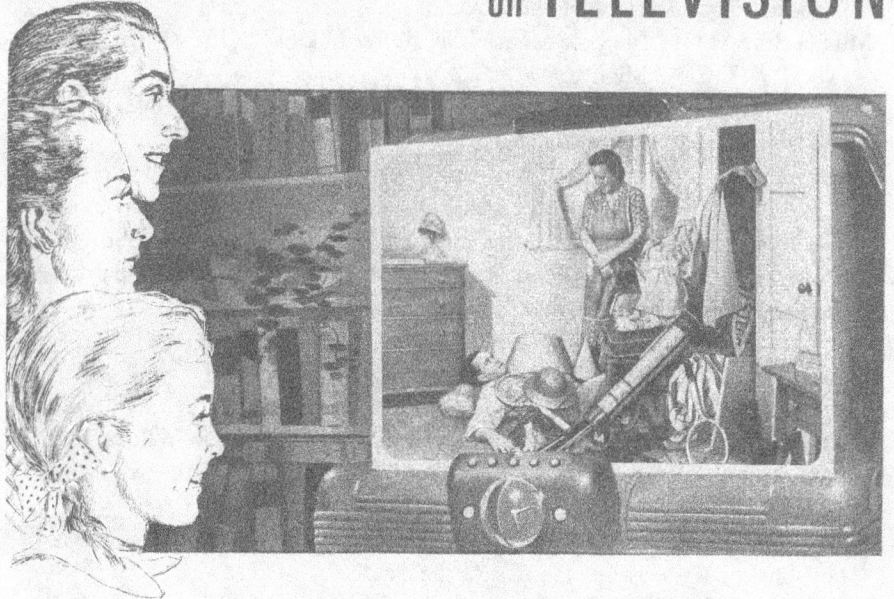

brought to you by NBC

Yes, on **NBC Television** that crowded closet at Wistful Vista—the foibles of lovable Fibber and the trials of patient Molly, for instance —could all become real visual experiences... experiences for you to *watch* as well as hear.

Think what television programs originating in studios of the National Broadcasting Company...such programs as the top-notch sound radio which has won NBC the distinction of America's most popular network...will add to home entertainment!

Already, plans—within the limitations imposed by wartime—have been placed in operation by NBC...plans which with the co-operation of business and government will result in extensive NBC television networks...

chains spreading from Eastern, Mid-Western and Western centers...gradually providing television after the war, to all of the nation.

Moderate-priced television receivers will provide your home with sight and sound programs consistent with the highest standards of NBC ...offer the most popular of the shows in this new, vastly improved field of entertainment. Look forward to other great NBC accomplishments such as FM, noise-free reception ...faithfulness of tone reproduction.

* * *

Look to NBC to lead in these new branches of broadcasting by the same wide margin that now makes it *"The Network Most People Listen to Most."*

National Broadcasting Company
America's No. 1 Network

This 1944 ad makes an impractical and unnecessary request because listeners could already picture Fibber and Molly most vividly in their mind's eye every Tuesday evening.

A 1945 ad that effectively combined a clever promotion for product and program with a patriotic appeal to buy war bonds.

The 1946 advertisement that inspired the November 25, 1952 episode, "Polishing Doc's Car."

Even in 1951 the recipe for fun remained the same: listen and laugh with that lovable Wistful Vista Gang.

Date: January 7, 1947
Title: New Radio
Cast: Jim Jordan (Fibber), Marian Jordan (Molly, Teeny), Harlow Wilcox, Bill Thompson (Wallace Wimple), Gale Gordon (Mayor LaTrivia), Arthur Q. Bryan (Doctor Gamble), Jim Backus (Mushmouth Bidwell), John Wald (announcer)
Summary: After Fibber hears a radio bulletin about a posse being formed to capture escaped convicts, he is torn between the desire to save face and the instinct to save his skin.
Music: Billy Mills: "Canadian Capers," "My Pretty Girl" (The King's Men, vocal), "For You, For Me, For Evermore"
Running Gags: "Bird book" (Wallace), hall closet opened by Fibber looking for shotgun
Comments: For the new year it's like old home week for not only does "Wing to Wing" return as the theme song but for this episode the original theme of "Save Your Sorrow for Tomorrow" is also brought back to lead into and out of the opening commercial. The writers again land some satiric jabs in the face of soap operas.

Date: January 14, 1947
Title: Package at the Post Office
Cast: Jim Jordan (Fibber), Marian Jordan (Molly), Harlow Wilcox, Bill Thompson (Wallace Wimple, Old Timer), Gale Gordon (Mayor LaTrivia), Arthur Q. Bryan (Doctor Gamble), Virginia Gordon (Old Timer's granddaughter)
Summary: Fibber goes to the post office in the midst of a blizzard to pick up a package.
Music: Billy Mills: "It's a Pity to Say Good Night," "Winter Wonderland" (The King's Men, vocal), "Love Is a Random Thing"
Running Gags: None
Comments: This episode features a clever introduction about a hunk of wood cracking merrily in the fireplace and a hunk on the davenport wisecracking merrily, and also quite likely the most vivid description of Aunt Sarah's miserliness ("That old dame is about as open-handed as 12 o'clock"). It also is built around one of the most improbable story lines in the show's history, that the post office would be open at night in a blizzard and that anyone (even Fibber) would go out in such weather to retrieve a parcel that could just as easily be picked up at a more convenient time under favorable conditions. Jim, who carries the bulk of the dialogue due to Marian's laryngitis, adds a bit of his own with an ad-lib about throwing one across the lake when conversing with Gamble and some improvised jabberwocky with Wimple.

Date: January 21, 1947
Title: House Alterations
Cast: Jim Jordan (Fibber), Marian Jordan (Molly, Teeny), Harlow Wilcox, Bill Thompson (Wallace Wimple), Gale Gordon (Mayor LaTrivia), Arthur Q. Bryan (Doctor Gamble), Jim Backus (Stanford Widdington Franless III)
Summary: The McGees seek advice from an architect as they plan alterations on the house.
Music: Billy Mills: "A Rainy Night in Rio," "Rickety Rickshaw Man" (The King's Men, vocal), "I'll Close My Eyes"
Running Gags: "Bird book" (Wallace), LaTrivia blowup over Greek fraternity
Comments: Teeny's plea on behalf of Miss Yeagley continues the string of references to the underpaid status of teachers on recent shows. The perspicacity of the writers is evident when Fibber dismisses his take on architects because it "wasn't very good anyway." A more quotable quote on the subject can be heard on the November 20, 1945 episode.

Date: January 28, 1947
Title: Trouble Boarding a Bus
Cast: Jim Jordan (Fibber), Marian Jordan (Molly), Harlow Wilcox, Bill Thompson (Wallace Wimple, Mahooney), Gale Gordon (Mayor LaTrivia), Arthur Q. Bryan (Doctor Gamble), Jim Backus (Jerry Babb)
Summary: In an act of uncivil disobedience, Fibber stands in front of a bus because the driver will not let the McGees on due to overcrowding.
Music: Billy Mills: "On the Other End of a Kiss," medley of "Zip-a-Dee-Do-Dah" and "Sooner or Later" (The King's Men, vocal), "And So to Bed"
Running Gags: None
Comments: All the action in this episode takes place away from 79 Wistful Vista. The appeal for the March of Dimes in the tag is another one couched in language that touches the heartstrings as much as the purse strings.

Date: February 4, 1947
Title: Minding Teeny
Cast: Jim Jordan (Fibber), Marian Jordan (Molly, Teeny), Harlow Wilcox, Bill Thompson (Wallace Wimple, announcer), Gale Gordon (Mayor LaTrivia), Arthur Q. Bryan (Doctor Gamble)
Summary: The McGees entertain Teeny while her parents play bridge.
Music: Billy Mills: "Serenade to a Wealthy Widow," "Managua, Nicaragua" (The King's Men, vocal), "Through a Thousand Dreams"
Running Gags: "Bird book" (Wallace), McGee blowup over $6.55
Comments: This is one of the uncommon episodes with considerable dialogue between Molly, Fibber, and Teeny in which there is not some contrived excuse for Molly's exit. This is also one of the program's most pun-filled episodes. Guitarist "Ace" [Perry] Botkin gets his name in the script again, this time from the announcer of the fictitious radio show *Bloodbath, Inc.*

Date: February 11, 1947
Title: Model Airplane
Cast: Jim Jordan (Fibber), Marian Jordan (Molly), Harlow Wilcox, Bill Thompson (Wallace Wimple), Gale Gordon (Mayor LaTrivia), Arthur Q. Bryan (Doctor Gamble), Gene Carroll (Lena)
Summary: Fibber works on an airplane he believes will revolutionize the aeronautics industry.
Music: Billy Mills: "The Anniversary Song," "The Gal in Calico" (The King's Men, vocal)
Running Gags: Mrs. Kladderhatch bit involving butterflies on stomach/tattoo (Gamble), LaTrivia blowup over a caterpillar club
Comments: Gamble gets his teeth into the Kladderhatch bit for the first time. For the second successive show a joke about the backside (*lobotomy* on February 4th, *mugwump* this week) is interrupted by Molly though listeners finish the gags in their minds. Gene Carroll makes his first appearance as Lena, shoehorning his way into the McGee house as obtrusively as Lena's entrances will be in the coming weeks. Lena's purpose is to serve as a feminine character until Bea Benaderet, recovering from injuries sustained in an automobile accident, can return to the program.

Date: February 18, 1947
Title: Collecting Doc's Bills
Cast: Jim Jordan (Fibber), Marian Jordan (Molly), Harlow Wilcox, Bill Thompson (Wallace Wimple), Gale Gordon (Mayor LaTrivia), Arthur Q. Bryan (Doctor Gamble), Gene Carroll (Lena), Virginia Gordon (Agatha Trilby)
Summary: The McGees eagerly go door-to-door collecting money owed to Doctor Gamble by his patients because they know they can keep half of the total amount received.
Music: Billy Mills: "Guilty," "The Leader Doesn't Like Music" (The King's Men, vocal), "Through a Thousand Dreams"
Running Gag: "Bird book" (Wallace)
Comments: The writers, who employed legal or medical jargon whenever the situation called for it, combine the two disciplines in Fibber's repetition of threatening deadbeats with a writ of *tramus mortimus* which sounds like the description of a deceased streetcar. For the purposes of this week's story, Wimple takes refuge in a love nest he shares with his bird book.

Date: February 25, 1947
Title: Replacing a Broken Window
Cast: Jim Jordan (Fibber), Marian Jordan (Molly, Teeny), Harlow Wilcox, Bill Thompson (Wallace Wimple), Gale Gordon (Mayor LaTrivia), Arthur Q. Bryan (Doctor Gamble), Gene Carroll (Lena)

Summary: Fibber spends the day putting panes of glass in a window frame and wondering why they fall out whenever someone slams the front door.
Music: Billy Mills: "It's a Good Day," "Wyoming" (The King's Men, vocal), "Beware My Heart"
Running Gags: Mrs. Kladderhatch bit involving swallowing pennies/get some sense (Gamble), "Bird book" (Wallace), "'Tain't funny, McGee" (Molly), LaTrivia blowup over "getting a little tight"
Comments: Quinn and Leslie again provide an important clue near the beginning of the show that is relevant to the denouement. Lena's remark about being told what to do with her music is about as blunt a line that the writers could get by the censors. The writers were flexible with the standard routines, willing to pull what Teeny calls "the old switcheroo" such as letting her ask the questions and Fibber provide the answers and, on occasion, having LaTrivia and Molly team up to force Fibber into the blowup.

Date: March 4, 1947
Title: Mail Service Complaint
Cast: Jim Jordan (Fibber), Marian Jordan (Molly), Harlow Wilcox, Bill Thompson (Wallace Wimple), Gale Gordon (Mayor LaTrivia), Arthur Q. Bryan (Doctor Gamble), Gene Carroll (Lena)
Summary: Fibber, upset that a letter he addressed to himself has not been delivered, takes his beef to the postmaster.
Music: Billy Mills: "Among My Souvenirs," "Polly, Put the Kettle On" (The King's Men, vocal), "Oh, But I Do"
Running Gags: Hall closet opened by Fibber looking for spats, word confusion involving *mastiff/bailiff/bay leaf/flyleaf* (Fibber, Molly), "Bird book" (Wallace), LaTrivia blowup over "cup of tea with relish"
Comments: The best LaTrivia blowups are those in which he gets himself hopelessly tied up in spoonerisms and this episode features a tasty one topped off with piccalilli. Mirthful similes abound on this show as well including Fibber's description of glue on stamps that tastes "like the underside of the last step on the back stairs of a tannery" and Gamble's appraisal of McGee's handwriting as looking "like it had been dictated to a left-handed baboon while he was skipping rope."

Date: March 11, 1947
Title: Physical Fitness
Cast: Jim Jordan (Fibber), Marian Jordan (Molly), Harlow Wilcox, Bill Thompson (Wallace Wimple), Gale Gordon (Mayor LaTrivia), Arthur Q. Bryan (Doctor Gamble), Gene Carroll (Lena)
Summary: After reading *Man's Untapped Energy*, Fibber becomes a tornado of activity around the house.
Music: Billy Mills: "The Maple Leaf Rag," "That's What Uncle Remus Said" (The King's Men, vocal), "That's Where I Came In"

Running Gags: Hall closet opened by Gamble who thinks it is the front door, word confusion involving *Corsicans/corpuscles/corporals/caporals/capital* (Fibber, Molly), "Bird book" (Wallace)

Comments: If this episode seems a bit familiar, listeners may recall the January 23, 1945 show in which Fibber was also bouncing all around. However, there are enough new wrinkles to make the dialogue seem fresh, including the cute gag that Fibber "has so much energy that if ants had pants, they've have McGees in them."

Date: March 18, 1947
Title: Meeting Someone in the Rain
Cast: Jim Jordan (Fibber), Marian Jordan (Molly), Harlow Wilcox, Bill Thompson (Wallace Wimple, Mahooney), Gale Gordon (Mayor LaTrivia), Arthur Q. Bryan (Doctor Gamble), Gene Carroll (Lena)
Summary: The McGees stand in front of a store waiting for a man whose identity Fibber refuses to reveal.
Music: Billy Mills: "Heartaches," "It's a Good Day" (The King's Men, vocal), "It's Dreamtime"
Running Gags: "'Tain't funny, McGee" (Molly), "Bird book" (Wallace)
Comments: A snapshot revealing that life with McGee could be entertaining and trying in the same frame is captured in the conversation with LaTrivia that the gabby one monopolizes. Puns abound in this episode, perhaps the biggest groaner being Wimple's declaration that it isn't "a fit night out for man or beets." Fibber's follow-up to that joke, indicating it would not reach 200 on the Colgate laugh meter, is a reference to *Can You Top This?* (In those years mentioning a product on the air which was not the sponsor of the show would often result in a generous supply of that product arriving the following week, although, with Fibber's luck, the gift package would have included no toothpaste and a gross of laugh meters.)

Date: March 25, 1947
Title: Home Power Plant
Cast: Jim Jordan (Fibber), Marian Jordan (Molly), Harlow Wilcox, Bill Thompson (Wallace Wimple), Gale Gordon (Mayor LaTrivia), Arthur Q. Bryan (Doctor Gamble), Gene Carroll (Lena)
Summary: Fibber thinks the Little Vulcan Home Power Plant he bought will allow him to manufacture his own electricity if he can just keep the device running.
Music: Billy Mills: "You Can't See the Sun," "I Got a Gal in North and South Dakota" (The King's Men, vocal), "We Could Make Such Beautiful Music"
Running Gags: None
Comments: Fibber vs. recalcitrant machine was also used on the May 29, 1945 show when McGee battled a lawn mower. One of the marvels of *Fibber McGee and Molly* is that, in retrospect, some of the funniest lines are

those not directly connected to jokes as in this episode with Molly's peerless delivery of the question "You gonna have to come down here and wail it with that rope forty times a day?"

Date: April 1, 1947
Title: Safe Driving Campaign
Cast: Jim Jordan (Fibber), Marian Jordan (Molly), Harlow Wilcox, Bill Thompson (Wallace Wimple, irate driver), Gale Gordon (Mayor LaTrivia), Arthur Q. Bryan (Doctor Gamble), Gene Carroll (Lena)
Summary: During the city's campaign to reduce crime and accidents, Fibber drives his car with extra caution to avoid receiving a ticket.
Music: Billy Mills: "April Showers," "Slow Down" (The King's Men, vocal)
Running Gag: "Bird book" (Wallace)
Comments: Although Quinn and Leslie created numerous original witticisms, they weren't above reaching for a chestnut (e.g., Fibber's response of "It's old enough" after Molly tells him the engine is smoking) or joining the hit parade by taking their turn at a topical subject nearly every other comedy program was aiming at like having Wilcox say that *The Lost Weekend* was hung over for another week.

Date: April 8, 1947
Title: Molly's Sprained Ankle
Cast: Jim Jordan (Fibber), Marian Jordan (Molly), Harlow Wilcox, Bill Thompson (Nick Depopolis), Gale Gordon (Mayor LaTrivia), Arthur Q. Bryan (Doctor Gamble), Gene Carroll (Lena)
Summary: After Molly twists her ankle, Fibber makes a mess of the living room trying to finish her housework.
Music: Billy Mills: "Waltz in Springtime," "Casey Jones" (The King's Men, vocal), "Love Is a Random Thing"
Running Gags: Word confusion involving *sacroiliac/Mackinac/mechanic/almanac* (Fibber, Molly), hall closet opened by Fibber looking for hot water bottle, LaTrivia blowup over his mother being presented at court
Comments: Nick, who tells one of his fractured stories by getting fairy tale characters mixed up, appears for the first time since the October 14, 1941 show. Also brought back for a curtain call is the delightful joke about Fibber darning a sock with string and a hammer, earlier used on the April 20, 1943 program.

Date: April 15, 1947
Title: Quarter from 1880
Cast: Jim Jordan (Fibber), Marian Jordan (Molly), Harlow Wilcox, Bill Thompson (Wallace Wimple), Gale Gordon (Mayor LaTrivia), Arthur Q. Bryan (cab driver, Doctor Gamble), Gene Carroll (Lena), Shirley Mitchell (Miss Dilgiprink)

Summary: The McGees chase all over town looking for an 1880 quarter Fibber accidentally used to buy cigars.

Music: Billy Mills: "I Got a Gal in North and South Dakota," "I Tipped My Hat and Slowly Rode Away" (The King's Men, vocal), "Beware My Heart"

Running Gags: "Get them brakes fixed" (Fibber), Mrs. Kladderhatch bit involving Willie/swallowing cigarette lighter/using matches (Gamble), LaTrivia blowup over "wild goose chase," word confusion involving *metaphor/semaphore/samovar* (Fibber, Molly, LaTrivia)

Comments: Jim flubs "blue peepers," then has some fun by saying, "bue pleepers." To get some sense of how coin values have changed, the average 1880 Seated Liberty quarter worth $10 in 1947 would fetch $200 or more today and a 1916 Standing Liberty quarter is worth at least $5,000 now compared with $60 cited in this episode.

Date: April 22, 1947
Title: Carnival
Cast: Jim Jordan (Fibber), Marian Jordan (Molly, Teeny), Harlow Wilcox, Bill Thompson (Wallace Wimple, Uncle Fred), Gale Gordon (numbers wheel barker), Arthur Q. Bryan (Doctor Gamble), Gene Carroll (Lena)
Summary: At the carnival Molly wins a prize at every game she wisely takes a crack at while Fibber just cracks wise.
Music: Billy Mills: "Little Rock Getaway," "Sawing a Woman in Half" (The King's Men, vocal), "Oh, You Beautiful Doll"
Running Gags: Hall closet opened by Fibber looking for his hat, "Where'd I put that hammer?" (Uncle Fred)
Comments: Uncle Fred is just Bill Thompson's take on Horatio K. Boomer kicking the gong around. Molly delivers one of those convoluted sentences that usually come from the mouth of her husband: "I'm so frightened of admitting I'm scared that I get so brave I'm frightened of my own courage." The affectionate dialogue at the top of the Ferris wheel ranks second only to the ice skating scene on the February 5, 1946 episode as the most romantic vignette heard on *Fibber McGee and Molly.*

Date: April 29, 1947
Title: Thelma Graham Visits
Cast: Jim Jordan (Fibber), Marian Jordan (Molly, Teeny), Harlow Wilcox, Bill Thompson (Wallace Wimple), Gale Gordon (Mayor LaTrivia), Arthur Q. Bryan (Doctor Gamble), Bea Benaderet (Thelma Graham), Gene Carroll (Lena)
Summary: When Thelma Graham, an old pal of Molly's, stops at the McGees for tea, she unloads a baggage of gags older than their friendship.
Music: Billy Mills: "Linda," "I Do, Do, Do Like You" (The King's Men, vocal), "We Could Make Such Beautiful Music Together"

Running Gags: "Bird book" (Wallace, Gamble), "'Tain't funny, McGee" (Molly)

Comments: Bea Benaderet returns, having recovered from injuries sustained in an automobile accident. In the midst of a show loaded with jokes, some throwaway lines are apt to be overlooked like this excuse from Fibber as he tries to get out of the house so he can paint the pool balls: "I'm one of the few who knows what color the eight ball is."

Date: May 6, 1947
Title: Grammar Improvement
Cast: Jim Jordan (Fibber), Marian Jordan (Molly, Teeny), Harlow Wilcox, Bill Thompson (Wallace Wimple), Gale Gordon (Mayor LaTrivia), Arthur Q. Bryan (Doctor Gamble), Gene Carroll (Lena)
Summary: Fibber and Molly make a $5.00 bet over which of them will be the first to say *ain't*.
Music: Billy Mills: "I Believe," "Ain't We Got Fun?" (The King's Men, vocal), "It's Dreamtime"
Running Gags: Cigar routine (Fibber, Harlow), "Bird book" (Wallace), LaTrivia blowup over tenses
Comments: Seasoned listeners to *Fibber McGee and Molly* know that before the show is over a connection will be drawn between the bet and the window shade. They also realize that a number of the songs performed by The King's Men in recent months are tied to the subject of the program (e.g. "Ain't We Got Fun?" for this episode, "Slow Down" for the one about driving, "It's a Good Day" for the rainy night program, "Sawing a Woman in Half" for the carnival show, and "You Can't Tell a Man By His Hat" for the May 13th program about men's clothing). A unique occurrence happens when Teeny receives applause upon entering, her appearances generally accepted routinely because Marian has already been introduced to the audience as Molly.

Date: May 13, 1947
Title: Irish Tweed
Cast: Jim Jordan (Fibber), Marian Jordan (Molly, Teeny), Harlow Wilcox, Bill Thompson (Wallace Wimple), Gale Gordon (Mayor LaTrivia), Arthur Q. Bryan (Doctor Gamble), Gene Carroll (Lena)
Summary: After Fibber buys three bolts of cloth from a man in an alley, he attempts to sell parts of his prize purchase to pals for a profit.
Music: Billy Mills: "Illusion," "You Can't Tell a Man By His Hat" (The King's Men, vocal), "Mi Vida"
Running Gags: "Bird book" (Wallace), LaTrivia blowup over *colander*
Comments: Gene Carroll appears for the last time. The cast has lots of fun with ad-libs: Jim and Arthur ride Preakness three times around the track and Jim follows his gaffe over hot chocolate with "cart before the horse" that breaks up Marian and Bill.

Date: May 20, 1947
Title: Interviewed at Home
Cast: Jim Jordan (Fibber), Marian Jordan (Molly, Teeny), Harlow Wilcox, Bill Thompson (Old Timer, Wallace Wimple), Gale Gordon (Mayor LaTrivia), Arthur Q. Bryan (Doctor Gamble), Bea Benaderet (Miss Cartwright)
Summary: When Miss Cartwright visits their home, the McGees assume she is a reporter interviewing them for a newspaper article.
Music: Billy Mills: "Smile Right Back at the Sun," "Country Style" (The King's Men, vocal), "That's Where I Came In"
Running Gags: "That ain't the way I heered it" (Old Timer), Miss Kladderhatch bit involving husband/buzzing in ears/keeps bees (Gamble), "Bird book" (Wallace), LaTrivia blowup over *hose*
Comments: This is a notable appearance for Bea in that she gets to use her normal voice for the part of Miss Cartwright. A Quinn and Leslie quote of note is Fibber's citing the political lesson to be learned from *The Spirit of '76*: "If you're on the left, you make shrill noises; if you're on the right, you get ready to beat it; and if you get caught in the middle, you start waving the flag."

Date: May 27, 1947
Title: Shrimps McGee
Cast: Jim Jordan (Fibber), Marian Jordan (Molly, Teeny), Harlow Wilcox, Bill Thompson (Old Timer, Wallace Wimple), Gale Gordon (Mayor LaTrivia), Arthur Q. Bryan (Doctor Gamble)
Summary: After Fibber finds an old recipe in the attic, he prepares a tasty dish and invites friends over for supper.
Music: Billy Mills: "My Adobe Hacienda," "The Possum Song" (The King's Men, vocal)
Running Gags: "That ain't the way I heered it" (Old Timer), Myrt bit involving working in laundry/iron while strike was hot (Fibber), "Bird book" (Wallace)
Comments: This episode shows Fibber at the peak of his inventive powers, the highlights being the involved recipe with acorns in which the ride is as much fun as being let off by a manhole cover, and his Kraniform system of measurement with its oodles, gobs, heaps, and loads of merriment.

Date: June 3, 1947
Title: Citizenship Test
Cast: Jim Jordan (Fibber), Marian Jordan (Molly, Teeny), Harlow Wilcox, Bill Thompson (Wallace Wimple), Gale Gordon (Mayor LaTrivia), Arthur Q. Bryan (Doctor Gamble)
Summary: Because he does not have a birth certificate, Fibber feels compelled to take an examination on how government works and U.S. history to prove he is an American.

Music: Billy Mills: "The Russian Rag," "Linda" (The King's Men, vocal), "Almost Like Being in Love"
Running Gags: None
Comments: The name of the judge is a takeoff on Judge Crater, the man whose unexplained disappearance was the subject of as many jokes in the thirties and forties as Jimmy Hoffa in recent times. Fibber is still spinning yarns and stretching them out to full length, the design most apparent in the Chinese gibberish he lays before Wilcox and the tale of two Keys for Teeny. The set of free initials is one of the very few mail-in premiums offered by Johnson's Wax on *Fibber McGee and Molly*.

Date: June 10, 1947
Title: Looking for Gold at Dugan's Lake
Cast: Jim Jordan (Fibber), Marian Jordan (Molly, Teeny), Harlow Wilcox, Bill Thompson (Old Timer, Wallace Wimple), Gale Gordon (Mayor LaTrivia), Arthur Q. Bryan (Doctor Gamble)
Summary: Because Gamble reveals that he lost gold coins at Dugan's Lake, McGee spends his time diving for them instead of enjoying a picnic.
Music: Billy Mills: "Cecelia," "Oh, Evaline" (The King's Men, vocal), "Fine Thing"
Running Gags: "That ain't the way I heered it" (Old Timer), "Gotta get them brakes fixed" (Fibber), "Bird book" (Wallace), LaTrivia blowup over "your honor"
Comments: The Old Timer's explanation after his catch phrase is accurate about a number of the jokes he tells: "It may not be funny, kids, but it's topical." His jest about Indians and Teeny's calling LaTrivia an Indian giver do not amuse listeners today as they once did for obvious reasons.

Date: June 17, 1947
Title: Homer Vickery
Cast: Jim Jordan (Fibber), Marian Jordan (Molly, Teeny), Harlow Wilcox, Bill Thompson (Old Timer), Gale Gordon (Mayor LaTrivia), Arthur Q. Bryan (Doctor Gamble), Homer Vickery (Lou Merrill)
Summary: The McGees play host to the owner of a vacuum cleaner company who wants to repay $3.00 he borrowed from Fibber.
Music: Billy Mills: "Across the Alley from the Alamo," "By the Watermelon Vine" (The King's Men, vocal), "Sleep"
Running Gags: "That ain't the way I heered it" (Old Timer), tongue twister starting with Flatfoot McGee (Fibber), LaTrivia blowup over *squash*, Mrs. Kladderhatch bit involving husband/Relapse, 112/horse (Gamble)
Comments: Harlow is so accustomed to reciting the credits in the usual pattern that he fluffs the sequence due to Frank Pittman getting a mention on the final show of the season. The mottoes quoted by Vickery throughout the episode should prepare listeners for the payoff. LaTrivia's blowup, the last

one to be heard until October 5, 1948, is a dandy, one of top ten on his fit parade. The Top Ten set to which the McGees refer contains four records of specially-recorded selections which, according to the liner notes, are "genuine collector's editions…the first phonograph records, as far as is known, especially recorded before a large studio audience." For the second consecutive year *The Fred Waring Show* replaces *Fibber McGee and Molly* for the summer.

Date: October 7, 1947
Title: Football Game Anniversary
Cast: Jim Jordan (Fibber), Marian Jordan (Molly, Teeny), Harlow Wilcox, Bill Thompson (Old Timer, Wallace Wimple, Joe), Gale Gordon (F. Ogden Williams), Arthur Q. Bryan (Doctor Gamble)
Summary: To commemorate the thirtieth anniversary of their first football date, Fibber prepares a surprise for Molly, unaware that she also has one planned for him.
Music: Billy Mills: "The Lady from Twenty Nine Palms" "Freedom Train" (The King's Men, vocal with spoken interlude by Fibber and Molly), "All of Me"
Running Gags: "That ain't the way I heered it" (Old Timer), "'Tain't funny, McGee" (Molly)
Comments: Jim ad-libs "What are we doing?" in response to Molly's declaration that "If I could turn my emotions on and off like that, I'd be doing soap operas." Rather than offend people by continuing with a character whose name closely resembled that of Fiorello LaGuardia who died on September 20th, Mayor LaTrivia is dropped for the 1947-1948 season as Gale Gordon becomes F. Ogden ("Foggy") Williams, a wishy-washy weatherman.

Date: October 14, 1947
Title: Cat Under the Porch
Cast: Jim Jordan (Fibber), Marian Jordan (Molly, Teeny), Harlow Wilcox, Bill Thompson (Old Timer, Wallace Wimple), Gale Gordon (F. Ogden Williams), Arthur Q. Bryan (Doctor Gamble)
Summary: When the cat Teeny brings to the house hides under the front porch, the McGees and friends try to rescue it.
Music: Billy Mills: "I Wonder Who's Kissing Her Now," "Tallahassee" (The King's Men, vocal), "Why Should I Cry Over You?"
Running Gags: "That ain't the way I heered it" (Old Timer), "'Tain't funny, McGee" (Molly)
Summary: As on a number of other occasions where the action commences with Fibber grumbling about some matter, this episode begins with McGee in medias rage: "And another thing…" A recorded version of "Why Should I Cry Over You?" will be used on a number of fifteen-minute episodes. Fibber's closing comment, "It's hard to hold that terrific pace right up to the end," may have been a truism for other series, but the writers of *Fibber McGee and Molly* kept the dialogue top-notch from start to finish for years to come.

Date: October 21, 1947
Title: Overdue Car Payment
Cast: Jim Jordan (Fibber), Marian Jordan (Molly, Teeny), Harlow Wilcox, Bill Thompson (Old Timer), Gale Gordon (F. Ogden Williams), Arthur Q. Bryan (Doctor Gamble), Jess Kirkpatrick (Carl Snarl)
Summary: The McGees rush downtown to make their September payment before the Wistful Vista Finance Company repossesses their car.
Music: Billy Mills: "Kate," "The Stanley Steamer" (The King's Men, vocal), "Why Should I Cry Over You?"
Running Gags: "I heered it in a slightly different way" (Old Timer), Fibber opens closet to get his hat
Comments: Bill Thompson, with some of the most versatile vocal chords in radio, even manages to get a little melody in his laugh leading up to the twist on his catch phrase. Harlow breaks up Jim and Marian with a whistle bit whose timing is off just a bit. The plug for the Community Chest in the tag effectively appeals to the conscience.

Date: October 28, 1947
Title: Apple Crop
Cast: Jim Jordan (Fibber), Marian Jordan (Molly), Harlow Wilcox, Bill Thompson (Old Timer, Wallace Wimple), Gale Gordon (F. Ogden Williams), Arthur Q. Bryan (Doctor Gamble), Jess Kirkpatrick (Tim Hays)
Summary: The McGees take a drive in the country to consummate a deal involving apples between Fibber and a farmer.
Music: Billy Mills: "Feudin' and Fightin'," "Shine On, Harvest Moon" (The King's Men, vocal), "Near You"
Running Gags: Myrt bit involving brother/false face/not wearing one (Fibber), cigar routine (Fibber, Williams), "That ain't the way I heered it" (Old Timer), "Gotta get them brakes fixed" (Fibber), "Bird book" (Wallace)
Comments: This episode is like a trip down memory lane as we see the bygone sites pointed out by the McGees: Burma Shave signs, three-sheet circus posters, and barns painted with ads for patent medicines. The writers permit Gamble to give voice to the amazing coincidences that happen on radio which allow continuing characters to run into one another no matter where they are.

Date: November 4, 1947
Title: Getting Weighed
Cast: Jim Jordan (Fibber), Marian Jordan (Molly, Teeny), Harlow Wilcox, Bill Thompson (Old Timer, Horatio K. Boomer), Gale Gordon (F. Ogden Williams), Arthur Q. Bryan (Doctor Gamble), Virginia Gordon (Rosie)
Summary: Because Fibber does not believe the reading of 177 pounds on his scale at home, he and Molly go to Kremer's Drugstore to get a second opinion on his weight.

Music: Billy Mills: "Naughty Angeline," "Civilization" (The King's Men, vocal), "The Best Things in Life Are Free"
Running Gag: "Where did I put that coaxer?" (Horatio)
Comments: A recorded version of "The Best Things in Life Are Free" will be used on numerous fifteen-minute episodes of this program. Doc Gamble's assessment of Fibber's appearance is a cap-a-pie dressing down in which the writers build to the topper of McGee looking like "a Malaysian headhunter turned loose in the men's locker room of a bowery flophouse." Fibber's recollection of when he last saw Boomer is a bit clouded; it was not two or three years ago as McGee mentioned but rather the previous year on April 2nd. The Jordans figuratively step to the footlights in the tag to look the audience in the eye and remind them of the urgent need to save people in Europe from starvation.

Date: November 11, 1947
Title: Raft of Troubles
Cast: Jim Jordan (Fibber), Marian Jordan (Molly), Harlow Wilcox, Bill Thompson (Horatio K. Boomer, Old Timer), Gale Gordon (F. Ogden Williams), Arthur Q. Bryan (Doctor Gamble)
Summary: The McGees get a close view of the effects of inflation when a sixteen-man raft fills their living room, leaving little room for living.
Music: Billy Mills: "Come to the Mardi Gras," "Save the Bones for Henry Jones" (The King's Men, vocal), "How Soon?"
Running Gag: "Where'd I put that Christmas list?" (Horatio)
Comments: This episode plays wonderfully on radio because, just as the raft fills the room, so the imaginations of listeners expand to their fullest to visualize the incongruous scene and the expressions on the faces of thunderstruck visitors. "The Curious Thing About Women" episode of *The Dick Van Dyke Show,* in which Laura Petrie opens a package which contains a life raft, is funny, but the raft doesn't consume the whole room as the McGee raft extends to all corners of our minds. Given Boomer's propensity for finding himself behind bars, perhaps the most valuable tidbit he ever extracts from his person when looking for some other object is the receipt he finds here entitling him to a petty larceny on the house which appears to be the equivalent of a "get out of jail free" card.

Date: November 18, 1947
Title: Missed Telephone Call
Cast: Jim Jordan (Fibber), Marian Jordan (Molly, Teeny), Harlow Wilcox, Bill Thompson (Old Timer, Horatio K. Boomer), Gale Gordon (F. Ogden Williams), Arthur Q. Bryan (Doctor Gamble), Virginia Gordon (Miss Eager)
Summary: Fibber, angered over making too many trips to the phone, stubbornly refuses to answer a call, then fears that the unknown caller might have had an important message for him.

Music: Billy Mills: "On the Avenue," "Sipping Cider on the Zider Zee" (The King's Men, vocal), "Sincerely Yours"

Running Gags: "That ain't the way I heered it" (Old Timer), Myrt bit involving uncle/pen point ball/out of prison (Fibber), "Where did I put those pennies?" (Horatio), hall closet opened by Horatio looking for the front door, Mrs. Kladderhatch bit involving cut out starches/in diet/in laundry (Gamble)

Comments: A recorded version of "Sincerely Yours" will be used on some of the fifteen-minute programs of the series. Bill Thompson adds to his repertoire by getting the tune of "Yankee Doodle Dandy" into the Old Timer's laugh. The writers through Gamble employ a clever switch on the "tall, dark, and handsome" cliché. The writers also include the McGee phone number on this broadcast so after dialing O for Myrt one can get M for Mirth by asking for 1073.

Date: November 25, 1947
Title: Painting the Kitchen
Cast: Jim Jordan (Fibber), Marian Jordan (Molly), Harlow Wilcox, Bill Thompson (Old Timer, Horatio K. Boomer), Gale Gordon (F. Ogden Williams), Arthur Q. Bryan (Doctor Gamble)
Summary: After Molly brings home a new bread box and canister set, Fibber decides to repaint the kitchen to match the new additions.
Music: Billy Mills: "The Stanley Steamer," "Pass That Peace Pipe" (The King's Men, vocal), "All of Me"
Running Gags: "That ain't the way I heered it" (Old Timer), "Letter, letter. Where did I put that—" (Horatio)
Comments: The mention of Fred Banks is an in-joke, a plug for the real painter by that name who assisted in the redecoration of Jim and Marian's home in Encino. Thompson's shortness of breath at the end of the long sentence adds to the humor of the line but is also in character for it is to be expected that an Old Timer would be coming up for air after such an outburst. As on the November 4th show when Fibber miscalculated the last time he met Boomer, the writers' math is off when Molly claims that the linoleum was installed when they moved in their house nine years ago. Actually the McGees moved in twelve years earlier on September 2, 1935.

Date: December 2, 1947
Title: Duck Hunting Plans
Cast: Jim Jordan (Fibber), Marian Jordan (Molly, Teeny), Harlow Wilcox, Bill Thompson (Horatio K. Boomer, Old Timer), Gale Gordon (F. Ogden Williams), Arthur Q. Bryan (Doctor Gamble)
Summary: As Fibber prepares to go hunting, he repeatedly pooh-poohs Molly's suggestion that she go along for the day.
Music: Billy Mills: "Tallahassee," "A Friend of Yours" (The King's Men, vocal), "Near You"

Running Gag: "Where did I put that address book?" (Horatio)

Comments: As usual, Quinn and Leslie pounce on handy puns whenever the subjects of guns (*caliber* and *bore*) or ducks (*cheese and quackers*) figure in the script. They also deal a winning hand to Fibber and Teeny who play another round of banter involving pooch and papa.

Date: December 9, 1947
Title: Newspaper Interview
Cast: Jim Jordan (Fibber), Marian Jordan (Molly), Harlow Wilcox, Bill Thompson (Old Timer, Horatio K. Boomer), Gale Gordon (F. Ogden Williams), Arthur Q. Bryan (Doctor Gamble,) Bea Benaderet (Clementine Clark)
Summary: The McGees give a reporter for *The Wistful Vista Gazette* a tour of their home while Fibber gives her a rundown of his life which is also rundown.
Music: Billy Mills: "Peggy O'Neill," "With a Hey, a Hi, and a Ho Ho Ho" (The King's Men, vocal), "How Soon?"
Running Gags: "That ain't the way I heered it" (Old Timer), "What did I do with that opener?" (Horatio)
Comments: The writers, not wanting to waste a good idea used earlier, tweaked the idea of an at-home interview used on May 20, 1947 and, with the same featured players, mined some more comic gold by picking at the subject from different angles. One of the richest veins struck is Fibber's throwaway line of "And a happier bunch of hillbillies..." which just might be the funniest words spoken that night.

Date: December 16, 1947
Title: Fruitcake
Cast: Jim Jordan (Fibber), Marian Jordan (Molly, Teeny), Harlow Wilcox, Bill Thompson (Old Timer, Horatio K. Boomer), Gale Gordon (F. Ogden Williams), Arthur Q. Bryan (Doctor Gamble), Jess Kirkpatrick (Carl Snarl)
Summary: Using a recipe from Aunt Sarah, Fibber concocts a batch of fruitcake.
Music: Billy Mills: "I'll Dance at Your Wedding," "Seven More Shopping Days Till Christmas" (The King's Men, vocal), "Why Should I Cry Over You?"
Running Gags: "That ain't the way I heered it" (Old Timer), "What did I do with— [cooker]" (Horatio)
Comments: For the second successive week the writers borrow an idea involving the same circumstances they used the previous spring. On May 27, 1947 the recipe found in the attic was for preparing shrimp. Fibber and Molly play a clever version of the shell game. For the purposes of this episode Quinn and Leslie make it seem that Fibber is Sarah's nephew. On all other occasions Sarah has been Molly's aunt.

Date: December 23, 1947
Title: Lost Keys
Cast: Jim Jordan (Fibber), Marian Jordan (Molly, Teeny), Harlow Wilcox, Bill Thompson (Old Timer, Wallace Wimple), Gale Gordon (F. Ogden Williams), Arthur Q. Bryan (Doctor Gamble)
Summary: Fibber shovels snow in search of a set of keys he lost.
Music: Billy Mills: "March of the Wooden Soldiers," "'Twas the Night Before Christmas" (The King's Men and Teeny, vocal)
Running Gags: None
Comments: Molly's description of Fibber's calamities after the last time he lost his keys pass so quickly that the audience hardly has time to visualize the scene of him tripping over the lamp, sticking his foot in the fishbowl, grabbing the drapes, falling on the end table, and rolling into the hallway. Another line that does not get what it deserves is the witty "I'm as bushed as the left-hand Smith Brother" which is greeted with a tiny laugh and scattered applause.

Date: December 30, 1947
Title: Gift Certificate for $10.00
Cast: Jim Jordan (Fibber), Marian Jordan (Molly), Harlow Wilcox, Bill Thompson (Old Timer, Wallace Wimple), Gale Gordon (F. Ogden Williams), Arthur Q. Bryan (Doctor Gamble), Jess Kirkpatrick (Carl Snarl)
Summary: The McGees shop at the Bon Ton for something to buy with a gift certificate from Aunt Sarah.
Music: Billy Mills: "There'll Be Some Changes Made," "What Are You Doing New Year's Eve?" (The King's Men, vocal), "The Stars Will Remember"
Running Gag: "That ain't the way I heered it" (Old Timer)
Comments: With eight floors of merchandise the Bon Ton can hold its own in that department with Macy's or Gimbels. Attentive listeners who carefully note the repeated mention of knitted socks are ready for the payoff. Quinn and Leslie shop the world for Doc's exotic descriptions of Fibber's taste in clothes with stops this week in East Mongolia and Brazil.

Date: January 6, 1948
Title: Magician McGee
Cast: Jim Jordan (Fibber), Marian Jordan (Molly, Teeny), Harlow Wilcox, Bill Thompson (Wallace Wimple, Old Timer), Gale Gordon (F. Ogden Williams), Arthur Q. Bryan (Doctor Gamble), Jess Kirkpatrick (Chet Morris)
Summary: Fibber performs some magic tricks in front of Molly and friends.
Music: Billy Mills: "How Soon?," "Evaline" (The King's Men, vocal), "Sincerely Yours"
Running Gags: "'Tain't funny, McGee" (Molly), "That ain't the way I heered it" (Old Timer), hall closet opened by burglar looking for silver

Comments: Quinn and Leslie perform a little magic of their own by taking the plot they used before on June 12, 1945 and displaying a different (though not necessarily new) set of situations and jokes before the audience. The highlight of this episode is when the Old Timer, trying to convince Fibber to go on living, talks himself into joining a necktie party.

Date: January 13, 1948
Title: Portable Radio
Cast: Jim Jordan (Fibber), Marian Jordan (Molly), Harlow Wilcox, Bill Thompson (Wallace Wimple, Old Timer), Gale Gordon (F. Ogden Williams), Arthur Q. Bryan (Doctor Gamble), Ken Christy (dispatcher)
Summary: Fibber works on his invention of a radio that can be used in automobiles and in homes.
Music: Billy Mills: "Pass That Peace Pipe," "I'm A-Comin' A-Courtin' Corabelle" (The King's Men, vocal), "The First Time I Kissed You"
Running Gag: "That ain't the way I heered it" (Old Timer)
Comments: Not content with a joke that ties the alphabet and two networks together, the writers let Fibber touch all the bases by saying that "If they give me hail, Columbia, I'll give it right back to them which will make it Mutual." Not content to let a slight delay in a sound effect go by which no one would have noticed, the cast milk it for a laugh when Jim tells Wilcox he's a little late and Harlow justifies his present existence with the excuse "I can't come in till the door opens."

Date: January 20, 1948
Title: Pickles at Women's Bazaar
Cast: Jim Jordan (Fibber), Marian Jordan (Molly, Teeny), Harlow Wilcox, Bill Thompson (Old Timer, Wallace Wimple), Gale Gordon (F. Ogden Williams), Arthur Q. Bryan (Doctor Gamble)
Summary: Rather than let Molly's pickles be purchased by a bidder at the women's bazaar, Fibber resorts to a stratagem that will allow him to keep the delicacy for himself.
Music: Billy Mills: "Golden Earrings," "Theresa" (The King's Men, vocal), "A Few More Kisses"
Running Gags: Mrs. Kladderhatch bit involving son/sew ear/letters on sweater (Gamble), "That ain't the way I heered it" (Old Timer)
Comments: Mrs. Williams appears for the only time, just long enough to do a "Good evening, probably" switch on her husband's exit line. Teeny joins in the appeal for a charity in the tag.

Date: January 27, 1948
Title: Missing Laundry
Cast: Jim Jordan (Fibber), Marian Jordan (Molly), Harlow Wilcox, Bill Thompson (Wallace Wimple, Old Timer), Gale Gordon (F. Ogden Williams), Arthur Q. Bryan (Doctor Gamble), Bea Benaderet (clerk)

Summary: Fibber, hot under the collar because his favorite shirt has not been cleaned and returned, takes his complaint to the owner of the laundry.
Music: Billy Mills: "I'm Looking Over a Four-Leaf Clover," "How Lucky You Are" (The King's Men, vocal), "You Were Meant for Me"
Running Gag: "Gotta get those brakes fixed" (Fibber), tongue twister starting with "wet wash" (Fibber)
Comments: Beginning with this episode, the running gag of tongue twister evolves from a name Fibber was known as in earlier days which was tied to an appropriate moniker preceding *McGee* into a less cadenced but still tricky string of phrases, many of them glimpses of Fibber's past that he was apparently revealing to Molly for the first time. The scene of Molly alternately dressing down Doc and Fibber plays very much like a mother scolding her two sons right down to the sotto voce comments of each man while the faults of the other are being exposed as if he is saying "There! She sure told you!"

Date: February 3, 1948
Title: Table Lamp
Cast: Jim Jordan (Fibber), Marian Jordan (Molly, Teeny), Harlow Wilcox, Bill Thompson (Old Timer, Wallace Wimple), Gale Gordon (F. Ogden Williams), Arthur Q. Bryan (Doctor Gamble)
Summary: While Fibber makes a lamp for Molly out of a pewter teapot, he tries to keep it a secret so he can surprise her.
Music: Billy Mills: "I've Got a Feeling I'm Falling," "The Secretary Song" (The King's Men, vocal), "The Stars Will Remember"
Running Gags: "That ain't the way I heered it" (Old Timer), tongue twister starting with "Mayor Moore" (Fibber)
Comments: The reference to former classmate little Charlie Correll is an in-joke about another Peorian, one of the stars on *Amos 'n' Andy*. The "she don't know what outta" line becomes a bit tiresome by the time Gamble arrives, but Jim freshens it up while breaking everyone up with his fluff of "she don't know outta how from what."

Date: February 10, 1948
Title: Sled from Childhood Days
Cast: Jim Jordan (Fibber), Marian Jordan (Molly), Harlow Wilcox, Bill Thompson (Old Timer, Wallace Wimple), Gale Gordon (F. Ogden Williams), Arthur Q. Bryan (Doctor Gamble)
Summary: Fibber repairs his childhood sled so he can use it again.
Music: Billy Mills: "All Dressed Up With a Broken Heart," "Mañana" (The King's Men, vocal), "Thoughtless"
Running Gags: "I heered it with a slight political twist" (Old Timer), Mrs. Kladderhatch bit involving husband/bit by worm/five feet long (Gamble), word confusion involving *neuralgia/nostalgia/nasturtiums/aspersions* (Fibber, Molly), tongue twister starting with "thin thicket" (Fibber)

Comments: That the players on *Fibber McGee and Molly* had some freedom to deviate slightly from the script to milk a laugh is evident three times in this episode: Bill ad-libs a kiss and "just a demonstration smacker"; Jim adds "Oh, that laid an egg" after his song about a tortoise dies; Harlow magnifies his blooper of *confused* by repeating the line with *fused*. In the tag when talking about the anniversary of the Boy Scouts, however, Jim is all business when he simply corrects his error of *83rd* to *38th* with no comment.

Date: February 17, 1948
Title: Money for Old Books
Cast: Jim Jordan (Fibber), Marian Jordan (Molly), Harlow Wilcox, Bill Thompson (Old Timer, K. Stanley Flyleaf), Gale Gordon (F. Ogden Williams), Arthur Q. Bryan (Doctor Gamble), Jess Kirkpatrick (bookshop owner)
Summary: The McGees visit the Book Nook to buy Horatio Alger novels they plan to resell to a book collector.
Music: Billy Mills: "Now Is the Hour," "Two Things to Worry About" (The King's Men, vocal), "The Stars Will Remember"
Running Gag: "That ain't the way I heered it" (Old Timer), tongue twister starting with "cash for cashmere" (Fibber)
Comments: The Old Timer's description of a candidate who is presidential timber is a Quinn and Leslie quote of note that uses just about every tree pun except possibly *out on a limb*: "He can look green and act grown, he ain't too sappy or shady, he don't mind getting the bird, he knows when to bow and leave and he can bark when necessary, spends a lot of time on the stump, keeps his trunk packed, and falls the right way when they give him the ax." If the first edition of *Uncle Tom's Cabin* used as a doorstop worth $200 in 1948 was the first printing in cloth published in two volumes in 1852, its current value would likely exceed $6,000.

Date: February 24, 1948
Title: Getting $7.00 Loan Back
Cast: Jim Jordan (Fibber), Marian Jordan (Molly, Teeny), Harlow Wilcox, Bill Thompson (Old Timer, Wallace Wimple), Gale Gordon (F. Ogden Williams), Arthur Q. Bryan (Doctor Gamble)
Summary: Fibber makes arrangements to speak via short wave to a man in the Philippines who owes him money.
Music: Billy Mills: "Papa, Won't You Dance With Me?," "The Little Old Mill" (The King's Men, vocal), "You Were Meant for Me"
Running Gags: "That ain't the way I heered it" (Old Timer), hall closet opened by Williams thinking it was the side door
Comments: Harlow's welcoming message of "Fibber and Molly join us in a moment" will become a frequent greeting heard before the first commercial in months to come. Fibber uses "He makes me tired" about Gamble for

the first time. Teeny borrows Fibber's "drag out the throw net" line. The plea on behalf of National Brotherhood Week is admirable, although somewhat discordant in a program that opens with the mention of "the savage Indian" sending smoke signals, a superfluous gag about the Indian on a penny blinking, and a closing joke about a husband wanting to hit his wife.

Date: March 2, 1948
Title: Jury Duty
Cast: Jim Jordan (Fibber), Marian Jordan (Molly), Harlow Wilcox, Bill Thompson (Old Timer), Gale Gordon (F. Ogden Williams), Arthur Q. Bryan (Doctor Gamble), Virginia Gordon (Miss Bagel), Jess Kirkpatrick (judge)
Summary: Fibber has a difficult time convincing anyone that he wants to volunteer to serve on a jury.
Music: Billy Mills: "Beg Your Pardon," "Betty Blue" (The King's Men, vocal), "Fool That I Am"
Running Gags: "That ain't the way I heered it" (Old Timer), tongue twister starting with "Russell wrestling" (Fibber)
Comments: The Old Timer has one of his best speeches in this episode with a wonderful array of legal gibberish and a resolution of the case that finds the judge convicted, the prosecuting attorney sentenced to jail, and the defendant awarded alimony and custody of the bailiff. Fibber's comment of "Save a lot of actors that way" seems to have been appreciated only by a few tittering cast members. The short plug for *Mr. District Attorney*, another NBC program, was not coincidental. In the tag the Jordans make doubly certain listeners get the message about Easter Seals.

Date: March 9, 1948
Title: Broken Card Table
Cast: Jim Jordan (Fibber), Marian Jordan (Molly, Teeny), Harlow Wilcox, Bill Thompson (Wallace Wimple, Old Timer), Gale Gordon (F. Ogden Williams), Arthur Q. Bryan (Doctor Gamble)
Summary: Fibber hopes to disguise the broken leg on Doc's card table while they play checkers.
Music: Billy Mills: "What'll I Do?," "You Don't Have to Know the Language" (The King's Men, vocal), "How Soon?"
Running Gag: "That ain't the way I heered it" (Old Timer)
Comments: Dr. Gamble's name of George is used for the first time in the series. Just when Fibber delivers what could have been the funniest line of the night ("What's money when you got a head like an apple?"), Gamble tops him with "Look who's asking."

Date: March 16, 1948
Title: Spearhead Commission
Cast: Jim Jordan (Fibber), Marian Jordan (Molly), Harlow Wilcox, Bill Thompson (Wallace Wimple, Old Timer), Gale Gordon (F. Ogden Williams), Arthur Q. Bryan (Doctor Gamble), Ken Christy (George Marshall), Herb Vigran (telegram delivery man, cab driver)
Summary: After Fibber receives a wire from George Marshall asking for his assistance, he assumes it is from the Secretary of State and makes plans to leave for Washington.
Music: Billy Mills: "The Big Brass Band," "Too-Ra-Loo-Ra-Loo-Ra" (The King's Men, vocal), "Thoughtless"
Running Gags: Myrt bit involving grandmother/lost her shirt on long shot/ Mort Toops (Fibber), tongue twister starting with "workman working on watches" (Fibber), "That ain't the way I heered it" (Old Timer)
Comments: Wilcox delivers the most colorful introduction ever heard on the program. The walking man in the Myrt bit is an allusion to the name of a contest offered on *Truth or Consequences*, another NBC program. Molly's boisterous laugh helps turn a miss into a hit when Gale accidentally starts to read one of his lines a second time.

Date: March 23, 1948
Title: Easter Dress
Cast: Jim Jordan (Fibber), Marian Jordan (Molly, Teeny), Harlow Wilcox, Bill Thompson (Old Timer), Gale Gordon (F. Ogden Williams), Arthur Q. Bryan (Doctor Gamble), Jess Kirkpatrick (Henri), Sandra Gould (Eloise)
Summary: The McGees visit a couturier to have a dress designed for Molly who won it in a contest she entered.
Music: Billy Mills: "Saturday Date," "Zip-a-Dee-Doo-Dah" (The King's Men, vocal), "Haunted Heart"
Running Gag: "That ain't the way I heered it" (Old Timer)
Comments: Sometimes the adage of the simplest things in life being the best (jokes included) is true as evidenced by Fibber's pithy comment on the Old Timer's short career of being shot out of a cannon: "You mean, they fired you and then you quit." In the tag Jim and Marian acknowledge the contribution of Ken Darby, who eventually will win three Oscars of his own, in helping "Zip-a-Dee-Doo-Dah" win the 1947 Academy Award for Best Song.

Date: March 30, 1948
Title: Overnight Trip Downtown
Cast: Jim Jordan (Fibber), Marian Jordan (Molly), Harlow Wilcox, Bill Thompson (Wallace Wimple, cigar clerk, Old Timer), Gale Gordon (F. Ogden Williams), Arthur Q. Bryan (Doctor Gamble), Walter Tetley (Small Fry Wilcox), Herb Vigran (Cravishaw)

Summary: The McGees check in at the Wistful Vista Plaza before they enjoy a night on the town.
Music: Billy Mills: "Ooh! Look-A There, Ain't She Pretty?," "Cincinnati" (The King's Men, vocal), "Passing Fancy"
Running Gag: Tongue twister starting with "sitter to sit" (Fibber)
Comments: Two concerns that undoubtedly occurred to faithful listeners are given voice in this episode when Molly complains that their visitors are always the same people and when Harlow asks Fibber "Vacation, pal? From what?"

Date: April 6, 1948
Title: Fixing Doc's Car
Cast: Jim Jordan (Fibber), Marian Jordan (Molly, Teeny), Harlow Wilcox, Bill Thompson (Wallace Wimple), Gale Gordon (F. Ogden Williams), Arthur Q. Bryan (Doctor Gamble)
Summary: Fibber, veering off from his intended task of cleaning the closet to tuning up Gamble's automobile, makes more of a mess in the driveway with tools and parts than ever tumbled into the hallway after opening his old nemesis.
Music: Billy Mills: "Hooray for Love," "Love Is So Terrific" (The King's Men, vocal), "My Sin"
Running Gags: Hall closet opened by Fibber looking for tools, tongue twister starting with "new zoo" (Fibber)
Comments: For the first time the writers allow Williams to lose his temper a la LaTrivia. Fibber's claim that he will have Gamble's car "humming like Jack Benny's quartet" is one of those thinking man's (or woman's) jokes that zips by too quickly before the audience can make the connection.

Date: April 13, 1948
Title: Fire Alarm Box
Cast: Jim Jordan (Fibber), Marian Jordan (Molly), Harlow Wilcox, Bill Thompson (Wallace Wimple, Old Timer), Gale Gordon (F. Ogden Williams), Arthur Q. Bryan (Doctor Gamble)
Summary: Fibber appoints himself guardian of the new alarm box in the neighborhood and seems most anxious to be the first person to use it.
Music: Billy Mills: "The Feathery Feeling," "The Fireman's Bride" (The King's Men and Marian, vocal), "Fool That I Am"
Running Gags: Word confusion involving *arsenic/arsonist/arson/Orson* (Fibber, Molly), tongue twister starting with "pop popcorn" (Fibber), "That ain't the way I heered it" (Old Timer)
Comments: A name game between the McGees and Williams is another step in making Gordon's character more assertive. The honorary degree mentioned in the tag to be presented at St. Joseph's College on April 15th demonstrates that the popularity of *Fibber McGee and Molly* extended beyond the home into academia.

Date: April 20, 1948
Title: Making a Vase
Cast: Jim Jordan (Fibber), Marian Jordan (Molly, Teeny), Harlow Wilcox, Bill Thompson (Old Timer), Gale Gordon (F. Ogden Williams), Arthur Q. Bryan (Doctor Gamble)
Summary: After Molly expresses interest in a vase at the Bon Ton, Fibber promises to produce one in their oven and manages to do just that.
Music: Billy Mills: "You Turned the Tables on Me," "It's a Quiet Town" (The King's Men and Marian, vocal), "My Sin"
Running Gags: "That ain't the way I heered it" (Old Timer), tongue twister starting with "proprietor of Peoria Pottery" (Fibber)
Comments: For once the sensible one gets top billing as Harlow brings the couple on with "Molly McGee and Fibber." Williams is given more dialogue than usual to chew on this week, though the chestnuts about lightning calculator and buoy/gull may have tasted a bit stale.

Date: April 27, 1948
Title: Passenger Pigeon
Cast: Jim Jordan (Fibber), Marian Jordan (Molly), Harlow Wilcox, Bill Thompson (Wallace Wimple, Old Timer, scoffer), Gale Gordon (F. Ogden Williams), Arthur Q. Bryan (Doctor Gamble)
Summary: Fibber builds a trap to capture a passenger pigeon he saw, ignoring the skepticism of those who claim the bird is extinct.
Music: Billy Mills: "Little White Lies," "The Dickey-Bird Song" (The King's Men, vocal), "Confess"
Running Gags: "Bird book" (Wallace), hall closet opened by Fibber looking for tools, tongue twister starting with "totaling tea" (Fibber), "'Tain't funny, McGee" (Molly)
Comments: Like a quarterback who wisely distributes passes among a number of receivers, Quinn and Leslie spread the bird and animal jokes around so that all the visitors (except Wimple who has his "bird book" bit) get a crack at a crack, the chief groaner of the bunch being Harlow's "people-toed pigeon."

Date: May 4, 1948
Title: Selling the House
Cast: Jim Jordan (Fibber), Marian Jordan (Molly, Teeny), Harlow Wilcox, Bill Thompson (Old Timer), Arthur Q. Bryan (Doctor Gamble)
Summary: Fibber wants to sell the house to a willing buyer, but Molly tries to convince him they should stay put at 79 Wistful Vista.
Music: Billy Mills: "But Beautiful," "Money, Money, Money" (The King's Men, vocal)
Running Gags: None

Summary: The selection of the professor's name is an in-joke, a tip of the hat to director Frank Pittman. Fibber's witticism about giving "this place eleven years of the best years of my wife" is light in more ways than one: *Fibber McGee and Molly* had been on the air just over thirteen years when this episode was broadcast. Jim also slips on a number when he says, "$18.00 papers" instead of "$18,000 papers." The citation presented to Jim and Marian indicates that, at least in 1948, popularity in the media and high moral values went hand-in-hand.

Date: May 11, 1948
Title: Fishing Bet with Gamble
Cast: Jim Jordan (Fibber), Marian Jordan (Molly, Teeny), Harlow Wilcox, Bill Thompson (Wallace Wimple), Gale Gordon (F. Ogden Williams), Arthur Q. Bryan (Doctor Gamble)
Summary: Gamble and Fibber wager $10.00 on who will catch the larger fish at Dugan's Lake by hook or by crook.
Music: Billy Mills: "I May Be Wrong," "Blue Shadows on the Trail" (The King's Men, vocal), "It Only Happens When I Dance With You"
Running Gag: Tongue twister starting with "fly-tying factory" (Fibber)
Comments: Jim's blooper on *saloon* breaks up Marian and the ad-lib of "plate slipped" tickles Arthur as well. Molly's excuse to leave the boat for cold cream is the most awkward and contrived way to clear the stage for Fibber and Teeny listeners will ever hear on *Fibber McGee and Molly*.

Date: May 18, 1948
Title: Baseball Cologne
Cast: Jim Jordan (Fibber), Marian Jordan (Molly, Teeny), Harlow Wilcox, Bill Thompson (Old Timer), Gale Gordon (F. Ogden Williams), Arthur Q. Bryan (Doctor Gamble)
Summary: Fibber tries to create a men's fragrance that captures the essence of a baseball game.
Music: Billy Mills: "Better Luck Next Time," "Casey, the Pride of Them All" (The King's Men, vocal)
Running Gags: None
Comments: This is a rare episode in that the outcome of Fibber's scheme is undisclosed at the end of the show as we leave the amateur chemist still at work with his table filled with concoctions. A Quinn and Leslie quote of note is Teeny's definition of cologne: "The stuff that girls put on their ears to keep boys on their toes."

Date: May 25, 1948
Title: Molly's Toothache
Cast: Jim Jordan (Fibber), Marian Jordan (Molly), Harlow Wilcox, Bill Thompson (Wallace Wimple, Old Timer), Gale Gordon (F. Ogden Williams),

Arthur Q. Bryan (Doctor Gamble), Ken Christy (officer), Herb Vigran (officer)

Summary: Fibber goes to any length to alleviate the discomfort Molly is suffering with her sore tooth.

Music: Billy Mills: "Tell Me A Story," "Pecos Bill" (The King's Men, vocal), "Yours"

Running Gags: Tongue twister starting with "senior seesaw salesman" (Fibber), "Gotta get them brakes fixed" (Fibber)

Comments: Breaking into Kremer's Drugstore does seem out of character for the McGees particularly in light of the award received just three weeks earlier for presenting entertainment with a high moral tone. The names employed for the supporting policemen (Needham, Louis and Brorby) is an in-joke for that is the name of the show's advertising agency.

Date: June 1, 1948
Title: Fibber's Tune
Cast: Jim Jordan (Fibber), Marian Jordan (Molly, Teeny), Harlow Wilcox, Bill Thompson (Old Timer), Gale Gordon (F. Ogden Williams), Arthur Q. Bryan (Doctor Gamble)

Summary: Fibber hopes to revive a song he wrote in 1916 by having it sung over radio station WVIS.

Music: Billy Mills: "A Fella With an Umbrella," "Fibber's Tune" (The King's Men, Vocal with a reprise by Fibber and Molly), "When You're Smiling"

Running Gags: "That ain't the way I heered it" (Old Timer), Mrs. Kladderhatch bit involving husband/lost his nose/counting votes (Gamble)

Comments: The character F. Ogden Williams appears for the last time. Frank Pittman is mentioned in the credits as he was for the final show of the 1946-1947 season. Jim and Bill add to the merriment with ad-libs, Thompson's being a natural extension of the song title the Old Timer recites which falls flat on its treble clef. Even though *Call the Police* starring George Petrie will be the summer replacement series in the *Fibber McGee and Molly* time slot, the program promoted by Jim, Marian, and Harlow is Fred Waring's twice-weekly morning show sponsored by Johnson's Wax.

Date: October 5, 1948
Title: Pants Pressed Downtown
Cast: Jim Jordan (Fibber), Marian Jordan (Molly, Teeny), Harlow Wilcox, Bill Thompson (Old Timer, Wallace Wimple), Gale Gordon (Mayor LaTrivia), Arthur Q. Bryan (Doctor Gamble), Herb Vigran (officer)

Summary: Because things are so dull around home, Fibber and Molly go to the tailor to have McGee's pants pressed.

Music: Billy Mills: "A Fella With an Umbrella," "The Mad Arranger" (The King's Men, vocal), "Bluebird of Happiness"

Running Gags: "Bird book" (Wallace), "'Tain't funny, McGee" (Molly), LaTrivia blowup over "cooked his goose"
Comments: The character of Mayor LaTrivia, last heard on the June 17, 1947 show, is again assumed by Gale Gordon. The elusive bluebird of happiness still has not found its way into the Wimple love nest.

Date: October 12, 1948
Title: Quits Smoking
Cast: Jim Jordan (Fibber), Marian Jordan (Molly, Teeny), Harlow Wilcox, Bill Thompson (Wallace Wimple), Gale Gordon (Mayor LaTrivia), Arthur Q. Bryan (Doctor Gamble).
Summary: After giving up cigars, Fibber feels so rejuvenated he begins tearing around the living room like a dynamo.
Music: Billy Mills: "You Call Everybody Darling," "It's a Most Unusual Day" (The King's Men, vocal), "In My Dreams"
Running Gags: LaTrivia blowup over "new broom sweeps clean," hall closet opened by LaTrivia seeking the front door, Mrs. Kladderhatch bit involving husband/rare case/house for rent (Gamble)
Comments: The writers, sparked by the untapped potential of the January 23, 1945 episode, blew a few smoke rings around Fibber's bundle of energy, and turned out a program that has a different feel from start to finish.

Date: October 19, 1948
Title: Radio Retrieved from Repairman
Cast: Jim Jordan (Fibber), Marian Jordan (Molly, Teeny), Harlow Wilcox, Bill Thompson (Wallace Wimple), Gale Gordon (Mayor LaTrivia), Arthur Q. Bryan (Doctor Gamble), Jess Kirkpatrick (Freddy)
Summary: The McGees visit Freddy's Audio and Video Studio to retrieve a portable radio Fibber left the previous spring in a dispute over the price of a battery.
Music: Billy Mills: "Hair of Gold," "Love Somebody" (The King's Men, vocal), "You Were Only Fooling"
Running Gag: Tongue twister starting with "two-toned tuna" (Fibber)
Comments: The tongue twister is one of the few that ever got the better of Jim as evidenced by Marian's remark of "Not even if you could say it again" which brings down the house and gets a hand. The joke about Fred Allen and *Stop the Music* is an allusion to the popular game show which was eroding listeners away from the comedian's show.

Date: October 26, 1948
Title: Planting Grass
Cast: Jim Jordan (Fibber), Marian Jordan (Molly), Harlow Wilcox, Bill Thompson (Old Timer, Wallace Wimple), Gale Gordon (Mayor LaTrivia), Arthur Q. Bryan (Doctor Gamble)

Summary: With his usual sense of bad timing, Fibber plants grass seed in the middle of fall.
Music: Billy Mills: "Lavender Blue" (The King's Men, vocal), "The 12th Street Rag," "Until"
Running Gags: "That ain't the way I heered it" (Old Timer), LaTrivia blowup over "playing possum"
Comments: Fibber leaves himself wide open when he says that "when I finish plowing, you'll find me harrowing," a straight line Molly has to fight off audibly. Fibber gives voice to what is a first for *Fibber McGee and Molly* and perhaps for radio, that of a Chinese Eskimo. The plea for the Community Chest in the tag appeals to both the heart and the head.

Date: November 2, 1948 Election Returns—No *Fibber McGee and Molly* broadcast.

Date: November 9, 1948
Title: Reupholstering Davenport
Cast: Jim Jordan (Fibber), Marian Jordan (Molly, Teeny), Harlow Wilcox, Bill Thompson (Old Timer, Wallace Wimple), Gale Gordon (Mayor LaTrivia), Arthur Q. Bryan (Doctor Gamble), Herb Vigran (Louis)
Summary: After Fibber's efforts to recover the sofa himself stall, the McGees seek the advice of a professional upholsterer.
Music: Billy Mills: "Little Girl," "Shine On, Harvest Moon" (The King's Men, vocal), "You Walk By"
Running Gags: "'Tain't funny, McGee" (Molly), Mrs. Kladderhatch bit involving glued hand to flat board/thirteen spades playing bridge (Gamble), LaTrivia blowup over "strike a happy medium"
Comments: An elephant and donkey appear in Fibber's "The Monkey and the Coconut" song to capitalize on the election held the previous Tuesday. When unexpected audience reaction temporarily keeps Bill from proceeding, he ad-libs a complaint all comedians would love to encounter: "Can't get a straight line into the laughs." When Fibber pulls the old/new gag with Wilcox and adds that "I haven't used that one for a long time," he speaks the truth: the last time was on November 27, 1945 when he switched "new car, old top" with "new top, old car."

Date: November 16, 1948
Title: Bowling Substitute
Cast: Jim Jordan (Fibber), Marian Jordan (Molly, Teeny), Harlow Wilcox, Bill Thompson (Old Timer), Gale Gordon (Mayor LaTrivia), Arthur Q. Bryan (Doctor Gamble), Herb Vigran (Fred Allen)
Summary: While Fibber searches for a fourth for bowling, Molly keeps dropping hints that she wants to fill the vacancy until she finally takes matters into her own hands.

Music: Billy Mills: "Buttons and Bows," "Bella Bella Marie" (The King's Men, vocal), "Lonesome"
Running Gag: Tongue twister starting with "beating batter" (Fibber)
Comments: During the tongue twister Jim utters the most famous blooper heard on the show, *bladder,* a word considered indelicate in 1948. However, he knew that booboos bring chuckles, not boos, so he is there later to magnify Harlow's slight stutter into "Yes, any-any minute now." The unseen character of Fifi Tremaine, whose presence in the Wistful Vista geography was felt in a number of 1946 episodes, is reintroduced to create some sparks of romantic rivalry between Gamble and LaTrivia. The name of the bowling establishment being Allen's Alley is mentioned in passing and the dialogue is carefully arranged so the owner's first name of *Fred* and surname of *Allen* are not used together, both of which comprise a tip of the fedora to radio's leading wit.

Date: November 23, 1948
Title: Pheasant Dinner
Cast: Jim Jordan (Fibber), Marian Jordan (Molly, Teeny), Harlow Wilcox, Bill Thompson (Old Timer, Wallace Wimple), Gale Gordon (Mayor LaTrivia), Arthur Q. Bryan (Doctor Gamble)
Summary: Fibber plans a special way of cooking pheasants by wrapping them in clay and roasting them in the fireplace.
Music: Billy Mills: "Every Day I Love You a Little Bit More," "I've Got 160 Acres" (The King's Men, vocal), "Powder Your Face With Sunshine"
Running Gags: "That ain't the way I heered it" (Old Timer), word confusion involving *prefabricate/prevaricate/eradicated/barricade* (Fibber, Molly), hall closet opened by Fibber looking for clay, LaTrivia blowup over "always had my nose in a book"
Comments: Ever since this episode aired listeners have undoubtedly been struck in the middle of the night with this question: "Why did Fibber have *three* basketball shoes?" At least on this occasion Fibber abandons his belief that Teeny is a midget as he grudgingly mutters "Precocious child" after her exit.

Date: November 30, 1948
Title: Streetlight
Cast: Jim Jordan (Fibber), Marian Jordan (Molly, Teeny), Harlow Wilcox, Bill Thompson (Old Timer), Gale Gordon (Mayor LaTrivia), Arthur Q. Bryan (Doctor Gamble), Herb Vigran (officer)
Summary: After Fibber gets no results from the city in having a streetlight bulb replaced, he decides to do the job himself.
Music: Billy Mills: "A Slow Boat to China," "Stick-To-It-Ivity" (The King's Men, vocal), "Bouquet of Roses"
Running Gag: Myrt bit involving brother/shakes/putting on roof (Fibber)

Comments: Jim turns a mistake by the sound effects man who needed three cracks at a bulb into the biggest laugh of the night with the ad-lib "It finally broke." Hot-tempered LaTrivia spews the oddest oath ever heard on the program when he exclaims "Sweet Genevieve in a marble scooter!"

Date: December 7, 1948
Title: Early Christmas Shopping
Cast: Jim Jordan (Fibber), Marian Jordan (Molly), Harlow Wilcox, Bill Thompson (Old Timer, Wallace Wimple), Gale Gordon (Mayor LaTrivia), Arthur Q. Bryan (Doctor Gamble)
Summary: The McGees hope to simplify their shopping at the Bon Ton by having the store employees wrap all their gifts.
Music: Billy Mills: "Only Fifteen Shopping Days Till Christmas" (The King's Men, vocal), "For You," "Rendezvous with a Rose"
Running Gag: LaTrivia blowup over "took the bull by the horns"
Comments: This episode features one of the best blowups by LaTrivia as his spoonerisms, explosion of temper, and delivery of "Why would I call on Miss Tremaine with a dead bull?" work to exquisite comic effect. An anachronism occurs when Molly declares that Fibber had caused the front step to become loose in 1932, three years before they moved into 79 Wistful Vista.

Date: December 14, 1948
Title: Wins a Salmon
Cast: Jim Jordan (Fibber), Marian Jordan (Molly, Teeny), Harlow Wilcox, Bill Thompson (Old Timer), Gale Gordon (Mayor LaTrivia), Arthur Q. Bryan (Doctor Gamble), Jack Kirkwood (Kremer), Herb Vigran (bus driver, man on street)
Summary: Fibber's premonition that this is his lucky day is reinforced when he wins a salmon in a fish market.
Music: Billy Mills: "A Little Bird Told Me," "Buttons and Bows" (The King's Men, vocal)
Running Gag: McGee and Molly blowup over "what's cooking"
Comments: The idea of McGee feeling lucky and the events of the day proving to be disastrous, first employed on February 13, 1940, received good results every time it was used.

Date: December 21, 1948
Title: Christmas Card from Elizabeth
Cast: Jim Jordan (Fibber), Marian Jordan (Molly, Teeny), Harlow Wilcox, Bill Thompson (Wallace Wimple, Old Timer), Gale Gordon (Mayor LaTrivia), Arthur Q. Bryan (Doctor Gamble)
Summary: The McGees are mystified by a Christmas card sent to Fibber from someone named Elizabeth.

Music: Billy Mills: Medley of Christmas melodies, "Let's Have an Old-Fashioned Christmas" (The King's Men, vocal), "Powder Your Face With Sunshine"
Running Gag: "'Tain't funny, McGee" (Molly)
Comments: Molly delivers a Quinn and Leslie quote of note when she defines the dangerous age for men as being "the period of time between when his pants get long and his wind gets short." The traditional "'Twas the Night Before Christmas" is omitted this year.

Date: December 28, 1948
Title: Country Club Dance
Cast: Jim Jordan (Fibber), Marian Jordan (Molly), Harlow Wilcox, Bill Thompson (Wallace Wimple, angry neighbor), Gale Gordon (Mayor LaTrivia), Arthur Q. Bryan (Doctor Gamble, Mike), Bea Benaderet (Genevieve MacDonald, angry neighbor), Jack Kirkwood (Walter Argebright)
Summary: The McGees spend a pleasant evening in high society as a guest of Mayor LaTrivia.
Music: Billy Mills: "You Were Only Fooling," "Pledge to Good Fellowship" (The King's Men, vocal), "I Love You So Much It Hurts Me"
Running Gags: Tongue twister starting with "Long Bong Tong" (Fibber), LaTrivia blowup over "going to sleep around the clock"
Comments: Fibber not only doesn't stand on formality, he actually squats on it by addressing the governor as Walt and Mrs. MacDonald as Gen immediately upon being introduced to them. A question that may not occur to listeners until after the program is over is why does Fibber go to the door after the bell rings when the McGees usually say, "Come in." (Fibber would probably answer that question by replying, "I was reading ahead and I knew it was a boy delivering flowers who had no lines.") Those same listeners are apt to do serious thinking concerning safety on the road after hearing Jim and Marian's warning about the consequences of careless driving.

Date: January 4, 1949
Title: Weather-Stripping the Door
Cast: Jim Jordan (Fibber), Marian Jordan (Molly), Harlow Wilcox, Bill Thompson (Old Timer, Wallace Wimple), Gale Gordon (Mayor LaTrivia), Arthur Q. Bryan (Doctor Gamble)
Summary: The house is frigid because Fibber forgot to order oil for the furnace so his method of making the place warmer is to take the front door off and put weather stripping on it.
Music: Billy Mills: *"Cuanto La Gusta,"* "Saskatchewan" (The King's Men, vocal), "That Certain Party"
Running Gags: None

Comments: The use of transcribed commercials for Johnson's Wax by a pitchman other than Wilcox will become more common in months to come. Not one of the program's better episodes, the biggest laugh of the night comes from the commercial line ("Pour it out/Spread it around/Let it dry") that the McGees steal from Wilcox.

Date: January 11, 1949
Title: Sleigh Ride With a Meal
Cast: Jim Jordan (Fibber), Marian Jordan (Molly), Harlow Wilcox, Bill Thompson (Old Timer, Wallace Wimple), Gale Gordon (Mayor LaTrivia), Arthur Q. Bryan (Doctor Gamble), Herb Vigran (sleigh driver)
Summary: The McGees arrange for a sleigh ride with their friends, but the best-sleighed plans of ice and men often go a-dray.
Music: Billy Mills: "Lavender Blue," "A Little Bird Told Me" (The King's Men, vocal)
Running Gags: Hall closet opened by Fibber looking for book with phone number, Myrt bit involving brother/beef with cops/beef on rye (Fibber), LaTrivia blowup over *hockey*
Comments: Molly's recollection of receiving her first kiss from Fibber on a sleigh ride contradicts the information she gave to her husband in the April 22, 1947 episode when she remembered that first buss occurring in a Ferris wheel. This week's audience, which grants applause to the Old Timer upon his entrance and to LaTrivia near the end of his tirade, seems more responsive than those attending the show the previous Tuesday who turned a cold shoulder to at least four gags.

Date: January 18, 1949
Title: Money in a Shoebox
Cast: Jim Jordan (Fibber), Marian Jordan (Molly, Teeny), Harlow Wilcox, Bill Thompson (Wallace Wimple), Gale Gordon (Mayor LaTrivia), Arthur Q. Bryan (Doctor Gamble), Herb Vigran (sergeant)
Summary: After Fibber brings home a shoebox filled with $5,000, he intends to keep the windfall while Molly insists that they find the person to whom the money belongs and return it.
Music: Billy Mills: "So in Love," "Galway Bay" (The King's Men, vocal), "One Has My Name"
Running Gags: None
Comments: When Fibber actually gets his hands on large amounts of money as he did when he found the fortune in a sofa on November 17, 1942, the promise of a life of real wealth is, like the currency, phony. This episode marks the fifth time someone makes a remark about what Fibber does for a living or his lack of a job.

Date: January 25, 1949
Title: Laundry to the Sudsomat
Cast: Jim Jordan (Fibber), Marian Jordan (Molly), Harlow Wilcox, Bill Thompson (Old Timer, Wallace Wimple), Gale Gordon (Mayor LaTrivia), Arthur Q. Bryan (Doctor Gamble), Ed Begley (Kremer)
Summary: After Fibber fixes their washing machine but (no) good, the McGees take their laundry to be cleaned at the sudsomat.
Music: Billy Mills: "I've Got My Love to Keep Me Warm," "Skyball Paint" (The King's Men, vocal)
Running Gag: LaTrivia blowup over *crow's nest*, "That ain't the way I heered it" (Old Timer), "'Tain't funny, McGee" (Molly)
Comments: Fibber may have stumbled on to the reason physicians prescribe a diet of vegetables for patients when he reports the medical examiner's reason for advising McGee to eat copious amounts of carrots: "It'll get rid of a lotta carrots and I hate 'em." The hint of Fibber buying something for the next holiday should tip off perceptive listeners as to what he has up his sleeve.

Date: February 1, 1949
Title: Learning How to Listen
Cast: Jim Jordan (Fibber), Marian Jordan (Molly, Teeny), Harlow Wilcox, Bill Thompson (Old Timer), Gale Gordon (Mayor LaTrivia), Arthur Q. Bryan (Doctor Gamble)
Summary: Fibber's resolution to stop interrupting people culminates in a bet with Gamble that requires him to control his bad habit for five minutes.
Music: Billy Mills: "Powder Your Face With Sunshine," "Siesta" (The King's Men, vocal)
Running Gags: Word confusion involving *aqueduct/adequate/etiquette* (Fibber, Molly), "'Tain't funny, McGee" (Molly)
Comments: Based upon the stories he has told, Fibber's claim that his life has been so much more interesting than anybody else's is hard to refute. And for imagery of noiselessness, Fibber's attempt to be "quieter than a rubber-heeled butterfly tiptoeing over twenty feet of wet moss" is hard to beat.

Date: February 8, 1949
Title: Date on the Calendar
Cast: Jim Jordan (Fibber), Marian Jordan (Molly, Teeny), Harlow Wilcox, Bill Thompson (Old Timer, Wallace Wimple), Gale Gordon (Mayor LaTrivia), Arthur Q. Bryan (Doctor Gamble)
Summary: Because Fibber believes the circled date on the calendar is Molly's birthday, he plans a surprise party for her.
Music: Billy Mills: "Here I'll Stay," "The Pussycat Song" (The King's Men, vocal)
Running Gag: LaTrivia blowup over "pay for a dead horse"

Comments: Molly's birthday moves around to fit the convenience of the writers. Her birth month in this episode is given as April which was actually correct for Marian as well who was born on April 15th. In 1951 Molly's birthday will be celebrated in October.

Date: February 15, 1949
Title: Looking for 1414 14th Street
Cast: Jim Jordan (Fibber), Marian Jordan (Molly), Harlow Wilcox, Bill Thompson (Englishman on street, Old Timer), Gale Gordon (Mayor LaTrivia), Arthur Q. Bryan (Doctor Gamble), Bea Benaderet (gabby woman), Dick LeGrand (janitor)
Summary: The McGees search all along 14th Street for the house of a dressmaker.
Music: Billy Mills: "Little Jack Frost, Get Lost," "Sunflower" (The King's Men, vocal), "As You Desire Me"
Running Gag: "Gotta get them brakes fixed" (Fibber)
Comments: This episode is loaded with vivid figures of speech like "she's got less sense of direction than a punch-drunk pigeon sitting on a weathervane in a Kansas tornado" that Fibber utters during his fits of pique.

Date: February 22, 1949
Title: Impressing Visitor from Canada
Cast: Jim Jordan (Fibber), Marian Jordan (Molly), Harlow Wilcox (train announcer), Bill Thompson (Crevice), Gale Gordon (Mayor LaTrivia), Bea Benaderet (information clerk), Howard Duff (Harry Sedgwick)
Summary: To impress a visitor, the McGees pretend that LaTrivia's house is their home.
Music: Billy Mills: "Far Away Places," "Oklahoma" (The King's Men, vocal), "Powder Your Face With Sunshine"
Running Gag: LaTrivia blowup over "won't let the cat out of the bag"
Comments: In passing Molly gives listeners a quick glance at their modest home: six rooms with a 72-inch driveway. Long-time listeners with good memories will recall a similar ruse employed by the McGees to impress a rich visitor on the December 26, 1939 program. This is a rare episode in which Bill Thompson does not assume the part of any of his regular characters.

Date: March 1, 1949
Title: Jalopy
Cast: Jim Jordan (Fibber), Marian Jordan (Molly, Teeny), Harlow Wilcox, Bill Thompson (Old Timer), Gale Gordon (Mayor LaTrivia), Arthur Q. Bryan (Doctor Gamble), Bea Benaderet (gabby woman)
Summary: The McGees try to dispose of an old car parked in front of their house.

Music: Billy Mills: "Brush Those Tears From Your Eyes," "It's What You Do With What You Got" (The King's Men, vocal), "Hold Me"
Running Gags: None
Comments: The joke about Milt Spilk sets up the appearance of a character by that name the following month. In an apparent move to put a little variety in the program, the writers short-circuited the running gags by giving the Old Timer the "I'll ignore it" switch on his catch phrase and having Myrt and LaTrivia play it straight. The "still think that kid's a midget" line is submerged under the music at the end.

Date: March 8, 1949
Title: Elks Club Mortgage
Cast: Jim Jordan (Fibber), Marian Jordan (Molly), Harlow Wilcox, Bill Thompson (Old Timer, Wallace Wimple), Gale Gordon (Mayor LaTrivia), Arthur Q. Bryan (Doctor Gamble), Bea Benaderet (gabby woman), Dick LeGrand (Ole Swenson)
Summary: Fibber, planning a speech to commemorate the burning of the mortgage held on the Elks clubhouse, goes at the job like a house afire.
Music: Billy Mills: "Someone Like You," "Clancy Lowered the Boom" (The King's Men, vocal), "Everywhere You Go"
Running Gags: LaTrivia blowup over "kept it under my hat," "I'm yust donating my time" (Ole)
Comments: Some recordings of this broadcast commence with the tinkle of the plastic glass hitting the floor used during the audience warm-up. (More explanation of this device is included in the comments of the May 3, 1949 show.) As Dick LeGrand makes his first appearance as Ole, almost the first words out of his mouth are those that will become his catch phrase. The "It's swarm/Take your coat off" wheeze may have been in circulation when the clubhouse was built in 1867.

Date: March 15, 1949
Title: Doc Gamble Day
Cast: Jim Jordan (Fibber), Marian Jordan (Molly, Teeny), Harlow Wilcox, Bill Thompson (Wallace Wimple), Gale Gordon (Mayor LaTrivia), Arthur Q. Bryan (Doctor Gamble), Dick LeGrand (Ole Swenson), Virginia Gordon (Miss Dalloway)
Summary: The citizens of Wistful Vista honor Doctor Gamble for his thirty years of service to the town thanks to modest McGee who lets everyone know "I thought it up."
Music: Billy Mills: "Red Roses for a Blue Lady," "Ohee-Ohi-Oho," (The King's Men, vocal), "My Dream Is Yours"
Running Gag: "I'm yust donating my time" (Ole)
Comments: Fibber shows his true affection for Gamble by risking his health to be with his friend at the end. For once a blooper by Jim makes sense when

he mistakenly says, "Drum and beagle corps from the big pound" instead of "Drum and bugle corps from the big pond."

Date: March 22, 1949
Title: Models a Dress for Molly
Cast: Jim Jordan (Fibber), Marian Jordan (Molly), Harlow Wilcox, Bill Thompson (Old Timer), Gale Gordon (Mayor LaTrivia), Arthur Q. Bryan (Doctor Gamble), Dick LeGrand (Ole Swenson), Virginia Gordon (Miss Armadel)
Summary: Because Fibber ruined Molly's dress form, he has to model the garment she is making which she hopes to wear to a convention in Chicago.
Music: Billy Mills: "You Was" (The King's Men, vocal), "Sunflower," "Someone Like You"
Running Gags: "I'm yust donating my time" (Ole), hall closet opened by Ole thinking it was the side door, LaTrivia blowup over upper and lower berths
Comments: The plot of this episode is quite similar to the one aired on June 18, 1940. A dramatic instance of how times change is the Old Timer's recollection that his sister who dressed in flour sacks was known as Madame XXX, a symbol of down-on-the-farm wholesomeness, whereas a woman with that title today would likely be a performer in pornographic movies.

Date: March 29, 1949
Title: Thousand Pound Inheritance
Cast: Jim Jordan (Fibber), Marian Jordan (Molly, Teeny), Harlow Wilcox, Bill Thompson (Wallace Wimple), Gale Gordon (Mayor LaTrivia), Arthur Q. Bryan (Doctor Gamble), Dick LeGrand (Ole Swenson), Bud Stefan (delivery man)
Summary: After McGee receives news of a legacy from the estate of a British uncle, Fibber puts on airs and his English accent in anticipation of receiving the money and a possible title.
Music: Billy Mills: "Rosewood Spinet," "I Wake Up Every Morning" (The King's Men, vocal)
Running Gags: "I'm yust donating my time," (Ole), "Bird book" (Wallace)
Comments: Bud Stefan appears for the first time. An indication of the strength of the dollar in 1949 (or the weakness of it now) is that Molly says that 1,000 pounds is equivalent to $4,000.

Date: April 5, 1949
Title: Cash Register at Kremer's
Cast: Jim Jordan (Fibber), Marian Jordan (Molly), Harlow Wilcox, Bill Thompson (Old Timer), Gale Gordon (Mayor LaTrivia), Arthur Q. Bryan (Doctor Gamble), Dick LeGrand (Ole Swenson), Bud Stefan (Milton Spilk)
Summary: Against Kremer's wishes Fibber attempts to repair the drugstore's cash register.

Music: Billy Mills: "Great Guns," "Lavender Blue" (The King's Men, vocal), "Candy Kisses"
Running Gags: "Yust donating my time" (Ole), LaTrivia blowup over "by way of shank's mare"
Comments: This is an uncommon episode in which all of the action occurs downtown. The two-part article by Robert Yoder appearing in *Saturday Evening Post* that is mentioned in the introduction and the tag is the most comprehensive study of *Fibber McGee and Molly* published during the years the program was on the air.

Date: April 12, 1949
Title: Smoking a Pipe
Cast: Jim Jordan (Fibber), Marian Jordan (Molly), Harlow Wilcox, Bill Thompson (Wallace Wimple), Gale Gordon (Mayor LaTrivia), Arthur Q. Bryan (Doctor Gamble), Dick LeGrand (Ole Swenson), Bud Stefan (Milton Spilk)
Summary: Fibber hopes to take up smoking a pipe if he can just light more tobacco than matches.
Music: Billy Mills: "No Orchids For My Lady," "If You Stub Your Toe on the Moon" (The King's Men, vocal), "You Broke Your Promise"
Running Gags: "He was yust donating his time" (Ole), Mrs. Kladderhatch bit involving wrinkles/prunes (Gamble)
Comments: Quinn and Leslie knew how to select *le mot juste*. By calling Fibber's tobacco Old Mustard Mouth no more needed to be said about its quality or fragrance, Molly's suggestion of Old Saddle Blanket finishing out of the money. This episode also features an exquisite insult, so striking that even Molly comments on its loveliness, coming from Gamble who portrays Fibber appearing "as intellectual as the third man from the bottom of a lightning-struck totem pole."

Date: April 19, 1949
Title: Fire Truck
Cast: Jim Jordan (Fibber), Marian Jordan (Molly, Teeny), Harlow Wilcox, Bill Thompson (Old Timer), Gale Gordon (Mayor LaTrivia), Dick LeGrand (Ole Swenson), Bud Stefan (Milton Spilk), Ken Christy (Mike Casey)
Summary: After Fibber dents a fender on the new fire truck, the McGees take it on the lam.
Music: Billy Mills: "Bali Ha'i," "The Beautiful Blonde from Bashful Bend" (The King's Men, vocal), "You'd Be Hard to Replace"
Running Gags: None
Comments: This is another episode in which all the events occur away from 79 Wistful Vista. More convoluted questions like the perplexing query Fibber asks of Wilcox will be asked in coming months with better comic effect than this one.

Date: April 26, 1949
Title: Organizing Housework
Cast: Jim Jordan (Fibber), Marian Jordan (Molly), Harlow Wilcox, Bill Thompson (Wallace Wimple), Gale Gordon (Mayor LaTrivia), Arthur Q. Bryan (Doctor Gamble), Dick LeGrand (Ole Swenson), Bud Stefan (Milton Spilk)
Summary: By taking over Molly's chores and finishing them according to a schedule, Fibber intends to show his wife how to work efficiently.
Music: Billy Mills: "I'm Gonna Wash That Man Right Out of My Hair," "I Want to Marry Mary" (The King's Men, vocal), "Once and For Always"
Running Gags: "Yust donating my time" (Ole), word confusion involving *epidermis/epidemic/hypodermic/hypochondriac* (Fibber, Molly, Gamble), LaTrivia blowup over "makes strange bedfellows," "Bird book" (Wallace)
Comments: Jim, Marian, and Arthur have some unscheduled fun when they step on each other's lines. Entrances are handled rather awkwardly in this episode with either Molly or Fibber identifying the people who come through the door as if the other spouse needs to reminded who these weekly visitors are.

Date: May 3, 1949
Title: Good Deeds
Cast: Jim Jordan (Fibber), Marian Jordan (Molly), Harlow Wilcox, Bill Thompson (Old Timer, Breen), Gale Gordon (Mayor LaTrivia), Arthur Q. Bryan (Doctor Gamble), Dick LeGrand (Ole Swenson), Bud Stefan (Milton Spilk)
Summary: Fibber tries to make up for all the good deeds he has not performed since taking his Boy Scout oath.
Music: Billy Mills: "Streets of Laredo," "Busy Doing Nothing" (The King's Men, vocal), "Where is the One?"
Running Gag: "'Tain't funny, McGee" (Molly) "I'm yust donating my time" (Ole)
Comments: Wilcox chokes during the opening commercial, yet recovers remarkably quickly to read the introduction to bring on Fibber and Molly. His remark of "I need a glass of water like Fibber had" refers to the warm-up routine preceding shows when, just before going on the air, Jim would drink some water and toss the container over his shoulder, causing the audience to explode with laughter when they saw that the glass was made of plastic. Fibber's comment of "I wish I could do something for him" about Ole after the janitor mentioned the problem of a leaky roof on his rented house points to the subject of the following week's show.

Date: May 10, 1949
Title: House for Ole
Cast: Jim Jordan (Fibber), Marian Jordan (Molly), Harlow Wilcox, Bill Thompson (Old Timer), Gale Gordon (Mayor LaTrivia), Arthur Q. Bryan

(Doctor Gamble), Dick LeGrand (Ole Swenson), Bud Stefan (Milton Spilk), Ed Begley (Marvin), Jess Kirkpatrick (Eck Conley)
Summary: After Ole is evicted, the Elks pitch in to build a house for him and his family in one day.
Music: Billy Mills: "Always True to You in My Fashion," "Riders in the Sky" (The King's Men, vocal), "Red Roses for a Blue Lady"
Running Gags: "Let's skip it" (switch by Old Timer), word confusion over the state fish hatchery (Fibber, Molly, LaTrivia), "You poor fellas yust been donating your time" (Ole)
Summary: As usual when there is a project to be done, Fibber contributes his biggest asset (his mouth) by bossing everybody around. The integrated commercial is skillfully crosscut with sound effects of saw and hammer to pound home its message. Early in the show Molly provides a clue about Ole owning a lot that becomes significant later.

Date: May 17, 1949
Title: Suit for Doc
Cast: Jim Jordan (Fibber), Marian Jordan (Molly, Teeny), Harlow Wilcox, Bill Thompson (Old Timer, irate driver), Gale Gordon (Mayor LaTrivia), Arthur Q. Bryan (Doctor Gamble), Dick LeGrand (Ole Swenson), Joseph Kearns (clerk)
Summary: After convincing Doc he needs to update his wardrobe, the McGees accompany Gamble to the Bon Ton to shop for a new suit.
Music: Billy Mills: "Some Enchanted Evening," "A, You're Adorable" (The King's Men, vocal), "It's Summertime Again"
Running Gags: "You're yust donating your time" (Ole), LaTrivia blowup over "I've killed two birds with one stone"
Comments: The idea of Fibber and Molly rejecting suits and making comments about fabrics had so much potential that it was expanded on the January 24, 1950 episode with Cliff Arquette as the harried clerk.

Date: May 24, 1949
Title: Writing Movie Script
Cast: Jim Jordan (Fibber), Marian Jordan (Molly), Harlow Wilcox, Bill Thompson (Wallace Wimple), Gale Gordon (Mayor LaTrivia), Arthur Q. Bryan (Doctor Gamble), Dick LeGrand (Ole Swenson), Bud Stefan (Milton Spilk)
Summary: McGee writes a scenario on the history of the typewriter.
Music: Billy Mills: "Careless Hands," "The Typewriter Serenade" (The King's Men, vocal)
Running Gags: None
Comments: The titles of both musical selections are in the same key as the show's theme this week. This is another of the pun-filled episodes right up to Fibber's closing line. Ideas come from many places, but if Charles Schulz

had listened to Fibber's mixture of disparate plotlines that never come together, the bit might have been filed away in his subconscious until awakened years later by a beagle sitting in front of a typewriter on a doghouse.

Date: May 31, 1949
Title: Canoeing
Cast: Jim Jordan (Fibber), Marian Jordan (Molly, Teeny), Harlow Wilcox, Bill Thompson (Old Timer), Gale Gordon (Mayor LaTrivia), Arthur Q. Bryan (Doctor Gamble), Dick LeGrand (Ole Swenson), Bud Stefan (Milton Spilk)
Summary: After expressing well wishes to their friends for the summer, Fibber and Molly go canoeing on Dugan's Lake.
Music: Billy Mills: "Five Foot Two," "Cruising Down the River" (The King's Men, vocal)
Running Gags: "I'm yust donating my time" (Ole), LaTrivia blowup over "I always pick a herringbone," hall closet opened by LaTrivia seeking the front door (misdirected by Fibber)
Comments: Director Frank Pittman is mentioned in the credits as he has been for the final show the previous two seasons. The writers tease listeners by having Fibber mention something in the closet twice before lowering the boom with LaTrivia. The Old Timer claims to be 116. Ken Darby and The King's Men host the summer replacement which features King for a Night, a musical guest star each week.

Date: September 13, 1949
Title: Fifteenth Anniversary Special
Cast: Jim Jordan (Fibber), Marian Jordan (Molly, Teeny), Harlow Wilcox, Bill Thompson (Wallace Wimple, Old Timer), Harold Peary (Throckmorton P. Gildersleeve), Gale Gordon (Mayor LaTrivia), Dick LeGrand (Ole Swenson), Dinah Shore, Robert Young, Phil Harris, Alice Faye, Perry Como, Irene Dunne, Dennis Day, William Bendix, Bob Hope
Summary: Movie and radio stars stop by to congratulate Fibber and Molly for fifteen years on NBC for Johnson's Wax.
Music: Billy Mills: "So in Love," "A Wonderful Guy" (Dinah Shore, vocal), "Give Me Your Hand" (Perry Como, vocal), "I'll Take You Home, Kathleen" (Dennis Day, vocal), medley of old-time songs consisting of "I'm Always Chasing Rainbows," "You Tell Me Your Dream," and "Side By Side" (The King's Men, vocal)
Running Gags: LaTrivia blowup over *dinosaur/Dinah Shore*, "'Tain't funny, McGee" (Molly), "Bird book" (Wallace), "I'm yust donating my time" (Ole), tongue twister starting with Long Under Ware McGee (Fibber)
Comments: This is the only sixty-minute episode in the program's history. The purpose of this special broadcast is primarily to promote NBC shows returning to the air for the new season. Bob Hope's comment, "There's only

a few of us left," refers to *The Jack Benny Program*, *Amos 'n' Andy*, and other shows which had moved to CBS. The Gildersleeve skit was not the only recycled material; the hand-me-down and necktie gags by the Old Timer and Fibber's tongue twister had also been used before.

Date: September 20, 1949
Title: Mustard Slogan
Cast: Jim Jordan (Fibber), Marian Jordan (Molly), Harlow Wilcox, Bill Thompson (Old Timer), Gale Gordon (Mayor LaTrivia), Arthur Q. Bryan (Doctor Gamble), Dick LeGrand (Ole Swenson), Bud Stefan (Milton Spilk)
Summary: Fibber works on a slogan for Middleton's Mustard that could win him $1,000.
Music: Billy Mills: "Hucklebuck," "The Merrily Song" (The King's Men, vocal)
Running Gags: "'Tain't funny, McGee" (Molly), hall closet opened by Milton looking for medicine, "You're yust donating your time" (Ole)
Comments: Extant recordings of this episode end after Doc's visit so modern listeners cannot hear if Fibber gets to meet Middleton. The script indicates McGee meets Middleton offstage and is disappointed after his suggestions have been rejected, but Molly saves the day by revealing a check for $1,000 because watching him lather hot dogs gave her the idea for the prizewinner: "Middleton's Mustard: it should happen to a dog."

Date: September 27, 1949
Title: Fish Dinner
Cast: Jim Jordan (Fibber), Marian Jordan (Molly, Teeny), Harlow Wilcox, Bill Thompson (Wallace Wimple), Gale Gordon (Mayor LaTrivia), Arthur Q. Bryan (Doctor Gamble), Dick LeGrand (Ole Swenson), Bud Stefan (Milton Spilk)
Summary: The McGees plan a dinner for friends because they believe Wimple is going to supply the main course for the meal.
Music: Billy Mills: "Fiddle Dee Dee," "Ichabod " (The King's Men, vocal), "You Told a Lie"
Running Gag: LaTrivia blowup over "hitting the ball"
Comments: Milton's last name was given the previous week. Quinn and Leslie, who loved switching nouns in idioms, had used "no use crying over Milt Spilk" before and now could hint at that gag each time the boy's name is given.

Date: October 4, 1949
Title: Umbrella Stand
Cast: Jim Jordan (Fibber), Marian Jordan (Molly), Harlow Wilcox, Bill Thompson (Old Timer), Gale Gordon (Mayor LaTrivia), Arthur Q. Bryan (Doctor Gamble), Dick LeGrand (bricklayer), Bud Stefan (delivery boy)

Summary: After an umbrella stand is delivered to them by mistake, the McGees take it to the Bon Ton where they find that returning it is not that easy.
Music: Billy Mills: "Toot, Toot, Tootsie," "Busy Doing Nothing" (The King's Men, vocal)
Running Gags: Myrt bit involving nephew/quarterback 90 yard run/gave quarter back (Fibber), LaTrivia blowup over iron ore
Comments: Molly's change of heart about the umbrella stand is too sudden to be credible. The entire script is not one of Quinn and Leslie's freshest, replete as it is with strained jokes (Wilcox changes a man's actual name to get into the middle commercial) and well-worn humor (the iron ore routine had been mined many times by comedians).

Date: October 11, 1949
Title: Paper into Cloth
Cast: Jim Jordan (Fibber), Marian Jordan (Molly, Teeny), Harlow Wilcox, Bill Thompson (Old Timer), Gale Gordon (Mayor LaTrivia), Arthur Q. Bryan (Doctor Gamble), Dick LeGrand (Ole Swenson), Bud Stefan (Milton Spilk)
Summary: Fibber, with nothing more than some old newspapers, a few chemicals, a washing machine, and a half-baked idea, tries to manufacture cloth out of paper.
Music: Billy Mills: "Lorabelle Lee," "Mischa, Yasha, Sasha, Tasha" (The King's Men, vocal), "Make Believe"
Running Gag: "He was yust donating his time" (Ole)
Comments: The "Fibber and Molly join us in a moment" line by Wilcox is given out of place just before the last commercial instead of after the credits are read at the beginning of the program. Molly's request for money to buy shirts, couched in terms of the episode's theme, concludes the program with a bit of wit rather than a big laugh which is not a bad tradeoff.

Date: October 18, 1949
Title: Community Chest Bazaar
Cast: Jim Jordan (Fibber), Marian Jordan (Molly, Teeny), Harlow Wilcox, Bill Thompson (Old Timer), Gale Gordon (Mayor LaTrivia), Arthur Q. Bryan (Doctor Gamble), Dick LeGrand (Ole Swenson), Bud Stefan (Milton Spilk)
Summary: Fibber is eager to sell kisses to raise money for the Community Chest, though Molly is not completely happy with the idea for obvious reasons.
Music: Billy Mills: "It's a Great Feeling," "That Lucky Old Sun" (The King's Men, vocal)
Running Gags: Mrs. Kladderhatch bit involving twitch coming back/put him to bed (Gamble), tongue twister starting with Collar Ad McGee (Fibber), LaTrivia blowup over "I'll be there with bells on"

Comments: Like the beginning of the April 20, 1948 episode, Harlow introduces the couple as "Molly McGee and Fibber." Doc's change of heart regarding Fibber offering his services in a booth should tip off listeners that something is afoot. In his conversation with the show's regular unseen patient, Gamble refers to her as Mrs. K., giving listeners an important start on the spelling of her last name. The tongue twister is a temporary return to the "knowed as" version of that gag. For a change of pace, Fibber is the one who says, "Heavenly days!"

Date: October 25, 1949
Title: Concert Tickets
Cast: Jim Jordan (Fibber), Marian Jordan (Molly), Harlow Wilcox, Bill Thompson (Old Timer), Gale Gordon (Mayor LaTrivia), Arthur Q. Bryan (Doctor Gamble), Dick LeGrand (Ole Swenson)
Summary: The McGees prepare to attend a symphony concert with tickets Fibber found at the airport.
Music: Billy Mills: "You're Breaking My Heart," "The Leader Doesn't Like Music" (The King's Men, vocal), "Someday"
Running Gags: LaTrivia blowup over "walking a tightrope all week," hall closet opened by LaTrivia seeking the front door
Comments: This is one of the racier episodes with jokes about falsies, "getting the hill out of there," and navels, but at least the closet comes clean just in time to provide the fresh shirt McGee needs. Fibber's hint in the tag about taking a ride on the streetcar points to the subject of the following week's program.

Date: November 1, 1949
Title: Trolley Riders
Cast: Jim Jordan (Fibber), Marian Jordan (Molly, Teeny), Harlow Wilcox, Bill Thompson (conductor, Old Timer), Gale Gordon (Mayor LaTrivia), Arthur Q. Bryan (Doctor Gamble), Dick LeGrand (Ole Swenson), Frank Hemingway (transit company representative)
Summary: The McGees ride the trolley to get ideas for the $100 prize offered by the transit company for ways to increase revenue.
Music: Billy Mills: "Georgia on My Mind," "The Trolley Song" (The King's Men, vocal), "Room Full of Roses"
Running Gag: "I'm yust donating my dime" (Ole)
Comments: Bill Thompson appears for the first time as the conductor who speaks in garbled tongues. His bit of getting on and off the streetcar is an ad-lib that breaks up Jim and Marian. All of the action until the tag takes place away from 79 Wistful Vista.

Date: November 8, 1949
Title: Cuckoo Clock
Cast: Jim Jordan (Fibber), Marian Jordan (Molly, Teeny), Harlow Wilcox, Bill Thompson (Old Timer), Gale Gordon (Mayor LaTrivia), Cliff Arquette (Bessie)
Summary: Fibber, trying to repair a clock Teeny brings to him, succeeds in making springs bust out all over in November.
Music: Billy Mills: "Dear Hearts and Gentle People," "Mule Train" (The King's Men, vocal)
Running Gags: LaTrivia blowup over grandfather's clock, "That ain't the way I heered it" (Old Timer)
Comments: Cliff Arquette, who last appeared on a 1936 broadcast, plays Bessie for the first time. OT and Bessie have been engaged since 1934, though it was not first betrothal for the Old Timer who will admit on the January 17, 1950 episode he was engaged to a lumberman's daughter named Mabel for almost 12 years. Listeners waiting for the hall closet door to be opened are not totally disappointed because they get to hear the clock fall apart four times.

Date: November 15, 1949
Title: Sidewalk Grating
Cast: Jim Jordan (Fibber), Marian Jordan (Molly), Harlow Wilcox, Bill Thompson (conductor, Old Timer), Arthur Q. Bryan (Doctor Gamble), Dick LeGrand (Ole Swenson), Cliff Arquette (Bessie, bystander)
Summary: After Fibber gets his hand stuck while trying to retrieve a coin, the McGees go to Gamble to have the grating removed.
Music: Billy Mills: "Ain't She Sweet?," "California Orange Blossom" (The King's Men, vocal), "You're Always There"
Running Gags: "'Tain't funny, McGee" (Molly), "That ain't the way I heered it" (Old Timer), "I'm yust donating my time" (Ole)
Comments: This episode includes the only time a single gag by Fibber prompts both the "'Tain't funny, McGee" response from Molly *and* the "That ain't the way I heered it" catch phrase from the Old Timer. The writers are obviously trying to open up the program for this is the fourth show of the season in which considerable action takes place away from the house.

Date: November 22, 1949
Title: Tax Bill
Cast: Jim Jordan (Fibber), Marian Jordan (Molly, Teeny), Harlow Wilcox, Bill Thompson (Gus), Gale Gordon (Mayor LaTrivia), Arthur Q. Bryan (Doctor Gamble), Dick LeGrand (Ole Swenson)
Summary: Fibber learns a lesson in citizenship after complaining about the amount of his property tax bill.
Music: Billy Mills: "Bye, Bye Baby," "The Last Mile Home" (The King's Men, vocal), "Happy Times"

Running Gag: McGee blowup over "no wick for the rested"

Comments: Dick LeGrand and Bill Thompson get a change of pace in this episode with Dick offering his interpretation of a Swede badly impersonating an Irishman and Bill delivering a serious patriotic message. After the joke involving *southpaw*, Jim acknowledges that the gag is dated by ad-libbing "Mrs. Bones." The importance of one letter to a joke's success is demonstrated when Jim uses *u* instead of *a* in the tag.

Date: November 29, 1949
Title: Inner Tube That's No Bargain
Cast: Jim Jordan (Fibber), Marian Jordan (Molly), Harlow Wilcox, Bill Thompson (Old Timer), Gale Gordon (Mayor LaTrivia), Arthur Q. Bryan (Doctor Gamble), Dick LeGrand (Ole Swenson), Cliff Arquette (Bessie)
Summary: The McGees experience considerable frustration as Fibber applies patch after patch to an inner tube that appears to have more holes than rubber.
Music: Billy Mills: "Now That I Need You," "Twenty-Two Shopping Days Till Christmas" (The King's Men, vocal), "Make Believe"
Running Gags: "You don't mind yust donating your time" (Ole), tongue twister starting with "patch" (Fibber), LaTrivia blowup over "birds of a feather flock together"
Comments: The writers reach back to Lena's days (and probably all the way back to vaudeville) for the Cuban heel gag. The pointed solution to the dilemma is also borrowed from an earlier episode, the November 11, 1947 adventure with living room inflation.

Date: December 6, 1949
Title: Painting Christmas Cards
Cast: Jim Jordan (Fibber), Marian Jordan (Molly, Teeny), Harlow Wilcox, Bill Thompson (Old Timer), Gale Gordon (Mayor LaTrivia), Arthur Q. Bryan (Doctor Gamble), Dick LeGrand (Ole Swenson)
Summary: Fibber gives way to his creative urges by painting his own Christmas cards and composing apposite verses for each card.
Music: Billy Mills: "She Wore a Yellow Ribbon," "Rudolph, the Red-Nosed Reindeer" (The King's Men and Teeny, vocal), "Dear Hearts and Gentle People"
Running Gags: Hall closet opened by LaTrivia looking for the front door, word confusion involving *specific/prolific/terrific* (Fibber, Molly)
Comments: As usual, when the subject of the program is art, Quinn and Leslie satirize surrealistic painting. Having LaTrivia confuse the closet door with the front door is pretty contrived, but by 1949 finding new ways of getting that gag in and the character out before the musical number began must have been harder than locating anything in that tumbling-down chamber of horrors in the hall.

Date: December 13, 1949
Title: Man of the Year
Cast: Jim Jordan (Fibber), Marian Jordan (Molly), Harlow Wilcox, Bill Thompson (conductor, Old Timer), Gale Gordon (Mayor LaTrivia), Arthur Q. Bryan (Doctor Gamble), Cliff Arquette (Bessie), Herb Vigran (chief of police), Peter Leeds (J. Worthington Grift)
Summary: Fibber forks over $77.50 for copies of a book that will show him as a man of the year despite Molly's warnings that the promotion is just a racket.
Music: Billy Mills: "The Johnson Rag," "The Old Master Painter" (The King's Men, vocal), "Dear Hearts and Gentle People"
Running Gag: LaTrivia blowup over "it's better to be a big toad in a little puddle..."
Comments: Peter Leeds appears for the first time. LaTrivia's bit about the bellows is a bit awkward, but it does allow Gordon to demonstrate what he did better than anyone in radio, i.e. blow his top.

Date: December 20, 1949
Title: Christmas Decorations
Cast: Jim Jordan (Fibber), Marian Jordan (Molly, Teeny), Harlow Wilcox, Bill Thompson (Old Timer), Gale Gordon (Mayor LaTrivia), Dick LeGrand (Ole Swenson), Cliff Arquette (Bessie), Herb Vigran (Herbert Appel)
Summary: Fibber buys loads of Christmas lights to put in front of the house so the McGees might have one of the best-decorated homes in Wistful Vista.
Music: Billy Mills: Medley of Christmas melodies, "'Twas the Night Before Christmas" (The King's Men and Teeny, vocal)
Running Gag: LaTrivia blowup over "Netcher for dogcatcher"
Comments: LaTrivia delivers a Quinn and Leslie quote of note when he draws this line of distinction: "A statesman is always out to get his country the best deal he can. A politician is always out to get his." The quirk given to Herb Vigran's character by the writers is to have him either push the last letters of words to the beginning of the next words or to squeeze two words together. Jim has trouble with his vowels like he did on the November 12th show when he spells the last four letters of *Christmas* as *t-m-u-s*. Cliff Arquette's rendering of Bessie's letter is a folksy foretaste of the style he would employ later as Charley Weaver reading missives from mama.

Date: December 27, 1949
Title: Trip to Aunt Sarah's
Cast: Jim Jordan (Fibber), Marian Jordan (Molly), Harlow Wilcox, Bill Thompson (Old Timer, porter), Gale Gordon (train conductor), Arthur Q. Bryan (train announcer), Dick LeGrand (Ole Swenson), Cliff Arquette (Bessie, cab driver)

Summary: The McGees board the Cinder Bucket for a trip to visit Aunt Sarah but get less than they bargained for.
Music: Billy Mills: "A Thousand Violins," "When You Dance the Old Year Out" (The King's Men, vocal), "A Dream is a Wish Your Heart Makes"
Running Gag: Myrt bit involving grandmother/right tackle/fishing (Fibber)
Comments: Attentive listeners will note that Ole does not ask over the phone what tickets are being offered nor does Fibber divulge that information. This episode provides a change of pace for Bryan, Gordon, and Thompson, allowing them to take their show on the (rail) road with different characters.

Date: January 3, 1950
Title: At Aunt Sarah's
Cast: Jim Jordan (Fibber), Marian Jordan (Molly), Harlow Wilcox, Bill Thompson (Oglesby), Gale Gordon (train conductor), Arthur Q. Bryan (Oster), Elvia Allman (Miss Longfeather)
Summary: Fibber takes advantage of Aunt Sarah's hospitality by ordering her staff around and by trying to take over her business affairs.
Music: Billy Mills: "Envy," "All the Bees Are Buzzing Round My Honey" (The King's Men, vocal), "Farewell, Amanda"
Running Gag: Sarah's hall closet opened by Fibber looking for riding crop
Comments: Oglesby delivers the pitch for Johnson's Wax in the middle of the show because it would too contrived to drop Wilcox into Aunt Sarah's. After Oglesby reads Ole's letter in Swedish, Jim accidentally calls him "Yogi," perhaps subconsciously thinking of Yogi Yorgesson, the Swedish comic character created by Harry Stewart whose widow Gretchen Jim would eventually marry the year after Marian died. Bryan and Gordon have their smallest parts since they became regulars on the show.

Date: January 10, 1950
Title: Walt's Malt Shop
Cast: Jim Jordan (Fibber), Marian Jordan (Molly, Teeny), Harlow Wilcox, Bill Thompson (Wallace Wimple, Old Timer), Gale Gordon (Mayor LaTrivia), Arthur Q. Bryan (Doctor Gamble), Dick LeGrand (Ole Swenson), Cliff Arquette (Walt, Bessie), Elvia Allman (customer), Herb Vigran (angry customer, Herbert Appel)
Summary: The McGees, temporarily in charge of Walt's restaurant, go at their jobs with a burning passion.
Music: Billy Mills: "Dear Hearts and Gentle People," "Bibbidi-Bobbidi-Boo" (The King's Men, vocal), "Stay Well"
Running Gag: Word confusion involving *epicat/epicure/pedicure/pedagogue/pollywog/pedigree* (Fibber, Molly, Gamble)

Comments: This is the second consecutive episode in which the action takes place away from 79 Wistful Vista. Allusions to "Ghost Riders in the Sky" and Hopalong Cassidy lock the episode in time just as topical references to rationing and "Rosie the Riveter" place those WWII shows in their period.

Date: January 17, 1950
Title: Cutting Firewood
Cast: Jim Jordan (Fibber), Marian Jordan (Molly), Harlow Wilcox, Bill Thompson (Old Timer), Gale Gordon (Mayor LaTrivia), Arthur Q. Bryan (Doctor Gamble), Dick LeGrand (Ole Swenson, critic), Herb Vigran (Herbert Appel), Elvia Allman (Mrs. Clammer), Cliff Arquette (tree surgeon)
Summary: Fibber cuts down an oak tree for a neighbor, hoping to get some free wood out of the good deed.
Music: Billy Mills: "Charley, My Boy," "I Said My Pajamas and Put On My Prayers" (The King's Men, vocal)
Running Gags: "I'm yust donating my time" (Ole), tongue twister starting with brother Hugh (LaTrivia)
Comments: This episode is atypical in that for the first five minutes none of the characters that regularly interact with the McGees appear. Usually the appeals for humanitarian causes delivered by Marian and Jim in the tags focus on reasons to donate, but this one raises the possibility of the Red Menace encircling the undernourished as consequences of not contributing to CARE.

Date: January 24, 1950
Title: Shopping for Fibber's Suit
Cast: Jim Jordan (Fibber), Marian Jordan (Molly), Harlow Wilcox, Bill Thompson (Wallace Wimple), Gale Gordon (Mayor LaTrivia), Arthur Q. Bryan (Doctor Gamble), Dick LeGrand (Ole Swenson), Elvia Allman (PA announcer), Cliff Arquette (Waldo Cuffington)
Summary: The McGees are not easy to please as they put a clerk through his paces showing them new suits and clothing samples.
Music: Billy Mills: "Chattanooga Shoe Shine Boy" (The King's Men, vocal)
Running Gags: None
Comments: This episode has a different musical sound to it. First, there is no featured instrumental by the orchestra. More significantly, several bridges are used to suggest changes of scene or flashbacks much in the vein of *The Milton Berle Show* and other programs which featured sketches rather than situation comedy.

Date: January 31, 1950
Title: Sleigh Ride in Snowstorm
Cast: Jim Jordan (Fibber), Marian Jordan (Molly, Teeny), Harlow Wilcox, Bill Thompson (Old Timer), Gale Gordon (Mayor LaTrivia), Arthur Q. Bryan

(Doctor Gamble), Dick LeGrand (Ole Swenson), Elvia Allman (Mrs. Clammer), Herb Vigran (Herbert Appel)

Summary: The McGees and their friends get caught in a blizzard while on a sleigh ride.

Music: Billy Mills: "All the Bees Are Buzzing Round My Honey," "I Want to Go Home with You" (The King's Men, vocal), "There's No Tomorrow"

Running Gags: Hall closet opened by Fibber in the dark, not knowing he was home

Comments: Wilcox never gets to finish the introduction, making this a unique episode in that regard. The writers were obviously trying to open up the program, this being the sixth consecutive show with action principally outside the home.

Date: February 7, 1950
Title: City Council Vacancy
Cast: Jim Jordan (Fibber), Marian Jordan (Molly), Harlow Wilcox, Bill Thompson (Wallace Wimple, Krobney), Gale Gordon (Mayor LaTrivia), Arthur Q. Bryan (Doctor Gamble), Dick LeGrand (Ole Swenson), Elvia Allman (Mrs. Clammer, Miss Gimlet)
Summary: Molly considers filling a position on the city council while Fibber, acting as her campaign manager, offers unsolicited advice.
Music: Billy Mills: "There's Something About a Hometown Band" (The King's Men, vocal), "Happy Times"
Running Gags: None
Comments: The "cut the ribbon" gag seems out of place given to LaTrivia when it is more in Myrt's line of banter. Like the January 24th show, there is no featured number by the orchestra.

Date: February 14, 1950
Title: Missing Radium
Cast: Jim Jordan (Fibber), Marian Jordan (Molly), Harlow Wilcox, Bill Thompson (Wallace Wimple, conductor), Gale Gordon (Mayor LaTrivia), Arthur Q. Bryan (Doctor Gamble), Dick LeGrand (Ole Swenson), Elvia Allman (Miss Gimlet, country woman), Herb Vigran (clerk, paper mill worker)
Summary: The McGees frantically chase all over town trying to locate some missing tubes of radium.
Music: Billy Mills: "A Dream Is a Wish Your Heart Makes," "The Cry of the Wild Goose" (The King's Men, vocal)
Running Gag: "Gotta get them brakes fixed" (Fibber)
Summary: It is somewhat surprising that a comedy program broadcast on February 14th does not even mention Valentine's Day. On the December 27, 1949 show listeners learned that there is an East Wistful Vista; in this episode Miss Gimlet expands our view of the program's geography by also

naming off North, West, and South Wistful Vista. Listeners who wonder why in 1950 McGee was still asking for people on the phone instead of dialing their numbers will notice that, through the miracle of radio, Fibber was connected immediately with the intended parties so letting his mouth do the talking was as fast as letting his fingers do the walking.

Date: February 21, 1950
Title: Mailman Bitten by Dog
Cast: Jim Jordan (Fibber), Marian Jordan (Molly, Teeny), Harlow Wilcox, Bill Thompson (Old Timer), Gale Gordon (Mayor LaTrivia), Arthur Q. Bryan (Doctor Gamble), Dick LeGrand (Ole Swenson)
Summary: Fibber is being sued by a mailman who was bitten by a dog on property owned by the McGees.
Music: Billy Mills: "Waiting for the Robert E. Lee," "The Whistler and His Dog" (The King's Men, vocal), "I Can Dream, Can't I?"
Running Gags: "I'm yust donating my time" (Ole), LaTrivia blowup over "a horse of a different color"
Comments: Fibber's torrent of jumbled syntax to Doc beginning with "You haven't ever been sued…" is probably the funniest of his convoluted sentences. "The Whistler and His Dog" completes a string of four consecutive shows in which the song by The King's Men is connected with the general theme of that week's episode.

Date: February 28, 1950
Title: LaTrivia's Party
Cast: Jim Jordan (Fibber), Marian Jordan (Molly), Harlow Wilcox, Bill Thompson (Old Timer), Gale Gordon (Mayor LaTrivia), Arthur Q. Bryan (Doctor Gamble), Dick LeGrand (Ole Swenson), Elvia Allman (Miss Gimlet), Cliff Arquette (Fosdick)
Summary: The McGees are happy to accept an invitation to a party at the country club, but Fibber is not pleased with the trouble he has catching up with the tuxedo he will wear to the affair.
Music: Billy Mills: "Happy Times," "Iowa Indian Song" (The King's Men, vocal)
Running Gags: Name game (Fibber, Molly, Fosdick), LaTrivia blowup over "on thin ice"
Comments: In this episode Fibber unequivocally gets the better of Gamble for the only time in the series by rendering him speechless. This is the first of a number of riotous episodes in which characters portrayed by Cliff Arquette confuse the McGees by addressing them with incorrect names. LaTrivia's blowup is one of his very best, memorable both for the "ating on thin skice" spoonerism and the heightened state of apoplexy he achieves.

Date: March 7, 1950
Title: Ole Kidnapped
Cast: Jim Jordan (Fibber), Marian Jordan (Molly, Teeny), Harlow Wilcox, Bill Thompson (Wallace Wimple), Gale Gordon (Mayor LaTrivia), Arthur Q. Bryan (Doctor Gamble), Dick LeGrand (Ole Swenson), Cliff Arquette (sergeant)
Summary: The McGees alert the police because they believe Ole has been abducted.
Music: Billy Mills: "Music, Music, Music" "The Cinderella Work Song" (The King's Men, vocal), "You Kissed Me"
Running Gags: None
Comments: Taken seriously, the McGees do not come off too nobly in this episode: they both jump to conclusions; Fibber allows Molly to carry groceries, wants to use his wife as a shield in a time of potential danger, and asks Gamble to use his car so the McGee auto will not receive any bullet holes; Molly calmly goes to sort laundry while a friend may be in desperate straits. Considered practically, listeners accept mistaken identities as a standard plot element, McGee's crass behavior and cowardice as part of his character, and Molly's exits as preludes for Teeny's entrances.

Date: March 14, 1950
Title: Guest House
Cast: Jim Jordan (Fibber), Marian Jordan (Molly), Harlow Wilcox, Bill Thompson (Old Timer), Gale Gordon (Mayor LaTrivia), Arthur Q. Bryan (Doctor Gamble), Dick LeGrand (Ole Swenson, Mort Postum), Cliff Arquette (Farnsworth Crandledance)
Summary: After the McGees are told they have to tear down a house because they did not get a building permit, they take their complaint to the city hall.
Music: Billy Mills: "Copper Canyon," "If I Knew You Were Coming, I'd've Baked a Cake" (The King's Men, vocal), "Oh, How I Miss You Tonight"
Running Gags: Name game (Fibber, Molly, Farnsworth), Myrt bit involving brother/cistern/sistern (Fibber), tongue twister starting with "seaweed seed" (Fibber)
Comments: This is an episode which asks for listener forbearance in accepting the fact that the dimensions for a house meant for a dog (regardless of the animal's size) could be mistaken for a habitation for humans. Listeners might also wonder how Molly could have suddenly forgotten who Myrt was and how Fibber could be connected instantaneously with his party simply by telling the operator "Give me Aunt Sarah, long distance." The garbled sentence Fibber speaks to LaTrivia is a dandy and the last one of that magnitude until the January 16, 1951 episode. Marian and Jim's appeal for Easter Seals in the tag using the image of freeing children from their wheelchairs would make any listener reach for wallet or purse.

Date: March 21, 1950
Title: Pruning a Tree
Cast: Jim Jordan (Fibber), Marian Jordan (Molly, Teeny), Harlow Wilcox, Bill Thompson (Old Timer), Gale Gordon (Mayor LaTrivia), Arthur Q. Bryan (Doctor Gamble), Dick LeGrand (Ole Swenson, bystander), Cliff Arquette (Elrod Nutwinkle III)
Summary: Fibber battles a persistent woodpecker as he trims a tree in the front yard.
Music: Billy Mills: "The Woodpecker Song" (The King's Men, vocal), "The Third Man Theme," "Stars and Stripes Forever"
Running Gags: Tongue twister starting with "Bruner's pruners" (Fibber), name game (Fibber, Molly, Elrod)
Comments: The joke Ole tells about Gustav being blown up is one of a number of gags that had been used over the years in which explosives or ammunition apparently brought fatal results. Some may consider such jests in bad taste, others will just place them in the same "anything for a laugh" category as the eye-poking and face-slapping performed by The Three Stooges. Concerns about juvenile delinquency and Communism, prevalent in the early 1950s, are present in this episode.

Date: March 28, 1950
Title: Flying Saucer
Cast: Jim Jordan (Fibber), Marian Jordan (Molly, Teeny), Harlow Wilcox, Bill Thompson (Sergei Petrasky), Gale Gordon (Mayor LaTrivia), Arthur Q. Bryan (Doctor Gamble), Dick LeGrand (policeman), Bud Stefan (lieutenant colonel), Elvia Allman (bystander, Rhoda Dendron), Herb Vigran (Shriner)
Summary: Fibber, a scoffer of those who claim to have seen flying saucers, suddenly becomes a believer when an object lands on his property which he hopes to turn into a cash cow.
Music: Billy Mills: "The Hot Canary," "Music, Music, Music" (The King's Men, vocal), "Enjoy Yourself"
Running Gags: Tongue twister starting with "raisin ranch" (Fibber), "'Tain't funny, McGee" (Molly)
Comments: Doc's joke about never hearing a Republican play "The Missouri Waltz" on a piano, a reference to Harry Truman, brings about Jim's ad-lib of "We're on the front burner now," acknowledging the first big laugh of the night. The writers cleverly pepper the middle commercial with appropriate astronomical terms like *cosmic dust* and *meteor showers*.

Date: April 4, 1950
Title: Census Taker
Cast: Jim Jordan (Fibber), Marian Jordan (Molly), Harlow Wilcox, Bill Thompson (Old Timer, butler), Arthur Q. Bryan (Doctor Gamble), Dick LeGrand

(Ole Swenson), Elvia Allman (Mrs. Cory), Cliff Arquette (Wilks-Farthington, Axelrod P. Baker), Jean Vander Pyl (wife of imprisoned man)
Summary: Molly accompanies Fibber as he asks census questions of Wistful Vista residents.
Music: Billy Mills: "If I Knew You Were Coming, I'd've Baked a Cake," "Have I Told You Lately That I Love You?" (The King's Men, vocal)
Running Gags: "That ain't the way I heered it" (Old Timer), name game (Fibber, Molly, Axelrod)
Comments: A Quinn and Leslie quote of note is the distinction Molly points out to Fibber between two similar words: "The census asks people what they do and the censor says they mustn't do it." The joke Fibber delivers about Gamble walking like a chapped duck receives a healthy laugh, maybe because listeners are either picturing a duck waddling in chaps or a quacker trying to keep its sore legs from touching one another.

Date: April 11, 1950
Title: General Store
Cast: Jim Jordan (Fibber), Marian Jordan (Molly), Harlow Wilcox, Bill Thompson (customer, Old Timer), Gale Gordon (Mayor LaTrivia), Arthur Q. Bryan (Doctor Gamble), Elvia Allman (Mrs. Heinz), Herb Vigran (crooked customer), Cliff Arquette (customer, Daniel Q. Offenback)
Summary: The McGees, running the general store for a day, wait on customers with the help of a cash register that thinks for itself.
Music: Billy Mills: "The Cannonball Rag," "The Merrily Song" (The King's Men, vocal), "With My Eyes Wide Open, I'm Dreaming"
Running Gags: "'Tain't funny, McGee" (LaTrivia), name game (Fibber, Molly, Daniel)
Comments: This episode abounds in self-referential fun including Fibber's looking up *aspirin* during rehearsal, Jim accenting Marian's fluff by repeating "and-and," reprising the *Smackout* greeting, "the shortest distance between two jokes is a straight line" gag, and the plug regarding the current issue of *Look*.

Date: April 18, 1950
Title: Car Trouble
Cast: Jim Jordan (Fibber), Marian Jordan (Molly, Teeny), Harlow Wilcox, Bill Thompson (Old Timer), Gale Gordon (Mayor LaTrivia), Dick LeGrand (Ole Swenson), Elvia Allman (Angelica Dennison), Cliff Arquette (Levinworth P. Eaton)
Summary: After Molly brings home an object she thinks fell off while she was driving, Fibber tries to figure out what it is and where it goes on the car.
Music: Billy Mills: "Sunshine Cake," "Stay With the Happy People" (The King's Men, vocal), "Are You Lonesome Tonight?"

Running Gags: Word confusion involving *obstetrician/octogenarian/optometrist/ optician* (Fibber, Molly, Ole), name game (Fibber, Molly, Levinworth)

Comments: This episode contains what is quite likely the best of the Arquette badinages because it allows Cliff's character to play upon the names of people *and* magazines to wonderful effect, leaving Fibber grumbling to himself. Gordon almost blows the climactic line in the script when he hesitates momentarily before selecting the correct possessive.

Date: April 25, 1950
Title: Elks Club Dance
Cast: Jim Jordan (Fibber), Marian Jordan (Molly), Harlow Wilcox, Bill Thompson (Old Timer, Emil), Gale Gordon (Mayor LaTrivia), Arthur Q. Bryan (Doctor Gamble), Dick LeGrand (Ole Swenson), Bud Stefan (telegram delivery boy), Elvia Allman (Angelica Dennison), Cliff Arquette (MacDonald), Jean Vander Pyl (Mrs. Curry)
Summary: Fibber, in charge of the big dance, overlooks one important detail but still saves the day (and his skin).
Music: Billy Mills: "Candy and Cake," "Dearie" (The King's Men and Betty Wand, vocal), "Paper My Walls with Your Love Letters"
Running Gags: Myrt bit involving brother/lost three fingers/root beer (Fibber), "I'm yust donating my time" (Ole), name game (Fibber, Molly, MacDonald)
Comments: The "little house" line spoken by Molly is another of those suggestive bits skillful writers hand to listeners so their minds can entertain country matters. Jim must have been late picking up his cue near the end because he says, "I got here just in time" and breaks up during his next speech. Betty Wand, who complements the King's Men nicely on "Dearie," was an unseen presence in a number of motion pictures, most notably dubbing songs for Leslie Caron in *Gigi* and Rita Moreno in *West Side Story.*

Date: May 2, 1950
Title: Fishing with Automatic Reel
Cast: Jim Jordan (Fibber), Marian Jordan (Molly), Harlow Wilcox, Bill Thompson (Old Timer, man with goggles), Gale Gordon (Mayor LaTrivia), Arthur Q. Bryan (Doctor Gamble), Dick LeGrand (Ole Swenson), Bud Stefan (lad fishing), Cliff Arquette (Carl, man on pier)
Summary: Fibber has trouble assembling the reel he hopes will help him catch a bigger bass than Doc Gamble does so he can win a $5.00 wager.
Music: Billy Mills: "Wilhelmina," "The Old Piano Roll Blues" (The King's Men, vocal)
Running Gag: "I'm yust donating my time" (Ole)
Comments: Jim milks an extra laugh out of the script just by feeding a line to Wilcox without pausing for a comma. Harlow provides an important

clue to set up the closer by saying that Doc has "an automatic reel just like yours." Cliff's Carl sounds more than a little like Charley Weaver. Old Muley, the fish that Fibber apparently caught back on May 7, 1946, returns briefly in this episode but will always be the one that got away in Wistful Vista lore.

Date: May 9, 1950
Title: Circus Day
Cast: Jim Jordan (Fibber), Marian Jordan (Molly, Teeny), Harlow Wilcox, Bill Thompson (Old Timer, Horatio K. Boomer), Gale Gordon (Mayor LaTrivia), Arthur Q. Bryan (Doctor Gamble), Bud Stefan (parking lot attendant), Cliff Arquette (pickpocket, Bascom W. Prentwhistle)
Summary: The McGees spend the day at the circus.
Music: Billy Mills: "Billboard March," "Hoop-De-Do" (The King's Men, vocal)
Running Gag: Name game (Fibber, Molly, Bascom)
Comments: The attraction Fibber and Molly visit is more like a carnival than a circus with concessions, barkers, and sideshows rather than a tent show featuring tightrope walkers, clowns, and animal acts. Perhaps because the writers had already taken the McGees to several carnivals before they wanted to put a different slant on this episode. Repeatedly mentioning Fred Nitney's name throughout the story should have prepared listeners for the revelation Fibber makes at the end. "The Great Gusto" persiflage is one of the better name games, accidentally enriched when Cliff muffs a line. The Mother of the Year award presented to Marian is another indication of how *Fibber McGee and Molly* kept the home fires glowing throughout America.

Date: May 16, 1950
Title: Picnic in the Country
Cast: Jim Jordan (Fibber), Marian Jordan (Molly), Harlow Wilcox, Bill Thompson (golfer, Old Timer), Gale Gordon (Mayor LaTrivia), Arthur Q. Bryan (Doctor Gamble), Dick LeGrand (Ole Swenson), Cliff Arquette (golfer, Oliver J. Bostwick III)
Summary: The McGees travel all over the countryside trying to find a peaceful place to have a picnic.
Music: Billy Mills: "The Cornball Rag," "Home Cooking" (The King's Men, vocal)
Running Gags: "Gotta get them brakes fixed" (Fibber), "I'm yust donating my time" (Ole), name game (Fibber, Molly, Oliver)
Comments: Listeners accept the coincidence of the McGees encountering their friends no matter where they go in the county because, as Fibber says to Wilcox, they regularly run into them "in the darnedest places."

Date: May 23, 1950
Title: Managing Ranch in Texas
Cast: Jim Jordan (Fibber), Marian Jordan (Molly), Harlow Wilcox, Bill Thompson (Old Timer, Newhouser), Gale Gordon (Mayor LaTrivia), Arthur Q. Bryan (Doctor Gamble), Dick LeGrand (Ole Swenson), Elvia Allman (PA announcer), Cliff Arquette (Marvin Doppelgong)
Summary: Fibber and Molly make preparations to take over Uncle Sycamore's ranch for the summer.
Music: Billy Mills: "Stay With the Happy People," "Hold That Critter Down" (The King's Men, vocal), "Let's Go to Church"
Running Gags: "I'm yust donating my time" (Ole), name game (Fibber, Molly, Marvin), hall closet opened by Fibber looking for calendar
Comments: This is the final episode of *Fibber McGee and Molly* sponsored by Johnson's Wax as the company moved more advertising dollars into television. *Head* is not a common word used when referring to turkeys who will soon lose theirs, but the writers make certain the letter states just "2500 head" and let Fibber jump to his own conclusions. This is the last episode directed by Frank Pittman. The replacement series are *The Penny Singleton Show* from May 30th through June 27th and *Presenting Charles Boyer* from July 4th through September 12th. *Fibber McGee and Molly* will return the third week in September, not the second week as Jim claims.

Date: September 19, 1950
Title: Chicken Barbeque
Cast: Jim Jordan (Fibber), Marian Jordan (Molly), Harlow Wilcox, Bill Thompson (Alsop, Old Timer), Gale Gordon (Mayor LaTrivia), Arthur Q. Bryan (Doctor Gamble), Dick LeGrand (Ole Swenson), Cliff Arquette (McSneed)
Summary: Fibber intends to feed the friends he has invited over for a barbeque in the backyard...if he can just keep the fire lit to cook the chickens.
Music: Billy Mills: "I Love the Guy," "The Picnic Song" (The King's Men, vocal), "Play a Simple Melody"
Running Gags: Name game (Fibber, Molly, McSneed), LaTrivia blowup over "where there's a will, there's a way"
Comments: This is the first episode sponsored by Pet Milk. Waxy Wilcox is now called Milcox or Milky by Fibber. The LaTrivia blowup is notable for several explosions by Gordon and the appropriate Hawaiian greeting by Fibber to go along with the Honolulu portion of the routine. Max Hutto is now director of the program.

Date: September 26, 1950
Title: Night School Chemist
Cast: Jim Jordan (Fibber), Marian Jordan (Molly), Harlow Wilcox, Bill Thompson (Old Timer, drunk, photographer), Gale Gordon (Mayor

LaTrivia), Arthur Q. Bryan (Doctor Gamble), Dick LeGrand (General Scully), Elvia Allman (PA announcer), Cliff Arquette (Spofford), Jean Vander Pyl (instructor)

Summary: Fibber goes back to school to study science so he can make a chemical discovery that will make the McGees rich.

Music: Billy Mills: "Sam's Song," "Let's Do It Again" (The King's Men, vocal), "Our Very Own"

Running Gags: Name game (Fibber, Molly, Spofford), "'Tain't funny, McGee" (Molly)

Comments: It only took two weeks for the writers to get the teacher's Pet pun in to promote the product. The writers slightly alter the gag used earlier about the fragrant steps and let LaTrivia deliver it this time.

Date: October 3, 1950
Title: Stomachache
Cast: Jim Jordan (Fibber), Marian Jordan (Molly, Teeny), Harlow Wilcox, Bill Thompson (Old Timer), Arthur Q. Bryan (Doctor Gamble), Bea Benaderet (Miss Fennimore), Dick LeGrand (Ole Swenson), Peter Leeds (Eddie)
Summary: Fibber, suffering from a stomachache he thinks is caused by appendicitis, becomes insufferable at the hospital.
Music: Billy Mills: "Don't Rock the Boat," "Good Night, Irene" (The King's Men, vocal), "Thinking of You"
Running Gags: "That ain't the way I heered it" (Old Timer), word confusion involving *monotony/monopoly/monogamy/mahogany* (Fibber, Molly)
Comments: Fibber's eating of "half a jar of Uncle Will Mills' Corn Relish" is an in-joke referring to an actual product distributed by bandleader Billy Mills who was a gourmet cook. The Bedouin joke is so awful and yet so awfully good it belongs in the *Fibber McGee and Molly* Hall of Famous Gags. An anachronism occurs when the records reveal that Gamble removed Fibber's appendix in 1934, a year before the nomadic McGees settled in Wistful Vista.

Date: October 10, 1950
Title: Wallet Racket
Cast: Jim Jordan (Fibber), Marian Jordan (Molly), Harlow Wilcox, Bill Thompson (conductor, Julep Jackson), Gale Gordon (Mayor LaTrivia), Arthur Q. Bryan (Doctor Gamble), Dick LeGrand (Ole Swenson), Herb Vigran (Greasy Gilbert), Cliff Arquette (teller)
Summary: Fibber wants to split a reward with a man who found a wallet, but Molly thinks the finder is a crook and that Fibber will be a weeper.
Music: Billy Mills: "I Don't Care if the Sun Don't Shine," "A Bushel and a Peck" (The King's Men, vocal), "Thinking of You"
Running Gag: Name game (Fibber, Molly, teller)

Comments: The McGees perceptively trace the mush-mouthed conductor's parentage to a telephone operator for a mother and a tobacco auctioneer for a father. This is the first episode in which the character played by Arquette pointedly flirts with Molly, giving Fibber more of a reason to lose his temper.

Date: October 17, 1950
Title: Photography Contest with $25 Prize
Cast: Jim Jordan (Fibber), Marian Jordan (Molly, Teeny), Harlow Wilcox, Bill Thompson (Old Timer, Charlie), Arthur Q. Bryan (Doctor Gamble), Dick LeGrand (Ole Swenson), Cliff Arquette (McIntyre)
Summary: Fibber, hoping to win a $25 contest sponsored by *The Wistful Vista Gazette*, keeps passing up photo opportunities until he finds one that really packs a wallop.
Music: Billy Mills: "Dream a Little Dream of Me," "Dig, Dig, Dig for Your Dinner" (The King's Men, vocal), "All of Me"
Running Gags: "That ain't the way it was originally recounted to me" (Old Timer), name game (Fibber, Molly, McIntyre), tongue twister starting with "making maps" (Fibber), hall closet opened by Teeny looking for Fibber's camera
Comments: The anthrax bit is a case of overkill in which a gag is run into the ground and the payoff at the end is meager. Using the name of a disease for satiric purposes is a rare case of bad judgment by the writers and as such the use of *anthrax* for the name of Fibber's camera dampens the humor in the 1953 episodes which also feature a snapshot contest.

Date: October 24, 1950
Title: Real Estate Deal
Cast: Jim Jordan (Fibber), Marian Jordan (Molly), Harlow Wilcox, Bill Thompson (Old Timer), Gale Gordon (Mayor LaTrivia), Dick LeGrand (Ole Swenson), Ken Christy (MacDonald), Cliff Arquette (Rasmussen)
Summary: Fibber checks over the legal ramifications of a deal he has pending with the Third National Bank.
Music: Billy Mills: "All My Love," "It's Deductible" (The King's Men, vocal), "It Looks Like a Cold, Cold Winter"
Running Gags: Myrt bit involving cousin/thrown off train/wedding rehearsal (Fibber), tongue twister starting with "people vs. Creepy Reeple" (Fibber), LaTrivia blowup over "first come, first served," name game (Fibber, Molly, Rasmussen)
Comments: Sometimes muffing a line is just what the cast needs to pick up a stagnant part of a script. When Jim stumbles trying to get out his joke about the bank taking blood, it throws off the timing of Harlow's entrance and the laughter snowballs from the comedy of errors.

Date: October 31, 1950
Title: Plays the Ukulele
Cast: Jim Jordan (Fibber), Marian Jordan (Molly), Harlow Wilcox, Bill Thompson (Old Timer, MC), Gale Gordon (Mayor LaTrivia), Arthur Q. Bryan (Doctor Gamble), Dick LeGrand (Ole Swenson, owner of nightclub), Perry Botkin
Summary: Fibber gets himself into a bind by promising to play the ukulele before his fellow Elks and, for the record, he manages to put on quite a performance.
Music: Billy Mills: "Goofus," "Halloween" (The King's Men, vocal), "Lover" (Perry Botkin, ukulele solo), "Pretty Red Wing"
Running Gags: None
Comments: It is no wonder LaTrivia balks at the attempt to catch him on "I'll be there with bells on." It had been just over a year (October 18, 1949) since he fell for the same line of malarkey.

Date: November 7, 1950
Title: Vision Problems
Cast: Jim Jordan (Fibber), Marian Jordan (Molly, Teeny), Harlow Wilcox, Bill Thompson (irate pedestrian, Old Timer), Arthur Q. Bryan (Doctor Gamble), Cliff Arquette (Freeling)
Summary: Fibber goes to an oculist because he is misidentifying people and things.
Music: Billy Mills: "If You Feel Like Singing, Sing" (The King's Men, vocal)
Running Gag: Name game (Fibber, Molly, Freeling)
Comments: There is no featured instrumental by the orchestra on this broadcast, an uncommon occurrence. The broken glass effect that closes the Teeny segment is an odd one for the front door which had been slammed countless times over the years would have to be made of wood to sustain all that abuse.

Date: November 14, 1950
Title: Stamp Worth $100,000
Cast: Jim Jordan (Fibber), Marian Jordan (Molly, Teeny), Harlow Wilcox, Bill Thompson (Old Timer, conductor), Gale Gordon (Mayor LaTrivia), Dick LeGrand (Ole Swenson), Danny Richards Jr. (Willie Toops)
Summary: When the McGees learn that Fibber may have given away a postage stamp worth $100,000, they search frantically to recover it.
Music: Billy Mills: "I'm Forever Blowing Bubbles," "The Thing" (The King's Men, vocal)
Running Gags: None
Comments: There is only one known example of the stamp in question, known as the British Guiana 1¢ magenta, last sold at over nine million dollars. A Quinn and Leslie specialty was the absurd analogy that heaped

one incongruous element upon another, often involving the names of far-away countries and animals to make the image more picturesque and ludicrous. The longest and perhaps the funniest of these gems occurs in this episode with LaTrivia's precise delineation of McGee's earning potential as a musician: "You couldn't pick up a split Peruvian penny playing 'The 1812 Overture' while juggling thirteen deep sea turtles blindfolded on a unicycle balancing a wheelbarrow full of pig iron on your nose and surrounded by fifty beautiful girls in bikini bathing suits waving American flags with their phone numbers tattooed on their knees."

Date: November 21, 1950
Title: Aunt Jennie
Cast: Jim Jordan (Fibber), Marian Jordan (Molly), Bill Thompson (puzzle editor, Wallace Wimple), Arthur Q. Bryan (Doctor Gamble), Dick LeGrand (Ole Swenson), Elvia Allman (Bertha), Cliff Arquette (Melvin J. Concannon)
Summary: Fibber takes over the advice column of *The Wistful Vista Gazette* for a day with Molly acting as his secretary.
Music: Billy Mills: "A Bushel and a Peck," "Baby, Won't You Say You Love Me?" (The King's Men, vocal)
Running Gags: Name game (Fibber, Molly, Melvin), "'Tain't funny, Aunt Jennie" (Molly)
Comments: Wallace Wimple appears for the first time this season. Early in the show Jim seems to be knocking down the fourth wall frequently by inviting the audience along when he ad-libs "Here we go, right into the bridge."

Date: November 28, 1950
Title: Parking Meters
Cast: Jim Jordan (Fibber), Marian Jordan (Molly), Bill Thompson (Wallace Wimple, policeman), Gale Gordon (Mayor LaTrivia), Dick LeGrand (Ole Swenson, Hibbard), Elvia Allman (PA announcer), Cliff Arquette (Courtney J. Gleep)
Summary: McGee takes his shaver to the Bon Ton to be repaired, then finds that he is living on borrowed time with a parking meter.
Music: Billy Mills: "It Looks Like a Cold, Cold Winter," "The Merrily Song" (The King's Men, vocal), "Dream Awhile"
Running Gags: LaTrivia blowup over "they're sticking to their guns," name game (Fibber, Molly, Courtney)
Comments: A subtle appeal for Christmas Seals is slipped in with the coin deposited in the parking meter and a more direct pitch is tossed into the tag. The Hemingway gag gets noticed by Fibber just like the "Win Placen Show" joke the Old Timer pulled three weeks earlier on the November 7th show and calls our attention to the witty, wacky way the writers wangle words.

Date: December 5, 1950
Title: Dinner at LaTrivia's House
Cast: Jim Jordan (Fibber), Marian Jordan (Molly, Teeny), Harlow Wilcox, Bill Thompson (butler, ambassador), Gale Gordon (Mayor LaTrivia), Arthur Q. Bryan (Doctor Gamble), Elvia Allman (Mrs. J. Withers Fetlock)
Summary: After the McGees are invited to LaTrivia's home, Fibber does everything he can to prevent the mayor from showing home movies to his dinner guests.
Music: Billy Mills: "The Best Thing for You," "Rudolph, the Red-Nosed Reindeer" (The King's Men and Teeny, vocal), "I'll Get By"
Running Gags: None
Comments: Fibber proves that being naturally unhandy can sometimes come in very handy. This is an uncommon episode in which Bill Thompson does not appear as any of his regular characters, although the ambassador is a reprise of the Flagerian character he assumed on *The Charlie McCarthy Show* in 1943 before entering the Navy.

Date: December 12, 1950
Title: Bank Night at the Movies
Cast: Jim Jordan (Fibber), Marian Jordan (Molly), Harlow Wilcox, Bill Thompson (ticket taker, Old Timer), Gale Gordon (Mayor LaTrivia), Dick LeGrand (Ole Swenson, heckler), Cliff Arquette (Kimberly), Tyler McVey (Marty Stiver)
Summary: The McGees go to the Bijou Theater on bank night, hoping to win the $3,000 prize.
Music: Billy Mills: "If I Were a Bell," "Orange Colored Sky" (The King's Men, vocal)
Running Gags: LaTrivia blowup over "coining money," name game (Fibber, Molly, Kimberly)
Comments: Owners of casinos would be wise to print Fibber's mantra in this episode above every bank of slot machines: "The longer you don't win, the sooner you gotta." 13 is a lucky number for Wilcox just as 131313 was a winner for the McGees in the house raffle fifteen years earlier.

Date: December 19, 1950
Title: Postman McGee
Cast: Jim Jordan (Fibber), Marian Jordan (Molly, Teeny), Harlow Wilcox, Bill Thompson (carrier number 7, Old Timer, Wallace Wimple), Gale Gordon (Mayor LaTrivia), Arthur Q. Bryan (Doctor Gamble), Dick LeGrand (carrier number 12, Ole Swenson), Ed Begley (postmaster), Cliff Arquette (Jim Kettle)
Summary: Molly accompanies Fibber on his mail route as he acts as temporary postal carrier during the busy Christmas delivery season.

Music: Billy Mills: "Sleigh Ride," "'Twas the Night Before Christmas" (The King's Men and Teeny, vocal)
Running Gags: "Gotta get them brakes fixed" (Fibber, three times), hall closet effect as Gamble opens door of car looking for a new stethoscope
Comments: Jeanette Nolan is mentioned in the credits but does not appear. Ole's surname is given for the first time.

Date: December 26, 1950
Title: Shoveling Snow
Cast: Jim Jordan (Fibber), Marian Jordan (Molly), Harlow Wilcox, Bill Thompson (NBC spokesman, Old Timer), Arthur Q. Bryan (Doctor Gamble), Dick LeGrand (Ole Swenson), Bud Stefan (insurance salesman), Cliff Arquette (Orville Pugsley)
Summary: While shoveling snow Fibber is repeatedly interrupted by phone calls that he never gets past the front porch to answer.
Music: Billy Mills: "Marshmallow World," "Hullabaloo" (The King's Men, vocal), "I've Never Been in Love Before"
Running Gags: Word confusion involving *cranium/curriculum/equilibrium/equestrian* (Fibber, Molly), name game (Fibber, Molly, Orville)
Comments: This episode illustrates how the writers could take the simplest idea (a man, a shovel, and a ringing phone) and build an entire show around it. Quibbling about why Fibber falls over the same shovel three times before someone moves it is pointless; this is the same stubborn man who would rather shove things back into a closet repeatedly than clean it up once and for all. The closing message cleverly incorporates the sponsor's selling points into well-wishes for the new year.

Date: January 2, 1951
Title: Teeny's Sled
Cast: Jim Jordan (Fibber), Marian Jordan (Molly, Teeny), Harlow Wilcox, Bill Thompson (Old Timer), Gale Gordon (Mayor LaTrivia), Arthur Q. Bryan (Doctor Gamble), Dick LeGrand (Ole Swenson), Danny Richards Jr. (boy), Peter Votrian (boy)
Summary: While in a fix-it mood Fibber gets himself into a fix by promising to repair Teeny's sled which has been run over by a streetcar.
Music: Billy Mills: "I'll Get By," "Get Out Those Old Records" (The King's Men, vocal), "You and Your Beautiful Eyes"
Running Gag: Tongue twister starting with "head tester for Ed Bestor" (Fibber)
Comments: Bigger parts must have originally been written for Danny and Peter for them to receive mention in the credits. As it is, they each have one line that is little more than crowd noise among the toys being dropped in the living room.

Date: January 9, 1951
Title: Circular Mailers
Cast: Jim Jordan (Fibber), Marian Jordan (Molly), Harlow Wilcox, Bill Thompson (Old Timer), Arthur Q. Bryan (Doctor Gamble), Dick LeGrand (Ole Swenson), Cliff Arquette (clerk)
Summary: With Molly's assistance Fibber assembles circulars promoting a combination potato peeler and button hook with the expectation of receiving five cents for every gadget sold.
Music: "Dear, Dear, Dear" (The King's Men, vocal), "Raggin' the Scale," "Frosty the Snowman"
Running Gags: Word confusion involving *toupee/touché/teepee/TV* (Fibber, Molly), name game (Fibber, Molly, clerk)
Comments: During the word confusion, Jim accidentally says the right word (*teepee*) instead of the wrong one (*toupee*) which works out fine because of the unexpected laughter and the ad-lib "What'd I say wrong in the first place—besides everything?" Jim's later ad-libs "I've been right here in my teepee."

Date: January 16, 1951
Title: Walking on Grass
Cast: Jim Jordan (Fibber), Marian Jordan (Molly), Harlow Wilcox, Bill Thompson (Old Timer, Rudy), Gale Gordon (Mayor LaTrivia), Bud Stefan (Claude Borgenhutz, Eddie), Dick Ryan (Biscaluz), John McIntire (Horowitz), Myra Marsh (Mrs. Y. Hamilton Dumphries)
Summary: After Fibber is issued a citation for walking on the grass, he pleads his case with the chief of police who is soon pleading with the persistent McGee to go home.
Music: Billy Mills: "Jing-a-Ling-a-Ling," "The Tennessee Waltz" (The King's Men, vocal), "Be My Love"
Running Gags: None
Comments: The last torrent of jumbled phrases ending in an unanswerable question was thrown at LaTrivia by Fibber on March 14, 1950. This time the big laugh comes seconds after the question is posed, probably caused by the facial expression of Gordon, a master of squeezing every ounce of humor out of a comical situation.

Date: January 23, 1951
Title: Belongings All Over Living Room
Cast: Jim Jordan (Fibber), Marian Jordan (Molly, Teeny), Harlow Wilcox, Bill Thompson (Old Timer), Arthur Q. Bryan (Doctor Gamble), Dick LeGrand (Ole Swenson)
Summary: When Fibber requests that his wife not pick up after him, the living room soon reaches capacity and Molly reaches the boiling point.

Music: Billy Mills: "Use Your Imagination," "Money, Money, Money" (The King's Men, vocal), "My Heart Cries for You"

Running Gags: Hall closet opened by Fibber looking for photo album, word confusion involving *subtitle/subtle/scuttle/shuttle/chateau* (Fibber, Molly, Gamble, Harlow)

Comments: The orchestra's number "Use Your Imagination" could serve as the theme of this episode as listeners visualize seashells being crushed underfoot, an avalanche of objects tumbling out of the closet, the head of a cross-eyed moose staring across a bedroom, a raft inflating before their ears, and umbrella stands, luggage racks, and other assorted knickknacks being kicked around the house.

Date: January 30, 1951
Title: Skating Party
Cast: Jim Jordan (Fibber), Marian Jordan (Molly), Harlow Wilcox, Bill Thompson (Old Timer, Wallace Wimple), Gale Gordon (Mayor LaTrivia), Arthur Q. Bryan (Doctor Gamble), Dick LeGrand (Ole Swenson), Myra Marsh (Gwendolyn Flack)
Summary: The McGees host a skating party for their friends at Dugan's Lake that turns into a roaring good time for everyone.
Music: Billy Mills: "Lullaby of Broadway," "Saskatchewan" (The King's Men, vocal), "Hullabaloo"
Running Gags: Myrt bit involving getting pinched/guy left elevator (Fibber), "I'm yust donating my time" (Ole), tongue twister starting with "Matt Black" (Fibber)
Comments: The repeated reference to the fire foreshadows how the party will go up in smoke. The message of the sponsor being given by Wilcox goes down a little easier when the audience is also attending to the stories being told by Doc, Fibber, and Ole. When Harlow asks the question "Hey, is anybody listening to me?" someone away from the microphone pipes in with an impromptu "I am."

Date: February 6, 1951
Title: Breakfast in Bed or in Kitchen?
Cast: Jim Jordan (Fibber), Marian Jordan (Molly), Harlow Wilcox, Bill Thompson (Old Timer), Gale Gordon (Mayor LaTrivia), Arthur Q. Bryan (Doctor Gamble), Dick LeGrand (Ole Swenson)
Summary: To commemorate National Pancake Day, Fibber concocts a breakfast for Molly that he can present to her in bed.
Music: Billy Mills: "My Heart Cries for You," "Yump Dee Dump Dee Dido" (The King's Men, vocal)
Running Gag: Word confusion involving *epitaph/epicure* (Fibber, Molly)
Comments: When Marian's voice cracks on "I'm starving," she sounds like she really *is* hungry. She cracks up in another way as Jim gets flagged for

speeding with an extra letter when he says, "You fling a flang into a flock of flapjacks."

Date: February 13, 1951
Title: Nasty Letter to Nitney
Cast: Jim Jordan (Fibber), Marian Jordan (Molly), Bill Thompson (Old Timer), Gale Gordon (Mayor LaTrivia). Arthur Q. Bryan (Doctor Gamble), Dick LeGrand (Ole Swenson), Harry Von Zell, Ken Christy (postal inspector), Cliff Arquette (pickpocket), Herb Vigran (officer)
Summary: Fibber, anxious to retrieve an ill-advised letter he sent, gets both arms stuck in a mailbox and is later arrested for tampering with the mail.
Music: Billy Mills: "You're Just in Love," "So Long, It's Been Good to Know You" (The King's Men, vocal), "It Is No Secret"
Running Gag: "I'm yust donating my time" (Ole)
Comments: Harry Von Zell substitutes for Harlow Wilcox. Gamble's memory is just a little off in the recollection of the grating incident which actually occurred in 1949, not "last year" in 1950. Fibber and Fred apparently had called a truce on their feud on May 9, 1950 when McGee wrestled Hydrogen Honsky (aka Nitney) and they split Fibber's $25.00 prize money.

Date: February 20, 1951
Title: Express Company Robbery
Cast: Jim Jordan (Fibber), Marian Jordan (Molly, Teeny), Harlow Wilcox, Bill Thompson (Old Timer), Gale Gordon (Mayor LaTrivia), Arthur Q. Bryan (Doctor Gamble), Dick LeGrand (Ole Swenson), John McIntire (Baby Face Williamson), Dick Ryan (Muggles)
Summary: Public enemy Baby Face Williamson, whose car breaks down in front of 79 Wistful Vista, convinces the McGees he is an official with the YMCA.
Music: Billy Mills: "You Love Me," "One of the Roving Kind" (The King's Men, vocal), "A Kiss and a Promise"
Running Gag: "'Tain't funny, McGee" (Molly)
Comments: The Old Timer's recollection of his wedding is a rare misfire in taste by the writers for his tale of a decapitation is too ghoulish to be amusing. The whole show seems disjointed and incomplete with a rapid exit by the Old Timer, an abrupt entry for LaTrivia who acts like a G-man, and no mention of what happens to the other robber.

Date: February 27, 1951
Title: Trip to Peoria
Cast: Jim Jordan (Fibber), Marian Jordan (Molly), Harlow Wilcox, Bill Thompson (Old Timer, train announcer), Gale Gordon (Mayor LaTrivia), Arthur Q. Bryan (Doctor Gamble), Dick LeGrand (Ole Swenson), Cliff Arquette (conductor), Tyler McVey (clerk)

Summary: The McGees take a train to Peoria to attend a convention of vaudevillians.
Music: Billy Mills: "Get Out Those Old Records," "If I Were a Bell" (The King's Men, vocal), "Zing Zing–Zoom Zoom"
Running Gag: Name game (Fibber, Molly, conductor)
Comments: Bill Thompson is given a chance to mix some of his garbled streetcar conductor language into the train announcer bit. The writers have considerable fun with names of trains (Cinder Bucket, Bone Shaker), places (Left Me Flat and the ever-popular Naked Jo, MO), and, of course, the acronym of Fibber's organization (SADPOOP).

Date: March 6, 1951
Title: Checkup for Molly
Cast: Jim Jordan (Fibber), Marian Jordan (Molly), Harlow Wilcox, Bill Thompson (Old Timer), Gale Gordon (Mayor LaTrivia), Arthur Q. Bryan (Doctor Gamble), Dick LeGrand (Ole Swenson), Dick Ryan (patient), Tyler McVey (John Tabloid), Lillian Lee (patient), Ann Diamond (nurse)
Summary: At McGee's insistence Molly agrees to have a checkup at Gamble's office where Fibber also comes under the watchful eye of the doctor.
Music: Billy Mills: "I am Loved," "Sparrow in the Treetop" (The King's Men, vocal), "And You'll Be Home"
Running Gags: None
Comments: A Quinn and Leslie quote of note is found in LaTrivia's definition of a committee: "A small group of the unfit appointed by the unthinking to undertake the utterly unnecessary." Gordon stumbles slightly over the next speech after his aphorism which gets another laugh, proving that a miscue is sometimes as productive as wit.

Date: March 13, 1951
Title: Antique Vase
Cast: Jim Jordan (Fibber), Marian Jordan (Molly), Harlow Wilcox, Bill Thompson (Old Timer, conductor), Gale Gordon (Mayor LaTrivia), Dick LeGrand (Ole Swenson), Cliff Arquette (Conrad), George Pirrone (Georgie Nothing)
Summary: The McGees have several close calls carrying home a vase they purchased at an antique shop.
Music: Billy Mills: "The Tennessee Waltz," "St. Patrick's Day Parade" (The King's Men, vocal), "That Old Gang of Mine"
Running Gag: "'Tain't funny, McGee" (Molly)
Comments: The writers put a twist on a batch of clichés in this episode including "strike while the iron is hot," "a face that would stop a clock," and "drunk with power."

Date: March 20, 1951
Title: Kindness to Strangers
Cast: Jim Jordan (Fibber), Marian Jordan (Molly), Harlow Wilcox, Bill Thompson (Old Timer), Arthur Q. Bryan (Doctor Gamble), Tyler McVey (Huntington J. Crumford), Norman Field (J. Merrill Moffat), Kay Lovel (shopper)
Summary: Fibber suddenly begins doing favors for people he does not know after he reads about a man who left his money to a kind stranger.
Music: Billy Mills: "By Heck," "Oh, What a Face" (The King's Men, vocal)
Running Gags: None
Comments: The writers take a good-natured swipe at their use of old jokes by having Fibber say to Molly, "If they fit, dig 'em up and use 'em again." This time the repeated mention of an object, the mackinaw, is a red herring that does not figure in the denouement.

Date: March 27, 1951
Title: Surprise Party
Cast: Harlow Wilcox, Bill Thompson (Wallace Wimple, Old Timer), Gale Gordon (Mayor LaTrivia), Arthur Q. Bryan (Doctor Gamble), Dick LeGrand (Ole Swenson), Herb Vigran (collector), Cliff Arquette (Crampton J. Truffles), Ann Diamond (nurse), Peggy Webber (clerk, Helga Swenson), Dave Willock (Herbershimer)
Summary: Fibber and Molly's friends prepare a surprise party for them while Wimple tries to tell them that the McGees will be staying longer at Aunt Sarah's house.
Music: Billy Mills: "Aba Daba Honeymoon," "That Old Gang of Mine" (The King's Men, vocal), "Peter Cottontail"
Running Gags: Mrs. Kladderhatch bit involving son/swallowed pennies/sense in him (Gamble), Myrt bit involving brother/shoot the mayor/billiards (Wallace), hall closet opened by Truffles looking for the front door, "We're yust donating our time" (Ole)
Comments: Jim's absence due to a bout with the flu gives some of radio's best supporting actors a chance to shine. When Gordon echoes Thompson's bugle call near the end, it is like two elks staking their claim to be king of the hill for at least one week.

Date: April 3, 1951
Title: Recuperating from Flu
Cast: Jim Jordan (Fibber), Marian Jordan (Molly, Teeny), Harlow Wilcox, Bill Thompson (Wallace Wimple, Old Timer), Gale Gordon (Mayor LaTrivia), Arthur Q. Bryan (Doctor Gamble), Dick LeGrand (Ole Swenson)
Summary: Fibber takes plenty of pills as he recovers from his battle with "various pneumonia."

Music: Billy Mills: "Mockin' Bird Hill," "The Hot Canary" (The King's Men, vocal), "I Whistle a Happy Tune"
Running Gag: LaTrivia blowup over *hothouse*
Comments: The connection between the pills and the pearls is a flimsy one because no groundwork has been laid for the pearls in the necklace being separated from the string nor for them being in a bottle which would have made the mix-up possible. Ole indicates that his wife's name is Genevieve; on the previous week's show (the only one in which she appears) he addresses her as Helga.

Date: April 10, 1951
Title: Gas Bill
Cast: Jim Jordan (Fibber), Marian Jordan (Molly), Harlow Wilcox, Bill Thompson (Old Timer), Arthur Q. Bryan (Doctor Gamble), Dick LeGrand (Ole Swenson), Ken Christy (Edgar P. Whom), Cliff Arquette (clerk), Tyler McVey (clerk), Jean Vander Pyl (Kitty MacDonald)
Summary: Fibber, enraged over a bill for $16.23, takes the matter directly to the gas company for satisfaction.
Music: Billy Mills: "It's a Lovely Day Today," "Never Been Kissed" (The King's Men, vocal), "Loveliest Night of the Year"
Running Gag: Name game (Fibber, Molly, clerk)
Comments: If someone is looking for a single episode containing statements which encapsulate Fibber's character, this is the one to save. Molly's "McGee, you're always in a fight with somebody" is his raison d'être, Doc's explanation that "a tornado is a hard blow and McGee is a vice versa" is his modus operandi, and Fibber's admission that he wants to act "before I cool off and realize how unreasonable I'm being" indicates that he knows he can be insufferable but he can't help himself. Fibber errs by two years when tells a clerk that he moved into his present residence in 1937.

Date: April 17, 1951
Title: Grocery Budget
Cast: Jim Jordan (Fibber), Marian Jordan (Molly), Harlow Wilcox, Bill Thompson (Old Timer), Gale Gordon (Mayor LaTrivia), Arthur Q. Bryan (Doctor Gamble), Dick LeGrand (Ole Swenson), Herb Vigran (butcher), Cliff Arquette (manager), John T. Smith (policeman), Charlie Smith (clerk)
Summary: Fibber accompanies Molly to the market, intent on showing her how to bring home the bacon on $15.00 a week.
Music: Billy Mills: "The Syncopated Clock," "The 'When You and I Were Young, Maggie' Blues" (The King's Men, vocal), "You Know You Belong to Somebody Else"
Running Gag: Name game (Fibber, Molly, manager)
Comments: What a difference a week makes. Last week the curtain parted on a McGee blasting the utility at full volume; this week opens with "the picture

of solid contentment" of a Fibber at peace…at least for forty seconds. Harlow's statement of "Men may be better at arithmetic than women…" may have been substantiated by statistical evidence, but even in 1951 such a sales pitch must have soured some females on Pet Milk.

Date: April 24, 1951
Title: Soapbox Derby
Cast: Jim Jordan (Fibber), Marian Jordan (Molly, Teeny), Harlow Wilcox, Bill Thompson (Old Timer), Gale Gordon (Mayor LaTrivia), Arthur Q. Bryan (Doctor Gamble), Dick LeGrand (Ole Swenson), Tyler McVey (PA announcer), Danny Richards Jr. (Willie Toops)
Summary: Fibber builds a soapbox racer for Teeny that he models on the one he made in Peoria as a boy.
Music: Billy Mills: "I Whistle a Happy Tune," "The Unbirthday Song" (The King's Men, vocal), "Mockin' Bird Hill"
Running Gag: "'Tain't funny, kiddo" (Fibber)
Comments: Fibber addresses LaTrivia as Homer for the first time. The digit 9 is repeatedly mentioned, reinforcing that number in the minds of listeners to set up the clincher: three times by McGee, once by LaTrivia announcing the 9th annual race, and once by Teeny when she hopes the racer will go 90 miles an hour.

Date: May 1, 1951
Title: Hitchhiking Bureau
Cast: Jim Jordan (Fibber), Marian Jordan (Molly), Harlow Wilcox, Bill Thompson (Old Timer), Gale Gordon (Mayor LaTrivia), Arthur Q. Bryan (Doctor Gamble), Dick LeGrand (Ole Swenson), Bud Stefan (Lars Swenson), Ed Begley (Tilford C. Cradfish)
Summary: Fibber hopes to make money by setting up a hitchhiking agency that will assure safety for drivers and provide certain rides for those traveling by thumb.
Music: Billy Mills: "Please Don't Talk About Me When I'm Gone," "Across the Wide Missouri" (The King's Men, vocal)
Running Gags: None
Comments: Listeners surely recognize the irony in Fibber's declaration that he plans to retire on the earnings from his new venture and do what he always wanted to do…nothing, which is exactly what he has been doing most of his life. The biggest laugh comes from LaTrivia's pause between *good* and *heavens*, proving that timing is indeed everything.

Date: May 8, 1951
Title: Art Class
Cast: Jim Jordan (Fibber), Marian Jordan (Molly), Harlow Wilcox, Bill Thompson (Old Timer), Gale Gordon (Mayor LaTrivia), Arthur Q. Bryan

(Doctor Gamble), Dick LeGrand (Ole Swenson), Cliff Arquette (Rembrandt J. Fink)
Summary: Fibber puts on smock, beret, and airs before attending an art class at the civic center where he is somewhat apprehensive about meeting the female model in her natural state.
Music: Billy Mills: "The Loveliest Night of the Year," "Just the Way You Are" (The King's Men, vocal), "The Kissing Song"
Running Gags: None
Comments: A throwaway line that might be the best in the script is Molly's admission that she saw a painting of McGee's when she "first came into the room and I have a stiff neck from trying not to look that way again." The horse in this episode may be one of a different color than the hayburner owned by the McGees for a few weeks in 1942, but the name (Lillian) is the same.

Date: May 15, 1951
Title: Hole in One
Cast: Jim Jordan (Fibber), Marian Jordan (Molly), Harlow Wilcox, Bill Thompson (Old Timer), Gale Gordon (Mayor LaTrivia), Arthur Q. Bryan (Doctor Gamble), Dick LeGrand (Ole Swenson), Bob Bruce (Sammy Snead)
Summary: Fibber gives Molly some pointers on golf, then they go to the course where McGee hopes to replicate his hole in one of 1923.
Music: Billy Mills: "How High the Moon," "Ezekiel Saw the Wheel" (The King's Men, vocal), "Love Is the Reason"
Running Gags: None
Summary: This is a very structured episodes with each of the three acts beginning in a different setting. The shrewd audience, familiar with McGee's financial dealings, anticipates his final revelation before he drops the other shoe.

Date: May 22, 1951
Title: Running a Red Light
Cast: Jim Jordan (Fibber), Marian Jordan (Molly), Harlow Wilcox, Bill Thompson (Eddie, Old Timer), Gale Gordon (Mayor LaTrivia), Dick LeGrand (Ole Swenson), Ken Christy (Flattery), Cliff Arquette (Ipso J. Facto), Peggy Knudsen (Miss Doberman)
Summary: After Fibber goes through a red light, he turns himself in but cannot find anyone willing to take his confession or his money.
Music: Billy Mills: "Fidoodin'," "Throw Him Out" (The King's Men, vocal), "Old Soldiers Never Die"
Running Gag: Name game (Fibber, Molly, Ipso, Flattery)
Comments: When Marian elides a line, Jim's ad-lib of "You tell him, Molly" breaks everyone up. Like most episodes, this one ends with a satisfactory

resolution: Fibber goes to his PTA meeting, Molly gets her soda. Peggy Knudsen was married to Jim Jordan Jr.

Date: May 29, 1951
Title: Nest in Mailbox
Cast: Jim Jordan (Fibber), Marian Jordan (Molly, Teeny), Harlow Wilcox, Bill Thompson (Wallace Wimple), Gale Gordon (Mayor LaTrivia), Arthur Q. Bryan (Doctor Gamble), Dick LeGrand (Ole Swenson)
Summary: The McGees try to recover a letter from the mailbox without disturbing a bird that has built a nest there.
Music: Billy Mills: "On Top of Old Smokey," "By the Watermelon Vine" (The King's Men, vocal), "Because of You"
Running Gag: "Bird book" (Wallace)
Comments: For some reason Fibber refers to the bird with masculine pronouns when it is obviously a female. His suggestion that plastering the wall would make a good show would be realized on February 3, 1953 when he installs a wall safe. This is the last episode in which Don Quinn is credited as writer. Quinn left *Fibber McGee and Molly* to devote more time to his other radio program, *The Halls of Ivy*.

Date: June 5, 1951
Title: Fish Bait
Cast: Jim Jordan (Fibber), Marian Jordan (Molly), Harlow Wilcox, Bill Thompson (Old Timer), Gale Gordon (Mayor LaTrivia), Arthur Q. Bryan (Doctor Gamble), Dick LeGrand (Ole Swenson), Cliff Arquette (renter of boats)
Summary: Fibber concocts McGee's Unbeatable Bait Balls which he hopes will reel in loads of fish and money.
Music: Billy Mills: "The Wang Wang Blues," "My Truly, Truly Fair" (The King's Men, vocal), "How Long Is Forever"
Running Gag: "Yust donating my time" (Ole)
Comments: This episode combines two themes that had been used separately several times, fishing and inventing. It also marks the only time McGee is unquestionably successful at catching fish. Phil Leslie receives sole writing credit for the first time.

Date: June 12, 1951
Title: Businessmen's Symphony
Cast: Jim Jordan (Fibber), Marian Jordan (Molly), Harlow Wilcox, Bill Thompson (Old Timer, Bert, Wallace Wimple), Gale Gordon (Mayor LaTrivia), Arthur Q. Bryan (Doctor Gamble), Dick LeGrand (Ole Swenson), Cliff Arquette (piccolo player)
Summary: Fibber composes an arrangement of "The Tennessee Waltz" for the Businessmen's Symphony that would make Spike Jones envious.

Music: Billy Mills: "The Cocky Cuckoo," "Back Home Again in Indiana" (The King's Men and Fibber, vocal)
Running Gags: Tongue twister starting with "mute the flute" (Fibber), "I'm yust donating my time" (Ole)
Comments: Jim reveals a pleasant voice in his number with The King's Men, giving listeners a taste of the kind of serious singing he did on *Smackout* and other early programs. The summer replacement series is *The Jack Pearl Show*.

Date: October 2, 1951
Title: Organizing Trip to Omaha
Cast: Jim Jordan (Fibber), Marian Jordan (Molly), Harlow Wilcox, Bill Thompson (Old Timer, Wallace Wimple), Gale Gordon (Mayor LaTrivia), Arthur Q. Bryan (Doctor Gamble), Dick LeGrand (Ole Swenson), Cliff Arquette (Rodney J. Wright, train announcer), Jean Vander Pyl (woman in prologue)
Summary: After he learns that LaTrivia is paying for the McGees' tickets to Omaha, Fibber invites his other friends to join them without informing the mayor that he will be footing the bill for the whole group.
Music: Billy Mills: "Love Is the Reason," "The Wondrous Word of the Lord" (The King's Men, vocal)
Running Gag: Name game (Fibber, Molly, Rodney)
Comments: This is the first script co-written by Phil Leslie and Keith Fowler. The cast knew how to feed off each other's ad-libs so when Jim stumbles over "come along," he magnifies the booboo with a repetition of "way-way-way" which Harlow echoes with "I'll be happy-happy-happy to."

Date: October 9, 1951
Title: Community Chest Rally in Omaha
Cast: Jim Jordan (Fibber), Marian Jordan (Molly), Harlow Wilcox, Bill Thompson (Pasquale, bellhop, Wallace Wimple, Old Timer), Gale Gordon (Mayor LaTrivia), Arthur Q. Bryan (Doctor Gamble), Dick LeGrand (Ole Swenson), Cliff Arquette (bellhop)
Summary: Fibber plans to deliver a speech for a Community Chest fundraiser if he can just find the coliseum where the event is being held.
Music: Billy Mills: "Because of You," "My Little Nebraska Town" (The King's Men, vocal), "Then I'll Be Happy"
Running Gags: Hall closet in hotel room is opened by Gamble thinking it is the door to the hallway, "Bird book" (Wallace), "'Tain't funny, McGee" (Molly), LaTrivia blowup over "when *Oklahoma* played Omaha"
Comments: Because they were taking the show on the road, the writers loaded the episode with running gags and names of old favorites like Fred Nitney to entertain the people of Omaha. The LaTrivia blowup is the funniest one since the "Where there's a will" explosion on September 19, 1950 because he gets all tangled up in the names of the cities.

Date: October 16, 1951
Title: Teeny's Tooth
Cast: Jim Jordan (Fibber), Marian Jordan (Molly, Teeny), Harlow Wilcox, Bill Thompson (Old Timer), Gale Gordon (Mayor LaTrivia), Arthur Q. Bryan (Doctor Gamble), Cliff Arquette (clerk), Tyler McVey (Doctor Durkin)
Summary: Fibber gives Teeny the royal treatment to take her mind off a loose tooth.
Music: Billy Mills: "The World Is Waiting for the Sunrise," "Oklahoma" (The King's Men, vocal), "Lonesome and Sorry"
Running Gag: Name game (Fibber, Molly, clerk)
Comments: There actually is a photo of Jim with curls circa 1898 that is somewhat like the one Fibber describes from his childhood days. Probably because of the badinage regarding *clairvoyant,* Jim fluffs a line by requesting a "nice, clair Havana."

Date: October 23, 1951
Title: Birthday Dinner for Molly
Cast: Jim Jordan (Fibber), Marian Jordan (Molly), Harlow Wilcox, Bill Thompson (Old Timer, conductor, Wallace Wimple), Gale Gordon (Mayor LaTrivia), Arthur Q. Bryan (Doctor Gamble), Dick LeGrand (Ole), Colleen Collins (Mrs. Toops)
Summary: The McGees invite their friends for a meal to be prepared by Fibber to celebrate Molly's birthday.
Music: Billy Mills: "In the Cool, Cool, Cool of the Evening," "Too Young" (The King's Men, vocal), "For All We Know"
Running Gag: Tongue twister starting with "party peach pie" (Fibber)
Comments: The biggest laugh of the night comes from just a single word, proving the incalculable value of a "yes" man like Bill Thompson who could condense all of Wimple's frustration at having the punch line of his joke whisked away from him into one guttural sound. Fibber's line regarding the potatoes of "Oh, boil them!" is borrowed from the Dennis Day school of daffy comebacks.

Date: October 30, 1951
Title: New Dog
Cast: Jim Jordan (Fibber), Marian Jordan (Molly), Harlow Wilcox, Bill Thompson (Old Timer), Gale Gordon (Mayor LaTrivia), Dick LeGrand (Ole Swenson), Ken Christy (officer), Cliff Arquette (telegraph clerk), Dallas McKinnon (dog)
Summary: Fibber has trouble making friends with the descendant of his childhood pet.
Music: Billy Mills: "Undecided," "Calla Calla" (The King's Men, vocal), "Me and My Shadow"
Running Gag: Name game (Fibber, Molly, clerk)

Comments: Like the mandolin episode of March 21, 1944 in which McGee was the only one who could not play the instrument, everyone except him gets along well with the dog, reinforcing the "me against the world" theme that makes for good fun. The "eyes-nose-tail" chestnut was a vaudeville staple that most radio comedies scraped up at least once.

Date: November 6, 1951
Title: Raccoon Coat
Cast: Jim Jordan (Fibber), Marian Jordan (Molly), Harlow Wilcox, Bill Thompson (Wallace Wimple, Old Timer), Gale Gordon (Mayor LaTrivia), Arthur Q. Bryan (Doctor Gamble), Dick LeGrand (Ole Swenson), Jean Vander Pyl (librarian)
Summary: The McGees search for a book that has a phone number in it that might lead to a buyer of Fibber's coat.
Music: Billy Mills: "Love Is Here to Stay," "Five Foot Two" (The King's Men, vocal)
Running Gag: "Bird book" (Wallace)
Comments: Two questions might occur to listeners: 1) What was Fibber doing with, in Molly's words, an "old collegiate coonskin" when he never attended college? 2) What is holding the uneven leg of the workbench after the book was returned to the library? Perry Botkin, who had performed banjo solos on "Waiting for the Robert E. Lee" and other numbers, gets credit for his work on "Five Foot Two."

Date: November 13, 1951
Title: Duck Hunting with Gamble and LaTrivia
Cast: Jim Jordan (Fibber), Marian Jordan (Molly), Harlow Wilcox, Bill Thompson (Old Timer), Gale Gordon (Mayor LaTrivia), Arthur Q. Bryan (Doctor Gamble)
Summary: Fibber looks forward to hunting with his pals, though Molly is not keen on the idea of shooting harmless ducks.
Music: Billy Mills: "When Buddha Smiles," "Bella Bimba" (The King's Men, vocal), "Bye Bye Blues"
Running Gag: Tongue twister starting with "coy decoy" (Fibber)
Comments: Molly must have had a change of heart regarding hunting because the last time McGee was to go out hunting (December 2, 1947), she went along and brought back four ducks herself.

Date: November 20, 1951
Title: Some Like It Hot
Cast: Jim Jordan (Fibber), Marian Jordan (Molly), Harlow Wilcox, Bill Thompson (Wallace Wimple, Old Timer, waiter), Arthur Q. Bryan (Doctor Gamble), Dick LeGrand (Ole Swenson), Ken Christy (furnace man)

Summary: Fibber is too cold, Molly is too hot, and the thermostat is right in the middle of this battle of the sexes.
Music: Billy Mills: "They Call the Wind Mariah" (The King's Men, vocal), "Down Yonder", "Ninety-nine out of a Hundred"
Running Gags: Myrt bit involving boyfriend/at airbase testing jet/water fountain (Fibber), tongue twister starting with "Hottentot hotshot" (Fibber)
Comments: Fibber states that the birth year to be engraved on his tombstone is 1903, making McGee seven years younger than Jim's actual age. The dessert ordered in the tag reinforces the lesson of the episode that compromise and common sense resolve most marital disputes.

Date: November 27, 1951
Title: Chaperones
Cast: Jim Jordan (Fibber), Marian Jordan (Molly), Harlow Wilcox, Bill Thompson (Old Timer), Gale Gordon (Mayor LaTrivia), Arthur Q. Bryan (Doctor Gamble), Mary Lou Harrington (Christina Swenson, girl), Gloria McMillan (girl, Marilyn Martin), Gil Stratton Jr. (Marvin), Jerry Farber (Flicker Krevetsky)
Summary: Fibber claims he is going to tear up the floor when the McGees chaperone a college dance, though Molly advises caution so he does not slip and land on his light fantastic.
Music: Billy Mills: "Charmaine," "I Get Ideas" (The King's Men, vocal), "Chances Are"
Running Gags: None
Comments: The Old Timer unleashes his first elegy to that "old gang of mine," that motley crew celebrated in cadenced roll calls that always seem to end with a character out of step both in rhythm and rhyme. The gem of the evening has the flavor of a Don Quinn joke so Phil Leslie had learned his lessons well from the master when he has Fibber remember "a soft shoe dance that was so quiet you couldn't even hear it. Then for an encore I'd have 'em turn out the lights so you couldn't see it either."

Date: December 4, 1951
Title: Floorwalker McGee
Cast: Jim Jordan (Fibber), Marian Jordan (Molly), Harlow Wilcox, Bill Thompson (customer, Old Timer), Gale Gordon (Mayor LaTrivia), Dick LeGrand (Ole Swenson), Cliff Arquette (cashier), Bud Stefan (customer), Herb Vigran (customer), Marian Richman (customer)
Summary: As floorwalker for a day at the Bon Ton, Fibber helps people while planning to help himself to an employee discount.
Music: Billy Mills: "Slow Poke," "Shrimp Boats" (The King's Men, vocal), "Chances Are"
Running Gags: None

Comments: When the recorded background noise ends too abruptly, Jim is right there with an ad-lib of "Hey, where'd the crowd go? Must have a lotta union customers in here." In the tag there is a switch in which Molly is the one who has to be pulled out of a torrent of words by Fibber.

Date: December 11, 1951
Title: Detective McGee After Prowler
Cast: Jim Jordan (Fibber), Marian Jordan (Molly, Teeny), Harlow Wilcox, Bill Thompson (Old Timer), Gale Gordon (Mayor LaTrivia), Arthur Q. Bryan (Doctor Gamble), Ed Begley (Hector Howell)
Summary: McGee uses his skills of deduction to track down a suspected prowler.
Music: Billy Mills: "Jalousie," "Let the Worry Bird Worry for You" (The King's Men, vocal), "Rose of the Rio Grande"
Running Gags: None
Comments: The color of Fibber's eyes seems to change with his moods; in this episode they are "piercing gray eyes." McGee creates a piercing image when he describes the efficiency of the police force: "Them lead-footed apple-snatchers couldn't track a Great Dane with muddy feet across a half-acre of bed sheets."

Date: December 18, 1951
Title: Pool Match
Cast: Jim Jordan (Fibber), Marian Jordan (Molly, Teeny), Harlow Wilcox, Bill Thompson (Old Timer), Gale Gordon (Mayor LaTrivia), Arthur Q. Bryan (Doctor Gamble), Dick LeGrand (Ole Swenson), Peter Leeds (Elmo Jones)
Summary: After the Elks select Fibber to represent them in a pool game, McGee is worried that his poor playing will make him a disgrace in front of his pals.
Music: Billy Mills: "Domino," "Rudolph, the Red-Nosed Reindeer" (The King's Men and Teeny, vocal), "I Love the Sunshine of Your Smile"
Running Gag: Tongue twister starting with "Paul Powell" (Fibber)
Comments: The Elks had already paid off their mortgage on the March 8, 1949 show and could hardly be working on the fourth mortgage on a new club in two years. The tongue twister gets stretched out when Fibber stops momentarily three times, prompting LaTrivia's remark that he feels he has known Paul Powell most of his life.

Date: December 25, 1951
Title: Spirit of Giving Presents
Cast: Jim Jordan (Fibber), Marian Jordan (Molly, Teeny), Harlow Wilcox, Bill Thompson (Old Timer, Wallace Wimple), Gale Gordon (Mayor LaTrivia), Arthur Q. Bryan (Doctor Gamble), Dick LeGrand (Ole Swenson)

Summary: As the McGees exchange gifts with their friends, Fibber preaches to Molly about the true spirit of Christmas while griping about the presents they receive.
Music: Billy Mills: "Christmas in Killarney" (The King's Men, vocal), "The Teddy Bears' Picnic," "Raggedy Ann" (The King's Men and Teeny, vocal), "Jingle Bells"
Running Gags: None
Comments: For some reason Wilcox, who has often referred to his wife over the years, is now a bachelor. This episode is unique in that the biggest laughs come during the middle commercial, not from exchanges with the regular characters.

Date: January 1, 1952
Title: New Year's Day Visiting
Cast: Jim Jordan (Fibber), Marian Jordan (Molly), Harlow Wilcox, Bill Thompson (Wallace Wimple, Old Timer), Gale Gordon (Mayor LaTrivia), Arthur Q. Bryan (Doctor Gamble), Dick LeGrand (Ole Swenson)
Summary: The McGees enjoy calling on their friends so much they really eat it up, especially Fibber.
Music: Billy Mills: "'S Wonderful," "Swinging Down the Lane" (The King's Men, vocal)
Running Gags: None
Comments: When Gamble dictates changes Fibber needs to make in his lifestyle, Jim skillfully uses an assortment of different vowel sounds to vocalize displeasure with the edict.

Date: January 8, 1952
Title: Rumors
Cast: Jim Jordan (Fibber), Marian Jordan (Molly, Teeny), Harlow Wilcox, Bill Thompson (Old Timer, Wallace Wimple), Gale Gordon (Mayor LaTrivia), Arthur Q. Bryan (Doctor Gamble), Dick LeGrand (Ole Swenson), Dick Ryan (O'Malley)
Summary: To prove to Molly the folly of listening to rumors, Fibber plants a false story with the Old Timer that comes back to haunt him.
Music: Billy Mills: "Manhattan," "There Is Nothing Like a Dame" (The King's Men, vocal)
Running Gags: None
Comments: The consequences of the discovery of America which Fibber enumerates in groups of three pass so quickly one might miss their alliterative effect: "Gin rummy, jitterbugs, and jam sessions; flagpole sitters, Florida real estate, and flying saucers; Bankhead, bebop, and banana burgers; hot rods, hitchhikers, and Hedda Hopper's hats; political platforms, plastic plumbing, and plunging necklines; smog, small-loan companies, and 'On Top of Old Smokey.'" The Old Timer's joke about a lake for people over the

age of thirty-five is an allusion to Serutan, a laxative whose selling point was that its name was *natures* spelled backwards.

Date: January 15, 1952
Title: Rummage Sale
Cast: Jim Jordan (Fibber), Marian Jordan (Molly), Harlow Wilcox, Bill Thompson (Old Timer), Gale Gordon (Mayor LaTrivia), Dick LeGrand (Ole Swenson), Myra Marsh (Miss Trotter), Colleen Collins (Mrs. MacDonald), Bob Bruce (bidder)
Summary: Fibber has difficulty selling items at the rummage sale for the Wistful Vista Women's Club until he goes hunting and lands some duds.
Music: Billy Mills: "Soliloquy," "Never" (The King's Men, vocal), "Let a Smile Be Your Umbrella"
Running Gags: "'Tain't funny, McGee" (Molly), "That ain't the way I heered it" (Old Timer)
Comments: The plug for Eddie Cantor's show in the tag is just one of a number that will be heard in the coming months as radio programs futilely try to combat the loss of their audience to television.

Date: January 22, 1952
Title: Locked Out
Cast: Jim Jordan (Fibber), Marian Jordan (Molly), Harlow Wilcox, Bill Thompson (Old Timer), Gale Gordon (Mayor LaTrivia), Arthur Q. Bryan (Doctor Gamble), Dick LeGrand (Ole Swenson)
Summary: The McGees try to get into the house after they return from the movies and discover they have forgotten the key to the front door.
Music: Billy Mills: "I Talk to the Trees," "Chattanooga Choo Choo" (The King's Men, vocal), "Anytime"
Running Gag: "'Tain't funny, McGee" (Molly), LaTrivia blowup over Eton College
Comments: Gamble deals listeners in on the peculiar rules of a card game invented by McGee which begins with "All spades are wild except the king which becomes a deuce of hearts..." and gets more convoluted after that. Fibber says, "I'd liked to have saw that" for the first time, an ungrammatical expression that will be spoken a number of times in the coming months by the McGees. For some reason the audience is tickled with the Old Timer's "hot spot" gag, laughing for almost fifteen seconds.

Date: January 29, 1952
Title: Matchmaker McGee
Cast: Jim Jordan (Fibber), Marian Jordan (Molly), Harlow Wilcox, Bill Thompson (Old Timer), Dick LeGrand (Ole Swenson), Gloria McMillan (Debbie Lynn), Gil Stratton Jr. (Ed Tatum)

Summary: While Fibber promotes the value of marriage to two lovebirds, he unintentionally demonstrates the traits of a poor husband.
Music: Billy Mills: "Grand Central Station," "Slow Poke" (The King's Men, vocal), "My One and Only Love"
Running Gags: Tongue twister starting with "Ada and Ida" (Fibber), hall closet opened by Fibber looking for budget book
Comments: The hall closet gag is brought out of mothballs after a long absence. It had been fourteen weeks since that noisy sound effect was heard and that was a closet in an Omaha hotel room. When the closet in Wistful Vista was opened on March 27, 1951, Jim and Marian were not on the show so one has to go back over a year to January 23, 1951 to find the last time Fibber touched that fateful door.

Date: February 5, 1952
Title: Paying Bills
Cast: Jim Jordan (Fibber), Marian Jordan (Molly), Harlow Wilcox, Bill Thompson (Old Timer, conductor), Gale Gordon (Mayor LaTrivia), Arthur Q. Bryan (Doctor Gamble), Dick LeGrand (Ole Swenson), Ed Begley (Kremer)
Summary: The McGees make several trips downtown to buy ink, envelopes, and a stamp so Fibber can finish paying his bills.
Music: Billy Mills: "Always," "Marshmallow Moon" (The King's Men, vocal), "I'd Like to Baby You"
Running Gags: LaTrivia blowup over "I've just been on a merry-go-round all day," "'Tain't funny, McGee" (Molly)
Comments: This episode is a good example of the "one darn thing after another" plots that makes *Fibber McGee and Molly* so much fun. Ed Begley's blooper breaks Jim up, though he recovers quickly to mimic the fluff by saying, "Liar fluid I don't need."

Date: February 12, 1952
Title: Braided Rug
Cast: Jim Jordan (Fibber), Marian Jordan (Molly), Harlow Wilcox, Bill Thompson (Wallace Wimple, Old Timer), Gale Gordon (Mayor LaTrivia), Arthur Q. Bryan (Doctor Gamble), Dick LeGrand (Ole Swenson), Jess Kirkpatrick (bill collector)
Summary: Friends of the McGees, mistakenly thinking their pals are down on their luck, bring them clothing and blankets which Fibber and Molly braid into a rug.
Music: Billy Mills: "Anytime," "Undecided" (The King's Men, vocal), "June Night"
Running Gag: "Bird book" (Wallace)
Comments: Long-time listeners will recall the February 25, 1941 show in which Uppy, Gildy, and other acquaintances also thought the McGees were

in dire need. This is the third consecutive show in which the featured instrumental is given a distinctive lively treatment by the Billy Mills Orchestra.

Date: February 19, 1952
Title: IRS Wants to See Fibber
Cast: Jim Jordan (Fibber), Marian Jordan (Molly), Harlow Wilcox, Bill Thompson (Old Timer), Gale Gordon (Mayor LaTrivia), Arthur Q. Bryan (Doctor Gamble), Dick LeGrand (Ole Swenson), Tyler McVey (C.J. Jones), Gloria McMillan (secretary)
Summary: Fibber is worried after receiving a letter asking him to meet with a representative of the Internal Revenue Service.
Music: Billy Mills: "The Little White Cloud That Cried," "Pittsburgh, Pennsylvania" (The King's Men, vocal), "I Hear a Rhapsody"
Running Gags: Hall closet opened by Fibber looking for receipts, "'Tain't funny, Mrs. McGee" (Fibber)
Comments: Fibber mentions records for mortgage payments, a strange deduction for a house that was won on a raffle in 1935. Vivid figures of speech were used during the Don Quinn years, but Leslie and Fowler came up with dandies of their own, including two from this episode: "He's more rattled than a gourd in a rumba band" and "I'm as nervous as a mother clam taking her kids past a chowder factory."

Date: February 26, 1952
Title: Pancake Day
Cast: Jim Jordan (Fibber), Marian Jordan (Molly), Harlow Wilcox, Bill Thompson (Old Timer, Wallace Wimple), Gale Gordon (Mayor LaTrivia), Arthur Q. Bryan (Doctor Gamble), Peter Leeds (photographer), Marian Richman (woman), Gloria McMillan (girl)
Summary: Fibber organizes a parade to celebrate National Pancake Day.
Music: Billy Mills: "Tulip and Heather," "Charmaine" (The King's Men, vocal)
Running Gag: Myrt bit involving sister/dogs all bit her/hot dogs, bitter (Fibber)
Comments: No episode in the series melds plot and sponsor's product as effectively as this one. No one suggests that a parade held on a February evening is apt to be a bit nippy nor mentions the improbability of planning and holding a parade in less than twelve hours.

Date: March 4, 1952
Title: Back Step
Cast: Jim Jordan (Fibber), Marian Jordan (Molly, Teeny), Harlow Wilcox, Bill Thompson (Old Timer), Arthur Q. Bryan (Doctor Gamble), Dick LeGrand (Ole Swenson), Jess Kirkpatrick (Frank Frink)
Summary: Fibber borrows trouble (not to mention boards from all over the house) when he sets out to replace a step on the back porch.

Music: Billy Mills: "The Wheel of Fortune" (The King's Men, vocal), "Be My Life's Companion"
Running Gags: Tongue twister starting with "sawed cedar" (Fibber), "'Tain't funny, McGee" (Molly)
Comments: The writers use Kirkpatrick's talented tongue to have him whistle while he works (and talks). The perceptive audience, knowing how Fibber operates from past shows, anticipates the appropriation of the ironing board before Molly reveals it and is well-prepared for McGee's next moves in this board game.

Date: March 11, 1952
Title: Candy from Joe
Cast: Jim Jordan (Fibber), Marian Jordan (Molly), Harlow Wilcox, Bill Thompson (Wallace Wimple), Gale Gordon (Mayor LaTrivia), Arthur Q. Bryan (Doctor Gamble), Gloria McMillan (Debbie Lynn), Dallas McKinnon (radio announcer), Jimmy Durante
Summary: Fibber, jealous after Molly receives a box of candy from someone named Joe, is anxious to find out the identity of the man he views as a home wrecker.
Music: Billy Mills: "Perfidia," "Retreat" (The King's Men, vocal)
Running Gags: "Bird book" (Wallace), LaTrivia blowup over "I scratch his back and he scratches mine"
Comments: The January 18, 1944 episode employed the same plot except flowers and Ralph were used instead of candy and Joe. Why this date was picked to celebrate Jim and Marian's twenty years on NBC is not clear. The first *Smackout* heard on an NBC affiliate (WMAQ) was in November 1931. In March 1931, when *Smackout* first began, WMAQ was owned by CBS. In any case, 1951 would have been the year to commemorate a twentieth anniversary, not 1952.

Date: March 18, 1952
Title: Buckshot McGee
Cast: Jim Jordan (Fibber), Marian Jordan (Molly), Harlow Wilcox, Bill Thompson (Old Timer, Eddie, Wallace Wimple), Gale Gordon (Mayor LaTrivia), Arthur Q. Bryan (Doctor Gamble), Dick LeGrand (Ole Swenson, bystander), Ken Christy (construction boss), Tyler McVey (officer), Gil Stratton Jr. (psychology student), Peggy Webber (Miss Merkle, bystander)
Summary: Fibber mounts a campaign to save the statue of his uncle before a construction crew destroys it.
Music: Billy Mills: "Dardanella," "Little David, Play on Your Harp" (The King's Men, vocal), "Be My Life's Companion"
Running Gag: Myrt bit involving brother/diving for pearls/Pearl's purse (Fibber)

Comments: The question that might occur to listeners at the conclusion of the show is why would members of the regiment raise funds to erect a monument to a nefarious cuss who victimized them. Fibber's answer might be "So we could get in all these gags about him almost ninety years later."

Date: March 25, 1952
Title: Running Kremer's Drugstore
Cast: Jim Jordan (Fibber), Marian Jordan (Molly), Harlow Wilcox, Bill Thompson (customer, Old Timer), Arthur Q. Bryan (Doctor Gamble), Dick LeGrand (Ole Swenson), Ed Begley (Kremer), Gloria McMillan (Debbie Lynn, customer), Gil Stratton Jr. (Ed Tatum)
Summary: McGee assumes control of Kremer's Drugstore without obtaining Kremer's permission so he can show Ed Tatum how to run a business.
Music: Billy Mills: "After I Say I'm Sorry," "The Gandy Dancer's Ball" (The King's Men, vocal)
Running Gags: Tongue twister starting with "Pringle and Dingle" (Fibber), "'Tain't funny, McGee" (Molly)
Comments: The confusion resulting from information the audience hears but McGee doesn't is brought back in his exchange with Ole about his son's chest but is not as elaborate or amusing as Fibber's confrontations with Mrs. Uppington over mix-ups involving furniture, clothing, and children.

Date: April 1, 1952
Title: Umbrellas on a Hot Day
Cast: Jim Jordan (Fibber), Marian Jordan (Molly), Harlow Wilcox, Bill Thompson (Old Timer, Myron), Gale Gordon (Mayor LaTrivia), Arthur Q. Bryan (Doctor Gamble), Dick LeGrand (Ole Swenson), Cliff Arquette (Blankensop), Jean Vander Pyl (Myron's wife, Gordon's mother), Joe Forte (Frisbee), Jeff Silver (Gordon)
Summary: Fibber, acting on a tip from the Old Timer that it is going to rain, buys rain gear that he hopes to resell to customers seeking relief from the storm.
Music: Billy Mills: "Song of the Bayou," "The Cowboy Song" (The King's Men, vocal), "Honest and Truly"
Running Gag: LaTrivia blowup over "a very good friend of mine to boot"
Comments: A heat wave in early spring is hard to believe, even on April Fools' Day. An unexpected laugh comes from Bill Thompson's muffled "goodbye" after the phone has been hung up.

Date: April 8, 1952
Title: Horoscope Keeps Fibber Inside
Cast: Jim Jordan (Fibber), Marian Jordan (Molly), Harlow Wilcox, Bill Thompson (Wallace Wimple), Gale Gordon (Mayor LaTrivia), Arthur Q. Bryan (Doctor Gamble), Dick LeGrand (Ole Swenson)

Summary: After Fibber reads a horoscope that forecasts an ominous day for him and fellow Scorpios, he refuses to budge from his living room chair.
Music: Billy Mills: "The Dipsy Doodle," "Singin' in the Rain" (The King's Men, vocal), "Whistle While You Work"
Running Gag: "Bird book" (Wallace)
Comments: In some episodes the characters mention items, expressions, places, events, or occasions that are now long gone or considered quaint and this one abounds in them, including doctors making house calls, establishments called beauty parlors, shotguns being used in forced marriages, punchboards, and crippled children.

Date: April 15, 1952
Title: All You Can Eat
Cast: Jim Jordan (Fibber), Marian Jordan (Molly), Harlow Wilcox, Bill Thompson (conductor, Old Timer), Gale Gordon (Mayor LaTrivia), Cliff Arquette (disc jockey), Gloria McMillan (Debbie Lynn), Gil Stratton Jr. (Ed Tatum), Lou Krugman (Tony Ippolito)
Summary: Against Molly's advice to exercise moderation, Fibber takes advantage of an all you can eat for $1.00 offer at a restaurant by staying all day and stuffing himself.
Music: Billy Mills: "The Moon Was Yellow" (The King's Men, vocal), "The Noodlin' Rag," "I May Hate Myself in the Morning"
Running Gag: LaTrivia blowup over "light eater"
Comments: The show opens with a clinker rather than a bang when Jim uses *hungry* instead of *empty*, but he quickly recovers himself by repeating the line correctly and ad-libbing "We better do 'em all twice." The lachrymose songs of Johnny Ray are wonderfully satirized in the titles given by the disc jockey.

Date: April 22, 1952
Title: Traffic Court
Cast: Jim Jordan (Fibber), Marian Jordan (Molly), Harlow Wilcox, Bill Thompson (Old Timer, officer), Gale Gordon (Mayor LaTrivia), Arthur Q. Bryan (Doctor Gamble), Dick LeGrand (Ole Swenson), Ken Christy (Judge Blake), Herb Vigran (bailiff)
Summary: After Molly gets a parking ticket, Fibber takes the matter to court and acts as her attorney.
Music: Billy Mills: "Blue Tango," "Around the Corner, Beneath the Berry Tree" (The King's Men, vocal), "Forgive Me"
Running Gag: Tongue twister starting with "Root to write a writ" (Fibber)
Comments: There is great fun in the confusion over numbers during the interrogation of Ole and in Fibber's putting words in the mouths of the Irish policeman. Attentive listeners will notice how Jim adds to the enjoyment by ad-libbing "What's that?" which almost breaks up Ken Christy. Mark this down as a rare episode in which McGee emerges triumphant by accomplishing exactly what he said he was going to do.

Date: April 29, 1952
Title: Plant and Pet Show
Cast: Jim Jordan (Fibber), Marian Jordan (Molly), Harlow Wilcox, Bill Thompson (Old Timer), Gale Gordon (Mayor LaTrivia), Arthur Q. Bryan (Doctor Gamble), Dick LeGrand (Ole Swenson)
Summary: Fibber mixes plant-growers with bug-killers on a geranium that he hopes will win top prize in the Potted Plant and Pet Show.
Music: Billy Mills: "Cumaná," "Roll Out the Wagon" (The King's Men, vocal)
Running Gag: LaTrivia blowup over "I took it with a grain of salt"
Comments: Listeners should have anticipated the end of this shaggy grasshopper story because Fibber usually gets things backwards. The salute to Carlton E. Morse and *One Man's Family* on the serial's twentieth anniversary at the end turns into a tamer version of the Myrt bit.

Date: May 6, 1952
Title: Picnic at Dugan's Lake
Cast: Jim Jordan (Fibber), Marian Jordan (Molly), Harlow Wilcox, Bill Thompson (Wallace Wimple), Arthur Q. Bryan (Doctor Gamble), Gloria McMillan (Debbie Lynn), Gil Stratton Jr. (Ed Tatum)
Summary: The McGees complete preparations for a picnic, then leave with their friends for a day at Dugan's Lake.
Music: Billy Mills: "The Blacksmith Blues," medley of old-time songs (The King's Men, vocal)
Running Gags: "'Tain't funny, McGee" (Molly, twice), hall closet opened by Fibber looking for swimming suit, Myrt bit involving brother/broken back/broke and back (Fibber), "Bird book" (Wallace)
Comments: This avalanche of items from the hall closet is one of the more prolonged ones, meriting a round of applause from the audience. Jim attempts to milk some laughs from the "down, boy, down" line used the previous week. Fibber's recollection of his first kiss with Molly contradicts information given on the April 22, 1947 show which indicated that that romantic event took place on a Ferris wheel.

Date: May 13, 1952
Title: Tunes the Piano Again
Cast: Jim Jordan (Fibber), Marian Jordan (Molly), Harlow Wilcox, Bill Thompson (Old Timer, delivery man), Gale Gordon (Mayor LaTrivia), Dick LeGrand (Ole Swenson), Gloria McMillan (Debbie Lynn), Gil Stratton Jr. (Ed Tatum)
Summary: Molly slyly gets Fibber to tune the piano, knowing that he will wreck it so they can buy a new one from the Bon Ton.
Music: Billy Mills: "Delicado," "Lady Love" (The King's Men, vocal), "Love Letters in the Sand"
Running Gag: "'Tain't funny, McGee" (Molly)

Comments: Listeners hoping to hear the closet door open get an effect just as noisy when the piano falls apart. The clever use of the musical scale to deliver the sponsor's message has the appearance of being spontaneous because of the way Wilcox is reaching to hit all the notes.

Date: May 20, 1952
Title: Carnival Head Man
Cast: Jim Jordan (Fibber), Marian Jordan (Molly), Harlow Wilcox, Bill Thompson (Wallace Wimple, wheel of fortune barker), Arthur Q. Bryan (Doctor Gamble), Dick LeGrand (Ole Swenson), Peter Leeds (George, Eddie), Marian Richman (Madame Cleo), Harry Lang (P.T. Wingding), Cliff Clark (barker)
Summary: At a carnival Fibber reminisces about his experiences on the midway when he was head man with P.T. Wingding.
Music: Billy Mills: "Goody, Goody," "Kiss of Fire" (The King's Men, vocal), "Ma, He's Making Eyes at Me"
Running Gag: "'Tain't funny, Mrs. McGee" (Fibber)
Comments: Sometimes in the midst of a show filled with give-and-take gags a line spoken in a still small voice carries a substantial wallop and Fibber delivers just such a knockout punch when he follows Madame Cleo's comment that the crystal ball is dim and cloudy with "Maybe you ought to go over it with a damp rag." Two years earlier the joke probably would have included some Glo-Coat on the rag.

Date: May 27, 1952
Title: Checkup Fibber Avoids
Cast: Jim Jordan (Fibber), Marian Jordan (Molly), Harlow Wilcox, Bill Thompson (Old Timer, conductor), Gale Gordon (Mayor LaTrivia), Arthur Q. Bryan (Doctor Gamble), Gil Stratton Jr. (Ed Tatum)
Summary: The McGees avoid Doctor Gamble because Fibber doesn't want to take a physical examination.
Music: Billy Mills: "I'll Walk Alone," "I'll Always Be Following You" (The King's Men, vocal), "Linger Awhile"
Running Gag: LaTrivia blowup over "I sat there just glued to my seat…"
Comments: Jim carries on through his "tumping thummys" blooper, gamely ignoring the giggling around him. He tosses in an extra *neigh* to the Old Timer's nag gag that finished out of the money.

Date: June 3, 1952
Title: Singing Commercial
Cast: Jim Jordan (Fibber), Marian Jordan (Molly), Harlow Wilcox, Bill Thompson (Old Timer), Gale Gordon (Mayor LaTrivia), Dick LeGrand (Ole Swenson), John McIntire (William Harding)

Summary: McGee plans a career as a singer of jingles after he receives an offer to use his voice in a commercial.
Music: Billy Mills: "Walking My Baby Back Home," "Lullaby of Broadway" (The King's Men, vocal)
Running Gag: "'Tain't funny, McGee" (Molly)
Comments: Harlow's use of musical voices, coming just three weeks after he climbed the scales, stretched that gimmick just about as far as it could go. The best howl of the evening is delivered by Molly at the end.

Date: June 10, 1952
Title: Political Campaign Manager
Cast: Jim Jordan (Fibber), Marian Jordan (Molly), Harlow Wilcox, Bill Thompson (Old Timer, Wallace Wimple), Gale Gordon (Mayor LaTrivia), Arthur Q. Bryan (Doctor Gamble), Dick LeGrand (Ole Swenson), Ken Christy (salesman), Ralph Edwards
Summary: Fibber begins working to get Senator Salesco elected after receiving a telegram asking him to handle the 1952 campaign.
Music: Billy Mills: "Popularity," summertime medley (The King's Men, vocal), "In the Good Old Summertime"
Running Gags: Hall closet opened by Fibber looking for typewriter, Myrt bit involving cousin/blew his head off/glass of beer (Fibber), tongue twister starting with "case of the vase" (Fibber), "'Tain't funny, McGee" (Molly), "Bird book" (Wallace)
Comments: This is the final episode sponsored by Pet Milk. The dates in Harlow's introduction are off: Roosevelt was already serving his second term in 1937 and his third term in 1941. After the rousing rendition of "Popularity," Jim gets a good laugh when he ad-libs, "There's nothing like a good old waltz." Ralph Edwards appears to promote the summer replacement series, *Truth or Consequences*.

Date: October 7, 1952
Title: Rich Friend Gert
Cast: Jim Jordan (Fibber), Marian Jordan (Molly), Harlow Wilcox, Bill Thompson (Old Timer), Gale Gordon (Mayor LaTrivia), Dick LeGrand (Ole Swenson), Joe Forte (Charles Jones), Mary Jane Croft (Gertrude Jones)
Summary: The McGees borrow LaTrivia's silver set and pretend to be wealthy to timpress an old friend who attended school with Molly.
Music: Billy Mills: "Sing a Little Song," "Polly, Put the Kettle On" (The King's Men, vocal), "The Best Things in Life Are Free"
Running Gag: "'Tain't funny, McGee" (Molly)
Comments: This is the first episode sponsored by Reynolds Aluminum. The nickname Fibber chooses for Wilcox this season is Lumy. A sign that television was taking over American living rooms is Harlow's pitch for a TV

show sponsored by Reynolds, the first of numerous such plugs to be heard in the coming months.

Date: October 14, 1952
Title: Stock in Transit Company
Cast: Jim Jordan (Fibber), Marian Jordan (Molly), Harlow Wilcox, Bill Thompson (conductor, Old Timer), Arthur Q. Bryan (Doctor Gamble), Dick LeGrand (Ole Swenson), Marvin Miller (Weatherhead), Betty Moran (Miss Nidelson, Eloise), Theodore von Eltz (Anderson)
Summary: The McGees visit the offices of the Wistful Vista Transit Company where Fibber, holder of one share of the firm's stock, proceeds to wreak havoc.
Music: Billy Mills: "Vanessa," "Jambalaya" (The King's Men, vocal), "This Can't Be Love"
Running Gag: "'Tain't funny, Mrs. McGee" (Fibber)
Comments: Jim's remarks concerning a waltz received a good response after the last lively number by the orchestra, but his ad-lib about mountain music goes unnoticed in this episode.

Date: October 21, 1952
Title: Post Office Box Key
Cast: Jim Jordan (Fibber), Marian Jordan (Molly), Harlow Wilcox, Bill Thompson (Old Timer), Gale Gordon (Mayor LaTrivia), Arthur Q. Bryan (Doctor Gamble), Dick LeGrand (Old Swenson), Cliff Arquette (Blatherton), Tyler McVey (postmaster), Gil Stratton Jr. (clerk)
Summary: The McGees have difficulty getting a letter out of their post office box after their box number has been changed.
Music: Billy Mills: "Somebody Loves Me," "Ezekiel Saw the Wheel" (The King's Men, vocal), "But Not for Me"
Running Gags: LaTrivia blowup over "keeping my nose to the grindstone," "'Tain't funny, McGee" (Molly)
Comments: Anyone who remembers licking stamps before the days of self-adhesives will appreciate Fibber's description that the last batch he had "tasted like a rubber floor mat out of the engine room of a diesel-powered Scandinavian tuna boat." Jim throws two ad-libs at Harlow, "Never started" and "Keeps the chicken in, too?," that the announcer steps right over while doing the commercial.

Date: October 28, 1952
Title: Grizzly Bear Article in Magazine
Cast: Jim Jordan (Fibber), Marian Jordan (Molly), Harlow Wilcox, Bill Thompson (Old Timer, Wallace Wimple), Arthur Q. Bryan (Doctor Gamble), Dick LeGrand (Ole Swenson), Gil Stratton Jr. (Ed Tatum)

Summary: Fibber is repeatedly interrupted while reading an article in *Partly True*.
Music: Billy Mills: "Meet Mr. Callahan," "Me and Marie" (The King's Men, vocal), "Make Believe (You Are Glad When You're Sorry)"
Running Gags: None
Comments: Ed's reason for breaking up with Debbie Lynn (played by Gloria McMillan) is that she got married. Actually, Gloria was busy doing episodes of *Our Miss Brooks* for television and radio as was Gale Gordon which is why Gordon appears in only thirteen *Fibber McGee and Molly* episodes during the 1952-1953 season and three of those are repeats of shows from previous years. Herb Vigran is listed in the credits but is not heard in this episode.

Date: November 4, 1952
Election Returns—No *Fibber McGee and Molly* broadcast.

Date: November 11, 1952
Title: Fruit Punch
Cast: Jim Jordan (Fibber), Marian Jordan (Molly), Harlow Wilcox, Bill Thompson (Old Timer), Arthur Q. Bryan (Doctor Gamble), Dick LeGrand (Ole Swenson), Jay Novello (Rocco)
Summary: Using his Uncle Sycamore's special recipe, Fibber makes a batch of fruit punch for Molly's Poetry and Pinochle Club.
Music: Billy Mills: "When You Wore a Tulip," "Blue Tail Fly" (The King's Men, vocal)
Running Gags: None
Comments: Recent bride Doris Callahan will become single again and the object of Gamble's affection in some of the fifteen-minute episodes. Listeners wondering why McGee makes the punch upstairs when he previously assembled concoctions in the kitchen or living room should have anticipated the ending. The Doctor Yak allusion is a reference to Doctor Yak-Yak Yancy, a character on *Honest Harold*, Hal Peary's series after he left *The Great Gildersleeve*.

Date: November 18, 1952
Title: Lost Umbrella
Cast: Jim Jordan (Fibber), Marian Jordan (Molly), Harlow Wilcox, Bill Thompson (Wallace Wimple, conductor), Arthur Q. Bryan (Doctor Gamble), Dick LeGrand (Ole Swenson), Cliff Arquette (J. Fraxton Potworthy), Gil Stratton Jr. (Ed Tatum), Mary Jane Croft (Miss Ogilvie)
Summary: The McGees search all over town for Fibber's umbrella.
Music: Billy Mills: "Lady of Spain," "Swinging Down the Lane" (The King's Men, vocal), "Zing Went the Strings of My Heart"

Running Gags: Myrt bit involving sister/Mrs. America/misses America (Fibber), hall closet opened by Fibber looking for umbrella

Comments: The writers get it right right off the bat as every married couple has gone through a question-and-question session that seems to go around in circles. The middle commercial proves again that no one on radio had as much fun while selling the product as Jim, Marian, and Harlow.

Date: November 25, 1952
Title: Polishing Doc's Car
Cast: Jim Jordan (Fibber), Marian Jordan (Molly), Harlow Wilcox, Bill Thompson (Old Timer), Gale Gordon (Mayor LaTrivia), Arthur Q. Bryan (Doctor Gamble)
Summary: McGee polishes a car blindfolded to win a $1.00 bet from Doctor Gamble.
Music: Billy Mills: "Jambalaya," "Get Out Those Old Records" (The King's Men, vocal), "Moonlight on the Ganges"
Running Gag: LaTrivia blowup over "have to pay the piper"
Comments: The image of darkness Fibber recites could be classified as vivid black humor: "I might as well be standing in a coal mine at midnight trying to hit a black cat with a handful of licorice." This episode, in which Fibber works for two laborious hours on the car, would not have been possible during the Johnson's Wax years when CarNu made such tasks a breeze.

Date: December 2, 1952
Title: Bowling or Canasta?
Cast: Jim Jordan (Fibber), Marian Jordan (Molly), Harlow Wilcox, Bill Thompson (Wallace Wimple), Arthur Q. Bryan (Doctor Gamble), Dick LeGrand (Ole Swenson), Elvia Allman (Minnie Beam), Gil Stratton Jr. (Ed Tatum)
Summary: Fibber attempts to keep Molly from remembering a previous engagement to play canasta so he can go bowling.
Music: Billy Mills: "Yours," "Open Up Your Heart" (The King's Men, vocal), "Avalon"
Running Gag: "'Tain't funny, McGee" (Molly)
Comments: The writers insert Molly's squelch of a Fibber gag up front even before Harlow finishes the introduction. Technically, Molly does not remember the canasta game before Fibber's bowling time because the clock strikes 8:00 before the reference to "right on the beam" jogs her memory so Fibber should be allowed to go out, but that would go against the established pattern of McGee as the chump who cannot get a break.

Date: December 9, 1952
Title: New Hat for Molly
Cast: Jim Jordan (Fibber), Marian Jordan (Molly, Teeny), Harlow Wilcox, Gale Gordon (Mayor LaTrivia), Dick LeGrand (Ole Swenson), Cliff Arquette (Armand Pierre Hammerschlag), Jean Vander Pyl (Madame Bertha), Gil Stratton Jr. (Ed Tatum), Mary Jane Croft (laughing woman, Mabel Toops)
Summary: After Fibber buys an atrocious hat for Molly, she does her best to have it put out of its and her misery.
Music: Billy Mills: "Takes Two to Tango," "You Don't Know What Lonesome Is" (The King's Men, vocal)
Running Gag: Name game (Fibber, Molly, Armand)
Comments: Bill Thompson, who had appeared on all the shows since his return from the Navy on January 15, 1946, is absent. A character played by Cliff Arquette once again engages in a name game (albeit a short one) for the first time since October 30, 1951. Mary Jane Croft appears as the character Mabel Toops for the first time. Teeny, out of sight since March 4, 1952, bumps into McGee downtown so listeners will get reacquainted with her and therefore not feel her singing the next two weeks contrived appearances of a character brought back solely for the sake of holiday tradition.

Date: December 16, 1952
Title: Exchanging Wimple's Gift
Cast: Jim Jordan (Fibber), Marian Jordan (Molly, Teeny), Harlow Wilcox, Bill Thompson (Old Timer, Wallace Wimple), Arthur Q. Bryan (Doctor Gamble), Elvia Allman (PA announcer), Cliff Arquette (exchange clerk)
Summary: The McGees keep exchanging items at a store until they find something they can sink their teeth into.
Music: Billy Mills: "Hindustan," "Rudolph, the Red-Nosed Reindeer" (The King's Men and Teeny, vocal), "I Saw Mommy Kissing Santa Claus"
Running Gags: Name game (Fibber, Molly, clerk), "'Tain't funny, McGee" (Gamble)
Comments: Jim breaks everybody up when he can't keep *fool* separate from *foulard*. The PA announcement concerning customers seeking advice about which cigarette to buy alludes to commercials by tobacco companies prevalent at the time which cited specious claims like "Three out of four doctors say _____ are less irritating to throat membranes than any other brand of cigarettes."

Date: December 23, 1952
Title: Party for Doc Gamble
Cast: Jim Jordan (Fibber), Marian Jordan (Molly, Teeny), Harlow Wilcox, Bill Thompson (Old Timer, Wallace Wimple), Arthur Q. Bryan (Doctor Gamble), Dick LeGrand (Ole Swenson)

Summary: The McGees get Doctor Gamble out of town on a ruse so they can decorate his house for a surprise Christmas party.
Music: Billy Mills: Medley of Christmas melodies, "'Twas the Night Before Christmas" (The King's Men and Teeny, vocal)
Running Gag: Myrt bit involving brother/became a poppa/popcorn popper (Fibber)
Comments: In just 90 seconds the Billy Mills Orchestra manages to meld bits of five different holiday favorites into a pleasant medley. Harlow's subtle mention of aluminum production going to "the defense of the nation" is the first time the Korean War is even hinted at on *Fibber McGee and Molly*. The writers use the inarticulate exchange between McGee and Gamble to realistically capture the affection the old battling buddies have for each other.

Date: December 30, 1952
Title: New Year's Eve Dance
Cast: Jim Jordan (Fibber), Marian Jordan (Molly), Harlow Wilcox, Bill Thompson (Old Timer, Frank), Arthur Q. Bryan (Doctor Gamble), Dick LeGrand (Ole Swenson), Gil Stratton Jr. (Ed Tatum)
Summary: The McGees prepare for attending the New Year's Eve dance at the country club as the guests of bank president MacDonald.
Music: Billy Mills: "Glow Worm," "Wonderful Copenhagen" and "No Two People" (The King's Men, vocal), "Rise and Shine"
Running Gag: Myrt bit involving brother/shot a wild lion down/while lying down (Fibber)
Comments: Faithful listeners will recall that Fibber had referred to Ole as "boy" on numerous occasions, but now Swenson takes umbrage at being called a child, probably for the practical reason that it will serve as a point of contention between the men in the coming weeks and thus punch up the dialogue.

Date: January 6, 1953
Title: Fred Nitney in Town
Cast: Jim Jordan (Fibber), Marian Jordan (Molly), Harlow Wilcox, Bill Thompson (Wallace Wimple, train announcer), Arthur Q. Bryan (Doctor Gamble), Dick LeGrand (Ole Swenson), Cliff Arquette (information clerk), Bob Sweeney (Fred Nitney)
Summary: Fibber reunites with old vaudeville crony Fred Nitney while his pal waits between trains.
Music: Billy Mills: "Don't Let the Stars Get in Your Eyes," "Winter Wonderland" (The King's Men, vocal), "Good News"
Running Gags: None
Comments: This is only episode in which the often-cited Fred Nitney actually appears as a speaking character. Bob Sweeney is the actor who assumed the

role of Fibber McGee on the television version of *Fibber McGee and Molly* that ran on NBC from September 15, 1959 through January 19, 1960.

Date: January 13, 1953
Title: Buying a Puppy
Cast: Jim Jordan (Fibber), Marian Jordan (Molly), Harlow Wilcox, Bill Thompson (Old Timer, parrot), Arthur Q. Bryan (Doctor Gamble), Dick LeGrand (Ole Swenson), Tyler McVey (MacDonald), Colleen Collins (customer), Jack Kruschen (Brokehausen, parrot)
Summary: The McGees watch a pet shop for the owner before Fibber can take possession of a dog he hopes to resell for a $40.00 profit.
Music: Billy Mills: "Chicago Style," "Ohee-Ohi-Oho" (The King's Men, vocal), "Love of My Life"
Running Gags: "'Tain't funny, McGee" (Molly), tongue twister starting with "Hu Down and Lu How" (Fibber)
Comments: The chaos in the pet shop sounds quite authentic, topped by the comic sight of rotund Gamble fleeing the premises with a screeching cat on his head.

Date: January 20, 1953
Title: Gossip Book
Cast: Jim Jordan (Fibber), Marian Jordan (Molly), Harlow Wilcox, Bill Thompson (Old Timer), Gale Gordon (Mayor LaTrivia), Dick LeGrand (Ole Swenson), Gil Stratton Jr. (Ed Tatum)
Summary: Fibber places an ad in the newspaper soliciting gossip with the intention of using the responses he gets as material for a book.
Music: Billy Mills: "Veradero," "Blow the Man Down" (The King's Men, vocal), "To See You"
Running Gags: Myrt bit involving uncle/below the Mexican border/under Carlos Hernandez (Fibber), LaTrivia blowup over "I took the role of the governor"
Comments: With this blowup Gale Gordon adds a double take like he had been doing on *Our Miss Brooks* in which he repeats a word or phrase (e.g. "Kate!") in a shrieking tone as if he cannot believe what he has just said. The fictitious book titles Fibber mentions are not as amusing as *Tom Swift and His Mechanical Lint Picker* and two others cited on December 23, 1952.

Date: January 27, 1953
Title: Icicle
Cast: Jim Jordan (Fibber), Marian Jordan (Molly, Teeny), Harlow Wilcox, Bill Thompson (Old Timer), Arthur Q. Bryan (Doctor Gamble), Dick LeGrand (Ole Swenson)
Summary: Fibber does his best to make certain a giant icicle hanging from the house stays there until 4:00 so he can win a $5.00 bet from Doc Gamble.

Music: Billy Mills: "Bye Bye Blues" "So in Love" (The King's Men, vocal)
Running Gags: Tongue twister starting with "Sickle's pickles" (Fibber), hall closet opened by Fibber looking for garden hose, Myrt bit involving father/tossed in jug/cider (Fibber)
Comments: Time seems to go backward at one point in the script. Molly greets Gamble by saying, "Good afternoon," yet after he leaves and the bridge indicates a passage of time she tells Fibber that it's half past eleven. Listeners might accept an icicle ten feet long hanging from the gutter of a tall house but will likely balk at swallowing Fibber's remark that he got a reading of -10° from a thermometer placed in the refrigerator.

Date: February 3, 1953
Title: Wall Safe
Cast: Jim Jordan (Fibber), Marian Jordan (Molly), Harlow Wilcox, Bill Thompson (Old Timer), Gale Gordon (Mayor LaTrivia), Arthur Q. Bryan (Doctor Gamble), Dick LeGrand (Ole Swenson)
Summary: Fibber makes a mess of the living room as he pokes holes in the wall so he can install a safe.
Music: Billy Mills: "Golden Gate," "By the Watermelon Vine" (The King's Men, vocal), "Brown Eyes, Why Are You Blue?"
Running Gags: "'Tain't funny, McGee" (Molly), Myrt bit involving little stranger/ten pounds/midget (Fibber), LaTrivia blowup over "lady in waiting"
Comments: This episode from San Francisco is the last one in which the cast leaves the studio to go on the road to another city. The audience anticipates Fibber's final predicament before it occurs to him because they know he often acts impulsively without considering consequences.

Date: February 10, 1953
Title: Courteous McGee
Cast: Jim Jordan (Fibber), Marian Jordan (Molly), Harlow Wilcox, Bill Thompson (Old Timer), Gale Gordon (Mayor LaTrivia), Arthur Q. Bryan (Doctor Gamble), Gil Stratton Jr. (Ed Tatum)
Summary: Reading a biography of Sir Walter Raleigh prompts McGee to act gallant like the knights of old.
Music: Billy Mills: "Second Star to the Right," "The Wondrous Word of the Lord" (The King's Men, vocal)
Running Gags: None
Comments: Although Fibber has put on airs a number of times speaking in a formal British dialect, this is the first time he adopts sixteenth-century language, the topper being his question after he breaks a knickknack: "What the hecketh was that?"

Date: February 17, 1953
Title: Minding Doc Gamble's Office
Cast: Jim Jordan (Fibber), Marian Jordan (Molly, patient), Harlow Wilcox, Bill Thompson (Wallace Wimple), Gale Gordon (Mayor LaTrivia), Arthur Q. Bryan (Doctor Gamble), Jack Kruschen (Tomlinson, delivery man), Paula Winslowe (patient)
Summary: After Molly offers to serve as Doc's receptionist for the day, Fibber stays as well to snoop in Gamble's files and meddle in his affairs.
Music: Billy Mills: "Who Cares?," "Pagan Love Song," "With a Song in My Heart" (The King's Men, vocal), "My Sin"
Running Gags: None
Comments: The dates from the 1930s Fibber reads off his record occurred long before he even met Gamble. Jim only misses one word in his line about Doc's running ability, but he repeats it, then ad-libs, "We better go back to the beginning and do the whole thing over."

Date: February 24, 1953
Title: Art Class (Repeat)
Cast: Jim Jordan (Fibber), Marian Jordan (Molly), Harlow Wilcox, Bill Thompson (Old Timer), Gale Gordon (Mayor LaTrivia), Arthur Q. Bryan (Doctor Gamble), Dick LeGrand (Ole Swenson), Cliff Arquette (Rembrandt J. Fink)
Summary: Fibber puts on smock, beret, and airs before attending an art class at the civic center where he is somewhat apprehensive about meeting the female model in her natural state.
Music: Billy Mills: "Love Is Sweeping the Country," "How Do You Speak to an Angel?," "The Martins and the Coys" (The King's Men, vocal), "This is a Very Special Day"
Running Gags: None
Comments: This is a repeat of the May 8, 1951 show. The main changes are that on this broadcast the cast credits are at the end and the commercials and musical numbers are different. The inflections, hesitations, laughs, and sound effects are otherwise identical so it appears that a transcription of the original show was used to produce this episode.

Date: March 3, 1953
Title: Breakfast in Bed or in Kitchen? (Repeat)
Cast: Jim Jordan (Fibber), Marian Jordan (Molly), Harlow Wilcox, Bill Thompson (Old Timer), Gale Gordon (Mayor LaTrivia), Arthur Q. Bryan (Doctor Gamble), Dick LeGrand (Ole Swenson)
Summary: To commemorate National Pancake Day Fibber concocts a breakfast for Molly that he can present to her in bed.
Music: Billy Mills: "New Sun in the Sky," "Side by Side," "Don't Let the Stars Get in Your Eyes" (The King's Men, vocal), "S'posing"

Running Gags: None
Comments: This is a repeat of the February 6, 1951 show. The main changes are that on this broadcast the cast credits are at the end and the commercials and musical numbers are different. Also the *pamper/hamper* joke, the confusion over *epicure* and *epitaph*, and the allusion to the Mary Lee Taylor cookbook do not appear in the 1953 show. The "fling a flang" blooper occurs in both broadcasts and the other elements like inflections and distinctive laughers in the audience indicate that a transcription of the earlier show was used to produce this episode.

Date: March 10, 1953
Title: Car Trouble (Repeat)
Cast: Jim Jordan (Fibber), Marian Jordan (Molly, Teeny), Harlow Wilcox, Bill Thompson (Old Timer), Gale Gordon (Mayor LaTrivia), Dick LeGrand (Ole Swenson), Elvia Allman (Angelica Dennison), Cliff Arquette (Levinworth P. Eaton)
Summary: After Molly brings home an object she thinks fell off while she was driving, Fibber tries to figure out what it is and where it goes on the car.
Music: Billy Mills: "But Not for Me," "Caravan," "It's Deductible" (The King's Men, vocal), "Tonight You Belong to Me"
Running Gags: Word confusion involving *obstetrician/octogenarian/optometrist* (Fibber, Molly, Ole), name game (Fibber, Molly, Levinworth)
Comments: This is a repeat of the April 18, 1950 show. The main differences are that on this broadcast the credits are at the end and the commercials and musical numbers are different. The story told to Teeny is also different, the 1950 tale being about rabbits because of it being closer to Easter and this story about cuckoos. Transcriptions of earlier shows were used to produce this episode. When Marian was still not well enough to return after three weeks of repeats, new shows were written.

Date: March 17, 1953
Title: Meeting Someone Downtown
Cast: Jim Jordan (Fibber), Harlow Wilcox, Bill Thompson (Wallace Wimple, conductor, Old Timer), Arthur Q. Bryan (Doctor Gamble), Dick LeGrand (Ole Swenson), Cliff Arquette (Claude J. Babbleton), Elvia Allman (PA announcer), John McIntire (Kremer), Mary Jane Croft (Mabel Toops, clerk), Dick Beals (messenger)
Summary: Fibber is directed all over town to meet someone who wants to thank him for performing a noble deed.
Music: Billy Mills: "There's a Great Day Coming Mañana," "Goofus," "Two Shillelagh O'Sullivan" (The King's Men, vocal), "Haven't Got a Worry"
Running Gags: None
Comments: Elvia Allman again rings up some good chuckles with her pungent delivery as the store announcer. It is probably because Jim is so used

to thinking of Tuesday as their broadcast night that he mistakenly gives the date of the upcoming Academy Awards as "next Tuesday night, March 19th" when he really meant to say "next Thursday night, March 19th."

Date: March 24, 1953
Title: Lucky Day
Cast: Jim Jordan (Fibber), Harlow Wilcox, Gale Gordon (Mayor LaTrivia), Arthur Q. Bryan (Doctor Gamble), Dick LeGrand (Ole Swenson), Herb Vigran (con man, Mike), John McIntire (Kremer), Jack Kruschen (Pete), Dick Beals (Cub Scout), Jim Nusser (MacDonald)
Summary: After Fibber reads a fortune card indicating that today is his lucky day, misfortune trips him up in just about every imaginable way.
Music: Billy Mills: "The Best Things in Life Are Free," "I'll Be Hanging Around," "Red River Valley" (The King's Men, vocal), "Downhearted"
Running Gag: LaTrivia blowup over "a fine kettle of fish"
Comments: Listeners with long memories will recall the February 13, 1940 show in which Fibber's luck after receiving an Egyptian good luck ring is anything but good. Jim slips in a sotto voce tip of the hat to his friend when he says, "Uncle Will Mills" after the featured orchestra number.

Date: March 31, 1953
Title: Hypnotism
Cast: Jim Jordan (Fibber), Harlow Wilcox, Arthur Q. Bryan (Doctor Gamble), Dick LeGrand (Ole Swenson), Cliff Arquette (J. Whistler Van Goo), Elvia Allman (Cora Burns), Jess Kirkpatrick (Walt), Tyler McVey (postmaster), Mary Jane Croft (Mabel Toops), Jack Kruschen (Whitey Addleton, Brokehausen), Bob Bruce (Oscar Swenson)
Summary: Fibber tries to put into practice the principles of hypnotism after he receives a book on the subject in the mail.
Music: Billy Mills: "Blow, Gabriel, Blow," "Keep it a Secret," "Get Along Home, Cindy" (The King's Men, vocal), "A Fool in Love"
Running Gags: Name game (Fibber, Van Goo), tongue twister starting with "French-fried fritters" (Fibber)
Comments: It appears that Fibber's idea for french-fried fritters is what we now call corn dogs. Fibber's reference to a three-stooler is a sly takeoff on the three-holer outhouse.

Date: April 7, 1953
Title: Vaudeville Show
Cast: Jim Jordan (Fibber), Harlow Wilcox, Bill Thompson (Wallace Wimple, Old Timer), Arthur Q. Bryan (Doctor Gamble), Dick LeGrand (Ole Swenson), John McIntire (Kremer), Bob Sweeney (Eddie), Jan Arvan (Cy Pierson), Jerry Hausner (man), Billy Mills

Summary: After Kremer and Gamble ask Fibber to take over the management of the upcoming vaudeville show, McGee orders everyone around in his usual tactless manner.
Music: Billy Mills: "I Feel a Song Coming On," "Hot Toddy," "Wild Horses" (The King's Men, vocal), "June Night"
Running Gag: Myrt bit involving brother/hot seat/father got up (Fibber)
Comments: The laugh generated by a tardy egg hitting the floor illustrates the impact of a well-timed sound effect. Just as on the December 18, 1951 episode in which his fellow Elks wanted McGee to represent them in a pool game, listeners undoubtedly expect right from the beginning that there is an ulterior motive in putting Fibber in charge of the show.

Date: April 14, 1953
Title: On the Lam
Cast: Jim Jordan (Fibber), Marian Jordan (Molly), Harlow Wilcox, Bill Thompson (Wallace Wimple, Old Timer), Arthur Q. Bryan (Doctor Gamble), Dick LeGrand (Ole Swenson), Elvia Allman (Cora Burns), Jess Kirkpatrick (Walt), Herb Vigran (Monahan), John McIntire (Kremer), Mary Jane Croft (Mabel Toops)
Summary: Fibber flees from a police officer after he accidentally sets off a fire alarm.
Music: Billy Mills: "Rise and Shine," "April in Portugal," "By the Light of the Silvery Moon" (The King's Men, vocal), "Rose of the Rio Grande"
Running Gags: None
Comments: Marian has a very limited role in this episode, her first appearance in almost two months. The writers undoubtedly planned most of the script around Fibber's misadventures as they had the past four weeks, presuming she might not return, and then added a small part for her when she was deemed healthy enough to appear. Harlow's narration is almost always limited to the introduction, but on this show he also sets the scene coming out of the band number. Mary Jane Croft must have been one of the highest paid supporting radio actresses on a per word basis, delivering about a dozen words in most of her laconic exchanges with Fibber when she played Mabel Toops.

Date: April 21, 1953
Title: Delivering a Cake
Cast: Jim Jordan (Fibber), Marian Jordan (Molly), Harlow Wilcox, Bill Thompson (Wallace Wimple), Arthur Q. Bryan (Doctor Gamble), Dick LeGrand (Ole Swenson), Tyler McVey (Bullets Brown), Myra Marsh (Mrs. Spradley), Mary Jane Croft (Mabel Toops)
Summary: By taking a roundabout route to deliver a tasty cake, Fibber meets an unsavory character.

Music: Billy Mills: "Fine and Dandy," "I'm Sitting on Top of the World," "The Leader Doesn't Like Music" (The King's Men, vocal), "Lonesome and Sorry"

Running Gags: "'Tain't funny, McGee," (Molly), hall closet opened by Fibber looking for his hat, "Gotta get them brakes fixed" (Fibber)

Comments: Molly again has a small part at the beginning and at the end of the show. The writers drop the name of Ken Darby, leader of The King's Men, into one of Gamble's jests. Having earlier met Briefcase Bronson (May 1, 1945) and Bullets Brannigan (March 26, 1946), Fibber takes a ride with Bullets Brown to complete his encounters with the killer Bs.

Date: April 28, 1953
Title: Swapping
Cast: Jim Jordan (Fibber), Marian Jordan (Molly), Harlow Wilcox, Bill Thompson (Old Timer, Wallace Wimple), Dick LeGrand (Ole Swenson), Elvia Allman (Cora Burns), Cliff Arquette (Professor Pickens), Jack Kruschen (Brokehausen), Mary Jane Croft (Mabel Toops)
Summary: Fibber spends the day trading one item for another.
Music: Billy Mills: "Of Thee I Sing," "Doggie in the Window," "Skyball Paint" (The King's Men, vocal), "When You're Smiling"
Running Gag: Tongue twister starting with "Pop Popper" (Fibber)
Comments: Molly again has a small part, although her absence during most of Fibber's swapping is necessary to set up her astonished reaction at the end. Considering Fibber's record as a lovable loser, any day in which he ends up with as much as he had at the beginning is a triumph.

Date: May 5, 1953
Title: Guilty Secret
Cast: Jim Jordan (Fibber), Marian Jordan (Molly), Harlow Wilcox, Bill Thompson (Old Timer), Arthur Q. Bryan (Doctor Gamble), Dick LeGrand (Ole Swenson), Elvia Allman (Cora Burns), Jean Vander Pyl (Mrs. O'Meara), Bob Bruce (Fogel)
Summary: After Fibber comes to the assistance of a woman on the street, he fears someone might have seen his action and report to Molly that he has been unfaithful.
Music: Billy Mills: "Oklahoma," "Anna," "I Believe" (The King's Men, vocal). "Ma, He's Making Eyes at Me"
Running Gags: None
Comments: For the fourth consecutive week since Marian's return Fibber carries most of the action as husband and wife again are separated for a portion of the show.

Date: May 12, 1953
Title: Ole's Brother
Cast: Jim Jordan (Fibber), Marian Jordan (Molly), Harlow Wilcox, Bill Thompson (Old Timer, conductor, Wallace Wimple), Arthur Q. Bryan (Doctor Gamble), Dick LeGrand (Ole Swenson), Elvia Allman (Cora Burns), Tyler McVey (airport announcer), Mary Jane Croft (Mabel Toops), Nestor Paiva (Sven Johnson)
Summary: In appreciation for his twenty years of service for the Elks, Ole's friends bring his brother from Sweden to surprise the janitor.
Music: Billy Mills: "Sing, My Heart," "Your Cheating Heart," "Just Another Polka" (The King's Men, vocal), "Bye Bye Blues"
Running Gag: "'Tain't funny, Mrs. McGee" (Fibber)
Comments: This episode features the best of the "old gang of mine" routines, memorable not only for the incongruity of Grandma Abercrombie being in the group but also for the fun generated from Bill's blooper of saying "powder room" instead of "powder house."

Date: May 19, 1953
Title: Old Tax Law
Cast: Jim Jordan (Fibber), Marian Jordan (Molly), Harlow Wilcox, Bill Thompson (Old Timer, photographer), Gale Gordon (Mayor LaTrivia), Dick LeGrand (Ole Swenson), Mary Jane Croft (city attorney, child), Jan Arvan (reporter)
Summary: Fibber discovers a statute in an old library book that he believes will exempt him from paying local taxes.
Music: Billy Mills: "You Do Something to Me," "I'm in Love," "Roll Out the Wagon" (The King's Men, vocal), "You Know You Belong to Somebody Else"
Running Gag: Myrt bit involving brother/swept out to sea/swept out dirt to see (Fibber)
Comments: Listeners may be surprised when Fibber says that Wistful Vista has over 40,000 residents as many followers of the show have pictured it as a smaller community in their minds. This episode features a rare instance of the Myrt routine taking place in a public phone booth rather than the McGee living room.

Date: May 26, 1953
Title: Hector Howell
Cast: Jim Jordan (Fibber), Marian Jordan (Molly), Harlow Wilcox, Bill Thompson (Wallace Wimple, Old Timer), Arthur Q. Bryan (Doctor Gamble), Elvia Allman (Cora Burns), Nestor Paiva (Hector Howell)

Summary: After Hector Howell punches him, Fibber uses the Hercules Body Builder to develop muscles which may enable him to get revenge on his neighbor.

Music: Billy Mills: "Flying Down to Rio," "Song from *Moulin Rouge*," "Coming Through the Rye" (The King's Men, vocal), "Yours"

Running Gags: Myrt bit involving cousin/took cyanide/Cy and Ida (Fibber), "'Tain't funny, McGee" (Molly)

Comments: In the conclusion facile Fibber goes from cowering to cagey to cadging in less than two minutes. Jim usually handled the rapid-fire tongue twisters with nary a slip of the lip, but some simple lines tripped him up such as when he says, "W-a-wix" instead of "W-a-x" in this episode.

Date: June 2, 1953
Title: Cats
Cast: Jim Jordan (Fibber), Marian Jordan (Molly), Harlow Wilcox, Bill Thompson (Old Timer), Dick LeGrand (Ole Swenson), Marian Richman (woman), Mary Jane Croft (woman), Walter Tetley (boy), Jan Arvan (man)
Summary: Due to an error in a newspaper ad, the McGees are besieged with people wanting to collect a reward for a lost cat.
Music: Billy Mills: "'S Wonderful," "Somebody Stole My Gal," "Hasta La Vista" (The King's Men, vocal), "Lonesome and Sorry"
Running Gag: Tongue twister starting with "pet cat Nat" (Fibber)
Comments: A woman in the audience with a distinctive laugh (Milton Berle's mother in the wrong studio?) can be heard after a number of jokes. Mary Jane Croft's baby talking character seems to be an ideal mate for Arthur Q. Bryan's Elmer Fudd.

Date: June 9, 1953
Title: Safe Driving Campaign (Repeat)
Cast: Jim Jordan (Fibber), Marian Jordan (Molly), Harlow Wilcox, Bill Thompson (Wallace Wimple), Gale Gordon (Mayor LaTrivia), Arthur Q. Bryan (Doctor Gamble), Jack Kruschen (officer)
Summary: During the city's campaign to reduce crime and accidents, Fibber drives his car with extra caution to avoid receiving a ticket.
Music: Billy Mills: "Bojangles of Harlem," "I'm Just Wild about Harry," "Iowa Indian Song" (The King's Men, vocal), "That Old Gang of Mine"
Running Gag: "Bird book" (Wallace)
Comments: This is a repeat of the plot used on the April 1, 1947 show with these main changes: the commercials and musical numbers are different, an exchange with Ole replaces the dialogue with Lena, Doc's ball-and-chain gag is dropped in favor of a catcher's mitt joke, and the months Fibber counts off at the end are different because the 1953 show aired two months later than the 1947 episode.

Date: June 16, 1953
Title: Date with Al Bennington
Cast: Jim Jordan (Fibber), Marian Jordan (Molly), Harlow Wilcox, Bill Thompson (Wallace Wimple), Arthur Q. Bryan (Doctor Gamble), Dick LeGrand (Ole Swenson), Paula Winslowe (Al Bennington)
Summary: After Molly accepts a luncheon date with old schoolmate Al Bennington, Fibber's jealousy causes him to spy on them at the Ritz Vista.
Music: Billy Mills: "Anything Goes," "Big Mamou," "Me and Marie" (The King's Men, vocal), "Sunny"
Running Gags: None
Comments: Fibber should have remembered that it was not quite ten years ago on October 5, 1943 that he made the same incorrect assumption about someone named Al. Since numerous shows have recounted anecdotes indicating that Molly and Fibber have known each other since childhood, the introduction of a classmate that McGee would not know should indeed be a surprise.

Date: June 23, 1953
Title: Civil Defense
Cast: Jim Jordan (Fibber), Marian Jordan (Molly), Harlow Wilcox, Bill Thompson (Wallace Wimple, Old Timer), Arthur Q. Bryan (Doctor Gamble), Dick LeGrand (Ole Swenson), Elvia Allman (Cora Burns)
Summary: Fibber scoffs at the efforts of Molly and others working for the Ground Observer Corps until a message from above changes his mind.
Music: Billy Mills: "Who Knows?," "No Other Love," "Keep It Gay" (The King's Men, vocal), "Let A Smile Be Your Umbrella"
Running Gag: Hall closet opened by Fibber looking for varnish
Comments: Just as some of the WWII shows have that forties feel because of themes relating to the conflict or rationing, so this episode with emphasis on cold war paranoia and an indirect reference to 3D movies places it squarely in the years we liked Ike.

Date: June 30, 1953
Title: Fishing With No Tall Tales
Cast: Jim Jordan (Fibber), Marian Jordan (Molly), Harlow Wilcox, Bill Thompson (Old Timer), Arthur Q. Bryan (Doctor Gamble), Dick LeGrand (Ole Swenson)
Summary: McGee goes fishing with his pals under a handicap, namely that he refrain from living up to his first name or else he will be tossed in Dugan's Lake.
Music: Billy Mills: "High and Low," "Maple Leaf Rag," "Tenderfoot" (The King's Men, vocal), "Linger Awhile"

Running Gag: "'Tain't funny, Mrs. McGee" (Fibber)

Comments: This is the last of the thirty-minute episodes and also the final show with musical numbers from an orchestra and vocal group performed before an audience. Although Wilcox tells listeners to watch local papers "for our return in the fall," he would not be part of the cast that assembled that October. *Cousin Willie*, featuring Bill Idelson, aired in the *Fibber McGee and Molly* slot from July 7 through September 29.

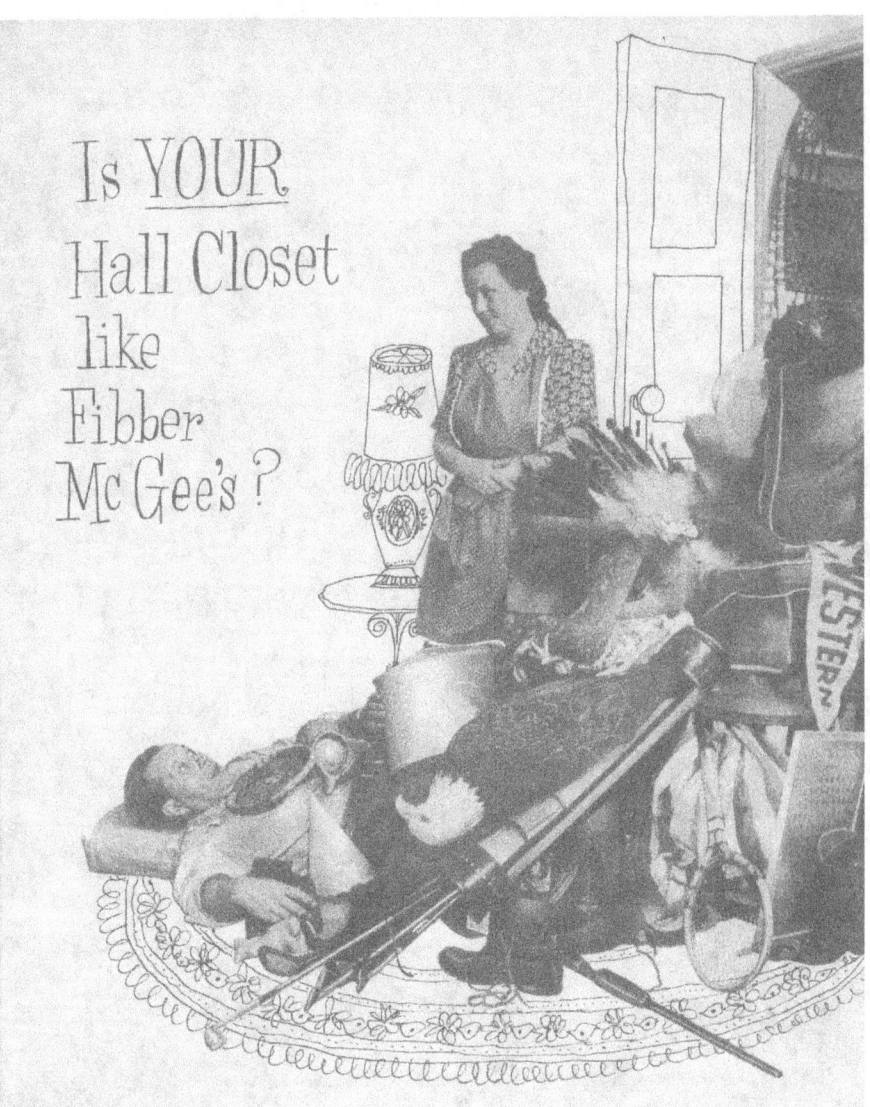

Attention-getting cover of 16-page booklet published in 1953 for "General Motors Men and Women by the Personnel and Employee Relations Staff."

The National Commanders Award of the Catholic War Veterans being presented to Marian and Jim by Charles Buckmeyer. Wording on the Award appears in the Comments section for the June 19, 1945 episode.

Fifteen-Minute Episodes

The fifteen-minute episodes were first broadcast on NBC Monday through Friday evenings at 10:00 Eastern. From August 29, 1954 through June 23, 1955 the shows ran Sunday through Thursday at the same time. From June 27, 1955 through the last episode on March 23, 1956 *Fibber McGee and Molly* was heard at 11:45 AM Monday through Friday with repeat broadcasts aired at 10:00 PM Monday through Thursday (boxing took over the Friday evening slot). There was no audience and the music was pre-recorded on these transcribed shows. The standard theme of "Wing to Wing" remained at the opening and closing with the songs after the final act usually being "The Best Things in Life Are Free," "Sincerely Yours," or "Why Should I Cry Over You?" John Wald replaced Harlow Wilcox as announcer. (Wald is listed among the cast members even if he only delivered the introduction, closing, and intermediate messages.) Bill Thompson and Arthur Q. Bryan were the only regular supporting actors retained from the half-hour series, and Max Hutto continued as director. The category of **Running Gags** is only listed for episodes on which such gags are used. Because different writers assisted Phil Leslie with many of these scripts, a separate category is listed for the **Writers** of each episode. The type of messages delivered by John Wald and others changed frequently so these are listed under **Sponsors** whether the show actually had a client or whether the show was sustained by NBC.

Date: October 5, 1953
Title: Hanging Aunt Sarah's Picture
Cast: Jim Jordan (Fibber), Marian Jordan (Molly, Teeny), John Wald, Bill Thompson (Wallace Wimple), Arthur Q. Bryan (Doctor Gamble)
Summary: Fibber has trouble finding the right tools to hang a picture.
Writer: Phil Leslie
Sponsors: Public Service Announcements for safe driving, CARE, savings bonds
Running Gag: Hall closet opened by Fibber looking for a hammer

Comments: This segment of the *Fibber McGee and Molly* saga begins with a typical story in which not much gets accomplished because of Fibber's inefficiency.

Date: October 6, 1953
Title: Letter to Postmaster
Cast: Jim Jordan (Fibber), Marian Jordan (Molly, Teeny), John Wald, Bill Thompson (Old Timer), Arthur Q. Bryan (Doctor Gamble)
Summary: Fibber plans to vent his dissatisfaction with the postal service after receiving a letter from the postmaster soliciting his opinion.
Writer: Phil Leslie
Sponsors: PSAs for Red Cross, racial tolerance, Ground Observer Corps
Comments: The Old Timer's shaggy beard story about his father is a gem that gets a groan from Fibber.

Date: October 7, 1953
Title: Buying a Parakeet
Cast: Jim Jordan (Fibber), Marian Jordan (Molly), John Wald, Bill Thompson (Wallace Wimple), Mary Jane Croft (clerk)
Summary: The McGees buy, lose, and recover a parakeet.
Writer: Phil Leslie
Sponsors: PSAs for CARE, savings bonds, safe driving
Running Gag: "'Tain't funny, McGee" (Molly)
Comments: The beat-out bunt gag and the story of a bird full of BBs had been used before, but they fit nicely with the circumstances of this adventure so they are worth resurrecting.

Date: October 8, 1953
Title: Teaching Parakeet to Talk
Cast: Jim Jordan (Fibber), Marian Jordan (Molly, Teeny), John Wald, Arthur Q. Bryan (Doctor Gamble), Elvia Allman (Cora Burns)
Summary: Fibber becomes possessive of the parakeet as he attempts to get the bird to repeat his words.
Writer: Phil Leslie
Sponsors: PSAs for racial tolerance, schools, Ground Observer Corps
Comments: Elvia Allman's part is no bigger than the speeches given to her during the years of the thirty-minute shows, but because of the shorter script her contribution seems greater as she provides the comic highlight of the program with her deadpan delivery.

Date: October 9, 1953
Title: Shampoo Bottle
Cast: Jim Jordan (Fibber), Marian Jordan (Molly), John Wald, Bill Thompson (conductor), Arthur Q. Bryan (Doctor Gamble), Howard McNear (Kremer)
Summary: After Fibber spills a bottle of shampoo, the McGees go to Kremer's to get a replacement.

Writer: Phil Leslie
Sponsors: PSAs for safe driving, CARE, savings bonds
Comments: Fibber gives their phone number as 1809, a change from the 1073 number during the thirty-minute era.

Date: October 12, 1953
Title: Call from Executives Club
Cast: Jim Jordan (Fibber), Marian Jordan (Molly), John Wald, Bill Thompson (Old Timer), Arthur Q. Bryan (Doctor Gamble)
Summary: Fibber waits anxiously for a phone call asking him to speak at a luncheon.
Writer: Phil Leslie
Sponsors: PSAs for schools, fire prevention; promo for NBC programs
Comments: It is an odd coincidence that the Old Timer's five silly don'ts are followed by Wald's five serious rules to prevent fires in the home. Eunice Petrosky is one of the delightful names that sounds too good to be untrue.

Date: October 13, 1953
Title: Preparing Speech
Cast: Jim Jordan (Fibber), Marian Jordan (Molly, Teeny), John Wald, Bill Thompson (Wallace Wimple)
Summary: Fibber works on the speech he plans to deliver to a group of business executives.
Writer: Phil Leslie
Sponsors: Tums; PSA for mail for military; promo for NBC programs
Running Gag: Myrt bit involving brother/washed him out/mouth with soap (Fibber)
Comments: Leslie has pun fun with proper nouns in this episode by inserting names from Fibber's past and present.

Date: October 14, 1953
Title: Buying a Suit for Luncheon
Cast: Jim Jordan (Fibber), Marian Jordan (Molly, Teeny), John Wald, Herb Vigran (Quigley)
Summary: Because Molly has given away Fibber's old suits, they shop for new duds downtown.
Writer: Phil Leslie
Sponsors: PSAs for savings bonds, schools; promo for NBC programs
Comments: Listeners should not be surprised at the ending for Leslie sets it up with Fibber's repeated admiration of Quigley's outfit.

Date: October 15, 1953
Title: Biography for Luncheon
Cast: Jim Jordan (Fibber), Marian Jordan (Molly), John Wald, Bill Thompson (Old Timer), Arthur Q. Bryan (Doctor Gamble), Marian Richman (Doris Callahan)

Summary: McGee, still working on his speech, prepares his life history for the man who will introduce him.
Writer: Phil Leslie
Sponsors: PSAs for fire prevention, mail for military; promo for NBC programs
Comments: Leslie slips in a sly joke with SAPS (The Society for the Advancement of Purchases in the Stores) even if it has to limp a little to get ten words into a four-letter acronym.

Date: October 16, 1953
Title: Hoarse from Practicing Speech
Cast: Jim Jordan (Fibber), Marian Jordan (Molly, Teeny), John Wald
Summary: Fibber tirelessly rehearses his speech.
Writer: Phil Leslie
Sponsors: None
Comments: This show is unique among the fifteen-minute episodes in that only Jim and Marian appear and musical interludes are played instead of commercials, PSAs, and promos.

Date: October 19, 1953
Title: Ribbon on Finger (Shorter Version)
Cast: Jim Jordan (Fibber), Marian Jordan (Molly), John Wald, Bill Thompson (Wallace Wimple), Arthur Q. Bryan (Doctor Gamble)
Summary: Fibber performs a variety of tasks, hoping that one of them is the reason for the ribbon on his finger.
Writer: Phil Leslie
Sponsors: PSAs for savings bonds, CARE; promo for NBC programs
Comments: This episode borrows heavily from the December 28, 1943 broadcast and includes the garage and wallpaper gags from that show.

Date: October 20, 1953
Title: Dining and Dancing
Cast: Jim Jordan (Fibber), Marian Jordan (Molly), John Wald, Arthur Q. Bryan (Doctor Gamble), Mary Jane Croft (Grace Goddard), Rolfe Sedan (waiter)
Summary: After Molly has a busy day cleaning, Fibber takes her out for food and footwork at the Ritz Vista.
Writer: Phil Leslie
Sponsors: Tums; PSA for safe driving; promo for NBC programs
Comments: One of Molly's tasks that would not have been mentioned during the Johnson's Wax years is mopping the kitchen floor. Today the entree at a fancy restaurant which also provides entertainment like the Sump Room would be more than the total bill paid by the McGees.

Date: October 21, 1953
Title: Luggage Shopping

Cast: Jim Jordan (Fibber), Marian Jordan (Molly), John Wald, Bill Thompson (Old Timer), Jack Kruschen (clerk)
Summary: The McGees look for new luggage at a store after receiving a telegram from Aunt Sarah inviting them for a visit.
Writer: Phil Leslie
Sponsors: PSAs for savings bonds, schools; promo for NBC programs
Comments: References to popular singers like Eddie Fisher and Gordon MacRae set these shows in their time period just as mentions of Frank Sinatra's effect on bobbysoxers did a decade earlier.

Date: October 22, 1953
Title: Packing for Aunt Sarah's
Cast: Jim Jordan (Fibber), Marian Jordan (Molly), John Wald, Bill Thompson (Wallace Wimple), Arthur Q. Bryan (Doctor Gamble), Richard Beals (paperboy)
Summary: After borrowing Doc's luggage, the McGees complete preparations for their trip.
Writer: Phil Leslie
Sponsors: PSAs for preventing fires, mail to military; promo for NBC programs
Comments: Once again Fibber and Molly will be taking the Cinder Bucket which seems to be the only train that goes where they want to go. The tag's salute to the National Safety Council is followed by an appropriate bit in which Fibber demonstrates carelessness.

Date: October 23, 1953
Title: Preparations for Trip to Aunt Sarah's
Cast: Jim Jordan (Fibber), Marian Jordan (Molly, Teeny), John Wald, Bill Thompson (train announcer), Arthur Q. Bryan (Doctor Gamble), Parley Baer (information clerk), Leroy Leonard (engineer)
Summary: Teeny and Doc Gamble help the McGees get to the station for their trip.
Writers: Phil Leslie, Ralph Goodman
Sponsors: PSAs for Community Chest, savings bonds; promo for NBC programs
Comments: This is the first show co-written by Ralph Goodman. There is no music on this show which in earlier years would have suggested this was a rehearsal, but there was no longer any need for recorded runthroughs because the shows were taped without an audience and therefore could be edited easily.

Date: October 26, 1953
Title: Lost on Train
Cast: Jim Jordan (Fibber), Marian Jordan (Molly), John Wald, Bill Thompson (foreign passenger), Jester Hairston (porter), Jewel Rose (woman), Gilbert Frye (Eddie)

Summary: On board the train Fibber becomes disoriented and has difficulty finding his way back to the proper compartment.
Writers: Phil Leslie, Ralph Goodman
Sponsors: PSAs for savings bonds, schools; promo for NBC programs
Comments: There is no music on this broadcast. Fibber's reaction to what some men would have interpreted as an invitation for extramarital dalliance is what we expect from our noble hero: an embarrassed shudder and a hasty retreat.

Date: October 27, 1953
Title: Searching for Aunt Sarah's House
Cast: Jim Jordan (Fibber), Marian Jordan (Molly), John Wald, Bill Thompson (Charles), Jess Kirkpatrick (Macauley), Parley Baer (Parkinson)
Summary: Thanks to the kindness of a stranger who gives them a ride from the railroad station in a rainstorm, the McGees arrive at what they believe is the right address.
Writers: Phil Leslie, Ralph Goodman
Sponsors: Tums; PSA for savings bonds; promo for NBC programs
Comments: McGee is careless by neglecting to wire ahead and forgetful Macaulay nearly becomes carless.

Date: October 28, 1953
Title: Wrong House
Cast: Jim Jordan (Fibber), Marian Jordan (Molly), John Wald, Bill Thompson (Marston), Elvia Allman (Mrs. Watson J. Wellington III), Parley Baer (Parkinson), Margaret Braden (Mrs. O'Brien)
Summary: Fibber acts like lord of the manor as he orders the hired help around in a mansion.
Writers: Phil Leslie, Ralph Goodman
Sponsors: PSAs for safe driving, Red Cross; promo for NBC programs
Comments: Some elements from the January 3, 1950 visit to Aunt Sarah's house are carried over into this episode including the slipper gag and the ice water threat. Bill Thompson appears in an uncredited bit for the fourth consecutive show.

Date: October 29, 1953
Title: Who is F.C.?
Cast: Jim Jordan (Fibber), Marian Jordan (Molly), John Wald, Bill Thompson (Old Timer), Arthur Q. Bryan (Doctor Gamble)
Summary: The McGees attempt to find out who left a note in their mailbox.
Writers: Phil Leslie, Ralph Goodman
Sponsors: PSAs for savings bonds, schools; promo for NBC programs
Running Gag: Myrt bit involving cousin/ruthless/wife home to mother (Fibber)
Comments: The McGees and Doc play their version of "Who Wants to be a Millionaire?" and answer the question with a very qualified "Not us."

Date: October 30, 1953
Title: Trick or Treating
Cast: Jim Jordan (Fibber), Marian Jordan (Molly, Teeny), John Wald, Bill Thompson (irate man)
Summary: Fibber joins Teeny for some trick or treating and related mischief.
Writers: Phil Leslie, Ralph Goodman
Sponsors: PSAs for savings bonds, mail for military; promo for NBC programs
Comments: Molly's doubts about Fibber growing up in the tag are reinforced by his actions that evening in which Teeny acts more mature than he does.

Date: November 2, 1953
Title: Burglar at Large
Cast: Jim Jordan (Fibber), Marian Jordan (Molly), John Wald, Arthur Q. Bryan (Doctor Gamble)
Summary: Fibber rigs a trap to catch a thief.
Writers: Phil Leslie, Ralph Goodman
Sponsors: PSAs for schools, preventing fires; promo for NBC programs
Comments: Doc and Fibber, staying true to their relationship, trade insults before greeting each other cordially. It is not coincidental that the writers have Kremer and Gamble robbed while *listening* to radio instead of *watching* the new intruder in America's living rooms.

Date: November 3, 1953
Title: Burglar Nabbed
Cast: Jim Jordan (Fibber), Marian Jordan (Molly), John Wald, Bill Thompson (Wallace Wimple), Arthur Q. Bryan (Doctor Gamble), William Conrad (Sergeant Peterson)
Summary: The McGees provide details of the burglary at their home to a police officer before receiving a visit from Gamble that puts an end to the case.
Writers: Phil Leslie, Ralph Goodman
Sponsors: Tums; PSA for savings bonds; promo for NBC programs
Comments: After the point was made for the second time that McGee's watch runs ten minutes slow, listeners should have suspected that the timepiece would bring about the crook's downfall.

Date: November 4, 1953
Title: Lock for Front Door
Cast: Jim Jordan (Fibber), Marian Jordan (Molly), John Wald, Arthur Q. Bryan (Doctor Gamble), Frank Gerstle (Joe)
Summary: After the recent brush with a burglar, the McGees purchase a lock which Fibber installs on the front door.
Writers: Phil Leslie, Ralph Goodman

Sponsors: PSAs for schools, savings bonds; promo for NBC programs

Comments: This is the first episode in which Molly is driving when both McGees are in the car. We can understand why she would not want to do it often because Fibber is a front seat passenger as bad as any backseat driver.

Date: November 5, 1953
Title: Shoes to be Repaired
Cast: Jim Jordan (Fibber), Marian Jordan (Molly, Teeny), John Wald, Bill Thompson (Old Timer)
Summary: Fibber's intention to have his shoes resoled is curtailed when Teeny asks him to fix her wagon.
Writers: Phil Leslie, Ralph Goodman
Sponsors: PSAs for National Guard, mailing early for military; promo for NBC programs
Comments: This is the only time Gamble is welcomed into the McGee home without Arthur Q. Bryan actually appearing on the show. In the tag Neil Herndon, vice-president of the National Association of Letter Carriers, presents Fibber with a card making him a honorary member of the NALC, entitling McGee to carry a heavy satchel, receive complimentary bites from neighborhood dogs, and buy air mail stamps at the current rate of six cents.

Date: November 6, 1953
Title: Parakeet's Preference
Cast: Jim Jordan (Fibber), Marian Jordan (Molly), John Wald, Bill Thompson (Old Timer, Wallace Wimple), Arthur Q. Bryan (Doctor Gamble)
Summary: Fibber and the Old Timer think the parakeet should be in the sunshine while Molly and Doc Gamble lean toward the shady side of the question.
Writers: Phil Leslie, Ralph Goodman
Sponsors: PSAs for savings bonds, Community Chest; promo for NBC programs
Comments: It is symptomatic of these shows in which not much action occurs that the simple repetition of "clatter-clatter-clatter" passes for the most amusing line spoken during the fifteen minutes.

Date: November 9, 1953
Title: Teeny's Gift at the Bon Ton
Cast: Jim Jordan (Fibber), Marian Jordan (Molly, Teeny), John Wald, Bill Thompson (flustered man), Elvia Allman (PA announcer), Cliff Arquette (clerk)
Summary: The McGees shop at the Bon Ton for Teeny's birthday present.
Writers: Phil Leslie, Ralph Goodman
Sponsors: PSAs for savings bonds, schools; promo for NBC programs

Comments: Molly again demonstrates that a cool head trumps a hot hand not only in her opting for a sensible gift instead of a dangerous one but also in asking a probing question in the tag so Fibber does not fall for the same ploy twice.

Date: November 10, 1953
Title: Duck Hunting Invitation
Cast: Jim Jordan (Fibber), Marian Jordan (Molly), John Wald, Bill Thompson (Old Timer), Arthur Q. Bryan (Doctor Gamble), Jack Mather (Colonel Wingate)
Summary: Gamble (with Fibber's help) accepts an offer from a patient to spend some time at his cabin.
Writers: Phil Leslie, Ralph Goodman
Sponsors: Tums; PSA for Community Chest; promo for NBC programs
Comments: McGee shows he has no shame by not only eavesdropping and inviting himself along but also, instead of offering to contribute something like transportation, insists that they will use Doc's car for the trip.

Date: November 11, 1953
Title: Hunting for Hunting License
Cast: Jim Jordan (Fibber), Marian Jordan (Molly), John Wald, Arthur Q. Bryan (Doctor Gamble), Elvia Allman (Cora Burns)
Summary: The McGees look all over the house for Fibber's hunting license.
Writers: Phil Leslie, Ralph Goodman
Sponsors: PSAs for hiring disabled veterans, savings bonds; promo for NBC programs
Comments: The effect of a duck call that sounds like a dyspeptic moose made for great fun on the October 31, 1944 show and will be used wonderfully throughout this foray after wild game as well.

Date: November 12, 1953
Title: Buying Groceries for Trip
Cast: Jim Jordan (Fibber), Marian Jordan (Molly, Teeny), John Wald, Ken Christy (Senator Harper), Jack Kruschen (butcher), Tony Michaels (clerk)
Summary: Fibber finds it difficult to buy groceries for three men with only $10.00 to spend.
Writers: Phil Leslie, Ralph Goodman
Sponsors: PSAs for Community Chest, CARE; promo for NBC programs
Comments: The second half of this episode bears a resemblance to the April 17, 1951 show in which the McGees also battled high prices at the grocery store. For purposes of the story a house payment is used for food, although such a payment should be unnecessary on a home won in a raffle.

Date: November 13, 1953
Title: Trip to Lake Wapahokey
Cast: Jim Jordan (Fibber), Marian Jordan (Molly), John Wald, Arthur Q. Bryan (Doctor Gamble), Parley Baer (Herb Travis)
Summary: Doc, Herb, and Fibber drive to their cabin in the woods.
Writers: Phil Leslie, Ralph Goodman
Sponsors: PSAs for savings bonds, schools; promo for NBC programs
Comments: The writers undoubtedly chose Wapahokey because it sounds like an Indian word meaning "a heap of corn."

Date: November 16, 1953
Title: Raining at Lake Wapahokey
Cast: Jim Jordan (Fibber), John Wald, Arthur Q. Bryan (Doctor Gamble), Parley Baer (Herb Travis)
Summary: The men in the cabin try to find diversions to keep their minds off the lousy weather.
Writers: Phil Leslie, Ralph Goodman
Sponsors: PSA for churches; Paper Mate; promo for NBC programs
Comments: The first commercial for Paper Mate is also the first one integrated right into the action of the fifteen-minute series of shows. This is one of the better quarter-hour episodes, featuring the hilarious blatting of the duck call and the tall tale of the frozen bullet.

Date: November 17, 1953
Title: Duck Hunting, Finally
Cast: Jim Jordan (Fibber), John Wald, Arthur Q. Bryan (Doctor Gamble), Jess Kirkpatrick (Klopinger), Parley Baer (Herb Travis)
Summary: The rain stops, allowing the hunters a chance to shoot some ducks and trade some barbs.
Writers: Phil Leslie, Ralph Goodman
Sponsors: Tums; PSA for National Guard; promo for NBC programs
Comments: Molly is not involved in the action at the lake for obvious reasons. Marian will again be featured in all episodes up to the uranium adventure and fishing trip in August 1954.

Date: November 18, 1953
Title: Hunter McGee Returns Home
Cast: Jim Jordan (Fibber), Marian Jordan (Molly), John Wald, Bill Thompson (Old Timer), Arthur Q. Bryan (Doctor Gamble), Mary Jane Croft (Mabel Toops), Paula Winslowe (Ginny)
Summary: Molly has lunch with two friends, then welcomes Fibber back from his hunting trip.
Writers: Phil Leslie, Ralph Goodman
Sponsors: PSA for savings bonds; Paper Mate; promo for NBC programs

Comments: The Old Timer reprises his hand-me-down recipe gag that seems to go through the family like the flu.

Date: November 19, 1953
Title: Early to Bed After Hunting
Cast: Jim Jordan (Fibber), Marian Jordan (Molly), John Wald, Bill Thompson (Old Timer), Arthur Q. Bryan (Doctor Gamble)
Summary: Fibber, worn out from hunting and a late-night argument with Doc, attempts to go to bed right after supper.
Writers: Phil Leslie, Ralph Goodman
Sponsors: PSAs for Community Chest, schools; promo for NBC programs
Comments: As happens on many occasions, Molly is more like an understanding mother to Fibber than a devoted wife as she tolerates his mood shifts and mollifies him with a bedtime story.

Date: November 20, 1953
Title: Christmas Fund
Cast: Jim Jordan (Fibber), Marian Jordan (Molly, Teeny), John Wald, Bill Thompson (Old Timer)
Summary: Fibber takes charge of Molly's fundraising for her club as he promises to run her $10 into $100.
Writers: Phil Leslie, Ralph Goodman
Sponsors: PSA for churches; Paper Mate; promo for NBC programs
Comments: Just as on the October 18, 1949 show, Fibber's opinion of selling kisses changes when there is a chance he will get in on the smooching.

Date: November 23, 1953
Title: Phony Ring Swindle
Cast: Jim Jordan (Fibber), Marian Jordan (Molly), John Wald, Arthur Q. Bryan (Doctor Gamble), William Conrad (H.J. Shopington)
Summary: Fibber gets conned out of $10.00, then tries to pull the same scam on Gamble.
Writers: Phil Leslie, Ralph Goodman
Sponsors: PSA for savings bonds; Paper Mate; promo for NBC programs
Comments: The scene in the alley is one of the few times a flashback has been used on the program.

Date: November 24, 1953
Title: Selling a Ring to Doc
Cast: Jim Jordan (Fibber), Marian Jordan (Molly), John Wald, Bill Thompson (Wallace Wimple), Arthur Q. Bryan (Doctor Gamble)
Summary: The McGees invite Wimple to stay until his wife returns, then Fibber sells a ring to Gamble.
Writers: Phil Leslie, Ralph Goodman

Sponsors: Tums; PSA for buying Christmas Seals; promo for NBC programs
Comments: Wonders never cease, including the one of Fibber placing an ad in a weekly periodical which is miraculously printed, mailed, received, and read by a subscriber in less than twenty-four hours.

Date: November 25, 1953
Title: Autumn Drive
Cast: Jim Jordan (Fibber), Marian Jordan (Molly), John Wald, Bill Thompson (Wallace Wimple), Jack Moyles (Otto Strunk)
Summary: The McGees take Wimple along to look at the foliage in the country where Wallace meets a fellow birdwatcher.
Writers: Phil Leslie, Ralph Goodman
Sponsors: PSA for CARE; Paper Mate; promo for NBC programs
Comments: Fibber, never a patient person, takes Wimple's nitpicking at the breakfast table for about a minute before making a not-too-subtle remark about when Wallace will be going home. How scenic a drive is on November 25th is questionable because the leaves are on the ground by that date.

Date: November 30, 1953
Title: Bad Luck with Mirrors (Shorter Version)
Cast: Jim Jordan (Fibber), Marian Jordan (Molly), John Wald, Bill Thompson (Old Timer, Wallace Wimple), Arthur Q. Bryan (Doctor Gamble), Marian Richman (clerk)
Summary: Superstitious Fibber is filled with trepidation when Molly asks him to take a mirror downtown to be resilvered.
Writers: Phil Leslie, Ralph Goodman
Sponsors: PSA for mail for military; Paper Mate; promo for NBC programs
Running Gag: "'Tain't funny, McGee" (Molly)
Comments: This is a condensed version of the script used on the October 19, 1943 show. Fibber's math is as bad as his luck: 8x7 is 56, not 65.

Date: December 1, 1953
Title: Photo Contest with $50 Prize
Cast: Jim Jordan (Fibber), Marian Jordan (Molly), John Wald, Bill Thompson (Wallace Wimple)
Summary: Fibber enters a contest that offers a $50 prize for the most unusual photograph.
Writers: Phil Leslie, Ralph Goodman
Sponsors: Tums; PSA for churches; promo for NBC programs
Comments: Without even a flash on his camera, Fibber runs thirty dollars down to 90 cents in a flash.

Date: December 2, 1953
Title: Candid Camera Fiend
Cast: Jim Jordan (Fibber), Marian Jordan (Molly), John Wald, Arthur Q. Bryan (Doctor Gamble), Joseph Kearns (bus driver)
Summary: Fibber is a shutterbug who shoots just about everything that moves before his lens in hopes of winning a photo contest.
Writers: Phil Leslie, Ralph Goodman
Sponsors: PSA for savings bonds; Paper Mate; promo for NBC programs
Comments: Falling out of a window in a bus is a neat trick for an adult, particularly one with Fibber's girth.

Date: December 3, 1953
Title: Processing Film
Cast: Jim Jordan (Fibber), Marian Jordan (Molly), John Wald, Bill Thompson (Old Timer, Wallace Wimple)
Summary: Fibber develops photographs with the hope that one of them will be a prizewinner.
Writers: Phil Leslie, Ralph Goodman
Sponsors: PSAs for Red Cross, fire prevention; promo for NBC programs
Comments: Molly puts her finger on why she has trouble following McGee's conversations ("I guess I don't listen fast enough"), though her solution to the situation might be hard to accomplish: "I'll have to have my ears speeded up." The Old Timer refrains from referring to the mutilated statue as Custer's Last Hand.

Date: December 4, 1953
Title: Photo Lost
Cast: Jim Jordan (Fibber), Marian Jordan (Molly, Teeny), John Wald, Bill Thompson (Wallace Wimple), Bob Bruce (Joseph Leslie), Jack Moyles (Otto Strunk)
Summary: Fibber tries to ward off the offerings of a man he thinks is trying to sell him insurance.
Writers: Phil Leslie, Ralph Goodman
Sponsors: PSA for schools; Paper Mate; promo for NBC programs
Comments: Marian closes with a reminder for listeners to go to church on Sunday.

Date: December 7, 1953
Title: Photo Found
Cast: Jim Jordan (Fibber), Marian Jordan (Molly, Teeny), John Wald, Marian Richman (Susan), Stuffy Singer (Freddy Fuller)
Summary: Fibber recovers a photo from the trash that he hopes to redeem for cash from an insurance salesman.

Writers: Phil Leslie, Ralph Goodman
Sponsors: PSA for mailing packages early; Paper Mate; promo for NBC programs
Comments: Unlike many of the fifteen-minute shows, this episode has some laugh-out-loud lines like the used spider salesman remark and the bizarre circumstances covered by the insurance policy.

Date: December 8, 1953
Title: Call from Washington, D.C.
Cast: Jim Jordan (Fibber), Marian Jordan (Molly, Teeny), John Wald, Arthur Q. Bryan (Doctor Gamble)
Summary: Fibber wonders why someone from Washington, D.C. called for him.
Writers: Phil Leslie, Ralph Goodman
Sponsors: Tums; PSA for National Guard; promo for NBC programs
Comments: A Leslie and Goodman quote of note is Fibber's description of a gourmet as "a guy who knows how to complain about the check in any language."

Date: December 9, 1953
Title: Call Missed
Cast: Jim Jordan (Fibber), Marian Jordan (Molly), John Wald, Bill Thompson (Wallace Wimple), Marian Richman (receptionist)
Summary: Fibber continues to wait for a long-distance call and he pays his overdue phone bill to make sure the call comes through.
Writers: Phil Leslie, Ralph Goodman
Sponsors: PSA for savings bonds; Paper Mate; promo for NBC programs
Comments: The record Wimple mentions is Stan Freberg's parody of *Dragnet* entitled "St. George and the Dragonet."

Date: December 10, 1953
Title: Party Line: Expecting Call
Cast: Jim Jordan (Fibber), Marian Jordan (Molly), John Wald, Bill Thompson (Wallace Wimple), Natalie Masters (woman on phone)
Summary: Fibber is thwarted while waiting for an important call by a talkative woman on the party line.
Writers: Phil Leslie, Ralph Goodman
Sponsors: PSAs for schools, CARE; promo for NBC programs
Comments: For the convenience of this episode the McGees are on a party line. Every other time Fibber picks up the phone he is connected immediately with an operator.

Date: December 11, 1953
Title: Call Comes Through

Cast: Jim Jordan (Fibber), Marian Jordan (Molly), John Wald, Bill Thompson (Old Timer), Arthur Q. Bryan (Doctor Gamble), Ken Christy (General Pearson)
Summary: Fibber finally receives a call from the War Department.
Writers: Phil Leslie, Ralph Goodman
Sponsors: PSA for savings bonds; Paper Mate; promo for NBC programs
Comments: One of the better gags passes by almost unnoticed when the Old Timer's reply to the headache remark is "Just the opposite."

Date: December 14, 1953
Title: Cleaning Lady
Cast: Jim Jordan (Fibber), Marian Jordan (Molly), John Wald, Natalie Masters (Mrs. Bates)
Summary: Fibber hires a woman to help Molly with the cleaning who provides no help at all.
Writers: Phil Leslie, Ralph Goodman
Sponsors: PSA for CARE; Paper Mate; promo for NBC programs
Comments: Natalie Masters, who was an energetic chatterbox on the phone just a few days ago, demonstrates her versatility by becoming a slow-talking and slower-moving shirker on this episode. Fibber's admission at the end about forgetting the joke he was supposed to use is a gimmick writers can use one time only like a free pass.

Date: December 15, 1953
Title: Lost Earring
Cast: Jim Jordan (Fibber), Marian Jordan (Molly), John Wald, Arthur Q. Bryan (Doctor Gamble)
Summary: Fibber shovels the front walk, hoping to find an earring Molly lost.
Writers: Phil Leslie, Ralph Goodman
Sponsors: Tums; PSA for savings bonds; promo to buy radios
Comments: The McGee house continues to be a marvel for we learn in this episode, in case protection is needed from the onslaught of detritus catapulting out of the hall closet, there is a breastplate in an upstairs closet suitable for the task.

Date: December 16, 1953
Title: Christmas Shopping at the Bon Ton
Cast: Jim Jordan (Fibber), Marian Jordan (Molly), John Wald, Bill Thompson (foreign customer, Old Timer), Arthur Q. Bryan (Doctor Gamble), Elvia Allman (PA announcer, Mabel Toops), Bob Bruce (clerk), Natalie Masters (clerk)
Summary: The McGees separate at the Bon Ton so they can buy presents for each other.
Writers: Phil Leslie, Ralph Goodman

Sponsors: PSAs for CARE, mailing packages early; Paper Mate
Comments: This is the first time Elvia Allman appears as Mabel Toops. Elvia's line as the announcer about her lunch being sold in a shoebox is a comic highlight of this episode.

Date: December 17, 1953
Title: Raises $31.90
Cast: Jim Jordan (Fibber), Marian Jordan (Molly), John Wald, Arthur Q. Bryan (Doctor Gamble)
Summary: Fibber has a plan to raise over $30 for Molly's club that has him running in and out of the house.
Writers: Phil Leslie, Ralph Goodman
Sponsors: PSAs for CARE, mailing packages early; promo for buying radios as gifts
Comments: Molly's convoluted admission that begins with "Just don't get me into another one…" passes quickly but makes comic sense upon review.

Date: December 18, 1953
Title: Tax Refund
Cast: Jim Jordan (Fibber), Marian Jordan (Molly, Teeny), John Wald, Bill Thompson (Wallace Wimple, Old Timer)
Summary: Fibber tries to retrieve a letter that fell through a sewer grating.
Writers: Phil Leslie, Ralph Goodman
Sponsors: PSA for savings bonds; Paper Mate; promo for buying radios as gifts
Comments: The hat incident with Wimple and the grating interlude with Teeny reinforce the theme of many shows, that Fibber is everybody's foil.

Date: December 21, 1953
Title: Mailing Aunt Sarah's Gift
Cast: Jim Jordan (Fibber), Marian Jordan (Molly), John Wald, Bill Thompson (Wallace Wimple), Jan Arvan (clerk)
Summary: Fibber goes to great lengths to insure that a vase to be sent to Aunt Sarah is safely packaged.
Writers: Phil Leslie, Ralph Goodman
Sponsors: PSA for churches; Paper Mate; promo for buying radios as gifts
Running Gag: "'Tain't funny, McGee" (Molly)
Comments: Fibber, using his own strange devices, takes *excelsior* as his motto.

Date: December 22, 1953
Title: Bargaining for Christmas Tree
Cast: Jim Jordan (Fibber), Marian Jordan (Molly), John Wald, Bill Thompson (tree salesman), Jack Moyles (Herman), Natalie Masters (Tex)
Summary: Fibber haggles with different sellers of Christmas trees to find one at his price.

Writers: Phil Leslie, Ralph Goodman
Sponsors: Tums, Paper Mate; promo for buying radios
Comments: This episode is distinctive in that there is no setting of the opening scene by John Wald and this is the first of the fifteen-minute shows with commercials for two different products.

Date: December 23, 1953
Title: Decorating the Tree
Cast: Jim Jordan (Fibber), Marian Jordan (Molly), John Wald, Arthur Q. Bryan (Doctor Gamble), Mary Jane Croft (Doris Callahan)
Summary: With the help of Doc and his girlfriend the McGees decorate their tree just in time for Christmas.
Writers: Phil Leslie, Bill Danch
Sponsors: PSA for safe driving; Paper Mate; promo for NBC programs
Comments: This is the first episode co-written by Bill Danch who also worked on scripts for *Honest Harold* and *Baby Snooks*.

Date: December 24, 1953
Title: Laura, the Lopsided Tree
Cast: Jim Jordan (Fibber), Marian Jordan (Molly, Teeny), John Wald, Bill Thompson (Old Timer)
Summary: The McGees bid yuletide greetings to the Old Timer, then Fibber tells Teeny a Christmas story.
Writers: Phil Leslie, Ralph Goodman
Sponsors: PSAs for savings bonds, churches; holiday greetings from NBC
Comments: The tale of Laura is one of the longest stories Fibber unfolds for Teeny, lasting four minutes. Leslie considered this his favorite script from the fifteen-minute era. Rather than exiting before Teeny's appearance as she usually did, Molly sits silently through the story. The recording of the choir singing "Silent Night" is a rare instance of a singing musical interlude during this period.

Date: December 25, 1953
Title: Christmas at Home
Cast: Jim Jordan (Fibber), Marian Jordan (Molly), John Wald, Bill Thompson (radio announcer, Wallace Wimple), Arthur Q. Bryan (Doctor Gamble)
Summary: The McGees welcome two of their friends while trying to decide where to go for Christmas dinner.
Writers: Phil Leslie, Ralph Goodman
Sponsors: PSAs for savings bonds, churches; promo for NBC programs
Comments: This episode opens just like the last one ended, with a Christmas carol. Knocking ornaments off the tree will become a regular activity over the next few weeks. McGee's joke about the maître d' cracking a whip breaks up Molly and also a male in the background, probably Bill Thompson.

Date: December 28, 1953
Title: Exchanging Ice Bucket
Cast: Jim Jordan (Fibber), Marian Jordan (Molly), John Wald, Bill Thompson (Old Timer), Arthur Q. Bryan (Doctor Gamble), Colleen Collins (clerk)
Summary: The McGees take the present Doc gave them for Christmas to the Bon Ton to trade for something they need.
Writers: Phil Leslie, Bill Danch
Sponsors: PSAs for American economic system, churches; promo for NBC programs
Comments: The Old Timer's bit about the Flying Ballerinos indicates he could fabricate on a moment's notice with the best of them who was Fibber.

Date: December 29, 1953
Title: Planning New Year's Eve Party
Cast: Jim Jordan (Fibber), Marian Jordan (Molly, Teeny), John Wald, Bill Thompson (Old Timer)
Summary: Fibber tries out some vaudeville material on Teeny and the Old Timer.
Writers: Phil Leslie, Ralph Goodman
Sponsors: Tums; PSA for schools; promo for NBC programs
Comments: Bill must have ad-libbed the "Yeah!" because it breaks up both Jim and Marian.

Date: December 30, 1953
Title: Reviving Vaudeville Act
Cast: Jim Jordan (Fibber), Marian Jordan (Molly), John Wald, Bill Thompson (Wallace Wimple)
Summary: Fibber auditions Wimple to be his straight man for the show at the Elks.
Writers: Phil Leslie, Ralph Goodman
Sponsors: PSAs for mail for military, safe driving; promo for NBC programs
Comments: The corny exchanges that fall flat offer a contrast to the genuinely funny reminiscence about Charlie Fu and his All-Geisha Orchestra.

Date: December 31, 1953
Title: Night of Vaudeville Show
Cast: Jim Jordan (Fibber), Marian Jordan (Molly), John Wald, Bill Thompson (monkey trainer, Wallace Wimple), Arthur Q. Bryan (Doctor Gamble), Peter Leeds (Horace Watson), Myra Marsh (Mrs. Spradley), Jack Kruschen (man backstage)
Summary: The McGees anxiously await their time to go onstage to perform a revival of Fibber's old act.
Writers: Phil Leslie, Ralph Goodman

Sponsors: PSAs for Red Cross, American economic system; promo for NBC programs

Comments: For the first time Wimple's height of five foot three is mentioned which, coupled with his timid personality, provides another explanation of why he is henpecked.

Date: January 1, 1954
Title: New Year's Day at Home
Cast: Jim Jordan (Fibber), Marian Jordan (Molly), John Wald, Bill Thompson (Old Timer), Arthur Q. Bryan (Doctor Gamble)
Summary: Fibber basks in the acclaim being showered on him resulting from his act at the vaudeville show.
Writers: Phil Leslie, Ralph Goodman
Sponsors: PSAs for fire prevention, churches; promo for NBC programs
Comments: The wishes for peace and tolerance, usually expressed by the Jordans in the tag, are voiced by Molly right before Wald's final message for NBC. Just how Fibber could reveal the secret of his tricks on the unicycle twenty-five years after his death is a question that would strike a happy medium.

Date: January 18, 1954
Title: Citizen X Contest Continues
Cast: Jim Jordan (Fibber), Marian Jordan (Molly), John Wald, Bill Thompson (Wallace Wimple, Old Timer), Arthur Q. Bryan (Doctor Gamble), Joe Forte (floorwalker)
Summary: Fibber's solution to the whereabouts of Citizen X is at odds with the opinion of others in search of the $300 prize.
Writers: Phil Leslie, Ralph Goodman
Sponsors: PSA for March of Dimes; Richard Hudnut; promo for NBC programs
Comments: Recordings have not surfaced for earlier episodes of the Citizen X saga which began on January 7th and concluded on January 26th, making it the longest-running series of episodes devoted to a single story line heard on *Fibber McGee and Molly*.

Date: January 19, 1954
Title: Fixing Toaster
Cast: Jim Jordan (Fibber), Marian Jordan (Molly), John Wald, Bill Thompson (Old Timer), Arthur Q. Bryan (Doctor Gamble)
Summary: Fibber turns the toaster into a bread-shooting weapon when he tries to repair it.
Writers: Phil Leslie, Bill Danch
Sponsors: Tums; PSA for National Guard; promo for NBC programs

Comments: Gamble should have learned from his experience with Fibber's ignition device on April 2, 1946 that being too close to any McGee project is dangerous.

Date: January 20, 1954
Title: Citizen X Contest Goes Airborne
Cast: Jim Jordan (Fibber), Marian Jordan (Molly), John Wald, Bill Thompson (Old Timer), Arthur Q. Bryan (Doctor Gamble), Herb Vigran (Flashton), Tyler McVey (J.B.)
Summary: The prize of $500 for finding Citizen X brings more attention to Fibber who earlier in the week was the only one on the right track.
Writers: Phil Leslie, Ralph Goodman
Sponsors: PSA for March of Dimes; Richard Hudnut; promo for NBC programs
Comments: In the days of live audiences with a full stage of performers, recruiting people to be murmurers for crowd scenes was easy. During the fifteen-minute era only a handful of actors were usually in the studio, yet in this episode the illusion of a front yard filled with prize-seekers was well-done, apparently without resorting to a recording of background noise.

Date: January 21, 1954
Title: Cigar Ashes (Shorter Version)
Cast: Jim Jordan (Fibber), Marian Jordan (Molly), John Wald, Bill Thompson (Old Timer), Arthur Q. Bryan (Doctor Gamble)
Summary: Fibber bets Gamble $5.00 he can keep three inches of ash on his cigar.
Writers: Phil Leslie, Ralph Goodman
Sponsors: PSAs for Radio Free Europe, tax preparation; promo for NBC programs
Comments: This is a condensed version of the script used on October 26, 1943. This time the fire takes place somewhere in the neighborhood instead of the McGee kitchen and Fibber does not receive a black eye. Like the icicle wager on January 27, 1953 and the fishing bet of May 11, 1948, Fibber bends the rules and pays for his perfidy.

Date: January 22, 1954
Title: Birthday Forgotten by Friends
Cast: Jim Jordan (Fibber), Marian Jordan (Molly), John Wald, Bill Thompson (Wallace Wimple, Old Timer), Arthur Q. Bryan (Doctor Gamble), Mary Jane Croft (Doris Callahan), Lou Krugman (Slugsy)
Summary: Fibber is saddened when it appears that all his pals have forgotten his birthday.
Writers: Phil Leslie, Ralph Goodman
Sponsors: PSAs for March of Dimes, churches; promo for NBC programs

Comments: Jack Benny may have skipped about twenty birthdays, but at least he stayed with Valentine's Day whereas the writers moved Fibber's date around to fit the occasion. On the December 12, 1939 show Fibber claimed his birthday was November 16th, in 1946 he celebrated it on February 6th, and in 1954 he observed it on January 22nd.

Date: January 25, 1954
Title: Citizen X Found
Cast: Jim Jordan (Fibber), Marian Jordan (Molly), John Wald, Arthur Q. Bryan (Doctor Gamble), Elvia Allman (Cora Burns), Rolfe Sedan (Frenchman in phone booth), Jack Mather (bus driver)
Summary: On the last day of the contest the identity of Citizen X is revealed right before Fibber's disbelieving eyes.
Writers: Phil Leslie, Ralph Goodman
Sponsors: PSA for March of Dimes; Richard Hudnut; promo for NBC programs
Comments: Molly again has to act like a mother to a childish Fibber at the end just as on January 21st when she advanced his allowance for the month and, in doing so, cut him off from funds for Roy Rogers movies for that period.

Date: January 26, 1954
Title: Chagrined After Contest
Cast: Jim Jordan (Fibber), Marian Jordan (Molly), John Wald, Bill Thompson (Old Timer, Wallace Wimple), Arthur Q. Bryan (Doctor Gamble)
Summary: Fibber is displeased with the outcome of the Citizen X contest until he is lauded for his ability to keep a secret.
Writers: Phil Leslie, Ralph Goodman
Sponsors: Tums; PSA for schools; promo for NBC programs
Comments: What a difference a day makes as Fibber agonistes on Monday becomes Magnifico McGee on Tuesday. Apropos of the comment above concerning yesterday's show, Molly compares the photos in the newspaper of Fibber circa 1918 and of her in 1954 with probably the funniest line of this episode: "I look like your mother."

Date: January 27, 1954
Title: Lawsuit over $3.00
Cast: Jim Jordan (Fibber), Marian Jordan (Molly), John Wald, Bill Thompson (Old Timer), Ken Christy (judge), Parley Baer (Homer Bates)
Summary: Fibber takes a man to court for damaging a picket in the McGee fence.
Writers: Phil Leslie, Ralph Goodman
Sponsors: PSA for March of Dimes; Richard Hudnut; promo for NBC programs

Comments: Fibber and the legal system were solid gold as his numerous brushes with police and judges made for some of the funniest episodes in the series, particularly when he took on legal terms and Latin expressions like sic transit gloria mundi.

Date: January 28, 1954
Title: Tickets to *South Atlantic*
Cast: Jim Jordan (Fibber), Marian Jordan (Molly, Teeny), John Wald, Bill Thompson (Old Timer)
Summary: Molly is reluctant to use a free ticket to see a show at the opera house because it will mean going without Fibber.
Writers: Phil Leslie, Ralph Goodman
Sponsors: PSAs for fire prevention, tax preparation; promo for NBC programs
Comments: The show opens with a funny parody of both westerns and science fiction.

Date: January 29, 1954
Title: Plumber McGee
Cast: Jim Jordan (Fibber), Marian Jordan (Molly), John Wald, Dick Ryan (plumber)
Summary: Fibber tries to unplug a stopped-up drain, then calls in a plumber.
Writers: Phil Leslie, Ralph Goodman
Sponsors: PSAs for March of Dimes, savings bonds; promo for NBC programs
Comments: The handcuff trick mentioned as far back as 1943 plays a key role in this episode.

Date: February 1, 1954
Title: Four Dollar Debt (Shorter Version)
Cast: Jim Jordan (Fibber), Marian Jordan (Molly), John Wald, Arthur Q. Bryan (Doctor Gamble), Jack Moyles (T. Orville White)
Summary: A man who returns $4.00 he borrowed from Fibber is focused more on making a score than evening one.
Writer: Phil Leslie
Sponsors: PSA for American economic system; Richard Hudnut; promo for NBC Programs
Running Gag: Cigar routine (Fibber, White)
Comments: This is a condensed version of the script used on the October 24, 1944 show.

Date: February 2, 1954
Title: Servicemen's Center Needs Redecorating
Cast: Jim Jordan (Fibber), Marian Jordan (Molly), John Wald, Arthur Q. Bryan (Doctor Gamble), Jess Kirkpatrick (Tracy)
Summary: When Molly's women's club has no funds to spruce up the servicemen's center, Fibber and Doc secretly decide to do the job themselves.

Writers: Phil Leslie, Bill Danch
Sponsors: Tums; PSA for churches; promo for NBC programs
Running Gag: Mrs. Kladderhatch bit (through Miss Ogilvie) involving something broken/radio (Gamble)
Comments: For a change a building is not at 14th and Oak but further downtown at 3rd and Oak. Kirkpatrick's Tracy leans toward the folksy, Titus Moody school of storekeeping.

Date: February 3, 1954
Title: Redecorating Servicemen's Center
Cast: Jim Jordan (Fibber), Marian Jordan (Molly), John Wald, Bill Thompson (Wallace Wimple, Old Timer), Arthur Q. Bryan (Doctor Gamble)
Summary: Fibber and his buddies put a new shine on the servicemen's center only to get disturbing news about the building from Molly.
Writers: Phil Leslie, Bill Danch
Sponsors: PSA for Radio Free Europe; Richard Hudnut; promo for NBC programs
Comments: Listeners should have known 14th and Oak was not going to take yesterday's snub without fighting for a change of venue.

Date: February 4, 1954
Title: Paying Bills with Teeny's Ink
Cast: Jim Jordan (Fibber), Marian Jordan (Molly, Teeny), John Wald
Summary: Fibber comes to regret paying bills with pen and ink borrowed from Teeny.
Writers: Phil Leslie, Ralph Goodman
Sponsors: PSAs for safe driving, National Guard; promo for NBC programs
Running Gag: "'Tain't funny, McGee" (Molly)
Comments: Molly's decision to tell the meter reader that her husband's name was Francis might have brought more ridicule than giving his real name considering the popularity of movies at that time featuring a talking mule.

Date: February 5, 1954
Title: Disposing of Christmas Tree
Cast: Jim Jordan (Fibber), Marian Jordan (Molly), John Wald, Arthur Q. Bryan (Doctor Gamble), Jack Moyles (trash man)
Summary: Fibber finds that getting rid of the Christmas tree is harder than throwing a boomerang away.
Writers: Phil Leslie, Len Levinson
Sponsors: PSAs for safe driving, Red Cross; promo for NBC programs
Comments: This is the first fifteen-minute episode co-written by Leonard (Len) Levinson who worked on some *Fibber McGee and Molly* scripts with Don Quinn before Leslie joined the show in 1943. Levinson also wrote for *The Great Gildersleeve* and *The Jack Carson Show*. Fibber disdains the

common comparison to a newborn babe employed by guilty parties with a distinctive declaration: "I'm as innocent as an unborn calf." How knowing a person's license plate number could lead a farmer to 79 Wistful Vista before the McGees returned from the country is a mystery almost as deep as how to plant an evergreen tree in February.

Date: February 8, 1954
Title: Dial Phone
Cast: Jim Jordan (Fibber), Marian Jordan (Molly), John Wald, Arthur Q. Bryan (Doctor Gamble), Nestor Paiva (phone installer)
Summary: After the McGees have a dial phone installed, Fibber gets a call from a mobile Doc Gamble that makes him envious.
Writers: Phil Leslie, Len Levinson
Sponsors: PSA for American economic system; Richard Hudnut; promo for NBC Programs
Running Gag: Myrt bit involving nephew/raising a beard/grandfather's beard (Fibber)
Comments: The new phone number at 79 Wistful Vista is 4366. Decades before cell phones began diverting the attention of drivers Gamble pays a price for gabbing and steering at the same time.

Date: February 9, 1954
Title: Neighbor Frank Ingram
Cast: Jim Jordan (Fibber), Marian Jordan (Molly), John Wald, Jack Moyles (Frank Ingram)
Summary: The McGees become rental agents for a neighbor's house when Fibber learns there is $20 a month in it for them.
Writers: Phil Leslie, Ralph Goodman
Sponsors: Tums; PSA for schools; promo for NBC programs
Comments: On this date "I Love Paris" and "Ricochet" make the FM&M hit parade. With his eagerness to give advice on everything from making pickles to renting homes, Fibber again gives those wiser than him the benefits of his inexperience.

Date: February 10, 1954
Title: Frank Ingram Leaves
Cast: Jim Jordan (Fibber), Marian Jordan (Molly), John Wald, Bill Thompson (Old Timer), Jack Moyles (Frank Ingram)
Summary: Ingram gives Fibber and Molly final instructions before leaving the house in their care to rent.
Writers: Phil Leslie, Ralph Goodman
Sponsors: PSA for safe driving; Richard Hudnut; promo for NBC programs
Comments: Bill Thompson, returning after an absence of four consecutive shows, picks up the comic tempo of the program considerably.

Date: February 11, 1954
Title: Ad for Renting House
Cast: Jim Jordan (Fibber), Marian Jordan (Molly), John Wald, Bill Thompson (Wallace Wimple, policeman), Virginia Gregg (ad clerk)
Summary: The McGees labor over the wording of an ad for the house next door.
Writers: Phil Leslie, Ralph Goodman
Sponsors: PSAs for blood drive, churches; promo for NBC programs
Comments: The comic highlight of this episode is Wimple's sputtering reading of the ad that breaks up Jim and Marian.

Date: February 12, 1954
Title: House Almost Rented
Cast: Jim Jordan (Fibber), Marian Jordan (Molly), John Wald, Jack Kruschen (J. P. Hartford, Professor Snable)
Summary: The McGees come close to finding a tenant for the house next door until the relationship hits some sour notes.
Writers: Phil Leslie, Ralph Goodman
Sponsors: PSAs for American economic system, churches; promo for NBC programs
Comments: Fibber has added some interesting imprecations to his vocabulary recently which have more power than ordinary curses. On February 4th he asks "Who the nickel-plated heck is Max?" and on this episode inquires "What the triple-deckered holy smoke is that?"

Date: February 15, 1954
Title: Showing House
Cast: Jim Jordan (Fibber), Marian Jordan (Molly), John Wald, Bill Thompson (meter reader), Natalie Masters (Mrs. Potts, Florence Clark), Parley Baer (Ray Clark)
Summary: The McGees almost rent the house until Fibber leads them into another dead end by leaving his mouth in gear.
Writers: Phil Leslie, Ralph Goodman
Sponsors: PSA for National Guard; Richard Hudnut; promo for NBC programs
Comments: Because Bill Thompson's normal voice was heard infrequently, he could be counted on to play a number of unbilled roles.

Date: February 16, 1954
Title: Installing Light in Hall Closet
Cast: Jim Jordan (Fibber), Marian Jordan (Molly), John Wald, Arthur Q. Bryan (Doctor Gamble)
Summary: Fibber puts a light in the hall closet so can see the pile of chaos better.

Writers: Phil Leslie, Len Levinson
Sponsors: Tums; PSA for schools; promo for NBC programs
Running Gag: Hall closet opened by Fibber looking for ear muffs
Comments: Fibber rightly declares that it has been a long time since he looked in the closet for it was last opened for our eyes and ears on October 5, 1953.

Date: February 17, 1954
Title: House Finally Rented
Cast: Jim Jordan (Fibber), Marian Jordan (Molly), John Wald, Bill Thompson (Old Timer), Arthur Q. Bryan (Doctor Gamble)
Summary: Fibber works on a sign advertising the rental next door, not knowing that Molly has already found tenants for the house.
Writers: Phil Leslie, Ralph Goodman
Sponsors: PSA for Radio Free Europe; Richard Hudnut; promo for NBC programs
Comments: Fibber's litany of disasters in the garage illustrates the havoc he can create doing the simplest task. John Wald delivers the first teaser in the quarter-hour era when he asks questions about the attic at the end.

Date: February 18, 1954
Title: Attic Mystery Solved
Cast: Jim Jordan (Fibber), Marian Jordan (Molly), John Wald, Bill Thompson (Wallace Wimple, Old Timer)
Summary: Fibber and the Old Timer visit the attic of the Ingram house where they discover someone lurking in the shadows.
Writers: Phil Leslie, Ralph Goodman
Sponsors: PSAs for mail for military, nurse recruitment; promo for NBC programs
Comments: The writers mingle westerns with horror in a funny parody that is all too short but will cause one question to arise in the minds of listeners: How can a headless monster issue a gurgling scream?

Date: February 19, 1954
Title: Watching *Two-Gun Justice*
Cast: Jim Jordan (Fibber), Marian Jordan (Molly), John Wald, Bill Thompson (Old Timer, Kincaid), Natalie Masters (ticket seller, Lil), Robert Easton (Utah), Anne Whitfield (popcorn girl)
Summary: The McGees watch a soporific western movie.
Writers: Phil Leslie, Ralph Goodman
Sponsors: PSAs for American economic system, tax preparation; promo for NBC programs
Comments: The only film title mentioned in this episode that is not fictitious is *Quo Vadis*. *Broadway Rhythm* was a 1943 MGM feature, but James Dunn and Helen Twelvetrees were not in the cast.

Date: February 22, 1954
Title: Washington's Birthday
Cast: Jim Jordan (Fibber), Marian Jordan (Molly, Teeny), John Wald, Bill Thompson (Old Timer)
Summary: Fibber invites Molly to take the day off from her chores to celebrate Washington's birthday.
Writers: Phil Leslie, Ralph Goodman
Sponsors: PSA for savings bonds; Richard Hudnut; promo for NBC programs
Comments: The Old Timer's story of Miss Rump Roast of 1954 is a delight despite the fact it is brought in from left field. It is one of those routines that could be dropped into any episode so, even though it has nothing to do with Washington's birthday, it still steals the show.

Date: February 23, 1954
Title: Tall Tale McGee
Cast: Jim Jordan (Fibber), Marian Jordan (Molly), John Wald, Bill Thompson (Wallace Wimple), Jess Kirkpatrick (Tracy), Mary Lou Harrington (Sally Nelson), Robert Easton (Lester Nelson)
Summary: Fibber entertains a newcomer with one of his fanciful stories.
Writers: Phil Leslie, Ralph Goodman
Sponsors: Tums; PSA for churches; promo for NBC programs
Comments: One day after a holiday commemorating a president known for his telling the truth Fibber unleashes a yarn about a nine-foot bear with ten-inch teeth, three eyes, and, if time allowed him further embellishment, McGee might have added that it had one horn and was a flying purple people-eater. Cast as Lester, the perfect dupe, is Robert Easton, an actor who made a career out of playing hayseeds.

Date: February 25, 1954
Title: Old Newspaper
Cast: Jim Jordan (Fibber), Marian Jordan (Molly, Teeny), John Wald, Bill Thompson (Old Timer)
Summary: Fibber dries out a newspaper he found outside in the rain so he can read it.
Writers: Phil Leslie, Len Levinson
Sponsors: PSA for blood drive; Richard Hudnut; promo for NBC programs
Comments: The mention of General Sarnoff is a tip of the hat to NBC's chairman of the board. The name of Esther Williams is invoked three times. In the old days mentioning the right name on a program meant that something wonderful would show up at the doorstep the next week, but...no, that would be wishful (or Wistful Vista) thinking.

Date: February 26, 1954
Title: Trophy
Cast: Jim Jordan (Fibber), Marian Jordan (Molly), John Wald, Bill Thompson (Old Timer), Arthur Q. Bryan (Doctor Gamble), Robert Easton (Lester Nelson)
Summary: Fibber brings a tarnished trophy down from the attic, then makes an unsettling discovery when he polishes it.
Writer: Phil Leslie
Sponsors: PSAs for CARE, schools; promo for NBC programs
Comments: Leslie borrowed the idea from the March 18, 1952 show, changed the statue to a trophy, and produced another winning effort with the same result: deflating Fibber's ego.

Date: March 1, 1954
Title: Parking Attendant Problems
Cast: Jim Jordan (Fibber), Marian Jordan (Molly), John Wald, Herb Vigran (officer), Jack Mather (attendant)
Summary: The McGees have difficulty getting their car out of a parking lot when the attendant cannot change a ten-dollar bill.
Writers: Phil Leslie, Ralph Goodman
Sponsors: PSA for schools; Richard Hudnut; promo for NBC programs
Comments: The writers put Fibber back where he thrives, as the underdog battling the justice system with a parade of legal malapropisms.

Date: March 2, 1954
Title: Tax Time
Cast: Jim Jordan (Fibber), Marian Jordan (Molly), John Wald, Arthur Q. Bryan (Doctor Gamble), Jack Moyles (Charles Harrison)
Summary: Fibber struggles with the tax form, then takes Gamble's advice to see a tax preparer.
Writers: Phil Leslie, Ralph Goodman
Sponsors: Tums; PSA for Radio Free Europe; promo for NBC programs
Running Gag: Myrt bit involving soaking in hot water/air mail stamp (Fibber)
Comments: Income tax presupposes income so why is Fibber even filling out a form? The shoebox must have been kept in the hall closet because a similar racket is caused when Fibber deposits its contents on Harrison's desk.

Date: March 3, 1954
Title: Interest in Ketchup Gun
Cast: Jim Jordan (Fibber), Marian Jordan (Molly), John Wald, Bill Thompson (Old Timer)
Summary: Fibber receives a letter from a company that is interested in the McGee Jet Ketchup Gun.
Writers: Phil Leslie, Len Levinson
Sponsors: Carter's Little Liver Pills, Richard Hudnut; promo for NBC programs

Running Gag: "'Tain't funny, McGee" (Molly)
Comments: Fibber's recipe for success still makes sense: "Invent something which sells for under a buck that everybody needs but uses up fast and has to buy a new one."

Date: March 4, 1954
Title: Inventing Ketchup Gun
Cast: Jim Jordan (Fibber), Marian Jordan (Molly), John Wald, Arthur Q. Bryan (Doctor Gamble)
Summary: Fibber uses the trial-and-lots-of-errors method to perfect his ketchup gun.
Writers: Phil Leslie, Len Levinson
Sponsors: PSAs for safe driving, Ground Observer Corps; promo for NBC programs
Comments: Molly has some great lines as she watches her husband putter and mutter. Wald's teaser is filled with as many leading questions as heard on soap operas.

Date: March 5, 1954
Title: Ketchup Representative Arrives
Cast: Jim Jordan (Fibber), Marian Jordan (Molly), John Wald, Bill Thompson (Old Timer, Wallace Wimple), Joseph Kearns (Miggins)
Summary: After looking at Fibber's invention, the representative from the Kitchican Ketchup Canning Kitchen has both bad and good news for the McGees.
Writers: Phil Leslie, Len Levinson
Sponsors: PSAs for American economic system, saving bonds; promo for NBC programs
Comments: The comic highlight of this episode occurs when the Old Timer asks Fibber if he is using his invention which resembles a gas can with a nipple to wean a baby Austin.

Date: March 8 1954
Title: Envelope Swindle
Cast: Jim Jordan (Fibber), Marian Jordan (Molly), John Wald, Bill Thompson (Old Timer), Arthur Q. Bryan (Doctor Gamble), Mary Lou Harrington (Sally Nelson)
Summary: Fibber warns Molly against falling for swindles, then acts presumptuously when he thinks she has paid $14.80 for worthless newspapers.
Writers: Phil Leslie, Ralph Goodman
Sponsors: PSA for Radio Free Europe; Richard Hudnut; promo for NBC programs
Comments: The Old Timer must be a sleight of hand wizard if he can palm $3.00 and slip Monopoly money into an envelope before two witnesses.

Date: March 9, 1954
Title: Variety Store Opportunity
Cast: Jim Jordan (Fibber), Marian Jordan (Molly), John Wald, Bill Thompson (Old Timer, mover), Natalie Masters (Miss Quilby)
Summary: Fibber, eager for a new enterprise, thinks he has found a great business venture when he comes across the struggling owner of a store.
Writers: Phil Leslie, Ralph Goodman
Sponsors: Tums; PSA for American economic system; promo for NBC programs
Comments: The acronym Fibber cites of MFLFS is a parody of Lucky Strike's LSMFT. The idea of two states denying ownership of a town called Nicotine is perhaps less funny but certainly more probable today than in 1954.

Date: March 10, 1954
Title: Managing Variety Store
Cast: Jim Jordan (Fibber), Marian Jordan (Molly), John Wald, Arthur Q. Bryan (Doctor Gamble), Bob Bruce (Snead)
Summary: Fibber's first day of running the store shows a profit despite his bungling.
Writers: Phil Leslie, Ralph Goodman
Sponsors: Carter's Little Liver Pills, Richard Hudnut; promo for NBC programs
Running Gag: "'Tain't funny, McGee" (Molly)
Comments: The mistaken identity gimmick, particularly when inflating or deflating the value of property, proved to be profitable on *The Great Gildersleeve*, *The Adventures of Ozzie and Harriet*, and many other programs, and pays handsome dividends on *Fibber McGee and Molly* as well.

Date: March 11, 1954
Title: Business Is Dull
Cast: Jim Jordan (Fibber), Marian Jordan (Molly, Teeny), John Wald, Bill Thompson (Old Timer, customer)
Summary: The slow activity at the store picks up a little when Fibber remembers to put the open sign facing the street.
Writers: Phil Leslie, Ralph Goodman
Sponsors: PSAs for fire prevention, schools; promo for NBC programs
Comments: Fibber should have been wary of the "I'll keep the extra sucker" bit Teeny pulls on him because he tried a similar routine on Kremer during the drugstore's one-cent sale.

Date: March 12, 1954
Title: Promoting Business
Cast: Jim Jordan (Fibber), Marian Jordan (Molly), John Wald, Bill Thompson (Harry), Arthur Q. Bryan (Doctor Gamble), Elvia Allman (customer), Natalie Masters (Florence), Dick Ryan (customer), Pat O'Brien

Summary: Fibber creates a contest that brings crowds of customers to the variety store.
Writers: Phil Leslie, Ralph Goodman
Sponsors: PSAs for safe driving, churches; promo for NBC programs
Comments: The bit about Hassad, Ahmed, and Ben Bay is one of the funniest segments of the fifteen-minute period. In recognition of the recordings Jim and Marian made for the National Safety Council, Pat O'Brien presents the couple with the Council's Public Interest Award for Exceptional Service to Safety.

Date: March 15, 1954
Title: Promoting Store on Radio
Cast: Jim Jordan (Fibber), Marian Jordan (Molly), John Wald, Bill Thompson (Wallace Wimple), Arthur Q. Bryan (Doctor Gamble), Jack Moyles (Marty Daugherty)
Summary: Fibber takes to the airwaves to get free advertising for the variety store.
Writers: Phil Leslie, Ralph Goodman
Sponsors: PSAs for Red Cross, fire prevention; promo for NBC programs
Comments: Like a number of the continued stories, this one ends unresolved with Fibber wishing he could raise money to buy the store and Miss Quilby stuck with a losing proposition.

Date: March 19, 1954
Title: Aids Molly's Luncheon Plans
Cast: Jim Jordan (Fibber), Marian Jordan (Molly), John Wald, Bill Thompson (O'Halloran, Old Timer), Arthur Q. Bryan (Doctor Gamble)
Summary: Fibber gets Doc out of a scrape, then is coy about plans to punch up Molly's luncheon.
Writers: Phil Leslie, Len Levinson
Sponsors: PSAs for churches, savings bonds; promo for NBC *Monitor*
Running Gag: Myrt bit involving brother/fell off deep end/pier (Fibber)
Comments: In the missing March 22nd episode Fibber raises funds by charging the ladies fifty cents a pound for what they ate at the luncheon and by rigging the scales. The promo is the first for the long-running NBC *Monitor* program.

Date: March 30, 1954
Title: Voting for Congressman
Cast: Jim Jordan (Fibber), Marian Jordan (Molly, Teeny), John Wald, Arthur Q. Bryan (Doctor Gamble)
Summary: The McGees vote after Fibber gives Molly a rundown on the candidates.

Comments: There is some good political satire as Fibber explains the (dis)qualifications of the candidates and his views on filibusters. There are no PSAs, commercials, or credits.

Date: March 31, 1954
Title: Thousand Bricks
Cast: Jim Jordan (Fibber), Marian Jordan (Molly), John Wald, Bill Thompson (Wallace Wimple, Old Timer)
Summary: Fibber buys bricks with the idea of selling them as doorstops, then decides to build a barbeque with them instead.
Comments: There are no PSAs, commercials, or credits.

Date: April 2, 1954
Title: Building a Barbeque
Cast: Jim Jordan (Fibber), Marian Jordan (Molly), John Wald, Arthur Q. Bryan (Doctor Gamble)
Summary: Gamble helps Fibber with the foundation of a barbeque.
Comments: There are no PSAs, commercials, or credits. As soon as Doc puts his watch down, an inner voice in listeners says, "Watch out!" and before long it's "Watch in!"

Date: April 5, 1954
Title: Wimple Helps With Barbeque
Cast: Jim Jordan (Fibber), Marian Jordan (Molly, Teeny), John Wald, Bill Thompson (Wallace Wimple, Old Timer)
Summary: Wimple helps McGee build the barbeque from the inside out.
Comments: There are no PSAs, commercials, or credits. A thought that might hit someone like a ton of bricks is that, exclusive of parties or special occasions, this is the first time that Wimple and the Old Timer have been at 79 Wistful Vista at the same time.

Date: April 7, 1954
Title: Sleepwalker McGee
Cast: Jim Jordan (Fibber), Marian Jordan (Molly), John Wald, Bill Thompson (Wallace Wimple), Arthur Q. Bryan (Doctor Gamble), Mary Lou Harrington (Sally Nelson), Robert Easton (Lester Nelson)
Summary: Fibber appears to have walked in his sleep after eating a treat that caused such behavior in the past.
Writers: Phil Leslie, Ralph Goodman
Sponsors: PSA for Easter Seals; Arrid; promo by Eddie Cantor for his NBC show
Comments: The dates Fibber provides put his age at forty, a favorable number that would earn Jack Benny's approval.

Date: April 8, 1954
Title: Button Lost
Cast: Jim Jordan (Fibber), Marian Jordan (Molly), John Wald, Bill Thompson (Sergeant O'Hara), Arthur Q. Bryan (Doctor Gamble), Robert Easton (Lester Nelson)
Summary: When Fibber hears about a robbery, he thinks he might have committed the crime while sleepwalking.
Writers: Phil Leslie, Ralph Goodman
Sponsors: PSAs for schools, savings bonds; promo for NBC programs
Running Gag: "'Tain't funny, Mrs. McGee" (Fibber)
Comments: Wald's teaser is one of the weakest written for him which does nothing for creating interest in the next episode.

Date: April 9, 1954
Title: Exchanging Buttons
Cast: Jim Jordan (Fibber), Marian Jordan (Molly), John Wald, Arthur Q. Bryan (Doctor Gamble), Tyler McVey (police lieutenant), Dick Ryan (officer)
Summary: Fibber hopes that by switching buttons at the police station he can divert suspicion from himself so he will not be connected to the jewel robbery.
Writers: Phil Leslie, Ralph Goodman
Sponsors: PSAs for safe driving, fire prevention; promo for NBC programs
Comments: Gamble's line about Fibber getting *Lum and Abner* on a safe is a gem better than anything Mrs. MacDonald lost in the robbery.

Date: April 12, 1954
Title: Turning Fibber In
Cast: Jim Jordan (Fibber), Marian Jordan (Molly), John Wald, Bill Thompson (delivery man, sergeant), Ken Christy (Chief Malone), Jess Kirkpatrick (Mugsy)
Summary: Fibber tells Molly about the sleepwalking incident, then they go to the police station with intentions of confessing to the authorities.
Writers: Phil Leslie, Ralph Goodman
Sponsors: PSAs for savings bonds, American Cancer Society (by Walter Pidgeon); promo by Dinah Shore for her NBC show
Comments: Fibber hides in the hall closet twice and, mirabile dictu, nothing happens either time he opens and slams the door. The voice Kirkpatrick uses for the prisoner is one unlike any of the others he employed on the show.

Date: April 13, 1954
Title: Hiring a Lawyer
Cast: Jim Jordan (Fibber), Marian Jordan (Molly), John Wald, Bill Thompson (Old Timer), Paul Frees (Clarence Barrow)

Summary: The McGees seek the advice of an attorney regarding Fibber's dilemma.
Writers: Phil Leslie, Ralph Goodman
Sponsors: Tums; PSA for Easter Seals; promo by Willard Waterman et al. for *The Great Gildersleeve*
Comments: Paul Frees, whose comic skills were underutilized on radio, makes the most of his part as the vacillating lawyer.

Date: April 14, 1954
Title: Robbery Solved
Cast: Jim Jordan (Fibber), Marian Jordan (Molly), John Wald, Elvia Allman (Millie Malone)
Summary: Molly explains Fibber's fears about involvement in the jewel theft to the wife of the police chief who eases her mind about the button that might incriminate McGee.
Writers: Phil Leslie, Ralph Goodman
Sponsors: PSA for American Cancer Society by Esther Williams; Carter's Little Liver Pills; promo by Eddie Cantor for his NBC show
Comments: It took seven weeks but Esther Williams *does* show up, albeit in recorded form, after getting mentioned three times on the February 25th show.

Date: April 15, 1954
Title: Freeway Ride
Cast: Jim Jordan (Fibber), Marian Jordan (Molly), John Wald, Bill Thompson (officer), Arthur Q. Bryan (Doctor Gamble, truck driver)
Summary: The McGees endure a harrowing experience trying to get off a freeway filled with fast-moving vehicles.
Writers: Phil Leslie, Len Levinson
Sponsors: PSAs for American economic system, Easter Seals; promo by Jay Stewart for *It Pays To Be Married*
Comments: This show was heard very early in the freeway era, at a time when McGee felt he was cruising at forty-five miles an hour, a speed motorists adopt on city streets today.

Date: April 16, 1954
Title: Dying Easter Eggs
Cast: Jim Jordan (Fibber), Marian Jordan (Molly), John Wald, Bill Thompson (Wallace Wimple, Old Timer), Arthur Q. Bryan (Doctor Gamble)
Summary: Fibber and his pals make colorful eggs and a mess at the same time in preparation for an Easter egg hunt.
Writers: Phil Leslie, Ralph Goodman
Sponsors: PSAs for schools, American Cancer Society); promo by Gordon MacRae for *Railroad Hour*

Comments: With their bickering over colors and other juvenile behavior, the dyers of the eggs act as puerile as the children who will be hunting them. After the tomfoolery is over, Jim and Marian deliver a heartfelt Easter greeting, expressing hopes for lasting peace and brotherhood.

Date: April 19, 1954
Title: Indian Scout McGee
Cast: Jim Jordan (Fibber), Marian Jordan (Molly, Teeny), John Wald, Richard Beals (Willie Toops)
Summary: Fibber's stories about his exploits with the Kickapoo Indians leads into an unwanted adventure.
Writers: Phil Leslie, Ralph Goodman
Sponsors: PSAs for Ground Observer Corps, American Cancer Society (by Susan Hayward); promo by Bill Goodwin for Bob Hope's morning show
Comments: This is one episode in which Teeny, a long-time exploiter of McGee, becomes his advocate. Bill Goodwin (or his writer) must have been listening to Fibber's tall tales because to call Hope's morning show, a fifteen-minute mixture of pseudo interviews and severely-edited exchanges with members of the audience aimed at diverting housewives before they swung over to the soaps, "one of the great comedy radio shows of all time" is an exaggeration even McGee would be embarrassed to make. The PSA by Susan Hayward seems poignant today for she herself died of cancer in 1975.

Date: April 20, 1954
Title: Preparing for Hike
Cast: Jim Jordan (Fibber), Marian Jordan (Molly), John Wald, Bill Thompson (Old Timer), Arthur Q. Bryan (Doctor Gamble), Richard Beals (Willie Toops)
Summary: Fibber tries to start a fire with two sticks while he frets about the upcoming nature hike.
Writers: Phil Leslie, Ralph Goodman
Sponsors: Tums; PSA for preventing fires; promo by Willard Waterman et al. for *The Great Gildersleeve*
Comments: As often happens, Bill Thompson steals the show with his rhythmic delivery of "I says" and his hilarious misadventures with Freddy Fuller. This is one time when a sound effect (two sticks being rubbed together) matches the sound described by the actor.

Date: April 21, 1954
Title: Hike at Dugan's Woods
Cast: Jim Jordan (Fibber), Marian Jordan (Molly, Teeny), John Wald, Richard Beals (Willie Toops), Peter Votrian (Ronald), Daws Butler (bus driver, Davey), Patricia Iannone (Suzy)

Summary: On the nature hike Fibber gives the children lessons in woodcraft by reading his cuffs and flying by the seat of his pants.
Writers: Phil Leslie, Ralph Goodman
Sponsors: PSA by Ted Williams for American Cancer Society; Arrid; promo by James Stewart for *The Six Shooter*
Comments: Fibber, the perpetual child, disciplines Willie with a water pistol.

Date: April 22, 1954
Title: Forty Thousand Copies of *Partly True*
Cast: Jim Jordan (Fibber), Marian Jordan (Molly), John Wald, Bill Thompson (Old Timer, Wallace Wimple), Peter Leeds (mailman)
Summary: Already upset that his monthly *Partly True* has not arrived, Fibber is stupefied when 40,000 copies of the magazine are delivered to him.
Writers: Phil Leslie, Len Levinson
Sponsors: PSAs for fire prevention, Radio Free Europe; promo by Dinah Shore for her NBC show
Comments: The story "Who'll Buy My Violence?" is a parody of the blood-and-thunder novels penned by Mickey Spillane and his ilk.

Date: April 23, 1954
Title: Unloading Copies of *Partly True*
Cast: Jim Jordan (Fibber), Marian Jordan (Molly, Teeny), John Wald, Arthur Q. Bryan (Doctor Gamble), Frank Nelson (Oofner)
Summary: A representative from *Partly True* arrives to pick up the copies of the May issue sent to Fibber by mistake.
Writers: Phil Leslie, Len Levinson
Sponsors: PSAs for savings bonds, American Cancer Society; promo by Gordon MacRae for *The Railroad Hour*
Comments: Long before blame for such colossal blunders could be placed on computers, Oofner tries to point the finger at modern machinery, but Molly knows that, as always, the ultimate responsibility lies with "human boneheads."

Date: April 26, 1954
Title: Suit to Salvation Army
Cast: Jim Jordan (Fibber), Marian Jordan (Molly), John Wald (newscaster), Jack Moyles (Rockhead Grogin), Eleanor Audley (Miss Brown)
Summary: The McGees visit a Salvation Army store intent on reclaiming a suit of Fibber's that Molly gave away.
Writers: Phil Leslie, Ralph Goodman
Sponsors: PSAs for schools, American Cancer Society); promo by Dinah Shore for her NBC show
Comments: It is a reflection of the times that even a do-nothing like McGee who has no job and no need to dress up still intends to wear a suit around the house on an ordinary Monday.

Date: April 27, 1954
Title: Stung by a Wasp
Cast: Jim Jordan (Fibber), Marian Jordan (Molly, Teeny), John Wald, Arthur Q. Bryan (Doctor Gamble), Parley Baer (Herb Travis), Jack Mather (Gus Felthammer)
Summary: Pain from a wasp sting isn't as agonizing to Fibber as the teasing he takes from friends about his black eye.
Writers: Phil Leslie, Len Levinson
Sponsors: Tums; PSA for mental health research; promo by Eddie Cantor for his NBC Show
Comments: The November 12, 1940 episode also involved a black eye, one Fibber got from a door. The ending of each show is similar with Fibber making a bad situation worse.

Date: April 28, 1954
Title: Tennis Racket
Cast: Jim Jordan (Fibber), Marian Jordan (Molly), John Wald, Bill Thompson (clerk, Old Timer), Arthur Q. Bryan (Doctor Gamble)
Summary: Fibber attempts to restring a tennis racket he found in the attic.
Writers: Phil Leslie, Len Levinson
Sponsors: PSA by Barbara Stanwyck for American Cancer Society; Carter's Little Liver Pills; promo by Roy Rogers and Dale Evans for *The Roy Rogers Show*
Comments: The repetition of "cat gut-sheep gut-beef gut" plays second fiddle to the sound effect of "zing went the strings of McGee's racket."

Date: April 29, 1954
Title: Oak Tree Must Come Down
Cast: Jim Jordan (Fibber), Marian Jordan (Molly), John Wald, Bill Thompson (Old Timer), Arthur Q. Bryan (Doctor Gamble), Chris O'Brien (Doctor Beechwood)
Summary: After a tree surgeon pronounces the McGee oak tree dead, Fibber tries to find someone to cut it down.
Writer: Phil Leslie
Sponsors: PSAs for nursing, research for mental health; promo by Bill Goodwin for Bob Hope's morning show
Comments: Leslie borrows much of the dialogue in the first half of this episode from the November 27, 1945 broadcast.

Date: April 30, 1954
Title: Cutting Down the Oak Tree
Cast: Jim Jordan (Fibber), Marian Jordan (Molly, Teeny), John Wald, Bill Thompson (Old Timer)
Summary: Fibber takes a break from chopping away at the oak tree to tell Teeny a story, then finishes the job.
Writer: Phil Leslie

Sponsors: PSAs for American Cancer Society (by Joe DiMaggio), safe driving; promo by Jay Stewart for *It Pays To Be Married*

Comments: In the second half of this episode Leslie borrows some dialogue and also the denouement of having a vehicle in the driveway from the November 27, 1945 show.

Date: May 3, 1954
Title: New Shoes
Cast: Jim Jordan (Fibber), Marian Jordan (Molly), John Wald, Bill Thompson (Stropolis), Arthur Q. Bryan (Doctor Gamble), Herb Vigran (Miller)
Summary: Molly convinces Fibber that his old shoes cannot be repaired and persuades him to shop for a new pair.
Writers: Phil Leslie, Ralph Goodman
Sponsors: PSA by George Murphy for United Cerebral Palsy; Plymouth; promo by Bill Goodwin for Bob Hope's morning show
Comments: Even in the throes of profound disappointment over his old shoes Fibber is still the inveterate quipster who cannot resist the "shod at sunrise" wheeze.

Date: May 4, 1954
Title: Hiccups
Cast: Jim Jordan (Fibber), Marian Jordan (Molly), John Wald, Bill Thompson (Wallace Wimple, Old Timer), Arthur Q. Bryan (Doctor Gamble)
Summary: The efforts of Molly, Wimple, and the Old Timer fail to stop Fibber's hiccups, but Gamble saves the day with a shocking treatment.
Writers: Phil Leslie, Ralph Goodman
Sponsors: Tums; PSA for savings bonds; promo by Willard Waterman et al. for *The Great Gildersleeve*
Comments: The "ebb tide" line is one of the best in this episode, made even more credible by the hiccup in the middle (with no mustard on top).

Date: May 5, 1954
Title: Orchid Plant for Doc
Cast: Jim Jordan (Fibber), Marian Jordan (Molly), John Wald, Bill Thompson (Wallace Wimple), Arthur Q. Bryan (Doctor Gamble), Marian Richman (Miss Ogilvie), Natalie Masters (florist)
Summary: The McGees purchase a plant for Gamble, then experience great difficulty getting to see the doctor to give it to him.
Writers: Phil Leslie, Len Levinson
Sponsors: Plymouth, Arrid; promo by James Stewart for *The Six Shooter*
Comments: Gamble may not have eaten hamburgers for lunch as he avowed on the May 4th show, but he liked hot dogs for that meal as evidenced by this episode and the January 10, 1950 show. No wonder Doc is so busy: his office is at 14th and Oak where all the other commercial buildings in Wistful Vista seem to be located.

Date: May 6, 1954
Title: Minding Teeny (Shorter Version)
Cast: Jim Jordan (Fibber), Marian Jordan (Molly, Teeny), John Wald, Arthur Q. Bryan (Doctor Gamble), Jack Moyles (Marvin Mayhem)
Summary: The McGees entertain Teeny while her parents play bridge.
Writer: Phil Leslie
Sponsors: PSAs for safe driving, research for mental health; promo by Dinah Shore for her NBC show
Comments: This episode is a condensed version of the February 4, 1947 show. The major change is that, to take advantage of the popularity of detective shows, *Marvin Mayhem, Private Snoop* replaces *Bloodbath, Inc.* as the radio program that captures Teeny's attention.

Date: May 7, 1954
Title: Coffee Slogan Contest
Cast: Jim Jordan (Fibber), Marian Jordan (Molly), John Wald, Bill Thompson (Old Timer, Williams), Arthur Q. Bryan (Doctor Gamble)
Summary: While shopping for groceries with Molly, Fibber gets sidetracked by a slogan contest that keeps him occupied the rest of the day.
Writers: Phil Leslie, Ralph Goodman
Sponsors: PSA by Walter Pidgeon for United Cerebral Palsy; Plymouth; promo by Gordon MacRae for *The Railroad Hour*
Comments: This episode really picks up comic speed after the McGees return home with some great banter and a line that does not make common sense but great nonsense: "Pipe down so I can shut up."

Date: May 10, 1954
Title: Plans to Attend Night School
Cast: Jim Jordan (Fibber), Marian Jordan (Molly), John Wald, Bill Thompson (Old Timer), Arthur Q. Bryan (Doctor Gamble)
Summary: Fibber is upset at the prospect of night school classes being discontinued, then considers enrolling at the school himself.
Writers: Phil Leslie, Ralph Goodman
Sponsors: PSA for research for mental health; Plymouth; promo by Jay Stewart for *It Pays To Be Married*
Comments: The Old Timer gives a classic example of how rumors get started and, considering his garrulity, the town will soon be talking about the principal ending up in the hospital after a fight with Fibber.

Date: May 11, 1954
Title: Clobberhead Jones
Cast: Jim Jordan (Fibber), Marian Jordan (Molly), John Wald, Bill Thompson (Old Timer), Marian Richman (registration clerk), Jack Kruschen (draft board clerk, Doctor Eisensutz), Robert Easton (Lester Nelson)

Summary: Fibber attends his first night school class, still smarting over the mistreatment he suffered as a schoolboy from Clobberhead Jones.
Comments: There are no PSAs, commercials, or credits on this truncated broadcast.

Date: May 13, 1954
Title: Coffeemaker Broken by Flash
Cast: Jim Jordan (Fibber), Marian Jordan (Molly), John Wald, Bill Thompson (Old Timer), Arthur Q. Bryan (Doctor Gamble), Herb Vigran (O.Z. Corner), Dick Ryan (Sergeant O'Hara), Pinto Colvig (Flash)
Summary: A dog is strangely attracted to McGee, causing the mutt's owner to believe Fibber is trying to steal the animal's affections from him.
Writers: Phil Leslie, Len Levinson
Sponsors: PSAs for Ground Observer Corps, United Cerebral Palsy; promo by Dinah Shore for her NBC show
Comments: With dogs Fibber can't win for losing. On February 21, 1950 a dog he doesn't even own gets him into trouble with a postman bitten on McGee's property. On October 30, 1951 a descendant of Fireball repeatedly growls and snaps at him. And now in 1954 when a dog finally likes him, that puppy love leads to a lawsuit.

Date: May 14, 1954
Title: Planning Defense for Trial
Cast: Jim Jordan (Fibber), Marian Jordan (Molly, Teeny), John Wald, Bill Thompson (Wallace Wimple), Arthur Q. Bryan (Doctor Gamble)
Summary: As Fibber ponders how to defend himself in court, Wimple offers to intercede in the hopes that the plaintiff will drop the lawsuit.
Writers: Phil Leslie, Len Levinson
Sponsors: PSA for savings bonds; Plymouth; promo by Bill Goodwin for Bob Hope's morning show
Comments: Listeners should know by now that when the writers let McGee blow his top they do it with an explosion of hyphenated adjectives, and on this show Flash gets the double-barreled treatment, described over the phone as "that slab-sided, mutton-headed, peanut-brained monster."

Date: May 17, 1954
Title: Trial of McGee Vs. Corner
Cast: Jim Jordan (Fibber), Marian Jordan (Molly), John Wald, Arthur Q. Bryan (Doctor Gamble), Ken Christy (Judge Birstock), Herb Vigran (O.Z. Corner), Dick Ryan (Sergeant O'Hara), Pinto Colvig (Flash)
Summary: Testimony is given by the plaintiff, O'Hara, and Gamble at McGee's trial.
Writers: Phil Leslie, Len Levinson

Sponsors: PSAs for nurse recruitment, mail for military; promo by Willard Waterman et al. for *The Great Gildersleeve*
Running Gag: "It ain't funny, McGee" (Judge)
Comments: This is one of the best of the fifteen-minute episodes for it allows Fibber to trample all over judicial procedure and jargon and it ends with a scene of courtroom chaos worthy of the Marx Brothers.

Date: May 18, 1954
Title: Returning Flash to Corner
Cast: Jim Jordan (Fibber), Marian Jordan (Molly), John Wald, Bill Thompson (Wallace Wimple), Herb Vigran (O.Z. Corner), Dick Ryan (Sergeant O'Hara), Robert Easton (Lester Nelson), Pinto Colvig (Flash)
Summary: The McGees get in more trouble when they take Flash back to his owner at night.
Writers: Phil Leslie, Len Levinson
Sponsors: Tums; PSA for mental health research; promo by George Fenneman for *You Bet Your Life*
Running Gag: "'Tain't funny, McGee" (Corner)
Comments: Molly attempts to replicate Fibber's twin-loaded style of swearing but only a short-tempered, silver-tongued, insult-wielding loudmouth like McGee can pull off such name-calling with his élan.

Date: May 19, 1954
Title: Chimes Are Stuck
Cast: Jim Jordan (Fibber), Marian Jordan (Molly, Teeny), John Wald, Bill Thompson (Old Timer, Wallace Wimple), Arthur Q. Bryan (Doctor Gamble)
Summary: Fibber gets stuck as he tries to unstick the door chimes.
Writers: Phil Leslie, Len Levinson
Sponsors: PSA for schools; Arrid; promo by Jay Stewart for *It Pays To Be Married*
Comments: For a change Teeny, not Molly, is the character exiting into another part of the house so Fibber alters his line from "There goes a good kid" to "There goes a cute kid." At the end Fibber utters what could be his epitaph: "I just can't win."

Date: May 20, 1954
Title: Flash Offered to Fibber
Cast: Jim Jordan (Fibber), Marian Jordan (Molly, Teeny), John Wald, Bill Thompson (truck driver), Robert Easton (Lester Nelson), Herb Vigran (O.Z. Corner), Pinto Colvig (Flash)
Summary: Corner tries to sell Flash to a reluctant Fibber.
Writers: Phil Leslie, Len Levinson

Sponsors: PSAs for United Cerebral Palsy, savings bonds; promo by Bill Goodwin for Bob Hope's morning show

Comments: Teeny's project of collecting newspapers almost sounds like an early example of recycling except that the sole purpose of the effort, filling classrooms with old issues, might make an ecologist mutter, "Aw, heck! Gee, phooey! Who cares anyhow?"

Date: May 21, 1954
Title: Phone Numbers in New Notebook
Cast: Jim Jordan (Fibber), Marian Jordan (Molly), John Wald, Bill Thompson (Wallace Wimple, Old Timer)
Summary: The McGees eliminate various names from their old phone register and record the ones they wish to retain in a new notebook Fibber bought at Kremer's Drugstore.
Writer: Phil Leslie
Sponsors: PSAs for American economic system, safe driving; promo for listening to NBC shows in the car
Running Gag: Word confusion involving *apathetic/alphabetic/automatic/aromatic/ operatic* (Fibber, Molly)
Comments: As funny as Wimple and the Old Timer are, the glow of the humor is diminished somewhat by the somber prospect of a person being dropped five stories from a balcony and the advice of gargling with kerosene.

Date: May 24, 1954
Title: Experiments in Garage
Cast: Jim Jordan (Fibber), Marian Jordan (Molly, Teeny), John Wald, Bill Thompson (Old Timer)
Summary: Fibber mixes various concoctions, hoping to invent something by chance.
Writers: Phil Leslie, Ralph Goodman
Sponsors: PSA for multiple sclerosis; Plymouth; promo by Eddie Cantor for his show
Running Gag: "'Tain't funny, McGee" (Molly)
Comments: Both Teeny and Molly know that Fibber has to be regarded as helpless, one so she can wheedle freebies out of him, the other so he doesn't injure himself slicing a frankfurter.

Date: May 25, 1954
Title: Fire in Garage
Cast: Jim Jordan (Fibber), Marian Jordan (Molly), John Wald, Bill Thompson (Wallace Wimple), Robert Easton (Lester Nelson)
Summary: Fibber's chemicals cause the garage to go to blazes.
Writers: Phil Leslie, Ralph Goodman

Sponsors: Tums; PSA for United Negro College Fund; promo by George Fenneman for *You Bet Your Life*
Comments: On these fifteen-minute shows just the sound effects of fire engines and of trucks departing along with the imagination of listeners can effectively convey action *and* avoid the expense of hiring actors to play bits as firefighters.

Date: May 26, 1954
Title: Invents Glue Accidentally
Cast: Jim Jordan (Fibber), Marian Jordan (Molly), John Wald, Bill Thompson (Old Timer), Arthur Q. Bryan (Doctor Gamble)
Summary: While dumping out chemicals to be thrown away, Fibber inadvertently invents a powerful adhesive.
Writers: Phil Leslie, Ralph Goodman
Sponsors: Plymouth, Carter's Little Liver Pills; promo by Roy Rogers and Dale Evans for *The Roy Rogers Show*
Comments: McGee's creativity with names matches that of his inventiveness with chemicals for no sooner is the tire iron attached to the pipe than he has dubbed the gooey mess in the bucket McGee's Steel Stickum.

Date: May 27, 1954
Title: Phoning About Invention
Cast: Jim Jordan (Fibber), Marian Jordan (Molly), John Wald, Bill Thompson (Old Timer), Mary Lansing (telephone supervisor), Ralph Moody (Admiral Farragut Halsted)
Summary: Confusion reigns when Fibber talks over the phone with a naval officer.
Writers: Phil Leslie, Ralph Goodman
Sponsors: PSAs for savings bonds, American economic system; promo by Dinah Shore for her NBC show
Comments: Fibber is now calling his invention McGee's Steel Seal. The name of the cruiser is an in-joke for mal de mer is seasickness.

Date: May 28, 1954
Title: Demonstrates Steel Seal at Home
Cast: Jim Jordan (Fibber), Marian Jordan (Molly, Teeny), John Wald, Arthur Q. Bryan (Doctor Gamble), Lloyd Perrin (Lieutenant Commander Smith)
Summary: Fibber repairs one of Teeny's skates for a naval officer to illustrate the efficacy of McGee's Steel Seal.
Writers: Phil Leslie, Ralph Goodman
Sponsors: PSA for preventing forest fires; Plymouth; promo by Bill Goodwin for Bob Hope's morning show
Comments: Gamble joins Fibber and Molly to bid good night to the audience, an uncommon occurrence.

Date: May 31, 1954
Title: Catching Flight to Philadelphia
Cast: Jim Jordan (Fibber), Marian Jordan (Molly), John Wald, Bill Thompson (plane announcer, Old Timer, Wallace Wimple), Arthur Q. Bryan (Doctor Gamble), Cliff Arquette (ticket clerk), Lou Krugman (stranger)
Summary: At the airport a suspicious stranger seems to be following the McGees.
Writers: Phil Leslie, Ralph Goodman
Sponsors: PSAs for CARE, preventing forest fires; promo by Willard Waterman et al. for *The Great Gildersleeve*
Comments: As Jimmy Durante often said, "Everybody wants to get into the act!" Now even a stranger gets to say "Good night" in the tag.

Date: June 1, 1954
Title: Flight to Philadelphia
Cast: Jim Jordan (Fibber), Marian Jordan (Molly), John Wald, Lou Krugman (Joseph Brock)
Summary: The McGees zealously protect their briefcase containing a sample of McGee's Steel Seal from a nosy man who follows them to their hotel in Philadelphia.
Writers: Phil Leslie, Ralph Goodman
Sponsors: Tums; PSA for savings bonds; promo by James Stewart for *The Six Shooter*
Comments: Not only does the stranger look like Peter Lorre but Krugman's interpretation of the role borrows a little from the Lorre school of creepy behavior in the hotel room with a sinister laugh and an ominous reading of "successful assignment."

Date: June 2, 1954
Title: Ride in a Jeep
Cast: Jim Jordan (Fibber), Marian Jordan (Molly), John Wald, Arthur Q. Bryan (Doctor Gamble), Bob Bruce (Lieutenant Hadley)
Summary: The McGees are chauffeured to a Navy shipyard where Fibber is to demonstrate his Steel Seal.
Writers: Phil Leslie, Ralph Goodman
Sponsors: PSA for mail for military; Arrid; promo by Eddie Cantor for his NBC show
Comments: Many military jeeps were open-air vehicles so a glass partition in one that opens and closes would offer little privacy. This is the only episode in which Molly is goosed by a telephone.

Date: June 3, 1954
Title: Demonstrates Steel Seal in Shipyard
Cast: Jim Jordan (Fibber), Marian Jordan (Molly), John Wald, Bob Bruce (Lieutenant Hadley), Joe Granby (G.B. Hull), Herb Ellis (workman)

Summary: The shipbuilders put McGee's adhesive to the test by comparing metal glued together with metal which has been riveted.
Writers: Phil Leslie, Ralph Goodman
Sponsors: PSAs for churches, nurse recruitment; promo by Jay Stewart for *It Pays To Be Married*
Comments: Molly's impatient "Do ya? Do ya?" inquiries have the urgency and rhythm of the rapid-fire questions Teeny throws at McGee.

Date: June 4, 1954
Title: Telegram for $3.81
Cast: Jim Jordan (Fibber), Marian Jordan (Molly, Teeny), John Wald, Bill Thompson (telegram delivery man), Arthur Q. Bryan (Doctor Gamble), Robert Easton (Lester Nelson)
Summary: The McGees scramble to collect the necessary funds to pay for a collect telegram.
Writers: Phil Leslie, Len Levinson
Sponsors: PSAs for savings bonds, American economic system; promo by Dinah Shore for her NBC show
Comments: Again wonders never cease in Wistful Vista, a place where track results appear in newspapers the same day the races are run.

Date: June 7, 1954
Title: Moving Heavy Crate
Cast: Jim Jordan (Fibber), Marian Jordan (Molly, Teeny), John Wald, Bill Thompson (Wallace Wimple), Arthur Q. Bryan (Doctor Gamble), Jack Kruschen (Tucker)
Summary: Fibber comes to the aid of a trucker who is trying to move a crate.
Writers: Phil Lester, Len Levinson
Sponsors: PSAs for savings bonds, churches; promo by Dinah Shore for her NBC show
Comments: The writers throw a curve right by the NBC censor when Wimple's spelling lesson ends in a K.

Date: June 8, 1954
Title: Losing His Hair?
Cast: Jim Jordan (Fibber), Marian Jordan (Molly, Teeny), John Wald, Bill Thompson (Old Timer), Arthur Q. Bryan (Doctor Gamble)
Summary: After finding hair in his comb, Fibber believes he is getting bald.
Writers: Phil Leslie, Ralph Goodman
Sponsors: Tums; PSA for Ground Observer Corps; promo by Roy Rogers and Dale Evans for *The Roy Rogers Show*
Running Gag: Word confusion involving *filigrees/follicles/monocle/manacle/barnacles* (Fibber, Molly, Gamble)
Comments: Wald's preview of Wednesday's show is wordier than most introductions and, at thirty seconds, the longest teaser in extant episodes.

Date: June 9, 1954
Title: Repairing Washing Machine
Cast: Jim Jordan (Fibber), Marian Jordan (Molly), John Wald, Tyler McVey (boss), Nestor Paiva (Louie), Jack Moyles (Marty)
Summary: Fibber accompanies repairmen to their shop so he can show them how to fix the McGees' washing machine.
Writers: Phil Leslie, Len Levinson
Sponsors: PSA for auto safety; Carter's Little Liver Pills; promo by George Fenneman for *You Bet Your Life*
Running Gag: Tongue twister starting with "wishy-washy washers" (Fibber)
Comments: Apparently it is not the sound effect but Jim's ad-lib of "I didn't know it was loaded" that cracks him up and Marian as well.

Date: June 10, 1954
Title: Barbeque
Cast: Jim Jordan (Fibber), Marian Jordan (Molly), John Wald, Bill Thompson (Old Timer, Wallace Wimple), Arthur Q. Bryan (Doctor Gamble)
Summary: McGee prepares spare ribs in the backyard for his friends.
Writers: Phil Leslie, Len Levinson
Sponsors: PSAs for forest fire prevention, savings bonds; promo by Bill Goodwin for Bob Hope's morning show
Comments: Even when one of Fibber's projects is a success he manages to spoil it for someone, in this case for himself. Marian seems particularly tickled over the line about paw paws and ice cream as if she had just read it for the first time.

Date: June 11, 1954
Title: Porch Swing (Shorter Version)
Cast: Jim Jordan (Fibber), Marian Jordan (Molly, Teeny), John Wald, Bill Thompson (Old Timer), Arthur Q. Bryan (Doctor Gamble)
Summary: As Fibber hangs the porch swing, various friends reclaim tools he borrowed from them.
Writer: Phil Leslie
Sponsors: PSAs for mail for military, Radio Free Europe; promo by James Stewart for *The Six Shooter*
Comments: This is a condensed version of the script used on the June 13, 1944 show. A major change is the introduction of the Stumpy Walker character who gave them the swing.

Date: June 14, 1954
Title: Fire Prevention
Cast: Jim Jordan (Fibber), Marian Jordan (Molly, Teeny), John Wald, Barney Phillips (Ed Barwell)

Fifteen-minute Episodes ♦ 359

Summary: Teeny, acting as a junior inspector, cites Fibber for various fire hazards that McGee tries to correct before a fireman arrives for an inspection.
Writers: Phil Leslie, Ralph Goodman
Sponsors: PSAs for auto maintenance, CARE; promo by Eddie Cantor for his NBC show
Comments: The "dum de dum dum" notes from the *Dragnet* theme that Fibber speaks should have been very familiar to Barney Phillips because he had a featured role on that show at one time. In the tag Jim and Marian are presented with a citation on behalf of the Firefighters of Los Angeles because they have "taken advantage of every opportunity to spread the gospel of fire prevention to their vast listening audience."

Date: June 15, 1954
Title: Gamble's Painting
Cast: Jim Jordan (Fibber), Marian Jordan (Molly), John Wald, Bill Thompson (Cecil), Arthur Q. Bryan (Doctor Gamble), Elvia Allman (Lady Dabley)
Summary: The McGees accompany Doc to an art gallery which is exhibiting one of Gamble's works.
Writers: Phil Leslie, Ralph Goodman
Sponsors: Tums; PSA for savings bonds; promo by Willard Waterman et al. for *The Great Gildersleeve*
Comments: Although Lady Dabley gives Gamble's middle initial as B, his middle name is never revealed in the series.

Date: June 16, 1954
Title: Hobby Show Director
Cast: Jim Jordan (Fibber), Marian Jordan (Molly), John Wald, Bill Thompson (Old Timer), Arthur Q. Bryan (Doctor Gamble)
Summary: The McGees gather merchandise from merchants for prizes in the upcoming hobby show.
Writers: Phil Leslie, Ralph Goodman
Sponsors: PSA for nurse recruitment; Arrid; promo by Roy Rogers and Dale Evans for *The Roy Rogers Show*
Comments: As if to make up for all the times Fibber has insulted him or been a nuisance, Gamble finally takes matters into his own feet by putting his stamp of disapproval on McGee in a physical way.

Date: June 17, 1954
Title: Hobby Show Entrants
Cast: Jim Jordan (Fibber), Marian Jordan (Molly), John Wald, Bill Thompson (clock collector), Arthur Q. Bryan (Doctor Gamble), Jack Kruschen (Harold Rover), Jack Moyles (captain), Natalie Masters (Eloise Van Rimple III)
Summary: Fibber and Molly register hobbyists for Friday's show.

Writers: Phil Leslie, Ralph Goodman

Sponsors: PSAs for savings bonds, Ground Observer Corps; promo by Dinah Shore for her NBC show

Comments: Fibber changes his standard complaint about Gamble from "He makes me tired" to "He makes me sick," a feeling that should assure a physician of steady employment. The lines in this episode are not particularly amusing, but eccentrics alone are almost always good for some laughs.

Date: June 18, 1954
Title: Hobby Show Opens
Cast: Jim Jordan (Fibber), Marian Jordan (Molly), John Wald, Bill Thompson (Wallace Wimple, Old Timer), Arthur Q. Bryan (Doctor Gamble), Jack Moyles (G.B. Axworthy), Nestor Paiva (Gus)
Summary: Fibber, with the unwanted help of Wallace, completes last-minute details and oversees the opening of the hobby show.
Writers: Phil Leslie, Ralph Goodman
Sponsors: PSAs for American economic system, safe driving; promo by Dave Garroway for his NBC show
Comments: Fibber, who compliments himself on his tact in mollifying Wimple, reverts to his usual strong-arm style of diplomacy by the time he is on the outside looking in.

Date: June 21, 1954
Title: Repairing Sewing Machine
Cast: Jim Jordan (Fibber), Marian Jordan (Molly), John Wald, Arthur Q. Bryan (Doctor Gamble), Mary Lansing (clerk)
Summary: Fibber attempts to fix a decrepit sewing machine until Doc Gamble suggests an alternative plan certain to please Molly.
Writers: Phil Leslie, Ralph Goodman
Sponsors: PSAs for fire prevention, savings bonds; promo by Bill Goodwin for Bob Hope's morning show
Comments: After living with Fibber for so many years, Molly has picked up McGee's method of inventing names for parts as she identifies the problem with the sewing machine as being the "framistat on the rigarole."

Date: June 22, 1954
Title: Umpire McGee
Cast: Jim Jordan (Fibber), Marian Jordan (Molly), John Wald, Bill Thompson (hardware store clerk, Old Timer), Arthur Q. Bryan (Doctor Gamble), Robert Easton (Lester Nelson), Jack Moyles (Morrie, announcer)
Summary: Fibber practices his calls of balls, strikes, and outs as he prepares to umpire a charity baseball game.
Writers: Phil Leslie, Len Levinson

Sponsors: Tums; PSA for mail for military; promo for listening to NBC shows in cars
Running Gag: "'Tain't funny, McGee" (Molly)
Comments: This is the first episode in which Doc Gamble does not appear until the tag.

Date: June 23, 1954
Title: Counterfeit $5.00 Bill?
Cast: Jim Jordan (Fibber), Marian Jordan (Molly), John Wald, Bill Thompson (Wallace Wimple), Arthur Q. Bryan (Doctor Gamble), Elvia Allman (Cora Burns)
Summary: The McGees try to find the source of a bill they believe is counterfeit.
Writers: Phil Leslie, Ralph Goodman
Sponsors: PSA for preventing forest fires; Carter's Little Liver Pills; promo for NBC programs
Comments: Characters in situation comedies (including the McGees) have often kept money in the sugar bowl. Why Molly put this $5.00 bill in the cookie jar is not explained. One wonders if the orders Cora barks to the cook are genuine hash house jargon or inventions of the writers, but the suspicion exists that if someone ordered a yo-yo on a string at a real eatery a sassy waitress would erupt with a comeback such as "Get outta here, you yo-yo, before I string *you* up."

Date: June 24, 1954
Title: Boating at Dugan's Lake
Cast: Jim Jordan (Fibber), Marian Jordan (Molly, Teeny), John Wald, Bill Thompson (Old Timer), Arthur Q. Bryan (Doctor McGee)
Summary: The McGees spend a relaxing day on Dugan's Lake where they meet Gamble with a boatload of children.
Writers: Phil Leslie, Len Levinson
Sponsors: PSAs for American economic system, nurse recruitment; promo by Bill Goodwin for Bob Hope's morning show
Running Gag: "'Tain't funny, McGee" (Old Timer)
Comments: This episode answers the question about the name of Dugan's Lake, although Fibber's answer may be blarnified. Even on a boat Fibber is dressed formally with a tie that he inconveniently dips in the gas tank.

Date: June 25, 1954
Title: Golden Rule
Cast: Jim Jordan (Fibber), Marian Jordan (Molly, Teeny), John Wald, Bill Thompson (Old Timer), Robert Easton (Lester Nelson), Marvin Miller (kind stranger), Lee Millar (accident victim), Gail Bonney (Aurelia Johns)
Summary: After a man returns his lost wallet to him, Fibber vows to live by the golden rule for a week.

Writers: Phil Leslie, Len Levinson

Sponsors: PSAs for savings bonds, Ground Observer Corps; promo by Dave Garroway for his NBC show

Comments: This is one of the more serious episodes with the sarcasm in Fibber's response to the Old Timer being only humor in the script. It may be that Marvin Miller's sincere performance as a conscientious benefactor who is happy to brighten the lives of others on this episode and the concluding segment in this six-part story about Bob Stanley on July 2nd had something to do with his landing the role a few months later of Michael Anthony, the dispenser of big checks authorized by John Beresford Tipton, *The Millionaire*.

Date: June 28, 1954
Title: Threats Get Nowhere with McGee
Cast: Jim Jordan (Fibber), Marian Jordan (Molly), John Wald, Arthur Q. Bryan (Doctor Gamble), Joseph Kearns (Johns), Jack Moyles (bailiff)
Summary: The McGees resist intimidation and bribery from a county commissioner and his wife regarding an accident Fibber witnessed.
Writers: Phil Leslie, Len Levinson
Sponsors: PSAs for American economic system, savings bonds; promo by Jay Stewart for *It Pays To Be Married*
Comments: The writers seem to have temporarily forgotten that *Fibber McGee and Molly* is a comedy show because each episode in this story seems like a chapter from a soap opera.

Date: June 29, 1954
Title: Golden Rule Spreads
Cast: Jim Jordan (Fibber), Marian Jordan (Molly), John Wald, Bill Thompson (Wallace Wimple), Arthur Q. Bryan (Doctor Gamble), Lee Millar (Bob Stanley)
Summary: Fibber is somewhat concerned that the McGees put up their home as security for Bob Stanley's bail but pleased that his "do unto others" philosophy is catching on around town.
Writers: Phil Leslie, Len Levinson
Sponsors: Tums; PSA for Ground Observer Corps; promo by Eddie Cantor for his show
Comments: Wimple's poem is the only light touch in the show and even that tale of his latest skirmish with his wife is tainted, as always, by the bittersweet knowledge of their mutually-abusive relationship. Wald's teaser now carries a personal element to entice listeners to tune in to the next chapter of what might be called *Fibber Faces Bankruptcy*.

Date: July 2, 1954
Title: Bob Stanley's Trial Concludes

Cast: Jim Jordan (Fibber), Marian Jordan (Molly), John Wald, Bill Thompson (Old Timer), Arthur Q. Bryan (Doctor Gamble), Ken Christy (judge), Marvin Miller (foreman), Lee Millar (Bob Stanley)
Summary: Stanley returns in time to save the McGee home and learn the verdict in his case.
Writers: Phil Leslie, Len Levinson
Sponsors: PSAs for savings bonds, safe driving; promo by Dave Garroway for his show
Comments: Listeners get as close as they ever will get to learning what state the McGees live in when Stanley says "Springfield" but is not allowed to supply the missing half. At the end the McGees are concerned about making a mortgage payment, an unnecessary worry about a house they won in a raffle in 1935. Recordings of two episodes in the Golden Rule saga are absent. On June 30th the McGees attempt to locate the missing Bob Stanley. The July 1st episode, which focuses on ways to raise funds because of the possible forfeiture of Bob's bail, includes an examination of the hall closet's contents after Wimple opens the door looking for an umbrella.

Date: July 5, 1954
Title: Lawn Mower on Loan
Cast: Jim Jordan (Fibber), Marian Jordan (Molly, Teeny), John Wald, Arthur Q. Bryan (Doctor Gamble)
Summary: When Fibber tries out a power lawn mower, it takes him for a ride.
Writers: Phil Leslie, Len Levinson
Sponsors: PSA for nurse recruitment; RCA; promo for NBC programs
Comments: After a week in unfamiliar Sudsville battling social injustice, the McGees return to the familiar territory of Fibber vs. machine. Teeny's cry of fear that becomes a squeal is the first time Marian exercised that effect which makes her sound a bit like Fanny Brice doing Baby Snooks.

Date: July 6, 1954
Title: Wood in Front Yard
Cast: Jim Jordan (Fibber), Marian Jordan (Molly, Teeny), John Wald, Bill Thompson (Old Timer, Wallace Wimple)
Summary: Fibber is upset with the pile of lumber someone left in his front yard until he devises a plan to make something constructive out of it.
Writers: Phil Leslie, Ralph Goodman
Sponsors: Tums; PSA for churches; promo for NBC programs
Comments: The reminiscing that the McGees do invokes one of the laws of nostalgia: nothing today tastes (or looks or smells or feels) as good as the way we remember it in our youth.

Date: July 7, 1954
Title: Lemonade Stand
Cast: Jim Jordan (Fibber), Marian Jordan (Molly, Teeny), John Wald, Bill Thompson (Old Timer), Arthur Q. Bryan (Doctor Gamble), Robert Easton (Lester Nelson), Parley Baer (Kevin Clark)
Summary: Fibber watches Teeny's lemonade stand until he runs afoul of the law.
Writers: Phil Leslie, Ralph Goodman
Sponsors: PSA for mail for military; Carter's Little Liver Pills; promo for NBC programs
Comments: Officer Clark's statement of "This was just a simple misunderstanding" underestimates McGee's ability to complicate matters for within minutes Fibber talks himself into and out of trouble several times.

Date: July 8, 1954
Title: Mesmerizing Molly
Cast: Jim Jordan (Fibber), Marian Jordan (Molly), John Wald, Arthur Q. Bryan (Doctor Gamble)
Summary: Fibber, using a technique he learned at a demonstration, practices hypnotism on Molly with startling results.
Writers: Phil Leslie, Len Levinson
Sponsors: L&M; PSA for preventing forest fires; promo for NBC programs
Running Gag: Myrt bit involving brother/going to night school/knight suit (Fibber)
Comments: A Leslie and Levinson quote of note is Fibber's definition of philosophy: "The science of being cheerful when bad luck happens to other people."

Date: July 9, 1954
Title: Jaywalking Is No Thrill
Cast: Jim Jordan (Fibber), Marian Jordan (Molly), John Wald, Bill Thompson (Old Timer), Tyler McVey (Slawson), Jack Moyles (Costello), William Conrad (Glover)
Summary: After the McGees receive tickets for jaywalking, Fibber gives officers a lesson in going by the book at the policemen's thrill circus.
Writers: Phil Leslie, Len Levinson
Sponsors: PSA for American economic system; RCA Victor; promo for NBC programs
Comments: It has to be a nod to a comedy team and not just coincidence that the name of the officer on the street is Costello and that the field where the show is being held is Fleugel (or Floogle) which is the name of the street sought after for years by Abbott and Costello as they gave the business to the Susquehanna Hat Company.

Date: July 12, 1954
Title: Planting Seeds, Finding a Bone
Cast: Jim Jordan (Fibber), Marian Jordan (Molly), John Wald, Bill Thompson (Old Timer), Arthur Q. Bryan (Doctor Gamble)
Summary: While digging in his backyard, Fibber discovers a bone that Gamble believes has historical significance.
Writers: Phil Leslie, Ralph Goodman
Sponsors: PSA for preventing forest fires; RCA Victor; promo for NBC programs
Comments: The writers give Bill Thompson another chance to demonstrate what a valuable member of the cast he is with a word game that provides the first laugh-out-loud moments in weeks.

Date: July 13, 1954
Title: Bone Verified
Cast: Jim Jordan (Fibber), Marian Jordan (Molly), John Wald, Bill Thompson (Wallace Wimple), Arthur Q. Bryan (Doctor Gamble), Joseph Kearns (Otto Von Kleinmetz)
Summary: McGee visits a professor of paleontology to authenticate the bone found in his backyard.
Writers: Phil Leslie, Ralph Goodman
Sponsors: Tums; PSA for nurse recruitment; promo for NBC programs
Comments: Joe Kearns makes the most of his opportunity to play a featured role in a series on which he was not a regular. The professor's house is a bit like the lair of the Flintstones, complete with a jawbone clock that sounds the hour like a defective gong.

Date: July 14, 1954
Title: Curator Visits
Cast: Jim Jordan (Fibber), Marian Jordan (Molly, Teeny), John Wald, Arthur Q. Bryan (Doctor Gamble), Mary Jane Croft (Doctor Eichelberger)
Summary: The McGees welcome the curator of the Wistful Vista Museum who examines the bone McGee found and the place where he found it.
Writers: Phil Leslie, Ralph Goodman
Sponsors: PSA for schools; Arrid; promo for NBC programs
Comments: This is the first time a sun porch in the McGee house is mentioned. This episode features a rare instance of a scheme planned by Gamble backfiring on him.

Date: July 15, 1954
Title: Theater Party Invitations
Cast: Jim Jordan (Fibber), Marian Jordan (Molly), John Wald, Bill Thompson (Old Timer, Wallace Wimple), Arthur Q. Bryan (Doctor Gamble), Robert Easton (Lester Nelson)

Summary: Fibber surprises everyone (including Molly) by inviting their acquaintances to a theater party.
Writers: Phil Leslie, Len Levinson
Sponsors: L&M; PSA for CARE; promo for NBC programs
Running Gag: Myrt bit involving sat on cactus/satin pattern on dress (Fibber)
Comments: Inquiring listeners may wonder how they can hear Wallace Wimple's voice at the other end of the phone but not that of Myrt or Miss Ogilvie. Judging by the responses Fibber receives to his offer to attend an unknown production at an unspecified location, the magic word in Wistful Vista is *free*.

Date: July 16, 1954
Title: Drive-In Theater
Cast: Jim Jordan (Fibber), Marian Jordan (Molly, Teeny), John Wald, Bill Thompson (Wallace Wimple, Old Timer), Arthur Q. Bryan (Doctor Gamble), Herb Vigran (theater manager), Robert Easton (Wild Will Wyoming)
Summary: The McGees and friends endure a number of disturbances while watching *Lasso Law* at the Moonbeam Drive-In.
Writers: Phil Leslie, Len Levinson
Sponsors: PSA for safe driving; RCA Victor; promo for NBC programs
Comments: The writers satirize Shane, Roy, Gene, Hoppy, and the other good guys who forestall retribution until the final reel with Wyoming's placid response of "We'll see about that" to every atrocity. No wonder the passengers are surly: three men (one of them obviously overweight) and a child in the back seat of a car is a full load, and stuffing them with popcorn is exceeding the feed limit.

Date: July 19, 1954
Title: Ham on the Radio
Cast: Jim Jordan (Fibber), Marian Jordan (Molly), John Wald, Jess Kirkpatrick (Stringbean Wilson), Jack Kruschen (Chin Lee)
Summary: Fibber dabbles with a friend's ham radio while Molly (to no avail) advises caution.
Writers: Phil Leslie, Ralph Goodman
Sponsors: PSA for preventing forest fires; RCA Victor; promo for NBC programs
Running Gag: "'Tain't funny, Mrs. McGee" (Fibber)
Comments: Minutes after being on a device new to him, Fibber, in typical fashion for one with illusions of grandeur, elevates himself to number one ham operator.

Date: July 20, 1954
Title: Keys Left in Car
Cast: Jim Jordan (Fibber), Marian Jordan (Molly), John Wald, Arthur Q. Bryan (Doctor Gamble), Mary Jane Croft (Mabel Toops), Natalie Masters (Eloise), Jack Moyles (sergeant)
Summary: Fibber reads Molly the riot act after she leaves keys in the car.
Writers: Phil Leslie, Ralph Goodman
Sponsors: Tums, RCA Victor; promo for NBC programs
Comments: NBC, which had lost *Amos 'n' Andy*, *The Jack Benny Program*, and other comedy shows to CBS, cannot help crowing about landing *Lux Radio Theatre*, a CBS reliable for almost twenty years, even though the first episode of what would be its final season would not air until September 14th.

Date: July 21, 1954
Title: Painting Bathroom
Cast: Jim Jordan (Fibber), Marian Jordan (Molly, Teeny), John Wald, Dick Ryan (clerk), Jack Kruschen (clerk)
Summary: Using paint purchased at a fire sale, Fibber paints the bathroom (and a fair share of himself as well).
Writers: Phil Leslie, Len Levinson
Sponsors: RCA Victor, Carter's Little Liver Pills; promo for NBC programs
Comments: The "good clean smell of paint" must have made Fibber a bit groggy because his decision to paint the linoleum with the same enamel he uses on the walls is going to make for a mighty slick surface that may have him screaming one day "Fire Sale! My busted, baby blue clavicle!"

Date: July 22, 1954
Title: Meeting the Upper Crust
Cast: Jim Jordan (Fibber), Marian Jordan (Molly), John Wald, Bill Thompson (Robert), Ed Begley (Harrison B. Chase), Gail Bonney (Mrs. Jay Manville Whitney III)
Summary: The McGees drive to the mansion of wealthy Mrs. Whitney who seeks their help in planning a surprise party for Doctor Gamble.
Writers: Phil Leslie, Ralph Goodman
Sponsors: L&M, RCA Victor; promo for NBC programs
Comments: Whether he actually does something purposely that brings positive results (rare) or whether he blunders serendipitously into and out of jams (often), Fibber is quick to do the four-flusher's salute which consists of patting himself on the back.

Date: July 23, 1954
Title: Formal Party for Doc Gamble
Cast: Jim Jordan (Fibber), Marian Jordan (Molly), John Wald, Bill Thompson (bellboy), Arthur Q. Bryan (Doctor Gamble)

Summary: The McGees desperately seek a way to lure Gamble to the Ritz Vista without letting the doctor know a surprise party awaits him there.
Writers: Phil Leslie, Ralph Goodman
Sponsors: PSA for auto maintenance; RCA Victor; promo for NBC programs
Running Gag: "'Tain't funny, McGee" (Molly)
Comments: This is a "much ado about nothing" show with a disappointing conclusion that, although probably reflective of what happens to physicians who are on call, leaves listeners believing the party was more important than the person who was to be honored at the party. Molly puts a twist on Fibber's frequent boast when she says, "Nothing any red-blooded American girl couldn't have done."

Date: July 26, 1954
Title: Postal Anniversary
Cast: Jim Jordan (Fibber), Marian Jordan (Molly, Teeny), John Wald, Bill Thompson (Old Timer, Wallace Wimple)
Summary: To commemorate the 179th anniversary of the founding of the United States Postal Service, Fibber gift-wraps a cigar for his mailman.
Writers: Phil Leslie, Ralph Goodman
Sponsors: PSA for American Cancer Society; RCA Victor; promo for NBC programs
Comments: Molly's follow-up to her Dr. Scholl's footpad gag in which she complains about getting in "a little corny joke now and then" seems to get lost in the footle.

Date: July 27, 1954
Title: Peach Preserves
Cast: Jim Jordan (Fibber), Marian Jordan (Molly), John Wald, Bill Thompson (Old Timer, Wallace Wimple), Arthur Q. Bryan (Doctor Gamble)
Summary: Wimple and Gamble help the McGees make twenty-four jars of peach preserves.
Writers: Phil Leslie, Ralph Goodman
Sponsors: Tums; PSA for CARE; promo for NBC programs
Comments: In this episode more than any other Molly becomes a mother figure not just for Fibber but for the other men as well as she chides them for their juvenile behavior. Yet, for all her maternal ways, at the end she shows she can be as flighty and forgetful at times as her husband.

Date: July 28, 1954
Title: Heat Wave
Cast: Jim Jordan (Fibber), Marian Jordan (Molly), John Wald, Bill Thompson (Old Timer), Arthur Q. Bryan (Doctor Gamble)
Summary: The McGees discover that they are not the only ones seeking relief from the warm weather in the city park.

Writers: Phil Leslie, Len Levinson
Sponsors: PSA for churches; Arrid; promo for NBC programs
Comments: Rarely has a sponsor's product matched the theme of an episode of *Fibber McGee and Molly* as well as this one. The Old Timer's far-fetched stories showing what the heat could cause could have gone one step beyond and recounted how one day in Parched Plain, Nevada it was so hot at high noon that the hour hand on a watch settled in the shade of the minute hand and wouldn't let it move on or give it the time of day.

Date: July 29, 1954
Title: Inventing Air Conditioner
Cast: Jim Jordan (Fibber), Marian Jordan (Molly, Teeny), John Wald, Bill Thompson (Wallace Wimple), Arthur Q. Bryan (Doctor Gamble)
Summary: After learning there are no air conditioners left for sale, Fibber assembles various elements in the living room so can invent his own cooling system.
Writers: Phil Leslie, Len Levinson
Sponsors: L&M; PSA for savings bonds; promo for NBC programs
Comments: A company that sells icebergs is a novelty for Wistful Vista or anyplace that is far removed from glaciers.

Date: July 30, 1954
Title: Cool House Attracts a Crowd
Cast: Jim Jordan (Fibber), Marian Jordan (Molly), John Wald, Bill Thompson (Old Timer, Wallace Wimple), Arthur Q. Bryan (Doctor Gamble), Mary Jane Croft (Mabel Toops), Robert Easton (Lester Nelson), Natalie Masters (rude lady)
Summary: The McGees are overwhelmed by the number of visitors who fill their cool house to escape the heat.
Writers: Phil Leslie, Len Levinson
Sponsors: PSA for schools; RCA Victor; promo for NBC programs
Comments: The Mighty Midget Monsoon is a rare McGee invention that actually works. The writers wisely do not mention the device again for homey heroes are noble but klutzy failures are funny.

Date: August 2, 1954
Title: Matinee for the Birds
Cast: Jim Jordan (Fibber), Marian Jordan (Molly, Teeny), John Wald, Jack Kruschen (pet shop owner)
Summary: Fibber and Molly's plans to attend a matinee are interrupted by phone calls and Teeny at the door.
Writers: Phil Leslie, Ralph Goodman
Sponsors: PSA for schools; RCA; promo for NBC programs
Comments: After all their verbal hassles, this is the first time Teeny gets physical with McGee. After all that has transpired, the McGees are still intent

on going to the theater, although it seems they will driving into the sunset before John Wayne rides into it.

Date: August 3, 1954
Title: Magnolia Manor Mix-up
Cast: Jim Jordan (Fibber), Marian Jordan (Molly), John Wald, Bill Thompson (Wallace Wimple), Arthur Q. Bryan (Doctor Gamble), Mary Lansing (Lana LaTour)
Summary: Fibber's rescue of a woman from a burning building makes him a goat instead of a hero.
Writers: Phil Leslie, Ralph Goodman
Sponsors: Tums; PSA for savings bonds; promo for NBC programs
Comments: This episode does produce a few minor chills with a storm and a car breakdown a la the *Suspense* thriller "On a Country Road." Unfortunately, it has far more foreboding thunderclaps than laughs, a deadly statistic for a comedy show.

Date: August 4, 1954
Title: Movie Offer
Cast: Jim Jordan (Fibber), Marian Jordan (Molly), John Wald, Bill Thompson (Cecil), Joseph Kearns (Duval)
Summary: A movie director hopes to save footage in the scene McGee spoiled by offering him a part in the film.
Writers: Phil Leslie, Ralph Goodman
Sponsors: PSA for safe driving; Carter's Little Liver Pills; promo for NBC programs
Comments: Directors of the DeMille and Von Stroheim school get a mild roasting in the exchanges between Duval and Cecil. Fibber's transformation from petulant recluse to insufferable prima donna is almost instantaneous and totally in character for the man with the weathervane personality.

Date: August 5, 1954
Title: Rehearsing Movie Role
Cast: Jim Jordan (Fibber), Marian Jordan (Molly), John Wald, Arthur Q. Bryan (Doctor Gamble), Robert Easton (Lester Nelson)
Summary: After Fibber brags to Nelson and Gamble about his value to the movie being shot nearby, the script arrives and he is dismayed at the size of his part.
Writers: Phil Leslie, Ralph Goodman
Sponsors: L&M; PSA for Ground Observer Corps; promo for NBC programs
Comments: Lester's first laugh line on the show, "Wonder it wasn't a stroke," passes without notice, probably deservedly so. Jim Jordan added zest to a mediocre script just by a hammy misreading of Shakespeare and a slight emphasis on a wrong initial for a movie star.

Date: August 6, 1954
Title: Movie Star McGee
Cast: Jim Jordan (Fibber), Marian Jordan (Molly), John Wald, Bill Thompson (Cecil), Arthur Q. Bryan (Doctor Gamble), Joseph Kearns (Duval), Frank Gerstle (electrician), Paul Frees (Brick Bronson)
Summary: On the movie set a nervous McGee delivers his sole speech, then stays too long to help Brick Bronson with the final scene of the film.
Writers: Phil Leslie, Ralph Goodman
Sponsors: PSA for preventing forest fires; RCA Victor; promo for NBC programs
Running Gag: "'Tain't funny, McGee" (Molly)
Comments: The title of the epic changed from *The Last of Magnolia Manor* on Wednesday to *The Secret of Magnolia Manor* by Friday. The name of the mogul who threatens to shut down production is a takeoff on Darryl F. Zanuck, kingpin at 20th Century-Fox.

Date: August 9, 1954
Title: Photo from Peoria Picnic
Cast: Jim Jordan (Fibber), Marian Jordan (Molly), John Wald, Bill Thompson (Wallace Wimple, Old Timer)
Summary: Fibber accuses Molly of being unfaithful when he thinks an old photograph they are looking at shows another man's arm around her at a picnic.
Writer: Phil Leslie
Sponsors: PSA for mail for military; RCA Victor; promo for NBC programs
Comments: This is one episode in which Fibber seems more short-tempered than usual as he snaps at both Molly and the Old Timer. Rodney and Agnes are new additions to the Peoria scrapbook, joining Otis, Fern, Leroy, and other members of that old gang.

Date: August 10, 1954
Title: Cleaning the Living Room
Cast: Jim Jordan (Fibber), Marian Jordan (Molly, Teeny), John Wald, Arthur Q. Bryan (Doctor Gamble)
Summary: Much to the surprise of Molly and Gamble, Fibber straightens up the living room.
Writer: Phil Leslie
Sponsors: Tums; PSA for nurse recruitment; promo for NBC programs
Comments: Over the years Tom Swift and the Rover Boys stay on Fibber's list of favorites with just the titles in the series changing to keep the gag fresh. The fall Tuesday night lineup Wald previews with pride is a far cry from the post-WWII years when listeners could hear *Amos 'n' Andy*, *Fibber McGee and Molly*, *The Bob Hope Show*, and *The Red Skelton Show*.

Date: August 11, 1954
Title: Safe Deposit Box
Cast: Jim Jordan (Fibber), Marian Jordan (Molly), John Wald, Bill Thompson (bank employee, Wallace Wimple), Arthur Q. Bryan (Doctor Gamble)
Summary: The McGees examine their safe deposit box with the intention of discarding any unneeded papers.
Writers: Phil Leslie, Len Levinson
Sponsors: PSA for churches; Arrid; promo for NBC programs
Running Gag: Word confusion involving *retroactive/retrospective/nostalgia/neuralgia* (Fibber, Molly)
Comments: Doc's "all the tripe I can stomach" slips by so quickly listeners may miss the effect of the pun. The 1913 Liberty Head nickel in McGee's box is actually worth a fortune because there were only five produced. 1913 was also the first year of the Buffalo nickel, not the next year as Fibber claims.

Date: August 12, 1954
Title: Old Newsboys' Day
Cast: Jim Jordan (Fibber), Marian Jordan (Molly), John Wald, Arthur Q. Bryan (Doctor Gamble), Myra Marsh (Mrs. Spradley)
Summary: Fibber sells newspapers to raise money for the Old Newsboys' Home and also for a chance to make a speech.
Writers: Phil Leslie, Len Levinson
Sponsors: L&M; PSA for savings bonds; promo for NBC programs
Comments: Listeners get a clue to the ending when Fibber comes out of the PSA in a hoarse voice. For a change Marian gets to deliver the closing for both of the stars.

Date: August 13, 1954
Title: Uranium Hunt Begins
Cast: Jim Jordan (Fibber), Marian Jordan (Molly), John Wald, Bill Thompson (Old Timer, PA announcer), Arthur Q. Bryan (Doctor Gamble), Bob Bruce (clerk)
Summary: Fibber wants in on the action when he learns that the Old Timer knows where a uranium deposit is located in Utah.
Writers: Phil Leslie, Len Levinson
Sponsors: PSA for Red Cross; RCA Victor; promo for NBC programs
Comments: As always, Fibber's imagination is at work for he has a name for the new venture (McGee Uranium Locating Enterprises) even before it gets off the ground.

Date: August 16, 1954
Title: Looking for Uranium Site
Cast: Jim Jordan (Fibber), John Wald, Bill Thompson (Old Timer), Arthur Q. Bryan (Doctor Gamble)

Summary: While Doc and McGee take turns driving their rented car in Utah, the Old Timer tries to remember the place where he found uranium fifty years ago.
Writers: Phil Leslie, Len Levinson
Sponsors: PSA for preventing forest fires; RCA Victor; promo for NBC programs
Running Gag: Word confusion involving *bazook/mazurka/berserk/bazooka* (Fibber, Old Timer, Gamble)
Comments: Doc's comment of "looks like the hind end of the world" passes without even a "if you'll pardon the expression." John Wald's prerecorded "Back to Wistful Vista in a minute" and "Fibber and Molly will be right back" must have left listeners wondering about time travel and teleportation.

Date: August 17, 1954
Title: Uranium Site Found
Cast: Jim Jordan (Fibber), John Wald, Bill Thompson (Old Timer), Arthur Q. Bryan (Doctor Gamble)
Summary: After McGee tells one of his long-winded tall tales, he and Doc locate a spot that actually seems to be loaded with uranium.
Writers: Phil Leslie, Len Levinson
Sponsors: Tums; PSA for American economic system; promo for NBC programs
Comments: McGee's shaggy sheep story goes a long way for a punny payoff. Gamble's passing remark that the land belongs to Uncle Sam is a clue that will become significant in the next two days.

Date: August 18, 1954
Title: Uranium Plans Foiled
Cast: Jim Jordan (Fibber), John Wald, Bill Thompson (Old Timer), Arthur Q. Bryan (Doctor Gamble), Tyler McVey (Atomic Energy Commission employee), Lou Krugman (Atomic Energy Commission employee)
Summary: Fibber, Doc, and the Old Timer are suspicious of two strangers who may be after their uranium strike.
Writers: Phil Leslie, Len Levinson
Sponsors: PSA for CARE; Carter's Little Liver Pills; promo for NBC programs
Comments: Even when gripped with fear, Fibber is resourceful enough to dip into his bag of tricks and pull out his cowpoke persona. The hunt for ore in Utah, like the hunting trip to Lake Wapohokey in November 1953 and the fishing trip later in August 1954, are "men only" adventures and thus Molly does not appear in them. The absent August 19th installment of this adventure reveals that the claim had been staked on the site of secret uranium storage of the Atomic Energy Commission.

Date: August 23, 1954
Title: *Beekeeper's Guide*
Cast: Jim Jordan (Fibber), Marian Jordan (Molly), John Wald, Bill Thompson (Old Timer), Arthur Q. Bryan (Doctor Gamble)
Summary: Fibber works on a letter ordering a subscription to *The Beekeeper's Guide* just to get the free premium that comes with each new subscription.
Writer: Phil Leslie
Sponsors: PSA for nurse recruitment; RCA Victor; promo for NBC program
Running Gag: "'Tain't funny, McGee" (Molly)
Comments: This is probably the best solo effort by Phil Leslie with funny lines and a visit with the Old Timer's old gang. Fibber's frustration as he repeatedly plays "Inka Dinka Doo" all over himself should be a tip-off as to what the subscription premium is going to be. Wald announces that *Fibber McGee and Molly* will be heard Sunday through Thursday beginning the next Sunday (August 29th).

Date: August 24, 1954
Title: Old Timer's Birthday?
Cast: Jim Jordan (Fibber), Marian Jordan (Molly), John Wald, Bill Thompson (Old Timer), Arthur Q. Bryan (Doctor Gamble), Jack Kruschen (waiter)
Summary: Because the McGees believe it is the Old Timer's birthday, they treat him to a meal and a movie.
Writers: Phil Leslie, Len Levinson
Sponsors: Tums; PSA for safe driving; promo for NBC programs
Comments: Fibber's statement of "If I ever get to be 91…" is prophetic for that is the age Jim Jordan was when he died in 1988. The Old Timer celebrates his birthday on January 1st and claims to be 89 years old. Judging by the cost of the dinner, an evening of food and film for three adults in 1954 was about $6.00, less than the price of admission for one at a cineplex today.

Date: August 25, 1954
Title: Watermelon
Cast: Jim Jordan (Fibber), Marian Jordan (Molly), John Wald, Bill Thompson (Wallace Wimple), Arthur Q. Bryan (Doctor Gamble), Jack Moyles (clerk), Jack Kruschen (bus driver)
Summary: The McGees buy a large watermelon downtown, then have difficulty changing an oversized two-dollar bill so they can take the bus home.
Writers: Phil Leslie, Len Levinson
Sponsors: PSA for Ground Observer Corps; Arrid; promo for NBC programs
Comments: For the convenience of the story the geography of the town is compressed at the end so that downtown and 79 Wistful Vista are not far apart. Two-dollar bills are so infrequently seen that someone today might also experience problems receiving change for one.

Date: August 26, 1954
Title: Mirror on Closet Door
Cast: Jim Jordan (Fibber), Marian Jordan (Molly), John Wald, Bill Thompson (Old Timer), Arthur Q. Bryan (Doctor Gamble), Robert Easton (Lester Nelson)
Summary: Fibber, Doc, and the Old Timer plan to surprise Molly with a mirror on the bedroom closet door if they can just keep her occupied until the door is hung.
Writers: Phil Leslie, Len Levinson
Sponsors: L&M; PSA for savings bonds; promo for NBC programs
Comments: Of all the episodes of *Fibber McGee and Molly*, this is the only one that takes in all levels of the house except the attic with scenes in the basement, kitchen, living room, and a bedroom upstairs.

Date: August 27, 1954
Title: Forgets Where Car Is Parked
Cast: Jim Jordan (Fibber), Marian Jordan (Molly, Teeny), John Wald, Bill Thompson (Wallace Wimple, violin teacher), Herb Vigran (officer), Robert Easton (Lester Nelson)
Summary: McGee searches all over downtown trying to find where he parked the car.
Writers: Phil Leslie, Len Levinson
Sponsors: PSA for American Cancer Society; RCA Victor; promo for NBC programs
Comments: Teeny displays that she has heart...the heart of a little gold digger who will be glad to help Fibber search for his car...when there is a reward.

Date: August 29, 1954
Title: Busy Sunday
Cast: Jim Jordan (Fibber), Marian Jordan (Molly), John Wald, Bill Thompson (Old Timer), Arthur Q. Bryan (Doctor Gamble), Myra Marsh (Mrs. Spradley), Natalie Masters (Mrs. Atherton), Peggy Knudsen (Aleene Cuddleson)
Summary: Fibber's plans for a quiet Sunday afternoon reading the funnies is destroyed when one visitor after another drops by 79 Wistful Vista.
Writer: Phil Leslie
Sponsors: PSAs for donating blood, schools; promo for NBC programs.
Comments: It is totally in keeping with the moral tone of the program that the first Sunday broadcast begins with the McGees at church. Fibber's remark about wearing his shoes out at the tops is a comic highlight of this episode.

Date: August 30, 1954
Title: Fishing Trip with Gamble and Wimple
Cast: Jim Jordan (Fibber), John Wald, Bill Thompson (Wallace Wimple), Arthur Q. Bryan (Doctor Gamble), Jess Kirkpatrick (Chadwick Potts)

Summary: Despite being warned that the lake they visit is fished out, Fibber, Doc, and Wimple row off in a leaky boat toward an island three miles from shore.
Writers: Phil Leslie, Ralph Goodman
Sponsors: PSA for CARE; RCA Victor; promo for NBC programs
Comments: This is one of the "to be continued" episodes that seems more interested in building a story than in creating laughs. Like the other masculine escapades at Lake Wapohokey and in Utah, there is no part for Molly in the script.

Date: August 31, 1954
Title: Stranded on Island
Cast: Jim Jordan (Fibber), Marian Jordan (Molly), John Wald, Bill Thompson (Wallace Wimple), Arthur Q. Bryan (Doctor Gamble), Jack Moyles (chef)
Summary: McGee, Gamble, and Wimple try to find a way to be rescued from the island on which they are stranded.
Writers: Phil Leslie, Ralph Goodman
Sponsors: Tums; PSA for savings bonds; promo for NBC programs
Comments: One disadvantage to continued narratives in a comedy program is that part of the dialogue at the beginning of episodes that might be used for humorous exchanges is devoted to recapping "the story up to now." It is telling that the most amusing feature of the two-day misadventure is the name of the lake, Winnahoppapoogie.

Date: September 1, 1954
Title: Day at the Office
Cast: Jim Jordan (Fibber), Marian Jordan (Molly, Teeny), John Wald, Bill Thompson (Old Timer), Arthur Q. Bryan (Doctor Gamble)
Summary: While Molly cleans the house, Fibber spends time in a realtor's office.
Writers: Phil Leslie, Len Levinson
Sponsors: PSA for churches; Carter's Little Liver Pills; promo for NBC programs
Comments: Just as Molly is lost without Fibber, McGee is at a loss of what to do at the office so it is fitting they end up at home where they can be lost together.

Date: September 2, 1954
Title: Repairing Radio
Cast: Jim Jordan (Fibber), Marian Jordan (Molly, Teeny), John Wald
Summary: Fibber tries to eliminate a whistling noise in the radio so he can invite friends over to listen to a boxing match.
Writers: Phil Leslie, Ralph Goodman

Sponsors: L&M, RCA Victor; promo for NBC programs

Comments: The reason for the change to a Sunday through Thursday schedule is now apparent as Friday night at 10:00 becomes boxing time on NBC radio as it already was on NBC television. Although they would not scare Mel Blanc into retirement with their impersonations, Jim and Marian make the most of their opportunity to mimic radio interference noises.

Date: September 5, 1954

Title: Back from Twin Rock Falls

Cast: Jim Jordan (Fibber), Marian Jordan (Molly, Teeny), John Wald, Bill Thompson (Wallace Wimple), Arthur Q. Bryan (Doctor Gamble), Robert Easton (Lester Nelson)

Summary: Fibber is anxious to talk about the trip the McGees took to Twin Rock Falls, but he cannot find any friend who will listen to him.

Writers: Phil Leslie, Ralph Goodman

Sponsors: PSAs for Red Cross, Ground Observer Corps; promo for NBC programs

Comments: This episode is reminiscent of the September 30, 1941 season-opener built around McGee's futile efforts to tell visitors about a summer vacation spent in Alaska.

Date: September 6, 1954

Title: Cat with Three Owners

Cast: Jim Jordan (Fibber), Marian Jordan (Molly), John Wald, Bill Thompson (Old Timer), Arthur Q. Bryan (Doctor Gamble), Jack Kruschen (cat)

Summary: The McGees, Old Timer, and Gamble claim ownership of a wandering cat.

Writers: Phil Leslie, Ralph Goodman

Sponsors: PSA for preventing forest fires; RCA; promo for NBC programs

Comments: The episode certainly has dramatic intensity with the three males bickering with each other. Unfortunately, it has no humor, a deadly shortcoming for a comedy program.

Date: September 7, 1954

Title: Cat Matter Resolved

Cast: Jim Jordan (Fibber), Marian Jordan (Molly, Teeny), John Wald, Bill Thompson (Old Timer), Arthur Q. Bryan (Doctor Gamble), Robert Easton (Lester Nelson), Jack Kruschen (cat)

Summary: After arguing all night about who owns a stray cat, Fibber, the Old Timer, and Gamble seem to find a solution to the problem when Teeny arrives.

Writers: Phil Leslie, Ralph Goodman

Sponsors: Tums; PSA for American Cancer Society; promo for NBC programs

Comments: None of the resolutions ring true to what has gone on before, including the one mentioned in the tag because Wimple's wife has repeatedly been touted as a formidable creature unafraid of man or beast.

Date: September 8, 1954
Title: Antique Bookend
Cast: Jim Jordan (Fibber), Marian Jordan (Molly), John Wald, Bill Thompson (Old Timer, train announcer), Elvia Allman (customer), Joe Forte (antique shop owner), Frank Gerstle (man in information booth)
Summary: Molly buys a bookend in a shop, then pursues a woman who accidentally walks out with her purchase.
Writers: Phil Leslie, Ralph Goodman
Sponsors: RCA Victor, Arrid; promo for NBC programs
Comments: This time Molly rather than Fibber carries the bulk of the action for a reason that becomes obvious when she gets home. Wald breaks up before the promo, a rare occurrence for him.

Date: September 9, 1954
Title: Returning Shirt to Bon Ton
Cast: Jim Jordan (Fibber), Marian Jordan (Molly), John Wald, Bill Thompson (Old Timer), Elvia Allman (PA announcer), Robert Easton (Lester Nelson), Natalie Masters (clerk)
Summary: The McGees visit the Bon Ton with the intention of returning a shirt Molly gave to Fibber which he considers effeminate.
Writers: Phil Leslie, Ralph Goodman
Sponsors: L&M, RCA Victor; promo for NBC programs
Comments: The PA announcer's plea for Mr. Ware has the flavor of one of Fibber's tongue twisters. Any royalty charged for the Old Timer's liberal borrowing from "Just One of Those Things" might have made up by considerations for the plug for *The High and the Mighty*.

Date: September 12, 1954
Title: Shuns Country Club Meeting
Cast: Jim Jordan (Fibber), Marian Jordan (Molly), John Wald, Arthur Q. Bryan (Doctor Gamble), Jack Kruschen (Wong), Herb Ellis (officer)
Summary: For some reason Fibber is apprehensive about going to the country club with Doc even before he reads an ominous fortune at a Chinese restaurant.
Writers: Phil Leslie, Ralph Goodman
Sponsors: PSA for fire prevention; RCA Victor; promo for NBC programs
Comments: It would not be long before Americans had more to fear from the man in the gray flannel suit than from one dressed in blue serge.

Date: September 13, 1954
Title: Joke Fibber Tries to Tell
Cast: Jim Jordan (Fibber), Marian Jordan (Molly), John Wald, Bill Thompson (Wallace Wimple, Old Timer), Arthur Q. Bryan (Doctor Gamble)
Summary: Fibber's attempts to tell an amusing story are interrupted by the Old Timer, Wimple, and Gamble who have gags of their own to share.
Writers: Phil Leslie, Ralph Goodman
Sponsors: PSA for savings bonds; RCA Victor; promo for NBC programs
Comments: It is not just the Wimple wheeze that has whiskers on it; versions of the rary jest appeared in a number of sources, including one of Bennett Cerf's collections of humor.

Date: September 14, 1954
Title: Molly Chairs Meeting
Cast: Jim Jordan (Fibber), Marian Jordan (Molly), John Wald, Bill Thompson (Old Timer), Arthur Q. Bryan (Doctor Gamble)
Summary: Fibber gives Molly a crash course in parliamentary procedure before she conducts a committee meeting of the Wistful Vista Women's Club.
Writers: Phil Leslie, Len Levinson
Sponsors: Tums, RCA Victor; promo for NBC programs
Comments: In the tag Bill Thompson gets a chance to speak in his normal voice as he accepts an award for his work on behalf of the Ground Observer Corps.

Date: September 15, 1954
Title: Water Shut Off
Cast: Jim Jordan (Fibber), Marian Jordan (Molly), John Wald, Bill Thompson (Old Timer, Wallace Wimple), Robert Easton (Lester Nelson)
Summary: When the water in their neighborhood is shut off for the day, a thirsty McGee goes in search of liquid refreshment from friends.
Writers: Phil Leslie, Ralph Goodman
Sponsors: RCA Victor, Carter's Little Liver Pills; promo for NBC programs
Comments: This is the first episode with a scene in the Nelson home since they moved in next door. Listeners familiar with Fibber's habits know that, sooner or later, he will express a desire for his favorite beverage, root beer.

Date: September 16, 1954
Title: Overdue Library Book
Cast: Jim Jordan (Fibber), Marian Jordan (Molly), John Wald, Arthur Q. Bryan (Doctor Gamble), Mary Jane Croft (Doris Callahan), Jack Kruschen (clerk)
Summary: The McGees search for a used copy of a book that Fibber can take to the library to replace the overdue book he cannot find.

Writers: Phil Leslie, Ralph Goodman
Sponsors: L&M, RCA Victor; promo for NBC programs
Comments: Gamble has become a rotund Romeo, dating both a librarian and a nurse. Once again Molly has to admonish her "boys" for their "childish nonsense."

Date: September 19, 1954
Title: Teeny's Hand Stuck in Phone
Cast: Jim Jordan (Fibber), Marian Jordan (Molly, Teeny), John Wald, Arthur Q. Bryan (Doctor Gamble), Joseph Kearns (Briny)
Summary: The McGees and Gamble combine resources to extricate Teeny's hand from a phone at Kremer's Drugstore.
Writers: Phil Leslie, Len Levinson
Sponsors: Murine, RCA Victor; promo for NBC programs
Running Gag: Myrt bit involving washed hair/can't do a thing with it/Belgian hare (Teeny)
Comments: Teeny uses all her wiles to take advantage of the situation. The principals may not win any phone booth stuffing contests, but three adults, a child, and a Gosh Awful Gooey in close quarters is a gosh awful mess.

Date: September 20, 1954
Title: Dinner at Ritz Vista
Cast: Jim Jordan (Fibber), Marian Jordan (Molly), John Wald, Arthur Q. Bryan (Doctor Gamble), Jack Moyles (chef), Fritz Feld (maître d')
Summary: Fibber takes Molly to the Sump Room where he finds the prices for food higher than he expected.
Writers: Phil Leslie, Len Levinson
Sponsors: PSA for schools; RCA; promo for NBC programs
Comments: The lines about base canard and the kitchen downstairs are two of the sly pleasures of this night on the town.

Date: September 21, 1954
Title: Frog Hunting
Cast: Jim Jordan (Fibber), Marian Jordan (Molly), John Wald, Bill Thompson (Old Timer), Robert Easton (Lester Nelson)
Summary: Fibber, Lester, and the Old Timer catch frogs at Dugan's Lake in expectation of selling them to the chef at the Ritz Vista.
Writers: Phil Leslie, Len Levinson
Sponsors: Tums, RCA Victor; promo for NBC programs
Comments: The Old Timer perceptively sizes up the situation when he acknowledges that the frogs are too smart for them and suggests they quit before "they steal our flashlight and net and put us in a sack."

Date: September 22, 1954
Title: Frogs in Bathroom
Cast: Jim Jordan (Fibber), Marian Jordan (Molly), John Wald, Bill Thompson (Wallace Wimple, Old Timer)
Summary: Because Molly wants the frogs Fibber brought home out of their bathtub, McGee builds a holding pen for them in the backyard.
Writers: Phil Leslie, Len Levinson
Sponsors: RCA Victor, Arrid; promo for NBC programs
Comments: This episode is a delight to the eyes and ears as we picture frogs raining (and reigning) in the bathroom like refugees from the plague in Egypt, savor the always amusing cowpoke banter, and chuckle at the new species Fibber invents, *frogus McGeeus wooglius*.

Date: September 23, 1954
Title: Frog Business Concluded
Cast: Jim Jordan (Fibber), Marian Jordan (Molly, Teeny), John Wald, Arthur Q. Bryan (Doctor Gamble), Robert Easton (Lester Nelson), Jack Moyles (chef)
Summary: When McGee realizes that the restaurant only wants the legs of the frogs and that he will have to serve as butcher, both he and Molly are anxious to find some way to get the frogs out of the backyard.
Writers: Phil Leslie, Len Levinson
Sponsors: L&M, RCA Victor, Murine
Running Gag: "'Tain't funny, McGee" (Molly)
Comments: Gamble's well-worn gag about the refrigerator is tossed in from left field as a time-filler. The frog franchise proved to be a failure, but business for *Fibber McGee and Molly* is picking up with two and often three sponsors per episode.

Date: September 26, 1954
Title: Trapped by Dog
Cast: Jim Jordan (Fibber), Marian Jordan (Molly), John Wald, Bill Thompson (Old Timer), Arthur Q. Bryan (Doctor Gamble), Mary Jane Croft (Mabel Toops), Fritz Feld (Tarzan)
Summary: When the McGees do a good turn for Mort and Mabel Toops by feeding their dog Tarzan while they are away, the brute holds them captive.
Writers: Phil Leslie, Ralph Goodman
Sponsors: Prudential, Murine, Jell-O
Comments: The scenes in the Toops house, like the situations Wimple describes in which he is imprisoned in the bedroom by his wife, carry the possibility of serious consequences that diminish the humorous effect somewhat. Fritz Feld could have lightened the mood a bit by ad-libbing one of his distinctive pops in place of a growl.

Date: September 27, 1954
Title: Party Line: Making Call
Cast: Jim Jordan (Fibber), Marian Jordan (Molly), John Wald, Bill Thompson (Old Timer), Arthur Q. Bryan (Doctor Gamble), Robert Easton (Lester Nelson), Mary Lou Harrington (Sally Nelson)
Summary: Fibber cannot call for a bowling substitute because a garrulous woman is using the party line.
Writers: Phil Leslie, Ralph Goodman
Sponsors: Prudential, RCA Victor, Jell-O
Comments: It stretches credulity a bit that Fibber would not recognize a neighbor's voice on the phone. The story about Miss Winemold of 1884 makes little sense to anyone too young to know that at the time of the broadcast a brewery annually named a comely lass Miss Rheingold.

Date: September 28, 1954
Title: Favor from Governor
Cast: Jim Jordan (Fibber), Marian Jordan (Molly), John Wald, Arthur Q. Bryan (Doctor Gamble), Herb Vigran (Sam), Jack Mather (Pottle), Hy Averback (Kenny Quinch)
Summary: When McGee learns that Governor Pottle is in town, he and Molly seek him out for a cushy job as compensation for a beaning Fibber got at a charity baseball game in June.
Writers: Phil Leslie, Len Levinson
Sponsors: Prudential, Tums, Jell-O
Comments: The brief exchange on the golf course after the McGees depart and the dialogue between Fibber and Molly in the tag are well-calculated to keep listeners in suspense to see who will get the last laugh.

Date: September 29, 1954
Title: Seeks State Job
Cast: Jim Jordan (Fibber), Marian Jordan (Molly), John Wald, Bill Thompson (Wallace Wimple), Arthur Q. Bryan (Doctor Gamble), Richard Beals (bellboy), Hy Averback (Kenny Quinch)
Summary: The McGees visit a representative of Governor Pottle in hopes of landing a job for Fibber as regent.
Writers: Phil Leslie, Len Levinson
Sponsors: Prudential, Carter's Little Liver Pills, Jell-O
Running Gag: "'Tain't funny, Mrs. McGee" (Fibber)
Comments: Molly's remark at the end that she is "just trying to get a laugh in here somewhere" is almost an admission by the writers that the jokes are getting farther apart. Jim and Marian are slightly farther apart (one year, five months) than the ages Fibber gives between him and Molly (one year, three months).

Date: September 30, 1954
Title: Rules for a Happy Marriage
Cast: Jim Jordan (Fibber), Marian Jordan (Molly), John Wald, Arthur Q. Bryan (Doctor Gamble), Elvia Allman (Cora Burns)
Summary: Fibber resolves to be more considerate of Molly after hearing Cora read ways to improve a marriage from a newspaper column.
Writers: Phil Leslie, Ralph Goodman
Sponsors: Prudential; PSA for American Cancer Society; Jell-O
Comments: This is the first time a conscience voice and a playback of earlier conversations are used. Fibber's hysterical laughter is out of register with the circumstances and Molly's trumped-up indignation at the end hits a false note as well because the McGees are not cut out for soap opera histrionics.

Date: October 3, 1954
Title: Forgotten Dinner Invitation
Cast: Jim Jordan (Fibber), Marian Jordan (Molly, Teeny), John Wald, Bill Thompson (Wallace Wimple, Old Timer), Arthur Q. Bryan (Doctor Gamble), Robert Easton (Lester Nelson), Mary Jane Croft (Mabel Toops)
Summary: As Molly tries to remember who invited the McGees for Sunday dinner, Teeny complicates matters by calling friends and asking them over to 79 Wistful Vista for a meal.
Writers: Phil Leslie, Len Levinson
Sponsors: Prudential; PSA for American economic system; *Better Farming*
Comments: An unfortunate consequence of the fifteen-minute format is that occasionally dialogue given to Jim and Marian takes up most of the story and, as happens in this episode, regulars Bryan and Thompson have only bit parts (in Thompson's case, two bits and no haircut).

Date: October 4, 1954
Title: Sitting in Chair
Cast: Jim Jordan (Fibber), Marian Jordan (Molly), John Wald, Bill Thompson (Old Timer), Arthur Q. Bryan (Doctor Gamble)
Summary: Fibber tells everyone that, because he read an article touting the health benefits of sitting still for an hour, he is not going to move from his chair for sixty minutes.
Writers: Phil Leslie, Ralph Goodman
Sponsors: Prudential, Murine; promo for NBC programs
Comments: Although indolent McGee never needed much of a reason to remain seated, this is the third time the writers gave him cause to stay put, the others being March 9, 1948 and April 8, 1952.

Date: October 5, 1954
Title: Discount Club
Cast: Jim Jordan (Fibber), Marian Jordan (Molly), John Wald, Peter Leeds (man with sink), Jack Mather (salesman), Leo Curley (Charlie)
Summary: Fibber and Molly use someone else's discount card to buy a new iron.
Writers: Phil Leslie, Ralph Goodman
Sponsors: Prudential, Tums, *Better Farming*
Summary: Years before Walmart and Sam's Club, Fibber is preaching the advantages of buying in volume, selling for less than competitors, and using a club which provides savings for members.

Date: October 6, 1954
Title: Wedding Invitation
Cast: Jim Jordan (Fibber), Marian Jordan (Molly), John Wald, Robert Easton (Lester Nelson), Jack Moyles (jewelry clerk), Bob Bruce (shoe clerk), Charlie Seel (man at church)
Summary: The McGees make hurried preparations to get dressed and buy a wedding gift when they receive an invitation an hour before the ceremony begins.
Writers: Phil Leslie, Len Levinson
Sponsors: Prudential, Arrid, RCA Victor
Comments: This is the first time in the series Nancy Horton is mentioned as a former neighbor. By the end of the show Fibber changes his tune from "I'll Dance at Your Wedding" to "Get Me to the [Right] Church on Time."

Date: October 7, 1954
Title: Feeling Peppy
Cast: Jim Jordan (Fibber), Marian Jordan (Molly), John Wald, Bill Thompson (Wallace Wimple, Old Timer), Parley Baer (book salesman), Dick Ryan (Pete)
Summary: Fibber begins the day with a rosy outlook that soon takes on a gloomy cast.
Writers: Phil Leslie, Len Levinson
Sponsors: Prudential, RCA, *Better Farming*
Comments: This is another episode with subtle reminders (a woman putting on a hat before leaving the house, egg shampoos, and an automobile repair bill under $30.00) of a bygone time. Fibber's barking at Lippy is a reference to Leo Durocher who had just won his only World Series title as manager, leading the New York Giants to a four-game sweep of the Cleveland Indians.

Date: October 10, 1954
Title: Selling the Car
Cast: Jim Jordan (Fibber), Marian Jordan (Molly), John Wald, Bill Thompson (Old Timer), Jack Kruschen (Harry Rayburn)

Summary: Although Fibber has a prospective buyer for their car, Molly has reservations about selling it.
Writers: Phil Leslie, Ralph Goodman
Sponsors: Prudential; PSA for fire prevention; *Better Farming*
Comments: The sentimental attachment the McGees have for the "old buggy" is understandable at a time when many Americans kept their vehicles for at least six years. Skillful actors Jim and Marian use a guilty cough or a nervous clearing of the throat as their mea culpas.

Date: October 11, 1954
Title: District Attorney Calls
Cast: Jim Jordan (Fibber), Marian Jordan (Molly), John Wald, Bill Thompson (Wallace Wimple), Arthur Q. Bryan (Doctor Gamble), Peggy Knudsen (secretary)
Summary: Fibber is fidgety when he learns the district attorney wants to talk with him.
Writers: Phil Leslie, Len Levinson
Sponsors: Prudential, Murine, RCA Victor
Comments: In typical McGee fashion, Fibber turns a day in which he breaks even on a bet and on stocks into a loss of his own making by imagining the worst.

Date: October 12, 1954
Title: Stolen Pants Recovered
Cast: Jim Jordan (Fibber), Marian Jordan (Molly), John Wald, Jess Kirkpatrick (Jess), Peter Leeds (officer), Jack Mather (sheriff), Les Tremayne (Witwilliger)
Summary: After the district attorney informs Fibber that his pants have been recovered from a cleaning store robbery, the McGees search for them among the other stolen goods.
Writers: Phil Leslie, Len Levinson
Sponsors: Prudential, Carter's Little Liver Pills; promo for NBC programs
Running Gag: "'Tain't funny, Mrs. McGee" (Fibber)
Comments: This almost becomes one of the "futility of it all" adventures with Fibber about to throw away what Hitchcock called the MacGuffin.

Date: October 13, 1954
Title: Returning Stolen Money
Cast: Jim Jordan (Fibber), Marian Jordan (Molly), John Wald, Bill Thompson (Old Timer), Arthur Q. Bryan (Doctor Gamble), Jess Kirkpatrick (Jess), Peter Leeds (officer), Jack Mather (sheriff), Les Tremayne (Witwilliger)
Summary: The McGees find that returning $84.00 taken in a robbery to the authorities is not a simple task.
Writers: Phil Leslie, Len Levinson

Sponsors: Prudential, RCA Victor, *Better Farming*
Comments: Peter Leeds, who had a tidbit part the previous day, fares slightly better here with half a dozen sentences. This episode is typical of a number of the fifteen-minute efforts which have more actors than action.

Date: October 14, 1954
Title: Missing Roller Skate
Cast: Jim Jordan (Fibber), Marian Jordan (Molly, Teeny), John Wald, Bill Thompson (Old Timer), Arthur Q. Bryan (Doctor Gamble)
Summary: The McGees help Teeny look for her missing skate so she can take part in a ritual that will entitle her to become an honorary boy.
Writers: Phil Leslie, Ralph Goodman
Sponsors: Prudential, Murine, *Better Farming*
Comments: For the first time Jim and Marian take part in two commercials for different products. Bill Thompson turns in a very brief appearance with three sentences and a couple moans.

Date: October 17, 1954
Title: Eating Pancakes Downtown
Cast: Jim Jordan (Fibber), Marian Jordan (Molly), John Wald, Arthur Q. Bryan (Doctor Gamble), Natalie Masters (Mrs. Atherton, waitress), Vivi Janiss (Mrs. Ingstrom)
Summary: Fibber and Molly bypass Walt's Malt Shop to try the breakfast fare at The Griddle.
Writers: Phil Leslie, Ralph Goodman
Sponsors: Prudential; PSA for savings bonds; promo for NBC programs
Comments: The odd couple here are not Felix and Oscar but rather Walt and Oscar whose presence is sensed more than expressed as the writers cleverly suggest their whereabouts. It is fitting that, just as listeners have all they can take of Fibber's story about the fabled, fabulous flapjacks, so McGee gets his fill of the real thing.

Date: October 18, 1954
Title: Shopping Runaround
Cast: Jim Jordan (Fibber), Marian Jordan (Molly), John Wald, Bill Thompson (clerk, Old Timer), Arthur Q. Bryan (Doctor Gamble), Elvia Allman (Lillian Stone)
Summary: McGee keeps running into the same short-tempered woman while at the Bon Ton.
Writers: Phil Leslie, Len Levinson
Sponsors: Prudential, RCA Victor, *Better Farming*
Running Gag: "'Tain't funny, McGee" (Molly)
Comments: Elvia Allman is given an opportunity to portray an irascible character like Mrs. Niles that she assumed on *The Abbott and Costello Show*.

Date: October 19, 1954
Title: Marital Advice
Cast: Jim Jordan (Fibber), Marian Jordan (Molly), John Wald, Robert Easton (Lester Nelson), Mary Lou Harrington (Sally Nelson)
Summary: Molly counsels Sally while Fibber instructs Les in conjugal matters.
Writers: Phil Leslie, Ralph Goodman
Sponsors: Prudential, Arrid; promo for NBC programs
Comments: Not surprisingly, the tenets espoused by the McGees of "Be firm" and "Let them think they are the boss" are still the battle cries of the sexes.

Date: October 20, 1954
Title: Who Was That Man?
Cast: Jim Jordan (Fibber), Marian Jordan (Molly), John Wald, Arthur Q. Bryan (Doctor Gamble), Jess Kirkpatrick (Mulligan)
Summary: After Fibber and Molly meet a familiar-looking man on the street downtown, they spend a restless afternoon and evening trying to recall his name.
Writers: Phil Leslie, Ralph Goodman
Sponsors: Prudential, RCA, *Better Farming*
Comments: The writers hit a mulligan here because the dour temperament of the milkman on the porch is not on course with the hail-fellow-well-met Molly and Fibber encounter downtown nor is it likely that the McGees would not remember a regular visitor to their back door.

Date: October 21, 1954
Title: Costume for Party
Cast: Jim Jordan (Fibber), Marian Jordan (Molly), John Wald, Bill Thompson (Old Timer, Wallace Wimple), Arthur Q. Bryan (Doctor Gamble)
Summary: Molly's costume for a party confuses visitors while Fibber delays revealing the identity of the character he will assume.
Writers: Phil Leslie, Ralph Goodman
Sponsors: Prudential, Murine, *Better Farming*
Comments: This is the second show in five days (the first was October 17) in which Bryan gets a chance to show he was a fair hand at foreign dialects.

Date: October 24, 1954
Title: Popcorn Machine Opportunity
Cast: Jim Jordan (Fibber), Marian Jordan (Molly), John Wald, Bill Thompson (Old Timer), Jean Vander Pyl (operator), Jack Kruschen (man on phone)
Summary: Fibber tries repeatedly to reach a party on the phone about a chance to run the popcorn concession in theaters.
Writers: Phil Leslie, Len Levinson
Sponsors: Prudential, Murine, *Better Farming*

Comments: As expected, Myrt does not appear but her absence is felt more than usual because her name is mentioned eight times. Once again, Fibber jabberwalks himself off of Easy Street.

Date: October 25, 1954
Title: Street Needs Repair
Cast: Jim Jordan (Fibber), Marian Jordan (Molly), John Wald, Bill Thompson (Old Timer, street department official), Joseph Granby (Councilman Glash)
Summary: Fibber gripes about the sorry state of the streets, then takes his cause to city hall to get action.
Writers: Phil Leslie, Len Levinson
Sponsors: Prudential, RCA Victor; promo for NBC programs
Comments: Fibber's earlier experience with asphalt mentioned in this episode is an allusion to his sticky misadventure on April 29, 1941.

Date: October 26, 1954
Title: Petition to Repair Street
Cast: Jim Jordan (Fibber), Marian Jordan (Molly, Teeny), John Wald, Bill Thompson (Old Timer), Robert Easton (Lester Nelson)
Summary: The McGees canvass the neighborhood in search of signatures on a petition to repair the pavement on Wistful Vista Street.
Writers: Phil Leslie, Len Levinson
Sponsors: Prudential, Carter's Little Liver Pills, *Better Farming*
Comments: The dialogue about the haunted vacant lot makes this episode stand out among so many of the quarter-hour shows that contain little genuine mirth.

Date: October 27, 1954
Title: Supervising Street Repair
Cast: Jim Jordan (Fibber), Marian Jordan (Molly, Teeny), John Wald, Bill Thompson (Joe, Wallace Wimple), Arthur Q. Bryan (Doctor Gamble), Jack Moyles (foreman)
Summary: As Fibber oversees the paving being done on Wistful Vista Street by advising the workers not to be wasteful, he hatches a plan for use of the leftover asphalt.
Writers: Phil Leslie, Len Levinson
Sponsors: Prudential, RCA Victor; promo for NBC programs
Comments: The depth of Teeny's intellect, which never ceases to dumbfound McGee, is displayed here in a matter of seconds as she displays her knowledge of movie characters, inventions, railroad history, supernatural literature, and best-sellers.

Date: October 28, 1954
Title: Renaming Wistful Vista Street
Cast: Jim Jordan (Fibber), Marian Jordan (Molly, Teeny), John Wald, Bill Thompson (Old Timer, Hennesey Williams), Arthur Q. Bryan (Doctor Gamble), Elvia Allman (Mrs. Finswabber, irate woman), Jack Carroll (Mr. Finswabber)
Summary: McGee hears the dismal results of his petition to rename the street where he lives to Fibber McGee Boulevard and receives even worse news when angry neighbors come to call.
Writers: Phil Leslie, Len Levinson
Sponsors: Prudential, *Better Farming*, Murine
Comments: Jim and Marian again do double duty as they take part in the first and third commercials. Hennesey Williams is a takeoff on the name of the famous playwright Tennessee Williams.

Date: October 31, 1954
Title: Mother Gamble Visits
Cast: Jim Jordan (Fibber), Marian Jordan (Molly), John Wald, Arthur Q. Bryan (Doctor Gamble), Kate McKenna (Mrs. Gamble)
Summary: When Gamble and his mother are invited to the McGees for a meal, there is food in the dining room and tomfoolery in the living room between Doc and Fibber.
Writers: Phil Leslie, Ralph Goodman
Sponsors: Prudential; PSA for United Fund and Community Chest; promo for NBC programs
Comments: The adventure of Fibber getting a fishbowl caught on his head while playing space cadet is one that is not recorded in an episode but one that sounds perfectly in keeping with the man whose daily lament is "Why does everything have to happen to me?"

Date: November 1, 1954
Title: Paperboy McGee
Cast: Jim Jordan (Fibber), Marian Jordan (Molly), John Wald, Arthur Q. Bryan (Doctor Gamble), Richard Beals (Richard)
Summary: When Fibber takes over the paperboy's route for a day, his delivery techniques are hardly more successful than they were in his younger days.
Writers: Phil Leslie, Ralph Goodman
Sponsors: Prudential, Dial, RCA Victor
Comments: McGee's slapstick takes second place to Molly who gets the two funniest lines with her rendering of *A Midsummer Night's Dream* in German and her comment about the width of handlebars then and now.

Date: November 3, 1954
Title: Duck Calls Irritate Neighbors
Cast: Jim Jordan (Fibber), Marian Jordan (Molly, Teeny), John Wald, Bill Thompson (Old Timer), Arthur Q. Bryan (Doctor Gamble), Robert Easton (Lester Nelson)
Summary: As Fibber tries out a variety of duck calls, he also tries the patience of everyone in the neighborhood, some of whom come calling to register their complaints.
Writers: Phil Leslie, Len Levinson
Sponsors: Prudential, RCA, Dial
Comments: Many of these quarter-hour shows could have aired a decade earlier or later without seeming out of place, but mentions of "It Takes Two to Tango," "Come On-a My House," and "Hernando's Hideaway" place this episode squarely in the 1950s. *Fibber McGee and Molly* was not heard the previous day (Tuesday) when election returns were broadcast.

Date: November 4, 1954
Title: Hunting for Clues with a Decoy
Cast: Jim Jordan (Fibber), Marian Jordan (Molly, Teeny), John Wald, Bill Thompson (Old Timer), Arthur Q. Bryan (Doctor Gamble), Robert Easton (Lester Nelson)
Summary: McGee uses his deductive skills as he tracks down the party who threw a decoy through his window.
Writers: Phil Leslie, Len Levinson
Sponsors: Prudential, Dial; promo for NBC programs
Comments: Another subtle instance of Marian being a good audience for Jim is apparent in her barely audible wheeze after Fibber's "easy bruise and slow heal" line. Listeners who have been along for the ride since the early years will recall that Teeny was also the culprit in another broken window mystery (January 13 and 20, 1942).

Date: November 7, 1954
Title: Gas Price War
Cast: Jim Jordan (Fibber), Marian Jordan (Molly), John Wald, Arthur Q. Bryan (Doctor Gamble), Jack Kruschen (Frank Fuller, Morgan), Natalie Masters (Mrs. Atherton)
Summary: While out for a drive, the McGees search for the lowest price in town during a gas war.
Writers: Phil Leslie, Ralph Goodman
Sponsors: Prudential; PSA for Community Chest; promo for NBC programs
Comments: This episode will remind Americans who now need thirty dollars to fill their tanks that there was a spot for one brief shining moment where gasoline was sixteen cents a gallon.

Date: November 8, 1954
Title: Cousin Gerry Coming to Visit
Cast: Jim Jordan (Fibber), Marian Jordan (Molly), John Wald, Arthur Q. Bryan (Doctor Gamble), Sam Edwards (Chick Bishop)
Summary: Fibber makes preparations to entertain a cousin he has never met.
Writers: Phil Leslie, Len Levinson
Sponsors: Prudential, Dial, RCA Victor
Running Gag: Myrt bit involving brother/fell on spikes/Spike Jones records (Fibber)
Comments: Sam Edwards, who appears for the first time on the series, assumes a brusque character not unlike those he portrayed frequently on *Gunsmoke, The Six Shooter,* and other westerns. The double meaning of Molly's quip about Fibber knocking wood with his skull may have gone over his head.

Date: November 9, 1954
Title: Cousin Gerry Arrives
Cast: Jim Jordan (Fibber), Marian Jordan (Molly), John Wald, Bill Thompson (Old Timer, foreign traveler), Arthur Q. Bryan (Doctor Gamble), Gloria McMillan (Geraldine McGee)
Summary: The McGees prepare the guest room for Fibber's cousin, then go to the train station to greet his relative.
Writers: Phil Leslie, Len Levinson
Sponsors: Prudential, Viceroy, Murine
Comments: The writers do a fair job of manipulating the dialogue so the revelation of Geraldine's identity is forestalled as long as possible. Much ado in error about a cousin was also the subject of the October 23, 1945 broadcast.

Date: November 10, 1954
Title: Dates for Cousin Gerry
Cast: Jim Jordan (Fibber), Marian Jordan (Molly), John Wald, Bill Thompson (Wallace Wimple, Old Timer), Arthur Q. Bryan (Doctor Gamble), Gloria McMillan (Geraldine McGee)
Summary: Fibber presumptuously arranges a busy day for Geraldine without consulting her schedule.
Writers: Phil Leslie, Len Levinson
Sponsors: Prudential, RCA Victor, Dial
Running Gag: Myrt bit involving sister/broke her neck/broker neck (Fibber)
Comments: It seems like old times with snappy banter between McGee and the Old Timer. Fink's Milk is a takeoff on Fink's Mules, the famous opening act in vaudeville.

Date: November 11, 1954
Title: Missing Wristwatch
Cast: Jim Jordan (Fibber), Marian Jordan (Molly), John Wald, Bill Thompson (Wallace Wimple), Robert Easton (Lester Nelson), Natalie Masters (Mrs. Atherton, bystander), Jack Moyles (policeman)
Summary: Fibber causes a traffic snarl when he looks for his $50 watch on the city streets.
Writers: Phil Leslie, Ralph Goodman
Sponsors: Prudential, Dial; promo for NBC sports programs
Comments: One hopes the watch is anti-magnetic for the search naturally takes place at Wistful Vista's lodestone, 14th and Oak. McGee's bumbling ways have fallen into such a predictable pattern that we, like Wald, have come to suspect misplaced items to turn up on his person eventually.

Date: November 14, 1954
Title: Dirtying and Cleaning the House
Cast: Jim Jordan (Fibber), Marian Jordan (Molly), John Wald, Bill Thompson (crewman, Wallace Wimple), Robert Easton (Lester Nelson)
Summary: After working on his car, Fibber creates one mess after another upstairs which, with the help of Les Nelson, he hopes to clean up before Molly returns from a meeting.
Writers: Phil Leslie, Len Levinson
Sponsors: Prudential; PSA for mailing packages early; promo for NBC programs
Comments: Jim seems to be doing his best James Stewart impression at the end as he drawls out *no* three times.

Date: November 15, 1954
Title: Stock Trading
Cast: Jim Jordan (Fibber), Marian Jordan (Molly), John Wald, Arthur Q. Bryan (Doctor Gamble)
Summary: Fibber comes to regret swapping shares of stock with Mort Toops.
Writers: Phil Leslie, Ralph Goodman
Sponsors: Prudential, Dial, RCA Victor
Running Gag: "'Tain't funny, Mrs. McGee" (Fibber)
Comments: Fibber, who cites Newton in this episode, proves his own third law of emotion: To every McGee action there is always an opposed and equal overreaction.

Date: November 16, 1954
Title: Stock Takeover
Cast: Jim Jordan (Fibber), Marian Jordan (Molly), John Wald, Bill Thompson (Old Timer), Arthur Q. Bryan (Doctor Gamble)
Summary: After learning of a possible takeover of the company in which he owns stock, McGee considers ways to reap financial gain out of the deal.

Writers: Phil Leslie, Ralph Goodman
Sponsors: Prudential, Viceroy, Buick
Comments: The Old Timer demonstrates that he is on the "eat as you go" plan.

Date: November 17, 1954
Title: Stock Talk on Train
Cast: Jim Jordan (Fibber), Marian Jordan (Molly), John Wald, Bill Thompson (train announcer, porter), Arthur Q. Bryan (Doctor Gamble), Shirley Mitchell (Alice Logan), Jack Mather (Frank Logan)
Summary: Blowhard McGee meets one of his own ilk on the train the McGees are taking to Chicago.
Writers: Phil Leslie, Ralph Goodman
Sponsors: Prudential, RCA Victor, Dial
Comments: Shirley Mitchell appears for the first time since the April 15, 1947 episode. Attractive Shirley, still a darling named Alice, employs the southern belle voice she beguiled Throcky with when she played Leila Ransome on *The Great Gildersleeve*.

Date: November 18, 1954
Title: Stockholder McGee Meets Bigwig
Cast: Jim Jordan (Fibber), Marian Jordan (Molly), John Wald, Bill Thompson (elevator boy, Harrison), Peggy Knudsen (Miss Quincy), William Conrad (J. Appleton Fonebocker)
Summary: In Chicago Fibber and Molly are welcomed by the financier they came to see.
Writers: Phil Leslie, Ralph Goodman
Sponsors: Prudential, Dial, Murine
Comments: Listeners learn that, among Fibber's many talents, he possesses the ability to make an invitation to breakfast sound like an important business deal. It is not surprising in these continuing narratives in which story supersedes humor that Peggy Knudsen's "back end" correction provides the most amusing moments in the broadcast.

Date: November 21, 1954
Title: Stockholder McGee Considers Options
Cast: Jim Jordan (Fibber), Marian Jordan (Molly), John Wald, Bill Thompson (bellboy), Arthur Q. Bryan (Doctor Gamble)
Summary: While he and Molly are ensconced in a luxury hotel suite, Fibber weighs offers for his three shares of Amalgamated Paper Clip stock.
Writers: Phil Leslie, Ralph Goodman
Sponsors: Prudential; PSA for Naval Air Reserve; promo for NBC programs
Comments: Perceptive listeners will beat McGee to discovering the identity of D.G. This is the first time Fibber's high blood pressure is mentioned, medication for which he can likely use during the tag.

Date: November 22, 1954
Title: Stockholders' Meeting
Cast: Jim Jordan (Fibber), Marian Jordan (Molly), John Wald, Bill Thompson (protector from reporters, stockholder), Jack Moyles (chauffeur, chairman), William Conrad (reporter, J. Appleton Fonebocker), Mary Lansing (reporter, stockholder)
Summary: Fibber considers the VIP treatment he received from Fonebocker, then announces to stockholders where he is placing his allegiance in the battle for control of Amalgamated Paper Clip.
Writers: Phil Leslie, Ralph Goodman
Sponsors: Prudential, Dial, RCA Victor
Comments: In this episode two supporting players get to stretch their characters a bit as Moyles offers a fair Ronald Colman impersonation and Conrad blows up at the end in the best Gale Gordon tradition.

Date: November 23, 1954
Title: Locked Out of Car
Cast: Jim Jordan (Fibber), Marian Jordan (Molly), John Wald, Bill Thompson (Old Timer), Arthur Q. Bryan (Doctor Gamble), Herb Vigran (locksmith)
Summary: After Fibber locks his keys in the car, he is determined to open it before his friends can tease him about the predicament.
Writers: Phil Leslie, Ralph Goodman
Sponsors: Prudential, Viceroy, Murine
Comments: Jim and Marian again do double duty for Prudential and Murine. At this time in his harried life Fibber has become the visible man for everyone can see right through him.

Date: November 24, 1954
Title: Hat Bet
Cast: Jim Jordan (Fibber), Marian Jordan (Molly), John Wald, Arthur Q. Bryan (Doctor Gamble), Mary Jane Croft (Mabel Toops), Natalie Masters (Madame Bertha)
Summary: Molly makes an agreement with a milliner that she can have a hat for nothing if McGee does not notice the new finery, then begins to wonder if Fibber is taking her for granted.
Writers: Phil Leslie, Len Levinson
Sponsors: Prudential, RCA Victor, Dial
Comments: Fibber never lets listeners down: after revealing he was still using the old bean, in the end he remains the old bean counter.

Date: November 25, 1954
Title: Mother McGee's Cranberry Super Sauce
Cast: Jim Jordan (Fibber), Marian Jordan (Molly), John Wald, Bill Thompson (Wallace Wimple, Old Timer), Arthur Q. Bryan (Doctor Gamble),

Robert Easton (Lester Nelson), Mary Lou Harrington (Sally Nelson), Kate McKenna (Mrs. Gamble)
Summary: As Molly welcomes guests for Thanksgiving dinner, McGee prepares an old family recipe from his mother's grandmother's great-grandmother's mother.
Writers: Phil Leslie, Len Levinson
Sponsors: Prudential, Dial, American Motors
Comments: Mark any episode that is built around one of Fibber's cooking concoctions with a star or asterisk for therein hilarity lies (with a few of his lies tossed in for flavoring). Alas, McGee's *succès fou* turns into success? phooey!

Date: November 28, 1954
Title: Vacuum Cleaner Salesman
Cast: Jim Jordan (Fibber), Marian Jordan (Molly), John Wald, Bill Thompson (Old Timer), Joseph Kearns (Oliver Dipswaddle)
Summary: The McGees seem to be getting the upper hand in turning away a persistent salesman until Fibber begins tinkering with their old vacuum cleaner.
Writers: Phil Leslie, Ralph Goodman
Sponsors: Prudential, RCA Victor, American Motors
Comments: No matter how cunning Molly is, Fibber may still get the last word as long as he has a screwdriver or some other tool in his hand.

Date: November 29, 1954
Title: Typewriter Ribbon
Cast: Jim Jordan (Fibber), Marian Jordan (Molly, Teeny), John Wald, Bill Thompson (Wallace Wimple), Arthur Q. Bryan (Doctor Gamble)
Summary: Fibber feverishly attempts to get a ribbon into his typewriter so he can begin working on a book about the sea.
Writer: Phil Leslie
Sponsors: Prudential, Dial, RCA Victor
Comments: Molly's description of her husband's memory being like a tea strainer is not entirely accurate for he recalls two novel ideas in this episode.

Date: November 30, 1954
Title: Dream Disturbs McGee
Cast: Jim Jordan (Fibber), Marian Jordan (Molly), John Wald, Arthur Q. Bryan (Doctor Gamble), Robert Easton (Lester Nelson)
Summary: Fibber is out of sorts as he sorts out the three parts of a foreboding nightmare.
Writers: Phil Leslie, Joel Kane
Sponsors: Prudential, Viceroy, RCA Victor

Comments: Nothing is impossible for McGee who manages to have a terrible dream and yet not get a wink of sleep all night. The callous treatment of his friends is not the least bit funny and cannot be ameliorated by the contrived happy ending.

Date: December 1, 1954
Title: Doctor Gamble to Elope?
Cast: Jim Jordan (Fibber), Marian Jordan (Molly), John Wald, Bill Thompson (Old Timer), Arthur Q. Bryan (Doctor Gamble), Kate McKenna (Mrs. Gamble)
Summary: Mrs. Gamble consults with the McGees after she overhears her son setting up what sounds like an elopement.
Writers: Phil Leslie, Ralph Goodman
Sponsors: Prudential, RCA Victor, Dial
Comments: By necessity this is one of the few fifteen-minute episodes in which neither Fibber nor Molly appear until the plot has been stirred. Kate McKenna makes the most of her larger part by bringing some soap opera dramatics into the story.

Date: December 2, 1954
Title: Sending Doctor Gamble Off at Station
Cast: Jim Jordan (Fibber), Marian Jordan (Molly), John Wald, Bill Thompson (Wallace Wimple, train announcer), Arthur Q. Bryan (Doctor Gamble), Robert Easton (Lester Nelson), Kate McKenna (Mrs. Gamble)
Summary: The McGees and a goodly crowd gather at the train station to surprise Doctor Gamble who everyone assumes is eloping with a nurse.
Writers: Phil Leslie, Ralph Goodman
Sponsors: Prudential, Dial, RCA Victor
Comments: The reprise of Gamble's words over the phone is not just for the benefit of those who missed the show the previous day. It also prepares listeners for Doc's revelation which spoils the celebration.

Date: December 5, 1954
Title: Avoiding Knucklehead Swayze
Cast: Jim Jordan (Fibber), Marian Jordan (Molly), John Wald, Bill Thompson (Old Timer), Arthur Q. Bryan (Doctor Gamble), Tyler McVey (Fred Swayze)
Summary: Fibber plays hard to find when Fred Swayze comes around because he thinks Swayze wants a favor from him.
Writers: Phil Leslie, Ralph Goodman
Sponsors: Prudential, RCA Victor; promo for NBC programs
Comments: Gamble's phone conversation is a variation of his routines with Mrs. Kladderhatch. For the first time bank executive MacDonald's first name is given as Prentice.

Date: December 6, 1954
Title: Party for John Cameron Swayze
Cast: Jim Jordan (Fibber), Marian Jordan (Molly, Teeny), John Wald, Bill Thompson (Wallace Wimple), Arthur Q. Bryan (Doctor Gamble), John Cameron Swayze
Summary: McGee takes Molly to a party to which they are not invited, hoping to find a way to get inside so they can meet the guest of honor.
Writers: Phil Leslie, Ralph Goodman
Sponsors: Prudential, Dial, RCA Victor
Comments: A guest star is a rarity during the fifteen-minute era. The crickets in Wistful Vista are a hearty breed, flourishing even in December to support the illusion that action is taking place outside.

Date: December 7, 1954
Title: Salesman on Bus
Cast: Jim Jordan (Fibber), Marian Jordan (Molly), John Wald, Bill Thompson (Wallace Wimple, officer), Jack Kruschen (bus driver, salesman)
Summary: A pushy salesman attempts to help the McGees with their Christmas shopping by offering them some of his wares.
Writers: Phil Leslie, Ralph Goodman
Sponsors: Prudential, Viceroy, RCA Victor
Comments: Cagey listeners will suspect that equally cagey Molly has a reason for her change of heart. Wandering Uncle Dennis, who never made much of his life, always serves a useful purpose when a tag is needed to close the show.

Date: December 8, 1954
Title: Safety Slogan Contest
Cast: Jim Jordan (Fibber), Marian Jordan (Molly), John Wald, Arthur Q. Bryan (Doctor Gamble), Robert Easton (Lester Nelson), Jack Moyles (radio announcer)
Summary: McGee is confident that his entry in a safe driving contest will be the winner.
Writers: Phil Leslie, Ralph Goodman
Sponsors: Prudential, RCA Victor, Dial
Comments: When Fibber turns out to be a winner in a traffic contest, it truly is an accident waiting to happen.

Date: December 9, 1954
Title: Picking Up Prize Money
Cast: Jim Jordan (Fibber), Marian Jordan (Molly), John Wald, Bill Thompson (Old Timer), Arthur Q. Bryan (Doctor Gamble), Parley Baer (Chamber of Commerce clerk)

Summary: The McGees go to the Chamber of Commerce office to accept the $25.00 prize for winning the slogan contest.
Writers: Phil Leslie, Ralph Goodman
Sponsors: Prudential, Dial, RCA Victor
Comments: Justice prevails as Fibber unfairly loses what rightfully was not his. Molly's "Wouldn't we all?" is a subtle reminder that all of us are apt to stretch the truth now and then.

Date: December 12, 1954
Title: Selecting Christmas Cards
Cast: Jim Jordan (Fibber), Marian Jordan (Molly), John Wald, Bill Thompson (Wallace Wimple), Arthur Q. Bryan (Doctor Gamble), Ken Christy (Kremer), Natalie Masters (Mrs. Crop)
Summary: Dissatisfied with the Christmas cards at Kremer's Drugstore, Fibber and Molly look over a selection brought to their home by one of Wallace Wimple's acquaintances.
Writer: Phil Leslie
Sponsors: Prudential, RCA Victor; promo for NBC programs
Comments: This episode brings back the "those were the days" feeling when only drugstores were open on Sundays and greeting cards cost a dime each.

Date: December 13, 1954
Title: Suggestions for Fibber's Present
Cast: Jim Jordan (Fibber), Marian Jordan (Molly), John Wald, Bill Thompson (Wallace Wimple, Old Timer), Arthur Q. Bryan (Doctor Gamble), Robert Easton (Lester Nelson)
Summary: Molly solicits gift suggestions for Fibber from his friends.
Writers: Phil Leslie, Ralph Goodman
Sponsors: Prudential, Dial, RCA Victor
Running Gag: Hall closet opened by Lester looking for shovel
Comments: It seems like old times when the hall closet gag and the Old Timer's famous chuckle return after long absences. The McGees set an example they hope is being emulated by listeners as they continue to make the radio a vital part of their daily life.

Date: December 14, 1954
Title: Government Job Recommendation
Cast: Jim Jordan (Fibber), Marian Jordan (Molly), John Wald, Bill Thompson (Wallace Wimple, clerk), Barney Phillips (investigator)
Summary: After providing a job reference for Wallace Wimple, McGee applies for a federal position himself.
Writers: Phil Leslie, Len Levinson
Sponsors: Prudential, Viceroy, RCA Victor

Comments: "Mort-wart-Doyle-boil" cannot stand with the involved, rhyming tongue twisters Fibber unleashed during the thirty-minute period, but it still provides the comic highlight of this episode.

Date: December 15, 1954
Title: Delivering Packages with Wimple (I)
Cast: Jim Jordan (Fibber), Marian Jordan (Molly), John Wald, Bill Thompson (Wallace Wimple), Tyler McVey (Roy Francen), Monte Masters (R.J. Barker)
Summary: While McGee and Wallace deliver parcels, Fibber plays by his irregular rules rather than by those of the postal service.
Writers: Phil Leslie, Len Levinson
Sponsors: Prudential, RCA Victor, Dial
Comments: Because Fibber and Wimple's adventures form the action of this episode, Molly does not appear until the last part of the story. Monte Masters, husband of frequent cast member Natalie, is better known for his work with her on *Candy Matson*.

Date: December 16, 1954
Title: Delivering Packages with Wimple (II)
Cast: Jim Jordan (Fibber), Marian Jordan (Molly), John Wald, Bill Thompson (Wallace Wimple), Arthur Q. Bryan (Doctor Gamble), Joseph Kearns (superintendent), Gail Bonney (Mrs. Jay Manville Whitney III)
Summary: Wimple and McGee fight hunger pains as they continue to make sure the mail gets through.
Writers: Phil Leslie, Len Levinson
Sponsors: Prudential, Dial, RCA Victor
Comments: Fibber calls Molly at 4366, a change from the 1809 number given on the October 9, 1953 episode. The climax stretches credulity a bit, but there was a time when local letters and parcels mailed in the morning would be delivered that afternoon.

Date: December 19, 1954
Title: Delivering Packages with Molly
Cast: Jim Jordan (Fibber), Marian Jordan (Molly, Teeny), John Wald, Bill Thompson (Wallace Wimple, Old Timer)
Summary: Molly fills in for an ailing Wimple as she helps McGee deliver packages.
Writers: Phil Leslie, Len Levinson
Sponsors: Prudential, RCA Victor; promo for NBC programs
Comments: The Old Timer, who claimed his name was Rupert Blasingame on January 29, 1946, now answers to Addleton P. Bagshaw. The two rather pointless stories about Uncle Dennis seem to be time fillers to set up the Old Timer's appellation revelation.

Date: December 20, 1954
Title: Christmas Shopping for Teeny
Cast: Jim Jordan (Fibber), Marian Jordan (Molly), John Wald, Bill Thompson (clerk, Old Timer), Arthur Q. Bryan (Doctor Gamble), Colleen Collins (doll, shopper)
Summary: As the McGees look for a present for Teeny in a new store, they are overwhelmed by the variety of toys for sale.
Writers: Phil Leslie, Ralph Goodman
Sponsors: Prudential, Dial; promo for NBC programs
Comments: This is one episode that takes place in a setting not unlike one that might be found today with four floors of toys, motor-driven playground equipment, slides and escalators, and dolls costing $67.50.

Date: December 21, 1954
Title: Advising Les after Accident
Cast: Jim Jordan (Fibber), Marian Jordan (Molly), John Wald, Arthur Q. Bryan (Doctor Gamble), Robert Easton (Lester Nelson), Jess Kirkpatrick (Calvin Clobber)
Summary: After Lester sustains a scratch falling over an ash can in an alley, Fibber demands that his neighbor seek legal action.
Writers: Phil Leslie, Joel Kane
Sponsors: Prudential, Viceroy; promo for NBC programs
Comments: Using the malapropisms *percolator* and *prefabricated* and going full speed ahead relentlessly, Fibber and the writers are in fine form as they usually are when McGee plays that old familiar strain "I fought the law and the law won."

Date: December 22, 1954
Title: Photograph for Christmas Gift
Cast: Jim Jordan (Fibber), Marian Jordan (Molly), John Wald, Bill Thompson (Old Timer), Arthur Q. Bryan (Doctor Gamble), Parley Baer (Lotsinger)
Summary: McGee takes advantage of a coupon offering $5.11 off so he can present a photo of himself to Molly for Christmas.
Writers: Phil Leslie, Len Levinson
Sponsors: Prudential; PSA for safe driving; Dial
Comments: A sepia-tinted 8x10 taken in 1954 by a professional photographer being ready in an hour during the busy holiday season sounds too good to be true to everyone but Fibber who, even in December, is the fall guy.

Date: December 23, 1954
Title: Patient Little Star
Cast: Jim Jordan (Fibber), Marian Jordan (Molly, Teeny), John Wald, Bill Thompson (Bagby, Old Timer)
Summary: The Old Timer delivers his present, then Fibber tells Teeny the story of a star that waited for just the right time to shine brightly.

Writers: Phil Leslie, Ralph Goodman
Sponsors: Prudential, Dial
Running Gag: Hall closet opened by Fibber looking for ornaments
Comments: Bill Thompson plays his version of "The Sidewalks of New York" with "Front door, back door, all around the house." The mystery of the ornaments is not how they got in the closet but how they survived the ride out amid all the other artifacts that go bump in the night when someone opens that door. Fibber's story is probably the most instructive one he tells Teeny, touching the bases of astronomy, kindness, humility, and patience before he reaches home with the message about the true meaning of Christmas.

Date: December 26, 1954
Title: Looking over Christmas Presents
Cast: Jim Jordan (Fibber), Marian Jordan (Molly, Teeny), John Wald, Bill Thompson (Wallace Wimple), Arthur Q. Bryan (Doctor Gamble)
Summary: The McGees and visitors assess the presents they received for Christmas.
Writers: Phil Leslie, Len Levinson
Sponsors: Prudential; PSA for schools; promo for NBC programs
Running Gag: "'Tain't funny, huh?" (Molly)
Comments: In this episode at least *Fibber McGee and Molly* is ahead of its time as Teeny acts kookier than Kookie at his ginchiest and Fibber mixes up a deviled marshmallow coffee fizzion many years before the latte crowd began roaming the malls.

Date: December 27, 1954
Title: Hole in the Wall
Cast: Jim Jordan (Fibber), Marian Jordan (Molly, Teeny), John Wald, Arthur Q. Bryan (Doctor Gamble)
Summary: After both Teeny and Gamble provide handiwork to cover a hole in the wall, the McGees face the option of hanging offensive art or offending friends.
Writers: Phil Leslie, Joel Kane
Sponsors: Prudential, Dial; promo for NBC programs
Comments: Molly's unfinished "The last time you did any plastering…" may refer to the incident of the wall safe in 1953 or the time a bird built a nest in their mailbox in 1951 or to some other bit of McGee mayhem unrecorded on audio.

Date: December 28, 1954
Title: Lester Seeks Public Relations Job
Cast: Jim Jordan (Fibber), Marian Jordan (Molly), John Wald, Bill Thompson (Old Timer), Robert Easton (Lester Nelson)
Summary: McGee decides to lend a hand after hearing neighbor Les express an interest in applying for a position in public relations.

Writers: Phil Leslie, Ralph Goodman
Sponsors: Prudential, Viceroy; promo for NBC programs
Running Gag: "'Tain't funny, McGee" (Molly)
Comments: Fibber, a stranger in the strange land of employment, adopts the disguise of a boss when he would be more at home impersonating a four-flusher, the role he has played all his life.

Date: December 29, 1954
Title: Pretending to be Lester's Boss
Cast: Jim Jordan (Fibber), Marian Jordan (Molly, Teeny), John Wald, Robert Easton (Lester Nelson), Parley Baer (Frisby)
Summary: McGee trowels the praise on in thick layers as he lauds Lester's abilities to a prospective employer.
Writers: Phil Leslie, Ralph Goodman
Sponsors: Prudential; PSA for safe driving; Dial
Comments: Teeny is in many ways a typical child as evidenced by her speech in the doorway showing the effects of the media upon her speech and psyche. Using the song "A Penny a Kiss, A Penny a Hug" as a guideline, Molly's estimate of affection received in the tag puts her weekly take at five cents.

Date: December 30, 1954
Title: Paying Back for Misdeeds
Cast: Jim Jordan (Fibber), Marian Jordan (Molly), John Wald, Bill Thompson (bus driver, Wallace Wimple), Joseph Kearns (Kremer)
Summary: Fibber decides to square accounts with those he wronged in 1954.
Writers: Phil Leslie, Ralph Goodman
Sponsors: Prudential, Dial; promo for NBC programs
Comments: Faithful listeners may be reminded of the May 3, 1949 episode in which McGee also made amends for past indiscretions.

Date: January 2, 1955
Title: Playing Cards with Mort and Mabel
Cast: Jim Jordan (Fibber), Marian Jordan (Molly), John Wald, Mary Jane Croft (Mabel Toops), Daws Butler (Mort Toops)
Summary: The McGees spend a long night in the company of Mort and Mabel Toops.
Writers: Phil Leslie, Len Levinson
Sponsors: Prudential; PSA for American economic system; promo for NBC programs
Comments: In this episode repeated fadeouts are used instead of musical bridges to indicate a passage of time. The oft-mentioned Mort Toops appears for the first time since the early days of the program when Jim played the role.

Date: January 3, 1955
Title: Tickets for Basketball Game
Cast: Jim Jordan (Fibber), Marian Jordan (Molly), John Wald, Robert Easton (Lester Nelson), Dick Ryan (Slim O'Reilly), Leo Curley (Fogerty)
Summary: After Fibber tells Les he can get tickets for an important game, he finds it painfully hard to deliver on his promise.
Writers: Phil Leslie, Joel Kane
Sponsors: Prudential, Dial; promo for NBC programs
Comments: Leo Curley, more accustomed to riding radio's range with Roy Rogers and Tom Mix, scores here as the gruff coach. This is one episode when Fibber has to answer Molly's "You asked for it" with "And how!"

Date: January 4, 1955
Title: War Surplus Auction
Cast: Jim Jordan (Fibber), Marian Jordan (Molly), John Wald, Bill Thompson (bidder, Wallace Wimple), Arthur Q. Bryan (Doctor Gamble), Mary Jane Croft (Mabel Toops), Eddie Marr (auctioneer)
Summary: Against Molly's better judgment, the McGees attend an auction with the intention of buying house paint at a bargain price.
Writers: Phil Leslie, Ralph Goodman
Sponsors: Prudential, Viceroy, *Better Farming*
Comments: Eddie Marr's character, both in delivery and attitude, sounds more like a carnival barker than an auctioneer. The trunk episode which soured Molly on auctions took place May 15, 1945.

Date: January 5, 1955
Title: Weather Balloon Promotion
Cast: Jim Jordan (Fibber), Marian Jordan (Molly), John Wald, Arthur Q. Bryan (Doctor Gamble), Stanley Farrar (Shelby Snodgrass)
Summary: Fibber is anxious to speak to the merchants of Wistful Vista about a plan to use the weather balloons he purchased at auction to increase their sales.
Writers: Phil Leslie, Ralph Goodman
Sponsors: Prudential; PSA for March of Dimes; Dial
Comments: To shed some light for those in the dark over two subtle gags used in the first act: Sally Rand employed balloons or fans as her only costume in her provocative dances and the caption that so tickles Gamble is…No, on second thought, readers need an explanation of that cartoon like a hole in the head.

Date: January 6, 1955
Title: Weather Balloon Promotion in Newspaper
Cast: Jim Jordan (Fibber), Marian Jordan (Molly), John Wald, Bill Thompson (Wilson, Old Timer), Arthur Q. Bryan (Doctor Gamble)

Summary: After Fibber sets up an interview with a reporter regarding his advertising idea, Molly hurriedly makes preparations to make herself presentable for the paper's photographer.
Writers: Phil Leslie, Ralph Goodman
Sponsors: Prudential, Dial, *Better Farming*
Comments: This episode is notable in that Fibber and Gamble, who have sometimes jokingly threatened each other, have a tussle of sorts in the doorway and McGee, who has been twitted on numerous occasions by the Old Timer, takes umbrage at the teasing he receives this time and refuses to divulge information he was formerly eager to tell. The newspaper switch involving Tommy Manville refers to the oft-married millionaire who, along with Zsa Zsa Gabor, served as prime celebrity fodder for comedians in the 1950s.

Date: January 9, 1955
Title: Weather Balloons Get Inflated
Cast: Jim Jordan (Fibber), Marian Jordan (Molly), John Wald, Bill Thompson (Old Timer, Wallace Wimple), Arthur Q. Bryan (Doctor Gamble)
Summary: McGee drafts Gamble and Wimple into holding down weather balloons as he prepares to launch his advertising campaign.
Writers: Phil Leslie, Ralph Goodman
Sponsors: Prudential; PSA for savings bonds; promo for NBC programs
Comments: The Old Timer's tale about the Widow Jackson might have sold as much family income plan insurance as the Prudential pitch that preceded it. Wimple apparently put on over 50 pounds since February 9, 1943 when he gave his weight as 78.

Date: January 10, 1955
Title: Weather Balloon Day
Cast: Jim Jordan (Fibber), Marian Jordan (Molly), John Wald, Bill Thompson (Wallace Wimple, Old Timer), Arthur Q. Bryan (Doctor Gamble), Mary Jane Croft (Mabel Toops), Peter Leeds (bystander), Jack Moyles (photographer)
Summary: Fibber prepares for his ascent in the weather balloons while Molly worries about his descent.
Writers: Phil Leslie, Ralph Goodman
Sponsors: Prudential, Dial; promo for NBC programs
Comments: Molly runs the gamut of melodramatic emotions from a(gony) to e(cstasy). Despite Fibber's claim that this is the first time he charged admission, he also tried to pocket some coins from the bystanders gawking at what they thought was a flying saucer in his yard on March 28, 1950.

Date: January 11, 1955
Title: Women Superior to Men?
Cast: Jim Jordan (Fibber), Marian Jordan (Molly), John Wald, Bill Thompson (McDermott, Old Timer), Arthur Q. Bryan (Doctor Gamble)

Summary: After Fibber scoffs at the claim that women are superior to men, Molly challenges him to the tune of "anything you can do, I can do better."
Writers: Phil Leslie, Joel Kane
Sponsors: Prudential, Viceroy, *Better Farming*
Comments: Carrying coals to Newcastle is nothing compared to the McGees who purchase a lawn mower in January and then carry rather than push it over a dozen blocks to a garage rather than drive the car to pick up the mower at the hardware store.

Date: January 12, 1955
Title: Diet Plan
Cast: Jim Jordan (Fibber), Marian Jordan (Molly), John Wald, Arthur Q. Bryan (Doctor Gamble), Marian Richman (Miss Ogilvie)
Summary: During Fibber and Molly's checkup with Gamble, the doctor's suggestion of going on a diet becomes contagious and all three become infected with the idea.
Writers: Phil Leslie, Len Levinson
Sponsors: Prudential; PSA for March of Dimes; Dial
Comments: As jokester McGee might say, "The best way to improve the shape of two cornballs and a tomato is to sweeten the pot with some lettuce."

Date: January 13, 1955
Title: Dieters Weaken
Cast: Jim Jordan (Fibber), Marian Jordan (Molly), John Wald, Bill Thompson (Wallace Wimple, Old Timer), Arthur Q. Bryan (Doctor Gamble), Robert Easton (Lester Nelson)
Summary: All three parties in the diet wager find it hard to resist tasty temptations.
Writers: Phil Leslie, Len Levinson
Sponsors: Prudential, Dial, *Better Farming*
Comments: Molly's declaration that "We'll get back on the diet tomorrow" is 1955's version of "I'm going to start my diet tomorrow."

Date: January 16, 1955
Title: Cheering a Shut-In
Cast: Jim Jordan (Fibber), Marian Jordan (Molly), John Wald, Arthur Q. Bryan (Doctor Gamble), Eleanor Audley (Mrs. Tolliver)
Summary: Fibber takes his gift of gab to entertain a sickly woman.
Writers: Phil Leslie, Len Levinson
Sponsors: Prudential, *Better Farming*; promo for NBC programs
Comments: Jim skillfully milks maximum humor out of his lines, especially when spewing out "cashew nut loaf with mock orange sauce with a side order of parsley" as if discarding a mouthful of the unappetizing stuff. Eleanor Audley is the perfect guest for this show's menu because she was without peer at playing sour pickles.

Date: January 17, 1955
Title: Diet Pills
Cast: Jim Jordan (Fibber), Marian Jordan (Molly), John Wald, Bill Thompson (Old Timer), Arthur Q. Bryan (Doctor Gamble)
Summary: McGee, acting upon an idea he gets when talking to the Old Timer, takes pills he believes will suppress his appetite.
Writers: Phil Leslie, Len Levinson
Sponsors: Prudential, Dial, Crosley
Comments: The clue of Fibber grabbing a handful of the pills without reading the directions fits with his impulsive nature and also makes the Old Timer's news at the table slightly more plausible. The addition of Crosley as a sponsor, rather than an admission of television's predominance now in American homes, could be viewed as a sign that the audience of *Fibber McGee and Molly* was still considered large enough to be worthy of targeting by advertising agencies.

Date: January 18, 1955
Title: Diet Contest Concludes
Cast: Jim Jordan (Fibber), Marian Jordan (Molly, Teeny), John Wald, Arthur Q. Bryan (Doctor Gamble), Marian Richman (Miss Ogilvie)
Summary: After Fibber tries to run off a little weight, he meets with Molly and Gamble at the doctor's office to see which one of them lost the most weight since January 12th.
Writers: Phil Leslie, Len Levinson
Sponsors: Prudential, Viceroy, *The Saturday Evening Post*
Running Gag: "'Tain't funny, McGee" (Molly)
Comments: For those who wonder when one is old enough to do kids' stuff, Teeny sets the mark at third grade. The tag proves that the McGees can't win even when they win.

Date: January 19, 1955
Title: Prescription Problems
Cast: Jim Jordan (Fibber), Marian Jordan (Molly, Teeny), John Wald, Bill Thompson (Wallace Wimple, irate druggist), Jack Kruschen (clerk)
Summary: Fibber's need for heartburn medication increases as he becomes infuriated over what he considers the high cost of a prescription.
Writers: Phil Leslie, Len Levinson
Sponsors: Prudential, Crosley, Dial
Running Gag: Word confusion involving *tribute/tribune/papyrus/bulrush/Bull Run* (Fibber, Molly)
Comments: That McGee whips himself into a state of apoplexy over tablets costing five or ten cents each demonstrates that he is the type who would nickel and dime himself to death.

Date: January 20, 1955
Title: Sleigh Ride Plans
Cast: Jim Jordan (Fibber), Marian Jordan (Molly), John Wald, Bill Thompson (Old Timer, Abel), Arthur Q. Bryan (Doctor Gamble)
Summary: After a big snowfall hits Wistful Vista, Gamble and the McGees organize a sleigh ride with their friends.
Writers: Phil Leslie, Ralph Goodman
Sponsors: Prudential, Dial, *Better Farming*
Running Gag: "'Tain't funny, Mrs. McGee" (Fibber)
Comments: Abel certainly lives up to his name, ably getting circulars in mailboxes just hours after the snow hits the ground. By stating that he was two at the time of the blizzard of 1888, the Old Timer must have been born in 1886. Depending on the month of his birth, that news would make him a not-so-old timer of 68 or 69 in 1955.

Date: January 23, 1955
Title: Sleigh Ride with Wiener Roast
Cast: Jim Jordan (Fibber), Marian Jordan (Molly, Teeny), John Wald, Bill Thompson (Wallace Wimple, Old Timer), Arthur Q. Bryan (Doctor Gamble), Robert Easton (Lester Nelson), Mary Lou Harrington (Sally Nelson)
Summary: The McGees and friends take a sleigh ride to Dugan's Lake to enjoy some fresh air, fellowship, and food.
Writers: Phil Leslie, Ralph Goodman
Sponsors: Prudential; PSA for engineer recruitment; promo for NBC programs
Comments: In Wistful Vista sleighs have the right of way on highways when snow flies, but when the pavement is clear sleighs are stranded on the road not taken.

Date: January 24, 1955
Title: Marriage Quiz
Cast: Jim Jordan (Fibber), Marian Jordan (Molly, Teeny), John Wald, Arthur Q. Bryan (Doctor Gamble), Mary Jane Croft (Mabel Toops)
Summary: Fibber and Molly try to change their habits after they fare poorly on the "Are You a Louse to Your Spouse?" test.
Writers: Phil Leslie, Joel Kane
Sponsors: Prudential, Dial, Crosley
Comments: This time Teeny really deserves her cookies because she gets the McGees back to normal with just a giggle and a couple words. The fade without music deftly indicates passage of time.

Date: January 25, 1955
Title: Tea Set Hunt
Cast: Jim Jordan (Fibber), Marian Jordan (Molly), John Wald, Bill Thompson (Wallace Wimple, butler), Arthur Q. Bryan (Doctor Gamble), Mary Jane Croft (Mabel Toops)

Summary: After learning that Aunt Sarah is coming for a visit, the McGees scurry all around town attempting to locate an elusive tea set she presented to them which they and numerous other recipients have given away.
Writers: Phil Leslie, Ralph Goodman
Sponsors: Prudential, Viceroy, *Better Farming*
Comments: In a time when nearly every home is overflowing with objects made in China, it is quaintly charming to remember that time when Outer Mongolia was considered the most remote spot on earth for the place of origin of weird or unwanted objects. Bill Thompson ably demonstrates how a bizarre pronunciation of a simple word like *Florida* can be the comedic high point of a show.

Date: January 26, 1955
Title: Donating Portrait
Cast: Jim Jordan (Fibber), Marian Jordan (Molly, Teeny), John Wald, Bill Thompson (Old Timer, Wallace Wimple)
Summary: After seeing a presidential portrait in a store window, Fibber purchases it with the intention of donating it to a local grammar school.
Writers: Phil Leslie, Len Levinson
Sponsors: Prudential, Crosley, Dial
Comments: It is appropriate that the person voted "lunk most likely to flunk" eight successive years would be attracted to an engraving of the only president (at the time) to be impeached. Significantly, Fibber provides an excuse for not unwrapping the portrait in front of Molly because she certainly would have taken the wind out of his sails, not to mention spoil the denouement.

Date: January 27, 1955
Title: Cappy Visits the McGees
Cast: Jim Jordan (Fibber), Marian Jordan (Molly), John Wald, Arthur Q. Bryan (Doctor Gamble), Joseph Kearns (Captain Clarence Wreskokoskowitz)
Summary: McGee's old commanding officer visits Wistful Vista and tells stories about Fibber's adventures in the Army during World War I.
Writers: Phil Leslie, Ralph Goodman
Sponsors: Prudential, Dial, *Better Farming*
Comments: Even when Fred Nitney is way out on the periphery of the story, his character (corny and niggardly) is front and center. One almost suspects Fibber of inventing the three-day pass excuse to divert attention from praise showered on him for his act of bravery.

Date: January 30, 1955
Title: Naval Expert McGee
Cast: Jim Jordan (Fibber), Marian Jordan (Molly), John Wald, Bill Thompson (Old Timer), Arthur Q. Bryan (Doctor Gamble), Jack Moyles (Marty Daugherty)

Summary: After McGee denigrates the movie *Torpedoes Away* for its inaccuracies, his habitual four-flushing comes back to haunt him.
Writers: Phil Leslie, Ralph Goodman
Sponsors: Prudential; PSA for Ground Observer Corps; promo for NBC programs
Comments: Fibber is probably the only adult in Wistful Vista who prefers a synopsis of a cartoon to that of a feature film.

Date: January 31, 1955
Title: Missing Garbage Can, Part 1
Cast: Jim Jordan (Fibber), Marian Jordan (Molly), John Wald, Arthur Q. Bryan (Doctor Gamble), Robert Easton (Lester Nelson), Herb Vigran (Sam), Barney Phillips (Dolan)
Summary: Fibber becomes a soft-boiled detective after his garbage can disappears.
Writers: Phil Leslie, Len Levinson
Sponsors: Prudential, Dial, *Woman's Home Companion*
Running Gag: Myrt bit involving high man in basketball game/8'6" (Fibber)
Comments: The stings, mysterioso music, overblown similes (e.g., "The dadratted cloud set off the sun like an unpaid light bill"), and sinister voiceovers all contribute to this merry lampoon of detective shows.

Date: February 1, 1955
Title: Missing Garbage Can, Part 2
Cast: Jim Jordan (Fibber), Marian Jordan (Molly, Teeny), John Wald, Bill Thompson (Wallace Wimple, garbage man)
Summary: McGee follows a tip from Wimple to continue his hunt for his garbage can.
Writers: Phil Leslie, Len Levinson
Sponsors: Prudential, Viceroy, *Woman's Home Companion*
Running Gag: Tongue twister starting with "catch-as-catch-can" (Fibber)
Comments: The McGees, solidly entrenched in the middle class, can at least boast of having a trash man who speaks in a tony English accent.

Date: February 2, 1955
Title: Missing Garbage Can, Part 3
Cast: Jim Jordan (Fibber), Marian Jordan (Molly), John Wald, Bill Thompson (clerk), Arthur Q. Bryan (Doctor Gamble), Robert Easton (Lester Nelson), Mary Lou Harrington (Sally Nelson)
Summary: Fibber employs the methods of novelist Hemingway Savage to solve the mystery that has been haunting him for three days.
Writers: Phil Leslie, Len Levinson
Sponsors: Prudential, *Better Farming*, Dial
Running Gag: Tongue twister starting with "*Case of the Missing Case*" (Fibber)

Comments: Even though the tongue twisters are now being slipped in with less fanfare, they can still be involved enough to leave Jim gasping for breath at the finish line.

Date: February 3, 1955
Title: Renewing License Plates
Cast: Jim Jordan (Fibber), Marian Jordan (Molly), John Wald, Bill Thompson (Phillips), Arthur Q. Bryan (Doctor Gamble, janitor)
Summary: When McGee uses Gamble's auto card to renew his plates for 1955, he impersonates the doctor and diagnoses a clerk's ailments.
Writers: Phil Leslie, Ralph Goodman
Sponsors: Prudential, Dial, *Woman's Home Companion*
Running Gag: "'Tain't funny, McGee" (Molly)
Comments: For a change Fibber does not dispute Molly's famous squelch of one of his puns. The dialects heard at the end suggest that humor of the minstrel show variety was still acceptable on radio in 1955.

Date: February 6, 1955
Title: Civil Defense Speech Preparations
Cast: Jim Jordan (Fibber), Marian Jordan (Molly), John Wald, Bill Thompson (Old Timer), Arthur Q. Bryan (Doctor Gamble), Charlie Seel (Harry Willoughby)
Summary: Fibber is worried about the reaction of the man he supplanted as speechmaker.
Writers: Phil Leslie, Ralph Goodman
Sponsors: Prudential; PSA for American Heart Association; promo for NBC programs
Comments: The Old Timer's description of a mayor's overreaction to disappointment is quite irritating to Molly, provoking her to utter a strong rebuke.

Date: February 7, 1955
Title: Civil Defense Speech at School
Cast: Jim Jordan (Fibber), Marian Jordan (Molly), John Wald, Bill Thompson (Wallace Wimple, chairman), Arthur Q. Bryan (Doctor Gamble)
Summary: As McGee prepares to leave for the school, he continues to doubt Mr. Willoughby's motives for stepping aside as speaker.
Writers: Phil Leslie, Ralph Goodman
Sponsors: Prudential, Dial, *Woman's Home Companion*
Comments: The drill sending people scurrying to the basement bomb shelter is a reminder of those "duck and cover" days during the Cold War.

Date: February 8, 1955
Title: Tiltmore Relaxing Chair

Cast: Jim Jordan (Fibber), Marian Jordan (Molly, Teeny), John Wald, Bill Thompson (Tyrone, Old Timer), Arthur Q. Bryan (Doctor Gamble), Jack Moyles (Marlin)
Summary: When Fibber has a chair delivered on trial, it becomes a trial to find a place for it in the living room.
Writers: Phil Leslie, Len Levinson
Sponsors: Prudential, Viceroy, *Woman's Home Companion*
Comments: An abbreviated version of "The Monkey and the Coconut" returns after a considerable absence.

Date: February 9, 1955
Title: Anniversary of First Meeting
Cast: Jim Jordan (Fibber), Marian Jordan (Molly), John Wald, Bill Thompson (Old Timer), Elvia Allman (Cora Burns)
Summary: Molly is upset because Fibber apparently has forgotten to observe an anniversary.
Writers: Phil Leslie, Ralph Goodman
Sponsors: Prudential, *Better Farming*, Dial
Comments: The concept of a couple celebrating the anniversary of their first meeting *twice* a year for thirty-five years in addition to commemorating their wedding anniversary is pretty far-fetched.

Date: February 10, 1955
Title: Furnace Needs Repair
Cast: Jim Jordan (Fibber), Marian Jordan (Molly, Teeny), John Wald, Arthur Q. Bryan (Charlie), Jack Moyles (Michael Brogan)
Summary: When the furnace goes on the fritz, McGee throws one of his fits after he discovers that Molly has given away a sweater containing a secret stash of cash.
Writers: Phil Leslie, Ralph Goodman
Sponsors: Prudential, Dial, *Woman's Home Companion*
Comments: Because of an important plot development, Molly and Teeny are left alone in the house for the first time in the series.

Date: February 13, 1955
Title: Phonograph Records from the Attic
Cast: Jim Jordan (Fibber), Marian Jordan (Molly), John Wald, Bill Thompson (Old Timer, Rafferty), Arthur Q. Bryan (Doctor Gamble)
Cast: The McGees, Doc, and the Old Timer play their version of "Get Out Those Old Records" with the intention of selling them to an interested party.
Writers: Phil Leslie, Ralph Goodman
Sponsors: Prudential; PSA for nurse recruitment; promo for NBC programs

Comments: By the end of this episode any desire to sell old records disappears because, to alter slightly the title of another record released later in 1955, memories are made of these.

Date: February 14, 1955
Title: Shopping for a Hat for Molly
Cast: Jim Jordan (Fibber), Marian Jordan (Molly), John Wald, Rolfe Sedan (Henri), Betty Lou Gerson (Mrs. Carter, Marie)
Summary: The McGees are difficult to please when they seek a new chapeau for Molly.
Writers: Phil Leslie, Ralph Goodman
Sponsors: Prudential, Dial; promo for NBC programs
Comments: Wald salutes Fibber and Molly for being voted Best Comedy Team in Radio by *Motion Picture Daily*, an honor the Jordans almost earned by default in the mid-fifties.

Date: February 15, 1955
Title: Planning to Paint a House
Cast: Jim Jordan (Fibber), Marian Jordan (Molly), John Wald, Bill Thompson (Old Timer), Jess Kirkpatrick (Tracy), Natalie Masters (Mrs. Morley), William Conrad (neighbor)
Summary: Fibber secretly solicits donations of supplies and labor as he handles arrangements for painting Mrs. Morley's house.
Writers: Phil Leslie, Len Levinson
Sponsors: Prudential, Viceroy, *Better Farming*
Comments: Even the casual listener might wonder why the precipitation in mid-February is not snow and why anyone would consider painting the exterior of a house less than a week after having a furnace repaired due to frigid weather.

Date: February 16, 1955
Title: Painting Mrs. Morley's House
Cast: Jim Jordan (Fibber), Marian Jordan (Molly), John Wald, Bill Thompson (Wallace Wimple, Old Timer), Arthur Q. Bryan (Doctor Gamble), Natalie Masters (Mrs. Morley), William Conrad (Hobson)
Summary: McGee supervises the painting of Mrs. Morley's house and then surprises the widow when the job is finished.
Writers: Phil Leslie, Len Levinson
Sponsors: Prudential, Nash, Dial
Comments: The writers may have purposely chosen the name of Conrad's character for it is obvious from the information Fibber reveals at the end that the landlord had been presented with a Hobson's choice.

Date: February 17, 1955
Title: Radio Interview Preparations
Cast: Jim Jordan (Fibber), Marian Jordan (Molly), John Wald, Bill Thompson (Wallace Wimple), Jack Moyles (Marty Daugherty)
Summary: Fibber gets ready for an interview on WVIS by dusting off phonograph records and stories about his days in vaudeville.
Writers: Phil Leslie, Ralph Goodman
Sponsors: Prudential, Dial, Nash
Comments: As McGee reminisces about his show biz career with Fred Nitney, we sense that those experiences were preparing him for his role in life, that of the patsy.

Date: February 20, 1955
Title: Library Committee Soirée
Cast: Jim Jordan (Fibber), Marian Jordan (Molly), John Wald, Bill Thompson (Wallace Wimple), Arthur Q. Bryan (Doctor Gamble), Gail Bonney (Mrs. Jay Manville Whitney III), Joseph Kearns (MacDonald)
Summary: Molly fears that Fibber will commit a solecism while they are guests at the home of a socialite.
Writers: Phil Leslie, Len Levinson
Sponsors: Prudential; PSA for Ground Observer Corps; promo for NBC programs
Comments: In this episode Fibber catches on by the end of the first act and catches it at the end of the second.

Date: February 21, 1955
Title: Washington Day Play
Cast: Jim Jordan (Fibber), Marian Jordan (Molly, Teeny), John Wald, Arthur Q. Bryan (Doctor Gamble), Mary Lansing (Miss Yeagley)
Summary: Fibber helps Teeny rehearse her part in a school play before leaving with Molly to see the patriotic drama.
Writers: Phil Leslie, Ralph Goodman
Sponsors: Prudential, Dial, *Woman's Home Companion*
Comments: This episode provides ample evidence that acting too big for his britches is nothing new for playful Fibber McGee.

Date: February 22, 1955
Title: Waffle-Weave Shirt
Cast: Jim Jordan (Fibber), Marian Jordan (Molly), John Wald, Bill Thompson (Old Timer), Arthur Q. Bryan (Doctor Gamble), Mary Lansing (demonstrator)
Summary: After McGee buys a miracle shirt at the Bon Ton, he takes it home where he proceeds to abuse it in front of his astonished spouse.

Writers: Phil Leslie, Len Levinson
Sponsors: Prudential, Viceroy, *Woman's Home Companion*
Comments: The game show described by the Old Timer sounds like *Truth or Consequences*, an apt selection for this episode because when the truth about the mix-up emerges, Fibber pays the consequence.

Date: February 23, 1955
Title: Valentine from Snooky
Cast: Jim Jordan (Fibber), Marian Jordan (Molly), John Wald, Bill Thompson (Wallace Wimple), Mary Jane Croft (Mabel Toops), Sam Edwards (employee for cleaners)
Summary: When Molly finds a Valentine in a coat she believes belongs to Fibber, she suspects that a flirtatious manicurist has designs on her husband.
Writers: Phil Leslie, Ralph Goodman
Sponsors: Prudential, *Better Farming*, Dial
Comments: This episode is a reminder of the time when people of both sexes were called Snooky and when domestic abuse was still an acceptable subject for humor on comedy programs.

Date: February 24, 1955
Title: Library Moving Day
Cast: Jim Jordan (Fibber), Marian Jordan (Molly), John Wald, Bill Thompson (Wallace Wimple, Murray), Arthur Q. Bryan (Doctor Gamble), Jean Vander Pyl (Miss Stackhouse), Gail Bonney (Mrs. Jay Manville Whitney III)
Summary: McGee devises an ingenious stratagem for moving books from the old library to the new one.
Writers: Phil Leslie, Len Levinson
Sponsors: Prudential, Dial, *Woman's Home Companion*
Comments: Mark this episode with an asterisk for two reasons: 1) it contains several laugh out loud lines in the first act; 2) the $500 bid from the Rock Bottom Moving Company of Rock Bottom, Illinois gives listeners a clue as to the whereabouts of Wistful Vista.

Date: February 27, 1955
Title: Lighter Racket
Cast: Jim Jordan (Fibber), Marian Jordan (Molly, Teeny), John Wald, Herb Vigran (peddler)
Summary: Fibber is upset after falling victim to the old switcheroo and is stuck with a defective lighter.
Writers: Phil Leslie, Len Levinson
Sponsors: Prudential; PSA for American Heart Association; promo for NBC programs
Comments: The first sale is consummated so quickly McGee doesn't even question how a man who lacks bus fare comes up with four dollars in change.

Date: February 28, 1955
Title: Five Dollars Given or Borrowed?
Cast: Jim Jordan (Fibber), Marian Jordan (Molly), John Wald, Arthur Q. Bryan (Doctor Gamble), Robert Easton (Lester Nelson), Bill Idelson (Frank Walker)
Summary: A dispute arises when Doc considers the five dollars he received from McGee a gift while Fibber maintains it was a loan.
Writers: Phil Leslie, Len Levinson
Sponsors: Prudential, Dial, *Woman's Home Companion*
Running Gag: Myrt bit involving picnic/through the ice/party at house (Fibber)
Comments: Jim's ad-lib of "How's your father?" upon being introduced to Frank Walker may be an in-joke referring to Bill Idelson's role on *One Man's Family*. The euphemistic oath "Interesting, my left funny bone" is a switch on the clavicle joke.

Date: March 1, 1955
Title: Mock Trial Begins
Cast: Jim Jordan (Fibber), Marian Jordan (Molly), John Wald, Bill Thompson (Old Timer), Arthur Q. Bryan (Doctor Gamble), Jack Mather (judge), Charlie Smith (Arnie Shayne), Bill Idelson (Frank Walker)
Summary: A recording and a reenactment lend credence to Gamble's argument that he did not ask McGee to loan him the five dollars in question.
Writers: Phil Leslie, Len Levinson
Sponsors: Prudential, Viceroy, *Woman's Home Companion*
Comments: When Fibber smells the stage of the courtroom, he shifts into high dudgeon, from his colorful declaration that Doc has the conscience of an "Abyssinian camel rustler" right up to sputtering amazement at his adversary's craftiness.

Date: March 2, 1955
Title: Mock Trial Continues
Cast: Jim Jordan (Fibber), Marian Jordan (Molly), John Wald, Bill Thompson (Wallace Wimple), Arthur Q. Bryan (Doctor Gamble), Jack Mather (judge), Charlie Smith (Arnie Shayne), Bill Idelson (Frank Walker)
Summary: After Wimple acts as dubious character witness for McGee, Fibber tries to assassinate Doc's character on the witness stand.
Writers: Phil Leslie, Len Levinson
Sponsors: Prudential, *Woman's Home Companion*, Dial
Comments: Fibber, who just three days ago played the sucker, proves he can still be a cagey counterpuncher by pulling his own switcheroo.

Date: March 3, 1955
Title: Mock Trial Concludes
Cast: Jim Jordan (Fibber), Marian Jordan (Molly), John Wald, Arthur Q. Bryan (Doctor Gamble), Jack Mather (judge), Charlie Smith (Arnie Shayne), Bill Idelson (Frank Walker)
Summary: Gamble attempts to stall the case, hoping that McGee will concede in order to make a bowling commitment.
Writers: Phil Leslie, Len Levinson
Sponsors: Prudential, Dial; promo for NBC programs
Comments: At least for one episode Fibber, the perpetual loser, becomes the all-American boy: a whiz at clandestine recording, a legal eagle who can cite chapter and verse from law books, and a bowling star.

Date: March 6, 1955
Title: Ten-Dollar Bill Spent
Cast: Jim Jordan (Fibber), Marian Jordan (Molly), John Wald, Bill Thompson (Wallace Wimple), Jack Kruschen (Ed Harper, flower salesman)
Summary: After Fibber breaks a ten-dollar bill to pay a forty-cent fine, his prediction that the remaining amount will go quickly comes true.
Writers: Phil Leslie, Ralph Goodman
Sponsors: Prudential; PSA for American economic system; promo for NBC programs
Comments: The McGees, though poorer in pocket at the end, leave their listeners richer in benevolence and compassion.

Date: March 7, 1955
Title: Observing Human Nature
Cast: Jim Jordan (Fibber), Marian Jordan (Molly, Teeny), John Wald, Bill Thompson (man on street, Old Timer)
Summary: While Molly is at the beauty shop, Fibber studies the people walking by with a hypercritical eye.
Writers: Phil Leslie, Len Levinson
Sponsors: Prudential, Dial; promo for NBC programs
Comments: Judging by the description of MacDonald's brother, his outfit resembles that of old Bob in "That's What I Like about the South." What listeners like about Wistful Vista is that the weather changes according to the whims of the writers: frigid yesterday when a warm coffee shop provided refuge from the elements, pleasant today when Fibber needed to spend four hours on the street.

Date: March 8, 1955
Title: Stock Certificate for India Company
Cast: Jim Jordan (Fibber), Marian Jordan (Molly), John Wald, Bill Thompson (Old Timer), Arthur Q. Bryan (Doctor Gamble), Charlie Seel (Appleheimer)

Summary: McGee hopes an old stock certificate he found is valuable.
Writers: Phil Leslie, Len Levinson
Sponsors: Prudential, Viceroy, *Saturday Evening Post*
Comments: Molly gets the last groan, but if Gamble got the last line it probably would have been "McGee shouldn't have to pay for the plate because he has more brass than anyone in town."

Date: March 9, 1955
Title: Raffle Ticket
Cast: Jim Jordan (Fibber), Marian Jordan (Molly, Teeny), John Wald, Bill Thompson (Wallace Wimple, telegram delivery boy), Arthur Q. Bryan (Doctor Gamble)
Summary: McGee sells shares in a raffle ticket on a car, trying to recoup the ten dollars he paid for it.
Writers: Phil Leslie, Joel Kane
Sponsors: Prudential; PSA for Red Cross; Dial
Comments: Whether the investment is shares or sodas, Teeny spends her quarters only on sure things.

Date: March 10, 1955
Title: Raffle Ticket Winners Meet
Cast: Jim Jordan (Fibber), Marian Jordan (Molly, Teeny), John Wald, Bill Thompson (Old Timer, Wallace Wimple), Arthur Q. Bryan (Doctor Gamble), Robert Easton (Lester Nelson)
Summary: The five shareholders meet at Doc's office to decide what to do with the $4,000 convertible they won.
Writers: Phil Leslie, Joel Kane
Sponsors: Prudential, Dial; promo for NBC programs
Comments: Marian's cold is scarcely noticeable until Fibber mentions it in separate conversations with Molly and Teeny. That at least five minutes pass after Teeny releases the hand brake before the auto starts its fateful roll might cause the critical listener to exclaim "Don't give the car a brake. Give me a break!"

Date: March 13, 1955
Title: Pennies for Little Shavers Fund
Cast: Jim Jordan (Fibber), Marian Jordan (Molly), John Wald, Bill Thompson (Prince Basil), Arthur Q. Bryan (Doctor Gamble), Joe Granby (Henry Lester)
Summary: Fibber is less than pleased when he discovers that his title of Chairman of the Elks Auxiliary Finances Committee entails emptying pennies from weighing machines.
Writers: Phil Leslie, Len Levinson
Sponsors: Prudential; PSA for Red Cross; promo for NBC programs

Comments: Bryan's part is so small he can literally phone it in. It isn't just trash collectors in Wistful Vista who speak like nobility (see February 1, 1955 episode); even hoboes on the street are eloquent princes who wear spats.

Date: March 14, 1955
Title: Pennies Removed from Scales
Cast: Jim Jordan (Fibber), Marian Jordan (Molly, Teeny), John Wald, Bill Thompson (Old Timer, Parker), Joseph Kearns (MacDonald)
Summary: The McGees take a sack filled with pennies removed from 93 scales to the bank where they hope to make a deposit but receive a disappointment instead.
Writers: Phil Leslie, Len Levinson
Sponsors: Prudential, Dial; promo for NBC programs
Comments: For a change a scene takes place at 3rd and Elm instead of the usual 14th and Oak. The Old Timer has so many wheezes in his repertoire he can even offer multiple-choice punch lines.

Date: March 15, 1955
Title: Pennies Counted
Cast: Jim Jordan (Fibber), Marian Jordan (Molly, Teeny), John Wald, Bill Thompson (Old Timer, officer), Joseph Kearns (MacDonald), Daws Butler (newsboy)
Summary: After being required to count the pennies taken from the weighing machines before depositing them, the McGees take all 19,342 of them to the bank.
Writers: Phil Leslie, Len Levinson
Sponsors: Prudential, Viceroy; promo for NBC programs
Comments: The Old Timer gets to the join the McGees in saying "Good night" to the listeners.

Date: March 16, 1955
Title: Gifts for Wives Switched
Cast: Jim Jordan (Fibber), Marian Jordan (Molly), John Wald, Robert Easton (Lester Nelson), Mary Lou Harrington (Sally Nelson)
Summary: Fibber has to do some quick thinking after Molly assumes a bottle of perfume is a present from McGee when actually it is a birthday gift from Lester to Sally.
Writers: Phil Leslie, Ralph Goodman
Sponsors: Prudential; PSA for nurse recruitment; Dial
Comments: Apparently in Wistful Vista men put their overshoes in ovens instead of closets.

Date: March 17, 1955
Title: Dalmatian Trouble
Cast: Jim Jordan (Fibber), Marian Jordan (Molly, Teeny), John Wald, Bill Thompson (Wallace Wimple), Jess Kirkpatrick (Harkins), Jack Moyles (Spot)
Summary: The McGees try to find the owner of a dog.
Writers: Phil Leslie, Ralph Goodman
Sponsors: Prudential, Dial; promo for NBC programs
Comments: Even though the wheeze about the fifth at the end creaks a bit, it is still welcome for it provides the only bright spot in this lackluster episode.

Date: March 20, 1955
Title: Stage Money
Cast: Jim Jordan (Fibber), Marian Jordan (Molly), John Wald, Arthur Q. Bryan (Doctor Gamble), Peggy Knudsen (Nancy Cuddleson)
Summary: Problems arise when Fibber thinks he passed a phony five-dollar bill at a restaurant.
Writers: Phil Leslie, Ralph Goodman
Sponsors: Prudential; PSA for Red Cross; promo for NBC programs
Comments: This is one time when a McGee prank truly does go up in smoke.

Date: March 21, 1955
Title: Jinxed
Cast: Jim Jordan (Fibber), Marian Jordan (Molly), John Wald, Bill Thompson (Wallace Wimple, officer), Arthur Q. Bryan (Doctor Gamble), Mary Lansing (clerk, shopper)
Summary: Because everything seems to be going wrong for him after he gets up, by mid-morning McGee is convinced he is jinxed for the day.
Writers: Phil Leslie, Ralph Goodman
Sponsors: Prudential, Dial, *Woman's Home Companion*
Comments: For a change Molly gets the clinching laugh when she decides that Fibber's jinx is contagious.

Date: March 22, 1955
Title: Buys a Homburg
Cast: Jim Jordan (Fibber), Marian Jordan (Molly), John Wald, Bill Thompson (Prince Basil), Arthur Q. Bryan (Doctor Gamble), Jack Moyles (Louie, hatter)
Summary: Prince Basil convinces Fibber to give up his well-worn fedora for a new homburg at a nearby haberdashery.
Writers: Phil Leslie, Len Levinson
Sponsors: Prudential, Viceroy, *Woman's Home Companion*
Comments: Even on one of his normal days McGee still is jinxed for in essence he pays fifteen dollars to get his own battered hat back.

Date: March 23, 1955
Title: Sales Resistance Questioned
Cast: Jim Jordan (Fibber), Marian Jordan (Molly), John Wald, Bill Thompson (salesman, Old Timer), Eddie Marr (Carges)
Summary: Regardless of whether salesmen approach from the front or the rear, McGee is unable to resist the pitches they throw at him.
Writers: Phil Leslie, Len Levinson
Sponsors: Prudential, *Woman's Home Companion*, Dial
Comments: The payoff in the tag regarding Easter Seals verifies what listeners always suspected: gullible Fibber is still lovable Fibber.

Date: March 24, 1955
Title: Moose or Mousse for Dinner?
Cast: Jim Jordan (Fibber), Marian Jordan (Molly), John Wald, Bill Thompson (Old Timer, Bilson), Arthur Q. Bryan (Doctor Gamble), Gail Bonney (Mrs. Jay Manville Whitney III)
Summary: Fibber is ridiculed after making a statement which seems to reveal he is unsophisticated.
Writers: Phil Leslie, Len Levinson
Sponsors: Prudential, Dial; promo for NBC programs
Comments: No one who hears this episode can doubt that it is set a long time ago in a galaxy far, far away when a light bill for $4.80 was considered high, $1.00 purchased a leather clutch bag, and people were encouraged to mail currency through the mail. Jim distinctly says, "Goom-Bye" instead of "Good-Bye" when Fibber angrily dismisses the Old Timer.

Date: March 27, 1955
Title: Cab Ride to Airport
Cast: Jim Jordan (Fibber), Marian Jordan (Molly), John Wald, Bill Thompson (Old Timer, officer), Arthur Q. Bryan (Doctor Gamble), Herb Vigran (George Frazier)
Summary: After Gamble leaves his airline ticket at their house, the McGees take a frantic taxi ride in hopes of finding the doctor before his plane leaves for Miami.
Writers: Phil Leslie, Len Levinson
Sponsors: Prudential; PSA for Radio Free Europe; promo for NBC programs
Comments: The writers make certain Fibber does not refer to Gamble by his first name to avoid confusion with the cabbie before they bring in the "Let George do it" saying and a wheeze about Washington.

Date: March 28, 1955
Title: Cab Driver McGee
Cast: Jim Jordan (Fibber), Marian Jordan (Molly), John Wald, Bill Thompson (officer, elderly man), Leo Curley (passenger), Mary Lansing (dispatcher)

Summary: Fibber learns some painful lessons when he substitutes for an incarcerated cab driver.
Writers: Phil Leslie, Len Levinson
Sponsors: Prudential, Dial, *Woman's Home Companion*
Running Gag: Tongue twister starting with "hack in Hackensack" (Fibber)
Comments: Naturally hard-luck McGee is driving cab 13 and invites more trouble by saying, "Now I'd like to see anything go wrong."

Date: March 29, 1955
Title: Texan Entertains McGee
Cast: Jim Jordan (Fibber), Marian Jordan (Molly), John Wald, Arthur Q. Bryan (Doctor Gamble), Jack Mather ("Tex"), Bob Bruce (Tom Pelton)
Summary: McGee is diverted from his duties driving a taxi by an ebullient passenger who appears to be a wealthy oilman.
Writers: Phil Leslie, Len Levinson
Sponsors: Prudential, Viceroy, *Woman's Home Companion*
Comments: That McGee unmasks a four-flusher proves the bromide "It takes one to know one."

Date: March 30, 1955
Title: Avoids the Elks
Cast: Jim Jordan (Fibber), Marian Jordan (Molly), John Wald, Bill Thompson (Wallace Wimple), Arthur Q. Bryan (Doctor Gamble), Tyler McVey (Henry Lester), Mary Lansing (dispatcher)
Summary: Because Fibber suspects his brother Elks are planning some mischief for him, he avoids driving his taxi near the clubhouse.
Writers: Phil Leslie, Len Levinson
Sponsors: Prudential, *Ladies' Home Journal*, Dial
Comments: By having McGee talk to himself at the outset, Phil and Len cogently summarize the situation for those who had missed the previous episodes in two sentences. At the end listeners use their imaginations to deduce where Fibber's tense spot is located.

Date: March 31, 1955
Title: Snowy Owl
Cast: Jim Jordan (Fibber), Marian Jordan (Molly), John Wald, Bill Thompson (Wallace Wimple), Arthur Q. Bryan (Doctor Gamble), Eddie Marr (radio MC)
Summary: After the McGees, Wimple, and Gamble see a snowy owl, Fibber reports the sighting to a radio station.
Writers: Phil Leslie, Len Levinson
Sponsors: Prudential, Dial, *Woman's Home Companion*
Running Gag: "'Tain't funny, McGee" (Molly)

Comments: Fibber must have been thinking of another white owl when he dubbed this bird *nicotine scantioctus*. The shellfish/unselfish line passes so quickly most listeners probably missed the pun.

Date: April 3, 1955
Title: Lost Boy at Airport
Cast: Jim Jordan (Fibber), Marian Jordan (Molly), John Wald, Bill Thompson (Old Timer), Arthur Q. Bryan (Doctor Gamble), Colleen Collins (Jerry O'Brien)
Summary: Fibber, Molly, Doc, and the Old Timer attempt to learn the identity of a playful, prevaricating youngster found in the waiting room at the Wistful Vista Airport.
Writers: Phil Leslie, Len Levinson
Sponsors: Prudential; PSA for American Cancer Society; promo for NBC programs
Comments: At long last: the partnership between McGee and Nitney pays a dividend! Colleen Collins, like Cecil Roy, could do juvenile voices of either sex with ease.

Date: April 4, 1955
Title: Searching for Raincoat
Cast: Jim Jordan (Fibber), Marian Jordan (Molly), John Wald, Bill Thompson (Old Timer), Arthur Q. Bryan (Doctor Gamble)
Summary: Fibber picks up other items that belong to the McGees as he looks all over town for his missing raincoat.
Writers: Phil Leslie, Len Levinson
Sponsors: Prudential, Dial; jingle promoting radio listening
Comments: Molly's stern, unfinished statement ("If the truth were known…") did not need completion; by ordering Fibber not to open the closet, she had just demonstrated she had a will of her own. At the close Wald erroneously credits Bill Thompson with also playing Wimple, who is not heard in this episode.

Date: April 5, 1955
Title: Lester Whistles Well
Cast: Jim Jordan (Fibber), Marian Jordan (Molly), John Wald, Robert Easton (Lester Nelson), Mary Lou Harrington (Sally Nelson), Tommy Cook (Kevin O'Shaughnessy)
Summary: After Fibber discovers Les is an expert whistler, he makes plans to manage the young man's career in show business.
Writers: Phil Leslie, Ralph Goodman
Sponsors: Prudential, Viceroy; promo for NBC programs
Comments: The opening commercial for the free baseball booklet is refreshing in that it makes absolutely no attempt to sell insurance. The name of Kevin's

song ("Let's Hey Ba-Ba Rebop at My House, Baby, We Just Sh-Boomed at Yours") would almost certainly earn the Stan Freberg Seal of Satiric Approval.

Date: April 6, 1955
Title: Lester Prepares for Audition
Cast: Jim Jordan (Fibber), Marian Jordan (Molly), John Wald, Arthur Q. Bryan (Doctor Gamble), Robert Easton (Lester Nelson), Larry Dobkin (Oscar Harris), Gene Conklin (Harry)
Summary: McGee hampers as much as helps Lester practice for his audition at the studios of Victory Record Company.
Writers: Phil Leslie, Ralph Goodman
Sponsors: Prudential; PSA for Radio Free Europe; Dial
Comments: Fibber brings back his "stuff like that there" line and stumbles around the studios in fine form as the know-nothing who thinks he knows everything.

Date: April 7, 1955
Title: Lester Missing on Recording Day
Cast: Jim Jordan (Fibber), Marian Jordan (Molly), John Wald, Arthur Q. Bryan (Doctor Gamble), Robert Easton (Lester Nelson), Mary Lou Harrington (Sally Nelson)
Summary: McGee panics because Les cannot be found on the day he is to whistle in a recording session.
Writers: Phil Leslie, Ralph Goodman
Sponsors: Prudential, Dial; jingle promoting radio listening
Comments: Gene Conklin's bit as the orchestra leader on April 6 becomes apparent in the credits for April 7: he was already there, standing by, wetting his whistle.

Date: April 8, 1955
Title: Mystery Movie at Bijou
Cast: Jim Jordan (Fibber), Marian Jordan (Molly), John Wald, Arthur Q. Bryan (Doctor Gamble), Jack Kruschen (man in theater), Natalie Masters (woman in theater)
Summary: Fibber frets all day about going to see *Murder Me Gently, My Love*, much to the displeasure of Molly.
Writers: Phil Leslie, Ralph Goodman
Sponsors: Prudential; PSA for Ground Observer Corps; promo for NBC programs
Running Gag: Myrt bit involving man of dreams/tough luck/finance man (Fibber)
Comments: This episode is noteworthy in that tolerant Molly's patience is so exhausted by the climax she is even more willing to throw a punch than her exasperated husband.

Date: April 11, 1955
Title: Bargain Day at Bon Ton
Cast: Jim Jordan (Fibber), Marian Jordan (Molly), John Wald, Bill Thompson (Old Timer), Arthur Q. Bryan (Doctor Gamble), Pauline Drake (customer buying suit, clerk), Arlene Harris (customer with bundles)
Summary: Fibber and Molly, battling the crowds while shopping, have a difficult time staying together.
Writers: Phil Leslie, Len Levinson
Sponsors: Prudential, Dial; promo for NBC programs
Comments: According to the May issue of *TV Radio Mirror* cited here, audiences still liked Fibber and Molly enough to vote them their favorite husband-and-wife radio team, although by this time the number of entries in the ratings race had diminished considerably.

Date: April 12, 1955
Title: Protesting Meters
Cast: Jim Jordan (Fibber), Marian Jordan (Molly, Teeny), John Wald, Bill Thompson (public works spokesman), Robert Easton (Lester Nelson)
Summary: McGee shifts into high dudgeon drafting a letter of protest after deducing that holes dug in the front yard mean the city plans to install parking meters along his street.
Writers: Phil Leslie, Len Levinson
Sponsors: Prudential, Viceroy, *Saturday Evening Post*
Comments: Only Fibber could heat up a tempest in a teapot (complete with marshmallows) consisting of six pages of typed vitriol beginning with the ingratiating salutation "Gentlemen (you rats):"

Date: April 13, 1955
Title: Mystery Caller
Cast: Jim Jordan (Fibber), Marian Jordan (Molly), John Wald, Bill Thompson (Old Timer), Arthur Q. Bryan (Doctor Gamble), Robert Easton (Lester Nelson)
Summary: Fibber is frustrated by a party who calls periodically but refuses to speak.
Writers: Phil Leslie, Ralph Goodman
Sponsors: Prudential; PSA for CARE; Dial
Comments: McGee's juvenile behavior is emphasized throughout this episode (a yo-yo, chemistry set, and junior G-man badge seem to be among his favorite playthings), culminating in the conclusion when "Mama" Molly offers him sweets to curtail his childish pouting.

Date: April 14, 1955
Title: Efficiency in the Kitchen
Cast: Jim Jordan (Fibber), Marian Jordan (Molly), John Wald, Arthur Q. Bryan (Doctor Gamble), Bill Idelson (Dave Eustice)

Summary: After meeting an efficiency expert downtown, Fibber decides to apply such time-saving techniques at home, much to Molly's chagrin.
Writers: Phil Leslie, Ralph Goodman
Sponsors: Prudential, Dial; promo for NBC programs
Comments: Walter Tetley delivered the best scoff heard on the airwaves whenever Leroy doubted one of Gildersleeve's statements, but Marian Jordan was not far behind at playing the scorn horn as the perfect derisive note she hits in this episode proves.

Date: April 17, 1955
Title: Letter Found in Attic
Cast: Jim Jordan (Fibber), Marian Jordan (Molly), John Wald, Bill Thompson (Old Timer, Wallace Wimple), Arthur Q. Bryan (Doctor Gamble)
Summary: After Fibber finds an unopened letter from 1935 offering the McGees a chance to do a radio program, the McGees reminisce about the last twenty years.
Writer: Phil Leslie
Sponsors: Prudential; PSA for savings bonds; promo for NBC programs
Running Gag: "Bird book" (Wallace)
Comments: The citation read by the president of the Loyola University student body at the conclusion of this episode says it all: "To Jim and Marian Jordan, who for twenty years in the radio characters of Fibber McGee and Molly have brought hours of happiness beyond number to countless millions of listeners and who in the personal character of their whole life have set an example of decency, dignity, patriotism, and integrity, the Associated Students of Loyola University of Los Angeles present this, a citation for their excellence as artists and a token of our affectionate admiration for them as people."

Date: April 18, 1955
Title: Washing Front Window
Cast: Jim Jordan (Fibber), Marian Jordan (Molly), John Wald, Bill Thompson (Old Timer), Arthur Q. Bryan (Doctor Gamble)
Summary: After Molly virtually abandons hope that McGee will ever wash the front window, Fibber finally does the task in an intriguing way.
Writers: Phil Leslie, Ralph Goodman
Sponsors: Prudential, Dial; promo for NBC programs
Comments: Fibber's appraisal of the reason Gamble insults others would have sounded more appropriate had McGee been sitting in front of a mirror instead of a window.

Date: April 19, 1955
Title: Driving Doc on House Calls
Cast: Jim Jordan (Fibber), Marian Jordan (Molly), John Wald, Arthur Q. Bryan (Doctor Gamble), Jean Vander Pyl (Mrs. Thomas)

Summary: As McGee drives Gamble around to see patients, he tests his friend's patience by diagnosing and prescribing promiscuously.
Writers: Phil Leslie, Len Levinson
Sponsors: Prudential, Viceroy; promo for NBC programs
Comments: Listeners hear both ends of the phone conversation between Fibber and Gamble and only Molly's half of the exchange with Doc's mother. The friendship between Fibber and "good ol' Doc" will always run deep, though we know from experience that it will never run silent.

Date: April 20, 1955
Title: Helping Teeny's Parents
Cast: Jim Jordan (Fibber), Marian Jordan (Molly, Teeny), John Wald, Bill Thompson (Old Timer), Mary Lansing (Mrs. Taylor)
Summary: When lost train tickets and changed plans of a babysitter seem to doom a trip for Teeny's folks, the McGees come to the rescue of their neighbors twice.
Writers: Phil Leslie, Ralph Goodman
Sponsors: Prudential; PSA for American Cancer Society; Dial
Running Gag: Hall closet in Taylor home opened by Fibber to hang up coat
Comments: This is the first episode in which Teeny's mother appears. Mrs. Taylor's first name is not given, but her husband is referred to as Mark and the baby as Michael. Teeny's real first name was provided in 1948; when the other shoe drops seven years later, the "pint-size atom bomb" is revealed to be Elizabeth Taylor.

Date: April 21, 1955
Title: Babysitting Teeny and Michael
Cast: Jim Jordan (Fibber), Marian Jordan (Molly, Teeny), John Wald, Mary Lansing (Mrs. Taylor)
Summary: Mrs. Taylor briefs the McGees on their babysitting duties before departing on a trip.
Writers: Phil Leslie, Ralph Goodman
Sponsors: Prudential, Dial; promo for NBC programs
Comments: Fibber's claim of Teeny being full of tricks fades seamlessly into a scene of one of her pranks in progress being terminated by Mrs. Taylor.

Date: April 24, 1955
Title: Beauty Contest Judge
Cast: Jim Jordan (Fibber), Marian Jordan (Molly), John Wald, Arthur Q. Bryan (Doctor Gamble), Robert Easton (Lester Nelson), Herb Vigran (contest official)
Summary: Fibber eagerly prepares to judge a beauty contest in place of Doctor Gamble.
Writers: Phil Leslie, Len Levinson

Sponsors: Prudential: PSA for Ground Observers Corps; promo for NBC programs
Running Gag: Tongue twister starting with "Peter Mudge got loaded on fudge" (Fibber)
Comments: Although the far-fetched storytelling aspect of McGee's character had virtually vanished from the program by this time, the AC/DC anecdote reveals that he could still spin a tall (albeit brief) tale.

Date: April 25, 1955
Title: Noise Abatement Committee
Cast: Jim Jordan (Fibber), Marian Jordan (Molly, Teeny), John Wald, Bill Thompson (Old Timer), Arthur Q. Bryan (Doctor Gamble), Jack Kruschen (Filbert McKee)
Summary: Fibber is loaded with ideas on how to reduce noise once he becomes convinced he has been chosen to serve on a committee for the city.
Writers: Phil Leslie, Len Levinson
Sponsors: Prudential, Dial, *Woman's Home Companion*
Comments: Appropriately, the sound of a loud ringing phone replaces Wald's usual introduction.

Date: April 26, 1955
Title: Golf Match Begins
Cast: Jim Jordan (Fibber), Marian Jordan (Molly), John Wald, Bill Thompson (Old Timer), Arthur Q. Bryan (Doctor Gamble)
Summary: Fibber and Gamble commence a long-distance golf contest from Wistful Vista to Springfield.
Writers: Phil Leslie, Len Levinson
Sponsors: Prudential, Viceroy, *Woman's Home Companion*
Comments: The Old Timer supplies probably the most vivid description of the topography of Wistful Vista and environs ever heard on the program. For a change Doc and the Old Timer join Fibber in closing the show with "good night."

Date: April 27, 1955
Title: Golf Match Continues in the Country
Cast: Jim Jordan (Fibber), Marian Jordan (Molly), John Wald, Bill Thompson (Old Timer), Arthur Q. Bryan (Doctor Gamble), Jack Moyles (farmer)
Summary: Doc and McGee raise the ire of a farmer while raising their golf scores as they hack their way through the countryside.
Writers: Phil Leslie, Len Levinson
Sponsors: Prudential, *Woman's Home Companion,* Dial
Comments: The writers provide Gamble with an amusing handful of medical and anatomical gibberish for him to spew out instead of actual vulgarities after his ball lands in the empty coal car.

Date: April 28, 1955
Title: Golf Match Concludes
Cast: Jim Jordan (Fibber), Marian Jordan (Molly), John Wald, Bill Thompson (Old Timer, Wallace Wimple), Arthur Q. Bryan (Doctor Gamble), Robert Easton (Lester Nelson), Barney Phillips (Pete Plummer)
Summary: A crowd and a radio reporter are on hand as golfers McGee and Gamble approach their goal, the Springfield Country Club.
Writers: Phil Leslie, Len Levinson
Sponsors: Prudential, Dial; promo for NBC programs
Comments: Plummer mistakenly indicates the difference between the golfers is twelve strokes instead of twenty-one. Fibber naturally commits a typical gaffe at the end and then issues his usual challenge rather than pay off.

Date: May 1, 1955
Title: Mystery Ladies' Society
Cast: Jim Jordan (Fibber), Marian Jordan (Molly, Teeny), John Wald, Arthur Q. Bryan (Doctor Gamble), Colleen Collins (Joan and Charlotte Hotchkiss), Marian Richman (Kathy Weaver), Margie Liszt (Susie Powell)
Summary: Teeny introduces Fibber to members of her secret organization, then leads him on a merry chase to find his missing pen.
Writers: Phil Leslie, Ralph Goodman
Sponsors: Prudential; PSA for savings bonds; promo for NBC programs
Comments: Somehow following a three-day, thirty-mile golf match with a far-fetched search for a pen does not seem that incredible for a show that employs three adult actresses to speak a couple lines each as giggling girls.

Date: May 2, 1955
Title: Phone Number in Wallet
Cast: Jim Jordan (Fibber), Marian Jordan (Molly), John Wald, Bill Thompson (Old Timer, Wallace Wimple)
Summary: After Fibber finds "Wistful Vista 9312" written on a paper in his wallet, he spends most of the day trying to find out the identity of the party at that number.
Writers: Phil Leslie, Len Levinson
Sponsors: Prudential; PSA for USO; *Ladies' Home Journal*
Running Gag: Myrt bit involving housepainter uncle/kicked the bucket/died (Fibber)
Comments: The plot of this script requires that McGee be kept from doing the obvious (dialing the number) for as long as possible so Bill Thompson provides some amusing chatter to forestall the inevitable.

Date: May 3, 1955
Title: Christmas Cards Confusion

Cast: Jim Jordan (Fibber), Marian Jordan (Molly, Teeny), John Wald, Bill Thompson (Old Timer, Wallace Wimple), Arthur Q. Bryan (Doctor Gamble)
Summary: Problems arise when Fibber assumes the new Christmas cards on his desk are the ones received by the McGees in 1954.
Writers: Phil Leslie, Len Levinson
Sponsors: Prudential, Viceroy; promo for NBC programs
Comments: Molly does not dominate the comedy or the action but she is certainly the one in charge as she lays down the law to Fibber twice, the closing of the door between their last words putting a final exclamation mark on her role as queen of the house.

Date: May 4, 1955
Title: Plumbing Problems
Cast: Jim Jordan (Fibber), Marian Jordan (Molly, Teeny), John Wald, Larry Dobkin (Crimp Herkemeier)
Summary: When a faucet needs repair, McGee wants to do the job himself, but Molly insists on bringing in a plumber.
Writers: Phil Leslie, Len Levinson
Sponsors: Prudential; PSA for Radio Free Europe; promo for NBC programs
Comments: Just when it looks like Fibber has moved to a favorable position on the marital seesaw through craftiness, he tumbles off ignominiously due to clumsiness.

Date: May 5, 1955
Title: Doc Orders Fibber to Rest
Cast: Jim Jordan (Fibber), Marian Jordan (Molly, Teeny), John Wald, Bill Thompson (Wallace Wimple, Old Timer), Arthur Q. Bryan (Doctor Gamble)
Summary: After Gamble states his opinion that Fibber doesn't look well, he orders McGee to stay at home for the day.
Writers: Phil Leslie, Len Levinson
Sponsors: Prudential; PSA for CARE; promo for NBC programs
Comments: The specious fingernail test should have tipped off listeners that Gamble had a hidden motive for mandating a day of rest. The doctor might be spending the next day resting and recovering from the shock he gets as he leaves the house.

Date: May 8, 1955
Title: Writing Letter to Congressman
Cast: Jim Jordan (Fibber), Marian Jordan (Molly), John Wald, Arthur Q. Bryan (Doctor Gamble)
Summary: When Fibber starts writing a letter to protest a legislative bill, Molly and Doc assume the cause of his anger is a proposal to cut funds for education.

Writers: Phil Leslie, Ralph Goodman
Sponsors: Prudential; PSA for savings bonds; promo for NBC programs
Comments: Fibber unconsciously indicates the pitfalls of censorship with his "Get rid of *Vampire Girl* but leave my *Zombie Comics* alone" attitude.

Date: May 9, 1955
Title: Jury Duty for Molly
Cast: Jim Jordan (Fibber), Marian Jordan (Molly, Teeny), John Wald, Bill Thompson (Wallace Wimple), Arthur Q. Bryan (Doctor Gamble)
Summary: Molly hopes that her ever-eager, ever-dependent spouse doesn't spoil her chance to finally serve on a jury.
Writers: Phil Leslie, Len Levinson
Sponsors: Prudential; PSA for savings bonds; promo for NBC programs
Comments: Only McGee could require a can opener to perform such activities as lighting the stove, getting into a piggy bank, smoking cigars, and handling ice cubes. Teeny must be growing less venal in her old childhood because she takes on the task Fibber assigns her without asking him to first cross her sticky palms with silver.

Date: May 10, 1955
Title: Bank Statement Examined
Cast: Jim Jordan (Fibber), Marian Jordan (Molly), John Wald, Bill Thompson (Wallace Wimple, Old Timer)
Summary: Fibber describes his method of bookkeeping to Molly as she checks over the monthly bank statement.
Writers: Phil Leslie, Ralph Goodman
Sponsors: Prudential, Viceroy; promo for NBC programs
Comments: The exchange between the McGees at the end suggests that, regardless of what the figures on the statement and those peculiar entries in Fibber's checkbook turn out to be, the bank always comes out on the short end because McGee loads up on freebies every time he visits the bank.

Date: May 11, 1955
Title: Business Cards Give Fibber the Business
Cast: Jim Jordan (Fibber), Marian Jordan (Molly), John Wald, Bill Thompson (license bureau official), Arthur Q. Bryan (Doctor Gamble), Arlene Harris (solicitor for charity), Art Jacobson (Watkins)
Summary: After McGee hands out cards that imply he is in business, he finds himself all wrapped up in red tape.
Writers: Phil Leslie, Len Levinson
Sponsors: Prudential; PSA for CARE; promo for NBC programs
Comments: Mark this as one of the best satiric quarter-hour episodes as Phil and Len hit the bull's eye with their shots at implacable bureaucracy and dubious charities.

Date: May 12, 1955
Title: Forgotten Tune Title
Cast: Jim Jordan (Fibber), Marian Jordan (Molly), John Wald, Bill Thompson (Old Timer), Arthur Q. Bryan (Doctor Gamble), Robert Easton (Lester Nelson), Jack Moyles (Combs)
Summary: Fibber is frustrated because neither he nor his friends can recall the name of a melody that has become his current obsession.
Writers: Phil Leslie, Ralph Goodman
Sponsors: Prudential; PSA for Radio Free Europe; promo for NBC programs
Comments: Jack Moyles slips into the role of English codger easily, although he does let his guard (and accent) down when he joins Fibber in an impromptu duet.

Date: May 15, 1955
Title: Purse Search in Theater
Cast: Jim Jordan (Fibber), Marian Jordan (Molly, lady in theater), John Wald, Bill Thompson (injured man), Paul Frees (Man Hunter), Rolfe Sedan (manager)
Summary: When Molly's handbag falls from the balcony during a movie, Fibber tries to recover the scattered remains and soothe the sore feelings of a man hit by the unsuspected flying object.
Writers: Phil Leslie, Len Levinson
Sponsors: Prudential; PSA for safe driving; promo for NBC programs
Running Gag: "'Tain't funny, McGee" (Molly)
Comments: The writers exploit the full possibilities of theater of the mind by allowing listeners to simultaneously watch Fibber fumble in the foreground and Man Hunter hunting Hot Lips on the screen in the distance.

Date: May 16, 1955
Title: Chili Recipe Found
Cast: Jim Jordan (Fibber), Marian Jordan (Molly), John Wald, Bill Thompson (Old Timer), Arthur Q. Bryan (Doctor Gamble)
Summary: The McGees prepare a batch of chili from a recipe Fibber finds among his valuable papers.
Writers: Phil Leslie, Len Levinson
Sponsors: Prudential; PSA on behalf of United Cerebral Palsy; promo for NBC programs
Comments: The incident of nine or ten years ago Fibber relates to Molly is not the kitchen misadventure from November 9, 1943 as listeners might suppose but rather some unrecorded gastronomic escapade.

Date: May 17, 1955
Title: Lock on Front Door Tested
Cast: Jim Jordan (Fibber), Marian Jordan (Molly), John Wald, Arthur Q. Bryan (Doctor Gamble)

Summary: Doc and McGee check the effectiveness of a new lock from the inside out and from the outside–out.
Writers: Phil Leslie, Len Levinson
Sponsors: Prudential, Viceroy; promo for NBC programs
Comments: Although the script offers little that is risible, Jim and Marian seem amused by something after the sound effect of tools falling on the floor is heard.

Date: May 18, 1955
Title: Plans to Operate Walt's Malt Shop
Cast: Jim Jordan (Fibber), Marian Jordan (Molly), John Wald, Bill Thompson (Wallace Wimple), Arthur Q. Bryan (Doctor Gamble)
Summary: After explaining to Molly how the Elks will take over Walt's Malt Shop for the weekend, Fibber is surprised to learn his assigned duty is not what he thought it would be.
Writers: Phil Leslie, Ralph Goodman
Sponsors: Prudential; PSA for nurse recruitment; promo for NBC afternoon programs
Comments: Molly slips one past McGee when her response to Gamble's threat to hit Fibber in the mouth with his satchel is how the act will disrupt the order of the doctor's pills, not how the blow will damage her husband's molars.

Date: May 19, 1955
Title: Waitress Tips at Walt's Malt Shop
Cast: Jim Jordan (Fibber), Marian Jordan (Molly), John Wald, Bill Thompson (officer), Arthur Q. Bryan (Doctor Gamble), Elvia Allman (Cora Burns), Mary Jane Croft (Mabel Toops), Myra Marsh (Mrs. Spradley)
Summary: Molly and two friends learn the tricks of serving customers from Cora Burns, then McGee and Gamble get behind the counter at Walt's Malt Shop.
Writers: Phil Leslie, Ralph Goodman
Sponsors: Prudential; PSA on behalf of United Cerebral Palsy; promo for NBC programs
Comments: Elvia Allman makes the most of her chance to shine as she serves up the tasty bits with relish.

Date: May 21, 1955
Title: Busy Day at Walt's Malt Shop
Cast: Jim Jordan (Fibber), Marian Jordan (Molly), John Wald, Bill Thompson (Wallace Wimple, Old Timer, Woof-Woof), Elvia Allman (Cora Burns), Myra Marsh (Mrs. Spradley)
Summary: While serving as chef at Walt's Malt Shop, Fibber cooks up an "all you can eat" scheme that works medium well.

Writers: Phil Leslie, Ralph Goodman
Sponsors: Prudential; PSA for Air Force recruitment; promo for NBC daytime programs
Comments: McGee learned his Cold War lesson well: when on the spot, use the threat of an H Bomb.

Date: May 23, 1955
Title: Belt for the Belly
Cast: Jim Jordan (Fibber), Marian Jordan (Molly), John Wald, Bill Thompson (Old Timer), Arthur Q. Bryan (Doctor Gamble), Jack Kruschen (salesman)
Summary: In an attempt to pull in his paunch, Fibber purchases a slimming belt he soon discovers fits too close for comfort.
Writers: Phil Leslie, Len Levinson
Sponsors: Prudential; PSA for savings bonds; promo for NBC programs
Comments: Fibber ends up a poorer but wider man.

Date: May 24, 1955
Title: Bee Problems
Cast: Jim Jordan (Fibber), Marian Jordan (Molly), John Wald, Bill Thompson (Wallace Wimple)
Summary: The McGees, after trying to rid their home of what appears to be a single pesky bee, seek advice from Wallace Wimple.
Writers: Phil Leslie, Ralph Goodman
Sponsors: Prudential, Viceroy; promo for NBC programs
Comments: Jim and Marian deliver a nicely-timed double double take on "Let's step outside." Fibber's "This is gonna be murder" points to a continuing story line.

Date: May 25, 1955
Title: Calling for Bee Relief
Cast: Jim Jordan (Fibber), Marian Jordan (Molly), John Wald, Bill Thompson (Old Timer), Arthur Q. Bryan (Doctor Gamble)
Summary: McGee makes many phone calls trying to find someone who will rid the backyard of a swarm of bees.
Writers: Phil Leslie, Ralph Goodman
Sponsors: Prudential; PSA on behalf of United Cerebral Palsy; promo for NBC programs
Running Gag: "'Tain't funny, McGee" (Molly)
Comments: "It'll be all over tomorrow" is almost as effective as Wald's concluding teaser as an inducement to bring listeners back for the denouement to "The McGees vs. the Bees."

Date: May 26, 1955
Title: Bees Removed from Backyard
Cast: Jim Jordan (Fibber), Marian Jordan (Molly, Teeny), John Wald, Arthur Q. Bryan (Doctor Gamble), Jess Kirkpatrick (Bekins), Scott Douglas (Perry)
Summary: Fibber becomes an instant bee-remover after watching a man rid 79 Wistful Vista of the annoying insects.
Writers: Phil Leslie, Ralph Goodman
Sponsors: Prudential; PSA for mail to military; promo for NBC programs
Comments: Fibber's promise of "I'll beezed there" almost slips by without notice amid all the commotion. Listeners are apt to be stung by the improbability of McGee's swift transformation from childish craven cowering by the window into masked mercenary actively seeking swarms for a quick buck.

Date: May 29, 1955
Title: Mistaken for Policemen
Cast: Jim Jordan (Fibber), Marian Jordan (Molly), John Wald, Bill Thompson (Wallace Wimple), Arthur Q. Bryan (Doctor Gamble), Jack Kruschen (crook), Mary Lansing (woman), Daws Butler (man)
Summary: McGee and Wimple, costumed in police uniforms while on their way to perform in a skit for the Elks, come to the rescue of imperiled citizens twice when mistaken for real officers.
Writers: Phil Leslie, Ralph Goodman
Sponsors: Prudential; PSA for safe driving; promo for NBC daytime programs
Comments: When Fibber and Wallace hit the streets as cops, the brogue and the blarney are sure to be there as well. The allusions to *Dragnet* in this episode were very familiar to Daws Butler, a voice actor who had helped make "St. George and the Dragonet" one of the popular novelty records of the period.

Date: May 30, 1955
Title: Pants Need Cleaning
Cast: Jim Jordan (Fibber), Marian Jordan (Molly), John Wald, Bill Thompson (Wallace Wimple), Jack Moyles (Ned), Barney Phillips (boss)
Summary: Fibber, while on his way to apply for a job, is sidetracked when he needs to have his soiled pants cleaned.
Writers: Phil Leslie, Len Levinson
Sponsors: Prudential; PSA on behalf of United Cerebral Palsy; promo for NBC programs
Comments: Phil and Len took the idea of a helpless and pantless McGee from the October 5, 1948 episode and put some new wrinkles into the farcical situation.

Fifteen-minute Episodes ♦ 435

Date: May 31, 1955
Title: Dress Mix-Up at Cleaners
Cast: Jim Jordan (Fibber), Marian Jordan (Molly), John Wald, Bill Thompson (cleaner), Mary Jane Croft (Mabel Toops)
Summary: After Fibber is given the wrong dress at the cleaners, Molly assumes it is a new one he purchased for her.
Writers: Phil Leslie, Ralph Goodman
Sponsors: Prudential, Viceroy; promo for NBC programs
Comments: This episode succinctly captures those bygone days in a quarter-hour time capsule with a reference to the male fantasy of being kidnapped by Marilyn Monroe, a job of racking pins in a bowling alley, the saying "This is for Ripley," and the presence of a handy sewing machine in the home.

Date: June 1, 1955
Title: Little Boy Lost
Cast: Jim Jordan (Fibber), Marian Jordan (Molly, Teeny), John Wald, Arthur Q. Bryan (Doctor Gamble), Richard Beals (Marvin)
Summary: The McGees and Gamble try to placate a crying boy with treats.
Writers: Phil Leslie, Ralph Goodman
Sponsors: Prudential; PSA for savings bonds; promo for NBC *Monitor*
Comments: It is appropriate that Teeny is inexplicit about Marvin's age because she herself has stayed "only about six" for the last twenty years.

Date: June 2, 1955
Title: Haircut
Cast: Jim Jordan (Fibber), Marian Jordan (Molly), John Wald, Bill Thompson (Wallace Wimple), Arthur Q. Bryan (Doctor Gamble), Fritz Feld (Pierre), Jay Novello (Joe)
Summary: Fibber agrees to have his hair cut by a new barber in town to avoid the errant scissors of the distraught clipper he usually patronizes.
Writers: Phil Leslie, Ralph Goodman
Sponsors: Prudential; PSA for American Cancer Society; promo for NBC *Monitor*
Comments: Feld leaves his distinctive mouth pop as a calling card. The writers intimate that the customer who just had his eyebrows trimmed is bushy-browed union leader John L. Lewis.

Date: June 5, 1955
Title: Ice Cream Tainted?
Cast: Jim Jordan (Fibber), Marian Jordan (Molly, Teeny), John Wald, Arthur Q. Bryan (Doctor Gamble), Robert Easton (Lester Nelson), Mary Jane Croft (Mabel Toops)
Summary: McGee suspects that the homemade ice cream he prepared for a lawn party is contaminated after he encounters Teeny complaining about pains in her stomach.

Writers: Phil Leslie, Len Levinson
Sponsors: Prudential; PSA for American Cancer Society; promo for NBC *Monitor*
Comments: Fibber demonstrates that a little knowledge is a dangerous thing and that he is out of his league when he goes one on one with either Teeny or Molly.

Date: June 6, 1955
Title: Daily Activity Guide
Cast: Jim Jordan (Fibber), Marian Jordan (Molly), John Wald, Bill Thompson (Old Timer), Arthur Q. Bryan (Doctor Gamble)
Summary: Fibber is convinced that the activity guide he bought for a dime reliably forecasts a person's daily fate.
Writers: Phil Leslie, Ralph Goodman
Sponsors: Prudential, *Ladies' Home Journal*; promo for NBC *Monitor*
Running Gag: Hall closet opened by Fibber looking for bowling shoes
Comments: The guide is as much decoder as horoscope which explains its appeal to the juvenile McGee. The pause that refreshes most in this episode is the one after Fibber announces that his sign is Taurus the Bull.

Date: June 7, 1955
Title: Exam Taken by Fibber and Gamble
Cast: Jim Jordan (Fibber), Marian Jordan (Molly, Teeny), John Wald, Arthur Q. Bryan (Doctor Gamble)
Summary: Gamble and McGee take an exam meant for twelve-year-olds to determine who is smarter.
Writers: Phil Leslie, Ralph Goodman
Sponsors: Prudential, Viceroy; promo for NBC *Monitor*
Comments: Teeny's sudden, unannounced appearance after the test is over is as questionable as the answer sheet in McGee's possession having no grade on it. Molly acts more like referee than proctor with her two middle-aged sixth-graders.

Date: June 8, 1955
Title: Spends Dime in Parking Meter
Cast: Jim Jordan (Fibber), Marian Jordan (Molly), John Wald, Bill Thompson (Old Timer, policeman), Arthur Q. Bryan (Doctor Gamble), Jess Kirkpatrick (Billy Keith)
Summary: The McGees discover that dawdling downtown can be costly after Fibber buys extra time on a parking meter.
Writers: Phil Leslie, Len Levinson
Sponsors: Prudential; PSA for safe driving; promo for NBC *Monitor*
Comments: On February 24, 1948 Billy Keith owed Fibber money, but this time McGee is the debtor. The message of the PSA fits perfectly with the

action on the street that preceded it. There is both rhyme and reason in the order of items Molly withdraws from her purse.

Date: June 9, 1955
Title: Night at the Copakabibble
Cast: Jim Jordan (Fibber), Marian Jordan (Molly), John Wald, Bill Thompson (Old Timer), Parley Baer (head waiter), Jack Moyles (waiter)
Summary: Fibber and Molly go to a new nightclub in town expecting to be treated but get tricked instead.
Writers: Phil Leslie, Len Levinson
Sponsors: Prudential; PSA for savings bonds; promo for NBC *Monitor*
Running Gag: Myrt bit involving Colorado uncle/struck gold/dentist (Fibber)
Comments: Those musical oddballs, Ish Kabibble and Jerry Colonna, were still riding high on the Wistful Vista hit parade in 1955.

Date: June 12, 1955
Title: Backyard Mischief
Cast: Jim Jordan (Fibber), Marian Jordan (Molly, Teeny), John Wald, Arthur Q. Bryan (Doctor Gamble), Robert Easton (Lester Nelson)
Summary: Teeny and Fibber cannot convince Molly and Gamble that they have found a playful creature in a hole in the McGee backyard.
Writers: Phil Leslie, Ralph Goodman
Sponsors: Prudential; PSA for preventing forest fires; promo for NBC *Monitor*
Comments: Molly's query at the end ("What'll they think of next and why?") could be addressed to the writers. Anything is possible in a town where practical jokers pull their gags in schools and offices of doctors.

Date: June 13, 1955
Title: Happy Icing on the Cake
Cast: Jim Jordan (Fibber), Marian Jordan (Molly), John Wald, Bill Thompson (Old Timer), Arthur Q. Bryan (Doctor Gamble), Mary Jane Croft (Mabel Toops)
Summary: A frustrated Fibber tries to determine what special occasion prompted Molly to bake a cake hidden in the broom closet.
Writers: Phil Leslie, Ralph Goodman
Sponsors: Prudential; PSA for CARE; promo for NBC *Monitor*
Comments: Mary Jane Croft hits a note that might make listeners suspect Jerry Colonna had been held over–a hot stove. They might also wonder why Gamble's voice but not Wimple's can be heard in Fibber's phone conversations.

Date: June 14, 1955
Title: Stock Certificate Found
Cast: Jim Jordan (Fibber), Marian Jordan (Molly, Teeny), John Wald, Bill Thompson (postal clerk, Old Timer), Natalie Masters (secretary), Herb Butterfield (Longworth J. Green)

Summary: McGee hopes to get a reward from a skinflint when he returns a stock certificate he found in the post office.
Writers: Phil Leslie, Ralph Goodman
Sponsors: Prudential, Viceroy; promo for NBC *Monitor*
Comments: Teeny makes a late appearance to remind everyone of Father's Day (June 19th). Fibber claims that Green is "so tight he squeaks," a bold accusation from someone who had just been comparison-shopping to find the best value in three-cent stamps.

Date: June 15, 1955
Title: Mysterious Knocker
Cast: Jim Jordan (Fibber), Marian Jordan (Molly), John Wald, Bill Thompson (Old Timer), Arthur Q. Bryan (Doctor Gamble)
Summary: Molly and Fibber are disturbed by rhythmic knocking in their front yard.
Writers: Phil Leslie, Ralph Goodman
Sponsors: Prudential; PSA for Air Force recruitment; promo for NBC *Monitor*
Comments: Marian's cadenced delivery of "Somebody was knocking, knocking on our front door" would not have been out of place in the studio when the Eldorados recorded "At My Front Door" that year.

Date: June 16, 1955
Title: Woodpecker Woes
Cast: Jim Jordan (Fibber), Marian Jordan (Molly, Teeny), John Wald, Bill Thompson (Wallace Wimple), Arthur Q. Bryan (Doctor Gamble)
Summary: After McGee's attempts to trap a noisy woodpecker fail, Teeny comes to the rescue with the aid of Miss McGillicuddy.
Writers: Phil Leslie, Ralph Goodman
Sponsors: Prudential; PSA for American economic system; promo for NBC *Monitor*
Comments: Fibber also matched wits with a woodpecker on March 21, 1950.

Date: June 19, 1955
Title: Old Timer Acts Lovesick
Cast: Jim Jordan (Fibber), Marian Jordan (Molly), John Wald, Bill Thompson (Wallace Wimple, Old Timer), Arthur Q. Bryan (Doctor Gamble)
Summary: Molly and Fibber visit the Old Timer with the intention of making him forget about girlfriend Bessie's absence by inviting him to go to the movies with them.
Writers: Phil Leslie, Ralph Goodman
Sponsors: Prudential; PSA for preventing forest fires; promo for NBC *Monitor*
Comments: The folks that Bessie visits must be residing at the old, old folks home. The lines written for the Old Timer after the McGees leave are

not particularly amusing, but Thompson's superb delivery of them is hilarious.

Date: June 20, 1955
Title: Persian Lamb Coat
Cast: Jim Jordan (Fibber), Marian Jordan (Molly), John Wald, Mary Jane Croft (Mabel Toops)
Summary: After Molly receives a coat sent by Aunt Sarah, McGee takes it downtown to put it in cold storage.
Writers: Phil Leslie, Len Levinson
Sponsors: Prudential; PSA for Women's Army Corps recruitment; promo for NBC programs
Running Gag: "'Tain't funny, McGee" (Molly)
Comments: Aunt Sarah gets royally roasted in this outing, even getting mentioned in the Prudential commercial.

Date: June 21, 1955
Title: Car Hit While Parked
Cast: Jim Jordan (Fibber), Marian Jordan (Molly), John Wald, Larry Dobkin (auto mechanic)
Summary: After their car has been hit downtown while they were shopping, the McGees take it to be repaired and also attempt to identify the hit-and-run culprit.
Writers: Phil Leslie, Ralph Goodman
Sponsors: Prudential, Viceroy; promo for NBC programs
Comments: It is peculiar that, on a program sponsored by an insurance company, the idea of contacting an insurance agent is not even suggested by any of the parties involved in the mishap or the repair of the vehicle.

Date: June 22, 1955
Title: Baseball Boasts Questioned
Cast: Jim Jordan (Fibber), Marian Jordan (Molly, Teeny), John Wald, Bill Thompson (Old Timer), Jack Kruschen (Mr. Parks), Richard Beals (Montgomery Parks)
Summary: McGee is on the spot when a youngster doubts that the baseball given to Teeny by Fibber was actually signed by Babe Ruth.
Writers: Phil Leslie, Ralph Goodman
Sponsors: Prudential; PSA for savings bonds; promo for NBC programs
Running Gag: "'Tain't funny, McGee" (Molly)
Comments: This is another instance of the Prudential commercial meshing perfectly with the theme of the action. Montgomery's baseball autographed by a bogus Babe Ruth belongs on a shelf next to the photograph signed by Rin Tin Tin.

Date: June 23, 1955
Title: Surprise Project in Kitchen
Cast: Jim Jordan (Fibber), Marian Jordan (Molly), John Wald, Bill Thompson (Wallace Wimple), Arthur Q. Bryan (Doctor Gamble), Mary Jane Croft (Mabel Toops)
Summary: Fibber tinkers in the kitchen while Molly worries in the living room about the surprise he has planned for her.
Writer: Phil Leslie
Sponsors: Prudential; PSA for safe driving; promo for daytime NBC programs
Running Gag: Hall closet opened by Fibber looking for yardstick
Comments: Jim ad-libs a salute to their steady scribe after the closet cacophony subsides: "There's Phil Leslie laying [sic] there." While the cast and writers take a break from June 27 through September 23, NBC will air reruns of selected episodes Monday through Friday at 11:45 am Eastern and repeats at 10:00 pm Sunday through Thursday.

Date: September 26, 1955
Title: Gasoline Saver Gimmick
Cast: Jim Jordan (Fibber), Marian Jordan (Molly), John Wald, Arthur Q. Bryan (Doctor Gamble), Jack Kruschen (Monk Martin)
Summary: Fibber attempts to defraud Gamble by selling him a worthless gas-saving device to prove to Molly that the doctor can be duped.
Writer: Phil Leslie
Sponsors: Alka-Seltzer, One-A-Day, Nervine
Comments: The schedule mentioned in the previous entry continues through the end of the series in March 1956 with usually four new episodes and one repeat a week. So *Fibber McGee and Molly* will not seem out of place if heard in the morning or at night the standard "Good night" and "Good night, all" are replaced with closings such as "See you later," "See you tomorrow," and "Goodbye, all."

Date: September 27, 1955
Title: Statue Presented to Elks
Cast: Jim Jordan (Fibber), Marian Jordan (Molly), John Wald, Bill Thompson (Wallace Wimple, Old Timer), Arthur Q. Bryan (Doctor Gamble), Peter Leeds (Marty), Jack Mather (Henry Lester), Kate McKenna (old lady)
Summary: McGee schemes to be elected Grand Exalted Ruler of the Elks by donating to the club an iron statue given to him for performing a good deed.
Writers: Phil Leslie, Len Levinson
Sponsors: Alka-Seltzer, One-A-Day
Comments: John Wald's diminished role during this final season of fifteen-minute episodes is evident in the pre-recorded bits like "In just a moment we'll try to straighten out the McGees" which are inserted before certain commercials whether they fit the action of the story or not.

Date: September 28, 1955
Title: Venetian Blinds Broken
Cast: Jim Jordan (Fibber), Marian Jordan (Molly, Teeny), John Wald, Bill Thompson (Old Timer)
Summary: Fibber attempts to repair Venetian blinds in the bedroom so Molly can have privacy at night and shade in the morning.
Writer: Phil Leslie
Sponsors: Alka-Seltzer, One-A-Day, Nervine
Comments: Marian's exclamations of shock and frustration are very credible. McGee's solution to life's problems was expressed musically a decade later: paint it black.

Date: September 29, 1955
Title: Nelsons in Need?
Cast: Jim Jordan (Fibber), Marian Jordan (Molly), John Wald, Bill Thompson (Wallace Wimple), Arthur Q. Bryan (Doctor Gamble), Robert Easton (Lester Nelson)
Summary: Thinking that the Nelsons are short on funds, McGee concocts a scheme whereby the couple will receive $20 from a fictitious benefactor.
Writers: Phil Leslie, Ralph Goodman
Sponsors: Alka-Seltzer, One-A-Day
Comments: Marian can be heard chuckling during the "olly olly oxen free" part of the letter. The plug for Alka-Seltzer at the close is a natural bonus.

Date: September 30, 1955
Title: Joke Fibber Tries to Tell (Repeat)
Cast: Jim Jordan (Fibber), Marian Jordan (Molly), John Wald, Bill Thompson (Old Timer, Wallace Wimple), Arthur Q. Bryan (Doctor Gamble)
Summary: Fibber's attempts to tell an amusing story are interrupted by the Old Timer, Wimple, and Gamble who have gags of their own to tell.
Writers: Phil Leslie, Ralph Goodman
Sponsors: Alka-Seltzer, One-A-Day, Tabcin
Comments: This is a repeat of the September 13, 1954 show. The only changes are the different commercials and the closing ("So long" and "Goodbye, all" replace "Good night" and "Good night, all").

Date: October 3, 1955
Title: Women's Club Shuns McGee
Cast: Jim Jordan (Fibber), Marian Jordan (Molly), John Wald, Bill Thompson (Old Timer), Mary Jane Croft (Mabel Toops), Myra Marsh (Mrs. Spradley), Natalie Masters (Monica Miller)
Summary: Molly and the members of her Women's Club do not appreciate McGee's presence at their meeting until he offers an interesting proposition for a fundraiser.
Writers: Phil Leslie, Ralph Goodman

Sponsors: Alka-Seltzer, One-A-Day
Comments: At one point the Old Timer appears to have grown another arm as he proves to be just as cagey around the grub as Fibber.

Date: October 4, 1955
Title: Seeing Shaw
Cast: Jim Jordan (Fibber), Marian Jordan (Molly), John Wald, Bill Thompson (Wadsworth), Arthur Q. Bryan (Doctor Gamble)
Summary: Molly pretends to be an Irish cook in order to meet reclusive author Stephen Shaw and ask him to deliver a speech on behalf of her Women's Club.
Writers: Phil Leslie, Ralph Goodman
Sponsors: Alka-Seltzer, Tabcin
Comments: Amid all the dialects the script's best line might pass unnoticed: "All our domestics are imported."

Date: October 5, 1955
Title: Painting Signs for Lecture
Cast: Jim Jordan (Fibber), Marian Jordan (Molly, Teeny), John Wald, Bill Thompson (Old Timer)
Summary: Fibber's peculiar spelling complicates matters as he prepares publicity signs for an upcoming speaking engagement at the high school.
Writer: Phil Leslie
Sponsors: Alka-Seltzer, One-A-Day
Comments: As a PR man, McGee was ahead of his time for in 1955 he was promoting a noted writer as "author and lecher."

Date: October 6, 1955
Title: Chowder for Lecturer
Cast: Jim Jordan (Fibber), Marian Jordan (Molly), John Wald, Arthur Q. Bryan (Doctor Gamble), Mary Jane Croft (Mabel Toops), Will Wright (Stephen Shaw)
Summary: When Gamble and McGee consume the clam chowder Molly prepared for a lecture guest, they scramble about trying to "put something in the pot."
Writer: Phil Leslie
Sponsors: Alka-Seltzer, One-A-Day, Tabcin
Comments: The unseen Aunt Sarah comes to the rescue once again with a handy recipe.

Date: October 7, 1955
Title: Antique Bookend (Repeat)
Cast: Jim Jordan (Fibber), Marian Jordan (Molly), John Wald, Bill Thompson (Old Timer, train announcer), Elvia Allman (customer), Joe Forte (antique shop owner), Frank Gerstle (man in information booth)

Summary: Molly buys a bookend in a shop, then pursues a woman who accidentally walks out with her purchase.
Writers: Phil Leslie, Ralph Goodman
Sponsors: Alka-Seltzer, Nervine
Comments: This is a repeat of the September 8, 1954 episode. The main changes are the different commercials and the closings by Jim and Marian.

Date: October 10, 1955
Title: New Shoes Too Tight
Cast: Jim Jordan (Fibber), Marian Jordan (Molly), John Wald, Bill Thompson (Old Timer), Arthur Q. Bryan (Doctor Gamble), Art Jacobson (clerk)
Summary: Fibber has five good reasons to regret his decision to let the Old Timer break in the pair of new shoes he bought at the Lucky Seven Shoe Sale.
Writers: Phil Leslie, Len Levinson
Sponsors: Alka-Seltzer, One-A-Day, Nervine
Comments: In the store Fibber tells the clerk he is going to carry the new shoes home, yet in the next scene he is painfully walking in the new pair.

Date: October 11, 1955
Title: Phone Booth Frenzy
Cast: Jim Jordan (Fibber), Marian Jordan (Molly, Teeny), John Wald
Summary: Molly has a difficult time finding Fibber who is impatiently waiting for her to pick him up near a phone booth.
Writers: Phil Leslie, Len Levinson
Sponsors: Alka-Seltzer, One-A-Day
Comments: This episode gives listeners a preview of the NBC *Monitor* shows for it shows what fun just Jim and Marian could create with confusion and great questions like "How are things in Glocca Morra?" and "Where between is it?"

Date: October 12, 1955
Title: Average Wistful Vista Couple
Cast: Jim Jordan (Fibber), Marian Jordan (Molly), John Wald, Bill Thompson (Wallace Wimple, Frank), Arthur Q. Bryan (Doctor Gamble), Parley Baer (Tom Collins)
Summary: After being informed they are the town's average couple, the McGees primp and clean the house in preparation for a visit by a journalist and photographer who will do a story about them for *The Wistful Vista Gazette*.
Writers: Phil Leslie, Joel Kane
Sponsors: Alka-Seltzer, One-A-Day, Tabcin
Comments: Fibber must be far above average because he introduces the visitor to Molly as "Mr. Collins" when the newspaperman never mentioned

his name. The incomplete reference to what Truman says about a senator's proposal is a peculiar allusion considering that Eisenhower had been in the White House since January 1953.

Date: October 13, 1955
Title: Five-Dollar Loan Letter
Cast: Jim Jordan (Fibber), Marian Jordan (Molly), John Wald, Bill Thompson (Old Timer), Arthur Q. Bryan (Doctor Gamble)
Summary: McGee spends the day composing a diplomatic letter requesting repayment of money loaned to Rocky Acres.
Writer: Phil Leslie
Sponsors: Alka-Seltzer, Nervine
Comments: There is no introduction into the action by Wald. The Old Timer's rib-tickling story about his father's forgetfulness makes this episode a memorable one.

Date: October 14, 1955
Title: Paperboy McGee (Repeat)
Cast: Jim Jordan (Fibber), Marian Jordan (Molly), John Wald, Arthur Q. Bryan (Doctor Gamble), Richard Beals (Richard)
Summary: When Fibber takes over the paperboy's route for a day, his delivery techniques are hardly more successful than they were in his younger days.
Writers: Phil Leslie, Ralph Goodman
Sponsors: Alka-Seltzer, One-A-Day
Comments: This is a repeat of the November 1, 1954 show. The primary changes are the different commercials and the farewells by Jim and Marian.

Date: October 17, 1955
Title: Movie Passes
Cast: Jim Jordan (Fibber), Marian Jordan (Molly, Teeny), John Wald, Bill Thompson (Old Timer, Wallace Wimple), Arthur Q. Bryan (Doctor Gamble), Eddie Marr (ticket taker)
Summary: Fibber, after being given movie passes from the owner of the Palace Theater, discovers that others in town have also received Annie Oakleys.
Writers: Phil Leslie, Joel Kane
Sponsors: Alka-Seltzer, Tabcin
Comments: The lure of 3-D and other gimmickry used to attract people to theaters prevalent in the mid-fifties is apparent in this episode. *Gold Diggers of 1949* starring Rin Tin Tin should be considered a lost film–and with good reason.

Date: October 18, 1955
Title: Burglary at 85 Wistful Vista?
Cast: Jim Jordan (Fibber), Marian Jordan (Molly), John Wald, Bill Thompson (Old Timer), Arthur Q. Bryan (Doctor Gamble)

Summary: Suspicious Fibber, thinking a break-in is taking place down the block, calls the police.
Writers: Phil Leslie, Ralph Goodman
Sponsors: Alka-Seltzer, Nervine
Comments: The influence of comic books and the effect of crime programs upon the susceptible minds of naïve people, hotly-debated topics in the 1950s, are evident throughout this episode.

Date: October 19, 1955
Title: Old Timer's Song
Cast: Jim Jordan (Fibber), Marian Jordan (Molly, Teeny), John Wald, Bill Thompson (Old Timer), Arthur Q. Bryan (Doctor Gamble)
Summary: The Old Timer pesters Fibber for three hours with verses of a song he believes will become a hit.
Writers: Phil Leslie, Ralph Goodman
Sponsors: Alka-Seltzer, One-A-Day
Comments: Marian can be heard softly laughing in response to Thompson's off-key warbling. At the end John Wald mistakenly credits Thompson as playing Wallace Wimple, who is not heard on this occasion.

Date: October 20, 1955
Title: Who Was That Man? (Repeat)
Cast: Jim Jordan (Fibber), Marian Jordan (Molly), John Wald, Arthur Q. Bryan (Doctor Gamble), Jess Kirkpatrick (Mulligan)
Summary: After Fibber and Molly meet a familiar-looking man on the street downtown, they spend a restless afternoon and evening trying to recall his name.
Writers: Phil Leslie, Ralph Goodman
Sponsors: Alka-Seltzer, One-A-Day, Nervine
Comments: This is a repeat of the October 20, 1954 show. The primary changes are the different commercials and the farewells by Jim and Marian.

Date: October 21, 1955
Title: Water Shut Off (Repeat)
Cast: Jim Jordan (Fibber), Marian Jordan (Molly), John Wald, Bill Thompson (Old Timer, Wallace Wimple), Robert Easton (Lester Nelson)
Summary: When the water in their neighborhood is shut off for the day, a thirsty McGee goes in search of liquid refreshment from friends.
Writers: Phil Leslie, Ralph Goodman
Sponsors: Alka-Seltzer, One-A-Day
Comments: This repeat of the September 15, 1954 show differs only in the commercials and farewells.

Date: October 24, 1955
Title: Beauty Parlor Palaver (Shorter Version)
Cast: Jim Jordan (Fibber), Marian Jordan (Molly, Teeny), John Wald, Arthur Q. Bryan (Doctor Gamble), Natalie Masters (Norma), Elvia Allman and Jean Vander Pyl (women)
Summary: Fibber, at first apprehensive about visiting a beauty salon with Molly, becomes amused by the chatter coming from women in an adjoining room.
Writer: Phil Leslie
Sponsors: Alka-Seltzer, One-A-Day
Comments: This is a condensed version of the script used on May 23, 1944. Leslie, knowing how effective the expectation of opening the hall closet can be, uses the open door policy repeatedly to set up listeners for the male gabfest at the end.

Date: October 25, 1955
Title: Wimple's Binoculars
Cast: Jim Jordan (Fibber), Marian Jordan (Molly), John Wald, Bill Thompson (Wallace Wimple)
Summary: Fibber and Molly spot what appears to be a strange creature in an attic while looking through binoculars left by Wallace Wimple.
Writers: Phil Leslie, Ralph Goodman
Sponsors: Alka-Seltzer, One-A-Day, Tabcin
Comments: Wimple's tall story about the swat bird sounds like it came from Fibber's book of legendary creations.

Date: October 26, 1955
Title: Mystery of Unanswered Phone Call
Cast: Jim Jordan (Fibber), Marian Jordan (Molly), John Wald, Bill Thompson (Old Timer), Arthur Q. Bryan (Doctor Gamble)
Summary: The McGees are unable to rest after their phone rings in the midnight hour.
Writers: Phil Leslie, Joel Kane
Sponsors: Alka-Seltzer, Nervine
Comments: Myrtle apparently provided 24/7 service long before the concept became fashionable because she is on the job in the wee small hours of the night.

Date: October 27, 1955
Title: Rotating Tires
Cast: Jim Jordan (Fibber), Marian Jordan (Molly), John Wald, Bill Thompson (Old Timer, Frank), Arthur Q. Bryan (Doctor Gamble), Robert Easton (Lester Nelson)
Summary: Fibber spends a trying day trying to switch tires on his car.
Writer: Phil Leslie

Sponsors: Alka-Seltzer, One-A-Day

Comments: Leslie revives the "two nickels for a dime" bit, employing "if it fits, use it" as his guide. The same motto must apply to tires in Wistful Vista, a place where commercial truck tires conveniently fit on passenger automobiles.

Date: October 28, 1955
Title: Molly's New Coat
Cast: Jim Jordan (Fibber), Marian Jordan (Molly), John Wald, Bill Thompson (Wallace Wimple), Mary Jane Croft (Mabel Toops), Mary Lansing (clerk)
Summary: Mabel Toops convinces Molly to purchase a coat which is on sale at the Bon Ton.
Writers: Phil Leslie, Ralph Goodman
Sponsors: Alka-Seltzer, One-A-Day, Nervine
Comments: This episode, in which Fibber is absent for most of the action, again demonstrates the essential part that character played in elevating the level of humor on the program.

Date: October 31, 1955
Title: Key Collection
Cast: Jim Jordan (Fibber), Marian Jordan (Molly), John Wald, Bill Thompson (Old Timer), Arthur Q. Bryan (Doctor Gamble)
Summary: At Molly's insistence Fibber sorts through his collection of 27 keys to weed out the inessential ones.
Writer: Phil Leslie
Sponsors: Alka-Seltzer, One-A-Day, Nervine
Running Gag: Mrs. Kladderhatch bit involving ant paste/pasted his aunt (Gamble)
Comments: Thompson's recitation of how the rustic makes sourdough bread breaks up both Jim and Marian.

Date: November 1, 1955
Title: Package from Aunt Sarah
Cast: Jim Jordan (Fibber), Marian Jordan (Molly, Teeny), John Wald, Bill Thompson (Margaret, box carrier), Arthur Q. Bryan (Doctor Gamble), Joseph Kearns (Franklin)
Summary: While on their way to pick up a package at the post office, the McGees stop at Teeny's school to assist her in a doggone matter.
Writers: Phil Leslie, Ralph Goodman
Sponsors: Alka-Seltzer, Nervine
Comments: In this episode Bill Thompson adds mutts to his menagerie of voices.

Date: November 2, 1955
Title: Luncheon Invitation from Gamble
Cast: Jim Jordan (Fibber), Marian Jordan (Molly), John Wald, Bill Thompson (patient, Frank Carlton), Arthur Q. Bryan (Doctor Gamble)

Summary: Fibber diagnoses a man's symptoms while waiting in the doctor's office to accompany Gamble to lunch.
Writers: Phil Leslie, Ralph Goodman
Sponsors: Alka-Seltzer, One-A-Day
Comments: Molly's short poem contains some nuggets about table etiquette that are just as timely today as they were in 1955.

Date: November 3, 1955
Title: Parking Meter Payback
Cast: Jim Jordan (Fibber), Marian Jordan (Molly), John Wald, Bill Thompson (Old Timer), Arthur Q. Bryan (Doctor Gamble), Jack Mather (Harper), Bill Idelson (young officer)
Summary: McGee thinks fast on his feet to combat a ticket-happy policeman.
Writers: Phil Leslie, Ralph Goodman
Sponsors: Alka-Seltzer, One-A-Day, Tabcin
Comments: The flashback, used infrequently on the program, is employed effectively on this occasion. Molly gets wound up after the quick turn of events when she imitates her husband's tirade against the officer.

Date: November 4, 1955
Title: Protesting Tax Assessment
Cast: Jim Jordan (Fibber), Marian Jordan (Molly), John Wald, Bill Thompson (Wallace Wimple), Jack Moyles (Calvis), Barney Phillips (Hennebury)
Summary: When he learns that Wimple's property taxes have nearly doubled in one year, Fibber challenges the assessment with the powers that be.
Writers: Phil Leslie, Len Levinson
Sponsors: Alka-Seltzer, One-A-Day
Comments: The street where the Wimples live, Valley View, is mentioned for the first time. On this occasion the ability of Sweetie Face to talk loudly and carry a big stick proves beneficial.

Date: November 7, 1955
Title: Auto Show with Midget Car Race
Cast: Jim Jordan (Fibber), Marian Jordan (Molly, Teeny), John Wald, Bill Thompson (Wallace Wimple), Arthur Q. Bryan (Doctor Gamble), Art Jacobson (Dribley)
Summary: The McGees observe how both Teeny and Gamble come up big at the auto show.
Writers: Phil Leslie, Ralph Goodman
Sponsors: Alka-Seltzer, Tabcin
Comments: The writers weave the names of real automobiles in with their creations and make them sound so appealing that some listeners might have called their local dealers to test drive a sporty Comparini.

Date: November 8, 1955
Title: Building Fire in Fireplace
Cast: Jim Jordan (Fibber), Marian Jordan (Molly), John Wald, Bill Thompson (Old Timer, Wallace Wimple), Robert Easton (Lester Nelson)
Summary: Fibber's efforts to start a fire in the fireplace create more smoke in the house than heat.
Writer: Phil Leslie
Sponsors: Alka-Seltzer, One-A-Day, Nervine
Comments: The Old Timer's story provides the necessary spark to ignite some laughs in this episode which follows a predictable pattern of McGee miscues.

Date: November 9, 1955
Title: Hunting for Hunting License (Repeat)
Cast: Jim Jordan (Fibber), Marian Jordan (Molly), John Wald, Arthur Q. Bryan (Doctor Gamble), Elvia Allman (Cora Burns)
Summary: The McGees look all over the house for Fibber's hunting license.
Writer: Phil Leslie
Sponsors: Alka-Seltzer, Tabcin
Comments: This repeat differs from the November 11, 1953 show in the commercials and Fibber's farewell. Ralph Goodman shared writing credit on the 1953 episode.

Date: November 10, 1955
Title: Buying Groceries for Trip (Repeat)
Cast: Jim Jordan (Fibber), Marian Jordan (Molly, Teeny), John Wald, Ken Christy (Senator Harper), Jack Kruschen (butcher), Tony Michaels (clerk)
Summary: Fibber finds it difficult to buy groceries for three men with only $10.00 to spend.
Writers: Phil Leslie, Ralph Goodman
Sponsors: Alka-Seltzer, One-A-Day
Comments: This repeat of the November 12, 1953 show has different commercials and farewells.

Date: November 11, 1955
Title: Trip to Lake Wapahokey (Repeat)
Cast: Jim Jordan (Fibber), Marian Jordan (Molly), John Wald, Arthur Q. Bryan (Doctor Gamble), Parley Baer (Herb Travis)
Summary: Doc, Herb, and Fibber drive to their cabin in the woods.
Writers: Phil Leslie, Ralph Goodman
Sponsors: Alka-Seltzer, One-A-Day, Tabcin
Comments: This repeat of the November 13, 1953 show differs only in the commercials and Fibber's farewell.

Date: November 14, 1955
Title: Raining at Lake Wapahokey (Repeat)
Cast: Jim Jordan (Fibber), John Wald, Arthur Q. Bryan (Doctor Gamble), Parley Baer (Herb Travis)
Summary: The men in the cabin try to find diversions to keep their minds off the lousy weather.
Writer: Phil Leslie
Sponsors: Alka-Seltzer, One-A-Day, Nervine
Comments: The repeat of the November 16, 1953 show has different commercials. Fibber's farewell replaces the earlier "Good Night" spoken by the three men. Ralph Goodman was given co-writing credit in 1953.

Date: November 15, 1955
Title: Duck Hunting, Finally (Repeat)
Cast: Jim Jordan (Fibber), John Wald, Arthur Q. Bryan (Doctor Gamble), Jess Kirkpatrick (Klopinger), Parley Baer (Herb Travis)
Summary: The rain stops, allowing the hunters a chance to shoot some ducks and trade some barbs.
Writers: Phil Leslie, Ralph Goodman
Sponsors: Alka-Seltzer, Tabcin
Comments: This repeat differs from the November 17, 1953 show only in the commercials.

Date: November 16, 1955
Title: Hunter McGee Returns Home (Repeat)
Cast: Jim Jordan (Fibber), Marian Jordan (Molly), John Wald, Bill Thompson (Old Timer), Arthur Q. Bryan (Doctor Gamble), Mary Jane Croft (Mabel Toops), Paula Winslowe (Ginny)
Summary: Molly has lunch with two friends, then welcomes Fibber back from his hunting trip.
Writers: Phil Leslie, Ralph Goodman
Sponsors: Alka-Seltzer, One-A-Day
Comments: This repeat of the November 18, 1953 episode has different commercials. Fibber adds "So Long, Everybody" to his 1953 farewell.

Date: November 17, 1955
Title: Early to Bed After Hunting (Repeat)
Cast: Jim Jordan (Fibber), Marian Jordan (Molly), John Wald, Bill Thompson (Old Timer), Arthur Q. Bryan (Doctor Gamble)
Summary: Fibber, worn out after hunting and a late-night argument with Doc, attempts to go to bed right after supper.
Writers: Phil Leslie, Ralph Goodman
Sponsors: Alka-Seltzer, One-A-Day, Tabcin

Comments: This repeat differs from the November 19, 1953 show in the commercials, farewells, and Wald's teaser at the end.

Date: November 18, 1955
Title: Sewing a Button
Cast: Jim Jordan (Fibber), Marian Jordan (Molly), John Wald, Bill Thompson (Old Timer), Robert Easton (Lester Nelson), Mary Jane Croft (Mabel Toops)
Summary: McGee is frustrated because he is unable to get a button sewed on a shirt, a task he considers of vital importance before he can have his hair cut.
Writer: Phil Leslie
Sponsors: Alka-Seltzer, Tabcin
Comments: Wald's closing comment that "We'll be back Monday for another chuckle or two" is an accurate assessment of the program's diminishing potential for laughs at this point. The Old Timer's simile about the beer truck might be considered the most amusing image in this study of contrived circumstances.

Date: November 21, 1955
Title: Practical Jokers
Cast: Jim Jordan (Fibber), Marian Jordan (Molly), John Wald, Bill Thompson (Wallace Wimple, Kremer), Arthur Q. Bryan (Doctor Gamble), Will Wright (Harrison Cromwell)
Summary: After Fibber is the victim of a hotfoot and dousing, he retaliates with a practical joke of his own that turns out to be more beneficial than harmful.
Writers: Phil Leslie, Ralph Goodman
Sponsors: Alka-Seltzer, One-A-Day, Tabcin
Comments: Gamble learns, much to his chagrin, that operator 23 and her mother have his number. Wald mistakenly credits Bill Thompson as playing the Old Timer instead of Wallace Wimple. Thompson has an uncredited bit as Kremer, a member of the Elks who may be the same Kremer who operates Wistful Vista's drugstore.

Date: November 22, 1955
Title: Remembering What to Do
Cast: Jim Jordan (Fibber), Marian Jordan (Molly, Teeny), John Wald, Bill Thompson (Wallace Wimple, Old Timer)
Summary: McGee is perplexed because he cannot remember what he had planned to do with his day.
Writer: Phil Leslie
Sponsors: Alka-Seltzer, One-A-Day
Comments: Fibber seems have to discovered the secret of perpetual (lack of) motion: spend every waking moment sitting around wondering what to do with the hours in that day.

Date: November 23, 1955
Title: Peanut Machine Troubles
Cast: Jim Jordan (Fibber), Marian Jordan (Molly), John Wald, Bill Thompson (man on street, policeman), Arthur Q. Bryan (Doctor Gamble), Gail Bonney (woman), Jack Moyles (man)
Summary: While waiting outside the Bon Ton, McGee confronts a stubborn machine and opinionated people.
Writer: Phil Leslie
Sponsors: Alka-Seltzer, Tabcin
Comments: This is one episode in which Fibber does not get his two cents in but still receives his money's worth.

Date: November 24, 1955
Title: Shopping for Turkey
Cast: Jim Jordan (Fibber), Marian Jordan (Molly), Bill Thompson (Wallace Wimple, clerk), Elvia Allman (shopper, Ma Goober), Jess Kirkpatrick (Elroy Goober)
Summary: The McGees look for a Thanksgiving turkey in town and in the country.
Writers: Phil Leslie, Ralph Goodman
Sponsors: Alka-Seltzer, One-A-Day, Tabcin
Comments: The presence of the formidable Mrs. Wimple is felt in an off-mike, offstage, in-our-minds fashion. The Goobers pull a novel twist on the bait and switch game, but Fibber gets the last laugh anyway.

Date: November 25, 1955
Title: Safeguarding Health
Cast: Jim Jordan (Fibber), Marian Jordan (Molly), John Wald, Bill Thompson (Old Timer), Arthur Q. Bryan (Doctor Gamble)
Summary: Claiming that remaining immobile will improve his well-being, McGee refuses to budge from his easy chair.
Writers: Phil Leslie, Ralph Goodman
Sponsors: Alka-Seltzer, One-A-Day, Nervine
Comments: This is one time when Fibber is not truly fibbing, for blocking his blunder with his body really does protect his health. Note the rugged schedule he details for Molly during her absence: after sitting for an hour, he plans to get up and take a nap.

Date: November 28, 1955
Title: Invents Bow-Maker
Cast: Jim Jordan (Fibber), Marian Jordan (Molly), John Wald, Bill Thompson (Old Timer, Wallace Wimple), Arthur Q. Bryan (Doctor Gamble)
Summary: Fibber demonstrates Secret Project X-R-5, a machine that makes Christmas bows, for Molly and their friends.

Writers: Phil Leslie, Ralph Goodman
Sponsors: Alka-Seltzer, Nervine
Comments: In typical fashion, McGee's first thought after sensing the impracticality of his invention is not to make it more efficient but to build more of the Rube Goldberg devices. Topical references are made to "Suddenly There's a Valley" and "Sixteen Tons," two recordings in the top ten on the music charts during this week in 1955.

Date: November 29, 1955
Title: Looking for Cigars
Cast: Jim Jordan (Fibber), Marian Jordan (Molly), John Wald, Bill Thompson (Old Timer), Arthur Q. Bryan (Doctor Gamble), Will Wright (Kremer)
Summary: After searching the premises for cigars, McGee buys a box of stogies and then stashes them all over the house.
Writers: Phil Leslie, Ralph Goodman
Sponsors: Alka-Seltzer, One-A-Day, Tabcin
Comments: Credulity is stretched more than a bit when listeners are expected to believe Fibber could forget a promise made the day before regarding the very object that is his current obsession.

Date: November 30, 1955
Title: Gives Up Cigars Briefly
Cast: Jim Jordan (Fibber), Marian Jordan (Molly), John Wald, Bill Thompson (Old Timer, Wallace Wimple), Arthur Q. Bryan (Doctor Gamble)
Summary: McGee employs a sneaky way to keep his promise not to touch a cigar until the end of the week.
Writers: Phil Leslie, Ralph Goodman
Sponsors: Alka-Seltzer, One-A-Day, Nervine
Comments: Judging by the Old Timer's story, Wistful Vista is not the only place where most of the action takes place at 14th and Oak. Given Fibber's gabby nature, there may be a double meaning to Molly's remark about his friends teasing him "that he shut himself up for the day."

Date: December 1, 1955
Title: Preparing for Mrs. Compost's Visit
Cast: Jim Jordan (Fibber), Marian Jordan (Molly), John Wald, Bill Thompson (Wallace Wimple), Arthur Q. Bryan (Doctor Gamble)
Summary: Fibber tries not to be a nuisance as Molly readies the house for the arrival of an important guest.
Writer: Phil Leslie
Sponsors: Alka-Seltzer, Tabcin
Running Gags: Tongue twister starting with Bud Booker (Fibber), hall closet opened by Fibber looking for shovel
Comments: The second Alka-Seltzer commercial is one designated for airing December 1st only. Molly's admonition of "Not in the living room" seems

to give tacit approval for Gamble to slug her husband elsewhere in the house. The tag seems to indicate the closet is virtually empty now, but, like the creatures in those Universal horror films who kept returning in sequels, the rumbling monster lurking in the hall would be heard from again.

Date: December 2, 1955
Title: Trapped by Dog (Repeat)
Cast: Jim Jordan (Fibber), Marian Jordan (Molly), Bill Thompson (Old Timer), Arthur Q. Bryan (Doctor Gamble), Mary Jane Croft (Mabel Toops), Fritz Feld (Tarzan)
Summary: When the McGees do a good turn for Mort and Mabel Toops by feeding their dog, the brute holds them captive.
Writers: Phil Leslie, Ralph Goodman
Sponsors: Alka-Seltzer, One-A-Day
Comments: This is a repeat of the September 26, 1954 episode with different commercials. The reference to Sunday from the earlier broadcast is omitted.

Date: December 5, 1955
Title: Mysterious Letter
Cast: Jim Jordan (Fibber), Marian Jordan (Molly), John Wald, Bill Thompson (Old Timer), Arthur Q. Bryan (Doctor Gamble)
Summary: When an envelope for Mary Ellen Strongheart is delivered to 79 Wistful Vista, the McGees become obsessed with determining the addressee's identity.
Writers: Phil Leslie, Ralph Goodman
Sponsors: Alka-Seltzer, One-A-Day
Comments: Actor Jack Moyles, heard frequently on the program during the fifteen-minute era, gets a salute from the writers as McGee mentions him as one of his radio heroes. Mary Ellen Strongheart is a takeoff on the name of mystery writer Mary Roberts Rinehart. Lawyers for Simon and Schuster may have groused a little after hearing of publishers Schuman and Shyster.

Date: December 6, 1955
Title: Who Is Mary Ellen Strongheart?
Cast: Jim Jordan (Fibber), Marian Jordan (Molly), John Wald, Bill Thompson (Old Timer), Arthur Q. Bryan (Doctor Gamble), Robert Easton (Lester Nelson), Mary Lou Harrington (Sally Nelson)
Summary: Molly, Fibber, and friends try to determine the identity of the pseudonymous Mary Ellen Strongheart.
Writers: Phil Leslie, Ralph Goodman
Sponsors: Alka-Seltzer, Tabcin
Comments: The promo for *Pepper Young's Family* at the conclusion is appropriate for this episode sounds more like a chapter from a serial than a comedy program.

Date: December 7, 1955
Title: Mary Ellen Strongheart Identified
Cast: Jim Jordan (Fibber), Marian Jordan (Molly), John Wald, Bill Thompson (Wallace Wimple)
Summary: Molly prepares for a tea party while Fibber concocts ways for the real author of *The Strangled Cat Murder Case* to reveal his or her identity.
Writers: Phil Leslie, Ralph Goodman
Sponsors: Alka-Seltzer, One-A-Day, Tabcin
Comments: Unlike most of the other Alka-Seltzer commercials that could be used anytime, this one is tailored specifically for airing this day of the week. The review of previous events in a rather cumbersome fashion is another measure of the serial format of this sequence of episodes.

Date: December 8, 1955
Title: Writing Book with Wimple
Cast: Jim Jordan (Fibber), Marian Jordan (Molly), John Wald, Bill Thompson (Wallace Wimple)
Summary: Fibber dictates while Wallace Wimple types as the two collaborate on a mystery novel.
Writers: Phil Leslie, Ralph Goodman
Sponsors: Alka-Seltzer, Nervine
Comments: Wald's prerecorded bridge to the middle commercial, "In just a moment we'll try to straighten out the McGees," is out of place on this occasion because Molly does not appear until the end. Love stories and mysteries were not the only cheap items available in 1955, a time when a typical home in Wistful Vista was valued at $9,000.

Date: December 9, 1955
Title: Gas Price War (Repeat)
Cast: Jim Jordan (Fibber), Marian Jordan (Molly), John Wald, Arthur Q. Bryan (Doctor Gamble), Jack Kruschen (Frank Fuller, Morgan), Natalie Masters (Mrs. Atherton)
Summary: While out for a drive, the McGees search for the lowest price in town during a gas war.
Writers: Phil Leslie, Ralph Goodman
Sponsors: Alka-Seltzer, Tabcin
Comments: This is a repeat of the November 7, 1954 episode with different commercials and farewells.

Date: December 12, 1955
Title: Christmas Shopping for Gamble
Cast: Jim Jordan (Fibber), Marian Jordan (Molly), John Wald, Arthur Q. Bryan (Doctor Gamble), Elvia Allman (PA announcer, shoplifter), Jack Kruschen (shoplifter), Larry Dobkin (silver salesman)

Summary: As the McGees look for a Christmas present for Doctor Gamble, Fibber consciously tries to put a price on friendship.
Writer: Phil Leslie
Sponsors: Alka-Seltzer, One-A-Day, Nervine
Comments: Fibber retains his unique character, complaining about the generosity of the person who is giving an expensive present to him and Molly and thus prompting them to reciprocate in kind.

Date: December 13, 1955
Title: Investment Plan
Cast: Jim Jordan (Fibber), Marian Jordan (Molly), John Wald, Bill Thompson (Wallace Wimple), Arthur Q. Bryan (Doctor Gamble), Colleen Collins (woman)
Summary: The McGee house is filled with capitalists after Fibber places an ad in the newspaper promising to return $15 on each $10 invested in McGee, Inc.
Writers: Phil Leslie, Ralph Goodman
Sponsors: Alka-Seltzer, Tabcin
Comments: The McGee phone number of 4366 now has a Vista prefix.

Date: December 14, 1955
Title: Investors Are Irate
Cast: Jim Jordan (Fibber), Marian Jordan (Molly, Teeny), John Wald, Bill Thompson (Old Timer, Wallace Wimple), Arthur Q. Bryan (Doctor Gamble), Mary Lansing (woman), Art Jacobson (Parker)
Summary: Investors in McGee, Inc. are clamoring for Fibber's head until he shows them a concrete way to make a profit.
Writers: Phil Leslie, Ralph Goodman
Sponsors: Alka-Seltzer, Tabcin
Comments: Fibber and Molly deliver the complete first commercial in a style that sounds much like a vignette from one of the scripts.

Date: December 15, 1955
Title: Investment Plan Succeeds
Cast: Jim Jordan (Fibber), Marian Jordan (Molly, Teeny), John Wald, Bill Thompson (Wallace Wimple, Boyce), Arthur Q. Bryan (Doctor Gamble), Robert Easton (Lester Nelson), Mary Jane Croft (Mabel Toops), Art Jacobson (Parker)
Summary: McGee gathers all the investors in McGee, Inc. together to demonstrate how they will benefit from his purchase of the Morgan mansion.
Writers: Phil Leslie, Ralph Goodman
Sponsors: Alka-Seltzer, Tabcin
Comments: This is one time when Fibber's plans purposely go up in smoke.

Date: December 16, 1955
Title: Vacuum Cleaner Salesman (Repeat)
Cast: Jim Jordan (Fibber), Marian Jordan (Molly), John Wald, Bill Thompson (Old Timer), Joseph Kearns (Oliver Dipswaddle)
Summary: The McGees seem to be getting the upper hand on turning away a persistent salesman until Fibber starts tinkering with the old vacuum cleaner.
Writers: Phil Leslie, Ralph Goodman
Sponsors: Alka-Seltzer, One-A-Day, Tabcin
Comments: This is a repeat of the November 28, 1954 episode with different commercials. The reference to Sunday at the beginning has been changed to "at all hours" and the farewells changed to reflect the daytime format.

Date: December 19, 1955
Title: Snowfall Upsets McGee
Cast: Jim Jordan (Fibber), Marian Jordan (Molly), John Wald, Bill Thompson (Old Timer, Wallace Wimple)
Summary: Fibber lets the heavy snowfall get him down and keep him housebound most of the day.
Writer: Phil Leslie
Sponsors: Alka-Seltzer, Tabcin
Comments: Molly adds a new spot to the Wistful Vista geography by mentioning a candy store just a block from 79 Wistful Vista. When Fibber gets to grumbling, the impracticality of his complaint that snow should fall during the summer months does not slow him down a bit.

Date: December 20, 1955
Title: Hiding Place
Cast: Jim Jordan (Fibber), Marian Jordan (Molly), John Wald, Arthur Q. Bryan (Doctor Gamble), Robert Easton (Lester Nelson)
Summary: McGee is in, out, and around the house but still hard to find so Molly and Gamble make a thorough search for him.
Writers: Phil Leslie, Ralph Goodman
Sponsors: Alka-Seltzer, One-A-Day, Tabcin
Comments: Molly hums the current hit "Love and Marriage" to start the episode and sings the seasonal "O Tannenbaum" to open the second act. Marian and Arthur get a rare chance to try their hand at dialects.

Date: December 21, 1955
Title: Christmas Sign
Cast: Jim Jordan (Fibber), Marian Jordan (Molly), John Wald, Bill Thompson (Wallace Wimple), Arthur Q. Bryan (Doctor Gamble)
Summary: McGee puts up a display of large electrified letters that soon spells trouble for him and Molly.

Writers: Phil Leslie, Ralph Goodman
Sponsors: Alka-Seltzer, Nervine
Comments: Leslie and Goodman dip into the reservoir of colorful descriptions by having Gamble invoke a cross-eyed fighter cast into the outer darkness of Mongolia.

Date: December 22, 1955
Title: Doc's Christmas Card
Comments: Jim Jordan (Fibber), Marian Jordan (Molly), John Wald, Arthur Q. Bryan (Doctor Gamble)
Summary: The McGees, believing they have forgotten to send Gamble a Christmas greeting, sneak into his residence so they can insert a card in a cancelled envelope.
Writers: Phil Leslie, Ralph Goodman
Sponsors: Alka-Seltzer, One-A-Day, Tabcin
Comments: Gamble, who for years lived in a house and had a housekeeper, is now living in an apartment building. The words of affection between Fibber and Doc show how much the friendly foes think of each other even though they feel more comfortable slinging brickbats than delivering compliments.

Date: December 23, 1955
Title: Patient Little Star (Repeat)
Cast: Jim Jordan (Fibber), Marian Jordan (Molly, Teeny), John Wald, Bill Thompson (Bagby, Old Timer)
Summary: The Old Timer drops off his present, then Fibber tells Teeny the story of a star that waited for just the right time to shine brightly.
Writers: Phil Leslie, Ralph Goodman
Sponsors: Alka-Seltzer, One-A-Day
Running Gag: Hall closet opened by Fibber looking for ornaments
Comments: This repeat of the December 23, 1954 episode differs in Wald's introduction and closing message, the commercials, and the mention of Miles Laboratories at the end.

Date: December 26, 1955
Title: Drill for Christmas Present
Cast: Jim Jordan (Fibber), Marian Jordan (Molly, Teeny), John Wald, Bill Thompson (Old Timer)
Summary: Molly regrets giving Fibber a drill for Christmas as he quickly makes himself a "holey" terror all over the house.
Writer: Phil Leslie
Sponsors: Alka-Seltzer, One-A-Day, Tabcin
Comments: It only takes Teeny one day to break a wheel on a Christmas present and McGee just a few minutes to deface it permanently.

Date: December 27, 1955
Title: Leftover Turkey Recipe
Cast: Jim Jordan (Fibber), Marian Jordan (Molly), John Wald, Bill Thompson (Wallace Wimple), Arthur Q. Bryan (Doctor Gamble)
Summary: While Molly is downtown shopping, McGee and Wimple concoct Turkey Maharajah, a recipe Fibber hopes will make the turkey left over from Christmas more appetizing.
Writer: Phil Leslie
Sponsors: Alka-Seltzer, Tabcin
Comments: Only Fibber would place an order over the phone to a grocery store asking for delivery of ingredients in the exact proportions called for in a recipe. McGee issues a sly pun when he is muttering about the turkey: "I don't know why I should start beefing at this late date."

Date: December 28, 1955
Title: Bank Robbery
Cast: Jim Jordan (Fibber), Marian Jordan (Molly), John Wald, Bill Thompson (officer), Jack Moyles (robber), Art Jacobson (teller)
Summary: While trying to get change for a $20.00 bill, the McGees inadvertently become involved in the robbery of a bank.
Writers: Phil Leslie, Ralph Goodman
Sponsors: Alka-Seltzer, One-A-Day, Tabcin
Comments: This long distance robbery is implausible, but at least on this occasion something good happens when Fibber is left holding the bag.

Date: December 29, 1955
Title: Plans for New Year's Eve
Cast: Jim Jordan (Fibber), Marian Jordan (Molly), John Wald, Bill Thompson (Old Timer), Arthur Q. Bryan (Doctor Gamble)
Summary: The plans Molly and Fibber have for celebrating New Year's Eve change several times in just a few minutes.
Writers: Phil Leslie, Ralph Goodman
Sponsors: Alka-Seltzer, Tabcin
Comments: Bill Thompson could have used some Alka-Seltzer and Tabcin because he sounds like he was suffering from a cold when this episode was recorded.

Date: December 30, 1955
Title: Party Line: Making Call (Repeat)
Cast: Jim Jordan (Fibber), Marian Jordan (Molly), John Wald, Bill Thompson (Old Timer), Arthur Q. Bryan (Doctor Gamble), Robert Easton (Lester Nelson), Mary Lou Harrington (Sally Nelson)
Summary: Fibber cannot call for a bowling substitute because a garrulous woman is using the party line.

Writers: Phil Leslie, Ralph Goodman
Sponsors: Alka-Seltzer, Nervine
Comments: This repeat of the September 27, 1954 episode has different commercials, farewells, and the addition of a new year's pitch for the March of Dimes by John Wald.

Date: January 4, 1956
Title: Electric Bill
Cast: Jim Jordan (Fibber), Marian Jordan (Molly), John Wald, Bill Thompson (frightened customer, Henry Watts), Arthur Q. Bryan (Doctor Gamble), Cliff Arquette (clerk), Marian Richman (secretary)
Summary: After the McGees receive a bill that is higher than usual, they take their complaint to the power company.
Writer: Phil Leslie
Sponsors: Alka-Seltzer, One-A-Day
Running Gag: Myrt bit involving aunt taking gun/threats/linen napkins (Fibber)
Comments: One wonders what colorful expressions McGee would use after receiving a bill today when an amount of $7.85 prompts a "throat-cutting, customer-cheating, short-changing collection of con men" tirade.

Date: January 5, 1956
Title: Dinner Wager
Cast: Jim Jordan (Fibber), Marian Jordan (Molly), John Wald, Arthur Q. Bryan (Doctor Gamble), Jeanne Bates (Miss Cuddleson), Fritz Feld (Pierre)
Summary: Gamble offers to treat the McGees to dinner at a posh restaurant if Fibber can control his temper all day.
Writers: Phil Leslie, Ralph Goodman
Sponsors: Alka-Seltzer, One-A-Day
Comments: This is one of the rare occasions when Fibber gets the better of Gamble until he discovers a way to outwit himself.

Date: January 6, 1956
Title: Marital Advice (Repeat)
Cast: Jim Jordan (Fibber), Marian Jordan (Molly), John Wald, Robert Easton (Lester Nelson), Mary Lou Harrington (Sally Nelson)
Summary: Molly counsels Sally while Fibber instructs Les in conjugal matters.
Writers: Phil Leslie, Ralph Goodman
Sponsors: Alka-Seltzer, One-A-Day
Comments: This repeat of the October 19, 1954 episode has different commercials and farewells.

Date: January 9, 1956
Title: Fur Coat Purchase
Cast: Jim Jordan (Fibber), Marian Jordan (Molly), John Wald, Arthur Q. Bryan (Doctor Gamble), Colleen Collins (clerk)

Summary: The McGees shop at the Bon Ton for a new coat with insurance money from Molly's Persian lamb that was damaged at a restaurant.
Writers: Phil Leslie, Ralph Goodman
Sponsors: Alka-Seltzer, One-A-Day
Comments: This episode suggests that persuaders in the mid-fifties were not all that hidden. McGee's promise to be "coming out fighting" and Wald's clever "watching the fur fly" remark are two of the most pleasing teasers of the fifteen-minute era.

Date: January 10, 1956
Title: Fur Coat Dispute
Cast: Jim Jordan (Fibber), Marian Jordan (Molly), John Wald, Bill Thompson (Old Timer), Arthur Q. Bryan (Doctor Gamble), Herb Butterfield (Hogan)
Summary: Fibber takes on lawyers for the Bon Ton over the Russian sable sold to the McGees by mistake.
Writers: Phil Leslie, Ralph Goodman
Sponsors: Alka-Seltzer, One-A-Day
Comments: McGee corners a spot in Ripley's Believe It or Not by claiming he didn't "hardly sleep a wink" because he "kept dreaming about the fur coat all night."

Date: January 11, 1956
Title: Coffee Table Purchase
Cast: Jim Jordan (Fibber), Marian Jordan (Molly), John Wald, Bill Thompson (Old Timer), Mary Jane Croft (Mabel Toops)
Summary: The McGees painfully discover that the coffee table Molly bought at a rummage sale is too big for their living room.
Writer: Phil Leslie
Sponsors: Alka-Seltzer, One-A-Day
Comments: In Hitchcockville callers dial M for murder; in Wistful Vista, as Fibber states, they dial O for Myrtle. Molly "darns" the table numerous times while Fibber characteristically employs his vivid "shin-busting, space-hogging" descriptions.

Date: January 12, 1956
Title: Coffee Table Has to Go
Cast: Jim Jordan (Fibber), Marian Jordan (Molly), John Wald, Arthur Q. Bryan (Doctor Gamble), Robert Easton (Lester Nelson), Jean Vander Pyl (Mrs. Croveney)
Summary: Fibber and Molly find that getting rid of the oversized coffee table is not an easy task.
Writer: Phil Leslie
Sponsors: Alka-Seltzer, One-A-Day

Comments: One unexplained detail is how a coffee table that is too big for a living room seems to fit compactly into automobiles for transport.

Date: January 13, 1956
Title: Missing Roller Skate (Repeat)
Cast: Jim Jordan (Fibber), Marian Jordan (Molly, Teeny), John Wald, Bill Thompson (Old Timer), Arthur Q. Bryan (Doctor Gamble)
Summary: The McGees help Teeny look for her missing skate so she can take part in a ritual that will entitle her to become an honorary boy.
Writers: Phil Leslie, Ralph Goodman
Sponsors: Alka-Seltzer, One-A-Day
Comments: This repeat of the October 14, 1954 episode has different commercials and farewells.

Date: January 16, 1956
Title: Consolation Prize
Cast: Jim Jordan (Fibber), Marian Jordan (Molly), John Wald, Bill Thompson (delivery man), Arthur Q. Bryan (Doctor Gamble)
Summary: The McGees endure freezing temperatures in their home while waiting for delivery of a prize Fibber won in a contest.
Writers: Phil Leslie, Ralph Goodman
Sponsors: Alka-Seltzer, One-A-Day
Comments: The film playing at the Bijou that the McGees are missing is *Roman Holiday*. This episode is replete with parodies of jargon used by repairmen and manufacturers (including Miles Laboratories).

Date: January 17, 1956
Title: Math Problem
Cast: Jim Jordan (Fibber), Marian Jordan (Molly, Teeny), John Wald, Bill Thompson (Old Timer, Clayburn), Arthur Q. Bryan (Doctor Gamble), Robert Easton (Lester Nelson), Charlie Seel (professor)
Summary: McGee, after working diligently on a problem in mathematics at home, seeks the help of a college professor.
Writer: Phil Leslie
Sponsors: Alka-Seltzer, One-A-Day
Comments: Bill Thompson has two roles to play but only a dozen words to speak.

Date: January 18, 1956
Title: Cheer-Up Visit
Cast: Jim Jordan (Fibber), Marian Jordan (Molly), John Wald, Bill Thompson (Sug Brown), Natalie Masters (Mrs. Brown)
Summary: Molly and Fibber visit a sickly woman who takes advantage of their generous nature.
Writer: Phil Leslie
Sponsors: Alka-Seltzer, One-A-Day

Comments: Natalie Masters, adept at assuming the parts of malingerers or shirkers, played another irritating character in the December 14, 1953 episode.

Date: January 19, 1956
Title: Shoes Repaired, Remembering Names
Cast: Jim Jordan (Fibber), Marian Jordan (Molly, Teeny), John Wald, Bill Thompson (cobbler, Old Timer), Jack Kruschen (boss)
Summary: Fibber tries to recall the identity of a man in a store while the McGees have their shoes repaired.
Writer: Phil Leslie
Sponsors: Alka-Seltzer, One-A-Day
Comments: A peppy, completely different musical bridge leads into and out of the final commercial. A more timely number for this episode would have been "Whatever Lola Wants."

Date: January 20, 1956
Title: Tea Set Hunt (Repeat)
Cast: Jim Jordan (Fibber), Marian Jordan (Molly), John Wald, Bill Thompson (Wallace Wimple, butler), Arthur Q. Bryan (Doctor Gamble), Mary Jane Croft (Mabel Toops)
Summary: After learning that Aunt Sarah is coming for a visit, the McGees scurry all around town attempting to locate an elusive tea set she presented to them which they and numerous other recipients have given away.
Writers: Phil Leslie, Ralph Goodman
Sponsors: Alka-Seltzer, One-A-Day
Comments: This repeat of the January 25, 1955 episode has different commercials and farewells. The reference to Sarah's arrival on a Tuesday is not altered even though this 1956 episode aired on a Friday.

Date: January 23, 1956
Title: Wedding Ring in Drainpipe
Cast: Jim Jordan (Fibber), Marian Jordan (Molly), John Wald, Bill Thompson (plumber), Arthur Q. Bryan (Doctor Gamble)
Summary: After Molly loses her ring in the laundry tub, the race is on to see if a plumber she called can retrieve it before Fibber returns with a Stillson wrench to perform his usual mayhem under the sink.
Writers: Phil Leslie, Ralph Goodman
Sponsors: Alka-Seltzer, One-A-Day
Comments: From her opening monologue right to the end Marian gives a wonderful lesson in how to act–naturally.

Date: January 24, 1956
Title: Moonstruck
Cast: Jim Jordan (Fibber), Marian Jordan (Molly), John Wald, Parley Baer (clerk)

Summary: After reading some pamphlets about staking claims, Fibber decides to shoot for the moon at the federal building.
Writers: Phil Leslie, Ralph Goodman
Sponsors: Alka-Seltzer, One-A-Day
Running Gag: "'Tain't funny, McGee" (Molly)
Comments: The most amusing portions of this episode occur in the wings: the pop-eyed expression on the clerk's face and the ruckus in the Wimple house.

Date: January 25, 1956
Title: Claiming the Moon
Cast: Jim Jordan (Fibber), Marian Jordan (Molly), John Wald, Bill Thompson (Wallace Wimple), Arthur Q. Bryan (Doctor Gamble), Parley Baer (clerk)
Summary: McGee takes Wimple with him to the federal building where he intends to complete the forms necessary to claim ownership of the moon.
Writers: Phil Leslie, Ralph Goodman
Sponsors: Alka-Seltzer, One-A-Day
Comments: The sequence of incomplete sentences in the commercial delivered by the Jordans is an amusing way to make listeners attend to the sales pitch. Fibber's watchword ("Remember the follies") could be the title of his autobiography.

Date: January 26, 1956
Title: Lost Purse
Cast: Jim Jordan (Fibber), Marian Jordan (Molly, Teeny), John Wald, Robert Easton (Lester Nelson)
Summary: The McGees, with the aid of neighbor Les, attempt to learn the identity of a woman whose purse was found by Teeny.
Writers: Phil Leslie, Ralph Goodman
Sponsors: Alka-Seltzer, One-A-Day
Comments: The contents of the purse falling on the coffee table sound like they could have tumbled out of the hall closet.

Date: January 27, 1956
Title: Cappy Visits the McGees (Repeat)
Cast: Jim Jordan (Fibber), Marian Jordan (Molly), John Wald, Arthur Q. Bryan (Doctor Gamble), Joseph Kearns (Captain Clarence Wreskokoskowitz)
Summary: McGee's old commanding officer visits Wistful Vista and tells stories about Fibber's adventures in the Army during World War I.
Writers: Phil Leslie, Ralph Goodman
Sponsors: Alka-Seltzer, One-A-Day
Comments: This is a repeat of the January 27, 1955 episode with different commercials.

Date: January 30, 1956
Title: Surprise for the House

Cast: Jim Jordan (Fibber), Marian Jordan (Molly), John Wald, Bill Thompson (Old Timer, phone installer), Mary Jane Croft (Mabel Toops)
Summary: Fibber keeps Molly in the dark about the new addition he has ordered for the home to make her life easier.
Writer: Phil Leslie
Sponsors: Alka-Seltzer, One-A-Day
Comments: McGee and the Old Timer provide a startling contrast, one wanting to save a million steps for his mate and the other not willing to take the first step with his date.

Date: January 31, 1956
Title: Phone Confusion
Cast: Jim Jordan (Fibber), Marian Jordan (Molly), John Wald, Bill Thompson (Old Timer, Wallace Wimple), Arthur Q. Bryan (Doctor Gamble)
Summary: Fibber and Molly have difficulty determining protocol for answering the new extension telephone.
Writers: Phil Leslie, Ralph Goodman
Sponsors: Alka-Seltzer, One-A-Day
Running Gag: Myrt bit involving uncle's estate/million francs/mildewed franks (Fibber)
Comments: This is one time when the prerecorded "We'll try to straighten out the McGees" is most appropriate. At the end Jim and Marian warn listeners that polio is still a present danger and encourage support of the March of Dimes.

Date: February 1, 1956
Title: Cat with Three Owners (Repeat)
Cast: Jim Jordan (Fibber), Marian Jordan (Molly), John Wald, Bill Thompson (Old Timer), Arthur Q. Bryan (Doctor Gamble), Jack Kruschen (cat)
Summary: The McGees, Gamble, and the Old Timer claim ownership of a wandering cat.
Writers: Phil Leslie, Ralph Goodman
Sponsors: Alka-Seltzer, One-A-Day
Comments: This is a repeat of the September 6, 1954 script with different sponsors.

Date: February 2, 1956
Title: Cat Matter Resolved (Repeat)
Cast: Jim Jordan (Fibber), Marian Jordan (Molly, Teeny), John Wald, Bill Thompson (Old Timer), Arthur Q. Bryan (Doctor Gamble), Robert Easton (Lester Nelson), Jack Kruschen (cat)
Summary: After arguing all night about who owns a stray cat, Fibber, the Old Timer, and Gamble seem to find a solution to the problem when Teeny arrives.

Writers: Phil Leslie, Ralph Goodman
Sponsors: Alka-Seltzer, One-A-Day
Comments: This is a repeat of the September 7, 1954 script. The first commercial makes the show sound fresh by including a reference to Groundhog Day.

Date: February 3, 1956
Title: Grocery Budget Scheme
Cast: Jim Jordan (Fibber), Marian Jordan (Molly), John Wald, Bill Thompson (Wallace Wimple, store manager), Elvia Allman (Cora Burns), Ken Christy (Walt), Mary Lansing (Helen)
Summary: Acting on a tip from Cora, Molly lets Fibber talk himself into demonstrating how to save money on the food budget.
Writers: Phil Leslie, Ralph Goodman
Sponsors: Alka-Seltzer, One-A-Day
Comments: The plot of McGee showing Molly how to economize at the grocery store had been used on April 17, 1951 with the same target of $15.00 a week. The writers slyly put Wimple's wife on the scene at the store yet conveniently out of the action.

Date: February 6, 1956
Title: Molly's Feigned Toothache
Cast: Jim Jordan (Fibber), Marian Jordan (Molly), John Wald, Bill Thompson (Old Timer, Silsley), Arthur Q. Bryan (Doctor Gamble), Colleen Collins (Miss Jackson)
Summary: Molly pretends to have a toothache so Fibber will accompany her to the dentist.
Writer: Phil Leslie
Sponsors: Alka-Seltzer, One-A-Day
Comments: The spat over nothing which opens the scene shows the argumentative side of McGee that makes his stubborn refusal to see the dentist seem a natural part of his character. Leslie borrowed the hot water bit and the Old Timer's tale about a brick from the May 25, 1948 broadcast when Molly actually did have a sore tooth.

Date: February 7, 1956
Title: Buried Package Mystery
Cast: Jim Jordan (Fibber), Marian Jordan (Molly), John Wald, Bill Thompson (Charlie), Tyler McVey (sergeant)
Summary: The McGees alert the police after they witness a surreptitious burial in their neighborhood.
Writers: Phil Leslie, Ralph Goodman
Sponsors: Alka-Seltzer, One-A-Day
Running Gag: "'Tain't funny, McGee" (Molly)

Comments: Although Myrt is on duty at daybreak, Fibber brushes her off, perhaps for the same reason he gives Molly when she rebuffs his gag: "It's too early in the morning for jokes."

Date: February 8, 1956
Title: Sub Gum Blooey
Cast: Jim Jordan (Fibber), Marian Jordan (Molly), John Wald, Bill Thompson (Wallace Wimple, delivery man), Arthur Q. Bryan (Doctor Gamble)
Summary: Fibber, who had a bad experience with Chinese food during WWI, changes his mind several times before agreeing to order some from a restaurant.
Writers: Phil Leslie, Ralph Goodman
Sponsors: Alka-Seltzer, One-A-Day
Comments: Fibber must have conveniently forgotten the September 12, 1954 adventure in which most of the action takes place in and around a Chinese restaurant. The casserole dish should have made McGee say "Phooey" to the notion that the blooey came from a restaurant kitchen.

Date: February 9, 1956
Title: Soap Carving Contest
Cast: Jim Jordan (Fibber), Marian Jordan (Molly, Teeny), John Wald, Bill Thompson (Old Timer), Arthur Q. Bryan (Doctor Gamble)
Summary: McGee whittles away at bars of soap in hopes of winning $500 in a contest.
Writers: Phil Leslie, Ralph Goodman
Sponsors: Alka-Seltzer, One-A-Day
Comments: Shrewd listeners accustomed to the modus operandi of the writers probably anticipated that the repeated reference to the incinerator would figure in the resolution to what turns out to be a sob story.

Date: February 10, 1956
Title: Anniversary of First Meeting (Repeat)
Cast: Jim Jordan (Fibber), Marian Jordan (Molly), John Wald, Bill Thompson (Old Timer), Elvia Allman (Cora Burns)
Summary: Molly is upset because Fibber apparently has forgotten to observe an anniversary.
Writers: Phil Leslie, Ralph Goodman
Sponsors: Alka-Seltzer, One-A-Day
Comments: This is a repeat of the February 9, 1955 script with different commercials.

Date: February 13, 1956
Title: Avoiding Clifford Parker
Cast: Jim Jordan (Fibber), Marian Jordan (Molly), John Wald, Bill Thompson (Wallace Wimple), Elvia Allman (Cora Burns)

Summary: When Fibber learns that an irksome schoolmate plans on stopping by 79 Wistful Vista, he and Molly avoid him by enjoying a long, long lunch at Walt's Malt Shop.
Writer: Phil Leslie
Sponsors: Alka-Seltzer, One-A-Day
Comments: When the McGees play their version of "I Remember It Well," Fibber recalls those "once there was a fleeting glimpse of glory–called Peoria" days when he got the best of his old rival, Otis Cadwallader.

Date: February 14, 1956
Title: Rolls Royce Ride
Cast: Jim Jordan (Fibber), Marian Jordan (Molly), John Wald, Bill Thompson (Crofton, Old Timer), Arthur Q. Bryan (Doctor Gamble), Art Jacobson (Clifford Parker)
Summary: The McGees hope all their friends see them after a rich acquaintance gives them the use of his chauffeured Rolls Royce for the day.
Writer: Phil Leslie
Sponsors: Alka-Seltzer, One-A-Day
Running Gag: Myrt bit involving cousin to Washington/Senator/second baseman (Fibber)
Comments: Jacobson also played a character named Parker in the Investment Plan episodes of December 14 and 15, 1955. The humor of the Myrt bit is best appreciated by those who remember the Major League Baseball franchise known as the Washington Senators. The joke about Eisenhower may escape those who do not recall that the headgear associated with Estes Kefauver, influential Democratic senator from Tennessee and a presidential candidate in 1952 and 1956, was a coonskin cap.

Date: February 15, 1956
Title: Searching for Shotgun
Cast: Jim Jordan (Fibber), Marian Jordan (Molly), John Wald, Bill Thompson (Old Timer), Arthur Q. Bryan (Doctor Gamble)
Summary: While Fibber frantically looks for his shotgun, Molly adamantly refuses to tell him where it is.
Writers: Phil Leslie, Ralph Goodman
Sponsors: Alka-Seltzer, One-A-Day
Running Gag: Hall closet opened by Fibber looking for shotgun
Comments: This time the Old Timer gets to mutter the "Here we go again" line. The hall closet has become the last place Fibber looks for missing articles instead of the first.

Date: February 16, 1956
Title: Deputy for a Day

Cast: Jim Jordan (Fibber), Marian Jordan (Molly), John Wald, Bill Thompson (Wallace Wimple, Officer Grogan), Arthur Q. Bryan (Doctor Gamble)
Summary: Acting as Litterbug Deputy, McGee issues citations to offenders on the sidewalk and in his car.
Writers: Phil Leslie, Ralph Goodman
Sponsors: Alka-Seltzer, One-A-Day
Comments: The name Doc gives to Fibber on the street seems most appropriate: Loudmouth Blubberhead McGee. Wald's signoff is not as warm as Wilcox's closing invitation to return the following week but accurately reflected the tenor of the time: "Hoping to have you with us again for more nonsense with Fibber McGee and Molly."

Date: February 17, 1956
Title: Valentine from Snooky (Repeat)
Cast: Jim Jordan (Fibber), Marian Jordan (Molly), John Wald, Bill Thompson (Wallace Wimple), Mary Jane Croft (Mabel Toops), Sam Edwards (employee for cleaners)
Summary: When Molly finds a Valentine in a coat she believes belongs to Fibber, she suspects that a flirtatious manicurist has designs on her husband.
Writer: Phil Leslie
Sponsors: Alka-Seltzer, One-A-Day
Comments: This is a repeat of the February 23, 1955 script with different commercials. Leslie *and* Ralph Goodman received credit for the 1955 episode.

Date: February 20, 1956
Title: *Fabulous Adventures* Article
Cast: Jim Jordan (Fibber), Marian Jordan (Molly), John Wald, Bill Thompson (Old Timer, Wallace Wimple), Arthur Q. Bryan (Doctor Gamble), Robert Easton (Lester Nelson)
Summary: Fibber, repeatedly interrupted while reading a magazine narrative, uses his connections to resolve the matter.
Writer: Phil Leslie
Sponsors: Alka-Seltzer, One-A-Day
Comments: Gamble delivers the equivalent of a Mrs. Kladderhatch bit without using the phone. Molly demonstrates again that Fibber's thirst for adventure can be supplanted by his appetite for food.

Date: February 21, 1956
Title: Elevator Ups and Downs
Cast: Jim Jordan (Fibber), Marian Jordan (Molly), John Wald, Bill Thompson (Old Timer), Jack Moyles (man in basement, man with toothache), Marian Richman (Miss Ogilvie)

Summary: The McGees experience difficulties using a self-service elevator as they attempt to get to the top floor of a new medical building.
Writers: Phil Leslie, Ralph Goodman
Sponsors: Alka-Seltzer, One-A-Day
Running Gag: "'Tain't funny, McGee" (Molly)
Comments: This is another "much ado about nothing" misadventure because Gamble decides to stay in his present office location. Fibber's conservative tie has more colors than can be found on the NBC peacock.

Date: February 22, 1956
Title: Avoiding Parking Ticket
Cast: Jim Jordan (Fibber), Marian Jordan (Molly), John Wald, Bill Thompson (Old Timer, officer), Robert Easton (Lester Nelson)
Summary: Fibber stubbornly tests the city ordinance against parking in the street by insisting that his car has a dead battery.
Writers: Phil Leslie
Sponsors: Alka-Seltzer, One-A-Day
Comments: Victims get little consideration on this Wacky Wednesday as the condition of the thermometer-swallowing patient and the wounded boss are unknown and Fibber is cited for a trivial one-inch violation.

Date: February 23, 1956
Title: Teeny's Aunt Catherine
Cast: Jim Jordan (Fibber), Marian Jordan (Molly, Teeny), John Wald, Bill Thompson (Old Timer), Arthur Q. Bryan (Doctor Gamble), Colleen Collins (Catherine)
Summary: Fibber and Molly are apprehensive about meeting Teeny's aunt when they learn that she reads books upside down and enjoys roller skating.
Writers: Phil Leslie, Ralph Goodman
Sponsors: Alka-Seltzer, One-A-Day
Comments: Dropping Charlie Addams into the conversation passes so quickly that listeners may not recognize the allusion to Charles Addams, creator of that macabre family of cartoon characters.

Date: February 24, 1956
Title: Gifts for Wives Switched (Repeat)
Cast: Jim Jordan (Fibber), Marian Jordan (Molly), John Wald, Robert Easton (Lester Nelson), Mary Lou Harrington (Sally Nelson)
Summary: Fibber has to do some quick thinking after Molly assumes a bottle of perfume is a present from McGee when actually it is a birthday gift from Lester to Sally.
Writers: Phil Leslie, Ralph Goodman
Sponsors: Alka-Seltzer, One-A-Day
Comments: This is a repeat of the March 16, 1955 episode with different commercials and farewells.

Date: February 27, 1956
Title: Icy Walk to Bus
Cast: Jim Jordan (Fibber), Marian Jordan (Molly), John Wald, Arthur Q. Bryan (Doctor Gamble), Jack Mather (bus driver), Art Jacobson (man)
Summary: Fibber, after assisting Molly along the hazardous street to the bus stop, appears to fall on the ice.
Writers: Phil Leslie, Ralph Goodman
Sponsors: Alka-Seltzer, One-A-Day
Comments: Listeners may grow suspicious about why sure-footed Fibber suddenly becomes Slippery Sam after Molly boarded the bus. McGee truly knows the best way to preserve frozen assets is to sit on them.

Date: February 28, 1956
Title: Wimple Going to Chicago
Cast: Jim Jordan (Fibber), Marian Jordan (Molly, Teeny), John Wald, Bill Thompson (Wallace Wimple, Old Timer), Arthur Q. Bryan (Doctor Gamble), Parley Baer (barber)
Summary: After Fibber learns that Wimple is leaving town, he organizes a group of friends to see him off first at the airport and then at the train station.
Writer: Phil Leslie
Sponsors: Alka-Seltzer, One-A-Day
Comments: This is one time when Fibber's conversation with Myrt sounds like an APB.

Date: February 29, 1956
Title: Sendoff for Wimple
Cast: Jim Jordan (Fibber), Marian Jordan (Molly), John Wald, Bill Thompson (Old Timer, Wallace Wimple), Arthur Q. Bryan (Doctor Gamble), Robert Easton (Lester Nelson), Mary Jane Croft (Mabel Toops), Jack Moyles (Mort Toops), Will Wright (Kremer)
Summary: The McGees and their friends gather at Union Station to present Wimple with a gift and good wishes before he departs for Chicago.
Writer: Phil Leslie
Sponsors: Alka-Seltzer, One-A-Day
Comments: The tricks played on Wimple described in the first act are never recorded in actual episodes because Wallace has always been the put-upon victim of domestic abuse who gets pity, not pranks, from Gamble and the McGees.

Date: March 1, 1956
Title: Haircut (Repeat)
Cast: Jim Jordan (Fibber), Marian Jordan (Molly), John Wald, Bill Thompson (Wallace Wimple), Arthur Q. Bryan (Doctor Gamble), Fritz Feld (Pierre), Jay Novello (Joe)

Summary: Fibber agrees to have his hair cut by a new barber in town to avoid the errant scissors of the distraught clipper he usually patronizes.
Writers: Phil Leslie, Ralph Goodman
Sponsors: Alka-Seltzer, One-A-Day
Comments: This is a repeat of the June 2, 1955 show with different commercials and farewells.

Date: March 2, 1956
Title: Dress Mix-Up at Cleaners (Repeat)
Cast: Jim Jordan (Fibber), Marian Jordan (Molly), John Wald, Bill Thompson (cleaner), Mary Jane Croft (Mabel Toops)
Summary: After Fibber is given the wrong dress at the cleaners, Molly assumes it is a new one he purchased for her.
Writers: Phil Leslie, Ralph Goodman
Sponsors: Alka-Seltzer, One-A-Day
Comments: This is a repeat of the May 31, 1955 episode with different commercials and farewells.

Date: March 5, 1956
Title: Looking at Cars with Wimple
Cast: Jim Jordan (Fibber), Marian Jordan (Molly), John Wald, Bill Thompson (Wallace Wimple), Art Jacobson (salesman)
Summary: Fibber and Wallace test various buttons and controls on new models in an automobile showroom.
Writers: Phil Leslie, Ralph Goodman
Sponsors: Alka-Seltzer, One-A-Day
Comments: Wimple, who puts his foot in it and sticks his neck out, could not have fared much worse if he had stayed home and tangled with his wife. The many color combinations and sophisticated controls cited contain more truth than exaggeration for in the mid-fifties two-toned exteriors and push button transmissions were very much in vogue.

Date: March 6, 1956
Title: Garbage Disposal
Cast: Jim Jordan (Fibber), Marian Jordan (Molly, Teeny), John Wald, Robert Easton (Lester Nelson)
Summary: Fibber grows impatient and frustrated when he cannot find any garbage to put in the new disposal unit.
Writers: Phil Leslie, Ralph Goodman
Sponsors: Alka-Seltzer, One-A-Day
Running Gag: "'Tain't funny, Mrs. McGee" (Fibber)
Comments: McGee, known for borrowing trouble, may be the only person in Wistful Vista and perhaps in all of radioland who tries to borrow garbage.

The thought doesn't occur to the McGees that without a garbage can they will need to find another place to deposit items like used paper plates, dirty rags, burned-out light bulbs, and the like.

Date: March 7, 1956
Title: License Plate
Cast: Jim Jordan (Fibber), Marian Jordan (Molly, Teeny), John Wald, Bill Thompson (Old Timer, clerk), Arthur Q. Bryan (Doctor Gamble), Barney Phillips (clerk)
Summary: The McGees learn that finders can be losers when they take a lost plate to the license bureau.
Writer: Phil Leslie
Sponsors: Alka-Seltzer, One-A-Day
Comments: A dog's life isn't so bad in Wistful Vista, a place where even a mutt can be a mister. The sentence handed down by the bureaucrats at this time is clear: 30 days or $3.00.

Date: March 8, 1956
Title: Out of Postage Stamps
Cast: Jim Jordan (Fibber), Marian Jordan (Molly), John Wald, Bill Thompson (Old Timer), Arthur Q. Bryan (Doctor Gamble)
Summary: The McGees, in search of stamps so Fibber can mail letters to relatives regarding his genealogy, search the house and beseech friends with little positive result.
Writers: Phil Leslie, Ralph Goodman
Sponsors: Alka-Seltzer, One-A-Day
Comments: The Old Timer's reference to Bridey Murphy relates to the movie and popular book of the time recounting the supposedly true account of a woman who may have had a prior existence. As usual, when the Old Timer regales the McGees with stories about his family tree or that "ol' gang of mine," it is the comic highlight of the show.

Date: March 9, 1956
Title: Stage Money (Repeat)
Cast: Jim Jordan (Fibber), Marian Jordan (Molly), John Wald, Arthur Q. Bryan (Doctor Gamble), Peggy Knudsen (Nancy Cuddleson)
Summary: Problems arise when Fibber thinks he passed a phony five-dollar bill at a restaurant.
Writers: Phil Leslie, Ralph Goodman
Sponsors: Alka-Seltzer, One-A-Day
Comments: This is a repeat of the March 20, 1955 show with different commercials and farewells.

Date: March 12, 1956
Title: Portrait for the Elks
Cast: Jim Jordan (Fibber), Marian Jordan (Molly), John Wald, Bill Thompson (Wallace Wimple, Old Timer), Arthur Q. Bryan (Doctor Gamble)
Summary: McGee and Wimple prepare a room at the Elks Club for a portrait of George Washington.
Writers: Phil Leslie, Ralph Goodman
Sponsors: Alka-Seltzer, One-A-Day
Comments: Wimple adapts "Sixteen Tons," still a top ten hit at the time, to the cast's source of revenue, NBC. The repetition of *life-size* is a clue as to the dimensions of the painting. Wald's closing is abrupt, ending immediately after the credits, with no invitation to listeners to tune in again.

Date: March 13, 1956
Title: Diverts Freeway for Old Timer
Cast: Jim Jordan (Fibber), Marian Jordan (Molly), John Wald, Bill Thompson (Old Timer), Arthur Q. Bryan (Doctor Gamble), Jack Mather (Crudley), Herb Butterfield (Jones), Bill Idelson (Pringle)
Summary: When the Old Timer learns that a freeway will dispossess him, he finds champions in Fibber, Molly, and Gamble so he can retain his residence.
Writers: Phil Leslie, Ralph Goodman
Sponsors: Alka-Seltzer, One-A-Day
Comments: Long before environmental studies and concern for endangered species halted construction projects, Molly finds another way to save wetlands by emphasizing the green: the long green. Fibber and Molly provide teasers to bring listeners back to see if 79 Wistful Vista becomes Interstate 79.

Date: March 14, 1956
Title: Diverts Freeway for Himself
Cast: Jim Jordan (Fibber), Marian Jordan (Molly), John Wald, Bill Thompson (Cropopolis, Old Timer), Arthur Q. Bryan (Doctor Gamble), Lou Krugman (Harry), Gail Bonney (wife's aunt, Miss Barry)
Summary: The McGees, disgusted with the poor results of their petition to stop a freeway, save their home when Fibber contacts an influential senator.
Writers: Phil Leslie, Ralph Goodman
Sponsors: Alka-Seltzer, One-A-Day
Comments: The kicker is that even when McGee appears to emerge triumphant, there is usually one final revelation that brings him down to earth. Gail Bonney expertly plays both insolent shrew and shrewd homeowner.

Date: March 15, 1956
Title: Spring Cleaning Plan
Cast: Jim Jordan (Fibber), Marian Jordan (Molly), John Wald, Bill Thompson (Wallace Wimple), Arthur Q. Bryan (Doctor Gamble), Robert Easton (Lester Nelson)
Summary: McGee devises a scheme that he believes will excuse him from helping with the spring cleaning if he can convince Molly and her friends to work together as a team.
Writer: Phil Leslie
Sponsors: Alka-Seltzer, One-A-Day
Comments: Fibber catches it in the catch-22 of womanhood which maintains a house needs to be cleaned before it can be seen by other women bent on cleaning said house. By cleaning the hall closet offstage, McGee made it a site for sore ears.

Date: March 16, 1956
Title: Dalmatian Trouble (Repeat)
Cast: Jim Jordan (Fibber), Marian Jordan (Molly, Teeny), John Wald, Bill Thompson (Wallace Wimple, Harkins' dog), Jess Kirkpatrick (Harkins), Jack Moyles (Spot)
Summary: The McGees try to find the owner of a dog.
Writers: Phil Leslie, Ralph Goodman
Sponsors: Alka-Seltzer, One-A-Day
Comments: This is a repeat of the March 17, 1955 episode with different commercials and farewells.

Date: March 19, 1956
Title: Boomerang
Cast: Jim Jordan (Fibber), Marian Jordan (Molly, Teeny), John Wald, Bill Thompson (Wallace Wimple, Grogin), Robert Easton (Lester Nelson), Mary Lou Harrington (Sally Nelson)
Summary: McGee regales the Nelsons and Wallace Wimple with tales of his boomerang prowess before demonstrating his talent in a roundabout way.
Writers: Phil Leslie, Ralph Goodman
Sponsors: Alka-Seltzer, One-A-Day
Comments: McGee could throw it with the best of them whether winding up in Melbourne or Wistful Vista. By the end of this flight of fancy it hits Wimple why Fibber performed before the crowned heads of Australia.

Date: March 20, 1956
Title: Knitting
Cast: Jim Jordan (Fibber), Marian Jordan (Molly), John Wald, Bill Thompson (Wallace Wimple), Arthur Q. Bryan (Doctor Gamble)

Summary: McGee knits a mystery garment that frustrates Molly because she cannot figure out what it is.
Writers: Phil Leslie, Ralph Goodman
Sponsors: Alka-Seltzer, One-A-Day
Running Gag: "'Tain't funny, McGee" (Molly)
Comments: With its emphasis on word play, this episode harks back to the 1940s heyday of the show. The tag gag is one of those brought in occasionally that has absolutely nothing to do with the first two acts.

Date: March 21, 1956
Title: Buying a Classic Book
Cast: Jim Jordan (Fibber), Marian Jordan (Molly), John Wald, Bill Thompson (Old Timer), Arthur Q. Bryan (Doctor Gamble), Mary Lansing (clerk)
Summary: Molly and Gamble are surprised by McGee's determination to purchase a notable work of fiction by Sir Walter Scott or Charles Dickens.
Writer: Phil Leslie
Sponsors: Alka-Seltzer, One-A-Day
Comments: The saga of Pancake Pete sounds like a scene from a slapstick comedy. The final request by Jim and Marian to support a worthwhile charity is delivered with the same heartfelt sincerity that marked all previous appeals.

Date: March 22, 1956
Title: Mystery Caller (Repeat)
Cast: Jim Jordan (Fibber), Marian Jordan (Molly), John Wald, Bill Thompson (Old Timer), Arthur Q. Bryan (Doctor Gamble), Robert Easton (Lester Nelson)
Summary: Fibber is frustrated by a party who calls periodically but refuses to speak.
Writers: Phil Leslie, Ralph Goodman
Sponsors: Alka-Seltzer, One-A-Day
Comments: This is a repeat of the April 13, 1955 episode with different commercials and farewells.

Date: March 23, 1956
Title: Efficiency in the Kitchen (Repeat)
Cast: Jim Jordan (Fibber), Marian Jordan (Molly), John Wald, Arthur Q. Bryan (Doctor Gamble), Bill Idelson (Dave Eustice)
Summary: After meeting an efficiency expert downtown, Fibber decides to apply such time-saving techniques at home, much to Molly's chagrin.
Writers: Phil Leslie, Ralph Goodman

Sponsors: Alka-Seltzer, One-A-Day

Comments: This is a repeat of the April 14, 1955 episode with different commercials and farewells. Fibber's final words to the listeners are "So long, everybody " and Molly closes with "Bye." It is fitting that the closing of the last fifteen-minute episode of *Fibber McGee and Molly* ends with a promotion of the NBC *Monitor* series for that will be the new venue for Fibber and Molly in 1957.

A press photo from November 1957 carries the caption "Fibber and Molly, the beloved McGees of 79 Wistful Vista, are regular visitors on NBC radio's MONITOR. Ten times each weekend the husband-wife team is heard in comedy-situation vignettes about the unusual happenings at the McGee Household."

Monitor Series

These bits of about three minutes each were heard on NBC *Monitor* on weekends from June 1, 1957 to September 6, 1959. Five of these vignettes were broadcast each Saturday and Sunday. Jim and Marian were the only actors, recording the programs at Radio Recorders in Hollywood with Cliff Thorsness providing the sound effects. The tapes were then shipped to New York for broadcast. There is no theme music nor any announcer setting the scenes. Tom Koch wrote all extant episodes.

Only a small fraction of these shows have been preserved in a recorded format and few of them have all five vignettes written for a specific Saturday or Sunday. Dating of a number of episodes is based on information given during the dialogue such as reference to a holiday, observance of a special week on the calendar, or birthday of a notable person. Episodes may have aired later than the events described.

Date: June 16, 1957
Title: Painting a Fly
Summary: Fibber, the artiste, dabbles away at a still life and scoffs at Molly's suggestion that he paint the front door.
Comments: With no introduction or musical cue Koch was adept at getting into the situation in the first ten seconds with opening lines like "McGee, would you mind telling me..." and "Gee whiz, Molly, I can't see why you wanted to come along with me on this hunting trip."

Date: July 27, 1957
Title: Lifeguard Memories
Summary: Fibber's recollections of his exploits as a lifeguard differ markedly from that of Molly's.
Comments: Just a few notes from a harp are all that is needed to signal time travel in Fibber and Molly's world.

Date: August 11, 1957
Title: Restaurant: First and Last Day
Summary: Fibber gets bad news from Doc Gamble over the phone about the restaurant the McGees have opened in their home.
Running Gag: Word confusion involving *exaggerated/exhaled* (Fibber, Molly)
Comments: This is the only extant vignette from the *Monitor* series in which a sponsor (Pepsi) is mentioned. This is the concluding segment of the five sketches about turning 79 Wistful Vista into an eatery.

Date: August 31, 1957
Title: Labeling Plants
Summary: Fibber explains the finer points of botany to Teeny who, fortunately for McGee, can identify only one plant he needs to avoid.
Comments: In these vignettes dialogue could be written solely for Fibber and Teeny and therefore excuses would not have to be made to get Molly out of the way.

Date: September 1, 1957
Title: First Meeting in Cribs
Summary: Fibber and Molly recall their first meeting while infants in the maternity ward.
Comments: Fibber was already boasting and stretching the truth before he got his first name. Molly's account of Fibber falling on his head in the crib might explain much of his behavior in later years.

Date: September 15, 1957
Title: Storm Windows
Summary: Fibber devises a plan to install storm windows with the use of suction cups on his feet that allow him to walk up the side of the house.
Comments: Fibber has put on twenty pounds since November 4, 1947 when he weighed in at 177.

Date: September 15, 1957
Title: Tree Shaker
Summary: Because Molly is skeptical that his invention to shake leaves off the elm tree will be successful, McGee gives her a demonstration.
Comments: Fibber's timetable is off a bit regarding the autumnal equinox.

Date: September 22, 1957
Title: Duck Hunting with Molly
Summary: Fibber teaches survival tactics to Molly.
Comments: Fibber's change from assured woodsman to craven shrieker is a bit abrupt but necessary given the brevity of these episodes.

Date: September 22, 1957
Title: Shooting a "Dirty Pheasant"
Summary: Somewhat out of desperation after Molly complains about lack of action, McGee takes aim at a bird more gamy than game.
Running Gag: Tongue twister starting with Dead Duck McGee (Fibber)
Comments: This tongue twister has the distinction of being the only one Fibber delivers in a stage whisper.

Date: September 22, 1957
Title: Teeny the Huntress
Summary: Teeny amazes Fibber with a report of her hunting prowess with a slingshot.
Comments: Fibber (through author Koch) resurrects his long-dormant "and stuff like that there" line.

Date: September 28, 1957
Title: Occupation: Professor
Summary: Fibber daydreams about what his life would have been like as a college professor.
Running Gag: "'Tain't funny, Dr. McGee" (Molly)
Comments: The "be that as it may or may not be or not" bit makes its way back into the McGee vernacular.

Date: September 28, 1957
Title: Occupation: Mandolinist
Summary: Fibber daydreams about how he might have fared as a bop mandolin plucker.
Comments: The McGees handle the hep talk in their square fashion superbly.

Date: September 28, 1957
Title: Occupation: Author
Summary: Fibber daydreams about what his life would have been like if he had been a writer.
Comments: It is safe to say that this is the first (and perhaps only) time the name of jurist Charles Evans Hughes was mentioned on a situation comedy.

Date: September 28, 1957, 1957
Title: Occupation: General
Summary: Fibber daydreams about what a career in the military he might have had.
Comments: Fibber's comment "I'd be at least a general" is an indirect hint that there are higher positions for military leaders including the one occupied by the resident at 1600 Pennsylvania Avenue at the time.

Date: September 28, 1957
Title: Occupation: Psychiatrist
Summary: Fibber daydreams about how he might have been a successful psychiatrist.
Comments: McGee belongs to the "It's My Party" school of psychiatrists: "It's my couch, Mrs. Fortnightly, and I'll lay on it if I want to."

Date: September 29, 1957
Title: Homework
Summary: After Fibber is interrupted by Teeny while doing his homework, he shows her how to solve math problems.
Comments: The shampoo bit doesn't go over because there is no payoff for Teeny. If Teeny pitches any product to McGee, there has to be some dough in it for her.

Date: October 19, 1957
Title: Publicity Seeker: Staying Awake
Summary: In order to get his name in the newspapers, Fibber vows he is going to break the record for consecutive hours without sleeping.
Running Gag: Myrt bit involving father/shot, hit on the nose/hole in one (Fibber)
Comments: A twenty-second Myrt bit, scarcely a blink of the eye in the half-hour era, becomes the most memorable part of brief skits like this one.

Date: October 19, 1957
Title: Publicity Seeker: Hot Air Balloon
Summary: To get an article written about him, Fibber creates a balloon made of old newspapers with which he hopes to reach high altitudes.
Running Gag: Tongue twister starting with Wind Bag McGee (Fibber)
Comments: Molly probably bit her tongue when McGee fed her a dandy straight line: "It's filled with hot air. I blew it up myself."

Date: October 19, 1957
Title: Publicity Seeker: Teeny is in Paper
Summary: While Fibber cogitates about finding a way to make news, Teeny tells him she already has made a splash for herself.
Comments: Teeny could have extended the Sam Hill joke by saying that Fibber was older than Sam's brother Bill as well, making him older than the Hills.

Date: October 19, 1957
Title: Publicity Seeker: Double Yolk
Summary: Fibber buys fifty dozen eggs in the hope that one of them will have a double yolk which will get his name in the papers.

Running Gag: Word confusion involving *obstruction/obstreperous/staccato* (Fibber, Molly)
Comments: Usually during the confusion with words Molly is on target with some of the terms, but in this episode both McGees need a dictionary.

Date: October 19, 1957
Title: Publicity Seeker: Swim Lake Michigan
Summary: Fibber attempts to swim across Lake Michigan to get his photo in the newspapers.
Comments: When Fibber says, "There goes a good kid," we almost expect Teeny to show up because that has been the cue for her entrance for so many years.

Date: October 27, 1957
Title: Lawyer: Applying for Course
Summary: Fibber decides to study law by enrolling in a correspondence course.
Comments: Unlike some of the vignettes that have scarcely a snicker in them, this one has several knee-slappers, the highlights being the napkin gag and the name of the bogus business.

Date: October 27, 1957
Title: Lawyer: Practicing Attorney
Summary: Now officially enrolled in a law course, Fibber tries out his new profession by interrogating Molly.
Comments: What McGee really needs to be practicing is how to recognize fly-by-nighters who should be grounded.

Date: October 27, 1957
Title: Lawyer: Courtroom Manner
Summary: Fibber pretends to defend a client with Molly acting as judge.
Comments: The puns of "almost before my clients don't know what hit them" and "the defense rests" may pass by unnoticed amidst all the other tomfoolery.

Date: October 27, 1957
Title: Lawyer: Summation
Summary: Fibber practices his final speech before Molly who pretends to be a juror.
Running Gag: Tongue twister starting with Electric Chair McGee (Fibber)
Comments: Koch, knowing how well McGee mangles legal jargon, gives him some dandies to mutilate. Fibber's straight-faced summation that indicts his client is one of the best bits during the *Monitor* years.

Date: October 27, 1957
Title: Lawyer: Finishes Course
Summary: As Fibber waits for his law diploma to arrive, he plans his first case.
Comments: It is too bad that Fibber did not continue on the path he described for Molly for he could have become a shy star of law. Shyster McGee he would have been known as in those days…

Date: November 2, 1957
Title: Tax Problems: Letter from IRS
Summary: Fibber's sunny disposition turns cloudy when he receives a letter from the Internal Revenue Service.
Comments: McGee's statement about Molly in lavender is inexplicable, but less than a minute later he has cause to consider how he will look in stripes.

Date: November 2, 1957
Title: Tax Problems: Deductions
Summary: Molly questions some of the deductions Fibber listed on tax returns he filed in previous years.
Running Gag: Tongue twister starting with Tax Dodge McGee (Fibber)
Comments: Even though these tongue twisters are not nearly as long as the ones that led into musical numbers during the program's first ten years, Jim, who has been on that course often, runs a little short of breath by the time be crosses the last T.

Date: November 2, 1957
Title: Tax Problems: Cancelled Checks
Summary: While looking for checks in the attic, Fibber finds his vaudeville trunk which brings back memories of those days in show business.
Running Gag: Word confusion involving *liniment/spearfish/clingstone* (Fibber, Molly)
Comments: This example of word confusion is different from most of the others in that each word is wrong in its context and Fibber and Molly never get back to "What'd I say wrong in the first place?"

Date: November 2, 1957
Title: Tax Problems: Still Checking
Summary: The McGees move their search for cancelled checks into the den with no more success than they had in the attic.
Comments: We are expected to complete Fibber's recitation of souvenirs from the 1933 World's Fair. "A feather from…" the savvy listener finishes with "…one of Sally Rand's fans."

Date: November 2, 1957
Title: Tax Problems: Fears Audit

Summary: McGee thinks he may face time in jail for tax indiscretions Molly considers insignificant.
Comments: Just what source of income earned in 1956 would entitle Fibber to a generous refund of $243.58 is a mystery. After learning that there is a Filbert McGee in town, Molly must have had to fight off the urge to ask, "You mean there's another nut named McGee in Wistful Vista?"

Date: November 9, 1957
Title: Trip to Peoria: Molly Going Alone
Summary: Molly, feeling an urge to travel, decides to visit her sister in Peoria.
Comments: This is the first time Molly's sister is mentioned in the series. It is odd that the sister's name is never given though her husband's name is bandied about freely.

Date: November 9, 1957
Title: Trip to Peoria: Bachelor Life
Summary: Fibber makes several phone calls to set up a card game with old pals during Molly's absence.
Comments: Doc Gamble would seem a logical person for Fibber to call, but he might be *too* accessible for the point of the vignette is to contact old friends who are now out of touch with the bachelor lifestyle.

Date: November 9, 1957
Title: Trip to Peoria: Cooking Dinner
Summary: McGee attempts to show Molly how self-sufficient he can be while she is away by preparing a meal for her.
Running Gag: Tongue twister starting with Cabbage Head McGee (Fibber)
Comments: More amazing than what Fibber does to Molly's kitchen is the knowledge that he served two weeks as a cook in the army and yet we still won World War I.

Date: November 9, 1957
Title: Trip to Peoria: Chores
Summary: Fibber sews and vacuums to demonstrate he can do household chores while Molly is away.
Comments: If "idle hands make rubble" as Fibber claims, his busy hands are a demolition crew.

Date: November 9, 1957
Title: Trip to Peoria: Day of Departure
Summary: Molly gives Fibber last-minute instructions as she prepares to leave on her trip to see her sister.
Comments: Fibber says he is looking forward to "just one long gay round of nothing" during the time Molly is gone. Isn't that what he had been doing most of his life?

Date: November 10, 1957
Title: Football Game: Outfit
Summary: Although Molly scoffs at the idea, Fibber plans to wear knickers and a raccoon coat to a football game.
Running Gags: Tongue twister starting with Fourth Down McGee (Fibber), "'Tain't funny, Mrs. McGee" (Fibber)
Comments: Due to the brevity of these episodes, getting two of the running gags in one three-minute segment did not happen often. The McGees would have made quite a pair if Fibber wore his 1920s garb and Molly her pastel pedal pushers.

Date: November 10, 1957
Title: Football Game: Gear
Summary: Molly is astounded by all the equipment Fibber plans to take to the football game.
Comments: For once Fibber is ahead of his time for he would have made a fine tail-gater if he had been allowed to set up in the parking lot outside the stadium.

Date: November 10, 1957
Title: Football Game: At Stadium
Summary: The McGees discover they are the only people at the Wistful Vista Normal football game.
Comments: If the McGees had waited long enough at the stadium, Andy Griffith might have ambled by to tell them "What it was wasn't football."

Date: November 16, 1957
Title: Thanksgiving: Reverse Albino
Summary: Molly doubts that the bird Fibber brings home for Thanksgiving dinner is a turkey.
Comments: This episode borrows the same idea and closing line from the September 22, 1957 episode "Shooting a 'Dirty Pheasant.'"

Date: November 16, 1957
Title: Thanksgiving: Pilgrims
Summary: Fibber tells his own version of the Pilgrim story to Teeny.
Comments: Teeny seems to have regressed: in November she was in the first grade and in this episode she indicates she was told the real story of the Pilgrims by her kindergarten teacher, although she could have heard that story the previous year.

Date: November 16, 1957
Title: Thanksgiving: Guests Considered
Summary: The McGees wonder if they should invite friends for Thanksgiving dinner.

Running Gag: Tongue twister starting with Sage Dressing McGee (Fibber)
Comments: Doc Gamble's name is used with some frequency on these *Monitor* episodes, but it is not common to hear the Wimples mentioned.

Date: November 16, 1957
Title: Thanksgiving: Pilgrim Diet
Summary: Fibber wants Molly to make authentic Pilgrim trimmings to go with the turkey.
Comments: Even though Fibber gets most of the good lines in these vignettes with malapropisms and a generous share of the jokes, Molly is given some gems now and then like her "wild Indian" comeback in this exchange.

Date: November 17, 1957
Title: Atlas: Texas
Summary: Fibber daydreams about what his life would have been like if he had lived in Texas.
Comments: Jim and Marian slip naturally into the cowboy dialect as they did about once a season during the half-hour series.

Date: November 17, 1957
Title: Atlas: New York
Summary: Fibber daydreams that he is an advertising executive in New York City.
Comments: Koch skewers Madison Avenue by mimicking adspeak and parodying slogans.

Date: November 17, 1957
Title: Atlas: Hollywood
Summary: Fibber daydreams about the career he might have had as a movie producer.
Comments: There is a bit of the old verbal fireworks between Teeny and Fibber that used to occur frequently in the McGee living room, though time restrictions cut it short.

Date: November 17, 1957
Title: Atlas: Wyoming
Summary: Fibber daydreams about how he would have fared as a gunslinger in Wyoming.
Comments: In McGee's world, mailmen are left holding the bag if they don't duck and cover.

Date: November 17, 1957
Title: Atlas: Wisconsin
Summary: Fibber daydreams about what might have happened if he had settled in Wisconsin and became part of the Chicago mob scene.

Comments: For some reason the camel's hair coat stays with McGee through a number of his mental meanderings with just the hat changing to suggest his identity of the moment.

Date: November 24, 1957
Title: Bowling: Buying Ball
Summary: After McGee decides to take up bowling again, he selects a ball that puzzles Molly.
Running Gag: Tongue twister starting with Rose Bowl McGee (Fibber)
Comments: Listeners may be reminded of the June 1, 1943 episode in which Fibber also found a ball with a tight fit.

Date: November 24, 1957
Title: Bowling: No Score
Summary: Fibber tries to explain the scoring system of bowling to Teeny.
Comments: When Teeny asks, "Do you bowl, Mister?" and "Do you, really, honest?," she is really asking two questions to which the answers are "Yes" and "Some of the time."

Date: November 24, 1957
Title: Bowling: Practicing
Summary: Fibber takes several cracks at rolling balls down an alley.
Comments: Whether duck hunting or bowling the only safe place to be when Fibber is around is out of firing range.

Date: November 24, 1957
Title: Bowling: One for the Books
Summary: Fibber keeps rolling the bowling ball in the gutter while Molly gives him words of encouragement.
Running Gag: Word confusion involving *subconscientious/consternation/consolation* (Fibber, Molly)
Comments: McGee may be the only bowler in history to put scorer and pinboy to sleep.

Date: November 24, 1957
Title: Bowling: League Begins
Summary: McGee prepares to leave for his his first night of league bowling.
Running Gag: "'Tain't funny, McGee" (Molly)
Comments: Considering all the damage Fibber would likely have caused at the alley, the McGees probably saved money by paying Doc Gamble for a house call.

Date: December 1, 1957
Title: Birthday: Breakfast in Bed

Summary: Fibber makes breakfast in bed and a mess in the kitchen on Molly's birthday.
Comments: This appears to be two vignettes melded together for it runs longer than most of the three-minute skits. Action has to be accelerated for it would be a trick even for McGee to get locked out, start a fire in the kitchen, and bring a tray of unappetizing food up to Molly in less than five minutes.

Date: December 1, 1957
Title: Birthday: Gifts
Summary: Fibber gives Molly birthday presents that are all distinctively masculine gifts.
Comments: Underslung Teachers is one of those names that sneaks up from behind and hits listeners when they least expect it.

Date: December 1, 1957
Title: Birthday: Teeny's Gift
Summary: Teeny gives an apron to Fibber as Molly's birthday gift.
Comments: Teeny should not be amazed that women (and Jack Benny) remain stuck on thirty-nine for she has been fixed on five or six for decades.

Date: December 8, 1957
Title: Uncle Elrod: Eureka! Uranium
Summary: Fibber invites his long-lost uncle to visit after he discovers the old man has struck it rich.
Comments: As with Aunt Sarah, Fibber is anxious to meet a relative as a sign of the times (the dollar sign).

Date: December 8, 1957
Title: Uncle Elrod: Old Diary
Summary: Fibber reads his diary to find clues into Uncle Elrod's habits.
Comments: Fibber's childishness is obvious in his regular viewing of the adventures of the Mickey Mouse Club and Rin Tin Tin.

Date: December 8, 1957
Title: Uncle Elrod: Teeny Wants Nickel
Summary: When Teeny asks for money, Fibber lectures her on the dangers of avarice.
Comments: This is the first time there is a mention of parking meters in front of the McGee house which, listeners have always assumed, is in a residential neighborhood.

Date: December 8, 1957
Title: Uncle Elrod: Auto Magnate
Summary: Fibber explains to Molly his plan for using Uncle Elrod's money to start an automobile factory.

Comments: Sometimes Fibber's malapropisms have more truth in them than he realizes for his good crackpot idea will almost certainly mean putting money in a slinking fund that will cause confusion with finance companies and might bring about a term of incarceration for all parties involved.

Date: December 21, 1957
Title: Memory Course: Awaiting Lesson
Summary: Fibber impatiently waits for his first lesson from the Apex Memory School.
Comments: This is one episode in which Molly truly gets the last laugh.

Date: December 21, 1957
Title: Memory Course: First Lesson
Summary: Fibber demonstrates for Molly, in his convoluted fashion, how the association of ideas espoused in the initial lesson of his memory course is helping him remember dates and events.
Comments: Comedy can be educational as name-droppers Fibber and Molly prove. How many people today can name two heroes of the War of 1812 much less employ their names in casual conversation?

Date: December 21, 1957
Title: Memory Course: Grocery List
Summary: Rather than rely on a written list to remember the groceries Molly wants, Fibber invents a mnemonic saying to help him remember the items.
Comments: It's a good thing Molly didn't ask McGee to buy a prism for he likely would have dragged home someone named Roy G. Biv.

Date: December 21, 1957
Title: Memory Course: Repetition
Summary: Teeny has some news for Fibber that he does not let her deliver until he lectures her on thought processes.
Comments: This one episode in which misdirection is really the direction Koch intended to fill the time.

Date: December 21, 1957
Title: Memory Course: By the Numbers
Summary: Fibber assigns numbers to objects to help him remember them.
Comments: Fibber is given most of the dialogue but Molly hits the gong and wins the kewpie doll with her take on hypothetical bread.

Date: December 22, 1957
Title: Prosperity: Attic Treasures
Summary: The McGees take inventory of items in the attic they hope can be sold to make them wealthy.

Comments: It is a sad but true fact that the books and magazines, dress form, coat, and other relics Fibber and Molly spot in the attic are worth little more now than they were in 1957.

Date: December 22, 1957
Title: Prosperity: Double or Nothing
Summary: McGee buys products that he hopes to return because of the "double your money back" guarantees.
Comments: Molly's remark that "You're too early to be Santa's helper" does not faze Fibber at all for it was never too late for him to be his spouse's hindrance.

Date: December 22, 1957
Title: Prosperity: Polishing Car
Summary: Molly and Fibber wax the car so they will appear prosperous.
Comments: The McGees' Whippet seems more decrepit than Jack Benny's Maxwell.

Date: December 22, 1957
Title: Prosperity: Cuts Hair
Summary: Fibber cuts his hair so he can sell it for eighty cents.
Comments: After all these years Molly finally asks McGee the dollar question: "Why don't you go out and get a job?"

Date: December 22, 1957
Title: Prosperity: Stock Plan
Summary: Fibber tells Teeny how he plans to buy stocks with the money he has made during National Prosperity Week.
Comments: Koch reaches way out on a limb for the "somebody else's purse" chestnut he then hands to Teeny. On this occasion McGee, accustomed to talking through his hat, learns too late that he has been talking through Molly's hat.

Date: January 5, 1958
Title: Renewing Vows: Invite Friends
Summary: Fibber suggests to Molly that, in observance of their anniversary, they invite those who were present at their wedding for a reenactment of that ceremony.
Comments: The Fred Nitney gag that is unfinished is a bit of a letdown for when Fibber forgets he usually invents.

Date: January 5, 1958
Title: Renewing Vows: Music
Summary: Fibber and Molly consider their musical options for the upcoming ceremony.

Comments: It was nice of Buford, who played at the wedding in Peoria many years ago, to move to Wistful Vista so Fibber wouldn't have to make a long-distance call when he needed his services as an organist.

Date: January 5, 1958
Title: Renewing Vows: Flower Girl
Summary: Fibber asks Teeny to serve as flower girl at the wedding reenactment.
Comments: Teeny is in the same kind of rut she accuses Fibber of being in for she has remained the same age since the 1930s.

Date: January 5, 1958
Title: Renewing Vows: Second Honeymoon
Summary: Fibber and Molly consider different places to go on their second honeymoon after their wedding ceremony.
Comments: This is one episode surely not treasured by members of the Niagara Falls Chamber of Commerce who would find little to laugh at in the McGees' description of their seedy hotel room in that city.

Date: January 5, 1958
Title: Renewing Vows: Big Day Arrives
Summary: Fibber and Molly assess their wedding guests as they await the beginning of the ceremony.
Comments: After all these years Fibber's body temperature remains the same: he passed out cold at the first wedding and he gets cold feet at the second one.

Date: February 23, 1958
Title: Efficiency Course: Last Choice
Summary: After considering financial opportunities offered in a magazine, Fibber decides to take an efficiency course by mail.
Comments: Fibber's closing remark is one instance of McGee, not Molly, pointing the finger at the source of his problems: himself.

Date: February 23, 1958
Title: Efficiency Course: First Lesson
Summary: Fibber puts into action the lessons he learned from the correspondence course he received by walking and eating more efficiently.
Comments: Two hilarious images stay in the mind long after the vignette has ended: Fibber striding like a frightened dachshund and Conrad sleeping standing up in his Murphy bed.

Date: February 23, 1958
Title: Efficiency Course: Rapid Reading
Summary: Fibber demonstrates for Molly how to read for speed, not for sense.

Running Gag: Tongue twister starting with Read Head McGee (Fibber)
Comments: Talk about a laugh riot: the speed-reading bit breaks up Marian, Jim, and a third party.

Date: February 23, 1958
Title: Efficiency Course: Saving Energy
Summary: Fibber gives unsolicited advice to Molly on how to do her housework more efficiently.
Comments: It's a good thing Fibber does not accompany Molly to the movies for he would surely insist that, rather than buy popcorn in a box that would have to be opened, she have the hot popcorn poured directly into her purse which would still be open from her paying for the tickets because it would take too much energy for McGee to unbutton his pants pocket to get his wallet.

Date: February 23, 1958
Title: Efficiency Course: Fast Day
Summary: Fibber discovers that by doing things too efficiently he has finished his day's activities right after breakfast.
Comments: In the first portion of this vignette Molly makes some rather cutting remarks about Fibber that hit the mark but do not cause any bruises because of the spirit in which they are spoken and the kind-hearted person who speaks them.

Date: March 1, 1958
Title: Florida: Homesick
Summary: The McGees, unable to get used to Florida, yearn to return to Wistful Vista.
Comments: Outside of visits to see Aunt Sarah and Uncle Dennis and the Steel Seal adventure, this is a rare instance of Fibber and Molly being away from home.

Date: March 2, 1958
Title: Contest Fever: Considering Prizes
Summary: McGee examines the merits of prizes awarded in various contests.
Comments: Molly's stated belief that Fibber "can't get into any trouble entering contests" itself should win an award in a Famous Last Words competition.

Date: March 2, 1958
Title: Contest Fever: Boxes Galore
Summary: Fibber brings home products from the grocery store solely because they offer contests that require proofs of purchase.
Comments: A slogan that would be on the lips of those guests to whom the McGees serve Foxy Fido on crackers: "It keeps me barking for more."

Date: March 2, 1958
Title: Contest Fever: Coffee Slogan
Summary: Fibber hopes to win a new house by entering the Dixie Bell Instant Coffee Contest.
Comments: This is probably the only episode in the series in which the most amusing line is delivered in the first ten seconds. The poke at a pig is another gem that occurs when Fibber gets warmed up.

Date: March 2, 1958
Title: Contest Fever: No Soap
Summary: Fibber works on a soap contest entry until Teeny stops him with some startling news.
Comments: The name of Teeny's brother Helen is emphasized twice, yet no explanation for the unusual moniker is sought by Fibber nor given by Teeny.

Date: March 2, 1958
Title: Contest Fever: Wins Prize
Summary: Fibber is elated to learn he has won a contest, then deflated when he finds out what his prize is.
Comments: Knowing Fibber's luck, the chicken brooder heated by solar energy would just have a hole in the top to let the sunshine through. A rarity: Fibber dials a number instead of giving it to the operator.

Date: March 23, 1958
Title: YMCA Week: Remembering Feats
Summary: Fibber tells Molly about his athletic exploits.
Running Gag: Tongue twister starting with Tall Paul Small (Fibber)
Comments: Only Fibber could tire himself out talking after just getting out of bed to such an extent he has to take a nap to recuperate.

Date: March 23, 1958
Title: YMCA Week: Swimming
Summary: Fibber seems reluctant to show off his swimming talents for Molly at the YMCA pool.
Comments: Fibber may be the only swimmer who swallows more water out of the pool than he displaces.

Date: March 23, 1958
Title: YMCA Week: Medicine Ball
Summary: Teeny tells Fibber about her activities at the YMCA.
Comments: Fibber seems to realize at the end that Teeny's been "playing popsy" with him for decades.

Date: March 23, 1958
Title: YMCA Week: Lifting Weights
Summary: Fibber shows Molly how to lift a dumbbell, then needs help to get it back on the floor.
Comments: Another milestone for McGee: he becomes the first man to bequeath possessions while holding a hundred pounds over his head.

Date: March 29, 1958
Title: Valentine from Old Girlfriend
Summary: Fibber wonders if he should send a valentine to an old flame until he receives one from her with some surprising news.
Running Gag: "'Tain't funny, McGee" (Molly)
Comments: Fern, who crops up occasionally in conversations about the past, has definitely been growing where she was planted.

Date: October 5, 1958
Title: New Car: Molly Wants One
Summary: Molly suggests they buy a new auto while Fibber believes the old one they have is adequate.
Comments: Fibber's sense of time is as awful as Jim's sense of timing is admirable. McGee wants to rush out immediately to buy an ice-making machine he does not need, yet he is willing to wait twenty-five years to accumulate enough green stamps to pay for a car to replace the broken-down vehicle in the garage.

Date: October 5, 1958
Title: New Car: Trade Offers
Summary: McGee calls dealers to determine how much his car is worth.
Comments: For a change Fibber, the frequent malcontent, is quite optimistic in this episode, indicating that oil on clothes will evaporate in time, leaving just a black, greasy scum and boldly declaring, in so many words, that there is nothing wrong with the old car that a new body and motor replacement cannot cure.

Date: October 5, 1958
Title: New Car: Auto Show
Summary: The McGees consider car options as they look over the new models at an auto show.
Comments: Koch is prescient by creating a car called the Firebird nine years before Pontiac rolled out its first example of that model. He also brilliantly satirizes the exotic names auto manufacturers invent for their car finishes and interior trim.

Date: October 25, 1958
Title: Dog Week: Past Pets
Summary: McGee tells Molly about the dogs of his youth.
Comments: Old Fireball, another dog from Fibber's past, is not mentioned here. It has been a while since McGee spun a tall tale and his yarn about Old Sport fits the bill.

Date: October 25, 1958
Title: Dog Week: New Pet?
Summary: Fibber considers buying a dog until Molly talks him out of it.
Comments: Again Molly proves to be the sensible one who is more far-sighted than her husband.

Date: October 25, 1958
Title: Dog Week: Poem
Summary: To commemorate National Dog Week Fibber composes an appropriate poem.
Comments: Fibber's way with poems is like his talent for spinning tall tales: he can think them up faster than he can recite them back to his audience.

Date: October 25, 1958
Title: Dog Week: Takes Walk
Summary: Fibber discusses dogs with Teeny when he meets her while out for a walk.
Comments: Teeny's male dog Margaret, mentioned here after a considerable absence, would be a natural companion for her brother Helen.

Date: October 25, 1958
Title: Dog Week: Dog at Door
Summary: McGee lets in a dog who quickly shows he is not McGee's best friend.
Comments: It is unfortunate there are no episodes about National Cantaloupe Week which Fibber mentions here for it would have been a natural fit for a tongue twister starting with Melon Head McGee.

Date: November 16, 1958
Title: Hi Fi: Getting the Facts
Summary: Molly explains high fidelity to a bewildered Fibber.
Comments: It is typical McGee behavior to be completely ignorant of a subject that he does not want to have anything to do with as he does here and then take up that subject as a hobby which he does in the next vignette.

Date: November 16, 1958
Title: Hi Fi: Buys a Set
Summary: Fibber plans to build a high fidelity set with the components he purchased.

Running Gag: Tongue twister starting with Flower Bulb McGee (Fibber)
Summary: Molly proves to be a prophet when she says, "More power to you."

Date: November 16, 1958
Title: Hi Fi: Record Store
Summary: Fibber cannot find any records at the store that are to his liking.
Comments: Despite his efforts to update the sound system in his home, Fibber reveals himself to be an old-fashioned prude.

Date: November 16, 1958
Title: Hi Fi: Record Purchase
Summary: McGee brings home a record to use on his new set but does not get a chance to play it.
Comments: As often happens, in the end Fibber finds that his troubles are behind him.

Date: November 16, 1958
Title: Hi-Fi: Classical Music
Summary: Fibber explains classical music to Teeny until she gives him some disturbing news.
Comments: The comparison of Molly to a barge is an uncomplimentary simile that misfires.

Date: November 22, 1958
Title: Letter Writing: Personal Mail
Summary: McGee is disappointed when the mail arrives with no personal letters for him.
Comments: The Apex Company has manufactured a number of products Fibber has ordered over the years. McGee's luck with them matches the fortunes of Wile E. Coyote with the Acme firm.

Date: November 22, 1958
Title: Letter Writing: Delivery Explained
Summary: Fibber clears up some misconceptions Teeny has about postal delivery.
Comments: Of all the excuses Molly gives for her departure before Teeny enters, fumigating Fibber's old suit is one of the least believable. Any fabric subject to McGee's cigar smoke over the years needs extermination, not fumigation.

Date: November 22, 1958
Title: Letter Writing: Aunt Sarah
Summary: Fibber writes a very factual letter to Aunt Sarah.
Comments: Naturally the programs Fibber has been watching are on NBC.

Date: November 22, 1958
Title: Letter Writing: To Friends
Summary: Fibber tries to think of friends he can write to during National Letter Writing Week.
Comments: Most people keep relics from the 1920s in the attic, but apparently at McGee Manor every drawer is an attic.

Date: November 22, 1958
Title: Letter Writing: Fred Nitney
Summary: McGee considers writing a letter to old pal Fred Nitney.
Comments: For once Molly throws Fibber off his narrative track which causes him to agree to something he quickly recants.

Date: November 23, 1958
Title: Poetry: Seize the Day
Summary: Fibber wants people in Wistful Vista to celebrate World Poetry Day.
Running Gag: Tongue twister starting with Type Writer McGee (Fibber)
Comments: This is the first time McGee's Uncle Otto is mentioned on the program.

Date: November 23, 1958
Title: Poetry: Preparing to Write
Summary: McGee finds it taxing as he assembles the tools necessary to write a poem.
Comments: The answer to the question "Why would anyone keep ink in such a hard-to-reach place as the top shelf of a bookcase?" is simple: so Fibber can climb on the chair with the cracked leg which will collapse under him so he will take a rest that will close the bit.

Date: November 23, 1958
Title: Poetry: Suffering
Summary: After reading that the great poets experienced deprivation, McGee tries hard to make his life miserable.
Comments: The line about the scholarship committee at Harvard holding Fibber's failure to finish high school against him is the icing on the cake in this vignette.

Date: November 23, 1958
Title: Poetry: Phoning Poets
Summary: Fibber calls Henry Wadsworth Longfellow and a Japanese poet on World Poetry Day.
Comments: As Shelley Berman and Bob Newhart also demonstrated, hilarity results from *not* hearing what the person on the other end of the phone is saying.

Date: November 23, 1958
Title: Poetry: Composing Poem
Summary: At bedtime Fibber writes "Ode to a Bird."
Comments: Something else owed to a bird: an apology.

Date: January 4, 1959
Title: Leaves: Equipment
Summary: Fibber plans to take many items Molly considers unnecessary for just a drive in the country.
Comments: The line of conversation about the camera and the thermos gets Fibber nowhere, yet he seems content to at least be back where he started.

Date: January 4, 1959
Title: Leaves: Color Change
Summary: Fibber explains to Teeny how leaves change color in the fall.
Comments: In the earlier episodes Teeny would have countered Fibber's nonsense with a scientific explanation, but time restrictions would not permit one of her lengthy comebacks.

Date: January 4, 1959
Title: Leaves: Final Preparations
Summary: Fibber loads the car with last-minute items preparatory to leaving for a drive in the country.
Running Gag: Tongue twister starting with Fall Guy McGee (Fibber)
Comments: Finally an excuse for years of inactivity: Fibber burned himself out *working* before the age of thirty.

Date: January 4, 1959
Title: Leaves: Drive
Summary: Molly enjoys the fall foliage while Fibber is concerned with other matters.
Comments: This time Fibber is preoccupied with food, cars, and himself.

Date: January 4, 1959
Title: Leaves: Photographs
Summary: The McGees study the photos Fibber took on their drive in the country.
Comments: The snapshots McGee took suggest he has a nose for news, a fetish for feet, and a martyr for a wife.

Date: February 14, 1959
Title: Blizzard: Big Wind of 1914
Summary: Fibber tells Teeny about a powerful storm from his youth.
Comments: Even tall tales can be taller so Fibber stretches the temperature twenty-one degrees in hopes of astonishing Teeny.

Date: February 14, 1959
Title: Blizzard: Inventory
Summary: The McGees take stock of their foodstuffs in anticipation of a blizzard Fibber fears is headed their way.
Comments: Sometimes even resourceful Fibber cannot think of of an explanation for his silly behavior so he just laughs it off and so should we. The eskimos living in town are a long way from their native land, but no matter how far people stray from home when they settle in Wistful Vista they end up near 14th and Oak.

Date: April 4, 1959
Title: Burbank: Celebrate Birth Date
Summary: After discovering that it is Luther Burbank's birthday, McGee wants to do something appropriate to commemorate the occasion.
Comments: Burbank was born March 7, 1849. If Fibber feels guilty because he has nothing to do on *this* day, his load of guilt for being idle up to this point would fill confessionals from the cozy cafes of Capri to the crowded corners of Calcutta. Marian cannot suppress a peachy giggle at the end.

Date: April 4, 1959
Title: Burbank: Flower Pots
Summary: McGee's experiments with weeds are not welcomed by Molly.
Comments: Fibber's enthusiasm over a new kind of weed-killer is not going to come as news to those who have been digging them out of the ground as he did.

Date: April 4, 1959
Title: Burbank: Planting Seeds
Summary: Fibber decides to put in a garden to celebrate Luther Burbank's birthday.
Comments: McGee vividly demonstrates how thoughtless he can be as he discards Molly's hint about buying her a bouquet, then makes her get all the tools and accompany him outside on a cold day.

Date: April 4, 1959
Title: Girl Scout Week
Summary: Fibber's attention veers from plants to people when he decides to do something to observe National Girl Scout Week.
Comments: Girl Scout Week always begins on a Sunday and includes March 12, the actual birthday of the Girls Scouts of America, so that week in 1959 would have commenced March 8 and ended March 14. As usual, whenever Fibber has time on his hands, it means more time on her feet for Molly.

Appendix A

ALPHABETICAL LIST OF EPISODES

Acting School Principal
September 6, 1937

Ad for Renting House
February 11, 1954

Advice Column
June 13, 1939

Advising Les after Accident
December 21, 1954

Aids Molly's Luncheon Plans
March 19, 1954

Alice on the Phone
April 17, 1945

Alice's Boyfriend
May 9, 1944

All You Can Eat
April 15, 1952

Amateur Show
October 14, 1935

Amusement Park
June 17, 1941

Anniversary of First Meeting
February 9, 1955

Anniversary of First Meeting (Repeat)
February 10, 1956

Antique Bookend
September 8, 1954

Antique Bookend (Repeat)
October 7, 1955

Antique Furniture
April 4, 1939

Antique Vase
March 13, 1951

Ants in Doc's House
November 2, 1943

Apple Crop
October 28, 1947

Architect McGee
November 20, 1945

Art Class
May 8, 1951

Art Class (Repeat)
February 24, 1953

At Aunt Sarah's
January 3, 1950

At the Racetrack
September 28, 1936

Atlas: Hollywood
November 17, 1957

Atlas: New York
November 17, 1957

Atlas: Texas
November 17, 1957

Atlas: Wisconsin
November 17, 1957

Atlas: Wyoming
November 17, 1957

Attic Mystery Solved
February 18, 1954

Auditioning for New Singer
November 8, 1937

Aunt Jennie
November 21, 1950

Aunt Sarah's Portrait
May 2, 1944

Author McGee
January 26, 1943

Auto License
February 9, 1943

Auto Show
October 31, 1939

Auto Show and an Appraisal
October 11, 1937

Auto Show with Midget Car Race
November 7, 1955

Autumn Drive
November 25, 1953

Average Wistful Vista Couple
October 12, 1955

Aviation Show
June 4, 1946

Avoiding Clifford Parker
February 13, 1956

Avoiding Knucklehead Swayze
December 5, 1954

Avoiding Parking Ticket
February 22, 1956

Avoids Scrubbing the Back Porch
September 23, 1935

Avoids the Elks
March 30, 1955

Babysitting Teeny
January 14, 1941

Babysitting Teeny and Michael
April 21, 1955

Back from Twin Rock Falls
September 5, 1954

Back from Vacation
October 1, 1940

Back from Vacation to Alaska
September 30, 1941

Back Step
March 4, 1952

Backyard Mischief
June 12, 1955

Bad Luck with Mirrors
October 19, 1943

Bad Luck with Mirrors (Shorter Version)
November 30, 1953

Bakes a Cake
May 20, 1941

Bank Night at the Movies
December 12, 1950

Bank Robbery
December 28, 1955

Bank Statement Examined
May 10, 1955

Barbeque
June 10, 1954

Barbershop Quartet
April 30, 1946

Bargain Day at Bon Ton
April 11, 1955

Bargaining for Christmas Tree
December 22, 1953

Barometer
May 11, 1943

Baseball Boasts Questioned
June 22, 1955

Baseball Cologne
May 18, 1948

Bean Contest
January 8, 1946

Beauty Contest Judge
April 24, 1955

Beauty Parlor Palaver
May 23, 1944

Beauty Parlor Palaver
(Shorter Version)
October 24, 1955

Beekeeper's Guide
August 23, 1954

Bee Problems
May 24, 1955

Bees Removed from Backyard
May 26, 1955

Belongings All Over Living Room
January 23, 1951

Belt for the Belly
May 23, 1955

Bergen and McCarthy Visit
November 11, 1941

Beulah Is Hired
March 14, 1944

Bicycle Ride and Cannibal Tale
October 7, 1935

Bills and a Budget
April 18, 1939

Billy Mills in the Hospital
January 12, 1943

Biography for Luncheon
October 15, 1953

Birthday Dinner for Molly
October 23, 1951

Birthday Forgotten by Friends
January 22, 1954

Birthday: Breakfast in Bed
December 1, 1957

Birthday: Gifts
December 1, 1957

Birthday: Teeny's Gift
December 1, 1957

Black Eye
November 12, 1940

Black Market Meat
April 27, 1943

Blizzard
January 27, 1942

Blizzard: Big Wind of 1914
February 14, 1959

Blizzard: Inventory
February 14, 1959

Boating at Dugan's Lake
June 24, 1954

Bob Stanley's Trial Concludes
July 2, 1954

Bone Verified
July 13, 1954

Boomerang
March 9, 1956

Boomer's Suitcase
March 3, 1942

Borrows Uppy's Car
May 18, 1943

Bowling Ball
June 1, 1943

Bowling or Canasta?
December 2, 1952

Bowling Substitute
November 16, 1948

Bowling: Buying Ball
November 24, 1957

Bowling: League Begins
November 24, 1957

Bowling: No Score
November 24, 1957

Bowling: One for the Books
November 24, 1957

Bowling: Practicing
November 24, 1957

Braided Rug
February 12, 1952

Breakfast in Bed for Molly
March 2, 1943

Breakfast in Bed or in Kitchen?
February 6, 1951

Breakfast in Bed or in Kitchen?
(Repeat)
March 3, 1953

Bridge Game
December 16, 1935

Briefcase Bronson
May 1, 1945

Broken Card Table
March 9, 1948

Broken Rib?
November 21, 1944

Broken Window, Part 1
January 13, 1942

Broken Window, Part 2
January 20, 1942

Bucking Bronco Contest
December 14, 1936

Buckshot McGee
March 18, 1952

Building a Barbeque
April 2, 1954

Building a Fireplace
February 7, 1938

Building Fire in Fireplace
November 8, 1955

Bull Moran
October 8, 1946

Bullets Brannigan
March 26, 1946

Burbank: Celebrate Birth Date
April 4, 1959

Burbank: Flower Pots
April 4, 1959

Burbank: Planting Seeds
April 4, 1959

Burglar at Large
November 2, 1953

Burglar Nabbed
November 3, 1953

Burglary at 85 Wistful Vista?
October 18, 1955

Buried Money in Backyard
September 20, 1937

Buried Package Mystery
February 7, 1956

Business Cards Give Fibber the Business
May 11, 1955

Business is Dull
March 11, 1954

Businessman McGee
January 4, 1944

Businessmen's Symphony
June 12, 1951

Busy Day at Walt's Malt Shop
May 22, 1955

Busy Sunday
August 29, 1954

Butler Gildersleeve
December 26, 1939

Button Lost
April 8, 1954

Buying a Classic Book
March 21, 1956

Buying a New Suit
February 4, 1941

Buying a Parakeet
October 7, 1953

Buying a Puppy
January 13, 1953

Buying a Suit for Luncheon
October 14, 1953

Buying Groceries for Trip
November 12, 1953

Buying Groceries for Trip (Repeat)
November 10, 1955

Buying Vegetables at Roadside Stand
November 25, 1935

Buys a Homburg
March 22, 1955

Cab Driver McGee
March 28, 1955

Cab Ride to Airport
March 27, 1955

Call Comes Through
December 11, 1953

Call from Executives Club
October 12, 1953

Call from Washington, D.C.
December 8, 1953

Call Missed
December 9, 1953

Calling for Bee Relief
May 25, 1955

Camera Left on Train
September 29, 1942

Campfire in Fireplace
February 29, 1944

Candid Camera Fiend
December 2, 1953

Candy from Joe
March 11, 1952

Cannery Job Offer
April 25, 1944

Canoeing
May 31, 1949

Cappy Visits the McGees
January 27, 1955

Cappy Visits the McGees (Repeat)
January 27, 1956

Captain of Ship
August 3, 1936

Car Hit While Parked
June 21, 1955

Car Missing a Fender
April 1, 1941

Car Reported Stolen
January 16, 1940

Car Reported Stolen Again
March 5, 1946

Car Trouble
April 18, 1950

Car Trouble (Repeat)
March 10, 1953

Carnival
April 22, 1947

Carnival Head Man
May 20, 1952

Cash Register at Kremer's
April 5, 1949

Cat Matter Resolved
September 7, 1954

Cat Matter Resolved (Repeat)
February 2, 1956

Cat Under the Porch
October 14, 1947

Cat with Three Owners
September 6, 1954

Cat with Three Owners (Repeat)
February 1, 1956

Catching Flight to Philadelphia
May 31, 1954

Cats
June 2, 1953

Census Taker
April 4, 1950

Chagrined After Contest
January 26, 1954

Chamber of Commerce Presidency
December 17, 1940

Changes Name to Homer K. Frink
May 4, 1943

Changes Name to Ronald McGee
March 25, 1941

Chaperones
November 27, 1951

Charity Bazaar
October 10, 1939

Charity Ends at Home
May 16, 1944

Checkroom Attendants
March 16, 1936

Checkup Fibber Avoids
May 27, 1952

Checkup for Molly
March 6, 1951

Cheering a Shut-In
January 16, 1955

Cheer-Up Visit
January 18, 1956

Chicken Barbeque
September 19, 1950

Chicken Soup for Fibber
December 28, 1936

Chili Recipe Found
May 16, 1955

Chili Sauce
November 9, 1943

Chimes Are Stuck
May 19, 1954

Chinchilla Coat
February 27, 1940

Chopping Down the Oak Tree
November 27, 1945

Chowder for Lecturer
October 6, 1955

Christmas at Home
December 25, 1953

Christmas Card from Elizabeth
December 21, 1948

Christmas Cards Confusion
May 3, 1955

Christmas Decorations
December 20, 1949

Christmas Fund
November 20, 1953

Christmas Shopping
December 9, 1935

Christmas Shopping at the Bon Ton
December 16, 1953

Christmas Shopping for Gamble
December 12, 1955

Christmas Shopping for Nephew
December 20, 1938

Christmas Shopping for Teeny
December 20, 1954

Christmas Sign
December 21, 1955

Cigar Ashes
October 26, 1943

Cigar Ashes (Shorter Version)
January 21, 1954

Circular Mailers
January 9, 1951

Circus
May 28, 1940

Circus Day
May 9, 1950

Citizen X Contest Continues
January 18, 1954

Citizen X Contest Goes Airborne
January 20, 1954

Citizen X Found
January 25, 1954

Citizenship Test
June 3, 1947

City Council Vacancy
February 7, 1950

Civil Defense
June 23, 1953

Civil Defense Speech at School
February 7, 1955

Civil Defense Speech Preparations
February 6, 1955

Claiming the Moon
January 25, 1956

Clay Investment Scheme
November 25, 1941

Clay Morgan for City Council
May 14, 1946

Cleaning Lady
December 14, 1953

Cleaning Closet for Millicent's Visit
June 5, 1945

Cleaning the Hall Closet
February 2, 1943

Cleaning the Living Room
August 10, 1954

Clobberhead Jones
May 11, 1954

Clothing Drive for European Relief
March 27, 1945

Club Banquet
February 21, 1939

Coffee Slogan Contest
May 7, 1954

Coffee Table Has to Go
January 12, 1956

Coffee Table Purchase
January 11, 1956

Coffeemaker Broken by Flash
May 13, 1954

Collecting Doc's Bills
February 18, 1947

College of Santa Clausing
November 29, 1937

Commission in WACs
October 12, 1943

Community Chest Bazaar
October 18, 1949

Community Chest Rally in Omaha
October 9, 1951

Concert Tickets
October 25, 1949

Consolation Prize
January 16, 1956

Contest Fever: Boxes Galore
March 2, 1958

Contest Fever: Coffee Slogan
March 2, 1958

Contest Fever: Considering Prizes
March 2, 1958

Contest Fever: No Soap
March 2, 1958

Contest Fever: Wins Prize
March 2, 1958

Converting Furnace
October 13, 1942

Convicts in the House?
May 30, 1939

Cool House Attracts a Crowd
July 30, 1954

Costume for Party
October 21, 1954

Counselor McGee
November 10, 1942

Counterfeit $5.00 Bill?
June 23, 1954

Country Club Dance
December 28, 1948

Courteous McGee
February 10, 1953

Courtroom of McGees
October 21, 1935

Cousin Ernest
October 23, 1945

Cousin Gerry Arrives
November 9, 1954

Cousin Gerry Coming to Visit
November 8, 1954

Crackshot McGee and Swordfish Tale
July 29, 1935

Crime Solver McGee
February 3, 1936

Cuckoo Clock
November 8, 1949

Curator Visits
July 14, 1954

Cutting Christmas Tree
December 16, 1941

Cutting Down Suit
January 5, 1943

Cutting Down the Oak Tree
April 30, 1954

Cutting Firewood
January 17, 1950

Daily Activity Guide
June 6, 1955

Dalmatian Trouble
March 17, 1955

Dalmatian Trouble (Repeat)
March 16, 1956

Dance Hall
September 14, 1936

Date on the Calendar
February 8, 1949

Date with Al Bennington
June 16, 1953

Dates for Cousin Gerry
November 10, 1954

Day at the Office
September 1, 1954

Deal with Mr. Carstairs
June 19, 1945

Decorating the Tree
December 23, 1953

Delivering a Cake
April 21, 1953

Delivering Packages with Molly
December 19, 1954

Delivering Packages with Wimple (I)
December 15, 1954

Delivering Packages with Wimple (II)
December 16, 1954

Delivering the Mail
April 11, 1939

Demonstrates Steel Seal at Home
May 28, 1954

Demonstrates Steel Seal in Shipyard
June 3, 1954

Deputy for a Day
February 16, 1956

Detective McGee
December 20, 1937

Detective McGee After Prowler
December 11, 1951

Dial Phone
February 8, 1954

Diamond Ring for $20.00
February 1, 1944

Dictionary in the Closet
March 5, 1940

Diet Contest Concludes
January 18, 1955

Diet Pills
January 17, 1955

Diet Plan
January 12, 1955

Dieters Weaken
January 13, 1955

Dining and Dancing
October 20, 1953

Dining Out
January 25, 1944

Dining Out with Doc Gamble
February 19, 1946

Dinner at LaTrivia's House
December 5, 1950

Dinner at Ritz Vista
September 20, 1954

Dinner Wager
January 5, 1956

Dinner with Miss Tremaine
October 29, 1946

Dirtying and Cleaning the House
November 14, 1954

Discount Club
October 5, 1954

Disposing of Christmas Tree
February 5, 1954

District Attorney Calls
October 11, 1954

Diverts Freeway for Himself
March 14, 1956

Diverts Freeway for Old Timer
March 13, 1956

Doc Gamble Day
March 15, 1949

Doc Gamble to Elope
December 1, 1954

Doc Orders Fibber to Rest
May 5, 1955

Doc's Christmas Card
December 22, 1955

Doc's Present to McGee
December 25, 1945

Dog License
March 19, 1940

Dog Trainer/Tutor Mixup
January 13, 1936

Dog Week: Dog at Door
October 25, 1958

Dog Week: New Pet?
October 25, 1958

Dog Week: Past Pets
October 25, 1958

Dog Week: Poem
October 25, 1958

Dog Week: Takes Walk
October 25, 1958

Doing the Laundry
January 10, 1938

Donating Portrait
January 26, 1955

Door Chimes
December 23, 1941

Drafted
March 18, 1941

Dream Disturbs McGee
November 30, 1954

Dress Mix-Up at Cleaners
May 31, 1955

Dress Mix-Up at Cleaners (Repeat)
March 2, 1956

Drill for Christmas Present
December 26, 1955

Drive-In Theater
July 16, 1954

Driving Doc on House Calls
April 19, 1955

Driving Lesson
November 13, 1945

Driving to Football Game
October 29, 1940

Driving Used Car Home
May 2, 1939

Duck Calls Irritate Neighbors
November 3, 1954

Duck Hunting Invitation
November 10, 1953

Duck Hunting Plans
December 2, 1947

Duck Hunting with Gamble
October 31, 1944

Duck Hunting with Gamble and LaTrivia
November 13, 1951

Duck Hunting with LaTrivia
November 3, 1942

Duck Hunting with Molly
September 22, 1957

Duck Hunting, Finally
November 17, 1953

Duck Hunting, Finally (Repeat)
November 15, 1955

Dude Ranch
October 12, 1936

Dying Easter Eggs
April 16, 1954

Early Christmas Shopping
December 7, 1948

Early 50th Anniversary
March 6, 1945

Early to Bed
February 18, 1941

Early to Bed After Hunting
November 19, 1953

Early to Bed After Hunting (Repeat)
November 17, 1955

Easter Dress
March 23, 1948

Eating Pancakes Downtown
October 17, 1954

Efficiency Course: Fast Day
February 23, 1958

Efficiency Course: First Lesson
February 23, 1958

Efficiency Course: Last Choice
February 23, 1958

Efficiency Course: Rapid Reading
February 23, 1958

Efficiency Course: Saving Energy
February 23, 1958

Efficiency in the Kitchen
April 14, 1955

Efficiency in the Kitchen (Repeat)
March 23, 1956

Egyptian Good Luck Ring
February 13, 1940

Eighteenth Wedding Anniversary
August 31, 1936

Electric Bill
January 4, 1956

Elevator Ups and Downs
February 21, 1956

Elks Club Dance
April 25, 1950

Elks Club Mortgage
March 8, 1949

Elope on Fifteenth Anniversary
September 12, 1939

Employment Agency
June 22, 1936

Encyclopedia Salesman
March 2, 1936

Envelope Swindle
November 23, 1943

Everyone Nice to Fibber
February 6, 1940

Exam Taken by Fibber and Gamble
June 7, 1955

Examining the Water
October 15, 1946

Exchanging Buttons
April 9, 1954

Exchanging Ice Bucket
December 28, 1953

Exchanging Wimple's Gift
December 16, 1952

Expecting Ronald Colman
November 12, 1946

Experiments in Garage
May 24, 1954

Express Company Robbery
February 20, 1951

Fabulous Adventures Article
February 20, 1956

Faking an Illness
September 26, 1939

Fall House Cleaning
October 21, 1941

Family Tree
October 20, 1942

Favor from Governor
September 28, 1954

Feeling Peppy
October 7, 1954

Fibber's Tune
June 1, 1948

Fifteenth Anniversary Special
September 13, 1949

Fifty Thousand Dollar Deal
October 7, 1941

Finance Company
November 28, 1939

Finds a Watch
December 31, 1940

Fire Alarm Box
April 13, 1948

Fire Commissioner McGee
October 14, 1941

Fire in Garage
May 25, 1954

Fire Prevention
June 14, 1954

Fire Truck
April 19, 1949

Fireball McGee
May 21, 1946

First Meeting in Cribs
September 1, 1957

Fish Bait
June 5, 1951

Fish Dinner
September 27, 1949

Fish Fry for Friends
September 5, 1939

Fishing Bet with Gamble
May 11, 1948

Fishing License
May 30, 1944

Fishing Trip with Gamble and Wimple
August 30, 1954

Fishing with Automatic Reel
May 2, 1950

Fishing With No Tall Tales
June 30, 1953

Five-Dollar Loan Letter
October 13, 1955

Five Dollars Given or Borrowed?
February 28, 1955

Five Tons of Coal
December 3, 1940

Fixing Christmas Toys
December 24, 1946

Fixing Doc's Car
April 6, 1948

Fixing the Radio
March 20, 1945

Fixing Toaster
January 19, 1954

Fix-It McGee
December 30, 1941

Flash Offered to Fibber
May 20, 1954

Flight to Philadelphia
June 1, 1954

Floorwalker McGee
December 4, 1951

Florida: Homesick
March 1, 1958

Flowers from Ralph
January 18, 1944

Flying a Kite
March 12, 1946

Flying Lessons
August 17, 1936

Flying Saucer
March 28, 1950

Football Game Anniversary
October 7, 1947

Football Game: At Stadium
November 10, 1957

Football Game: Gear
November 10, 1957

Football Game: Outfit
November 10, 1957

Football Play
November 19, 1946

Football Ringer
November 15, 1937

Footstool
March 10, 1942

Forgets Where Car Is Parked
August 27, 1954

Forgotten Dinner Invitation
October 3, 1954

Forgotten Tune Title
May 12, 1955

Forgotten Wedding Anniversary
May 28, 1946

Formal Party for Doc Gamble
July 23, 1954

Fortune Told and Furniture Tale
August 12, 1935

Forty Percent Discount
December 9, 1941

Forty Thousand Copies of "Partly True"
April 22, 1954

Four Dollar Debt
October 24, 1944

Four Dollar Debt (Shorter Version)
February 1, 1954

Frank Ingram Leaves
February 10, 1954

Fred Nitney in Town
January 6, 1953

Freeway Ride
April 15, 1954

Frog Business Concluded
September 23, 1954

Frog Hunting
September 21, 1954

Frogs in Bathroom
September 22, 1954

Frozen Water Pipes
February 14, 1939

Fruit Punch
November 11, 1952

Fruitcake
December 16, 1947

Fudge
November 6, 1945

Fur Coat Dispute
January 10, 1956

Fur Coat Purchase
January 9, 1956

Furnace Needs Repair
February 10, 1955

Gamble's Painting
June 15, 1954

Games for the Army
May 6, 1941

Garbage Disposal
March 6, 1956

Gardening Urge
April 5, 1937

Gas Bill
April 10, 1951

Gas Price War
November 7, 1954

Gas Price War (Repeat)
December 9, 1955

Gas Rationing
December 1, 1942

Gasoline Saver Gimmick
September 26, 1955

General Store
April 11, 1950

Get Out the Vote
November 5, 1940

Getting $7.00 Loan Back
February 24, 1948

Getting Bald
March 21, 1939

Getting in Shape
November 24, 1942

Getting Out of Lease
July 5, 1937

Getting Photo Taken
June 10, 1941

Getting Weighed
November 4, 1947

Gift Certificate for $10.00
December 30, 1947

Gift from Aunt Sarah
January 2, 1945

Gifts for Wives Switched
March 16, 1955

Gifts for Wives Switched (Repeat)
February 24, 1956

Gildersleeve as Supper Guest
December 29, 1942

Gildersleeve Girdle Quiz Show
January 23, 1940

Gildersleeve Helps Pack
June 25, 1940

Gildersleeve Returns
March 28, 1944

Gildersleeve's Diary
October 22, 1940

Gildersleeve's Ladder
May 27, 1941

Gildersleeve's Party
October 24, 1939

Gildersleeve's Suit
January 9, 1940

Girl Scout Week
April 4, 1959

Gives Up Cigars
October 8, 1940

Gives Up Cigars Briefly
November 30, 1955

Glasses
April 25, 1939

Going to Be Rich
May 19, 1942

Going Western
March 13, 1945

Golden Rule
June 25, 1954

Golden Rule Spreads
June 29, 1954

Golf Match Begins
April 26, 1955

Gold Match Concludes
April 28, 1955

Golf Match Continues in the Country
April 27, 1955

Good Deeds
May 3, 1949

Gossip Book
January 20, 1953

Gossip Column
September 19, 1939

Government Job Recommendation
December 14, 1954

Governor's Pal
December 11, 1945

Grammar Improvement
May 6, 1947

Great Lakes Esposition
July 27, 1936

Grizzly Bear Article in Magazine
October 28, 1952

Grocery Budget
April 17, 1951

Grocery Budget Scheme
February 3, 1956

Grumpy McGee at Christmastime
December 22, 1942

Guest House
March 14, 1950

Guilty Secret
May 5, 1953

Haircut
June 2, 1955

Haircut (Repeat)
March 1, 1956

Halloween Party
October 28, 1935

Ham on the Radio
July 19, 1954

Hamburger Stand
March 7, 1939

Hand Stuck in Bottle
January 28, 1941

Handcuffed
December 14, 1943

Handwriting Analysis
February 15, 1944

Hanging a Picture
April 23, 1940

Hanging Aunt Sarah's Picture
October 5, 1953

Hanging Curtains and Shoe Tree Tale
September 16, 1935

Happy Face McGee
June 8, 1943

Happy Icing on the Cake
June 13, 1955

Hat Bet
November 24, 1954

Health Foods
April 23, 1946

Heat Wave
July 28, 1954

Hector Howell
May 26, 1953

Heir to Estate with Oil Wells
December 27, 1937

Helping Teeny's Parents
April 20, 1955

Hi Fi: Buys a Set
November 16, 1958

Hi Fi: Classical Music
November 16, 1958

Hi Fi: Getting the Facts
November 16, 1958

Hi Fi: Record Purchase
November 16, 1958

Hi Fi: Record Store
November 16, 1958

Hiawatha
November 7, 1939

Hiccups
May 4, 1954

Hiding Place
December 20, 1955

Hike at Dugan's Woods
April 21, 1954

Hip Boots
October 10, 1944

Hiring a Lawyer
April 13, 1954

Hitchhiking Bureau
May 1, 1951

Hoarse from Practicing Speech
October 16, 1953

Hobby Show Director
June 16, 1954

Hobby Show Entrants
June 17, 1954

Hobby Show Opens
June 18, 1954

Hole in One
May 15, 1951

Hole in the Wall
December 27, 1954

Home Movies
February 17, 1942

Home Power Plant
March 25, 1947

Homecoming after Lux
April 9, 1940

Homecoming after Making Movie
July 19, 1937

Homer Vickery
June 17, 1947

Homework
September 29, 1957

Horoscope
March 16, 1943

Horoscope Keeps Fibber Inside
April 8, 1952

Horse in the Garage
February 24, 1942

Hospital Room
March 30, 1936

Hot Dogs and a Blowout
April 30, 1935

House Almost Rented
February 12, 1954

House Alterations
January 21, 1947

House Finally Rented
February 17, 1954

House for Ole
May 10, 1949

Houseboat on Dugan's Lake
June 26, 1945

Housing Survey
May 8, 1945

Human Cannonball
June 28, 1937

Hundred Dollar Bill
January 7, 1941

Hunter McGee Returns Home
November 18, 1953

Hunter McGee Returns Home (Repeat)
November 16, 1955

Hunting for Clues with a Decoy
November 4, 1954

Hunting for Hunting License
November 11, 1953

Hunting for Hunting License (Repeat)
November 9, 1955

Hypnotism
March 31, 1953

Ice Cream
February 8, 1944

Ice Cream Tainted?
June 5, 1955

Ice Skating
February 5, 1946

Icicle
January 27, 1953

Icy Walk to Bus
February 27, 1956

Ignition Release Invention
April 2, 1946

Impressing Visitor from Canada
February 22, 1949

Income Tax Return
January 11, 1944

Indian Scout McGee
April 19, 1954

Indian Trouble
May 3, 1937

Ink on the Rug
April 16, 1940

Inner Tube That's No Bargain
November 29, 1949

Installing Light in Hall Closet
February 16, 1954

Interest in Ketchup Gun
March 3, 1954

Interviewed at Home
May 20, 1947

Interviewing Vaudeville Talent
March 22, 1937

Inventing Air Conditioner
July 29, 1954

Inventing Ketchup Gun
March 4, 1954

Invents Bow-Maker
November 28, 1955

Invents Glue Accidentally
May 26, 1954

Investment Plan
December 13, 1955

Investment Plan Succeeds
December 15, 1955

Investors Are Irate
December 14, 1955

Irish Tweed
May 13, 1947

IRS Wants to See Fibber
February 19, 1952

Jalopy
March 1, 1949

Jaywalking Is No Thrill
July 9, 1954

Jewelry Store Robbery
December 12, 1939

Jinxed
March 21, 1955

Job in Grand Rapids
February 10, 1936

Joke Fibber Tries to Tell
September 13, 1954

Joke Fibber Tries to Tell (Repeat)
September 30, 1955

Judge of Domestic Relations Court
September 7, 1936

Jury Duty
March 2, 1948

Jury Duty for Molly
May 9, 1955

Justice of the Peace
February 14, 1938

Ketchup Representative Arrives
March 5, 1954

Key Collection
October 31, 1955

Keys Left in Car
July 20, 1954

Killer Canova's Autograph
October 3, 1939

Kindness to Strangers
March 20, 1951

Knitting
March 20, 1956

Labeling Plants
August 31, 1957

LaTrivia's Party
February 28, 1950

Laundry to the Sudsomat
January 25, 1949

Laura, the Lopsided Tree
December 24, 1953

Lawn Care
October 17, 1939

Lawn Mower a No-Goer
May 29, 1945

Lawn Mower on Loan
July 5, 1954

Lawsuit over $3.00
January 27, 1954

Lawyer: Applying for Course
October 27, 1957

Lawyer: Courtroom Manner
October 27, 1957

Lawyer: Finishes Course
October 27, 1957

Lawyer: Practicing Attorney
October 27, 1957

Lawyer: Summation
October 27, 1957

Learning How to Listen
February 1, 1949

Learning the Restaurant Business
January 27, 1936

Leaves: Color Change
January 4, 1959

Leaves: Drive
January 4, 1959

Leaves: Equipment
January 4, 1959

Leaves: Final Preparations
January 4, 1959

Leaves: Photographs
January 4, 1959

Leaving for Hollywood
June 24, 1941

Leftover Turkey Recipe
December 27, 1955

Lemonade Stand
July 7, 1954

Lester Missing on Recording Day
April 7, 1955

Lester Prepares for Audition
April 6, 1955

Lester Seeks Public Relations Job
December 28, 1954

Lester Whistles Well
April 5, 1955

Letter Found in Attic
April 17, 1955

Letter to Postmaster
October 6, 1953

Letter Writing: Aunt Sarah
November 22, 1958

Letter Writing: Delivery Explained
November 22, 1958

Letter Writing: Fred Nitney
November 22, 1958

Letter Writing: Personal Mail
November 22, 1958

Letter Writing: To Friends
November 22, 1958

Library Book Overdue
November 21, 1939

Library Committee Soiree
February 20, 1955

Library Moving Day
February 24, 1955

License Plate
March 7, 1956

Life on a Modern Farm
August 2, 1937

Lifeguard Memories
July 27, 1957

Lighter Racket
February 27, 1955

Lighting Furnace with Gasoline
November 18, 1935

Little Boy Lost
June 1, 1955

Loan for Summer Trip
June 27, 1939

Lock for Front Door
November 4, 1953

Lock on Front Door Tested
May 17, 1955

Locked Out
January 22, 1952

Locked Out of Car
November 23, 1954

Looking at Cars with Wimple
March 5, 1956

Looking for Cigars
November 29, 1955

Looking for 1414 14th Street
February 15, 1949

Looking for Gold at Dugan's Lake
June 10, 1947

Looking for Uranium Site
August 16, 1954

Looking over Christmas Presents
December 26, 1954

Losing His Hair?
June 8, 1954

Lost Boy at Airport
April 3, 1955

Lost Collar Button
January 24, 1939

Lost Earring
December 15, 1953

Lost Engagement Ring
February 3, 1942

Lost Keys
December 23, 1947

Lost on Train
October 26, 1953

Lost Purse
January 26, 1956

Lost Umbrella
November 18, 1952

Lucky Day
March 24, 1953

Luggage Shopping
October 21, 1953

Luncheon Invitation from Gamble
November 2, 1955

Magic Act
June 12, 1945

Magician McGee
January 6, 1948

Magnolia Manor Mix-up
August 3, 1954

Mail Service Complaint
March 4, 1947

Mailing Aunt Sarah's Gift
December 21, 1953

Mailing Christmas Packages
December 10, 1940

Mailman Bitten by Dog
February 21, 1950

Making a Dress for Molly
April 20, 1943

Making a Vase
April 20, 1948

Making Dinner for 30 People
December 6, 1937

Man of the Year
December 13, 1949

Man on the Street Interview
October 18, 1937

Managing Candy Company
October 25, 1937

Managing Drugstore
January 20, 1936

Managing Food Store
July 26, 1937

Managing Hardware Store
March 15, 1937

Managing Jewelry Store
December 7, 1936

Managing Night Club
April 12, 1937

Managing Ranch in Texas
May 23, 1950

Managing Travel Bureau
January 3, 1938

Managing Variety Store
March 10, 1954

Mandolin
March 21, 1944

Maple Syrup
October 17, 1944

Marital Advice
October 19, 1954

Marital Advice (Repeat)
January 6, 1956

Marriage Quiz
January 24, 1955

Mary Ellen Strongheart Identified
December 7, 1955

Masquerade
November 29, 1938

Matchmaker McGee
January 29, 1952

Math Problem
January 17, 1956

Matinee for the Birds
August 2, 1954

Matrimonial Bureau
December 13, 1937

Mayor Doesn't Leave
November 18, 1941

Measles Quarantine
March 11, 1941

Meeting Someone Downtown
March 17, 1953

Meeting Someone in the Rain
March 18, 1947

Meeting the Upper Crust
July 22, 1954

Memory Course
March 14, 1939

Memory Course: Awaiting Lesson
December 21, 1957

Memory Course: By the Numbers
December 21, 1957

Memory Course: First Lesson
December 21, 1957

Memory Course: Grocery List
December 21, 1957

Memory Course: Repetition
December 21, 1957

Merchant Marine
January 30, 1945

Mesmerizing Molly
July 8, 1954

Military Maneuvers
January 31, 1939

Militia Camp
August 10, 1936

Minding Doc Gamble's Office
February 17, 1953

Minding Teeny
February 4, 1947

Minding Teeny (Shorter Version)
May 6, 1954

Minding the Baby
January 24, 1938

Mirror on Closet Door
August 26, 1954

Missed Telephone Call
November 18, 1947

Missing $15.00
December 15, 1942

Missing Garbage Can, Part 1
January 31, 1955

Missing Garbage Can, Part 2
February 1, 1955

Missing Garbage Can, Part 3
February 2, 1955

Missing Laundry
January 27, 1948

Missing Pen
February 26, 1946

Missing Radium
February 14, 1950

Missing Roller Skate
October 14, 1954

Missing Roller Skate (Repeat)
January 13, 1956

Missing Screwdriver
October 15, 1940

Missing Wristwatch
November 11, 1954

Mistaken for Policemen
May 29, 1955

Mock Trial Begins
March 1, 1955

Mock Trial Concludes
March 3, 1955

Mock Trial Continues
March 2, 1955

Model Airplane
February 11, 1947

Modeling a Dress
June 18, 1940

Models a Dress for Molly
March 22, 1949

Molly Chairs Meeting
September 14, 1954

Molly's Card Party
January 29, 1946

Molly's Feigned Toothache
February 6, 1956

Molly's New Coat
October 29, 1955

Molly's Sprained Ankle
April 8, 1947

Molly's Toothache
May 25, 1948

Money for Old Books
February 17, 1948

Money Hidden in Sofa
November 17, 1942

Money in a Shoebox
January 18, 1949

Moonstruck
January 24, 1956

Mother Gamble Visits
October 31, 1954

Mother McGee's Cranberry Super Sauce
November 25, 1954

Motorcycle Cop and Judge
April 16, 1935

Moose or Mousse for Dinner?
March 24, 1955

Mouse Frightens Big Game Hunters
February 28, 1939

Mouse in the House
June 16, 1942

Movie Offer
August 4, 1954

Movie Passes
October 17, 1955

Movie Star McGee
August 6, 1954

Movies Mix-up
September 28, 1943

Moving Heavy Crate
June 7, 1954

Mushrooms
January 9, 1945

Mustache
December 2, 1941

Mustard Slogan
September 20, 1949

Mysterious Knocker
June 15, 1955

Mysterious Letter
December 5, 1955

Mystery Caller
April 13, 1955

Mystery Caller (Repeat)
March 22, 1956

Mystery Ladies' Society
May 1, 1955

Mystery Movie at Bijou
April 8, 1955

Mystery of Unanswered Phone Call
October 26, 1955

Nasty Letter to Nitney
February 13, 1951

Naval Expert McGee
January 30, 1955

Neighbor Frank Ingram
February 9, 1954

Nelsons in Need?
September 29, 1955

Nest in Mailbox
May 29, 1951

New Car: Auto Show
October 5, 1958

New Car: Molly Wants One
October 5, 1958

New Car: Trade Offers
October 5, 1958

New Dog
October 30, 1951

New Furniture
November 4, 1941

New Hat for Molly
December 9, 1952

New Radio
January 7, 1947

New Roomer
October 5, 1943

New Shoes
May 3, 1954

New Shoes Too Tight
October 10, 1955

New Suits for Fibber and Friends
February 12, 1946

New Tools
January 2, 1940

New Year's Celebration
December 30, 1935

New Year's Day at Home
January 1, 1954

New Year's Day Visiting
January 1, 1952

New Year's Eve Dance
December 30, 1952

Newspaper Interview
December 9, 1947

Newspaperman McGee
August 16, 1937

Night at the Copakabibble
June 9, 1955

Night of Vaudeville Show
December 31, 1953

Night Out with Gildersleeve
April 22, 1941

Night School
November 14, 1944

Night School Chemist
September 26, 1950

No Hot Water
January 16, 1945

No Newspaper
April 10, 1945

No Pep
April 6, 1943

No Train Reservations
October 16, 1945

Noise Abatement Committee
April 25, 1955

Oak Tree Must Come Down
April 29, 1954

Observing Human Nature
March 7, 1955

Occupation: Author
September 28, 1957

Occupation: General
September 28, 1957

Occupation: Mandolinist
September 28, 1957

Occupation: Professor
September 28, 1957

Occupation: Psychiatrist
September 28, 1957

Offer from 4th National Bank
December 3, 1946

Officer of the Bank
April 19, 1937

Old Muley Caught?
May 7, 1946

Old Newsboys' Day
August 12, 1954

Old Newspaper
February 25, 1954

Old Suit
January 30, 1940

Old Tax Law
May 19, 1953

Old Timer Acts Lovesick
June 19, 1955

Old Timer on the Lam
October 27, 1942

Old Timer's Birthday?
August 24, 1954

Old Timer's Song
October 19, 1955

Ole Kidnapped
March 7, 1950

Ole's Brother
May 12, 1953

On the Lam
April 14, 1953

Orchid Plant for Doc
May 5, 1954

Organizing Housework
April 26, 1949

Organizing Trip to Omaha
October 2, 1951

Otis Cadwallader Calls
October 6, 1942

Out of Gas on Broadway
May 7, 1935

Out of Postage Stamps
March 8, 1956

Overdue Car Payment
October 21, 1947

Overdue Library Book
September 16, 1954

Overnight Trip Downtown
March 30, 1948

Package at the Post Office
January 14, 1947

Package from Aunt Sarah
November 1, 1955

Package from Uncle Sycamore
December 19, 1939

Appendix A: Alphabetical List of Episodes ♦ **525**

Packing for Aunt Sarah's
October 22, 1953

Packing for Summer Vacation
June 23, 1942

Painter McGee
April 9, 1946

Painting a Fly
June 16, 1957

Painting Bathroom
July 21, 1954

Painting Christmas Cards
December 6, 1949

Painting Mrs. Morley's House
February 16, 1955

Painting Signs for Lecture
October 5, 1955

Painting the Kitchen
November 25, 1947

Pal of Your Wife
March 12, 1940

Pancake Day
February 26, 1952

Pants Need Cleaning
May 30, 1955

Pants Pressed Downtown
October 5, 1948

Paper into Cloth
October 11, 1949

Paperboy McGee
November 1, 1954

Paperboy McGee (Repeat)
October 14, 1955

Paperhanging
June 11, 1940

Parade Plans
April 14, 1942

Parakeet's Preference
November 6, 1953

Parking Attendant Problems
March 1, 1954

Parking Meter Payback
November 3, 1955

Parking Meters
November 28, 1950

Parking Ticket
November 14, 1939

Parrot or Stork?
May 23, 1939

Party for Doc Gamble
December 23, 1952

Party for John Cameron Swayze
December 6, 1954

Party Line: Expecting Call
December 10, 1953

Party Line: Making Call
September 27, 1954

Party Line: Making Call (Repeat)
December 30, 1955

Passenger Pigeon
April 27, 1948

Patient Little Star
December 23, 1954

Patient Little Star (Repeat)
December 23, 1955

Patrolman McGee
May 10, 1937

Pawn Broker
March 7, 1938

Paying Back for Misdeeds
December 30, 1954

Paying Bills
February 5, 1952

Paying Bills with Teeny's Ink
February 4, 1954

Paying Water Bill
November 16, 1943

Peach Preserves
July 27, 1954

Peanut Machine Troubles
November 23, 1955

Pennies Counted
March 15, 1955

Pennies for Little Shavers Fund
March 13, 1955

Pennies Removed from Scales
March 14, 1955

Persian Lamb Coat
June 20, 1955

Petition to Repair Street
October 26, 1954

Pheasant Dinner
November 23, 1948

Phone Booth Frenzy
October 11, 1955

Phone Confusion
January 31, 1956

Phone Number in Wallet
May 2, 1955

Phone Numbers in New Notebook
May 21, 1954

Phoning About Invention
May 27, 1954

Phonograph Records from the Attic
February 13, 1955

Phony Ring Swindle
November 23, 1953

Photo Contest with $25 Prize
October 17, 1950

Photo Contest with $50 Prize
December 1, 1953

Photo Found
December 7, 1953

Photo from Peoria Picnic
August 9, 1954

Photo Lost
December 4, 1953

Photograph for Christmas Gift
December 22, 1954

Photographer a Spy?
May 12, 1942

Physical Fitness
March 11, 1947

Picking Up Prize Money
December 9, 1954

Pickles at Women's Bazaar
January 20, 1948

Picnic at Dugan's Lake
May 6, 1952

Picnic in the Country
May 16, 1950

Picnic Outing
May 24, 1937

Pickpockets on the Bus
March 9, 1936

Pickpockets on the Bus (Revised Version)
March 1, 1937

Pioneer Day
January 22, 1946

Planning Defense for Trial
May 14, 1954

Planning for Ranch Life
June 20, 1944

Appendix A: Alphabetical List of Episodes ♦ **527**

Planning New Year's Party
December 29, 1953

Planning to Paint a House
February 15, 1955

Planning Vacation at Dugan's Lake
June 22, 1943

Plans for New Year's Eve
December 29, 1955

Plans to Attend Night School
May 10, 1954

Plans to Operate Walt's Malt Shop
May 18, 1955

Plant and Pet Show
April 29, 1952

Planting a Hedge
March 26, 1940

Planting Grass
October 26, 1948

Planting Seeds, Finding a Bone
July 12, 1954

Play about Julius Caesar
September 13, 1937

Playing Cards with Mort and Mabel
January 2, 1955

Plays the Piano
January 21, 1941

Plays the Ukulele
October 31, 1950

Plumber McGee
January 29, 1954

Plumbing Problems
May 4, 1955

Poet McGee
April 3, 1945

Poetry: Composing Poem
November 23, 1958

Poetry: Phoning Poets
November 23, 1958

Poetry: Preparing to Write
November 23, 1958

Poetry: Seize the Day
November 23, 1958

Poetry: Suffering
November 23, 1958

Poker Game
February 23, 1943

Policeman's Ball
June 3, 1941

Polishing Doc's Car
November 25, 1952

Political Campaign Manager
June 10, 1952

Pool Match
December 18, 1951

Popcorn Machine Opportunity
October 24, 1954

Porch Swing
June 13, 1944

Porch Swing (Shorter Version)
June 11, 1954

Portable Radio
January 13, 1948

Portrait for the Elks
March 12, 1956

Post Office Box Key
October 21, 1952

Post Office Job
December 21, 1936

Postal Anniversary
July 26, 1954

Postman McGee
December 19, 1950

Pot Roast
June 9, 1942

Practical Jokers
November 21, 1955

Preparations for Trip to Aunt Sarah's
October 23, 1953

Preparing for a Night Out
January 6, 1942

Preparing for Hike
April 20, 1954

Preparing for Mrs. Compost's Visit
December 1, 1955

Preparing Speech
October 13, 1953

Preparing to Leave for Hollywood
April 26, 1937

Prescription Problems
January 19, 1955

Presenting Vaudeville Show
March 29, 1937

Presents in the Closet
December 19, 1944

Pressing a Pair of Pants
December 5, 1944

Pretending to be Lester's Boss
December 29, 1954

Processing Film
December 3, 1953

Promoting a Feud
December 10, 1946

Promoting Business
March 12, 1954

Promoting Store on Radio
March 15, 1954

Prosperity: Attic Treasures
December 22, 1957

Prosperity: Cuts Hair
December 22, 1957

Prosperity: Double or Nothing
December 22, 1957

Prosperity: Polishing Car
December 22, 1957

Prosperity: Stock Plan
December 22, 1957

Protection Begins at Home
October 28, 1941

Protesting Meters
April 12, 1955

Protesting Tax Assessment
November 4, 1955

Prowler at Fifi's House
November 26, 1946

Pruning a Tree
March 21, 1950

Publicity Seeker: Double Yolk
October 19, 1957

Publicity Seeker: Hot Air Balloon
October 19, 1957

Publicity Seeker: Staying Awake
October 19, 1957

Publicity Seeker: Swim Lake Michigan
October 19, 1957

Publicity Seeker: Teeny is in Paper
October 19, 1957

Purse Search in Theater
May 15, 1955

Quarter from 1880
April 15, 1947

Quits Smoking
October 12, 1948

Quiz Program
December 12, 1944

Raccoon Coat
November 6, 1951

Radio Interview Preparations
February 17, 1955

Radio Retrieved from Repairman
October 19, 1948

Raffle Ticket
March 9, 1955

Raffle Ticket Winners Meet
March 10, 1955

Raft of Troubles
November 11, 1947

Raining at Lake Wapahokey
November 16, 1953

Raining at Lake Wapahokey (Repeat)
November 14, 1955

Raises $31.90
December 17, 1953

Reading *The Case of the Cross-Eyed Cat*
February 6, 1945

Real Estate Agent
January 17, 1938

Real Estate Deal
October 24, 1950

Record Player
December 24, 1940

Recovering from Pneumonia
April 4, 1944

Recuperating from Flu
April 3, 1951

Red Cross Captain
March 19, 1946

Red Cross Drive
February 27, 1945

Red Cross Volunteer
March 23, 1943

Redecorating Servicemen's Center
February 3, 1954

Redeeming Bottles
February 25, 1941

Rehearsing Movie Role
August 5, 1954

Remembering What to Do
November 22, 1955

Renaming Wistful Vista Street
October 28, 1954

Renewing License Plates
February 3, 1955

Renewing Vows: Big Day Arrives
January 5, 1958

Renewing Vows: Flower Girl
January 5, 1958

Renewing Vows: Invite Friends
January 5, 1958

Renewing Vows: Music
January 5, 1958

Renewing Vows: Second Honeymoon
January 5, 1958

Repairing Doc's Car
June 15, 1943

Repairing Radio
September 2, 1954

Repairing Sewing Machine
June 21, 1954

Repairing Washing Machine
June 9, 1954

Replacing a Broken Window
February 25, 1947

Resort Hotel Visit
August 23, 1937

Restaurant: First and Last Day
August 11, 1957

Returning Flash to Corner
May 18, 1954

Returning Shirt to Bon Ton
September 9, 1954

Returning Stolen Money
October 13, 1954

Reupholstering Davenport
November 9, 1948

Reviving Vaudeville Act
December 30, 1953

Ribbon on Finger
December 28, 1943

Ribbon on Finger (Shorter Version)
October 19, 1953

Rich Friend Gert
October 7, 1952

Ride in a Jeep
June 2, 1954

Ride to Elks Club
April 24, 1945

River Moonlight and Circus Tale
June 18, 1935

Robbery Solved
April 14, 1954

Rolls Royce Ride
February 14, 1956

Rotating Tires
October 27, 1955

Rules for a Happy Marriage
September 30, 1954

Rummage Sale
January 15, 1952

Rumors
January 8, 1952

Running a Hardware Store
May 21, 1940

Running a Red Light
May 22, 1951

Running Kremer's Drugstore
March 25, 1952

Safe Deposit Box
August 11, 1954

Safe Driving Campaign
April 1, 1947

Safe Driving Campaign (Repeat)
June 9, 1953

Safeguarding Health
November 25, 1955

Safety Slogan Contest
December 8, 1954

Sales Resistance Questioned
March 23, 1955

Salesman on Bus
December 7, 1954

Salmon Dinner
May 13, 1941

Salute to D-Day Invasion
June 6, 1944

Salvador Fixes Furniture
April 16, 1946

Scandinavian Sweepstakes Winner
November 22, 1937

School of Dramatic Arts
May 17, 1937

School Pal Visits
February 22, 1944

Scrap Drive
April 7, 1942

Sculptor McGee
October 30, 1945

Searching for Aunt Sarah's House
October 27, 1953

Searching for Raincoat
April 4, 1955

Searching for Shotgun
February 15, 1956

Searching for Summer Cottage
June 14, 1937

Seeing Shaw
October 4, 1955

Seeks State Job
September 29, 1954

Selecting Christmas Cards
December 12, 1954

Selling a Ring to Doc
November 24, 1953

Selling the Car
October 10, 1954

Selling the House
May 4, 1948

Sending Doctor Gamble Off at Station
December 2, 1954

Sendoff for Wimple
February 29, 1956

Servicemen's Center Needs Redecorating
February 2, 1954

Seventh War Loan Drive
May 22, 1945

Sewing a Button
November 18, 1955

Shampoo Bottle
October 9, 1953

Shoes Repaired, Remembering Names
January 19, 1956

Shoes to be Repaired
November 5, 1953

Shooting a "Dirty Pheasant"
September 22, 1957

Shopping for a Christmas Tree
December 21, 1943

Shopping for a Hat for Molly
February 14, 1955

Shopping for a Used Car
October 9, 1945

Shopping for Clothes
October 5, 1936

Shopping for Fibber's Suit
January 24, 1950

Shopping for Shoelaces
October 22, 1946

Shopping for Turkey
November 24, 1955

Shopping Runaround
October 18, 1954

Shoveling Snow
December 26, 1950

Showing House
February 15, 1954

Shrimps McGee
May 27, 1947

Shuns Country Club Meeting
September 12, 1954

Sidewalk Grating
November 15, 1949

Singing Commercial
June 3, 1952

Sitting in Chair
October 4, 1954

Skating Party
January 30, 1951

Skilled War Workers Needed
February 16, 1943

Sled from Childhood Days
February 10, 1948

Sleepwalker McGee
April 7, 1954

Sleigh Ride in Snowstorm
January 31, 1950

Sleigh Ride Plans
January 20, 1955

Sleigh Ride with a Meal
January 11, 1949

Sleigh Ride with Wiener Roast
January 23, 1955

Smoking a Pipe
April 12, 1949

Snowfall Upsets McGee
December 19, 1955

Snowy Owl
March 31, 1955

Soap Carving Contest
February 9, 1956

Soap Contest
March 31, 1942

Soapbox Derby
April 24, 1951

Solving a Mystery as Detectives
August 24, 1936

Some Like It Hot
November 20, 1951

Songwriter McGee
March 24, 1942

Spaghetti Dinner
June 4, 1940

Spearhead Commission
March 16, 1948

Speech for the Red Cross
March 7, 1944

Spends Dime in Parking Meter
June 8, 1955

Spirit of Giving Presents
December 25, 1951

Sports Reporter
August 30, 1937

Spring Cleaning
March 23, 1936

Spring Cleaning Plan
March 15, 1956

Spy Across the Street
April 18, 1944

Stage Director
April 30, 1940

Stage Money
March 20, 1955

Stage Money (Repeat)
March 9, 1956

Stamp Worth $100,000
November 14, 1950

Statue Presented to Elks
September 27, 1955

Stock Certificate for India Company
March 8, 1955

Stock Certificate Found
June 14, 1955

Stock in Transit Company
October 14, 1952

Stock Talk on Train
November 17, 1954

Stock Takeover
November 16, 1954

Stock Trading
November 15, 1954

Stockholder McGee
Considers Options
November 21, 1954

Stockholder McGee Meets Bigwig
November 18, 1954

Stockholders' Meeting
November 22, 1954

Stolen Pants Recovered
October 12, 1954

Stomachache
October 3, 1950

Store Adjusters
December 5, 1939

Storm Windows
September 15, 1957

Stranded on Island
August 31, 1954

Straw Hat
April 28, 1942

Streamliner Back to Wistful Vista
July 12, 1937

Street Inverview
December 2, 1935

Street Needs Repair
October 25, 1954

Streetcar Motorman McGee
April 20, 1936

Streetlight
November 30, 1948

Stuck in Pavement
April 29, 1941

Stung by a Wasp
April 27, 1954

Sub Gum Blooey
February 8, 1956

Sugar Substitute
May 5, 1942

Suggestions for Fibber's Present
December 13, 1954

Suit for Doc
May 17, 1949

Suit to Salvation Army
April 26, 1954

Summer Fishing Plans
June 11, 1946

Sun Lamp
December 17, 1946

Supervising Street Repair
October 26, 1954

Supervisor at State Fair
October 4, 1937

Supper Party for Friends
March 4, 1941

Surprise for the House
January 30, 1956

Surprise Party
March 27, 1951

Surprise Project in Kitchen
June 23, 1955

Swapping
April 28, 1953

Swimming by Ocean and
Lifeguard Tale
July 15, 1935

Table Lamp
February 3, 1948

Take Me Out to the Ball Game
April 21, 1942

Taking Over Hotel Desk
April 13, 1936

Tall Story Contest
January 1, 1946

Tall Tale McGee
February 23, 1954

Tax Bill
November 22, 1949

Tax Problems: Cancelled Checks
November 2, 1957

Tax Problems: Deductions
November 2, 1957

Tax Problems: Fears Audit
November 2, 1957

Tax Problems: Letter from IRS
November 2, 1957

Tax Problems: Still Checking
November 2, 1957

Tax Refund
December 18, 1953

Tax Time
March 2, 1954

Tea Set Hunt
January 25, 1955

Tea Set Hunt (Repeat)
January 20, 1956

Teaching Parakeet to Talk
October 8, 1953

Teeny the Huntress
September 22, 1957

Teeny's Aunt Catherine
February 23, 1956

Teeny's Gift at the Bon Ton
November 9, 1953

Teeny's Hand Stuck in Phone
September 19, 1954

Teeny's Missing Dog
November 30, 1943

Teeny's Sled
January 2, 1951

Teeny's Tooth
October 16, 1951

Telegram for $3.81
June 4, 1954

Telegram to Sponsor
March 8, 1937

Telescope
April 8, 1941

Ten-Dollar Bill Spent
March 6, 1955

Temper Under Control
December 26, 1944

Tennis Racket
April 28, 1954

Texan Entertains McGee
March 29, 1955

Thanksgiving: Guests Considered
November 16, 1957

Thanksgiving: Pilgrim Diet
November 16, 1957

Thanksgiving: Pilgrims
November 16, 1957

Thanksgiving: Reverse Albino
November 16, 1957

Theater Party Invitations
July 15, 1954

Thelma Graham Visits
April 29, 1947

Thousand Bricks
March 31, 1954

Thousand Pound Inheritance
March 29, 1949

Threats Get Nowhere with McGee
June 28, 1954

Tickets for Basketball Game
January 3, 1955

Tickets to "South Atlantic"
January 28, 1954

Tiltmore Relaxing Chair
February 8, 1955

Tire Trouble and Gondola Tale
May 21, 1935

To Catch a Train
February 20, 1945

To Tell the Truth
February 20, 1940

Toll Bridge and Diving Tale
June 11, 1935

Too Much Energy
January 23, 1945

Toothache Sends Fibber to Dentist
June 20, 1939

Trading in Car
April 6, 1936

Traffic Court
April 22, 1952

Trailer Camp
July 20, 1936

Train Tickets Difficult to Get
May 25, 1943

Trapped by Dog
September 26, 1954

Trapped by Dog (Repeat)
December 2, 1955

Treasure Map
January 15, 1946

Tree Shaker
September 15, 1957

Trial of McGee Vs. Corner
May 17, 1954

Trick or Treating
October 30, 1953

Trimming Drugstore Window
November 1, 1937

Trip to Aunt Sarah's
December 27, 1949

Trip to Lake Wapahokey
November 13, 1953

Trip to Lake Wapahokey (Repeat)
November 11, 1955

Trip to Peoria
February 27, 1951

Trip to Peoria: Bachelor Life
November 9, 1957

Trip to Peoria: Chores
November 9, 1957

Trip to Peoria: Cooking Dinner
November 9, 1957

Trip to Peoria: Day of Departure
November 9, 1957

Trip to Peoria: Molly Going Alone
November 9, 1957

Trolley Riders
November 1, 1949

Trophy
February 26, 1954

Trouble Boarding a Bus
January 28, 1947

Trunk of Trouble
May 15, 1945

Tunes the Piano
February 13, 1945

Tunes the Piano Again
May 13, 1952

Turning Fibber In
April 12, 1954

Typewriter Ribbon
November 29, 1954

Umbrella Stand
October 4, 1949

Umbrellas on a Hot Day
April 1, 1952

Umpire McGee
June 22, 1954

Uncle Dennis is Missing
May 26, 1942

Uncle Dennis Still Missing
June 2, 1942

Uncle Dennis Visits
November 26, 1940

Uncle Elrod: Auto Magnate
December 8, 1957

Uncle Elrod: Eureka! Uranium
December 8, 1957

Uncle Elrod: Old Diary
December 8, 1957

Uncle Elrod: Teeny Wants Nickel
December 8, 1957

Uncle Sycamore on the Radio
April 13, 1943

Unloading Copies of "Partly True"
April 23, 1954

Uppy Wants to Join the WACs
January 19, 1943

Uranium Hunt Begins
August 13, 1954

Uranium Plans Foiled
August 18, 1954

Uranium Site Found
August 17, 1954

Vacuum Cleaner Salesman
November 28, 1954

Vacuum Cleaner Salesman (Repeat)
December 16, 1955

Valentine from Old Girlfriend
March 29, 1958

Valentine from Snooky
February 23, 1955

Valentine from Snooky (Repeat)
February 17, 1956

Valentine's Day Candy
February 10, 1942

Variety Store Opportunity
March 9, 1954

Vaudeville Show
April 7, 1953

Venetian Blinds Broken
September 28, 1955

Vision Problems
November 7, 1950

Visit to Oculist
April 15, 1941

Visit to Racine
November 5, 1946

Visiting Fire Station
February 17, 1936

Visiting the Dairy
March 9, 1943

Visiting Uncle Dennis
November 19, 1940

Visiting Washington and G-Man Tale
July 8, 1935

Voting for Congressman
March 30, 1954

Waffle-Weave Shirt
February 22, 1955

Waiting for Radio Repairman
February 24, 1936

Waitress Tips at Walt's Malt Shop
May 19, 1955

Walk to Dugan's Lake
December 4, 1945

Walking on Grass
January 16, 1951

Wall Safe
February 3, 1953

Wallet Racket
October 10, 1950

Walt's Malt Shop
January 10, 1950

War Surplus Auction
January 4, 1955

Washing Front Window
April 18, 1955

Washing Machine
March 30, 1943

Washington Day Play
February 21, 1955

Washington's Birthday
February 22, 1954

Watch Salesman
February 11, 1941

Watching Gildersleeve's House
April 2, 1940

Watching "Two-Gun Justice"
February 19, 1954

Water Fight
May 14, 1940

Water Shut Off
September 15, 1954

Water Shut Off (Repeat)
October 21, 1955

Watermelon
August 25, 1954

Weather Balloon Day
January 10, 1955

Weather Balloon Promotion
January 5, 1955

Weather Balloon Promotion in Newspaper
January 9, 1955

Weather-Stripping the Door
January 4, 1949

Wedding Invitation
October 6, 1954

Wedding Ring in Drainpipe
January 23, 1956

Welcoming LaTrivia Home
October 2, 1945

Whims Cured with Placebos
October 1, 1946

Whipped Cream
April 11, 1944

White Christmas Tree
December 18, 1945

Who Is F.C.?
October 29, 1953

Who Is Mary Ellen Strongheart?
December 6, 1955

Who Was That Man?
October 20, 1954

Who Was That Man? (Repeat)
October 20, 1955

Wimple Going to Chicago
February 28, 1956

Wimple Helps with Barbeque

April 5, 1954

Wimple Home on Leave
November 28, 1944

Wimple's Binoculars
October 25, 1955

Win House in Wistful Vista
August 26, 1935

Window Shade
February 7, 1939

Wins a Salmon
December 14, 1948

Wins Drawing
December 7, 1943

Women in the Workforce
December 8, 1942

Women Superior to Men?
January 11, 1955

Women's Club Play
May 7, 1940

Women's Club Shuns McGee
October 3, 1955

Wood in Front Yard
July 6, 1954

Woodpecker Woes
June 16, 1955

World Cruise Plans
March 28, 1939

World's Fair Plans
May 9, 1939

Wrestler McGee
June 6, 1939

Writing Book with Wimple
December 8, 1955

Writing Letter to Congressman
May 8, 1955

Writing Movie Script
May 24, 1949

Wrong House
October 28, 1953

YMCA Week: Lifting Weights
March 23, 1958

YMCA Week: Medicine Ball
March 23, 1958

YMCA Week: Remembering Feats
March 23, 1958

YMCA Week: Swimming
March 23, 1958

Zither
May 16, 1939

Appendix B

RATINGS AND RANKINGS SUMMARY FOR *FIBBER MCGEE AND MOLLY*

Season	Rating	Ranking
1935-1936	6.6	Not among top 20 shows
1936-1937	13.0	Not among top 20 shows
1937-1938	14.8	16th
1938-1939	16.7	Tied for 14th
1939-1940	30.8	3rd
1940-1941	27.4	4th
1941-1942	33.3	2nd
1942-1943	37.7	3rd
1943-1944	31.9	1st
1944-1945	30.8	2nd
1945-1946	30.8	1st
1946-1947	30.2	Tied for 1st
1947-1948	27.7	2nd
1948-1949	26.9	2nd
1949-1950	16.9	Tied for 11th
1950-1951	13.7	Tied for 7th
1951-1952	10.7	14th
1952-1953	7.4	Tied for 15th
1953-1954	3.6	Not among top 20 shows
1954-1955	3.0	Not among top 20 shows
1955-1956	2.2	Not among top 20 shows

Ratings are Hooper through the 1948-1949 season, Nielsen beginning with the 1949-1950 season.

Source: *A Thirty-Year History of Programs Carried on National Radio Networks in the United States 1926-1956* edited by Harrison B. Summers. Arno Press, 1971.

The hall closet had become so firmly connected with *Fibber McGee and Molly* that this photograph was distributed to news sources to announce Jim and Marian's return for the 1942-1943 season beginning September 29th.

Appendix C

HALL CLOSET GAGS

1. March 5, 1940: opened by Molly looking for dictionary
2. March 5, 1940: Fibber looking for dictionary
3. October 15, 1940: Fibber looking for screwdriver
4. October 22, 1940: Fibber looking for gloves
5. October 29, 1940: Fibber looking for road maps
6. November 5, 1940: Abigail looking for voting booth
7. November 12, 1940: Fibber trying to hide from Abigail
8. December 3, 1940: Fibber looking for coat
9. December 17, 1940: Fibber looking for hat and coat
10. December 24, 1940: Fibber looking for scissors
11. January 7, 1941: Fibber looking for slippers
12. January 14, 1941: Fibber looking for pipe
13. January 28, 1941: Fibber looking for heating pad
14. February 11, 1941: Fibber looking for spats
15. February 18, 1941: Fibber looking for dictionary
16. March 11, 1941: Gildersleeve seeking front door
17. March 25, 1941: Fibber looking for birth certificate
18. May 6, 1941: Fibber looking for ping pong set
19. May 20, 1941: Fibber in disbelief because Molly had opened it soundlessly

20. June 3, 1941: Fibber who has been hiding there
21. June 17, 1941: Fibber during "The Sound Effects Man" song
22. June 24, 1941: Fibber looking for bill of sale
23. September 30, 1941: Gildersleeve looking for lawn mower
24. October 7, 1941: Fibber looking for shorthand book
25. October 21, 1941: Fibber wanting to lock himself in
26. November 18, 1941: LaTrivia seeking front door
27. December 9, 1941: Fibber looking for checkbook
28. January 27, 1942: Fibber looking for shovel
29. March 3, 1942: Old Timer seeking front door
30. April 7, 1942: Fibber looking for scrap
31. April 7, 1942: Fibber showing [failed] results of cleaning
32. April 21, 1942: Fibber looking for glove and ball
33. May 26, 1942: Fibber during "The Sound Effects Man" song
34. June 23, 1942: Meredith Willson because he asked to do it
35. October 20, 1942: Fibber looking for hat
36. October 27, 1942: Old Timer looking for hiding place
37. February 2, 1943: Wimple looking for typewriter
38. February 2, 1943: Molly looking for tablecloth
39. March 23, 1943: Fibber trying to prove closet has been cleaned
40. April 27, 1943: Teeny seeking front door
41. June 22, 1943: Abigail seeking front door
42. October 5, 1943: Fibber looking for hat
43. November 16, 1943: Fibber looking for hat
44. December 28, 1943: Fibber looking for hat
45. January 11, 1944: Fibber looking for telephone book
46. January 25, 1944: Fibber looking for derby hat
47. February 29, 1944: Eddie Cantor seeking front door
48. March 21, 1944: Fibber looking for electric cord
49. March 21, 1944: Fibber to see where mandolin will fall
50. March 28, 1944: Leroy seeking basement door

Appendix C: Hall Closet Gags ♦ **543**

51. April 11, 1944: Fibber looking for thermos bottle
52. April 25, 1944: Fibber during "The Sound Effects Man" song
53. May 2, 1944: Alice looking for portrait
54. May 16, 1944: Hogan looking for clues
55. June 13, 1944: Gamble looking for porch swing chains
56. October 10, 1944: Fibber looking for boots
57. October 24, 1944: Fibber to hang up guest's hat
58. November 14, 1944: Fibber looking for leather strap
59. November 28, 1944: Old Timer seeking front door
60. December 19, 1944: Fibber looking for presents
61. January 9, 1945: Fibber looking for cookbook
62. January 23, 1945: Fibber looking for plans for bicycle
63. February 13, 1945: piano tuner seeking back door
64. March 20, 1945: Fibber looking for tire tape
65. May 1, 1945: Mr. Davis (insurance man) as directed by Fibber
66. June 5, 1945: Millicent Carstairs seeking back stairs door where hall closet stuff is
67. October 2, 1945: Fibber looking for helmet
68. October 23, 1945: Fibber looking for Parcheesi board
69. October 30, 1945: Fibber looking for wrapping paper
70. November 13, 1945: Gamble looking for hat
71. November 27, 1945: tree surgeon looking for hat
72. December 11, 1945: Millicent seeking front door
73. December 25, 1945: Alice looking for present
74. January 29, 1946: LaTrivia looking for hat
75. March 12, 1946: Molly looking for writing paper
76. April 2, 1946: Gamble seeking front door
77. May 21, 1946: Wimple seeking front door
78. October 8, 1946: Fibber looking for glasses
79. October 22, 1946: Fibber looking for muffler
80. November 5, 1946: Fibber to hang up hats and coats in Herbert Johnson's closet

81. November 26, 1946: Fibber looking for helmet
82. January 7, 1947: Fibber looking for shotgun
83. March 4, 1947: Fibber looking for spats
84. March 11, 1947: Gamble seeking front door
85. April 8, 1947: Fibber looking for hot water bottle
86. April 22, 1947: Fibber looking for hat
87. October 21, 1947: Fibber looking for hat
88. November 18, 1947: Horatio seeking front door
89. January 6, 1948: burglar looking for silver
90. February 24, 1948: Williams believing it was a side door exit
91. April 6, 1948: Fibber looking for tools borrowed from Williams
92. April 27, 1948: Fibber looking for tools
93. October 12, 1948: LaTrivia seeking the front door
94. November 23, 1948: Fibber looking for modeling clay
95. January 11, 1949: Fibber looking for book with phone number
96. March 22, 1949: Ole seeking side door
97. May 31, 1949: LaTrivia seeking front door
98. September 20, 1949: Milton looking for medicine
99. October 25, 1949: LaTrivia seeking front door
100. December 6, 1949: LaTrivia seeking front door
101. January 3, 1950: Fibber looking for riding crop
102. January 31, 1950: Fibber in the dark, not knowing he was home
103. May 23, 1950: Fibber looking for calendar
104. October 17, 1950: Teeny looking for Fibber's camera
105. December 19, 1950: Gamble looking for stethoscope in crowded car
106. January 23, 1951: Fibber looking for photo album
107. March 27, 1951: Truffles seeking front door
108. October 9, 1951: Gamble seeking hallway door in hotel
109. January 29, 1952: Fibber looking for budget book
110. February 19, 1952: Fibber looking for receipts
111. May 6, 1952: Fibber looking for swimming suit

112. June 10, 1952: Fibber looking for typewriter
113. November 18, 1952: Fibber looking for umbrella
114. January 27, 1953: Fibber looking for garden hose
115. April 21, 1953: Fibber looking for hat
116. June 23, 1953: Fibber looking for varnish
117. October 5, 1953: Fibber looking for hammer
118. February 16, 1954: Fibber looking for ear muffs
119. July 1, 1954: Wimple looking for umbrella
120. December 13, 1954: Lester looking for shovel
121. December 23, 1954: Fibber looking for ornaments
122. April 20, 1955: Fibber in Taylor home to hang up coat
123. June 6, 1955: Fibber looking for bowling shoes
124. June 23, 1955: Fibber looking for yardstick
125. December 1, 1955: Fibber looking for snow shovel
126. December 23, 1955: Fibber looking for ornaments
127. February 15, 1956: Fibber looking for shotgun

Breakdown of Hall Closet Gags By Seasons

1939-1940 2
1940-1941 20
1941-1942 12
1942-1943 7
1943-1944 14
1944-1945 11
1945-1946 11
1946-1947 9
1947-1948 6
1948-1949 5
1949-1950 6
1950-1951 4
1951-1952 5
1952-1953 4
1953-1956 11
1957-1959 0

Total 127

JIM & MARIAN JORDAN
Co-stars of "Fibber McGee and Molly" NBC-Radio
BOTH BORN IN PEORIA, ILL.

Two pioneers of radio, Jim and Marian Jordan have been portraying "Fibber McGee and Molly" for 19 years. Marian was a piano teacher and Jim a salesman when they began to sing at local clubs. They entered radio as singers but soon were doing situation comedy which developed into their now famous "Fibber and Molly Show." They have two grown children. Son is a television producer. The Jordans own a 1000 acre ranch in Encino, California.

TELEVISION & RADIO STARS OF N.B.C.

B. G., H. L. I., Printed in U. S. A.   No. 16

It was still in the cards for Jim and Marian in 1952 as they were saluted for being two of the Television and Radio Stars of NBC.

Appendix D

NOTABLE OCCURRENCES ON *FIBBER MCGEE* AND *MOLLY*

First and Last Appearances

Cast:

Bea Benaderet, June 28, 1937; October 3, 1950
Arthur Q. Bryan, February 2, 1943; March 23, 1956
Gene Carroll, February 11, 1947; May 13, 1947
Gale Gordon, December 26, 1939; June 9, 1953
Marlin Hurt, January 25, 1944; June 26, 1945
Richard (Dick) LeGrand, May 16, 1944; June 30, 1953
Shirley Mitchell, February 17, 1942; November 17, 1954
Harold Peary, July 19, 1937; September 13, 1949
Isabel Randolph, January 13, 1936; June 22, 1943
Ransom Sherman, September 28, 1943; June 20, 1944
Hugh Studebaker, August 12, 1935; January 24, 1939
Bill Thompson, January 27, 1936; March 22, 1956
Harlow Wilcox, April 16, 1935; June 30, 1953

Characters:

Beulah, January 25, 1944; June 26, 1945
Horatio K. Boomer, July 20, 1936; May 9, 1950
Millicent Carstairs, March 27, 1945; December 24, 1946
Alice Darling, October 5, 1943; January 1, 1946
Nick Depopolis, January 27, 1936; April 8, 1947
Uncle Dennis Driscoll, October 5, 1943; January 25, 1944

Doctor Gamble, April 6, 1943; March 23, 1956
Throckmorton P. Gildersleeve, October 3, 1939; September 13, 1949
Mayor LaTrivia, October 14, 1941; June 9, 1953
Lena, February 11, 1947; May 13, 1947
Myrt, June 22, 1943 (only appearance)
Old Timer, September 13, 1937; March 22, 1956
Ole Swenson, March 8, 1949; June 30, 1953
Abigail Uppington, September 13, 1937; June 22, 1943
Silly Watson, November 18, 1935; January 24, 1939
Sigmund Wellington, September 28, 1943; June 20, 1944
F. Ogden Williams, October 7, 1947; June 1, 1948
Wallace Wimple, April 15, 1941; March 20, 1956

Running Gags:

"Bird book," December 17, 1946; April 17, 1955
Cigar routine, September 16, 1935; February 1, 1954
"Gotta get them brakes fixed," April 30, 1935; April 21, 1953
Hall closet, March 5, 1940; February 15, 1956
LaTrivia blowup, February 10, 1942; March 24, 1953
"Love that man," March 7, 1944; June 26, 1945
Mrs. Kladderhatch bit, February 11, 1947; October 31, 1955
Myrt bit, January 10, 1938; November 23, 1957
Name game, February 28, 1950; March 31, 1953
"'Tain't funny, McGee," April 16, 1935; April 27, 1958
"That ain't the way I heered it," February 7, 1938; January 15, 1952
Tongue twister, October 28, 1935; February 7, 1959
"Where'd I put that" May 10, 1937; December 2, 1947
Word confusion, October 1, 1940; December 29, 1957
"You're a harrrrd man, McGee," February 13, 1940; April 22, 1941
"Yust donating my time," March 8, 1949; June 12, 1951

Sponsors:

Johnson's Wax, April 16, 1935; May 23, 1950
Pet Milk, September 19, 1950; June 10, 1952
Reynolds Aluminum, October 7, 1952; June 30, 1953

Fibber Firsts

Says "Stuff like that there," January 24, 1939
Takes on city hall, March 19, 1940
Creates a mess, April 16, 1940

Reveals first name is Fimmer, March 25, 1941
Says "Flung a fang into," June 4, 1940
Assumes a phony English accent, December 2, 1941
Uses "scoff, deride" expression, March 24, 1942
Invokes "my clavicle" oath, October 6, 1942
Mentions vaudeville act with Fred Nitney, April 20, 1943

Miscellanea

Rare instances when Molly addresses husband as Fibber, *September 23, 1935; January 2, 1940; April 9, 1940*
Only time Harlow Wilcox's wife appears, *May 21, 1940*
First episode with "Wing to Wing" as theme song, *December 24, 1940*
First time Wallace Wimple calls his wife Sweetie Face, *October 7, 1941*
First script with Phil Leslie as co-writer, *March 9, 1943*
Teeny gives age as six, May 2, 1944; says she is six going on eight, *February 20, 1951*
References to what Fibber does for a living: *June 27, 1939; May 9, 1944; November 13, 1945; March 2, 1948; January 18, 1949*
First relative of Harlow's referred to as "Big ____ Wilcox," *December 19, 1944*
Order of objects in hall closet explained, *January 9, 1945*
First time all regular cast members mentioned in opening credits, *January 15, 1946*
First time Bill Thompson plays mumbling conductor, *November 1, 1949*
Rare episode in which Fibber emerges triumphant, *April 22, 1952*

A one-sheet poster from Jim and Marian's final feature film released in 1944 by RKO.

Appendix E

GUEST APPEARANCES ON OTHER RADIO PROGRAMS

Paramount Is On The Air. October 1937.

This radio preview of *This Way Please* contains a scene of Fibber and Molly by a ship reminiscing about their honeymoon. Teeny also appears in a bit.

   Carryovers from *Fibber McGee and Molly:* Tongue twister starting with Seagoing McGee, "'Tain't funny, McGee."

Gulf Screen Guild Theater. May 28, 1939.

Fibber and Molly engage in some banter with Roland Young and some mild flirtation with Ann Sheridan and Douglas Fairbanks Jr.

   Carryovers from *Fibber McGee and Molly:* "Heavenly days," "'Tain't funny, McGee," "That ain't the way I heered it," "Oh, pshaw!"

Lux Radio Theatre. April 8, 1940.

Jim and Marian star as Wilbur and Jessie Todd in "Mama Loves Papa," an adaptation of the 1933 Paramount film which featured Charles Ruggles and Mary Boland. The tale is one of mistaken identity that gets Wilbur appointed commissioner of parks, arrested, and exonerated. Host Cecil B. DeMille calls the Jordans Fibber and Molly and also refers to them as "two of America's foremost actors."

   Carryovers from *Fibber McGee and Molly:* "'Tain't funny, Wilbur," "Oh, pshaw!"

Lux Radio Theatre. February 24, 1941.

Jim and Marian again portray characters named Wilbur and Jessie in "The Whole Town's Talking," an adaptation of the 1935 Columbia picture starring

Edward G. Robinson. The story is built around the complications that occur because meek Wilbur looks like Killer Manion, public enemy number one.

Carryovers from *Fibber McGee and Molly*: "Dadratit," "Oh, pshaw," "Stuff like that there," "'Tain't funny, Wilbur," "Heavenly days," hall closet opened by Wilbur looking for sweater with sound effect after which Wilbur says, "Gotta straighten out that closet one of these days," "Jughead Jones I was knowed as in those days…"

Gulf Screen Guild Theater. March 9, 1941.

Edward Arnold mistakes Fibber and Molly for butler and maid at a dinner party he is hosting for Joan Bennett, Gary Cooper, and Frances Langford. The original story was written by Sam Perrin, Don Quinn, and Leonard Levinson.

Carryovers from *Fibber McGee and Molly*: broom closet opened by Edward followed by small sound effect and Arnold adding "Gotta straighten out that closet some of these days," "Dadratit," word confusion among Fibber, Molly, and Edward involving *manual/menu/menial*, "You're a harrrrd man, McGee."

The Chase and Sanborn Program. November 2, 1941.

Jim and Marian appear to promote *Look Who's Laughing*, the RKO film they made with Edgar Bergen and Charlie McCarthy.

The Great Gildersleeve. January 10, 1943.

When the McGees visit Gildersleeve and family in Summerfield, Fibber uses his discovery of Throcky's engagement to Leila Ransome to taunt his old chum.

Carryovers from *Fibber McGee and Molly*: Molly points out Gildy's neatly-arranged hall closet to Fibber, "Heavenly days," ". . . your clavicle," "Good night, all."

Kraft Music Hall. April 22, 1943.

The McGees are intent on asking Bing Crosby to perform at the Wistful Vista Elks Club.

Carryover from *Fibber McGee and Molly*: hall closet

Command Performance. December 9, 1944.

Fibber tells Molly about some of his war experiences, asks a cousin of Harlow's who is on leave many nosy questions, and then receives a lecture from Wilcox about keeping mum regarding military matters.

Carryovers from *Fibber McGee and Molly*: "The big war," cigar routine (Fibber, soldier).

G.I. Journal. January 12, 1945.

Fibber and Molly help Frank Sinatra edit the *G.I. Journal* as they welcome Doc Gamble, Teeny, Ginger Rogers, Connie Haines, and Mel Blanc.
 Carryovers from *Fibber McGee and Molly*: "Heavenly days," "'Tain't funny, McGee," "There goes a good kid."

Birds Eye Open House. May 3, 1945.

Dinah Shore visits 79 Wistful Vista with Harry Von Zell to receive an award from Fibber as the outstanding female singer of 1945.
 Carryovers from *Fibber McGee and Molly*: "Heavenly days," hall closet opened by Fibber looking for silver cup.

Here's to Veterans. Circa 1946.

Harlow Wilcox provides information for veterans before and after an excerpt from the October 2, 1945 episode of *Fibber McGee and Molly*.

Amos 'n' Andy. February 4, 1947.

While Andy (Charles Correll) is looking for Amos, he runs into Fibber McGee and Molly. There is an in-joke when Fibber indicates Andy looks familiar and asks him if he was ever in Peoria. Correll, like the Jordans, was born in Peoria.
 Carryovers from *Fibber McGee and Molly*: word confusion involving *manacles/monocle/barnacle/binnacle/pinochle* (Fibber, Molly, Andy), hall closet opened by Andy looking for Amos, "Gotta straighten out that closet one of these days."

Lady Esther Screen Guild Theater. February 10, 1947.

In this adaptation of the 1944 RKO film *Heavenly Days*, the McGees visit Washington, D.C. where Fibber takes up the cause of the average man on the Senate floor.
 Carryovers from *Fibber McGee and Molly*: "There goes a good kid," Myrt bit involving "how's your family?"/tried all over town and couldn't/house her family, hall closet opened by Fibber looking for suitcase, "Heavenly days."

Here's to Veterans. Circa 1947.

A special introduction and closing recorded by Jim and Marian about the G.I. Bill act as bookends for an excerpt from the June 17, 1947 episode of *Fibber McGee and Molly*.

Family Theater. October 30, 1947.

After Doc Gamble's secretary breaks up with her boyfriend, Fibber becomes a matchmaker who eventually saves the day in "Advice to the Lovelorn." Regular cast member Arthur Q. Bryan appears as Gamble. Jess Kirkpatrick and Tyler McVey, who made numerous appearances on *Fibber McGee and Molly*, also have parts in this production.

Carryovers from *Fibber McGee and Molly*: "'Tain't funny, McGee," Myrt bit involving brother/disc jockey/riding a plow, "about half past," word confusion involving *privateer/profiteer/porter*, "Heavenly days," Mrs. Kladderhatch is mentioned.

The Bob Hope Show. November 18, 1947.

While Bob is enroute to England, a number of NBC stars fill in including Jim and Marian in a bit with the McGees that has Fibber tinkering with the radio.

Carryover from *Fibber McGee and Molly*: word confusion involving *manacle/monocle/chronicle/bronchial/bronco*.

Philco Radio Time. April 14, 1948.

The McGees discuss Bing's career, then go to ask Crosby if he will sing at a local amateur show. All three join in a harmonic version of "I Had a Dream, Dear." Near the end of the show is a rare instance when the host of a program actually addresses Jim and Marian by their own names, not as Fibber and Molly.

Guest Star. June 20, 1948.

Molly does not want to hear about Fibber's plan to invest their life savings because she fears it is another of his get-rich schemes. Harlow Wilcox, Doc Gamble (Arthur Q. Bryan), and the Old Timer (Bill Thompson) appear in this program on behalf of U.S. Security Bonds. The orchestra of Billy Mills plays "Better Luck Next Time." Don Quinn and Phil Leslie are given writing credit.

Sealtest Variety Theater. December 16, 1948.

Fibber and Molly perform in a skit with Dorothy Lamour on a train.
Carryovers from *Fibber McGee and Molly:* Fred Nitney, Cinder Bucket.

Suspense. February 3, 1949.

In "Backseat Driver" Jim and Marian play a couple held captive by a killer who has hidden in the backseat of their car while they were watching a movie.

Carryovers from *Fibber McGee and Molly*: After the play is over, Jim calls Harlow Wilcox "Waxy" and starts on a tongue twister that only gets as far as "masterful miracles of manufacturing magnificence."

Guest Star. September 25, 1949.

Fibber has a plan to make money by returning soup that comes with a "double your money back" guarantee. Harlow Wilcox and Mayor LaTrivia (Gale Gordon) also appear in this program on behalf of U.S. Savings Bonds.

Carryover from *Fibber McGee and Molly*: LaTrivia blowup over *minor/miner*.

Family Theater. October 18, 1950.

"The Windbag" tells the story of the trouble D.J. Latimer (Jim) causes for himself and his wife Martha (Marian) when he takes credit for radio plays written by his son-in-law.

Suspense. February 22, 1951.

The Jordans repeat their performance from February 3, 1949.

25th Anniversary of NBC. December 15, 1951.

Fibber has rewired his radio so he and Molly can tune in old radio shows as a salute to NBC's silver anniversary. Teeny pays a visit to listen to some of the programs.

The Big Show. March 9, 1952.

Jim and Marian deliver a prerecorded message to commemorate their twenty years on NBC.

Carryovers from *Fibber McGee and Molly*: Uncle Dennis's drinking, "'Tain't funny, McGee."

Family Theater. February 6, 1957.

In this fantasy entitled "Genie with the Light Green Hair," Jim (Wallace) and Marian (Agnes) play tourists in Egypt where Wallace encounters an absent-minded genie who grants his wishes in a rather odd way. The stars are announced as "Jim and Marian Jordan, better known as Fibber McGee and Molly."

Carryover from *Fibber McGee and Molly*: "Dadratit."

Look who's laughing: It is only fitting that Marian and Jim have the last laugh.

Selected Bibliography

Brooks, Elston. *I've Heard Those Songs Before*. Morrow Quill, 1981.

Dunning, John. *On the Air: The Encyclopedia of Old-Time Radio*. Oxford University Press, 1998.

Firestone, Ross, ed. *The Big Radio Comedy Program*. Contemporary Books, 1978.

Gaver, Jack, and Dave Stanley. *There's Laughter in the Air!* Greenberg, 1945.

Mott, Robert L. *Radio Sound Effects*. McFarland, 1993.

Price, Tom. *Fibber McGee's Closet*. Thomas A. Price, 1987.

Schaden, Chuck. *Speaking of Radio*. Nostalgia Digest Press, 2003.

Smith, Mickey. *How Fibber McGee and Molly Won World War II*. BearManor Media, 2010.

Stumpf, Charles, and Ben Ohmart. *Fibber McGee's Scrapbook*. BearManor Media, 2002.

Stumpf, Charles, and Tom Price. *Heavenly Days!* The World of Yesterday, 1987.

Summers, Harrison B., ed. *A Thirty-Year History of Programs Carried on National Radio Networks in the United States, 1926-1956*. Arno Press, 1971.

Wertheim, Arthur Frank. *Radio Comedy*. Oxford University Press, 1979.

Yoder, Charles. "The McGees of Wistful Vista," *The Saturday Evening Post*, April 9 and 16, 1949.

Index

Abbott and Costello 130, 134, 147, 364
Abbott and Costello Show, The 126, 386
Ace, Goodman 194
Ace, Jane 194
Addams, Charles 470
Adventures of Ozzie and Harriet, The 342
Air Scouts, The 19
Alan Young Show, The 205
Alec Templeton Show, The 84
Allen, Fred 14, 188, 235, 237
Allen, Gracie 13, 96
Allman, Elvia 21, 79, 143, 178, 255-258, 260-262, 264, 265, 268, 269, 297, 298, 303-307, 309, 314, 318 320, 321, 327, 328, 333, 342, 359, 361, 378, 383, 386, 389, 411, 432, 442, 446, 449, 452, 455, 466, 467
Amos 'n' Andy 9, 159, 227, 249, 367, 371, 553
Annie Get Your Gun 200
Arnold, Edward 552
Arquette, Cliff 13, 24, 49, 50, 247, 252-256, 258-271, 273-281, 283, 290, 291, 295, 296, 298, 299, 302, 303, 306, 320, 356, 460
Arvan, Jan 304, 307, 308, 328
Attorney at Law 73
Audley, Eleanor 338, 405
Averback, Hy 382

Baby Snooks 329
Backus, Jim 8, 146, 193, 194, 195, 201, 210, 211
Baer, Parley 21, 317, 318, 322, 333, 337, 349, 364, 384, 397, 400, 402, 437, 443, 449, 450, 463, 464, 471
Bates, Jeanne 460
Beals, Dick (Richard) 303, 304, 317, 347, 382, 389, 435, 439, 444
Begley, Ed 241, 247, 269, 277, 284, 287, 390, 367
Benaderet, Bea 10, 18, 20, 61, 75, 83, 91, 113, 177-186, 188-205, 212, 216, 218, 224, 226, 239, 242, 243, 265, 547
Bendix, William 248
Bennett, Joan 552
Benny, Jack 14, 79, 231, 333, 344, 489, 491
Bergen, Edgar 43, 123, 552
Berle, Milton 308
Berman, Shelley 498
Berner, Sara 85, 90, 91, 93, 94, 101, 108, 111, 112
Beulah Show, The 7, 184
Big Show, The 555
Birds Eye Open House 553
Blanc, Mel 73-80, 82-86, 92, 93, 96 98 109, 126, 377, 553

Bob Hope Show, The 371, 554
Boland, Mary 551
Bolen, Joe 44
Bonney, Gail 361, 367, 399, 413, 414, 420, 452, 474
Borge, Victor 184
Botkin, Perry 191, 211, 267, 282
Braden, Margaret 318
Brice, Fanny 363
Broadway Rhythm 338
Brown, Bob 51, 52
Bruce, Bob 278, 286, 304, 306, 325, 327, 342, 356, 372, 384, 421
Bryan, Arthur Q. 10, 18, 20, 144, 147-205, 210-309, 313-338, 340-353, 355-383, 385-401, 403-417, 419-438, 440-471, 473-476, 547, 554
Burbank, Luther 500
Busse, Henry 62
Butler, Daws 347, 402, 418, 434
Butterfield, Herb 437, 461, 474

Call, Audrey 41, 42, 43, 46, 47, 48, 49, 50
Call the Police 234
Can You Top This? 214
Candy Matson 399
Cantor, Eddie 79, 162, 285, 354, 356, 359, 362, 542
Carroll, Gene 20, 212-217, 547
Carroll, Jack 389
Cerf, Bennett 379
Charlie McCarthy Show, The 269
Chase and Sanborn Program, The 552
Christy, Ken 74, 111, 141, 142, 150, 151, 160, 161, 166, 170, 174, 176, 177, 179, 185, 187, 203, 226, 230, 234, 245, 266, 273, 276, 278, 281, 282, 289, 291, 294, 321, 333, 334, 345, 352, 363, 398, 449, 466
Clark, Cliff 258
Clef Dwellers 42, 43
Cohan, George M. 136, 168
Colbert, Claudette 148, 149
Collins, Colleen 281, 286, 300, 330, 400, 422, 428, 456, 460, 466, 470
Colman, Benita 9
Colman, Ronald 125, 203, 204, 394

Colonna, Jerry 437
Colvig, Pinto 352, 353
Command Performance 552
Como, Perry 20, 51, 52-59, 63-68, 184, 248
Conklin, Gene 423
Conrad, William 319, 323, 364, 393, 394, 412
Cook, Tommy 185, 422
Cooper, Gary 552
Correll, Charles 227, 553
Cousin Willie 310
Croft, Mary Jane 294, 296, 298, 303, 304-308, 314, 322, 329, 332, 365, 367, 369, 379, 381, 383, 394, 402, 403, 404, 414, 432, 435, 437, 439, 440, 441, 442, 447, 450-454, 456, 461, 463, 465, 471, 472
Crosby, Bing 552, 554
Curley, Leo 384, 403, 420

Danch, Bill 10, 12, 329, 330, 331, 335
Darby, Ken 21, 120, 142, 230, 248, 306
D'Arcy, Emery 45
Day, Dennis 9, 248, 284
DeMille, Cecil B. 551
Dennis, Clark 47, 68, 69, 70, 71, 72, 73
Diamond, Ann 274, 275
Dick Van Dyke Show, The 222
DiMaggio, Joe 349
Dobkin, Larry 423, 429, 439, 455
Dodson, Jon 21
Donna, Kay 43, 44, 45
Douglas, Scott 434
Dragnet 326, 359, 434
Drake, Pauline 424
Duff, Howard 242
Dunn, James 338
Dunne, Irene 248
Durante, Jimmy 289, 356
Durocher, Leo 385

Easton, Robert 338, 339, 344, 345, 351, 353, 354, 357, 360, 361, 364, 365, 366, 369, 370, 375, 377-383, 387, 388, 390, 392, 395-398,

400-403, 405, 407, 409, 415, 417, 418, 422-424, 426, 428, 431, 437, 441, 445, 446, 449, 451, 456, 457, 459-461, 464, 465, 469-472, 475, 476
Easy Aces 194
Eddie Cantor Show, The 159
Edwards, Ralph 294
Edwards, Sam 391, 414, 469
Eisenhower, Dwight 444, 468
Ellis, Herb 356, 378
Evans, Dale 349, 355, 357, 359

Fairbanks, Douglas, Jr. 551
Family Theater 553, 555
Farber, Jerry 283
Farrar, Stanley 403
Faye, Alice 248
Feld, Fritz 380, 381, 435, 454, 460, 471
Felton, Verna 76, 78, 98, 116, 118, 141
Fenneman, George 355, 358
Fibber McGee and Company 20, 70
Field, Norman 275
Fields, W.C. 75
Fisher, Eddie 317
Forte, Joe 290, 294, 331, 378, 442
Four Notes 76-84
Fowler, Keith 12, 250, 288
Fraser, Monty 21, 174
Freberg, Stan 326, 423
Fred Waring Show, The 200, 220
Frees, Paul 345, 346, 371, 431
Frye, Gilbert 317

Gabor, Zsa Zsa 404
Garroway, Dave 360, 362
Gerson, Betty Lou 42, 412
Gerstle, Frank 319, 371, 378, 442
Gibbs, Parker 51, 53, 56
G.I. Journal 553
Goff, Norris 135
Gone With the Wind 97
Goldberg, Rube 136, 453
Goodman, Ralph 12, 317-348, 350, 351, 354-357, 359-361, 363-371, 376-387, 389, 390, 392-398, 400-404, 407, 408, 410-414, 416, 418, 419, 422-426, 428, 430-439, 441-476
Goodwin, Bill 347, 349, 350, 352, 353, 354, 360, 361
Gordon, Gale 10, 18, 20, 91-93, 100, 101, 103-106, 108-111, 113-117, 119-140, 145, 146, 152, 153, 155, 157, 158, 184-205, 210-298, 300-304, 307, 308, 547, 555
Gordon, Virginia 140-147, 150-512, 154, 156, 157, 174, 176, 177, 186-188, 195, 201, 202, 210, 221, 222, 229, 243, 244
Gould, Sandra 230
Granby, Joe 356, 388, 417
Great Gildersleeve, The 7, 121, 335, 342, 347, 350, 353, 356, 359, 393, 552
Gregg, Virginia 337
Grier, Jimmy 59-62
Griffith, Andy 486
Guest Star 554, 555
Gulf Screen Guild Theater 551, 552
Gunsmoke 391

Haines, Connie 553
Hairston, Jester 317
Halls of Ivy, The 279
Hanan, Bob 47
Hap Hazard 120
Harrington, Mary Lou 283, 339, 341, 344, 382, 387, 407, 409, 418, 422, 423, 454, 459, 460, 470, 475
Harris, Arlene 424, 430
Harris, Phil 248
Harris, Tommy 60, 61, 62
Hausner, Jerry 304
Hayward, Susan 347
Hearn, Sam 74
Heavenly Days 171, 172, 550, 553
Hemingway, Frank 251
Here We Go Again 137
Here's to Veterans 553
Herndon, Neil 320
High and the Mighty, The 378
Hitchcock, Alfred 385
Hitler, Adolph 181
Hodges, Joy 59
Honest Harold 296, 329

Hope, Bob 79, 102, 165, 178, 248, 347, 349, 350, 352, 354, 360, 361, 554
Hughes, Charles Evans 481
Hurt, Marlin 20, 160-184, 195, 547
Hutto, Max 21, 264, 313

Iannone, Patricia 347
Idelson, Bill 310, 415, 416, 424, 448, 474, 476
It Pays To Be Married 350, 351, 357, 362

Jack Benny Program, The 9, 89, 101, 145, 198, 200, 249, 367
Jack Carson Show, The 335
Jack Pearl Show, The 280
Jacobson, Art 430, 443, 448, 456, 459, 468, 471, 472
Janiss, Vivi 386
Johnson Merrymen 40, 41, 42
Jones, Spike 184, 279
Jordan, Jim 4, 6, 8, 9, 13-16, 18,22-32, 37-205, 209-479, 481, 484, 492, 540, 546, 550-556
Jordan, Jim, Jr. 179, 180, 182-185, 189, 190, 193-195, 198-200
Jordan, Marian 4, 6, 8, 9, 13-16, 18-30, 32, 37-68, 80-205, 210-303, 304-479, 481, 484, 540, 546, 550-556

Kabibble, Ish 437
Kane, Joel 12, 395, 400, 401, 403, 405, 407, 443, 444, 446
Kearns, Joseph 177, 180, 190, 247, 325, 341, 362, 365, 370, 371, 380, 395, 399, 402, 408, 413, 418, 447, 457, 464
Kefauver, Estes 468
King's Men, The 20, 21, 94-205, 210-309
Kirkpatrick, Jess 196, 221, 224, 225, 229, 230, 235, 247, 287, 288, 304, 305, 318, 322, 334, 335, 339, 345, 366, 375, 385, 387, 400, 412, 419, 434, 436, 445, 450, 452, 475, 554
Kirkwood, Jack 238, 239
Knotts, Don 14

Knudsen, Peggy 278, 279, 375, 385, 393, 419, 473
Koch, Tom 12, 479, 481, 487, 491, 495
Kraft Music Hall 552
Krugman, Lou 291, 332, 356, 373, 474
Kruschen, Jack 300, 302, 304, 306, 308, 316, 317, 321, 330, 337, 351, 357, 359, 366, 367, 369, 374, 377, 378, 379, 384, 388, 390, 397, 406, 416, 423, 427, 433, 434, 439, 440, 449, 455, 463, 465

Lady Esther Screen Guild Theater 553
LaGuardia, Fiorello 220
Lamour, Dorothy 554
Lang, Harry 293
Langford, Frances 552
Lansing, Mary 355, 360, 370, 394, 413, 419, 420, 421, 426, 434, 447, 456, 466, 476
Lauck, Chester 135
LaVere, Charlie 43, 46, 48
Lee, Lillian 274
Leeds, Peter 254, 265, 284, 288, 293, 330, 348, 385, 404, 440
LeGrand, Dick 10, 20, 166, 242-309, 547
Leonard, Leroy 317
Leslie, Phil 9-12, 18, 146, 148, 150, 159, 163, 165, 166, 171, 179, 189, 204, 213, 215, 218, 224, 225, 226, 228, 232, 233, 239, 245, 249, 250, 253, 254, 261, 268, 274, 279, 280, 283, 288, 313-476, 549, 554
Levinson, Len 12, 335, 336, 338-341, 343, 346-350, 352, 353, 357, 358, 360-364, 366, 367, 369, 372-376, 379-392, 394, 395, 398-402, 405, 406, 408, 409, 411-422, 424, 426-434, 436, 437, 439, 440, 443, 448, 552
Lewis, Cathy 21
Lewis, John L. 435
Linn, Bud 21
Liszt, Margie 428
Longfellow, Henry Wadsworth 498
Look Who's Laughing 120, 123, 552

Index ♦ **563**

Lorre, Peter 356
Lost Weekend, The 215
Lovel, Kay 275
Luke and Mirandy 19
Lum and Abner 16, 59, 135
Lux Radio Theatre 97, 98, 367, 551
MacRae, Gordon 317, 346, 348, 351
Mansfield, Ronnie 41
Manville, Tommy 404
Marcelli, Rico 20, 37-50
Marian and Jim in Songs 19
Marr, Eddie 403, 420, 421, 444
Marsh, Myra 271, 272, 286, 305, 330, 372, 375, 432, 441
Martin, Lynn 39, 40, 41, 42
Masters, Monte 399
Masters, Natalie 326-329, 337, 338, 342, 350, 359, 367, 369, 375, 378, 386, 390, 392, 394, 398, 412, 423, 437, 441, 446, 455, 462, 463
Mather, Jack 321, 333, 340, 349, 382, 384, 385, 393, 415, 421, 440, 448, 471, 474
Max, Ed 202
McIntire, John 271, 273, 293, 303, 304, 305
McKenna, Kate 389, 395, 396, 440
McKinnon, Dallas 251, 289
McMillan, Gloria 283, 286, 288, 289, 290, 291, 292, 296, 391
McNear, Howard 315
McVey, Tyler 269, 273-277, 281, 288, 289, 295, 300, 304, 305, 307, 332, 345, 358, 364, 373, 396, 399, 421, 466, 554
Meredith Willson's Musical Revue 103
Merrill, Lou 219
Michaels, Tony 321, 449
Millar, Lee 361, 362, 363
Miller, Marvin 295, 361, 362, 363
Millionaire, The 362
Mills, Billy 18, 20, 32, 71-205, 210-309, 554
Milton Berle Show, The 256
Mr. District Attorney 229
Mitchell, Shirley 18, 20, 135, 153, 154-190, 215, 393, 547

Mix, Tom 403
Monroe, Marilyn 435
Moody, Ralph 355
Moore, Clement Clarke 142
Moran, Betty 295
Moreno, Rosita 144, 145, 146, 148
Morse, Carlton E. 292
Moyles, Jack 324 325, 328, 334, 335, 336, 340, 343, 348, 351, 357, 359, 360, 362, 364, 367, 374, 376, 380, 381, 384, 388, 392, 394, 397, 404, 408, 411, 413, 419, 427, 431, 434, 437, 448, 452, 454, 471, 475
Murder at Midnight 10

Needham, Louis and Brorby 93, 234
Nelson, Frank 77, 78, 80, 85, 89, 90, 111, 112, 114, 116, 117, 121-123, 127-129, 131-134, 137, 140, 148, 151, 348
Nesbitt, John 136, 153
Newhart, Bob 498
Nolan, Jeanette 270
Novello, Jay 296, 435, 471
Novis, Donald 20, 73-89
Nusser, Jim 304

O'Brien, Chris 349
O'Brien, Pat 3342, 343
O'Henry Twins, The 19
One Man's Family 292, 415
Our Miss Brooks 296, 300

Page, Gale 38, 39
Paiva, Nestor 307, 336, 358, 360
Paramount Is On The Air 551
Passing Parade, The 153
Paul Taylor Choristers 88
Peary, Harold 10, 20, 32, 63-122, 126, 142, 163, 184, 248, 547
Penny Singleton Show, The 264
Pepper Young's Family 454
Perrin, Lloyd 355
Perrin, Sam 551
Peters, Susan Leslie 9
Petrie, George 234
Philco Radio Time 554

Phillips, Barney 358, 359, 398, 409, 428, 434, 448, 473
Pidgeon, Walter 351
Pirrone, George 271
Pittman, Frank 18, 21, 195, 219, 233, 234, 248
Pitts, ZaSu 20, 75-79
Porter, Cole 178
Post, Tom 44
Presenting Charles Boyer 264

Quinn, Don 5, 9, 18-26, 31, 32, 37, 48, 51, 53, 56, 72, 75, 77-79, 82 85, 86, 88-90, 93, 95, 98, 100, 102, 104, 108, 113, 114, 116, 119, 121, 126, 128, 130, 134, 135, 138, 139, 143, 145, 146, 148, 150, 159, 163, 165, 166, 174, 179, 189, 213, 215, 218, 224-226, 228, 232, 239, 245, 249, 250, 253, 254, 261, 268, 274, 279, 283, 288, 552, 554
Quo Vadis 338

Railroad Hour, The 346, 348, 351
Rand, Sally 403, 484
Randolph, Isabel 20, 32, 45, 46, 50, 57, 62-67, 69, 73-152, 547
Ray, Johnnie 291
Reagan, Ronald 203
Red Skelton Show, The 371
Reimer, Virgil 21, 120
Rhymer, Paul 145
Richards, Danny, Jr. 267, 270, 271
Richman, Marian 283, 288, 293, 308, 315, 324-326, 350, 351, 405, 406, 428, 460, 469
Rinehart, Mary Roberts 454
Robinson, Edward G. 552
Robinson, Rad 21
Rogers, Buddy 59
Rogers, Ginger 553
Rogers, Roy 333, 349, 355, 357, 359, 403
Roman Holiday 429
Ronnie and Van 37, 38
Roosevelt, Franklin 180
Rose, Jewel 317

Ross, Earle 195
Roy, Cecil 422
Roy Rogers Show, The 349, 355, 357, 359
Ruggles, Charles 551
Ruth, Babe 439
Ryan, Dick 271, 273, 274, 334, 342, 345, 352, 367, 384, 403

Schulz, Charles 247
Sealtest Variety Theater 554
Sears, Charlie 62
Sedan, Rolfe 316, 333, 412, 431
Seel, Charlie 384, 410, 416, 462
Shauer, Mel 145
Sheridan, Ann 551
Sherman, Ransom 20, 121, 153-168, 547
Shields, Jimmy 89-94
Shore, Dinah 248, 348, 352, 355, 357, 360, 553
Silver, Jeff 290
Sinatra, Frank 317, 553
Singer, Stuffy 325
Six Shooter, The 350, 356, 358, 391
Skelton, Red 188
Smackout 19, 33, 261, 289
Smith, Charlie 276, 415, 416
Smith, John T. 276
Snow White and the Seven Dwarfs 78
Song of Hiawatha, The 89
Spillane, Mickey 348
Stanwyck, Barbara 349
Stefan, Bud 244-250, 260, 262, 263, 270, 271, 277, 283
Stewart, Gretchen 255
Stewart, Harry 255
Stewart, James 350, 356, 358, 392
Stewart, Jay 350, 351, 357, 362
Stop the Music 235
Stratton, Gil, Jr. 283, 286, 289-293, 295-301
Studebaker, Hugh 20, 40, 43-46, 48-50, 52, 53, 55-58, 61-67, 69-74, 547
Suspense 370, 554, 555
Swayze, John Cameron 397
Sweeney, Bob 21, 299, 304

Tanner, Elmo 50, 56-59, 63-71
Templeton, Alec 84
Tetley, Walter 75, 76, 104, 163, 202, 230, 308, 425
This Way Please 4, 59, 60, 145, 551
Thompson, Bill 10, 16, 18, 20, 21, 31, 32, 46-153, 172, 190-205, 210-309, 313-476, 547, 549, 554
Thorsness, Cliff 479
Tilton, Martha 122-126
Tollefson, Bud 21
Tremayne, Les 385
Truman, Harry 180, 260, 444
Truth or Consequences 230, 294, 414
Tucker, Tommy 46
Tuttle, Lurene 115, 167, 177, 192
Twelvetrees, Helen 338

Uncle Tom's Cabin 228
Underwood, Cecil 21, 69

Van Doren, Carl 159
Vander Pyl, Jean 261, 262, 265, 276, 280, 282, 290, 298, 306, 388, 414, 425, 446, 461
Vic and Sade 16, 145, 164, 172
Victor Borge Show, The 184
Vigran, Herb 21, 230, 234, 236-238, 240, 254-257, 260, 265, 273, 275, 276, 283, 291, 296, 304, 305, 315, 332, 340, 350, 353, 366, 375, 382, 394, 409, 414, 420, 426
von Eltz, Theodore 295
Von Zell, Harry 158, 159, 163, 273, 553

Votrian, Peter 270, 347

Wald, John 21, 198, 199, 203, 210, 313-476
Wand, Betty 262
Waring, Fred 200, 205, 234
Waterman, Willard 347, 350, 353, 356, 359
Wayne, John 370
Weaver, Doodles 41
Webber, Peggy 275, 289
Weems, Ted 20, 50-59, 62-72
Wells, Kathleen 37, 38
Whitfield, Anne 338
Wilcox, Harlow 10, 18, 21, 31-205, 210-309, 313, 547, 549, 552, 553, 554
Williams, Esther 339, 346
Williams, Tennessee 389
Willock, Dave 275
Willson, Meredith 103, 136
Wilson, Charlie 41
Winkler, Betty 20, 67-72, 74
Winslowe, Paula 302, 309, 322, 450
Words at War 169
Wright, Frank Lloyd 80
Wright, Will 442, 451, 453, 471

Yoder, Robert 245
You Bet Your Life 355, 358
Young, Robert 248
Young, Roland 551

Zanuck, Darryl F. 371
Zaputo, Frankie 86, 87

www.ingramcontent.com/pod-product-compliance
Lightning Source LLC
Chambersburg PA
CBHW060758230426
43667CB00010B/1620